The Nature of International Law

The Library of Essays in International Law
General Editor: Robert McCorquodale

Titles in the Series

International Human Rights Law
Michael Addo

International Law and Indigenous Peoples
Stephen James Anaya

Law of the Sea
Hugo Caminos

Humanitarian Law
Judith Gardam

International Economic Regulation
Jane Kelsey

Sources of International Law
Martti Koskenniemi

Self-Determination in International Law
Robert McCorquodale

International Dispute Settlement
Mary Ellen O'Connell

International Crimes
Nikos Passas

International Environmental Law
Paula M. Pevato

State Responsibility in International Law
René Provost

Jurisdiction in International Law
W. Michael Reisman

Title to Territory
Malcolm Shaw

The Nature of International Law
Gerry Simpson

Collective Security
Nigel White

The Nature of International Law

Edited by

Gerry Simpson

The London School of Economics and Political Science

Routledge
Taylor & Francis Group
LONDON AND NEW YORK

First published 2001 by Darthmouth Publishing Company and Ashgate Publishing

Reissued 2018 by Routledge
2 Park Square, Milton Park, Abingdon, Oxon OX14 4RN
711 Third Avenue, New York, NY 10017, USA

Routledge is an imprint of the Taylor & Francis Group, an informa business

A Library of Congress record exists under LC control number: 00060591

ISBN 13: 978-1-138-70606-4 (hbk)
ISBN 13: 978-1-138-70603-3 (pbk)
ISBN 13: 978-1-315-20200-6 (ebk)

Contents

Acknowledgements

The editor and publishers wish to thank the following for permission to use copyright material.

The American Society of International Law for the essays: Anne-Marie Slaughter Burley (1993), 'International Law and International Relations Theory: A Dual Agenda', *The American Journal of International Law*, **87**, pp. 205–39; L. Oppenheim (1908), 'The Science of International Law: Its Task and Method', *The American Journal of International Law*, **2**, pp. 313–56; Hans J. Morgenthau (1940), 'Positivism, Functionalism, and International Law', *The American Journal of International Law*, **34**, pp. 260–84; W. Michael Reisman (1992), 'The View from the New Haven School of International Law', *American Society of International Law Proceedings*, pp. 118-25; Thomas M. Franck (1988), 'Legitimacy in the International System', *The American Journal of International Law*, **82**, pp. 705–59. Reproduced with permission from *The American Journal of International Law*. Copyright © The American Society of International Law.

Blackwell Publishers for the essay: David Armstrong (1999), 'Law, Justice and the Idea of a World Society', *International Affairs*, **75**, pp. 547–61.

Cambridge University Press for the essay: Martin Wight (1987), 'An Anatomy of International Thought', *Review of International Studies*, **13**, pp. 221–27. Copyright © 1987 Review of International Studies.

Columbia University for the essay: Fernando R. Tesón (1992), 'The Kantian Theory of International Law', *Columbia Law Review*, **92**, pp. 53–102. Copyright © 1992 Columbia Law Review. This article originally appeared at 92 Colum. L. Rev. 53 (1992). Reprinted by permission.

Harvard University for the essays: James Boyle (1985) 'Ideals and Things: International Legal Scholarship and the Prison-House of Language', *Harvard International Law Journal*, **26**, pp. 327–69; Martti Koskenniemi (1991), 'The Future of Statehood', *Harvard International Law Journal*, **32**, pp. 397–410; Antony Anghie (1999), 'Finding the Peripheries: Sovereignty and Colonialism in Nineteenth-Century International Law', *Harvard International Law Journal*, **40**, pp. 1–80. Copyright © the President and Fellows of Harvard College and the Harvard International Law Journal.

Kluwer Law International for the essay: Deborah Z. Cass (1996), 'Navigating the Newstream: Recent Critical Scholarship in International Law', *Nordic Journal of International Law*, **65**, pp. 341–83. Copyright © 1996 Kluwer Law International. With kind permission of Kluwer Law International.

MIT Press Journals for the essay: Joseph M. Grieco (1988), 'Anarchy and the Limits of Cooperation: A Realist Critique of the Newest Liberal Institutionalism', *International Organization*, **42**, pp. 485–507. Copyright © World Peace Foundation and the Massachusetts Institute of Technology.

Northwestern University School of Law for the essay: Anthony D'Amato (1985), 'Is International Law Really "Law"?', *Northwestern University Law Review*, **79**, pp. 1293–314. Copyright © 1985 Anthony D'Amato. Reprinted with special permission of Northwestern University School of Law.

Oxford University Press for the essays: Martti Koskenniemi (1990), 'The Politics of International Law', *European Journal of International Law*, **1**, pp. 4–32; Susan Marks (1997), 'The End of History? Reflections on Some International Legal Theses', *European Journal of International Law*, **8**, pp. 449–77.

University of Nebraska for the essay: Harold Hongju Koh (1996), 'Transnational Legal Process', *Nebraska Law Review*, **75**, pp. 181–207. Copyright © 1996 Harold Hongju Koh and Nebraska Law Review.

University of Notre Dame for the essay: Thomas M. Franck (1989), 'Is Justice Relevant to the International Legal System?', *Notre Dame Law Review*, **64**, pp. 945–63. Copyright © 1989 Notre Dame Law Review, University of Notre Dame. Reprinted with permission.

Every effort has been made to trace all the copyright holders, but if any have been inadvertently overlooked the publishers will be pleased to make the necessary arrangement at the first opportunity.

Personal Acknowledgements

The work on this book was completed while I was a Visiting Researcher at Harvard Law School. I would like to thank the Law Faculty at the Australian National University for providing financial support during my stay in Boston and Harvard Law School for making that stay a productive and enjoyable one.

Series Preface

Open a newspaper, listen to the radio or watch television any day of the week and you will read or hear of some matter concerning international law. The range of matters include the extent to which issues of trade and human rights should be linked, concerns about refugees and labour conditions, negotiations of treaties and the settlement of disputes, and decisions by the United Nations Security Council concerning actions to ensure compliance with international law. International legal issues have impact on governments, corporations, organisations and people around the world and the process of globalisation has increased this impact. In the global legal environment, knowledge of international law is an indispensable tool for all scholars, legal practitioners, decision-makers and citizens of the 21st century.

The Library of Essays in International Law is designed to provide the essential elements for the development of this knowledge. Each volume contains essays of central importance in the development of international law in a subject area. The proliferation of legal and other specialist journals, the increase in international materials and the use of the internet, has meant that it is increasingly difficult for legal scholars to have access to all the relevant articles on international law and many valuable older articles are now unable to be obtained readily. These problems are addressed by this series, which makes available an extensive range of materials in a manner that is of immeasurable value for both teaching and research at all levels.

Each volume is written by a leading authority in the subject area who selects the articles and provides an informative introduction, which analyses the context of the articles and comments on their significance within the developments in that area. The volumes complement each other to give a clear view of the burgeoning area of international law. It is not an easy task to select, order and place in context essays from the enormous quantity of academic legal writing prublished in journals – in many languages – throughout the world. This task requires professional scholarly judgment and difficult choices. The editors in this series have done an excellent job, for which I thank and congratulate them. It has been a pleasure working with them.

ROBERT McCORQUODALE
General Series Editor
Faculty of Law
The Australian National University

Introduction

Purpose

My purpose in this collection is to provide a map of some of the great theoretical debates within the discipline of international law. In doing so, I do not claim to have presented a definitive account of the development of international law or some revelation concerning its essence. Indeed, this collection could be relabelled *The Natures of International Law* for this is an area of study that contains multitudes. So, in the following pages I have compiled some key moments in the international law story with a view to bringing together a number of diverse and conflicting perspectives on the function, purpose and meaning of the international legal order.

There are a number of ways in which I could have approached a project like this. I might have collected together the leading essays in the area according to their influence, intrinsic merit or other analogous, and no doubt contested, criteria. Alternatively, I might have attempted a chronological story about the development of thinking in the discipline. Another possibility was to present a series of essays reflecting one particular position that I believed best explained the nature of international law. I have chosen to adopt none of these approaches, although I do hope that there is some sense of historical development conveyed in the essays.

Instead, I have presented international law as an argument among a number of competing positions on different international legal controversies. More specifically, I have adopted a dialectical style in choosing the essays. I want these groups of essays to function as conversations between theorists on concrete subjects. Sometimes, and usually unjustly, theory gets a bad name. In Ian Brownlie's contentious phrase, it is said to be '...a bank of fog on a still day' with little to say about the 'business of legal investigation' (Brownlie, 1983, p. 627). The point of this collection is to present theory as contribution to our thinking about specific legal and political problems. The writers I have chosen to include argue over the most important and profound issues facing international lawyers today.

This collection comprises six groups of essays on pivotal legal and political matters preceded by three introductory essays in which the nature of international law or, in the case of Martin Wight, international studies, is set out in survey form. Each of the groups following these introductory pieces can be read as a sort of Socratic dialogue between a number of positions.[1] This dialogue will often be obvious, and at other times implicit. Sometimes there will be surprising areas of agreement and sometimes the participants will appear to be talking about separate problems. In this respect, these conversations simply resemble the sorts of disagreement and discussion we might witness at a gathering of international lawyers. In this sense, I have imagined myself to be organizing a conference on international legal theory in much the same way as others might fantasize about their ideal dinner-party guests.

Like all successful conference organizers, I have had to limit the scope of subject matter and this has profoundly shaped my choice of essays. The nature of international law is a potentially expansive topic. After all, everything written in international law says something about the nature of the system. I have focused on essays that are explicit in their appraisal of the theoretical underpinnings of the system. The system with which I am concerned is the public international legal order in general, so I have tended to disregard often authoritative and persuasive material on the international economic order or regional societies such as the European Union or sub-sets of the public international law system such as the human rights scheme. I also have tried to include only essays that operate at a certain level of abstraction. This has meant leaving out essays that are more concerned with sources or structure than the overall nature of the system. In any case, separate collections in this series survey these areas of international law and I wish to avoid any overlap.[2]

As a consequence of all this, much has been omitted that might otherwise have been included in a more conventional collection. Limitations associated with length, as well as a preference for work published in essay form over that found in edited books, also results in the exclusion of some important work. Finally, I have tried to include unfamiliar work (from more obscure journals) in order to give these important essays visibility and exposure.

In the light of all these restrictions and because of my desire to tell some sort of coherent story about international law, I cannot claim any canonical status for this collection. Most notably, it provides only references to and descriptions of the work of the great international law scholars of the pre-modern era. There is no Grotius, no Suarez, no Gentili, no Lorimer and no Wheaton. Much published in languages other than English is missing. This is the nature of international law through predominantly Anglo-American eyes. Important schools of international legal scholarship are absent – for example, Kelsen and the Vienna School, Stone and the sociological school, Richard Falk and the World Order Model Project and Marxist international law (see Rigaux, 1998; Carty, 1998; Falk, 1989, 1992; Jones, 1935; McWhinney, 1990; Chimni, 1993). Missing, too, is some scholarship prized for its revolutionary impact on schools that *are* represented here – for example, David Kennedy's path-breaking scholarship (1980, 1993), Charlesworth, Chinkin and Wright's explosive essay on feminist methods (1991), Myres McDougal's *oeuvre* (McDougal and Lasswell, 1959), Louis Sohn's work (Clark and Sohn, 1966). Illuminating studies by the likes of Hedley Bull (1977) and Robert Keohane (1989) working in other disciplines also merit inclusion. I have also omitted a number of important essays on the sources of international law. Indeed, James Boyle's essay (Chapter 10) is the only contribution from this perspective. The nature and sources of international law are closely linked, of course. A separate collection in this series, edited by Martti Koskenniemi, features work on sources that would otherwise have been included here. I refer to essays by David Kennedy (1980), John Tasioulis (1996), Prosper Weil (1983) and James Watson (1980). Finally, there are those essays whose power and individuality have made them rather difficult to place in a collection such as this. These include Philip Allott's 'Language, Method and the Nature of International Legal Scholarship' (1971) and a number of Tony Carty's essays (for example, Carty, 1991). I recommend these to those curious about the discipline.

Ultimately, then, what follows are a series of conversations conducted among individuals who have reflected on their discipline in interesting ways and who have tried to provide an account of that discipline.

Structure

This collection is structured around a series of questions that have animated international legal studies for a long time. So that the reader can approach these questions armed with some sort of picture of international legal theory, I have prefaced the various conversations with three overviews of the discipline. Each of these survey pieces is both descriptive and analytic. The authors make genuine contributions to the continuing development of international law as well as supplying maps of some fragments of international studies.

The first conversation piece concerns that hardy perennial, 'Is international law, law?'. Despite Tom Franck's admonition to the effect that we are in a post-ontological age in international legal studies, it is surely the case that arguments will continue to rage over what sort of law or beast is international law. The six essays included here each answer the question in a different way. Sometimes that answer will be resoundingly affirmative as it is for Oppenheim and D'Amato (Chapters 4 and 5); at other times, it is suffused with ambivalence. Each essay answers the question in a confident and distinctive manner.

The collection then goes on to investigate the sources of law. Although this is the subject of another collection in the series, I have chosen to focus on it because it brings into relief the most ancient of all disagreements over the nature of international law – that is, that between natural lawyers (naturalists) and positivists.

In thinking about the nature of international law, we must inevitably consider the nature of the participants themselves. Here, again, we engage with a familiar debate in the discipline. Does international law regulate the behaviour of states alone? Is it, in effect, interstate law? Or is personality disparate? Are non-governmental organizations, international organizations and even individuals, actors within the system? What effects might these actors have?

The collection concludes with three more specific questions about the normative aspirations of the international legal order. Is it netural? Is it just? Is it democratic? Here, I first consider a traditional question concerning justice. This resembles the debate between naturalists and positivists but is updated by Tom Franck's Rawlsian re-workings. A more recently theorized debate concerns the relationship of politics (here defined much more widely than the realists would define it) and law. Is law ideologically neutral? Can it be? The challenge to the notion of neutrality or impartiality comes from critiques based on gender, language and culture. The final pair of essays is suitably millennial in tone. These concern the so-called democracy norm. Assessed here are implications for international law of neo-Kantian views about republican transnationalism and Fukuyama's end of history.

Three Overviews

The first three essays provide a panoramic view of the field, although in each case the field is somewhat different. In the opening essay, Martin Wight, the British international relations specialist, brings his distinctive powers of description and analysis to bear on the field of international studies. His typologies of the philosophies of international order are rightly celebrated for their clarity and independence of mind. These international relations theories (which are also, in effect, ways of approaching international law) are linked more explicitly to international law in Anne-Marie Slaughter's influential essay (Chapter 2). The remaining essay in Part I is more narrowly focused on international law scholarship alone. In it, Deborah Cass distinguishes Newstream and Mainstream international legal thought in order to present an analysis, history and navigation of the former.

Wight's essay (Chapter 1) discusses three theories of international thought.[3] His argument is that international studies (which I take to encompass both international law and international relations) can be approached from one of three distinctive philosophical perspectives, which he terms 'realist', 'rationalist' and 'revolutionist'. These three perspectives provide a useful, if partial, introduction to the various essays included in this collection.

According to Wight, each of these three theories (or patterns of thought) corresponds to an ingredient or condition of the international legal order. Realism emphasizes the condition of international anarchy (the absence of a world sovereign). The processes of state interaction (including those regulated by law) are stressed in the rationalist approach to international studies. Finally, notions of moral solidarity or global society find expression in theories variously known as revolutionist or cosmopolitan.

The realist tradition is represented in Wight's scheme by Machiavelli, Hobbes and Spinoza and takes as its focus the idea of international relations as a lawless state of nature, a *bellum omnium contra omnes*. Power is the dominant force here. There can be no justice, no society and very little law in a political environment in which power is anterior. States must, and will, inevitably seek security, power, prestige, status and, ultimately, survival in this hostile environment. Neither compliance with law (rationalism) nor the promotion of moral solidarity or democracy or human rights (revolutionism) is likely to be uppermost in the minds of statesmen steering their states through the system.[4] Nor should it be, according to the realists. This realist tradition is represented in this collection by Morgenthau (Chapter 6) and Grieco (Chapter 7).

The rationalist tradition, or the classical international law conception, accepts that international affairs occur in a state of nature but takes a kinder, gentler view of this state. Of these thinkers, Locke and Grotius are the masters. Locke argued that the state of nature was the place of sociability and goodwill. This state, then, was deemed capable of generating the sort of minimal social contract upon which an international legal order can be based (Locke, 1954; Grotius, 1925). The traditions of thought described below as positivist, Grotian and statist (despite their differences) belong in this category. Natural lawyers hover somewhere between this rationalist view and the revolutionists discussed next.

Those who emphasize moral solidarity, individual rights or world citizenship Wight describes as revolutionists because they wish to do away with what is seen as an illegitimate state of affairs operating in international order (p. 6). The interstate system and anarchy (givens for rationalists and realists) are temporary aberrations on the path to enlightened federative unions (Kantianism), political revolution (Marx) or world government or cosmopoli of varying strengths (Zolo, Falk). In its darker moments this revolutionism takes Stalinist or fascist forms. Wight is very sceptical of revolutionisms describing them as 'doctrinal imperialisms' and tracing them from Philip II of Spain to Nikita Krushchev. He contrasts two forms of revolutionism – catastrophic and evolutionary. I have included no catastrophic revolutionisms in this collection (Marxist international law is absent) but among the evolutionary revolutionists (we must forgive the oxymoron) are included the liberal internationalists (for example, Tesón and Slaughter).

A number of scholars fit rather uneasily into any of Wight's categories. Feminism is difficult to characterize although it undoubtedly contains elements of both rationalism and revolutionism. Koh's 'transnationalism' is basically rationalist but it rejects rationalism's fixation on the interstate system (and, to that extent, it contains traces of revolutionism). Meanwhile, Newstream scholars (Koskenniemi and Anghie) are uncategorizable, though Anghie's critique of international law is mildly revolutionist.

Wight concludes with two provocative lines of inquiry. The first maps these theoretical preferences on to psychological dispositions in the manner of Max Weber. For the purposes of this collection one might say that Morgenthau and Grieco are merely displaying a sense of proportion, Oppenheim a feeling of responsibility and Tesón and Slaughter a passionate devotion to cause. I suspect things are more complicated. The second consists of Wight's very tentative attempt to apply these theories to living politics. How much do these patterns of thought tell us about behaviour? This should perhaps be the test of subsequent readings in this collection.

In coming to an understanding of the nature of international law one must situate it more fully within the general literature on international studies summarized by Wight in this first essay. The relationship between international law and international relations has not been a particularly happy one. Although both disciplines explore the same set of social phenomena, there has been very little in the way of a fruitful dialogue between them.

In an essay, published in 1993, Anne-Marie Slaughter (Chapter 2) advocates greater interdisciplinary dialogue. This dialogue, she argues, can most productively occur around two positions characterized as institutionalist (a form of rationalism) and liberal (a form of 'evolutionary revolutionism'). Each of these programmes of belief can be seen as a response to the realist mainstream in international studies. Slaughter's essay is interesting because it takes a modified version of Wight's categories and locates international law more fully in them (see also Slaughter *et al.*, 1998; Scott, 1994).

In the first section of the essay, she characterizes the postwar political realism of scholars such as Morgenthau as a reaction to certain forms of international law idealism (in particular Woodrow Wilson's liberal internationalism) found in the interwar period. This debate was one conducted between realism and revolutionism (to translate into Wight's categories). Wilson wished to change the world by abolishing war and recourse to secret treaties and by establishing bodies like the League of Nations. When this project failed with the rise of fascism and the Second World War, realists believed they had found confirmation for their chief presupposition (that the international order is anarchical and threatening). The postwar debate revolved round this newly ascendant political realism and a chastened, rationalist international law. However, both fields became more fluid as the postwar era proceeds. A group of rationalist international relations scholars known as regime theorists or institutionalists came to embrace the idea that international norms and organizations can modify state behaviour and provide some measure of cooperation.[5] This has the potential to give rise to a sort of rationalist/Lockean consensus between international lawyers and institutionalists (each concerned with mitigating the worst effects of the state of nature).

Slaughter welcomes this development but concludes by calling for a liberal internationalist approach to international law – one that takes seriously preferences internal to the state and builds on the empirical insights of the democratic peace school (arguing that democratic states are less likely to go to war – see, for example, Tesón, Chapter 18). This is a move towards what Wight characterizes as evolutionary revolutionism although it is more grounded in empirically testable developments in international affairs than the revolutionism of, say, Wilson or Lenin.

Both Slaughter's and Wight's taxonomies operate in the modernist tradition. For all their differences, realists, rationalists and various revolutionists (liberal internationalists, cosmopolitans, Wilsonian idealists, Marxists) all derive their core assumptions from the political philosophies of the Enlightenment. Each of them is prescriptive, each operates in epistemologically positivist mode and each purports to describe a world 'out there'. The complications of indeterminacy, language, signification and culture are not yet present in these writings.

In her essay, Deborah Cass (Chapter 3) describes this modernist tradition as the 'Mainstream'. Each of Wight's and Slaughter's divergent patterns of thought is captured in this single phrase. Cass is mainly concerned with the rationalist limb of the Mainstream (that is, the classic positivist and pragmatist traditions in international law). However, there is little doubt that her references to the Mainstream can also apply to more radical variants of this stream, such as liberal internationalisms and cosmopolitanisms .

According to Cass, the Newstream scholars (see Boyle, Koskenniemi, Knop and Anghie (Chapters 10, 12–15)) can be distinguished from their Mainstream counterparts on a number of grounds. First of all, they demonstrate a concern for the cultural determinants of international law that is mostly missing in the work of their Mainstream counterparts. Second, they have interrogated notions of sovereignty thought to be stable and secure by the Mainstream. For the Newstream, sovereignty is a historically contingent concept developed out of a particular cultural and political matrix (see Anghie, Chapter 15). Third, they employ the insights of postmodern thought to show the constitutive, as opposed to the merely descriptive, nature of language. Thus, the discourse of international law becomes critical along with the argumentative structures (Kennedy, 1980; Koskenniemi, 1990) used to suppress its political, cultural and gendered foundations (Koskenniemi, Chapter 12; Boyle, Chapter 10; Anghie, Chapter 15; Knop, Chapter 14).

The differences between Newstream and Mainstream scholarship are not simply matters of substance or philosophy. As Cass demonstrates nicely, Newstream writers tend to adopt a personal style mostly alien to the more traditional writers. In the hands of some Newstream writers, international law becomes more personal quest than objective science (Kennedy, 1980; cf. Oppenheim, Chapter 4). There is little doubt that Newstream thought, for all its enigmatic qualities, represents one of the more exciting developments in international law. Its freshness of perspective and innovative methods have challenged traditional modes of thought in the discipline.

Is International Law, Law?

The study of international law poses some fascinating jurisprudential questions. The very nature or essence of legality becomes an issue as soon as one begins examining this highly distinctive legal order. How are compliance, legitimacy and efficacy ensured in a system with no centralized enforcement mechanisms? How are the validity and content of rules to be ascertained in the absence of an authoritative law-creating body or sovereign?

These questions have given rise to a number of interesting and divergent answers. I have identified five prominent responses here. To a certain extent, the differences between these various schools can be overstated. Realists and the Newstream each take politics seriously. The New Haven approach and legitimacy theory each attempt to escape semantic considerations of the meaning of law. Regime theorists and legalists share a belief in the modifying and constraining role of law and institutions.

I begin with the legalists. In one of the first essays published in the *American Journal of International Law*, Oppenheim (Chapter 4) lays down his views on the task and method of international law.[6] I have described this as the legalist approach although Oppenheim himself would have disliked the label. It is legalist in the sense that it sees the primary task of the lawyer as rule exposition. The nature of international law is that of a rule-bound system of interstate intercourse. Oppenheim's legalism comes through strongly in his advocacy of arbitral and judicial methods for resolving interstate disputes and in his general optimism about legal methods. This can be compared with some of the other essays in Part II, which emphasize regimes or language or power over rules.

Oppenheim is keen to promote a science of international law. The word 'science' is crucial. By 'science' Oppenheim means an international legal order capable of generating validity, objectivity and determinacy. The best method for achieving this is the positivist method, and he has much to say about the merits of this method. He compares positivism (the science of international law) with two other approaches – natural law and scepticism. Natural law is rejected as anachronistic and imprecise. Those who deny the very existence of international law (sceptics) are criticized for having failed to see the many forms law can take in a political order.

Oppenheim is distinguishable from Morgenthau on many counts. He wants to rid the system of political bias (for Morgenthau this is an impossibility), he believes in the efficacy of written rules and, at one point, he describes the triumph of international law over anarchy (Morgenthau and the realists argue the opposite). Nonetheless, Morgenthau would have had some sympathy for many of Oppenheim's concerns. In particular, Oppenheim's advocacy of an international law situated in history, practice and political context would ring true for both realists and members of the more critical schools discussed later in this Introduction. Oppenheim was no naive idealist. His legalism was a rigorous, 'realistic' science rather than empty sloganeering.

Anthony D'Amato's essay (Chapter 5) is a sterling and explicit defence of international law's 'lawness' (see also Brownlie, 1981; Watts, 1993). Against those who would question international law's claim to be a living legal order, D'Amato advances three arguments. First, he shows that law does not depend on enforcement for its legitimacy. Compliance in most functioning legal orders is automatic, resulting not from a fear of sanction but from habit, reciprocity and respect. International law is no different. True, some states break the law (and sometimes with apparent impunity) but this is no different from domestic criminal law where laws are broken and the perpetrators remain at liberty. Second, states and diplomats speak the language of law in their communications with each other. Many international lawyers assert that it would seem absurd to deny these communications the label, 'law', according to some abstract, hypothetical test divorced from social or intersubjective reality. Third, D'Amato believes that the strongest argument is one based on 'reciprocal entitlements'. According to this view, international law is enforced, albeit in a diffuse, decentralized and, often, bilateral manner. States that break the law are 'punished' through a loss of legal entitlements – for example, a state that uses force against another state might find that its own rights to territorial integrity are seriously impaired or a state that violates rules of diplomatic immunity might lose control over its financial deposits abroad.

In contrast, realists have been hostile to international law, believing it to be deficient both instrumentally and morally. Realism, as a science of international politics, grew out of a profound disillusionment with the international law idealism of the interwar years. To paraphrase E.H. Carr (1946, p. 10), by 1939 international law had become associated with wishing; and realism with thinking. Realists believed international lawyers to be immersed either in an irrelevant scholasticism (deciphering the meaning of legal texts, which had little impact on real international affairs) or in utopian speculation (proposing solutions for unattainable new world orders) and institution-building (the League of Nations). All this was described by leading realists as legalistic moralism. This is an important and damaging critique. Realists were not simply saying that international law was marginal or merely moral aspiration, they were also arguing that it encouraged a lack of prudence and restraint in international affairs that led to a neglect of power politics and a tendency to appease the evil manifestations of this politics.

Hans Morgenthau was regarded as a leading exponent of this brand of classical realism.[7] However, Morgenthau had begun his professional life as an international lawyer, and concern for, and understanding of, law is found in his writings. Many of the realist themes mentioned above are found in his 1940 essay, reproduced here as Chapter 6. Morgenthau is scathing about the proliferation of ineffective international organizations and the dominance, in international law scholarship, of a positivism detached from the facts of international social life.[8] This legal positivism is criticized for lacking social and political context, for failing to appreciate its own metaphysical foundations (even while attempting their obliteration) and for underestimating the significance of interpretation in changing the meaning of legal texts situated in history (p. 170). What is remarkable about these criticisms is that they closely mirror the assault on legal liberalism/positivism led by the critical legal studies Newstream half a century later (see Koskenniemi, (Chapter 13)).

Morgenthau, unlike the neo-realists who followed him, was not so dismissive of law that he could not see a way of rehabilitating it. His solution, propounded in this essay, was to adopt a functional approach.[9] This was basically an attempt to marry realism to international law, but the marriage was an unsatisfactory one viewed from the perspective of the legal partner. According to Morgenthau, international law existed either where states possessed 'identical interests' or where such rules could be enforced by major powers through the balance of power. Their validity could be assessed only through an empirical examination of likely or actual compliance. Here, to the dismay of international lawyers, international law is reduced to politics. It becomes, in Martti Koskenniemi's words, pure 'apology' (Koskenniemi, 1989).

In Chapter 7 Joseph Grieco picks up these realist insights and develops them further, telling us a great deal about the modern neo-realist conception of international law (in part by failing to mention international law at all). In order to appreciate the relevance of Grieco's essay to this collection one can usefully substitute international law for his term, 'liberal institutionalism' (even though they are not identical – see Slaughter, Chapter 2). Here, Grieco sets out the central ideas of the realist approach to international order and compares them to the one that he characterizes as liberal institutionalism, which encompasses a number of different approaches: functionalism, neo-functionalism and certain forms of regime theory.

For our purposes, it is important to understand liberal institutionalism as a theory of international relations sympathetic to international law. For institutionalists, law (along with, for example, organizations, expectations and norms) makes a difference to the way in which states behave. States collaborate in institutions because the collective benefits of such collaboration are large. International lawyers often explain states' readiness to comply with international law in similar terms. International law works because states benefit from it and enjoy absolute gains as a result of adhering to its rules. Grieco challenges these assumptions from a realist standpoint. The most important insight of the essay draws on the consequence of anarchy in the international system. Anarchy in the international order represents the absence of a centralized, vertical structure of law creation and enforcement. For realists, anarchy is the single most important structural feature in the international system – hence the use of the term 'structural realists' to describe Kenneth Waltz (1979) and his followers. Anarchy is a defining phenomenon of world order because it makes the system one in which survival and security are the central concerns of states.

International lawyers have responded to this insight in a number of different ways. Some have argued that the system is not anarchical in that the General Assembly, Security Council and International Court of Justice represent, at least incipient, central authorities (MacDonald, 1987), and others have argued that the realist focus on states is misleading (see Schreuer, 1993; Koh, Chapter 11). The international order is said to be constituted by a number of different actors for whom survival and security are not primary concerns. The most typical legalist response to the anarchy problem is to argue that the system is anarchical but that states, in well designed regimes and institutions, can pursue collective goals in a cooperative manner. So cooperation and anarchy are compatible.

Grieco argues that the absolute gains enjoyed by states in cooperative regimes may not satisfy their need for survival. This is because security and survival are relational. States can only survive if they maintain a certain degree of strength vis-à-vis their competitor states. Accordingly, State A and State B could enjoy absolute gains from participation in the international legal process or international organizations but it is likely that one state (say, State A) will gain more than the other (State B). For realists, this means that, while State B has made absolute gains (it is better off as measured against its previous performance), it has incurred a relative loss and is weaker in the context of an international system marked by anarchy. These relative losses can result in strong disincentives to participate in international law and international regimes. Grieco's argument is one that works even when international law works. Indeed, it is the very success of cooperative legal schemes that produces a different set of security dilemmas and existential anxieties among states.[10]

For the New Haven School, law is neither power (as for the realists) nor rules (as for the positivists and legalists). Instead, it is a process of rational decision-making in pursuit of community goals underpinned by a commitment to the promotion of human dignity. Law consists of decisions that are authoritative (being the product of right or legitimate process) and effective. And these laws are assessed not for their conformity to some written text but rather for their capacity to meet certain desirable ends and goals. We can see that, in looking at a legal order, New Haven scholars take a much wider view than the typical positivist.

Advocates of the New Haven approach will tend to examine social processes as a whole rather than separate some obviously legal elements and study them. In Michael Reisman's phrase, theirs is a 'cultural anthropology' of law (p. 212). This has important implications for the way the relevant participants in the international legal process are viewed (See Part IV). Clearly, scholars of the New Haven School regard international law as more than simply interstate law (in which respect they depart from positivists and realists alike). They argue that, in order to understand the international legal process, it is necessary to observe all the different types of participant – for example, non-governmental organizations, individuals and pressure groups (see, further, McDougal *et al.*, 1968; Falk, 1989; McDougal, 1985–86).

Ultimately, the New Haven approach is one immersed in social science techniques applied to law. The facts of social life are manifold. In this sense, the New Haven approach is 'superpositivism' or sociological positivism – a positivism that analyses and describes more than simply legal rules and processes. In another sense, the New Haven approach resembles an updated naturalism. The references to community values and world order goals give a flavour of this neo-naturalism. It is this combination of secular naturalism and sociological positivism that makes the New Haven approach distinctive and significant.

Tom Franck draws on the New Haven concern with process over rule in his intellectually powerful defence of international law, *The Power of Legitimacy Among Nations* (1990). The ideas in this book are given an earlier airing in the essay reproduced here as Chapter 9. In Franck's view, the debates about whether international law is a fundamentally rule-oriented or policy-oriented system ought now to be set aside in favour of a concept of law that measures legitimacy instead of legality (Watson, 1980) or strict validity (as advocated by Kelsen). The question becomes not whether a rule exists or whether a text is law but rather whether a particular norm has attained legitimacy and effectiveness. To put it more simply, why is it that states in a system dependent on voluntary compliance with law continue to obey the law even when such obedience runs contrary to the state's immediate self-interest? Or, to narrow the question still further, why is that some laws exert more pull to compliance than others? What do these rules possess that other rules lack?

For Franck, the answer lies in an examination of legitimacy. Legitimacy is important because only legitimate rules or norms (that is, rules created in accordance with right process) will have sufficient pull to compliance. In other words, states will obey only laws or norms or texts or rules that exhibit certain positive qualities. For Franck, these qualities are fourfold. First, a norm ought to have a certain degree of *textual determinacy*. It ought to possess clarity and transparency. Of course, all good norms carry a certain amount of flexibility and detail also but, at the very least, states must be able to tell what a particular rule permits or mandates. This determinacy is found in the text itself and is strengthened by the presence of processes and institutions capable of authoritatively interpreting ambiguous texts. Second, norms must possess *pedigree* or symbolic validation. They must be created according to some sort of right process, and that process will be more effective if it is accompanied by a set of rituals or legitimating signals that have meaning within the system. These are often venerable rituals designed to establish the authority of the norms created – for example, titles and prerogatives found in diplomatic practice. Third, norms ought to be *coherent*. They ought to treat like cases alike and make exceptions on a rational and principled basis. A norm ought also to be consistent with the network of rules and principles within which it is embedded. Finally, the particular norm in question is much more likely to be accorded legitimacy if it possesses *adherence* – that is, if it conforms to rules, principles and norms above it on the international law hierarchy. In particular, the norm must make sense in an international order defined by at least some embryonic notions of community.

The implications of Franck's thesis are considerable. If he is correct, then it demands that international lawyers leave aside questions of ontology and continue instead with the pressing task of perfecting a system of rules and norms with maximum legitimacy and, therefore, pull to compliance.

David Kennedy doubts whether international law in its current state of crisis is capable of perfecting itself in the manner described by Franck. In an occasionally recondite essay entitled 'Theses About International Law Discourse' (included in a companion collection on *The Sources of International Law*), Kennedy was the first consciously to apply to international law ideas derived from the critical legal studies movement and was influential in creating the international law Newstream.[11] According to Kennedy, international law is best understood by focusing on its discursive patterns as opposed to, say, its effect on diplomatic practice. As these patterns or structures of argument constitute the discipline, his focus is on the categories or styles of argumentation that repeat themselves across all areas of international law. These patterns come in binary form and ultimately rest on the inherent contradiction in international legal doctrine (and liberal theory generally) between autonomy and community. All arguments couched in international law talk are arranged around this opposition. Kennedy, anticipating the later work of Martti Koskenniemi, emphasizes that this contradiction is not capable of resolution. This is what makes international law manipulable, indeterminate and ideological. This indeterminacy results in a legal system that cannot determine or control outcomes. It cannot produce strictly legal results – that is, results mandated by the legal materials.

Many of these arguments have become familiar through caricature and others have been misrepresented. It is therefore important to understand what Kennedy is not saying in his essay. First, he is not making the claim that legal argument fails to convince (p. 357). Clearly it does. Decisions are made, judgements rendered and clients are satisfied. However, for Kennedy and the Newstream, the plausibility or, rather, the conclusiveness of these outcomes rests not on their legal accuracy or definitiveness but on other qualities – for example, the skill of the advocate, the aesthetic appeal of the argument. '"Being convinced", then, is a matter of giving up the fight, or of accepting the unstated moral and/or political values which lie beneath a line of reasoning' (p. 357). Second, Kennedy is not arguing that diplomats disregard international law. He is not a political realist in this sense. The argument, instead, is that international law could not plausibly constrain diplomats. Of course, states do obey but for reasons other than the force of legal argument. Finally, and most importantly, Kennedy does not argue that it is 'all politics' or that international legal argument is unconstrained and anarchic. In fact, the essay is an intricate description of a highly patterned form of argumentation. Only highly skilled practitioners can manage it. International law discourse has a structure and that structure is endemic in argumentation but the structure, by its very nature, cannot generate definitive outcomes.

Ultimately for Kennedy, the crisis in international law could give rise to a productive scholarship focusing not on perfecting the system (Franck) or developing a science of international law (Oppenheim, Chapter 4) or on choosing positivism (Watson, 1980) over naturalism (MacDonald, 1987) but on studying the discursive patterns reproduced in international law argument with a view to transforming that discourse and uncovering '...the structure of the dilemma which lies beneath' (at p. 391).

What is the Source of Law?

International law, for much of the pre-modern period, was a subject *constituted* by the differences between naturalists and positivists (see Nussbaum, 1947; Purvis, 1991). This debate has been somewhat superseded by recent theoretical developments. Nonetheless, it remains a discipline-defining dispute, and even theoretical literature that goes well beyond the parameters of the 'classical' period often contains traces of this argument – see, for example, Martti Koskenniemi's *From Apology to Utopia* (1989) and Thomas Franck's *Fairness in International Law and Institutions* (1995).

It is important to recognize, too, that both schools remained firmly in the legalist camp, so both naturalism and positivism are arguments *against* a realist approach to international relations. This is not always apparent. Realists in international relations are often described as having adopted a positivist epistemology while James Watson (1980), in a defence of legal positivism, describes his position as 'realistic jurisprudence'. The critical distinction to keep in mind here is that between a scepticism as to the reality, efficacy or existence of international law (realism) and arguments about the source of a law that is assumed to already exist (positivism and naturalism). This debate between naturalists and positivists can be traced through the scholarship of modern writers such as James Watson (1980) and Ronald MacDonald (1987). A characterization of the debates between natural lawyers and positivists can be found in the essay by Boyle, which is included as Chapter 10 of this collection.

The positivists' credo is based on a belief that international law is a human creation, discoverable by scientific method, capable of being defined with some certainty and with an identifiable content. Law, then, is the product of right process combined with authoritative institutional interpretation and sanction. Its normative status is derived from state consent (to treaties, to customary law), and this state consent is a sociological fact. Accordingly it can be analysed, described and ascertained with a degree of detachment, objectivity and rigour. This is the gist of James Watson's argument in a provocative and forthright essay (Watson, 1980). Watson laments the tendency among international lawyers to indulge in wishful thinking about what the law ought to be, particularly when this tendency carries over into utopian prescription (the law ought to be like this) or, worse, inaccurate description (this, despite what states actually do, is what the law is). This almost exactly parallels similar complaints made by Oppenheim in 1908 when he described the 'book rules' of many treatises as 'mere fancies' (p. 114, this volume). International lawyers ought to restrict themselves to modest analysis and description of the law as reflected in the practice of states. It is this practice, reflective of state consent, which provides the test for a putative norm of international law.

International law, according to positivists, is decentralized, reciprocal and consensual. Naturalists imagine it to be hierarchical, centralized and coercive whereas, according to positivists, international law possesses none of these qualities (although one is free to wish that it did). In this decentralized system – that is, one without world government or law-generating legislature, it is critical that norms be certain in order to ensure compliance (see Franck, Chapter 9). This is especially so in a system where the temptation to depart from legal standards is so great. States will only obey laws that are precise, certain and determinate. Laws postulated on the basis of community values or world order or 'value judgements' (Watson, 1980, p. 269) will be vague and inefficacious. Typical of what Watson disparages as 'New Approaches' are writings that derive international law from General Assembly Resolutions or community standards or International Court of Justice 'Activism'. Only those laws embedded in state consent and practice have any hope of achieving, what Tom Franck calls, 'legitimacy'.

These are important and often neglected arguments. Prosper Weil (1983) in another defence of positivism (see also 'The Sources of International Law', ed. Koskenniemi), offers a more detailed and theoretical account of the alleged deficiencies of the modern, neo-naturalist approaches. These writings cannot be dismissed lightly and yet positivism has been widely derided in recent years. Rare is the essay that engages fully with the positivist agenda, although two later essays do precisely this. One is John Tasiouslas's combative reply to Weil and the other is Alain Pellet's response to Weil (Weil, 1983; Tasioulas, 1996 (included in *The Sources of International Law*, ed. Koskenniemi); Pellet, 1992). This modern debate around two ancient traditions has been one of the most fascinating and scholarly in recent literature.

Naturalism in international law can be defined as a philosophical commitment to the existence of certain higher values within the international legal system. These values have their source not in state consent or behaviour but in some normative universe existing above states. These values can be used to judge state behaviour against some objective normative standard. Naturalism manifests itself in at least three distinct periods in international legal development. First, there is a religious phase during which values derived from Scripture take their place as the highest norms in the international order. Second, there is the secularization of natural law where human reason provides access to certain immutable and core principles of international order. Finally, there is the modern communitarian period in which natural or higher principles are derived from the needs of the international order, from the overall spirit of that order or from basic, foundational ideas central to that order.

Some writers have put the case for a continuing natural law influence in international law, along communitarian lines and expressed through the existence of higher norms or a hierarchy of principles. It is this hierarchy that Weil (1983) refers to, disapprovingly, as 'relative normativity'. Natural law sympathizers contend that reference to higher laws, universal moral standards or natural law norms has occurred throughout the history of international law notwithstanding the absence of much concern for these norms in the theory of international law. So, while, Suarez, Vitoria and the Nuremburg Trials may represent high water marks of the natural law tradition, international law, in all its phases, is replete with naturalism (MacDonald, 1987).

These higher norms can be found in several areas of the international legal order. First, the United Nations Charter can be said to represent some sort of higher law for the international community, based on the applicability of its principles to non-members (Article 103) and its quasi-legislative capacity. Second, the recent history of the *jus cogens* norm, the idea of obligations *erga omnes* and objective treaty regimes are evidence of the persistence of some sort of supernormativity in the international legal order. Each of these doctrines or principles is founded on the notion of a coercive moral order standing above states and capable of being used to determine the lawfulness of their behaviour. Most importantly, these norms represent the glue that might hold the system together. They represent the initial stages in building a system in which fairness and legitimacy are enhanced (MacDonald, 1987).

There have been attempts to transcend this debate between naturalists and positivists or, at least, to reconcile the positions within it. Many of these projects are described as 'Grotian', after Hugo Grotius. Grotius' classic text, *De jure belli ac pacis* fuses, or at least leans on, elements of both the natural law and the positivist tradition in attempting to systematize international law.[12] However, the use of the term 'Grotian' can lead to some confusion. In international studies it has come to signify four different things. First, 'Grotianism' is the term used to describe international legal philosophy that incorporates elements of natural law and positivism. In that sense, the Grotian perspective belongs here in Part II about the sources of international law. Second, it is used in international relations literature to stake out a middle ground between realism and cosmopolitanism. Here, Grotianism is used as a byword for the whole project of regulating international affairs using liberal legal techniques. It is neither revolutionary (like cosmopolitanism) nor is it entirely political (like realism). Grotius is situated between Kant and Hobbes on this spectrum (see, generally, Martin Wight). Third, the term 'Grotianism' is applied to conceptions of world order that allow for the coexistence of states (in the dominant role) and other entities (such as individuals and non-governmental organizations). In this sense, the Grotian perspective could be seen as a compromise between Koh's end of the state and realism's celebration of it (see Part IV). Fourth, and finally, 'Grotian' can be used to describe Grotius' own idiosyncratic approach to international law (Lauterpacht, 1946).

If Grotius effects a partial compromise between the natural law and positivist positions, James Boyle (Chapter 10) urges international lawyers to turn their backs on the search for essences or definitions or ultimate sources altogether. For him, the debate between naturalists and positivists is not just mistaken or misplaced but damaging to the discipline. International legal scholarship in this mode lacks a social theory capable of explaining its effects on the social world. Instead, what these endless argumentative and philosophical moves accomplish is the reification of contested political preferences. In other words, such preferences are transformed by international law scholarship and doctrine from ideas into apparently neutral truths or facts.

To take an example, naturalists and positivists both converge in their belief that international law has some essence or purpose that can help determine doctrine and shape the future of international law. The disagreement lies in the particular form of these essences or the concrete purpose that might direct international law. For all their differences, positivists and naturalists rely on the same assumptions about the existence of essence or purpose. But these assumptions are not part of the debate. They are self-standing 'facts' or ideas given the status of facts. The question, 'What is the purpose of international law?' 'reifies' the idea that there is a purpose, thereby closing off debate on this issue (while permitting debate only on the content of that purpose).

Worse, neither positivism nor naturalism is coherent on its own (reified) terms, and Boyle shows how each depends on a form of reasoning derived from the other. These reversibility arguments will be familiar from the work of David Kennedy. Positivism must demonstrate why consent or autonomy or sovereignty are central to the legitimating concepts of the system. Yet to do so would be to lapse into the sort of naturalism they decry. Equally, natural lawyers, if they are to avoid 'hopeless idealism' (p. 286), must ground their project on consent or state practice – that is, the very practices which their higher normative structures are purporting to judge.

This problem with the classic positions is replayed in later arguments between neo-naturalists (such as McDougal and the New Haven School) and modern positivists (such as Weil and Watson). Each is required to privilege a certain purpose – human dignity (McDougal) or stability (Watson) – but cannot explain from where this purpose is derived or why a universal value should carry so much weight in a scientific appraisal of behaviour. Those who seek to avoid value claims by simply studying the behaviour of states (for example, Henkin, 1979) cannot, according to Boyle, then explain how law comes to have any normative role in regulating this behaviour.

Who Are the Primary Actors?

Traditionally, the fundamental nature of the international legal system has been conceived of as statist. This view, associated with positivist conceptions, has been dominant from the Peace of Westphalia until relatively recently. One can see in the writings of realists like Morgenthau and positivists such as Oppenheim that the statist image of the international order had a powerful hold over even modern writers.

Of course, non-statist models of international order have existed prior to Westphalia and the vestiges of these systems remained in place until quite late in the nineteenth century. In the second half of the twentieth century, there existed another set of challenges to this statist model but, this time, not from some overarching empire or nascent world government but rather from the sheer range and diversity of participants in the international system. The impact of sub-state entities, international institutions and confederate structures indicate that the state is no longer the only game in town. This all has implications for international legal processes. International organizations enter into treaties, sub-state entities contribute to the formation of custom and federal units influence the development of general principles. The relationship between domestic law and international law is complicated by this move to diverse participation, and territory and membership have become much more contested terms.

Harold Koh in his 1994 Roscoe Pound Lecture at the University of Nebraska, (reproduced as Chapter 11) expands on some of these ideas and suggests that statist conceptions of international law are under challenge from a fully theorised accompaniment to the waning of the state: transnational legal process. This transnational legal process is defined as:

> ...the theory and practice of how public and private actors – nation-states, international organizations, multinational enterprises, non-governmental organizations, and private individuals – interact in a variety of public and private, domestic and international fora to make, interpret, enforce, and ultimately, internalize rules of international law. (pp. 313–14).

This is a complete rejection of the statist view of international law. The relevant actors in the international system are all the participants in that system. International law norms are disseminated and absorbed by all these actors operating in different capacities and spheres. The Security Council, the International Committee of the Red Cross, the Basle Club, the World Trade Organization, Greenpeace, and even Koh's Human Rights Clinic at Yale University, play a part in developing and influencing the legal system.

Koh's essay is about more than simply the range of participants in the international legal order; it is also about how compliance is secured in this decentralized system among this diffuse collection of actors. So, Koh can be read as a response to Watson and Slaughter, as well as to Koskenniemi. According to Koh, the regime theorists (described by Slaughter as institutionalists) have made progress in alerting us as to why states obey law in certain spheres, such as trade and arms control, but they have little to tell us about the role of non-state actors nor can they explain what ensures compliance in areas such as human rights law or debt relief. The liberal internationalists, like Slaughter and Tesón, do a better job of assessing the role of non-state actors and domestic politics, yet they are less good at explaining why international law secures compliance among non-democratic states or how domestic political positions are themselves constituted. In these areas, transnational legal process provides the tools. In the vast majority of cases compliance with international law is assured through a process of learning and interaction combined with the internalization of the rules and processes produced through interaction.

In Chapter 12 Martti Koskenniemi expands on these various critiques of the state. The state is under challenge from several directions. First, it is viewed as morally unsound – the tendency for centralized territorial power to lead to abuse of rights is much remarked upon. Second, a statist conception of international order seems at odds with sociological insights into globalization, the proliferation of non-state actors and the need to adopt global responses to global issues. Third, the rise of nationalism suggests that other more authentic communities than states exist and are eager for recognition.

However, Koskenniemi tempers enthusiasm about the end of state by pointing to its continuing robustness as a form (see, for example, the defence of undemocratic Kuwait (p. 339)) and the absence of any agreement on alternatives. According to Koskenniemi, human rights, global values and nationalism are not ideas or structures capable of replacing the state. Human rights remain controversial and indeterminate. Furthermore, in the absence of world government only the state is capable of providing protection and remedy in the area of human rights. Global values remain loosely defined and intangible. Certainly there are global agendas (such as the environment and trade). Alas, as Koskenniemi says, 'Shared vocabulary does not necessarily entail unity of purpose' (p. 346). Finally, the nation hardly seems like an auspicious alternative to the state, since nationalism has tended to take on a rather frightening, violent and exclusionary aspect in recent times. In any case, many national groups challenge a state and not the idea of statehood. They wish themselves to be states. All this points to the fact that statehood is an acceptable 'second-best' – a social structure necessary to protect us from the authoritarian impulses that would require allegiance to a set of beliefs associated with a particular version of human rights, an expansionary nationalism or an adherence to one particular set of global values.

Is International Law Neutral?

Many of the writings discussed so far have assumed that international law is somehow insulated or separable from politics or culture or gender. Oppenheim refers to a science of international law with all the connotations of objectivity and detachment that phrase carries and Watson advocates an international law that conforms to some predetermined external 'reality' – for example, the practice of states. Meanwhile, Koh puts his faith in transnational legal process capable of deployment by a multitude of groups both powerful and powerless, with the special power of law being heavily emphasized. In Franck's system, pseudo-scientific tests of legitimacy are paramount.

These various grammars of the international legal order have little to say about women in particular or the racial roots of the international legal system or the political preferences at the core of international legal argument. The three essays in Part V each challenge, though in different ways, what they perceive to be international law's complacency. Each of them is very loosely allied with the critical new stream movement in international law discussed in Cass's essay (Chapter 3). However, they each carve out an individual agenda drawing on sources of inspiration far removed from the American critical legal studies movement. Koskenniemi's work is infused with more overt European influences and he takes very seriously indeed international law's classical traditions. Knop's work contains a strongly feminist agenda while Anghie reaches as much to the likes of Anand (1986) and Weeramantry (1992) for inspiration as he does to Roberto Unger (1976) and Duncan Kennedy (1997).

Martti Koskenniemi's book *From Apology to Utopia: The Structure of International Legal Argument* (1989) is changing the way in which a generation of international lawyers view the discipline. The essay included here as Chapter 13, along with a companion piece from 1990 ('The Normative Force of Habit: International Custom and Social Theory'), are condensed versions of some of the major themes taken up in that book. Koskenniemi argues that liberal international law, with its commitment to the idea of a rule of law in international affairs, is a failed attempt to escape politics. For Koskenniemi, politics comes in two forms – the politics of natural justice or normativity (utopian politics) and the politics of state preference (apologetic politics). International law is caught between these two politics. Attempts to escape one invariably end up trapped in the other. New Haven's references to world order values are utopian, while positivism's science of state consent is apologetic. Meanwhile, the pragmatic, intermediate position proceeds in happy ignorance of its own incoherence. Ultimately, international law argument is inconclusive. It cannot come too close to either of these extreme political positions without descending into mere politics. On the other hand, middle positions are inconclusive. As I have stated elsewhere:

> According to Koskenniemi all this occurs because international legal argument is structured around a series of endlessly deferred and irresolvable oppositions between the naturalist quest for normativity and the positivist demand for certainty and concreteness. These ascending patterns of justification derived from state practice (positivism) and descending patterns derived from notions of justice or international morality (naturalism) manifest themselves as apologetic (the creation of rules that simply countenance and reflect state practice and do not seek to modify it) or utopian (the drafting of principles and ideals which reflect scholarly or non-state prejudices but have little hope of gaining state support). In common with the critical legal studies project generally, the deconstruction of these patterns of argument is designed to prove that international law cannot

> escape international politics and retreat into objectivity. The rule of law cannot exist in international politics despite the best intentions of international lawyers. International law is either too close to state practice (therefore reflecting exactly the political predilections of states) or too far from state practice (therefore reliant on the politicised foundations of subjective natural justice(s)). (Simpson, 1994, p. 111)

In some ways, Koskenniemi can be read as a response to both positivism and neo-naturalism. These two positions are dependent on each other and in perpetual opposition to each other. Positivism (the concern to assess externally observable legal behaviour) requires a neo-naturalist or political or psychological explanation as to what behaviour will be deemed legally relevant. Naturalism requires the certainties and clarity of positivism in order that it can be applied (see Boyle, Chapter 10). Koskenniemi shows how this operates in relation to a series of doctrinal arguments before concluding that law cannot generate results liberated from politics; '...in the end, legitimising or criticising state behaviour is not a matter of applying formally neutral rules but depends on what one regards as politically right, or just' (p. 382) or, as he puts it in 'The Normative Force of Habit' (1990, p. 152), 'The Rule of Law is part and parcel of the politics which it hopes to constrain and arguments about the law are arguments of political preference'.

Karen Knop's essay (Chapter 14) broke ground in international law scholarship by combining the important work of Charlesworth, Chinkin and Wright on feminist approaches to international law (1992) with a Newstream sensibility. These two essays remain landmarks in the ongoing attempt to build a feminist theory of international law. Knop's essay is an exploration of the gendered nature of international law. As she points out in her introduction, 'Feminist approaches to international law... draw attention to the male environment in which international legal principles are created and applied [and] the predominantly male elites who formulate policy in foreign ministries...' (p. 386). It is clear from this that feminist international law, for all the diversifying that has occurred within it, accepts that international law is not neutral. These are critically important insights and if they seem overfamiliar today then this is a tribute to the success of feminism in gaining a foothold in the discipline. What was once ridiculed as gauche radicalism is now dismissed as cliché. This represents something of a triumph for feminist approaches (see, for example, Charlesworth, 1992; Charlesworth and Chinkin, 1993; Charlesworth, Chinkin and Wright, 1992; also Tesón, 1993).

Knop moves the feminist agenda onwards from these initial positions. Essentially it complicates both feminism and international law by examining the puzzle of statehood. It rejects monolithic views of law and statism (for example, the idea that the state is 'bad' for women). What she shows us is that the state is imagined in a number of quite different ways and the social structures generated by these imaginings have a quite varied impact on women and can be used by women to pursue diverse ends. Democratic governance theory can be employed to argue for meaningful participation on the part of disfavoured groups. Transgovernmental perspectives (see Koh, Chapter 11) can be used to buttress the idea of an international civil society into which women can insert their various agendas. The state can be reconceptualized using metaphors drawn from feminist social theory so that it ceases to be seen as a monolithic force of oppression (or liberation). Ultimately, Knop is ambivalent about the state but this ambivalence should be read as strategic opportunity rather than intellectual hesitation.

In the two major classical traditions in international law, culture, like gender, is absent. Both natural law and positivism portray international law as a system above or beyond culture. For natural lawyers, the normative foundations of the system are found in transcendental and universal precepts. These foundations are characterized as culturally neutral or transcultural. Positivists, meanwhile, developed a science of international law with general application. This technocratic tendency is designed to achieve neutrality through the objective assessment of regimes of consent. Again, the system is cleansed of both natural law's mysticism and cultural preference and foundation. This pseudo-scientific perspective carries over into modern attempts to reconstruct the international legal system by founding it on universalizable processes or organizations. Needless to say, this perspective has been challenged by writers who argue that international law is a product of a particular style of thought or a set of cultural biases or a period of Western hegemony, with international law growing out of the Western tradition. Even where this tradition has been inclusive, it cannot help but reflect its cultural roots. Another view holds that international law may achieve some sort of formal neutrality or objectivity but that its application favours powerful Western interests.

Anthony Anghie's work is a radical reassessment of these arguments. He accepts that international law was used to justify colonial expansion and is thus complicit in the maintenance of ongoing inequalities. However, Anghie's thesis goes further than this by asserting that, from the nineteenth century onwards, international law was *constituted* by its encounters with the peripheries and by the process of colonialism that ensued. In other words, the nature of international law can only be understood by reference to the relationship between positivist doctrines of international law and politico-legal techniques and norms of colonial expansion.

Anghie's essay (Chapter 15) begins with an examination of the naturalist–positivist debate already encountered in this collection. He supplements these readings by engaging in a scholarly analysis of the writings of nineteenth-century positivists. This supplies some important historical and conceptual background to the essay by Oppenheim (Chapter 4). Anghie then challenges the scienticism of the positivist approach by pointing to its reliance on foundational, sociological concepts drawn from history. While positivists worked towards abstraction – scientific, apolitical – the requirement for fundamental, legitimizing principles kept drawing them back to politics, to history and to society.

Central to Anghie's thesis is the idea that this self-styled science of human affairs was able to provide the organizing concepts for distinguishing civilized from uncivilized social groups. Thus, nineteenth-century international law became an exercise in validating colonial conquest and cultural superiority: 'The primitive was not outside international law awaiting its ordering ministrations, but rather was within the very heart of the discipline' (p. 470). Anghie's essay is important because it suggests that the dominant image of international law – the projection of order in an anarchic environment made up of equal sovereign states – tells only half the story about the nature of international law. The other half is found in international law's 'other' image. This is the image of a legal system that defines sovereignty on the basis of race and culture, and thereby deprives 'uncivilized' peoples of that sovereignty – a system that then proceeds to regulate the relationship between sovereign and non-sovereign peoples. Anghie concludes with the provocative thought that certain elements of democratic peace scholarship, neo-Kantianism and liberal internationalism threaten to reproduce the categories of distinction found in nineteenth-century international legal positivism.

What each of these essays point to is the general loss of faith in either pre-Enlightenment (naturalist) ideals or Enlightenment (positivist) science as the basis for a coherent, distinctively (or exclusively) *legal* system of law-making and law application at the international level. Law is forced to embrace context, history and equity. Only by abandoning international law's pretensions to formality, logic and autonomy can the discipline survive and grow. Philosophically indefensible certainty must give way to a postmodern condition of candid uncertainty.

Is International Law Just?

Thomas Franck's essay (Chapter 16) answers his own question in the negative. According to Franck, the international legal order is distinguishable from domestic legal systems because it lacks 'institutionalized, rule-supported coercion' and because compliance in the international system depends wholly on a rule's legitimacy, whereas in the domestic legal order legitimacy *and* justice play a part in ensuring compliance. The absence or limited relevance of justice is demonstrated on both theoretical and operational grounds. In theoretical terms, justice is unattainable in a system of sovereign states because such a system is based on the legitimacy of an unjust and arbitrary distribution of life chances. For Franck, the advantages and disadvantages conferred upon us by birth and nationality as citizens of states are accepted because these states and the interstate system offer us, or are believed to offer us, a measure of security and predictability in a hostile world. The promotion of justice might entail a diminution in state power or, at least, a less stable international order.

Operationally, justice cannot be applied to states because to do so would be to treat states as unified legal persons capable of directly experiencing pleasure and pain. This is clearly not the case. Only individuals can suffer injustice and receive just treatment. This is Franck's basic contention. But why cannot states agree to be bound by principles of justice applying to all their citizens? The answer seems to be that, while this may be theoretically possible, it simply would not happen in the present international order. Franck uses Rawls' veil of ignorance to show that state representatives placed in an hypothetical original position would tend to choose principles and rules that might seem intuitively unjust. The examples he uses are non-intervention and self-determination. In the case of non-intervention, Franck imagines representatives of the governments of the world gathering to determine what to do about a state pursuing a genocidal policy against its population. He argues that such representatives would advocate a rule of non-intervention because, from behind the veil of ignorance, they could not be certain that their own state at some point in the future would not be subject to intervention under a different rule. A similar result arises in the case of a group suffering from human rights abuses within a state. States generating principles from behind the veil of ignorance would tend not to develop a generalized right to self-determination (regardless of the justice of the present case) in case minorities within their jurisdiction began to agitate for independence.

There are three main points to make in relation to Franck's arguments. First, he assumes a statist paradigm in constructing his views on justice. As he recognizes, non-statist models might lead to different results. However such models, he argues, could not plausibly imitate present conditions. Second, it is unclear why the restrictions on the right to self-determination and the non-intervention norm are 'unjust'. Franck depends on notions of intuitive justice to measure these state responses, but the point of Rawls' argument is to expel such notions from a framework of justice. The principles generated from behind the veil of ignorance are principles of justice, not norms or policies to be judged against an already existing principle of justice. Third, Franck himself has moved on somewhat from the position he takes in this essay, in his important treatise, *Fairness in International Law and Institutions* (1995), where he discerns, in the present system, the beginnings of a system of fair and legitimate norms.

Not everyone agreed with Franck's original view of the role of justice in international order. Richard Falk's work, for example, is animated by the promise of better worlds, a more equitable international order, a global ethos and an integrated system of cosmopolitan justice. His has been a constant voice calling for change in the international order. Falk's dissatisfaction with static positivisms and cynical realisms come through strongly in his numerous writings.

What Falk calls the progressivist account of international social change (what Wight would call evolutionary revolutionism), 'envisages steady progress toward a well-ordered international community premised on moves toward the supranational implementation of human rights – inherently interventionist – the prohibition of recourse to war and the accountability of leaders' (Falk, 1992, p. 414). This can be contrasted with a minimalism (encompassing both rationalists and realists) that accepts the limitations of the present order and seeks to secure modest cooperative goals within it (see Franck, Chapter 16). Clearly, the progressivist version is more sympathetic to the incorporation of justice as a component of the international legal order. Falk describes three adaptations of this progressivist approach. The first is the World Peace through World Law School developed by Clark and Sohn in the mid-1960s. This school attempted to transform the conditions of world order through the United Nations (Clark and Sohn, 1966). A second strand of this progressivist approach is neo-Kantianism or liberal internationalism (see the work of Tesón and Slaughter). The third adaptation, and the one preferred by Falk, can be characterized as human governance and fits loosely into the World Order Model Project developed at Princeton and Yale (see, for example, Mendlovitz, 1975; Falk, 1975). This final approach is more resolutely normative, prescriptive and transformative than the former approaches.

However, several obstacles lie in the path of developing this just and humane world order. These can be divided into three: the logic of statism (see Franck, Chapters 9 and 16 and Koskenniemi, Chapters 12 and 13), the logic of realism (see Morgenthau, Chapter 6 and Grieco, Chapter 7) and the logic of the market. While states continue to be seen as the dominant actors in international law, while realists obsessed with security and power continue to dominate foreign policy in these states and while neo-liberal values continue to prevail in domestic and international political economies, justice will find less than fertile ground for development. Falk remains optimistic, though. He sees the portents of a humane world order in at least five developments. These are the approaching obsolescence of war, the emergence of transnational networks dedicated to improving planetary conditions (Koh, Chapter 11), the spread of democracy (Tesón, Chapter 18 and Slaughter, Chapter 2), the newly minted system of individual accountability (such as international criminal courts) and the challenges to the nation-state from regional integration and self-determination for local groups. All this enhances the prospects for justice in the present and future world order.

In assessing these contrasting claims of justice and fairness, one could do worse than simply look to the evidence accumulating in international legal doctrine. This is, in effect, what David Armstrong does in his essay (Chapter 17). In doing so, he finds some support for the progressivist (liberal) view that international law is moving towards a more redistributive and justice-based system of normativity. The rise of human rights, the acceptance of development rights and the use of equitable principles all suggest a consolidation of this system. However, Armstrong also relates the sceptics' tale drawn from the writings of the Newstream and the realists. According to these sceptics, international law remains mired in ideology and partiality (Newstream) or merely works round the edges of conventional doctrine in order to produce limited change (realists, positivists). Armstrong's view is the classic middle position. He argues that international law remains an interstate system (cf. realists, positivists) but believes that the nature of the state has changed. No longer are states preoccupied with their position in the state of nature. Instead, social interaction between states and democratic developments within them have created the conditions for the development of a fairness norm with mutually constitutive components both inside and outside the state (see Franck, 1995).

Is International Law Democratic?

Fernando Tesón's essay (Chapter 18) belongs in the broader traditions of cosmopolitanism and natural law. It is cosmopolitan to the extent that it envisages some sort of republican federalism operating between states that share not just the common anxieties of realism or the minimal cooperative tendencies of legalism but a richer, deeper common tradition of democratic law and values. It is naturalist to the extent that it commits international law to a set of values derived not from states but from the idea of rights. The protection of individual human rights is regarded as the central aspiration of a normative regime, so Tesón's essay is an argument against those who would deny the applicability of justice to the international system and against those who would deny that there is sufficient agreement among states or individuals as to the meaning of justice.

In Tesón's view, justice is not just possible in the international legal system but mandated. The just community, whether international or domestic, is the purpose of all social life and juridical arrangement. A just community is one in which individual human flourishing is valued above stability or order. For Tesón, as for Kant, the liberal-democratic state is the only polity capable of advancing this conception of justice. Closely associated with this assumption is the belief that liberal-democratic states are peace-loving and committed to the rule of law. A radical prescription arising from this is the principle that only liberal-democratic states should be admitted to the family of nations. Accordingly, the basic principles of international governance are that the civil constitution of every nation should be republican (or 'constitutional democracies') and that international law shall be based on a federation of free states.

There is a necessary connection between the requirements of peace and the maintenance of a system that guarantees individual liberty. This is because representative democracies ('republican states') are most likely to observe human rights standards and least inclined to engage in hostilities. Tesón offers an explanation for this and a great deal of empirical evidence. Representative democracies are founded on the consent of individuals. There is, therefore, presumed consent between the government and the people. In common with other contractarian theorists, Tesón argues that humans are rational, free and peaceable. When these traits are reflected in the formation of the constitution, governments will inherit or derive these attributes from the citizenry. When governments are despotic, autocratic or authoritarian, the state will display contempt for individual autonomy in the domestic sphere and will act in an irrational manner internationally. The key to restraint in the international sphere is the moderating influence of public opinion. The force of public opinion is supplemented by a free press and protected by a Bill of Rights while the separation of powers ensures that a system of checks and balances mitigates the tendency of executive government to act rashly, unilaterally or belligerently. Self-governing states are disinclined to go to war because the effects of war are felt by the people who, when represented in the decision-making process, will seek to avoid the privations associated with their role in the war. Finally, liberal states, in favouring a global free market, have invested too much in peace to risk it all in war. For Tesón, the free exchange of goods and persons has the dual effect of spreading common ideas and pacifying the international culture though rational communication (Simpson, 1994, pp.116–18).[13]

Tesón's work is the most radically cosmopolitan of a larger group of writings that belong in a camp variously described as liberal internationalism (Slaughter), democratic governance theory (Franck) or neo-Kantianism (Tesón) (see Slaugher, 1995). In the final chapter, Marks describes this general movement as liberal millenarianism. It is liberal in that it advocates the adoption of explicitly liberal and democratic values in international legal institutions and norms. The millenarianism is derived from Francis Fukuyama's popularization of these ideas in his studies of the end of history where he argues, suggestively, that liberal democracy is the final and ultimate form of human government (Fukuyama, 1989). Liberal democracy, according to Fukuyama, has prevailed over its contenders in the realm of political ideas (for example, Marxism, socialism and Islam). The twenty-first century and all future centuries are likely to be the centuries of liberal triumph. The work of Tesón and Franck fall into this category of thought. These international lawyers comment on the increasing incidence of democracy among world states, the normative foundations for the idea in international law, the practice of the United Nations and other international organizations in promoting elections and the moral imperatives associated with it derived from Kant: human rights and human dignity.

Susan Marks, though, has some doubts about these recent trends in international legal thought. Her doubts are fourfold. First, liberal democracy is often presented in these writings as a 'monocular' phenomenon. The diversity of practices associated with democracy is missed and the potential conflict between the liberal and democratic components of liberal democracy is underplayed. Second, democracy is too often associated with a thin, attenuated and excessively formalistic version of democratic practice which itself revolves round participation in elections. Other forms of representation are rarely considered. Third, the various critiques of liberal democracy are given short shrift in these writings. The failure of many liberal democracies to offer genuine political choice and some measure of economic equality or security is rarely referred to. Fourth, the cultural roots of democracy and their implications for the universalizability of the norm merit only passing reference in many of these writings.

Conclusion

The debate surrounding democratic governance, like many of the others documented in this collection, is unlikely to be decided quickly. Perhaps David Kennedy is right in suggesting that international law would disappear if it resolved its interminable contradictions and tensions. The discipline thrives precisely because of its ambivalence about world order. As well as this ambivalence, international law is marked by a sort of intellectual openness that, I trust, is apparent in the essays I have chosen for this collection.

Notes

1 For an example of this method as employed in international relations see Der Derian, (1994).

2 An obvious exception is the debate between naturalists and positivists about the source of legal authority to be featured in the Collection on Sources of law.

3 Martin Wight, along with the work of Hedley Bull, helped define what is known as the 'English School'. The essay included here is based on a lecture given just prior to his death and is a summary of the views found in *International Theory*, an indispensable collection of his lectures published posthumously in 1991. See Wight (1991).

4 Interestingly, Wight describes this realist view as the 'governing conception' of the United Nations Charter. For contrasting views see Slaughter, (1994).

5 Wight's terminology is not universally accepted. It is quite common to find realists and institutionalists referred to as rationalists in international relations literature in counterpoint to scholars who work in a constructivist or poststructural mode. See Cass, Chapter 3 in this volume.

6 Lassa Oppenheim was the leading English international lawyer of his generation. His text, *International Law*, is regarded as the leading work in the area; a recent edition, reworked by Arthur Watts and Robert Jennings, is the closest thing in international law to a definitive treatise.

7 The primary realist texts of the classical era are thought to be Morgenthau (1978); Kennan (1951); Niebuhr (1932).

8 Morgenthau, in common with many realists, overstates the degree to which international lawyers are said to be out of touch with reality. He says at one point, that positivists have 'no solution' to the problem of system in which, 'there are valid rules of international law other than the rules embodied in written documents' (p. 164). This is simply wrong. Positivists have long been concerned with the elaboration of unwritten customary rules. Ironically, Morgenthau sounds a little like James Watson (a positivist) in his desire for '...a criterion to distinguish, in an objective way, between *seemingly* and *actually* valid rules of international law' (p. 165, emphasis in original).

9 For a slightly different understanding of functionalism as it applies to international law see Johnston (1988).

10 For the views of at least one eminent politician see Geoffrey Howe (1984).

11 For a general bibliography of these self-styled new approaches see Kennedy and Tennant (1994); Kennedy (1988).

12 The most significant recent collection on Grotian approaches to international law and international relations is Bull, Kingsbury and Roberts (1990). See also Yasuaki (1993), especially 'Introduction' at pp. 1–10 and Tadashi, T., 'Grotius's Method' at pp. 32–57. Grotius's own great contribution to international law is, of course, *De jure belli ac pacis* (1625).

13 This description is drawn from Simpson (1994, pp. 116–18).

References

Allott, Philip (1971), 'Language, Method and the Nature of International Legal Scholarship', *British Yearbook of International Law*, **45**, pp. 79–135.
Anand, Ram Prakash (1986), *International Law and the Developing Countries*, New Dehli: Banyan Publications.
Brownlie, Ian (1981), 'The Reality and Efficacy of International Law', *British Yearbook of International Law*, **52**, pp. 1–8.
Brownlie, Ian (1983), 'Recognition in Theory and Practice' in Ronald MacDonald and Douglas Johnston (eds), *The Structure and Process of International Law*, Oxford: Clarendon Press, pp. 627–41.
Bull, Hedley (1977), *The Anarchical Society*, London: Macmillan.
Bull, Hedley, Kingsbury, Benedict and Roberts, Adam (1990), *Hugo Grotius and International Relations*, Oxford: Clarendon Press.
Carr, Edward Hallett (1946), *The Twenty Years Crisis, 1919–1939: An Introduction to the Study of International Relations*, (2nd edn), London: Macmillan.
Carty, Anthony (1991), 'Critical International Law: Recent Trends in the Theory of International Law', *European Journal of International Law*, **2**(1), pp. 66–96.
Carty, Anthony (1998), 'The Continuing Influence of Kelsen on the General Perception of the Discipline of International Law', *European Journal of International Law*, **9**(2), pp. 344–54.
Charlesworth, Hilary (1992), 'The Public/Private Distinction and the Right to Development in International Law', *Australian Yearbook of International Law*, **12**, pp. 190–204.
Charlesworth, Hilary and Chinkin, Christine (1993), 'The Gender of Jus Cogens', *Human Rights Quarterly*, **15**(1), pp. 63–76.
Charlesworth, Hilary, Chinkin, Christine and Wright, Shelley (1991), 'Feminist Approaches to International Law', *The American Journal of International Law*, **85**(4), pp. 613–45.
Chimni, B.S. (1993), *International Law and World Order: A Critique of Contemporary Approaches*, New Dehli: Sage Publications.
Clark, Grenville and Sohn, Louis B. (1966), *World Peace Through World Law*, Cambridge Mass.: Harvard University Press.
Der Derian, James (1994), *International Theory: Critical Investigations*, New York: New York University Press.
Falk, Richard A. (1975), *A Study of Future Worlds*, New York: Free Press.
Falk, Richard A. (1989), *Revitalizing International Law*, Ames: Iowa State University Press.
Falk, Richard A. (1992), 'The Pursuit of International Justice: Present Dilemmas and An Imagined Future', *Journal of International Affairs*, **52**(2), pp. 409–44.
Franck, Thomas M. (1990), *The Power of Legitimacy Among Nations*, New York: Oxford.
Franck, Thomas M. (1995), *Fairness in International Law and Institutions*, Oxford: Clarendon Press.
Fukuyama, Francis (1989), 'The End of History?', *The National Interest*, **16**, pp. 3–18.
Grotius, H. (1925), *De jure belli ac pacis libri tres*, [1625] in J.B. Scott (ed.), *Classics of International Law*, translation F.W. Kelsey and an Introduction by James Brown Scott.
Henkin, Louis (1979), *How Nations Behave: Law and Foreign Policy*, (2nd edn), New York: Columbia University Press.
Howe, Geoffrey (1984), 'The Role of International Law in World Affairs', *International and Comparative Law Quarterly*, **33**, p. 739.
Jennings, R. and Watts, A. (1992), *Oppenheim's International Law, Vol. I, Peace*, Harlow: Longman.
Johnston, Douglas (1988), 'Functionalism in the Theory of International Law', *Canadian Yearbook of International Law* 26: pp. 3–60.
Jones, Walter (1935), 'The "Pure" Theory of International Law', *British Yearbook of International Law*, **16**, pp. 5–19.
Kennan, George (1951), *American Diplomacy 1900–1950*, Chicago: University of Chicago Press.
Kennedy, David (1980), 'Theses about International Law Discourse', *German Yearbook of International Law*, **23**, pp. 353–91.
Kennedy, David (1988), 'A New Stream of International Law Scholarship', *Wisconsin International Law Journal*, **7**(1), pp. 1–49.

Kennedy, David (1993), 'Autumn Weekends: An Essay on Law and Everyday Life', in Sarat and Kearns, *Law and Everyday Life*, p. 28.

Kennedy, David and Tennant, Chris (1994), 'New Approaches to International Law: A Bibliography', *Harvard International Law Journal*, **35**(2), pp. 417–60.

Kennedy, Duncan (1997), *A Critique of Adjudication: Fin de Siècle*, Cambridge, Mass.: Harvard University Press.

Keohane, Robert O. (1989), *International Institutions and State Power*, Boulder, Col: Westview Press.

Koskenniemi, Martti (1989), *From Apology to Utopia: The Structure of International Legal Argument*, Helsinki: Finnish Lawyers Publishing Company.

Koskenniemi, Martti (1990), 'The Normative Force of Habit: International Custom and Social Theory', *Finnish Yearbook of International Law*, **1**, pp. 77–153.

Lauterpacht, Hersch (1946), 'The Grotian Tradition in International Law', *British Yearbook of International Law*, **23**, pp. 1–53.

Locke, John (1954), *Essays on the Law of Nature*, [1696], ed. W. von Leyden, Oxford: Clarendon Press.

MacDonald, Ronald (1987), 'Fundamental Norms in Contemporary International Law', *Canadian Yearbook of International Law*, **25**(1), pp. 115–50.

McDougal, Myers (1985–86), 'McDougal's Jurisprudence: Utility, Influence, Controversy', *American Society of International Law Proceedings*, **79–80**, pp. 283–86.

McDougal, Myers and Lasswell, Harold (1959), 'The Identification and Appraisal of Diverse Systems of Public Order', *The American Journal of International Law*, **53**(1), pp. 1–29.

McDougal, Myers, Lasswell, Harold and Reisman, W. Michael (1968), 'Theories about International Law: Prologue to a Configurative Jurisprudence', *Virginia Journal of International Law*, **8**(2), pp. 188–299.

McWhinney, Edward (1990), 'The New Thinking in Soviet International Law: Soviet Doctrine and Practice in the Post-Tunkin Era', *Canadian Yearbook of International Law*, **28**, pp. 309–36.

Mendlovitz, Saul (1975), *On the Creation of a Just World Order*, New York: Free Press.

Morgenthau, Hans J. (1978), *Politics Among Nations: The Struggle for Power and Peace*, (5th edn), New York: Alfred A. Knopf.

Niebuhr, Reinhold (1932), *Moral Man and Immoral Society: A Study in Ethics and Politics*, New York: Scribner's Sons.

Nussbaum, A. (1947), *A Concise History of the Law of Nations*, New York: Macmillan.

Pellet, Alain (1992), ' The Normative Dilemma: Will and Consent in International Law-Making', *Australian Yearbook of International Law*, **12**, pp. 22–53.

Purvis, Nigel (1991), 'Critical legal studies in public international law', *Harvard International Law Journal*, **32**(1), pp. 81–127.

Rigaux, François (1998), 'Hans Kelsen on International Law', *European Journal of International Law*, **9**(2), pp. 325–43.

Schreuer, Christoph (1993), 'The Waning of the Sovereign State', *European Journal of International Law*, **4**(4), pp. 447–71.

Scott, Shirley (1994), 'International Law as Ideology: Theorizing the Relationship between International Law and International Politics', *European Journal of International Law*, **5**(3), pp. 313–25.

Simpson, Gerry (1994), 'Imagined Consent: Democratic Liberalism in International Legal Theory', *Australian Yearbook of International Law*, **15**, pp. 103–28.

Slaughter, Anne-Marie (1994), 'The Liberal Agenda for Peace: International Relations Theory and the Future of the United Nations', *Transnational Law and Contemporary Problems*, **4**, pp. 377–419.

Slaughter, Anne-Marie (1995), 'International Law in a World of Liberal States', *European Journal of International Law*, **6**(4), pp. 503–38.

Slaughter, Anne-Marie, Tulumello, Andrew S. and Wood, Stepan (1998), 'International Law and International Relations: A New Generation of Inter-Disciplinary Scholarship', *The American Journal of International Law*, **92**, pp. 367–97.

Tasioulas, John (1996), 'In Defence of Relative Normativity: Communitarian Values and the *Nicaragua* Case', *Oxford Journal of Legal Studies*, **16**(1), pp. 85–128.

Tesón, Fernando (1993), 'Feminism and International Law: A Reply', *Virginia Journal of International Law*, **33**(3), pp. 647–84.
Unger, Roberto (1976), *Law in Modern Society: Towards a Criticism of Social Theory*, New York: Free Press.
Waltz, Kenneth (1979), *Theory of International Politics*, New York: Random House.
Watson, James (1980), 'A Realistic Jurisprudence', *Yearbook of World Affairs*, **30**, pp. 265–85.
Watts, Arthur (1993), 'The International Rule of Law', *German Yearbook of International Law*, **36**, pp. 15–45.
Weeramantry, Christopher (1992), *Nauru: Environmental Damage under International Trusteeship*, Melbourne: Oxford University Press.
Weil, Prosper (1983), 'Towards Relative Normativity in International Law?', *The American Journal of International Law*, **77**(3), pp. 413–42; also in M. Koskenniemi (ed.) (2000) *The Sources of International Law*, Aldershot: Ashgate.
Wight, Martin (1991), *International Theory: The Three Traditions*, Leicester: Leicester University Press.
Yasuaki, O. (ed.) (1993), *A Normative Approach to War*, Oxford: Clarendon Press.
Zolo, Danilo (1997), *Cosmopolis* (trans. David McKie), Cambridge: Polity Press.

Part I
Three Overviews

[1]

Review of International Studies (1987), *13*, 221–227 *Printed in Great Britain*

An anatomy of international thought

Martin Wight*

This is an attempt at analysing the political philosophy of international relations in a very short span of time, so I do not propose to discuss questions of method. Indeed I may sound dogmatic, but that is merely because I shall not have the time to exhibit my diffidence.

You might say there is no such thing as the political philosophy of international relations; I have therefore played safe and called it 'international thought' in my title to use the least pretentious phrase describing speculation about international relations. International thought is what we find in the discussions of the man-in-the-street or in the popular press. International theory is what we find in the better press and hope to find in diplomatic circles and foreign offices. The political philosophy of international relations is the fully-conscious, formulated theory, illustrations of which you may find in the conduct of some statesmen, Wilson, probably Churchill, perhaps Nehru; and it may be expressed by serious writers, for example Kant or Kennan, Machiavelli or Morgenthau. The differences between thought, theory and philosophy are partly in the precision with which they are formulated, and partly in the degree of their profundity. But I am not concerned with these and ignore them.

To help us examine international thought let us first consider international relations themselves, the state of affairs which produces international theory. As a preamble to our philosophical analysis a sociological analysis will ask the following question: what *is* this condition which we study under the name of international relations? What does it consist of, what are its ingredients? It has three component social elements:

1. *International anarchy*: the multiplicity of sovereign states acknowledging no political superior. Politics here are not 'government'; they presuppose the absence of government.
2. *Habitual intercourse*: expressed in the institutions of diplomacy, international legal rules, commerce, etc.
3. *Moral solidarity*: the communion deeper than politics and economics, it is psychological and cultural, expressed in such phrases as the 'society of states', the 'family of nations', 'world public opinion', 'mankind'.

To each of these elements there corresponds a way of looking at international relations. It may be by temperament and bias, it may be by intellectual conviction. Everybody is inclined to give greater importance and value to one or another of these three elements and in consequence one can trace three, at least three, coherent

* This is the text of a lecture that the late Professor Wight gave at the Institut Universitaire de Hautes Etudes Internationales in Geneva in 1960. The widespread use of Wight's categories of Realists, Rationalists and Revolutionists (see, e.g. Hedley Bull, 'Martin Wight and the Theory of International Relations', *British Journal of International Studies*, 2 (1978)) makes this previously unpublished paper of particular interest. Ed.

0260-2105/87/03/0221-07/$03.00 © 1987 *Review of International Studies*

patterns of thought about international relations, two of which are indeed self-conscious intellectual traditions. To illustrate this, let us enquire into the nature of international society.

The first pattern

The most fundamental question you can ask in international theory is, What is international society?, just as the central question in political theory is, What is a State? Thinkers who emphasize the element of international anarchy in international relations answer this quite simply: Nothing. A fiction. An illusion. *Non est.* The first to make it explicit is probably Hobbes. Hobbes was certainly the first to make the equation between international relations and the state of nature. In the famous thirteenth chapter of *Leviathan* he anticipates the question, whether the state of nature, as he describes it, ever existed. He points first to American Indians, and second to 'Kings, and Persons of Soveraigne authority, (who) because of their Independency, are in continuall jealousies, and in the state and posture of Gladiators'.[1] This equation, that the state of nature = international relations, that sovereign states in their mutual relations are in a pre-contractual condition, passes from Hobbes into the general stream of public law and political theory.

But there is a second equation: international relations may = the state of nature, but what is the state of nature? *Bellum omnium contra omnes.* The state of nature = international relations = the war of all against all, therefore there cannot be an international society. Society is established by the contract, international relations is pre-contractual, the term 'Society of Nations' is contradictory. This is implicitly the position of Machiavelli and Bodin and explicitly that of Spinoza, Rousseau, Kant, Hegel, Fichte and most legal positivists.

Bismarck, for example, showed impatience when the words 'Christendom' or 'Europe' were introduced into diplomatic language. Once, when Gorchakov was urging on him the view that the Eastern Question was not a German or Russian but a *European* question, Bismarck replied: 'I have always found the word Europe on the lips of those politicians who wanted something from other Powers which they dared not demand in their own names.'[2] At the core of this pattern of thought is the doctrine that power is anterior to society, law, justice and morality. E. H. Carr in *The Twenty Years' Crisis* restates the Hobbesian position: 'Any international moral order must rest on some hegemony of power.'[3] Here is Hobbes: '. . . before the names of Just, and Unjust can have place, there must be some coercive Power.'[4] This position is also expressed by Morgenthau, when he says: 'Above the national societies there exists no international society so integrated as to be able to define for them the concrete meaning of justice or equality, as national societies do for their individual members.'[5] For this line of thought, the question: What is international society? admits of only one answer: Nothing!—until there is a world state.

This was the governing conception behind the United Nations Charter. The essentials of the Charter were agreed and drafted at the Dumbarton Oakes Conference in September 1944, when international relations were a state of war. The Third Reich and Japanese Empire were raging undefeated and nobody was confident of peace within a year. Hobbes argued that the only remedy for the state of war was an unlimited contract, whereby we all reduce our wills to one will, and appoint one man, or assembly of men, to act on our behalf in those things which concern the common peace and safety.[6] This is precisely what signatories of the Charter did by Articles 24, 25 and 48. The Smutsian preamble to the Charter, which is in another tradition of thinking, was tacked on later; and it was only later again that it appeared that the Hobbesian sovereign of the UN was a schizophrenic paralytic incapable of action, so that the UN has never worked as it was intended.

The second pattern

But the two Hobbesian equations I have mentioned are not inseparable. It is possible to accept the identification of international relations with the state of nature without accepting the description of the state of nature as *bellum omnium contra omnes.* This is what Locke apparently does in the *Second Treatise of Civil Government.* He repeats Hobbes' argument that if you are sceptical about a state of nature ever having existed you need only look at inter-state relations,[7] but he goes on to argue, for a whole chapter, that whereas the state of war is a state of enmity and mutual destruction, the state of nature is a state of goodwill and mutual assistance. I say 'what Locke *apparently does*' because Professor Richard Cox's book on Locke[8] has placed a large question mark over the traditional interpretation of Locke, but perhaps we may still accept the public Locke at his face value.

Grotius likewise conceded that the social condition was inaugurated by the social contract but argued that the pre-contractual state of nature was the condition of sociability—the capacity for becoming social. Suarez argued that although every state is a perfect community, it is none the less a member of a universal body, this membership being the basis of international law, and with nice precision he described the universal body as 'unitas quasi politica et moralis'.[9]

This is the sort of answer you will expect from those who emphasize our second component of international relations, habitual intercourse, institutions of diplomacy and law. Sovereign states, they will say, do form a society; they do not exist in a political or cultural vacuum, but in continuous political relations with one another. It is a society which must be understood on its own terms and not by comparison with domestic society, a society governed less by force, as the thinkers of the first group may hold, than by custom. It is a society with a system of law that is crude and not centrally enforced but still true law, a society without a government but regulated by certain special institutions such as diplomacy, the balance of power and alliances.

Locke's conception of the state of nature leads to a different kind of contract from Hobbes'. If the state of nature is not so beastly, civil society need not be so severe, and the social contract can be limited as was the Covenant compared with the Charter. The men who drafted the Covenant (excluding Wilson) did not think international life had broken down, only that it had suffered unusual interruption, and had shown it was deficient in means for the pacific settlement of international disputes, and what was needed was (Locke's words) 'umpirage . . . for . . . ending all the differences that may arise amongst' states.[10] For this a limited contract was sufficient. Signatories did not surrender their natural liberties, their sovereignty; states simply undertook to limit the exercise of their sovereignty, the unanimity rule was not abrogated. If we can detect the sardonic smile of Hobbes between the lines of the Charter, in the Covenant we may discern the more bland and amiable assumptions of traditional Locke.

The third pattern

Now there is a third, quite distinct way of conceiving of international society and it is related to those who tend to emphasize in international relations the element of moral solidarity. They will answer the question, What is international society? in such a fashion as this: international society is none other than mankind, encumbered and thwarted by an archaic fiction of an international society composed of sovereign states. States are *not* persons, they have no wills but the wills of the individuals who manage their affairs, and behind the legal façade of the fictitious Society of Nations is the true international society composed of men. Now, this much is not in contradiction with the second complex of ideas which we have just been noticing: you will find Grotius speaking of *societas generis humani* more often than of *societas gentium*.

But this third pattern of ideas is distinguished by two master-premises: firstly, that the existing state of affairs, the existing arrangements of international life, are invalid and illegitimate; secondly, that they are going to be modified or swept away by the course of events itself. Both these premises are religious in nature. The first expresses the impulse to eradicate sin and suffering, which are condemned by being identified, or that austere moral concern which made Kant argue, in *Rechtslehre*, that if nations were in the state of nature it was their duty to pass out of it, and 'all international rights . . . are purely *provisional* until the state of nature has been abandoned'.[11] The second premise, that the course of events itself is tending to bring about desired change, shows a desire for a theodicy. Every age has wanted to vindicate the justice of the universe in view of the existence of evil, but it is a peculiar modern manifestation of this desire, to believe that this vindication will be accomplished by the historical process itself. The belief in progress, historical inevitability, in the linear development of human affairs, whether evolutionary or catastrophic, is now often named 'historicism'.

'Historicism' is a word that has changed its meaning since Meinecke wrote the history of *Historismus*. Then it had its original sense, of the doctrine that all values are historically conditioned, that reality itself is a historical process, and that history can teach nothing except philosophical acceptance of change. Now it has a new sense: the doctrine that history has a purpose and direction, that its movement is largely predictable, and that it can (under proper interpretation) teach everything we need to know about life and prescribe our duties. In this new sense it is a label for Hegel and Marx, Spengler and Toynbee.

There are two historical agencies which, in this pattern of thinking, promote desirable international change. Kant, who is responsible for so much else in modern thought, was as far as I know the first to describe these historical agencies in this context.

First, was what he called 'the commercial spirit', 'which cannot exist along with war, and which sooner or later controls every people'.[12] We should probably translate it as the growing material interdependence of mankind, due to the economic unification of the world and industrialization. Its greatest English prophet was Cobden whose motto was 'Free Trade, Peace, Goodwill among Nations' and in whose political writings and speeches the expected consequences of growing material interdependence are made plain.

Secondly, was what Kant called 'the spirit of enlightenment'. 'Enlightenment . . . must ever draw mankind away from the egoistic expansive tendencies of its rulers once they understand their own advantage.'[13] We might translate it as the growing moral interdependence of mankind due to education, cultural exchange and intellectual standardization. It is manifested in the formation of a world public opinion, which some see as the animating principle of the United Nations.

Kant's imaginary treaty of Perpetual Peace contained a secret article, that before going to war, governments must consult the maxims of the philosophers. It is not to be expected (he says) that kings should philosophize or philosophers become kings, but kings can let philosophers speak freely, 'because this is indispensable for both in order to clarify their business.'[14] Kant was the subject of a Prussian monarch whose minister of education had not allowed him to speak freely: he himself would have liked to be on the Brains Trust of a President F. D. Roosevelt or on the Democratic Advisory Council, Committee on Foreign Policy, of a President Kennedy. This 'secret article' is the expression and possibly the direct inspiration, of the Wilsonian belief that enlightened public opinion, instructed public opinion in all countries, will promote peace and goodwill in international affairs.

It must be noticed here that this third pattern of ideas is not characterized by *recognizing* these two historical agencies. The growing material and moral interdependence of mankind as historical tendencies or trends would scarcely be denied by any thinker. But while a thinker of the first class might suppose that these trends would lead to more savage internecine conflicts culminating in a world despotism, and a thinker of the second class would believe that they posed continually new and agonizing problems, the historicist believes that these trends carry within themselves the solution of the problems they pose and will lead in the desired direction.

Given these premises, our question 'What is international society?' appears foolishly academic: 'The philosophers have only *interpreted* the world differently, the point is to change it.'[15] Very well then: change it how? By bringing out its essential nature, by making explicit what is implicit, by eradicating evil and making it virtuous, by clearing away the irrelevant historical clutter of states and forms to produce the regularity, uniformity and homogeneity of virtue. That is, by redrawing the map.

What kind of uniformity? Here there are two answers. Firstly, to assimilate all existing states, members of international society, to a pattern of conformity to which alone confers legitimacy and to eradicate inconsistencies. An early example is Kant's *Perpetual Peace.* He works out an ideal, make-believe treaty of eternal peace. Its first definitive article is that the constitution of each state should be republican, that is what we should call constitutional. But the principle that members of international society should be doctrinally uniform can be used by ideologists of more than one kind.

Kant's principle was put into effect in a counter-revolutionist sense by Alexander and Metternich, in the Holy Alliance, and for purposes of political theory it is necessary to define counter-revolutionism as a mode of revolutionism. Mazzini gave the principle a violent push in the opposite direction, so that it swung to a more extreme point than Kant; that there would be no valid international society till all its members were nation-states. This was the principle of national self-determination which triumphed in 1919. It was connected with Wilson's original demand that the League be a league of democratic states, which had its counterpart in the initial idea that the United Nations was to be a league of peace-loving states; this produced as a by-product the attempted international ostracism of Spain in 1946. Both the League and the United Nations were originally exclusive and limited bodies, whose membership depended on a qualifying test; both became inclusive and unlimited bodies, admission to which depended on no scrutiny and thus became degraded.

The same principle gave its driving force to Afro-Asian anti-colonialism. As Sukarno, host at the Bandung Conference of 1955 said then: 'Wherever, whenever and however it appears, colonialism is an evil thing and one which must be eradicated from the earth.'[16] One is not surprised to learn that Mazzini was held in respect by Nehru, and is widely read in South East Asia. But there is an alternative to the Kantian and Mazzinian line of reducing all members of international society to uniformity.

A more radical change and more drastic uniformity lies in the direction of the

Cosmopolis. A Cosmopolis too is immanent in the existing state-structure. Behind the empirical historical members of international society lies mankind, the City of Man, the City of the World, the Great Society, Civitas Maxima, the Parliament of Man, the Federation of the World. The supreme exponent of this view is Dante. *De Monarchia* presents a tight argument, a completely satisfying piece of intellectual architecture.

1. Mankind is a unity, united by the faculty of reason, capable of pursuing the same ends through the same channels: 'humanity'.
2. Mankind can only fulfil itself under a single government.
3. Providence designed for this rule the Roman Empire.

Today we accept the first two points, and can easily substitute for the Roman Empire either the United States or the Soviet Union. If we accept Gilson's view, Dante was the first person to conceive of mankind as a universal *temporal* community, a university community capable of and requiring a World Federation or the World State.[17]

This idea, whether directly from Dante or not, has haunted international thought. In Victoria, the earliest international theorist after Machiavelli,[18] and Alberiens Gentili[19] you have the idea of mankind as a great society whose majority vote can override individual nations. In Calvin and *Vindiciae contra Tyrannos* you have the idea of this great society having a right of intervention against a non-conformist member,[20] and Christian Wolff who was Professor at Halle 1679–1754 made the fiction of the *civitas maxima*, of which states were citizens and which could exercise authority over them, the basis of his theory of international law.[21] Kant too finds the idea of human progress in a 'continuously growing state consisting of various nations' to which 'the federative unions of states' of the *Perpetual Peace* is a second-best.[22]

Philip II of Spain believed it his duty to suppress heresy and impose doctrinal uniformity not only in his own vast dominions but throughout Christendom as well, and there hovered before the eyes of some of his diplomats and propagandists the mirage of a 'monarquia del mundo'. The first French Republic imposed Rights of Man wherever its armies could conquer. Hitler and after him Stalin, did the same in the parts of Europe they conquered. The same aim, of imposing uniformity on the state-system by transforming it into a universal satellite state-system, and this as a preliminary to absorbing the satellite state-system into a universal state has inspired, however dimly, the successive waves of doctrinal imperialism that have characterized international history from Philip II of Spain down to Mr Khrushchev.[23]

Patterns and traditions

If we speak of each of these three types of international theory as *patterns of thought* we approach them from a philosophical standpoint. We shall be likely to note the logical inter-relation, the logical coherence of the complex of thought and how acceptance of any one unit-idea is likely to entail logically most of the others, so that the whole is capable of being a system of political philosophy. If we speak of them as *traditions of thought* we consider them historically as embodied in and handed down by writers and statesmen. Here we are more likely to notice illogicalities and discontinuities because exigencies of political life often override logic. We shall find all kinds of intermediate positions. Interesting academic questions arise, such as whether Rousseau's international theory is contradictory to his political theory; how Kant, starting from acceptance of the Hobbesian doctrine of the state of nature reached totally opposite conclusions; why it is that you so often find the jump from a shrewd realistic appraisal of international politics to a sentimental idealism, even pacifism: in Tolstoy, Kennan or Butterfield.

It is tempting to develop a psychological typology supposing that each pattern of thought corresponds to a temperament. Coleridge has a tripartite distinction between the politics of sensation (Hobbes), of reason (Rousseau) and of understanding (S. T. Coleridge and W. Wilson). Max Weber analyses three qualities in a politician: a passionate devotion to cause, a feeling of responsibility and a sense of proportion. If we brought all this in we might speedily have a comprehensive psychological theory on which to base the understanding of international relations. But I speak of this as a temptation. I only feel capable of analysing political ideas—not psychologies—and when I scrutinize my own psyche I seem to find all these three ways of thought within me.

All I am saying is that I find these traditions of thought in international history dynamically interweaving, but always distinct, and I think they can be seen in mutual tension and conflict underneath the formalized ideological postures of our present discontents. It may be that China is passing out of her first revolutionary fervour into the phase where Machiavellian postulates of national interest will predominate over revolutionary expansion and this may be more dangerous for the rest of the world. The United States may yet prove itself a more Kantian society than the Soviet Union in its formal policies, as it seemed to be doing in Dulles' time. The Russia of Khrushchev may show itself more Grotian than the United States or Britain in its acceptance of the principle of seeking a common interest in the limitation of war. Perhaps the mere possibility of formulating such hypotheses implies a faint ray of hope.

References and notes

1. T. Hobbes, *Leviathan* (London, 1914), p. 65.
2. Quoted by A. J. P. Taylor in *Bismarck: the Man and the Statesman* (London, 1955), p. 167.
3. E. H. Carr, *The Twenty Years' Crisis, 1919–1939* (London, 1939), p. 213.
4. Hobbes, *Leviathan*, p. 74.
5. H. J. Morgenthau, *In Defense of the National Interest* (New York, 1951), p. 34; cf. Morgenthau, *Dilemmas of Politics* (Chicago, 1958), pp. 80–1.
6. Hobbes, *Leviathan*, p. 89.
7. J. Locke, *Two Treatises of Civil Armament* (London, 1924), para. 14, p. 124.
8. R. H. Cox, *Locke on War and Peace* (Oxford, 1960).
9. F. Suarez, *Tractatus de Legibus et Legislatore Deo*, Lib. 11, D 9, in *Selections from Three Works of Francisco Suarez*, Vol. I (Oxford, 1944), p. 190.
10. Locke, *Two Treatises*, para. 212, p. 225.
11. E. Kant, *The Metaphysics of Morals*, sect 61 in H. Reiss (ed.), *Kant's Political Writings* (Cambridge, 1970), p. 171.
12. Kant, *Perpetual Peace* (Liberal Arts edition, 1957), p. 32.
13. Kant, *Idea for a Universal History*, 8th principle, ed. C. J. Friedrich (New York, 1949), p. 128.
14. Kant, *Eternal Peace*, ed. C. J. Friedrich (New York, 1919), p. 456.
15. K. Marx, *Theses on Feuerbach*, no. 11, in Marx and F. Engels, *The German Ideology*, Pts I & III (London, 1938), p. 199.
16. President Sukarno's opening speech at the Bandung Conference, 22 April 1955, *Keesing's Contemporary Archives*, 1955/6, p. 14181.
17. E. Gilson, *Dante the Philosopher* (London, 1952), pp. 164–6.
18. See J. Brown Scott, *The Spanish Origins of International Law: Francisco de Victoria and his Law of Nations* (Oxford, 1934), p. 165 and Appendix C.
19. A. Gentili, *De Jure Belli* (1588).
20. See O. Gierke, *Natural Law and the Theory of Society, 1500–1800*, ed. E. Barker (Cambridge, 1934), p. 283, note 62.
21. C. Wolff, *Institutiones Jures Naturae et Gentium* (Halle, 1754), pp. 1090–2.
22. Kant, *Perpetual Peace*, pp. 19, 31.
23. See E. R. Goodman, *The Soviet Design for a World State* (New York, 1960).

[2]

INTERNATIONAL LAW AND INTERNATIONAL RELATIONS THEORY: A DUAL AGENDA

*By Anne-Marie Slaughter Burley**

INTRODUCTION

Writing in 1968 on the "relevance of international law," Richard Falk described his efforts as part of the larger endeavor of "liberating the discipline of international law from a sense of its own futility."[1] In 1992 that task appears to have been accomplished. International legal rules, procedures and organizations are more visible and arguably more effective than at any time since 1945. If the United Nations cannot accomplish everything, it once again represents a significant repository of hopes for a better world. And even as its current failures are tabulated, from Yugoslavia to the early weeks and then months of the Somali famine, the almost-universal response is to find ways to strengthen it. The resurgence of rules and procedures in the service of an organized international order is the legacy of all wars, hot or cold.

For international lawyers, both practitioners and professors, this is the end of a long journey. As Thomas Franck proclaims, we are finally in a "post-ontological" era.[2] But the existential limbo of the decades since 1950 took its toll in many ways, from the open disdain of highly visible public figures,[3] to deeper damage to the ability of the discipline to renew itself by attracting younger scholars. A particular casualty was the opportunities and prospects for sustained interdisciplinary collaboration with international relations scholars in political science.

Just as constitutional lawyers study political theory, and political theorists inquire into the nature and substance of constitutions, so too should two disciplines that study the laws of state behavior seek to learn from one another. At the very least, they should aspire to a common vocabulary and framework of analysis that would allow the sharing of insights and information.[4] If social science has any validity at all, the postulates developed by political scientists concerning patterns and regularities in state behavior must afford a foundation and framework for legal efforts to regulate that behavior. For instance, if it could be reliably shown

* Assistant Professor of Law and International Relations, University of Chicago. I am grateful to Andrew Moravcsik for much valuable discussion and helpful readings of several early drafts. Abram Chayes, Robert Keohane and Jay Westbrook contributed their insights. Thanks are also due to Sarah Fandell for excellent research assistance and to the Lee and Brena Freeman Faculty Research Fund at the University of Chicago Law School for financial support.

[1] Richard A. Falk, *The Relevance of Political Context to the Nature and Functioning of International Law: An Intermediate View*, *in* THE RELEVANCE OF INTERNATIONAL LAW 133, 142 (Karl W. Deutsch & Stanley Hoffmann eds., 1968).

[2] Thomas M. Franck, Principles of Fairness in International Law (paper presented at Annual Meeting of American Political Science Association, Chicago, IL, September 1992).

[3] *See, e.g.*, Robert Bork, *The Limits of 'International Law,'* NAT'L INTEREST, Winter 1989/90, at 3.

[4] In probably the most successful effort to bridge this disciplinary divide, Louis Henkin lamented that "the student of law and the student of politics . . . purport to be looking at the same world from the vantage point of important disciplines. It seems unfortunate, indeed destructive, that they should not, at the least, hear each other." LOUIS HENKIN, HOW NATIONS BEHAVE: LAW AND FOREIGN POLICY 4 (2d ed. 1979).

that a great-power condominium was the best guarantee of international peace, then international law and organization should accommodate and support an arrangement that confers special privileges on a group of great powers. On the other hand, if the prospects for peace hang on some other set of state characteristics, then international security organizations and norms designed to regulate the use of force should be reshaped accordingly. From the political science side, if law—whether international, transnational or purely domestic—does push the behavior of states toward outcomes other than those predicted by power and the pursuit of national interest, then political scientists must revise their models to take account of legal variables.

Notwithstanding the logic and intellectual appeal of this vision, interdisciplinary efforts fell victim for most of the postwar era to the "Realist challenge": the defiant skepticism of Political Realists such as George Kennan, Hans Morgenthau and, more recently, Kenneth Waltz that international law could ever play more than an epiphenomenal role in the ordering of international life. Much of the theoretical scholarship in both international law and international relations can be understood as either a response to or a refinement of this challenge. Many international lawyers attempted to reconceptualize international law in relation to international politics, seeking to relate the two disciplines without sacrificing one entirely. Political scientists by and large paid little attention, preferring to contest Realist methodology along various lines and to build increasingly abstract "systemic" theories of state behavior.

Beginning in the late 1970s, however, an important group of mainstream international relations theorists laid the foundation for a more fundamental attack on core Realist propositions concerning the role and relevance of international institutions. The result was a new emphasis on the role and impact of international "regimes," the principles, norms, rules and decision-making procedures that pattern state expectations and behavior. As international lawyers soon realized, this was international law by another name. By the end of the 1980s, regime theory had been subsumed under the more general rubric of Institutionalism, a powerful, although often complementary, alternative to Realism.

Part I of this article maps this postwar trajectory, seeking to delineate the major features of the interdisciplinary landscape and to provide an introduction to the relevant literature for scholars in both disciplines. A second and equally important goal, however, is to provide the necessary background for an exploration of interdisciplinary options in the 1990s. Happily, the dawning of a new era in global politics coincides with what may be greater convergence in some areas of international law and international political science than ever before. The result is a dual agenda in interdisciplinary scholarship, bridging to two distinct theoretical traditions in political science: Institutionalism and Liberalism.

Part II describes the Institutionalist agenda, a research program already being pursued by prominent scholars in both disciplines. Institutionalists and international lawyers subscribe to a common ontology of the international system: the actors, the structure within which those actors act, and the process of their interaction. Both groups, separately and together, are describing a common agenda focused on the study of improved institutional design for maximally effective international organizations, compliance with international obligations, and international ethics.

Although a broad avenue with many promising vistas, the Institutionalist road to interdisciplinary collaboration is only one possible route, with an inevitably limited set of destinations. Part III proposes another path, equally promising, but considerably more challenging. This new interdisciplinary bridge involves the application of "Liberal" international relations theory to law within and among nations. Liberals focus not on state-to-state interactions, at least not in the first instance, but on an analytically *prior* set of relationships among states and domestic and transnational civil society. The "black box" of sovereignty becomes transparent, allowing examination of how and to what extent national governments represent individuals and groups operating in domestic and transnational society. Democracies, or, more precisely, "liberal states," are presumed to behave differently from dictatorships, not only domestically but also internationally. Their relations with one another are shaped in important ways by domestic, transnational and international law, as are their relations with nonliberal states. Liberal international relations theory offers a way of conceptualizing the contributions of these bodies of law to the traditional goals of international order, while highlighting important patterns and breaks in current legal doctrines.

The Liberal agenda will require international lawyers to revise their most fundamental conceptions of the international system. The rewards are worth it, however; this approach permits the construction of a comprehensive legal framework that links factors and trends of interest to the widest possible spectrum of international lawyers, from traditional specialists on questions such as national self-determination, to human rights activists, environmental lawyers, trade experts and international litigators and deal makers. Moreover, the Liberal agenda *complements* the Institutionalist agenda as the study primarily of law among liberal states. Many of the world's most pressing problems are left to the Institutionalists. In sum, the dual agenda is a unified agenda, offering powerful tools and a cornucopia of research opportunities for all students of international law and politics.

I. The Postwar Trajectory

The Realist Challenge

The discipline of international relations was born after World War I in a haze of aspirations for the future of world government. These were quickly dimmed by World War II. The fledgling discipline was thus weaned on Political Realism, articulated and systematized by scholars such as Hans Morgenthau, Georg Schwarzenberger, E. H. Carr and George Kennan.[5] These seasoned observers of the interwar period reacted against Wilsonian liberal internationalism, which presumed that the combination of democracy and international organization could vanquish war and power politics. They believed instead in the polarity of law and power, opposing one to the other as the respective emblems of the domestic versus the international realm, normative aspiration versus positive description, cooperation versus conflict, soft versus hard, idealist versus realist. Regardless of their domestic colors, states in the international realm were champions only of their own national interest. "Law," as understood in the domestic sense, had no place in this world. The only relevant laws were the "laws of politics," and politics was "a struggle for power."[6]

[5] Some other notable Realists were Reinhold Niebuhr, Arnold Wolfers and Robert Strausz-Hupé.

[6] HANS J. MORGENTHAU, POLITICS AMONG NATIONS: THE STRUGGLE FOR POWER AND PEACE 4–5, 25–26 (4th ed. 1967). Although many of the fathers of the United Nations would have argued that it was founded precisely on a Realist recognition of the necessities of power politics—hence the special privileges for the great powers sitting on the Security Council—Morgenthau specifically cites "the great attempts at organizing the world, such as the League of Nations and the United Nations," as

From the Realist perspective, Woodrow Wilson and his followers were the high priests of the "legalist-moralist" tradition in American foreign policy, a tradition naively projecting the ordered domestic existence of a liberal state onto the inherent anarchy of the international system.[7] By trying to guarantee peace through an international organization dedicated to the high-minded ideals of Wilson's Fourteen Points, the Wilsonians disarmed themselves in the face of rising fascist power. More generally, wrote Kennan, they misunderstood the relative functions and capacities of law and diplomacy:

> History has shown that the will and the capacity of individual peoples to contribute to their world environment is constantly changing. It is only logical that the organizational forms (and what else are such things as borders and governments?) should change with them. The function of a system of international relationships is not to inhibit this process of change by imposing a legal straitjacket upon it but rather to facilitate it: to ease its transitions, to temper the asperities to which it often leads, to isolate and moderate the conflicts to which it gives rise, and to see that these conflicts do not assume forms too unsettling for international life in general. *But this is a task for diplomacy, in the most old-fashioned sense of the term. For this, law is too abstract, too inflexible, too hard to adjust to the demands of the unpredictable and the unexpected.*[8]

This, then, was the Realist challenge to international lawyers: a challenge to establish the "relevance" of international law.[9] International legal theorists had long grappled with the theoretical conundrum of the sources of international legal obligation—of law being simultaneously "of" and "above" the state. Yet the endless debates on this question nevertheless assumed that international legal rules, however derived, had some effect on state behavior, that law and power *interacted* in some way, rather than marking opposite ends of the domestic-international-spectrum. Political Realists, by contrast, gave no quarter. Their challenge struck at the heart of the discipline, claiming that international law was but a collection of evanescent maxims or a "repository of legal rationalizations."[10]

The Realist challenge was not merely academic posturing. It was mounted by one of the major architects of postwar foreign policy and formulated in terms of

---

efforts to implement the wrongheaded "conviction that the struggle for power can be eliminated from the international scene." *Id.* at 10.

Morgenthau did imagine some role for international law, as Francis Boyle has also noted, but few scholars or practitioners have read him or his fellow Realists this way. *See* Hans J. Morgenthau, *Positivism, Functionalism, and International Law*, 34 AJIL 260 (1940); FRANCIS A. BOYLE, WORLD POLITICS AND INTERNATIONAL LAW 3–16 (1985). Georg Schwarzenberger also defended the possibility of international law and organization in those limited contexts in which power politics did not rule.

[7] GEORGE KENNAN, AMERICAN DIPLOMACY, 1900–1950 (1951). Kennan linked the "legalist-moralist" approach, a term he coined, to the predominance of lawyers among American foreign-policy makers, in addition to a broader effort to "transpose the Anglo-Saxon concept of individual law into the international field and to make it applicable to governments as it is applicable here at home," to establish world order as we had once established a revolutionary national order. *Id.* at 95. *See also* Arnold Wolfers, *Introduction: Political Theory and International Relations*, *in* THE ANGLO-AMERICAN TRADITION IN FOREIGN AFFAIRS at ix (Arnold Wolfers & Laurence W. Martin eds., 1956).

[8] KENNAN, *supra* note 7, at 95 (emphasis added).

[9] This was the title of an excellent 1968 *Festschrift* in honor of Leo Gross, which was edited by two noted political scientists and included both international lawyers and political scientists. *See supra* note 1.

[10] Falk, *supra* note 1, at 138.

policy prescriptions that ignored law and lawyers. The efforts to answer it shaped the evolution of postwar international legal scholarship.

The Legal Response: Reconceptualizing Law and Politics

The chief legal or jurisprudential response to the Realist challenge was the reconceptualization of the relationship between international law and politics. Different international legal scholars obviously responded differently. Yet all their efforts share certain characteristics. First, all sought to relate law more closely to politics, pushed not only by the challenge of the Political Realists, but also by that of the Legal Realists, who had decisively demonstrated that legal doctrines inevitably reflected underlying policy choices.[11] Second, as part of this mission, all redefined the form of law, moving in some measure from rules to process.[12] Third, all reassessed the primary functions of law. Whereas rules guide and constrain behavior, providing triggers for sanctions, processes perform a wider range of functions: communication, reassurance, monitoring and routinization.[13]

Each of the sections that follow addresses a school of thought that can be identified as a distinct response to the Realist challenge. However, no effort is made to offer a comprehensive intellectual history of either discipline. The point is rather to provide a road map of self-conscious efforts to reconceptualize international law in a way that would demonstrate its relevance to international politics, and thus to rebuild a foundation for interdisciplinary scholarship.

Law as policy science. The first and most comprehensive response to the Realist challenge was that of Myres McDougal and Harold Lasswell, a brilliant team at

[11] There is a rich irony here. Both the Legal Realists and the Political Realists can be understood, in their extreme form, as having argued that law is indistinguishable from politics. Yet the Legal Realists argued that law subsumed politics; the Political Realists claimed that politics proceeded entirely independently of law. The difference, of course, is that the Legal Realists sought to demythologize a legal system in which legal *institutions*—lawyers and judges—unquestionably wielded great power. Political Realists, on the other hand, sought to demythologize a legal system in a society in which legal institutions were weak. The response to both critiques could thus be exactly the same, a move that endowed law with less autonomous power than thought by the formalists but more than perceived by the Realists of either stripe.

[12] David Kennedy is the great chronicler of this shift, although he conceptualizes it somewhat differently as a "preoccupation . . . with a process which might convince us of international law's *being* by imagining it in relationship to something else—often thought of as 'political authority.' " David Kennedy, *A New Stream of International Law Scholarship*, 7 WIS. J. INT'L L. 1, 2 (1988). His account is a more self-referential description of the collective psychology of the discipline, describing what I call the Realist challenge as an internal identity crisis.

[13] This redefinition of legal function was accomplished in two contradictory, but similarly motivated, maneuvers. On the one hand, some scholars argued that international law is like domestic law, but that domestic law operates in far more complex and subtle ways than by simply restraining behavior. *See, e.g.*, ABRAM CHAYES, THOMAS EHRLICH & ANDREAS F. LOWENFELD, INTERNATIONAL LEGAL PROCESS: MATERIALS FOR AN INTRODUCTORY COURSE at xiii–xv (1968) (domestic law is not so court-driven as we might suppose, and thus the absence of effective judicial institutions in the international realm is a difference in degree rather than kind); Roger Fisher, *Bringing Law to Bear on National Governments*, 74 HARV. L. REV. 1130 (1961) (domestic *private* law is enforceable by the power of the state, but not so domestic *public* law such as constitutional and administrative law; thus, absence of coercive enforcement option does not differentiate international law from many important types of domestic law); William Coplin, *International Law and Assumptions About the State System*, 17 WORLD POL. 615 (1965) (both international and domestic law communicate society's conception of itself). On the other hand, an equally ardent group of scholars have argued that the domestic analogy is false and misleading; international law must be understood as law in a very different context. *See, e.g.*, RICHARD A. FALK, THE STATUS OF LAW IN INTERNATIONAL SOCIETY (1970); *Introduction* to INTERNATIONAL LAW AND ORGANIZATION 1 (Richard A. Falk & Wolfram F. Hanrieder eds., 1968).

Yale Law School that had assumed the mission of training domestic lawyers as policy makers, equipping them to play a far more active role in leading a great nation through the vicissitudes of the postwar world.[14] As the Cold War began, McDougal and Lasswell found international lawyers similarly sidelined by the Political Realists' emphasis on "the importance of naked power."[15] In response, they reinvented international jurisprudence, creating a comprehensive framework within which international lawyers, retrained as public policy experts, could use empirical data and theoretical insights from political science and a range of other disciplines to ascertain and critique existing law. This entire enterprise was in turn to be subordinate to the international lawyer's ultimate function of inventing and promoting better law, a world public order that would advance human dignity.[16]

For McDougal, law itself became a political process. Having thus dissolved the traditional law-politics distinction, he turned to a particular conception of the political process, that developed by Harold Lasswell. Lasswell defined politics as the adversarial process of decision about the distribution of values in society.[17] McDougal and Lasswell then together defined law as the subset of this flow of decisions that could be said to be both "authoritative" and "effective." "Effective" means "controlling," thus *re*introducing an element of power; "authorita-

[14] This famous plan for the wholesale reconceptualization of American legal education was set forth in Harold D. Lasswell & Myres S. McDougal, *Legal Education and Public Policy: Professional Training in the Public Interest*, 52 YALE L.J. 203 (1943). Lasswell was a professor of both law and political science at Yale Law School.

[15] Myres S. McDougal, *International Law, Power and Policy: A Contemporary Conception*, 82 RECUEIL DES COURS 137, 157 (1953 I).

[16] Most of McDougal's most important early work is collected in MYRES S. MCDOUGAL & ASSOCIATES, STUDIES IN WORLD PUBLIC ORDER (1960), although in many ways McDougal's Hague lectures, *supra* note 15, provide more insight into the development of his unique framework. Other important articles, although only a limited selection from a vast corpus, include: Myres S. McDougal, *Law as a Process of Decision: A Policy-Oriented Approach to Legal Study*, 1 NAT. L. F. 53 (1956); Myres S. McDougal, *Some Basic Theoretical Concepts about International Law: A Policy-Oriented Framework of Inquiry*, 4 J. CONFLICT RESOL. 337 (1960); Myres S. McDougal & W. Michael Reisman, *The World Constitutive Process of Authoritative Decision*, 19 J. LEGAL EDUC. 253 (1967); Myres S. McDougal, Harold D. Lasswell & W. Michael Reisman, *Theories about International Law: Prologue to a Configurative Jurisprudence*, 8 VA. J. INT'L L. 188 (1968); Myres S. McDougal, *International Law and Social Science: A Mild Plea in Avoidance*, 66 AJIL 77 (1972); Myres S. McDougal & W. Michael Reisman, *International Law in Policy-Oriented Perspective*, *in* THE STRUCTURE AND PROCESS OF INTERNATIONAL LAW 103 (Ronald St. J. Macdonald & Douglas M. Johnston eds., 1983) [hereinafter *Policy-Oriented Perspective*]. On the contributions of his many students, see the *Festschrift* published on the occasion of his retirement: TOWARD WORLD ORDER AND HUMAN DIGNITY (W. Michael Reisman & Burns H. Weston eds., 1976) [hereinafter TOWARD WORLD ORDER], also containing a complete bibliography of works by and relating to McDougal.

For those unwilling to struggle with the specialized vocabulary of McDougal-Lasswell-Reisman jurisprudence, Richard Falk has done an excellent job of translation and explication. *See especially* Richard A. Falk, Book Review, 8 NAT. L. F. 171 (1963) (reviewing MYRES S. MCDOUGAL & FLORENTINO P. FELICIANO, LAW AND MINIMUM WORLD PUBLIC ORDER (1961)); and FALK, *supra* note 13, App. C. An insightful account of McDougal's work with particular attention to its social science origins is Oran R. Young, *International Law and Social Science: The Contributions of Myres S. McDougal*, 66 AJIL 60 (1972).

[17] *Cf.* Harold Lasswell's famous question: "Who gets what, when, how?" HAROLD D. LASSWELL, POLITICS: WHO GETS WHAT, WHEN, HOW (1936). The process is political because it inevitably involves power, both as a value in itself and as an instrument to attain other values. For a useful overview of Lasswell's scholarship and its relation to that of other "distributive" political theorists, see ORAN R. YOUNG, SYSTEMS OF POLITICAL SCIENCE 65–78 (1968). For the specific relationship between McDougal's theory of law and Lasswell's broader work, see Young, *supra* note 16, and, more recently, Gray L. Dorsey, *The McDougal-Lasswell Proposal to Build a World Public Order*, 82 AJIL 41 (1988).

tive" means in conformity with community values and expectations, as verified by the techniques of social science.[18] Thus redefined as a flow of authoritative and effective decisions, law merges with the political and social processes that ultimately determine its content, yet retains a distinctive identity as law.[19]

In a genuine community bound together by common values, "the law" can be identified as the authoritative expression of those values. But in the international system, said McDougal, no such community of values exists. In such an arena, law shifts in function as well as form: "legal norms are understood to support the realization of values rather than the restraint of behavior."[20] And if international law was an ideological battleground, international lawyers were on the front lines. McDougal, Lasswell and their associates[21] exhorted international lawyers to use a range of policy skills to determine which law, or which system of laws, best furthers "human dignity," and to distinguish such systems (public orders) from those that deny human dignity. After classifying the public orders in the world on the basis of these criteria, they proclaimed that the next step was to "invent and recommend" the principles and procedures necessary to a *world* public order consonant with the dignity and desires of all mankind.[22]

Law as systemic policy science. Some of McDougal's students—scholars such as Richard Falk, Saul Mendlovitz and Burns Weston—absorbed his conceptual medium without his substantive message. They recognized the importance of understanding law as the expression of social and political values but disagreed with McDougal's rejection of the possibility of a community of values at the systemic level in an ideologically charged world. Falk, for instance, hailed the contribution made by the McDougal-Lasswell framework to contextualizing the law but ultimately found that it veered too far toward politics, opening the door to national opportunism, denying the possibility of legitimate pluralism, and encouraging adversary confrontation in the face of a fragile nuclear balance. He sought instead to strike his own balance between the pure autonomy of a Kelsen, on the one hand, and the tainted relevance of a McDougal, on the other.[23]

[18] The legal process itself is thus subject to restraints flowing from a modern version of natural law, "substitut[ing] the empirical generalizations of social science for the metaphysically based propositions of reason and religion." Falk, Book Review, *supra* note 16, at 172.

[19] For an accessible discussion of the McDougalites' understanding of the relationship between authority and control, see Rosalyn Higgins, *Integration of Authority and Control: Trends in the Literature of International Law and International Relations, in* TOWARD WORLD ORDER, *supra* note 16, at 79.

[20] FALK, *supra* note 13, at 14.

[21] McDougal has collaborated with many distinguished scholars, some of whom are listed as his associates in STUDIES IN WORLD PUBLIC ORDER, *supra* note 16. See also the contributors to TOWARD WORLD ORDER, *supra* note 16.

Although many of his students profited from his insights when turned to their own purposes, McDougal's most prominent disciple and heir to his jurisprudential approach is W. Michael Reisman. *See, e.g.*, W. Michael Reisman, *A Theory about Law from the Policy Perspective, in* LAW AND POLICY 75 (D. N. Weisstub ed., 1976), *reprinted as abridged in* MYRES S. MCDOUGAL & W. MICHAEL REISMAN, INTERNATIONAL LAW ESSAYS: A SUPPLEMENT TO INTERNATIONAL LAW IN CONTEMPORARY PERSPECTIVE 1 (1981); and the coauthored works cited in note 16 *supra*.

[22] Myres S. McDougal & Harold D. Lasswell, *The Identification and Appraisal of Diverse Systems of Public Order, in* MCDOUGAL & ASSOCIATES, *supra* note 16, at 39. World public order is defined as "those features of the world social process, including both goal values and implementing institutions, which are protected by law." For McDougal and his associates, the supreme value to be promoted by international lawyers is the protection and furtherance of human dignity.

[23] FALK, *supra* note 13, at 41–49. An earlier version of this essay was published in THE RELEVANCE OF INTERNATIONAL LAW, *supra* note 1. Falk teaches in a political science department, and his ability to

Falk and his fellow participants in the World Order Models project thus developed their own response to the Realist challenge, compounding a distinctive mixture of Legal Realism and global idealism. They continued the McDougalite mission of studying and promoting law "from a policy perspective," but from the perspective less of human dignity than of systemic stability. In a nuclear world system, stability was a prerequisite for survival. Within this framework, law could be conceived either as rules or as process, either as an "international code of conduct" formulated in response to "the living needs of international society,"[24] or as a flow of authoritative and effective decisions made by a hypothetical "supranational" decision maker.[25] The result was the same, a transcendent order that served to "advance the values and interests of the overall world community rather than to promote the more special and diverse interests and values of national actors who are components of that system."[26] Law was thus redefined in relation to politics, but the politics in question flowed not from contending ideologies, but from an autonomous systemic logic.

Falk understood that adopting a "systemic orientation" meant setting up "an ideal form," but he concluded that it offered a better hope of international legal order than proposals for radical systemic change such as world government. The strength and relevance of such an order was enhanced by his de-emphasis of the constraint function of international law in favor of a host of other functions that international legal norms can and often do perform in international relations. These included: (1) the specification of "the constituents of minimum world order"—the basic rules of the international game that define the boundaries of acceptable action even when violated; (2) the provision of a process of communication in crisis through competing claims of right; (3) the underpinning of stable expectations for routine transactions by providing rules for "law-oriented bureaucracies" to follow; (4) the enabling of "cooperative regimes" in technical areas from telecommunications to health;[27] and (5) the positing of "criteria by which national governments and other actors can act reasonably, if so inclined."[28]

In sum, the exponents of world order followed McDougal in conceding the constraint function of international law, thereby blunting the sharpest point of the Realist challenge. They accepted the need to tie law closely to the political interplay of power and interest. Yet within this framework they set out to show how international legal norms and rules perform functions that are indeed in the

---

bridge both disciplines, as well as his unparalleled capacity to digest and disseminate vast quantities of material, makes him an invaluable resource for anyone engaged in an interdisciplinary enterprise.

[24] FALK, *supra* note 13, at 49. [25] *Id.* at 57.

[26] *Id.* at 18. Falk was influenced here by the development of systems approaches in international relations theory, discussed *infra,* which allowed him to conceptualize the operation of international law independently of state actors. Rosalyn Higgins later questioned whether systems theory could indeed be used "to identify universal values" distinct from the values of "sub-universal systems" such as "corporations, regions, organizations." Higgins, *supra* note 19, at 91.

[27] This function inspired an entire category of legal scholarship on "nonpolitical" international legal regimes that Falk has described elsewhere as "functionalism," analogous to the functionalism of David Mitrany. Scholars such as Percy Corbett, Wolfgang Friedmann, C. Wilfred Jenks and Julius Stone concentrated on the growth of law and legal organization in areas perceived as not of vital interest to nation-states, on the assumption that the growth of, and growing confidence in, these institutions would gradually feed the growth of law in areas of increasingly vital interest as well. *See* Richard A. Falk, *New Approaches to the Study of International Law,* 61 AJIL 477, 491–93 (1967); Higgins, *supra* note 19, at 89–90.

[28] FALK, *supra* note 13, at 52–59.

rational self-interest even of powerful actors interacting within a self-contained political system.[29]

Pragmatism and legal process. McDougal understood international law as an integral part of ongoing political and social processes; Falk conceptualized international law in relation to those processes on a systemic level. Abram Chayes, Thomas Ehrlich and Andreas Lowenfeld also recast international law as process, but as "international *legal* process."[30] In lieu of "the definition, elaboration and analysis of asserted rules or norms," the study of international legal process concerns itself with the question: "How—and how far—do law, lawyers, and legal institutions operate to affect the course of international affairs?"[31]

In U.S. domestic law, the legal process school pioneered by Henry Hart, Albert Sachs and Herbert Wechsler was another response to Legal Realism, a response built on the idea that emphasis on the process and institutional place of legal decision making could maximize the democratic legitimacy of judicial lawmaking, if judicial lawmaking there must be.[32] Attention to the details of legal process was thus intended and designed to constrain the autonomous power of lawyers and judges. In the international realm, by contrast, the purpose of the international legal process approach was, again, the prior aim of demonstrating that lawyers and legal norms had any impact at all on political processes. In direct response to Kennan's charge, Chayes, Ehrlich and Lowenfeld affirmed: "In none of the problems presented in this book is law determinative of every issue. But in all of them law is relevant and the role of lawyers is important."[33]

A corollary to the international legal process approach is the collection of empirical evidence demonstrating the role of international law in specific international crises. Abram Chayes's documentation of the way legal norms helped shape the decision-making process during the Cuban missile crisis is a classic of this genre, part of a series commissioned by the American Society of International Law to study the role of international law in international crises.[34] The animus of this series was to learn "not *how much* did law affect a given decision, but *how*. What are the different ways in which law and legal institutions affect what happens in international affairs?"[35]

Chayes traced the functions of law as "constraint, justification, and organization" in one specific crisis.[36] Louis Henkin addressed this "how" question on a far

[29] The casebook produced by three leading members of this school, BURNS H. WESTON, RICHARD A. FALK & ANTHONY D'AMATO, INTERNATIONAL LAW AND WORLD ORDER (2d ed. 1990), seeks to introduce students to this insight by asking them to work through a wide range of international political problems so as to understand the role of law in their solution.

[30] CHAYES, EHRLICH & LOWENFELD, *supra* note 13.

[31] *Id.* at xii. A more recent work in this vein is DANIEL G. PARTAN, THE INTERNATIONAL LAW PROCESS (1992).

[32] For an excellent short overview of the sources and principal tenets of the legal process school, see Akhil R. Amar, *Law Story*, 102 HARV. L. REV. 688 (1989) (reviewing HART AND WECHSLER'S THE FEDERAL COURTS AND THE FEDERAL SYSTEM (Paul M. Bator et al. eds., 1988)).

[33] CHAYES, EHRLICH & LOWENFELD, *supra* note 13, at xii.

[34] ABRAM CHAYES, THE CUBAN MISSILE CRISIS (1974). Other works in this series are THOMAS EHRLICH, CYPRUS, 1958–1967 (1974); and ROGER FISHER, POINTS OF CHOICE (1978).

[35] Roger Fisher, *Foreword* to CHAYES, *supra* note 34, at v. Fisher chaired a panel of ASIL members involved in the series.

[36] Chayes later applied his method to the workings of arms control agreements, concluding that the standard "rational actor" approach employed in strategic theory overlooked the importance of "consensus, concession, and commitment" on the part of a multitude of bureaucratic actors involved in the negotiation and ratification of a treaty as forces for compliance. Chayes also argued that legal

broader scale, in the one book on international law virtually all political scientists have read. *How Nations Behave* proceeds from the now-familiar proposition that international law remains condemned "constantly [to] defend its existence" and "[e]ven more earnestly . . . its relevance to world events."[37] Henkin sought to convince the Realists that "law *is* a major force in world affairs," while persuading international lawyers to "think beyond the substantive rules of law to the function of law, the nature of its influence, the opportunities it offers, the limitations it imposes."[38] Law provides the "submerged" rules of international relations, the definition of a state and the provision of the instruments of its interaction and communication with other states;[39] it establishes "common standards where they seem desirable";[40] customary law and international agreements "avoid the need for negotiating anew in every new instance";[41] and both "create justified expectation[,] warrant confidence as to how others will behave"[42] and facilitate cooperation in the pursuit of common interests.[43]

This pragmatic approach, examining law as nations see it rather than as scholars understand and reimagine it,[44] is the strategy recommended by Francis Boyle to overcome Realist skepticism.[45] Boyle, an international lawyer also trained as a political scientist, understands the evidentiary hurdle that must be surmounted if this approach is to be effective. "Relevance," for Political Realists, means causal relevance to how nations behave. It means a demonstration that international legal rules provide incentives or constraints capable of producing outcomes significantly *different from* those that a pure power theory would predict. Boyle outlines a detailed protocol to meet these standards.

The Political Response: Refining and Modifying Realism

Although it may have been dominant, Morgenthau Realism was hardly the last word in political science. Subsequent international relations theorists sought to refine Realism as a theory of international politics. Some of these theorists also returned to asking how law could be accommodated within the framework of power politics. Specifically, the question animating political scientists interested in international law in the 1960s was how the dramatic postwar changes in the

provisions designed to require the furnishing of information on demand, now known as "transparency" provisions, could play as important a role in compliance as the standard model of verification and sanctions in noncompliance. Abram Chayes, *An Inquiry into the Workings of Arms Control Agreements*, 85 HARV. L. REV. 905, 934, 954–55 (1972).

[37] HENKIN, *supra* note 4, at ix (preface to 1st ed. 1968, reprinted in 2d ed. 1979). Part 4, entitled "The Law in Operation," specifically examines the role of law in foreign-policy decision making in four case studies: Suez, the Eichmann abduction, the Cuban missile crisis and Vietnam. The rest of the book explores the role and functions of law in a broader frame. *See also* Louis Henkin, *International Organization and the Rule of Law*, 23 INT'L ORG. 656 (1969) (describing how international organizations contribute to international lawmaking, influence the disposition of states to comply with their international commitments, and conform to the interests of the United States).

[38] HENKIN, *supra* note 4, at 4–5. Henkin, too, felt compelled to rebut Kennan's charge of the irrelevance and unsuitability of international law. *See id.* at 322–29.

[39] *Id.* at 21.

[40] *Id.* at 29.

[41] *Id.*

[42] *Id.*

[43] *Id.* at 20.

[44] This is Henkin's criticism of the McDougal school, a view of law "not as is but always as becoming" from some Archimedean perspective. *Id.* at 40; *see also* Louis Henkin, *Force, Intervention, and Neutrality in Contemporary International Law*, 57 ASIL PROC. 147, 168 (1963).

[45] BOYLE, *supra* note 6.

international political system had changed the nature and potential effectiveness of international legal norms. A decade later, norms were once again read out of the equation with the introduction of "Structural Realism" or "Neo-Realism." Yet this last swing of the pendulum generated its own strong response, culminating in the modification of Realism on its own terms and the reestablishment of a strong theoretical argument for the function and effectiveness of international law.

Systematizing the international system. While lawyers were trying to demonstrate the relevance of law to the shaping of politics, several prominent international relations theorists undertook to determine the impact of politics on law. Stanley Hoffmann was originally trained as an international lawyer; Morton Kaplan collaborated with Nicholas Katzenbach, a recognized scholar in private international law.[46] Both Hoffmann and Kaplan were early "systems theorists," scholars who sought to apply the insights of domestic systems theory to international politics.[47] Once they had conceptualized state interaction over time in terms of a typology of "international systems," the question became how the distinctive characteristics of different systems found expression in international law.[48] They regarded the international law of a particular era as both a reflection of the reigning political system and a repository of normative efforts to regulate and shape it.[49] An understanding of this interrelationship was crucial to any analysis of the potential effectiveness of those norms.

Hoffmann analyzed and compared the relationships between international law and world politics in three historical political systems: the balance of power system from the Peace of Westphalia to the French Revolution, the century balance of power system, and "the present revolutionary system."[50] Kaplan took a more

[46] Stanley Hoffmann, *International Systems and International Law, in* THE INTERNATIONAL SYSTEM 205 (Klaus Knorr & Sydney Verba eds., 1961), *reprinted in* INTERNATIONAL LAW AND ORGANIZATION, *supra* note 13, at 89 (all citations herein are to the latter version); MORTON A. KAPLAN & NICHOLAS KATZENBACH, THE POLITICAL FOUNDATIONS OF INTERNATIONAL LAW (1961). Other important systems theorists include RICHARD N. ROSECRANCE, ACTION AND REACTION IN WORLD POLITICS (1963), who distinguished nine separate historical systems, and Oran Young. As discussed above, Richard Falk also drew on the insights of systems theory, but as a means of conceptualizing an *international legal system.*

[47] This effort was part of the ongoing struggle to define international relations as an "autonomous discipline." On the relationship between this effort and the conceptualization of international politics as constituting part of a distinct system, see CONTEMPORARY THEORY IN INTERNATIONAL RELATIONS 1-3 (Stanley Hoffmann ed., 1960).

For a brief, but useful, overview of the evolution of systems theory from the behavioral sciences, sociology, and cybernetics to domestic and, finally, international political science, see CONTENDING THEORIES OF INTERNATIONAL RELATIONS 102-37 (James E. Dougherty & Robert L. Pfaltzgraff eds., 1st ed. 1971). A more sophisticated review is YOUNG, *supra* note 17. For a particularly thoughtful effort to describe what a developed systems theory might look like, see ORAN R. YOUNG, A SYSTEMIC APPROACH TO INTERNATIONAL POLITICS (Princeton Research Monograph No. 33, 1968), which also features an exhaustive bibliography of systems literature.

[48] Each systems theorist uses a slightly different definition of "system," but all agree that the analytic concept of a system requires study of the *interaction* of states with one another within a particular structure and in accordance with established patterns of behavior.

[49] A quite different "systems approach" was that of political scientist William Coplin, *supra* note 13, who argued that international law should be thought of as a system of authoritative communication, particularly communication to actors within the system about the nature and structure of the system. Coplin's analogy between this function of international law and the function of domestic law in socialization processes bears striking resemblance to the arguments advanced a decade later by critical legal theorists in both domestic and international law.

[50] Hoffmann, *supra* note 46, at 107.

abstract approach, constructing six models of hypothetical international systems.[51] He and Katzenbach integrated this approach with McDougal-Lasswell jurisprudence, analyzing international legal norms as related to and constrained by the underlying institutions, values and interests in the political system they purport to govern. They sought particularly to explicate the differences between the international law of the nineteenth-century balance of power system and that of the contemporary "loose bipolar" system.[52]

These proponents of systems theory met the Realist challenge from within political science by articulating at least a potential role for international law. For international lawyers of the era, however, seeking to evaluate current prospects for practicing their trade, the results were decidedly mixed. From Hoffmann's point of view, the prospects for international law were dim as long as the current "revolutionary" system precluded any genuine political consensus or community of interests necessary to ensure at least minimum compliance with the rules of the game.[53] Kaplan and Katzenbach were considerably more positive, finding that "the United States and the Soviet Union have a joint interest in maintaining those minimal normative standards that permit each to live tolerably in a world in which the other is powerful."[54] Yet they also admitted that "more than one normative structure may be consistent with the present facts of international politics."[55]

From the perspective of traditional international lawyers, law conditioned on the polarities of power and any number of other political, economic and social variables was distressingly indeterminate;[56] moreover, "minimal normative standards" were a far cry from the carefully drawn rules of the Charter. It would have been reasonable to conclude that the effort to uncover the political roots of

[51] MORTON A. KAPLAN, SYSTEM AND PROCESS IN INTERNATIONAL POLITICS (1962).

[52] In contrast to this deliberate application of McDougal's principles, Hoffmann explicitly distanced himself from "deniers or cynics" "disguised as 'policy-oriented' theorists who dissolve rules and principles into a maze of processes, messages, and alternatives." Hoffmann, *supra* note 46, at 116. Yet a number of his conclusions strikingly accord with McDougal's analysis, notably his claim that in revolutionary systems, "gaps and ambiguities [in the law] become wedges for destruction or subversion of the international order in the interest of any of the actors." *Id.* at 98. This argument echoes McDougal's pleas for the avoidance of a "false universalism" in a system in which states with very different values can exploit ambiguities to their own advantage. The difference between the two thinkers is that Hoffmann saw these difficulties as limiting the relevance and usefulness of international law in certain political circumstances; McDougal sought to *use* the law to help change these political circumstances. *See* Stanley Hoffmann, *International Law and the Control of Force, in* THE RELEVANCE OF INTERNATIONAL LAW, *supra* note 1, at 21 [hereinafter *Control of Force*].

[53] *See* Hoffmann, *Control of Force, supra* note 52. As Hoffmann explained, his analysis led him to the regretful conclusion that "the plight of international law in the present international milieu is particularly serious," and that "the relevance of legal rules to the control of the use of force among states will . . . remain limited in the near future." *Id.* at 21. Contrary to the suggestion of some of his critics in the international legal community, however, he did not abandon hope for a future international legal order or advocate passivity until the system changed. He argued, instead, for pursuing the development of international law in areas other than the control of force, and in that area to develop practices that might operate as "quasi-law." *Id.* at 45.

[54] KAPLAN & KATZENBACH, *supra* note 46, at 348. This approach earned Falk's praise for using systems analysis to make a case for the value and potential effectiveness of international norms. FALK, *supra* note 13, at 486–87. Another international relations theorist, writing roughly contemporaneously with Kaplan and Katzenbach, who reached similar conclusions from staunchly Realist premises is JOHN H. HERZ, INTERNATIONAL POLITICS IN THE ATOMIC AGE (1959).

[55] KAPLAN & KATZENBACH, *supra* note 46, at 351.

[56] Even McDougal reached this conclusion, notwithstanding Kaplan and Katzenbach's acknowledged debt to his conceptual apparatus and professed efforts to apply it. *See* McDougal & Reisman, *Policy-Oriented Perspective, supra* note 16, at 112.

positive law undermined the autonomous legal foundations of normative law. In retrospect, however, such approaches were the high-water mark in interdisciplinary conceptions of international law and politics, at least until the early 1980s. The new generation of systems theorists proved far less congenial to international law.

Kenneth Waltz, one of the most influential international relations theorists of the 1980s, first distinguished among individual, unit-level and systemic levels of analysis in *Man, the State and War,* published in 1958. Over the next twenty years, he crafted a powerful and precise critique and redefinition of systems theory, redefining Political Realism in the process.[57] Waltz attacked earlier theorists such as Hoffmann and Kaplan for completely confusing "unit-level" with true systemic explanations. Their "systems" were no more than the sum total of the motives and actions of the actors within them. A true systemic explanation, by contrast, relies on the "structure" within which those actors act. It assumes that structural elements dictate channels of actor interaction and ultimately determine the outcomes of that interaction. The components of that structure, in turn, are threefold: an ordering principle, the differentiation and functional specification of the units, and the distribution of capabilities across units.

A comprehensive description of Waltz's theory, variously known as "Structural Realism" or "Neo-Realism," is beyond the scope of this article. The key point here is that from an international lawyer's perspective, his vision of the international system is extremely narrow. Unlike the structure of domestic political systems, Waltz argued, the structure of the *international* political system contains only two of the three potential components: anarchy (the ordering principle) and the number of great powers within the system (the distribution of capabilities across units). From this "positional picture" could the basic laws of international politics be deduced.[58] Whereas the missing component (the differentiation and functional specification of the units) permits some role for law in domestic political systems, its absence from Waltz's conception of the international system affords no comparable role for international law.

Waltz's was a brilliant and lasting achievement. In a discipline hungry for the theoretical apparatus that accompanies self-definition, he systematized the international system. But he left no room whatsoever for international law. If the earlier systems theorists had understood international legal norms to be inevitably conditioned and ultimately constrained by politics, they at least recognized international law as an autonomous variable in the international system, of differing strength under specified conditions. For Waltz, norms of any sort, qua norms, lacked independent causal force.

Modifying Structural Realism. Ironically, help came from a camp of political scientists, scholars who had been explicitly distancing themselves further and further from anything called "law" for twenty years. These were the students of international organization, or, more broadly, "international governance," defined as "the coordination of group activities so as to conduct the public business . . . consistent with national sovereignty."[59] As chronicled by Friedrich Kratochwil and John Ruggie in an insightful review of the field since its inception in the interwar period, the scholarly focus in this area shifted from a preoccupa-

[57] KENNETH N. WALTZ, THEORY OF INTERNATIONAL POLITICS (1979).

[58] *Id.* at 99.

[59] Friedrich Kratochwil & John G. Ruggie, *International organization: a state of the art on an art of the state,* 40 INT'L ORG. 753, 754 (1986).

tion with formal institutions, to an emphasis on institutional processes, to a more general inquiry into how international organizations work in a larger process of international governance. The last step in this progression was the reconceptualization of the entire field of international organization as the study of "international regimes," defined as the "principles, norms, rules, and decision-making procedures around which actor expectations converge in a given issue-area."[60]

This trajectory rescued the field of international organization from "irrelevance, if not obscurity,"[61] transforming it into one of the most vibrant and exciting areas of general international relations theory. By the late 1970s and early 1980s, the regime theorists were willing to challenge the Realists directly. The problem was how to explain the continued existence and relative strength of international institutions following the perceived decline of American hegemony.[62] Realists, both traditional and structural, had explained the existence of these institutions as a corollary of dominant U.S. power, and now had to argue either that U.S. power was not declining or that institutions from the General Agreement on Tariffs and Trade to the International Monetary Fund were suddenly tottering.

The alternative explanation favored by the regime theorists was that these institutions served a valuable purpose in their own right. The majority subgroup of these theorists, dubbed "modified structural realists," developed a theory of regimes that proceeded explicitly from neo-Realist premises, accepting the standard assumption of states as rational egoists and acknowledging the primary importance of the structure of the international system as a determinant of state behavior.[63] Robert Keohane took this approach one step further. Drawing on rational-choice techniques from the same microeconomics literature venerated by Waltz, he elaborated a "functional" theory of regimes that explains their pervasiveness and persistence in international politics as a result of rational calculations by participating states.

In *After Hegemony,* Keohane argues that international regimes

> enhance the likelihood of cooperation by reducing the costs of making transactions that are consistent with the principles of the regime. They create the

[60] Kratochwil and Ruggie trace every step of this progression with copious citations, and follow up with a critique of current trends in regime theory. For anyone interested in political science writing on international organization generally and regime theory in particular, this is necessary reading, as is the 1982 special issue of *International Organization* on international regimes, republished as INTERNATIONAL REGIMES (Stephen D. Krasner ed., 1983). Krasner's introduction provides an overview of the various approaches to regimes encompassed in the volume, ranging from Structural Realist skepticism to what he terms a "Grotian" position, advanced by Oran Young and Hopkins and Puchala, who regard regimes as the model status of international life. In between is the majority position in the volume, exemplified by the contributions of Robert Keohane and Arthur Stein, who proceed from Structural Realist premises but argue that regimes can maximize cooperation under specified conditions. Stephen D. Krasner, *Structural causes and regime consequences: regimes as intervening variables, in id.* at 1.

Two excellent reviews of the literature since then are Stephan Haggard & Beth A. Simmons, *Theories of International Regimes,* 41 INT'L ORG. 491 (1987); and Oran R. Young, *International Regimes: Toward a New Theory of Institutions,* 39 WORLD POL. 104 (1986). A valuable overview of the basic concepts of regime theory written especially for international lawyers is Kenneth W. Abbott, *Modern International Relations Theory: A Prospectus for International Lawyers,* 14 YALE J. INT'L L. 335 (1989).

The definition of regimes in the text is in Krasner, *supra,* at 2.

[61] Kratochwil & Ruggie, *supra* note 59, at 753.

[62] *See* Krasner, *supra* note 60; and ROBERT O. KEOHANE, AFTER HEGEMONY: COOPERATION AND DISCORD IN THE WORLD POLITICAL ECONOMY 8–10 (1984).

[63] *See* Krasner, *supra* note 60. See also discussion *supra* note 60.

> conditions for orderly multilateral negotiations, legitimate and delegitimate different types of state action, and facilitate linkages among issues within regimes and between regimes. They increase the symmetry and improve the quality of the information that governments receive.[64]

International regimes also enhance compliance with international agreements in a variety of ways, from reducing incentives to cheat and enhancing the value of reputation, to "establishing legitimate standards of behavior for states to follow" and facilitating monitoring, which creates "the basis for decentralized enforcement founded on the principle of reciprocity."[65]

This "functionalist" or, as it would later come to be known, "rationalist" view of regimes has provided a tool for the study of international cooperation that extends beyond the traditional "low politics" of international political economy, long thought a more fertile area for cooperative action than the "high politics" of security studies, where most Realists were concentrated.[66] As a group of international political economists and security scholars subsequently demonstrated, the approach was equally applicable to explaining cooperation under conditions of conflict.[67] Here the regime theorists were challenging the neo-Realists on their own ground.[68] And indeed, taken as a whole, Keohane's brand of regime theory constitutes not only a modification of Structural Realism, but also a critique, arguing that information must be added to power on the list of systemic variables.[69] Institutions that provide valuable information must thus be factored into systemic explanations of state behavior independently of structure.[70]

Rediscovering international law (and refusing to recognize it). Keohane is careful to distinguish these functions of regimes from world government, or even "centralized quasi-governments."[71] Rejecting a view of institutions based on " 'peace through law' or world government," he argues that "institutions that facilitate cooperation do not mandate what governments must do; rather, they help governments pursue their own interests through cooperation."[72] In a word, institutions "*empower* governments rather than shackling them."[73]

This was an insight new only to political scientists.[74] As discussed above, international lawyers had spent the previous three decades defining international law as something *other* than an Austinian constraint system. "World government" was international legal scholarship circa 1960, when scholars such as Inis Claude warned international lawyers to focus more on the "peace among groups" aspect

[64] KEOHANE, *supra* note 62, at 244. *See also* ORAN R. YOUNG, INTERNATIONAL COOPERATION: BUILDING REGIMES FOR NATURAL RESOURCES AND THE ENVIRONMENT (1989).

[65] KEOHANE, *supra* note 62, at 244–45.

[66] For elaboration on this point, see Kratochwil & Ruggie, *supra* note 59, at 762.

[67] *See* Robert Jervis, *Security Regimes*, *in* INTERNATIONAL REGIMES, *supra* note 60, at 173; COOPERATION UNDER ANARCHY (Kenneth A. Oye ed., 1986).

[68] For a collection of critiques of Neo-Realism, see NEO-REALISM AND ITS CRITICS (Robert O. Keohane ed., 1986).

[69] KEOHANE, *supra* note 62, at 14, 245.

[70] This was the "modification" of Structural Realism. Keohane also criticized the neo-Realists for relying too heavily on systemic approaches, arguing that, although valuable as a "first cut," such approaches must ultimately be supplemented by "unit-level" explanations drawn from domestic politics.

[71] KEOHANE, *supra* note 62, at 244.

[72] *Id.* at 246.

[73] *Id.* at 13.

[74] In an extensive bibliography, Keohane lists only one international law source, Henkin's *How Nations Behave*, which he cites for the proposition that regimes are fragmentary, and for "go[ing] so far as to say that 'almost all nations observe almost all principles of international law and almost all of their obligations almost all of the time.' " *Id.* at 88, 98 (quoting HENKIN, *supra* note 4, at 47).

TABLE 1

INTERNATIONAL NORMS AND INSTITUTIONS FROM THE PERSPECTIVE OF REGIME THEORISTS AND INTERNATIONAL LAWYERS

Functions and Benefits of International Regimes	Functions and Benefits of International Law
lowering transaction costs	providing rules of the game; fostering stable expectations (Falk, Henkin, Chayes)
creating conditions for orderly multilateral negotiations	establishing efficient baselines: avoiding the need for constant renegotiation and establishing common standards where they seem desirable (Henkin)
legitimating and delegitimating types of state action	positing criteria by which national governments and others can act reasonably and justify their action (Falk, Chayes)
	providing a process of communication in crisis (Falk)
increasing symmetry and improving quality of information	
	creating opportunities for intermeshing of national and international bureaucracies (Falk)
facilitating linkages	
enhancing compliance by creating conditions for decentralized enforcement: monitoring; enhancing value of reputation; establishing legitimate standards of behavior	enhancing compliance by embedding international agreements in domestic political and bureaucratic processes, improving transparency and fostering routinized "habits of compliance" (Chayes, Henkin)

of domestic legal structure.[75] Keohane followed this advice, but so had the audience for which it was intended. The international lawyers discussed above, among others, had spent two decades emphasizing the *facilitative* properties of international law. A comparison of a prototypical "functionalist" regime theorist's list of the attributes of international regimes with a summary of the functions and uses of international law, as identified by various international lawyers, is instructive (see table 1 above).

The overlap is not complete, the language and focus often still divergent. Nevertheless, the overall message is clear. Political scientists have rediscovered international law, explaining its function and value to their fellow scholars in terms very similar to those long used by international lawyers.

II. THE FRUITS OF CONVERGENCE: THE INSTITUTIONALIST AGENDA

Although frustrating to many international lawyers, the early regime theorists' insistence on deriving a theory of international institutions from Realist premises was a clever strategic move within political science. Reinventing international law in rational-choice language stopped the traditional "Realist-Idealist" debate cold. "Efficiency and transparency" are hardly legalist-moralist sentiments. They are the language of rational calculation, effective not only with political science Realists but also with a large and growing number of international lawyers' domestic colleagues.

[75] INIS L. CLAUDE, POWER AND INTERNATIONAL RELATIONS 255–71 (1962).

Further, modified Structural Realism added a valuable precision to the more general formulations of the "functions" of international law developed by international lawyers. While international lawyers may complain that regime theorists are simply restating the obvious—that international legal rules, norms and decision-making procedures facilitate cooperation—regime theorists may legitimately respond that international lawyers have been all too willing to accept this premise as an article of faith rather than as a theoretically deducible and empirically verifiable phenomenon. As noted, the overlap between the two sides of table 1 is not complete: regime theorists have elaborated much more detailed theories about the value of information to international cooperation and the ways that institutionalization shapes multilateral negotiations. Finally, the development of a "theory" of regimes permits regime theorists to predict "the demand" for international regimes, and thus the relative strength of different regimes according to fluctuations in the underlying demand.[76]

In the end, disciplinary one-upmanship must remain secondary to the central point: even without coercion and thus the requirement of central enforcement, legal rules and decision-making procedures can be used to structure international politics.[77] Regime theorists have elucidated this process in ways both familiar and unfamiliar to international lawyers. More important, however, they have reached a point where they are likely to be far more receptive to the lessons international lawyers can teach them about the functions of international law, particularly regarding the international legal emphasis on the role of law in providing focal points for the crystallization and stabilization of expectations.[78]

As the regime theorists won adherents, they differentiated themselves further from Realism, in both its classic and structural varieties. Keohane recast modified Structural Realism as "Neoliberal Institutionalism," a theoretical approach that begins by recognizing "the fact that world politics at any given time is to some extent institutionalized," both through "[f]ormal international organizations and codified rules and norms ('international regimes')" and through less-formalized patterns of behavior "recognized by participants as reflecting established rules, norms, and conventions."[79] Briefly, Neo-Liberal Institutionalism asserts "that con-

[76] *See, e.g.*, Robert O. Keohane, *The Demand for International Regimes*, *in* INTERNATIONAL REGIMES, *supra* note 60, at 141.

[77] This is the role that even Kenneth Waltz attributes to law in the domestic setting. Waltz analogizes the international system to a domestic market, in which the constituent units are governed by the law of unintended consequences and thus can be analyzed independently of their actual intentions. He claims that the analogy ends, however, because domestic markets are structured by laws channeling individual interests into productive uses, such as electoral laws, securities and banking regulation, antitrust laws, etc. WALTZ, *supra* note 57, at 91. In his words:

> To say that the two realms are structurally similar is not to proclaim their identity. Economically, the self-help principle applies within governmentally contrived limits. Market economies are hedged about in ways that channel energies constructively. One may think of pure food-and-drug standards, antitrust laws, securities and exchange regulations, laws against shooting a competitor, and rules forbidding false claims in advertising. International politics is more nearly a realm in which anything goes. International politics is structurally similar to a market economy insofar as the self-help principle is allowed to operate in the latter.

Id.

[78] *See* Geoffrey Garrett & Barry R. Weingast, *Ideas, Interests and Institutions: Constructing the EC's Internal Market*, *in* IDEAS AND FOREIGN POLICY (Judith Goldstein & Robert O. Keohane eds., forthcoming 1993).

[79] ROBERT O. KEOHANE, INTERNATIONAL INSTITUTIONS AND STATE POWER at vii (1989). This volume is a collection of Keohane's essays on institutions through the 1980s. For those seeking to find

ventions in world politics are as fundamental as the distribution of capabilities among states."[80] Thus formulated, Neo-Liberal Institutionalism stands more for a set of questions than for any particular answers, and offers a strong generic framework for any number of collaborative enterprises between international lawyers and political scientists.[81]

These opportunities for interdisciplinary collaboration expand even further when Keohane's "rationalist" critique of Neo-Realism is supplemented by an emerging "reflectivist" or "constructivist" critique. This approach focuses even more explicitly on the role of international legal norms in shaping state behavior. It forsakes rational-choice analysis for an exploration of the "intersubjective" quality of regimes and the auto-construction of both identities and interests.[82] It correspondingly focuses on the power of process and institutions to *transform* the self-perceptions of participants, and thus to reshape their calculation of interests. From this perspective, a shared understanding of international law as law is integral to its effectiveness.

Components of an Institutionalist Interdisciplinary Dialogue

Valuable lines of inquiry within Institutionalism include the following, all of which currently engage international lawyers and political scientists who are working along very similar lines and who could usefully participate in direct interdisciplinary debate.

Distinguishing legal regimes from nonlegal regimes. As international lawyers will not need to be reminded, Keohane's catholic definition of "international institutions" seems to track the customary and conventional sources of international law.[83] Yet the concept of international institutions is clearly broader than that of international law. A new question on the agenda thus concerns the difference between "legal" regimes and other regimes and their differential impact on state

---

their way through the bewildering maze of theoretical labels, the introductory essay offers a useful overview of the distinctions among Neo-Liberal Institutionalism, Neo-Realism, and Liberalism. However, Keohane's summation of the Liberal tradition differs considerably from the Liberal paradigm described in the second half of this article. He defines Liberalism "as a set of guiding principles for contemporary social science." Yet his preferred subset of these principles closely resembles Institutionalism. Thus, "Neoliberal institutionalists accept a version of liberal principles that . . . emphasizes the pervasive significance of international institutions without denigrating the role of state power." *Id.* at 11.

[80] *Id.* at 8.

[81] For an even more comprehensive approach to international relations theory that accords international law and institutions a central role, see Charles Lipson, The Centrality of Contract in International Relations (paper presented at Annual Meeting of the American Political Science Association, Chicago, IL, September 1992). Lipson advocates reconceptualizing all problems of international politics as "problems of contract."

[82] Kratochwil and Ruggie advocate this approach in the conclusion to their survey, pointing out that a definition of regimes that includes the element of convergent expectations necessarily has an intersubjective dimension. Kratochwil & Ruggie, *supra* note 59, at 763–71. *See also* FRIEDRICH KRATOCHWIL, RULES, NORMS, AND DECISIONS (1989); NICHOLAS G. ONUF, WORLD OF OUR MAKING: RULES AND RULE IN SOCIAL THEORY AND INTERNATIONAL RELATIONS (1989); Alexander Wendt, *Anarchy is What States Make of It*, 46 INT'L ORG. 391 (1992). The "rationalist/reflectivist" dichotomy was coined by Keohane in his 1988 presidential address to the International Studies Association. Robert O. Keohane, *International Institutions: Two Approaches*, 32 INT'L STUD. Q. 379 (1988).

[83] *Cf.* INTERNATIONAL COURT OF JUSTICE, STATUTE Art. 38 (instructing the Court to apply "international conventions, whether general or particular, establishing rules expressly recognized by the contesting states" and "international custom, as evidence of a general practice accepted as law").

behavior.[84] In remarks at the 1992 Annual Meeting of the American Society of International Law, Oran Young proposes a collaborative focus on several issues of mutual interest to political scientists and international lawyers.[85] One of the functional distinctions he proposes intersects recent work in both political science and law on the uses of "soft law" or informal agreements.[86] Yet he also emphasizes more traditional jurisprudential distinctions based on the source of legal obligation and, in particular, the distinctive nature of legal reasoning.[87] This latter line of inquiry might draw on the insights of recent critical scholarship.[88]

Organizational design. Another important area of potential collaboration is the question of organizational design, a subject targeted by Kratochwil and Ruggie as a way to bring the theory of international relations back to the practice of international organizations.[89] Enhancing our understanding of how different institutions can best perform a range of international problems is of equal interest to political scientists and lawyers.[90] Further, the "reflectivist" or intersubjective emphasis on the ways that organizations fulfill requirements of *transparency* and *legitimation* directly coincides with several important streams of international legal scholarship.[91]

Compliance. Many important studies of the phenomenon of compliance with international agreements are currently under way. Abram and Antonia Chayes have argued for decades that treaty "compliance" provisions are more effective at

[84] Keohane, following Haggard and Simmons, now limits the definition of regimes to "institutions with explicit rules, negotiated by states." KEOHANE, *supra* note 79, at 4, 17 n.5 (1989). It seems safe to assume that this definition of regimes will be virtually coextensive with Young's category of "legal regimes."

[85] Oran R. Young, Remarks, 86 ASIL PROC. 172 (1992). On the same panel, Kenneth Abbott went so far as to call for a new joint discipline, possibly called "the study of organized international cooperation," to take full advantage of shared understandings between international relations and international law. Kenneth W. Abbott, *Elements of a Joint Discipline*, *id.* at 167, 168.

Keohane has also called for further inquiry into the distinctions among different types of international institutions: formal organizations, regimes, and informal institutions or practices. KEOHANE, *supra* note 79, at 13–14. He explicitly poses the question whether "alliances ever develop norms that are not subject to calculations of interest, and that are therefore genuine normative commitments for participants." *Id.* at 15.

[86] Examples of legal writing on this issue include Anthony D'Amato, *What 'Counts' As Law?*, *in* LAWMAKING IN THE GLOBAL COMMUNITY 83 (Nicholas G. Onuf ed., 1982); and Peter S. Thacher, *Alternative Legal and Institutional Approaches to Global Change*, 1 COLO. J. INT'L ENVTL. L. & POL'Y 101 (1990). The most sophisticated treatment of this subject in political science is Charles Lipson, *Why are some international agreements informal?*, 45 INT'L ORG. 495 (1991).

[87] Young's arguments here track those of Friedrich Kratochwil. *See* KRATOCHWIL, *supra* note 82.

[88] *See, e.g.*, Kennedy, *supra* note 12; MARTTI KOSKENNIEMI, FROM APOLOGY TO UTOPIA: THE STRUCTURE OF INTERNATIONAL LEGAL ARGUMENT (1989).

[89] Kratochwil & Ruggie, *supra* note 59, at 772–73.

[90] A recent paper by Kenneth Abbott offers an exemplar of this approach, using an interdisciplinary framework to investigate the "rational design hypothesis" with respect to provisions governing the production of information in arms control agreements. Kenneth W. Abbott, *The Production of Information in Arms Control Treaties and Other International Agreements*, 26 CORNELL INT'L L.J. 701 (1993). *See also* Lipson, *supra* note 86.

[91] On transparency, see the work of Abram and Antonia Chayes outlining a noncriminal model of compliance that specifically addresses questions of organizational design. Abram Chayes & Antonia H. Chayes, *Regime Architecture—Elements and Principles* (Brookings Institution ed. volume, forthcoming 1993); *see also* Abram Chayes & Antonia H. Chayes, *On Compliance*, INT'L ORG. (forthcoming 1993). On the "compliance pull" of legitimacy, and for a serious effort to specify the content and dimensions of legitimacy, see THOMAS M. FRANCK, THE POWER OF LEGITIMACY AMONG NATIONS (1990).

specifying venues and structuring processes for dispute resolution than at "enforcing" compliance.[92] A group of younger scholars have used regime theory to conceptualize and measure compliance with international human rights regimes,[93] arms control treaties[94] and regimes governing the use of force.[95] On the political science side, Robert Keohane complements this insight by showing how rational state actors have plenty of incentives to agree to such provisions at the outset.[96] By drawing on insights and perspectives from scholars in both fields, it should be possible to formulate a set of questions to which both sides can contribute factual information and theoretical insight. The results of inquiries from both perspectives could then be synthesized in a common framework that would highlight the overlap of both disciplines and the comparative advantage of each.

International ethics. The final candidate in this brief and admittedly partial list is a renewed focus on direct normative inquiry in international politics. International ethics is an obvious area of overlap for international political theorists and international lawyers, but one that has suffered a fate similar to that of international law in international relations theory.[97] One way to strengthen this subfield is to argue *against* the uniqueness of the international realm, which would open the door to applying the same moral criteria to international political arrangements as to domestic political arrangements.[98]

[92] *See* Chayes & Chayes, *Regime Architecture, supra* note 91. Other interesting interdisciplinary work on compliance includes J. H. Ausubel & D. G. Victor, *Verification of International Environmental Agreements,* 17 ANN. REV. ENERGY & ENV'T 1 (1992); RONALD B. MITCHELL, FROM PAPER TO PRACTICE: IMPROVING ENVIRONMENTAL TREATY COMPLIANCE (1992); GLOBAL ENVIRONMENTAL CHANGE: UNDERSTANDING THE HUMAN DIMENSIONS (Paul C. Stern et al. eds., 1992); ORAN R. YOUNG, COMPLIANCE AND PUBLIC AUTHORITY: A THEORY OF INTERNATIONAL APPLICATIONS (1979); ROBERT O. KEOHANE, SOVEREIGNTY, INTERDEPENDENCE AND INTERNATIONAL INSTITUTIONS (1991); Robert O. Keohane, *Compliance with International Commitments: Politics within a Framework of Law,* 86 ASIL PROC. 176 (1992).

[93] Diane F. Orentlicher, *The Power of an Idea: The Impact of United States Human Rights Policy,* 1 TRANSNAT'L L. & CONTEMP. PROBS. 43 (1991) (uses regime theory to develop a model of the effectiveness of international human rights law, placing "norm-generating and compliance-directed activities" "along a spectrum of regime activities, ranging from weak to comparatively strong measures of promoting certain behavior"; *id.* at 64).

[94] Edwin M. Smith, *Understanding Dynamic Obligations: Arms Control Agreements,* 64 S. CAL. L. REV. 1549 (1991) (connects regime theory with relational contract literature to conceptualize and interpret a new class of international obligations that are defined within the context of a formal international agreement but that cannot be defined at the time the agreement is executed).

[95] Francis A. Boyle, *International Law and the Use of Force: Beyond Regime Theory, in* IDEAS AND IDEALS: ESSAYS ON POLITICS IN HONOR OF STANLEY HOFFMANN (forthcoming 1993).

[96] Robert O. Keohane, U.S. Compliance with Commitments: Reciprocity and Institutional Enmeshment (paper presented at Program on International Politics, Economics, and Security (PIPES), University of Chicago, Oct. 24, 1991).

[97] Notable exceptions include STANLEY HOFFMANN, DUTIES BEYOND BORDERS (1981); and CHARLES R. BEITZ, POLITICAL THEORY AND INTERNATIONAL RELATIONS (1979). Michael Doyle is currently working on a major project seeking to reconnect Kant's political and moral theories.

[98] Lea Brilmayer is pioneering this effort, arguing first that governmental treatment of foreigners should be subject to the same moral and political criteria as the treatment of citizens, and now that the "legitimacy of international hegemony" depends on the same criteria as the legitimacy of domestic government. *See* LEA BRILMAYER, JUSTIFYING INTERNATIONAL ACTS (1989); Lea Brilmayer, The Legitimacy of International Hegemony (unpublished draft). *See also* FRANCK, *supra* note 91. Franck is currently exploring ways to apply the fairness principles developed by John Rawls to the evaluation of international legal norms. Franck, *supra* note 2. In an equally philosophical tradition, Fernando Tesón is working to revive the Kantian moral tradition in international law. *See* Fernando Tesón, *The Kantian Theory of International Law,* 92 COLUM. L. REV. 53 (1992); Fernando Tesón, *Realism and Kantianism in International Law,* 86 ASIL PROC. 113 (1992).

Deficiencies of the Institutionalist Agenda

The above account is ultimately one of increasing convergence between international political science and international law, uniting scholars working in the most vigorous and dynamic areas of their respective fields. Moreover, in the wake of the Cold War and the dramatic revitalization of the United Nations, international law is enjoying a resurgence of interest from all sides.[99]

Why not stop here? The answer is that Institutionalism, however formulated, remains theoretically inadequate in many ways. Like all international relations theories, it is admittedly a partial theory. There is much of the world that it does not explain; and some of what it purports to explain, it explains poorly. Some of its deficiencies are of direct concern to international lawyers.

First, as Institutionalists themselves admit, regime theory cannot yet account for the creation of regimes in the first place, and how and when they are likely to change. The starting point for the applicability of regime theory is the assumption that, to the extent that states have mutual interests, the perceived benefits of cooperation will outweigh the costs; in such a case the existence of a regime will facilitate cooperation in all the ways outlined above. But when will the perceived benefits outweigh the costs? Who is doing the perceiving? For international lawyers, the answers are important. They are different ways of asking, What are the optimal conditions for the functioning of international law?

These problems are likely to be exacerbated to the extent that the "rationalist" approach to institutions remains dominant. The intellectual blinders imposed by an insistent "rationalism" may be most hampering precisely when trained on periods of the greatest change in international relations, when human endeavors are self-consciously "transformative."[100] Here the flaw in Institutionalism, for international lawyers, is its inability to relate positive description to normative aspiration. What nations "want," in either material or ideal terms, is irrelevant. The system, whether institutionalized or noninstitutionalized, dictates what they can get.[101]

Second, Institutionalism cannot take account of individual-state relations, either domestic or transnational, or transnational individual-individual relations. It thus cannot provide a politico-economic theory to help conceptualize and analyze the law that regulates these relations. This deficit is considerable, because such areas of law include human rights law, transnational litigation and arbitration law, and the law regulating international business transactions. Such law regulates domestic and transnational actors, which in regime theory are once again subsumed beneath the state.[102]

Third, *neither* Institutionalism *nor* international legal scholarship can take account of, much less use, evidence of the "democratic peace": evidence that "with

[99] This author has recently been approached by the editors of two well-respected journals in international political science seeking advice on how to increase the number of articles they publish on international law.

[100] I am indebted here to John Gerard Ruggie's remarks on a panel entitled "Neorealism and Neoliberal Institutionalism" at the September 1992 American Political Science Association Annual Meeting in Chicago.

[101] For a fuller explication of this difference, see Andrew Moravcsik, Liberalism and International Relations Theory (working paper, Center for International Affairs, Harvard University, 1992).

[102] For an explanation of this shift away from an emphasis on transnational actors in international relations back toward state-centric modes of analysis by one of its principal architects, see KEOHANE, *supra* note 79, at 8.

only marginal exceptions, democratic States have not fought each other in the modern era."[103] As Bruce Russett puts it, drawing on a growing pile of studies of increasing statistical rigor, "This is perhaps the strongest non-trivial or non-tautological statement that can be made about international relations."[104] These same studies strongly suggest that the correlation is not spurious, that a *causal* link exists between reciprocal peaceful behavior and the internal social, political and economic configuration of states.

Leading Institutionalists have emphasized the need to turn to theories of domestic politics to supplement regime theory.[105] Their interest, however, is limited to using domestic political factors to explain outstanding questions of regime creation and change. This overriding emphasis on the link between the level of *institutionalization* and international cooperation precludes them from taking account, in any systematic fashion, of evidence on sources of peace and cooperation unrelated to institutions. International lawyers, on the other hand, are hamstrung by their disciplinary insistence on what Hoffmann has described as the "formal homogeneity of a legal system whose members are supposedly equal."[106] The inability to differentiate between different types of state on the basis of domestic regime type has been implicit in international law since Grotius. It is grounded in the very concept of "sovereign states" as the equal and identical subjects of international law, and buttressed by the affirmative norms of sovereign equality and nonintervention.

In sum, whether convergent or divergent on the relevance and function of international law and institutions, mainstream international relations theory and international legal scholarship share a set of fundamental analytical assumptions. Theirs is a "top-down" analysis, beginning with standard Realist assumptions that unlike entities (states) can be treated as like for analytical purposes, by virtue of the constraints and incentives imposed by the international system. Whether that system includes patterns of institutionalized behavior, shaped and conditioned by law and international organizations, is a secondary question. At its core, the model of "how nations behave" is a "black box" or "billiard ball" model of the international system, in which states are regarded as identical in form and function and opaque with regard to domestic regime type and state-society relations.[107]

III. A New Paradigm: The Liberal Agenda

A rich vein of collaborative scholarship between Neo-Liberal Institutionalists and international legal scholars thus waits to be mined. Considerable common ground exists already; many remaining obstacles are matters as much of semantics as of conviction. But many international relations scholars and international law-

[103] Bruce Russett, *Politics and Alternative Security: Toward a More Democratic, Therefore More Peaceful, World*, *in* ALTERNATIVE SECURITY: LIVING WITHOUT NUCLEAR DETERRENCE 107, 111 (Burns H. Weston ed., 1990).

[104] *Id.*

[105] *See* KEOHANE, *supra* note 79, at 14, 173–74; Helen Milner, *International Theories of Cooperation among Nations: Strengths and Weaknesses*, 44 WORLD POL. 466 (1992).

[106] Hoffmann, *supra* note 46, at 113.

[107] Arnold Wolfers coined the "billiard ball model" as a description of Realist assumptions. He was less interested in the opacity of the individual units, however, than in explicating the Realist assumption that states were the only international actors whose actions mattered, notwithstanding evidence of proliferating supra- and subnational actors. ARNOLD WOLFERS, DISCORD AND COLLABORATION: ESSAYS ON INTERNATIONAL POLITICS 19–24 (1962).

yers alike will want to push further. They will want answers to the various questions posed above. And above all, they will want a theoretical framework that takes account of increasing evidence of the importance and impact of so many factors excluded from the reigning model: individuals, corporations, nongovernmental organizations of every stripe, political and economic ideology, ideas, interests, identities and interdependence. It must be a framework that will take account of and explain the democratic peace, that will focus on the striking differences in the international realm over time, as well as the similarities. Such a framework would improve the quality of debate within both disciplines and forge a new interdisciplinary bridge between them.

An alternative framework can be found in international relations theory. It is Liberalism. A wide variety of "liberal" theories have long been offered as alternatives to or critiques of both Neo-Realism and Neo-Liberal Institutionalism, but "Liberal" theory as a whole has been conceptualized as a grab bag or "tradition" of loosely linked beliefs and approaches. It has never been reduced to a theoretical template or "paradigm," a set of core propositions from which a wide array of subtheories could be deduced. Its utility as a *competitor* to Realism and Neo-Liberal Institutionalism has been correspondingly reduced, since it has often been difficult for international political scientists to pinpoint where Realist or Neo-Liberal Institutionalist explanations end and Liberal theories begin.

These conceptual problems are being remedied. The core propositions of "Liberal theory," or a "Liberal theoretical framework," have been distilled as an explicit alternative to reigning theories.[108] The remainder of this article sets out the core assumptions of Liberal theory and explores their very different implications for interdisciplinary scholarship in international law and international relations.

The Core Assumptions of Liberal Theory

Three fundamental assumptions shared by all Liberal theories are the following.

(1) "*The fundamental actors in politics are members of domestic society, understood as individuals and privately constituted groups seeking to promote their independent interests. Under specified conditions, individual incentives may promote social order and the progressive improvement of individual welfare.*"[109] Here Liberal theory rejects a foundational premise of both Realism and Institutionalism: that the structure of the international system, whether defined to take account of institutionalized state practices or not, is the primary determinant of state behavior. Liberals analyze state behavior primarily as a function of the constraints placed on state actors by being embedded in domestic and transnational civil *society*. Note that Liberals do not seek to rule out the state as the primary *agent* of international action; once state interests are determined, governments do pursue them in a rational unitary fashion. But the underlying source of those interests is social rather than systemic.

[108] Moravcsik, *supra* note 101. For an effort to identify and organize the group of theorists working "within the Liberal tradition," see Mark Zacher & Richard Matthew, Liberal International Theory: Common Threads, Divergent Strands (paper presented at American Political Science Association Annual Meeting, September 1992). Zacher and Matthew explicitly recognize that Liberalism's "propositions cannot be simply deduced from its assumptions," precisely the task that Moravcsik sets himself.

[109] Moravcsik, *supra* note 101, at 6.

(2) "*All governments represent some segment of domestic society, whose interests are reflected in state policy.*"[110] Here is the link between the individual and group actors in domestic and transnational society and state behavior. Liberals begin by identifying patterns of interests that are determined by the purposive actions of individuals and groups. The next step is to determine which particular interests—which segment of society—are represented by a particular state government. The answer depends on the type of government in question, ranging from military dictatorship or oligarchies to democracies.

(3) "[*T*]*he behavior of states—and hence levels of international conflict and cooperation—reflects the nature and configuration of state preferences.*"[111] The determination of the precise social interests represented by a particular government permits the specification of that government's "preferences"—the agenda that it will seek to promote in international bargaining. It is about the bargaining process that Liberalism makes its third fundamental assumption. Where Realists claim that power will determine bargaining outcomes, and Institutionalists argue that it is power as conditioned by institutionalized practices, Liberals claim, straightforwardly enough, that "what states do is determined by what they want."[112] More formally, the strength and intensity of a particular preference will determine how much the state is willing to concede to obtain that preference, which in turn will determine its likelihood of success in achieving the bargaining outcomes it desires. This is a counterintuitive claim, here stated in a stronger form than is necessarily subscribed to by all Liberals. Nevertheless, its formulation here represents the Liberal antipode to Realist and Institutionalist claims about the determining power of the international system.

A Liberal Reconceptualization of the Role of Law in International Politics

The premises from which Liberal analyses of international relations proceed suggest a very different agenda for interdisciplinary work on common questions of international peace and cooperation. International lawyers seeking to build on insights from international relations theory will discover a new conceptual apparatus with which to analyze both old and new areas of law. On the other hand, political scientists interested in the impact of law on international relations will find that Liberal theory either points in the direction of bodies of law they may have been unaware of or presents familiar legal phenomena in a very different light. The interdisciplinary agenda outlined below briefly reviews potential implications from the perspective of both fields.

Comparative constitutional law and international order. The Liberal emphasis on domestic and transnational civil society and the representation of patterns of interests emerging from that society points to the importance of domestic constitutional law as a determinant of international behavior. To the extent that a government and its relationship with the society it governs are in fact constituted by a constitution, the limitations placed on that government will establish the boundaries of its ability to encumber or foster the ongoing development of civil society both within and across state borders. The constitution will also determine the extent to which and how resulting social interests (including economic interests) are represented, both by ensuring protections for minority rights and by structuring elections.

[110] *Id.* at 9.

[111] *Id.* at 10.

[112] *Id.* at 11.

Comparative constitutional law offers a rich lode of information on questions such as the relative advantages of parliamentary versus presidential systems, different electoral schemes and separation of powers arrangements.[113] *Which* questions international lawyers might decide to pursue depends on their international area of interest and the subtheory in political science that specifies the causal mechanism between a domestic variable and an international behavioral trend. For instance, international lawyers interested in the law of force would research the literature on the "democratic peace." Maoz and Russett have recently distilled the findings of a wide range of studies in this area into two competing causal models, a "structural" model and a "normative" model. The structural model argues that democracies require complex political mobilization processes to engage in conflict.[114] The normative model claims, by contrast, that "states externalize—to the extent possible—the norms of behavior that are developed within and characterize their domestic political processes and institutions," and that the democracies resolve conflict under norms of compromise that promote "a fundamental sense of stability at the personal, communal, and national levels."[115]

Armed with one or both of these hypotheses, an international lawyer could then conduct a study in comparative constitutional law with an eye to how different constitutional provisions can create checks and balances that make complex mobilization processes necessary, and/or the ways that both constitutional and statutory law can inculcate norms of cooperation and compromise. Here the paralysis that is often associated with divided government in a presidential system may appear in a new light, accustoming political actors to the need for compromise. Other promising lines of inquiry include the relationship between a well-functioning judicial system and the inculcation of stable expectations among private citizens,[116] and the impact of the "juridicization" of legislative politics through the institution of judicial review.[117] In conducting such a study, an international lawyer would be probing questions familiar to constitutional lawyers, but with a distinctive agenda directly relevant to the establishment and maintenance of world order.

The third normative implication of Liberal analysis is recognition of the "sovereignty paradox" in connection with the relations between liberal states and nonliberal states. The reconceptualization of sovereignty described above is based on phenomena observable primarily in relations among liberal states. Relations with

[113] *See, e.g.*, Juan J. Linz, *Transitions to Democracy*, WASH. Q., Summer 1990, at 143 (explores these issues in different contexts). The interest in comparative constitutional issues has been so strong in recent political science that it has even spawned a journal, *The Journal on Democracy*.

[114] Zeev Maoz & Bruce Russett, *Normative and Structural Causes of Democratic Peace, 1946–1986*, *in* GRASPING THE DEMOCRATIC PEACE: PRINCIPLES FOR A POST-COLD-WAR WORLD (forthcoming 1993) (manuscript at 6–7, on file with the author).

[115] *Id.* at 4.

[116] By comparing the evolution of judicial systems in well-established liberal states with the emergence of judicial systems in transitional states, we may be able to learn more about the link between domestic law and international order.

[117] One of the pioneers of this type of analysis is Martin Shapiro, a political scientist trained in comparative politics who teaches in a law school. *See* MARTIN SHAPIRO, COURTS: A COMPARATIVE AND POLITICAL ANALYSIS (1981). This type of analysis has also spawned a growing literature on courts in liberal societies, analyzing questions such as the growth of judicial review in France in the face of a long tradition of parliamentary sovereignty and comparing the political role of courts in France and Germany. *See* ALEC STONE, THE BIRTH OF JUDICIAL POLITICS IN FRANCE: THE CONSTITUTIONAL COUNCIL IN COMPARATIVE PERSPECTIVE (1992); Alec Stone, *Judging Socialism: Constitutional Politics in France and Germany*, COMP. POL. STUD. (forthcoming 1993).

nonliberal states, by contrast, are more likely to be conducted by the political branches. The result is that *in court,* pleas of the prerogatives of sovereignty are more likely to be honored with respect to nonliberal states than with respect to liberal states. Just as family members are often freer with one another and less respectful of the boundaries of politeness than they might be with strangers or new acquaintances, so too with members of the family of liberal nations. Their legal relations, at least, reflect a similar type and degree of conflict, conducted in the context of underlying commonality and unity of interest.

A theoretical framework for transnational law. Liberal theory provides a powerful theoretical framework for the analysis of transnational law. Using the term more narrowly than the classic definition advanced by Philip Jessup,[118] I define transnational law to include all municipal law and a subset of intergovernmental agreements that directly regulate transnational activity between individuals and between individuals and state governments.[119] Although this area of law is growing apace,[120] it remains a definition and a category without a theory. The result is a seemingly random hodgepodge of doctrines and topics connected as a field only by a common "international" or "foreign" element.[121] As a reviewer of a leading casebook in the area queried, "Is there a field in this class?"[122]

From a Liberal standpoint, transnational law helps structure patterns of individual and group interaction in transnational society, patterns that in turn generate interests that shape and constrain state action. Transnational law is also likely to contribute to the "fundamental sense of stability" identified by Maoz and Russett as a distinctive characteristic of liberal societies that buttresses the probability of peace with other liberal societies. How and to what extent transnational law performs these functions is a subject for political scientists working within the Liberal paradigm. At the same time, the Liberal emphasis on the social interaction of individuals and groups as the underlying determinants of state behavior recasts transnational law as a primary contributor to world order. If, to take one definition, the criterion for a functional "field" of law is whether it seeks " 'to realize some underlying kind of justice,' "[123] then transnational law, whether subdivided into international litigation, international business transactions or traditional private international law, seeks to accomplish the very same aims long pursued by the

[118] PHILIP C. JESSUP, TRANSNATIONAL LAW (1956).

[119] This definition subsumes traditional private international law but does not embrace all of public international law.

[120] As I define it, "transnational law" includes subjects labeled international litigation, international practice, and much of international business transactions. Casebooks in this area are proliferating, written by both practitioners and academics.

[121] To complain of the absence of an overriding organizing principle or conception that would provide identity and cohesion to this subject area as a *field* is not to say that the material itself does not have common elements. Born and Westin, for instance, identify five "recurrent themes": interest balancing, foreign relations, federalism, public international law and international comity. GARY B. BORN & DAVID WESTIN, INTERNATIONAL CIVIL LITIGATION IN UNITED STATES COURTS: COMMENTARY AND MATERIALS 3 (1st rev. ed. 1990).

[122] Stephen B. Burbank, *The World in Our Courts,* 89 MICH. L. REV. 1456 (1991) (reviewing BORN & WESTIN, *supra* note 121 (1st ed. 1989)). Teachers of international business transactions similarly warn students of the conceptual incoherence of the field. Private communication from Professor Jay Westbrook, University of Texas Law School (Dec. 7, 1992).

[123] Burbank, *supra* note 122, at 1458 (quoting Michael Moore, *A Theory of Criminal Law Theories,* *in* TEL AVIV STUDIES IN LAW (Daniel Friedmann ed., 1991)).

practitioners of public international law, and may arguably do so with greater success.[124]

Within this unified framework, a number of questions should prove of interest to both international lawyers and political scientists. First, how do domestic legal doctrines encourage or discourage transnational economic interaction? Private international lawyers have pointed out connections between a country's stance on personal jurisdiction doctrines and its friendliness or hostility to international trade.[125] In the United States, the Supreme Court has decided an entire line of cases concerning forum selection and the enforceability of arbitral awards on the assumption that an overly "parochial" attitude toward enforcement of U.S. law or insistence on litigation in U.S. courts would handicap U.S. business in international transactions.[126] Beyond the judicial system, legislative and executive positions on the enforcement of U.S. laws abroad have softened, paying at least lip service to the values of comity and reciprocity.

A second line of inquiry would link the political findings on the value of stability to the traditional system of conflicts of law, which long recognized the importance of stable expectations in fostering transnational commerce. From Story and Dicey forward, conflicts scholars have understood that a central purpose of a conflicts system is to give individuals some way to know the rules that govern their conduct, on the premise that it is unfair and irrational to let those rules be determined after the fact by the happenstance of the tribunal's location. National courts must thus be prepared to adopt general principles allowing them to apply each other's law when fairness and predictability so require.[127] As Dicey observed, "The growth of rules for the choice of law is the necessary result of the peaceful existence of independent nations combined with the prevalence of commercial intercourse."[128]

The use of Liberal theory to illuminate the study of private international law, and vice versa, would also extend to the fast-growing law of international com-

[124] Note that the proposed contribution of transnational law to world order differs from the model developed in RICHARD A. FALK, THE ROLE OF DOMESTIC COURTS IN THE INTERNATIONAL LEGAL ORDER (1964). Falk saw private international law as constituting a "horizontal" international legal order that operated by stabilizing *state* expectations. Liberalism, by contrast, focuses on the stabilization of *individual* expectations.

The Liberal approach should equally be distinguished from more eclectic efforts to supplement or amend an essentially state-centric analysis by taking transnational actors into account. Such efforts are best exemplified in political science by Robert Keohane and Joseph Nye's model of "complex interdependence," which begins with the state and then supplements state action with inquiry into the transnational activities of individuals and interest groups. ROBERT O. KEOHANE & JOSEPH S. NYE, JR., POWER AND INTERDEPENDENCE (1977). Similarly, a growing number of international lawyers have called for formal acknowledgment of the increasing importance of individuals and groups as subjects of public international law and for a move away from traditional state centrism. See, most recently, Mark W. Janis, *International Law?*, 32 HARV. J. INT'L L. 363 (1991) (arguing that we should return to the "law of nations" in place of the overly state-centric "*inter-national* law").

[125] *See* Arthur T. von Mehren, *Adjudicatory Jurisdiction: General Theories Compared and Evaluated*, 63 B.U. L. REV. 280 (1983).

[126] *See* The Bremen v. Zapata Off-Shore Co., 407 U.S. 1 (1972); Scherk v. Alberto-Culver Co., 417 U.S. 506 (1974); Mitsubishi Motors Corp. v. Soler Chrysler-Plymouth, Inc., 473 U.S. 614 (1985).

[127] Judge Cardozo similarly insisted, "courts are not free to refuse to enforce a foreign right at the pleasure of the judges, to suit the individual notion of expediency or fairness." Loucks v. Standard Oil Co., 120 N.E. 198, 201–02 (N.Y. 1918).

[128] A. V. DICEY, A DIGEST OF THE LAW OF ENGLAND WITH REFERENCE TO THE CONFLICT OF LAWS 8 (2d ed. 1908).

mercial arbitration. A Liberal analysis would highlight the intersection of the public and private spheres underpinning a law that formally regulates individual merchants outside national legal systems but is ultimately dependent on them.[129] This law is developed by international arbitral tribunals, a private hybrid of public international law, different national laws and general equitable principles. Further, the process of international commercial arbitration itself

> begins as a private arrangement between the parties. It continues by way of private proceedings, in which the wishes of the parties are of great importance. Yet it ends with an award which has binding legal force and effect and which, on appropriate conditions being met, the courts of most countries of the world will be prepared to recognise and enforce. *The private process has a public effect, implemented by the support of the public authorities of each state expressed through its national law.*[130]

Here is perhaps the quintessential Liberal regime: a body of rules regulating transnational society that fosters the creation of transnational patterns of interest likely to shape state action, but that depends at the same time on the performance of certain state functions. On this foundation of domestic and transnational state-society relations rests part of the architecture of a Liberal international system.

A third and final question is the extent to which transnational law can be understood as a distinctive feature of law among liberal states. I have sketched such an argument elsewhere with respect to the act of state doctrine, arguing that the doctrine helps circumscribe a zone of "legitimate difference" among liberal states within which foreign laws can either be applied as law or overturned in accordance with mutually recognized legal principles.[131] Many other transnational legal doctrines lend themselves to a similar analysis, revealing internal fissures that upon closer examination appear related to objectively identifiable differences between liberal and nonliberal states. Adequate forum requirements in forum selection and *forum non conveniens* cases, for instance, are applied consistently with the liberal-nonliberal divide; the evolution of public policy exceptions in choice-of-law doctrines and recognition and enforcement of foreign judgments may yield insights about the dynamic of liberal interdependence; and the rise of interest-balancing tests in areas ranging from extraterritoriality[132] to personal jurisdiction[133] to treaty application[134] may be characteristic of a density of transnational interaction found primarily among liberal states.

A Liberal analysis of public international law. Liberal theory also has important implications for the analysis of international institutions, including, although not

[129] Susan Strange has written of the undermining of national authority by the spread of the "international business civilization." Susan Strange, *The Name of the Game*, *in* SEA-CHANGES: AMERICAN FOREIGN POLICY IN A WORLD TRANSFORMED 238 (Nicholas X. Rizopoulos ed., 1990). At the same time, however, she notes that "a central concern of th[is] civilization is the securing of property rights, for individuals and for firms." *Id.* at 263. It is time that international political economists purveying such perspectives factored transnational law into their global equations.

[130] ALAN REDFERN & MARTIN HUNTER, LAW AND PRACTICE OF INTERNATIONAL COMMERCIAL ARBITRATION 7 (1986) (emphasis added).

[131] Anne-Marie Burley, *Law Among Liberal States: Liberal Internationalism and the Act of State Doctrine*, 92 COLUM. L. REV. 1907 (1992).

[132] *See* Timberlane Lumber Co. v. Bank of America, N.T. & S.A., 549 F.2d 597 (9th Cir. 1976); Mannington Mills v. Congoleum Corp., 595 F.2d 1287 (3d Cir. 1979); U.S. DEPARTMENT OF JUSTICE, ANTITRUST ENFORCEMENT GUIDELINES FOR INTERNATIONAL OPERATIONS (1988) (for private antitrust actions).

[133] Asahi Metal Indus. Co. v. Superior Court of California, Solano County, 480 U.S. 102 (1987).

[134] Societe Nationale Industrielle Aerospatiale v. U.S. District Court, 482 U.S. 522 (1987).

limited to, customary and conventional international legal regimes and international organizations. On the one hand, a Liberal approach fills many of the acknowledged gaps in current regime theory by providing the tools to determine when there will be mutual interests that can be furthered by international cooperation, hence specifying the preconditions that Institutionalists hold necessary for strong and effective institutions. On the other hand, Liberal theory also suggests that in many instances institutions will be epiphenomenal; by pinpointing underlying interests, it will permit Institutionalists to isolate hard cases in which institutions caused an outcome that could not have been predicted by patterns of underlying interests. To the extent that the "institution" in question is a legal institution, a Liberal approach will permit a more rigorous demonstration of the impact of law.

This debate is a *causal* debate, of primary interest to political scientists. For international lawyers who wish to proceed from the assumption that international law exists and matters, Liberal theory offers an equally interesting, and, from a traditional international lawyer's point of view, heretical, proposition. From a Liberal perspective, regimes governing liberal states are likely to be more effective in accomplishing their professed aims than regimes governing liberal and nonliberal states (other than purely technical regimes such as international traffic agreements). This proposition generates a radical and stimulating research agenda, calling for a new comparative look at regimes ranging from the United Nations to the International Monetary Fund to, above all, the European Community. Indeed, one of the most powerful reorienting effects of Liberal analysis is the transformation of the Community from anomaly to archetype. In the remainder of this section, I will offer a very preliminary Liberal account of the evolution of the Community as a prototype for the role of public international law among liberal states.

The Treaty of Rome was concluded in 1957 as an *international* treaty. The fathers of the European Community never intended to make its provisions directly effective in the courts of the member states.[135] Nor, for that matter, did they intend to have the European Court of Justice play a particularly prominent role in the shaping and administration of the Community.[136] Yet the "constitutionalization" of the Treaty has been the Court's achievement, and the Court's alone.[137] As the Community takes another leap forward with the adoption of a new set of plans for economic and political union, the power and strength of Community law is such that Great Britain announced publicly that it sought separate treaties for European Monetary Union and European Political Union to avoid the jurisdiction of the Court of Justice.[138]

[135] *See* HJALTE RASMUSSEN, ON LAW AND POLICY IN THE EUROPEAN COURT OF JUSTICE 249–50 (1986).

[136] Rasmussen argues that the drafters of the Treaty of Rome intended the new European Court of Justice to have even less power than was exercised by the Court of the European Coal and Steel Community. *Id.* at 220–22.

[137] Eric Stein, *Lawyers, Judges and the Making of a Transnational Constitution*, 75 AJIL 1 (1981). As Stein and others have pointed out, the Court has often taken its cue from the Commission as regards the political climate in the member states to determine just how far it should go. Numerous political scientists have concluded that the Court was careful not to transgress the bounds of the political consensus of the Community. Nevertheless, its incremental style and successful wooing of the national courts both to expand its jurisdiction and to secure the enforcement of its judgments gradually pushed the bounds of Community law steadily forward.

[138] *Countdown to Maastricht*, Fin. Times (London), Nov. 18, 1991, §1, at 8.

Surely, it will be argued, the European Court was able to give the international law of the Treaty equivalent status to domestic law by relying on the initial political commitment of the member states to *unite,* to become some kind of a polity under law. As witnessed by the relaunching of the single market in 1985, however, and the still-tentative steps toward political union over thirty years after the original compact, the initial commitments were vague indeed. Beneath the clouds of rhetoric, the Treaty of Rome could have been interpreted much like any other economic treaty. The Court's famed "teleological" method of interpretation relies on "giving effect" to the original intentions of the parties as construed by the Court, even where those same parties had apparently failed to supply what the Court considers to be the necessary means to achieve those ends. On that basis the International Court of Justice should have been able to establish world peace by now.

A Liberal theorist would argue that the difference lies in the receptivity of the national courts of the Community's member states to accepting the possibility of supranational law as *law,* as a body of rules interpreted and applied by a nonpolitical entity. It is not simply that the member states are relatively homogeneous. It is that the substance of that homogeneity is a particular set of political and economic beliefs and institutions that are uniquely congenial to the independent operation of the rule of law. More concretely, the liberal institution of an independent judiciary charged with administering the rule of law permits the maintenance of a meaningful distinction between law and politics, even in tandem with widespread recognition of how political beliefs and values can influence legal choices. In this setting, international tribunals can enjoy a measure of the same legitimacy as domestic courts, and carry on a dialogue with domestic courts independent of the political authorities.[139]

The nations of Europe will retain their identity and "sovereignty," however defined, as separate nations. At the same time, the fate of the Maastricht Treaty notwithstanding, European governments will increasingly set national policy at a supranational level. They will implement these policies as Community law. From a Liberal perspective, this law will not be a hybrid law suspended between the traditional poles of domestic and international law. It will be, and is now, a rich and fascinating paradigm for international law, finally made flesh within a deliberately and self-consciously defined community of liberal states.[140] Joseph Weiler recently suggested that his theory of the "bidirectional" relationship between

[139] This is a highly stylized account of the European Court of Justice, without reference to the extensive lobbying effort undertaken by the Court for support from the national courts, or its own political balancing act in gradually advancing its agenda. For such an alternative account, see Anne-Marie Burley & Walter Mattli, *Europe before the Court: A Political Theory of Legal Integration,* 47 INT'L ORG. 41 (forthcoming 1993). Nevertheless, I would argue that the existence of a common liberal culture and institutions provided the context in which such efforts and concerns were even possible.

[140] The Preamble to the Treaty of Rome commits the members of the European Community to "pool[] their resources to preserve and strengthen peace and liberty," and "call[s] upon the other peoples of Europe who share their ideal to join in their efforts." It should be noted that, in keeping with the liberal principles on which these states are based, the supranational lawmaking process will increasingly have to conform to democratic principles. Paradoxically, this will mean the devolution of some lawmaking power *away* from Community organs, under the principle of subsidiarity or other federalist (in the American sense) doctrines. It is also likely to mean greater transparency in Community decision making and greater input not only from the Community Parliament, but from *national* parliaments.

legal and political processes in the transformation of Community law from "soft" (international) to "hard" (domestic) law "could even be part of a general theory of international lawmaking."[141] It could, indeed, as could the work of many other Community scholars—when combined with a general theory of lawmaking in liberal states.[142]

Rethinking the rules of the game. A Liberal approach to international relations and international law opens the door to a new normative agenda in international law that in turn could change the conceptual apparatus employed by international relations theorists.[143] The evolution of what Henkin calls the "submerged rules of

[141] Joseph Weiler, *The Transformation of Europe*, 100 YALE L.J. 2403, 2426 (1991).

[142] The Community could equally provide a rich lode of experience on institutional and organizational design. A Liberal analysis would emphasize the desirability of "embedding" public international institutions in domestic society, not only, as Ruggie has argued, to allow states to remain part of these institutions, but also to strengthen the institutions themselves by reshaping private expectations. *See* John G. Ruggie, *International Regimes, Transactions, and Change: Embedded Liberalism in the Postwar Economic Order*, 36 INT'L ORG. 379 (1982). It is interesting to compare Keohane's notion of "sovereign enmeshment," arguing for the compliance-enhancing role of institutions in terms of their link to domestic legal and political processes. Keohane's analysis proceeds from a strict and relatively static division between the systemic and unit levels of analysis, without taking into account individual and group actors or interests. *See* Keohane, *supra* note 96. The Liberal approach, by contrast, builds from a more holistic vision of state responses to domestic and transnational pressures.

[143] For some readers, Liberal analysis may appear to have much in common with McDougal-Lasswell jurisprudence. Both schools look beyond the state and emphasize the importance of individual and group actors as principal actors in world politics. Both schools posit that the internal characteristics of states determine their external behavior, leading both to emphasize the distinctive attributes of "liberal" states and the concomitant importance of comparative law, particularly comparative constitutional law. Both schools thus reject the positive and normative universalism projected by Realism, Institutionalism and traditional international law, substituting a differential analysis based on an underlying convergence of interests and values.

Appearances notwithstanding, these similarities belie important differences. First, McDougal's projection of Lasswell's model political decision-making process onto international politics (the "world power process" and the "world social process") identifies *all* the possible participants in this process indiscriminately, without attempting to specify the causal relationships and the generative orderings among them. Liberal theory, by contrast, deliberately sets out to build a model of the international system that will serve as a carefully specified alternative to Waltzian Neo-Realism. It marries theories of interest formation in domestic and transnational society with theories of international bargaining. The result is a model that can specify, as a generative model should, how changes in one part of the model will affect actors and processes in another part, with a precise claim about how the causal arrows run.

A second basic category of differences between the two schools rests on the relative vulnerability of McDougal-Lasswell analysis and Liberal analysis to subjective manipulation. As some McDougal students have pointed out, the popular critique of McDougal-Lasswell jurisprudence for its supposed identification of the "law" with the subjective values of individual decision makers is based on a crude misreading or fundamental misunderstanding of McDougal's work. Nevertheless, one such defender himself goes on to deplore the ultimate subjectivity of the various applications of this theory by McDougal himself and many of his associates. Falk, *supra* note 1, at 138–41. Many others in both law and political science have taken a similar view. *See, e.g.*, CLAUDE, *supra* note 75, at 255–71; Hoffmann, *supra* note 46, at 116.

From the Liberal perspective, such critiques seem an inevitable concomitant of a theory in which lawyers themselves become policy scientists. McDougal and Lasswell promptly enlisted their theories as positive means to normative ends. In place of a false universalism, they urged differentiation in word and in fact—of *all* systems of public order: international, regional and potentially national. They devoted their efforts to teaching lawyers how to undertake this process—how to "appraise" systems of public order so as to distinguish the good from the bad and consequently elevate the good. In practice, they "urg[ed] the use of international law as a strategy to attain the goals of the democratic public order states and to frustrate the designs of their totalitarian adversaries." Falk, *supra* note 1, at 142.

the game," fundamental concepts such as sovereignty and statehood, would result in a different analytical and operative construction of international reality. Liberal theory both buttresses and illuminates this agenda, as illustrated by the following three examples.

First, international lawyers are amending the traditional definition of statehood. Scholars such as Thomas Franck and Gregory Fox are working to establish the international legal pedigree for a right of democratic governance.[144] If individuals do have a right to govern themselves, a government founded on any principle other than some form of self-government should no longer qualify for recognition as an independent state. The current criterion of "government" as one of the elements of statehood[145] must logically give way to "democratic government." Franck and Fox recognize these implications, and already advocate the application of some form of democratic criteria in the recognition process, although they favor proceeding with great caution.

A Liberal analysis of international law offers a new positive ontology to fit this new normative agenda. From the Liberal perspective, state behavior is best analyzed as a function of domestic and transnational behavioral patterns for which liberal and nonliberal states serve as an excellent proxy. To the extent that positive behavioral differences can be identified on the basis of this division, they will reinforce the intelligibility and utility of a normative distinction. Conversely, a norm of democratic governance helps to justify the positive Liberal distinction between liberal and nonliberal states.[146]

A second reconceptualization illuminated by Liberal analysis is of the nature of territorial and jurisdictional sovereignty among liberal states. Empirical evidence suggests that, as a practical matter, the higher volume of exchanges of all kinds among liberal states creates a web of interrelationships that in turn make judicial infringements or "violations" of sovereignty much more likely.[147] Territorial boundaries become increasingly meaningless, so that situs analysis cedes its place to interest analysis. Indeed, the willingness to subject the matter in dispute to judicial scrutiny at all—even in the face of considerable political controversy—is significantly greater if the state in question is a liberal state.[148]

In this conception, lawyers perform their own social science in the guise of policy science. The artificial and wavering line between positive and normative, between "is" and "ought," cannot long withstand such fusion. No independent check exists on the lawyers' findings. In the Liberal model, by contrast, it is left to the political scientists to uncover the links between domestic and transnational social patterns and distinctive patterns of state behavior. The lawyers must be bound by the results of this research, both in ascertaining what the law is and in thinking about what it should be. The Liberal approach to interdisciplinary collaboration thus maintains the separate identities and functions of both disciplines. But it harnesses them on a common track, one that remains largely unexplored.

[144] Gregory H. Fox, *The Right to Political Participation in International Law,* 17 YALE J. INT'L L. 539 (1992); Thomas M. Franck, *The Emerging Right to Democratic Governance,* 86 AJIL 46 (1992). *See also* Theodor Meron, *Democracy and the Rule of Law,* 153 WORLD AFF. 22 (1990); Henry J. Steiner, *Political Participation as a Human Right,* 1 HARV. HUM. RTS. Y.B. 77 (1988) (arguing for the right of political participation as a "programmatic right").

[145] *See, e.g.,* IAN BROWNLIE, PRINCIPLES OF PUBLIC INTERNATIONAL LAW 75 (3d ed. 1979).

[146] There is indeed a difference between "liberal states" and "democracies," in that the definition of a liberal state requires constitutional protections and private property rights in addition to self-governance. In practice, however, I know of no genuine democracy that does not also at least aspire to these other attributes.

[147] I use the term "violation" of sovereignty because that is how certain judicial decisions are often perceived by the representatives of the foreign government in question.

[148] *See* Burley, *supra* note 131.

On the other hand, relations among liberal states are more likely to be conducted on a principle of "legitimate difference" or mutual recognition of each other's laws, on the implicit ground that sufficient commonality exists to render many country-specific differences along a wide range of policy choices irrelevant. In both directions, the figurative baseline of territorially defined absolute sovereign power seems increasingly inapposite. Within the liberal zone, then, the all-purpose powers and privileges currently denoted by sovereignty may in fact attach to different states in different issue-areas as a function of strength of interest and regulatory purpose. As the "dynamic density" of individuals and issues increases within this zone, rendering the inadequacy and irrelevance of traditional concepts of sovereignty apparent, Liberal analysis and prescription could highlight an alternative baseline for legal relations based on reciprocal recognition of mutual interest rather than exclusive zones of power.[149]

Potential Deficiencies in a Liberal Analysis

Although many theories of international relations have adopted or been tagged with the rubric "liberal," the nonutopian Liberal theoretical framework presented here is a new effort to challenge the dominance of Realism. Only time, scholarly debate and practical application will determine its long-term power and utility. Several potential difficulties already loom on the horizon.[150] The brief discussion of some of these problems below helps illuminate not only likely points of dispute between the Institutionalist and the Liberal agendas, but also how in the end these agendas fit together.

Liberals operating within this framework must be able to deduce substantive theoretical propositions from its core assumptions. The leading example of such a proposition is the claim that liberal states do not go to war with one another. My various hypotheses about how the legal relations of liberal states are likely to vary from legal relations between liberal and nonliberal states would also meet this requirement. Nevertheless, Liberal international relations theorists using this framework will be required by their Realist and Institutionalist colleagues to demonstrate its utility in generating a wider range of more specific propositions. To the extent they succeed, they will produce coherent empirical research programs from which international lawyers working within the same analytical framework stand to profit. Should they fail, the eclecticism, incoherence and utopianism that has long plagued Liberalism is likely to continue.

A second problem concerns the *relative* power of Liberalism versus Realism and Institutionalism. Even assuming that Liberals do succeed in formulating substantive theoretical propositions, under what conditions will those propositions explain *more* than Realism and Institutionalism? In other words, even if Liberal

[149] Ruggie has emphasized the importance of the Durkheimian concept of "dynamic density," defined as "the quantity, velocity, and diversity of transactions that go on within society," to the changing definition of sovereignty. John G. Ruggie, *Continuity and Transformation in the World Polity: Toward a Neorealist Synthesis*, 35 WORLD POL. 261, 281–85 (1983). Kratochwil has taken these insights further in his work on the nature of boundaries and the resurrection of the Roman concept of dominion. Friedrich Kratochwil, *Of Systems, Boundaries, and Territoriality: An Inquiry into the Formation of the State System*, 39 WORLD POL. 27 (1986). *See also* Note, *Constructing the State Extraterritorially: Jurisdictional Discourse, the National Interest, and Transnational Norms*, 103 HARV. L. REV. 1273 (1990).

[150] I am indebted to Robert Keohane for a personal communication highlighting many of these points.

propositions offer a more accurate *description* of empirical phenomena, do they ultimately add anything to our ability to explain and predict such phenomena?[151] If not, why displace the relative parsimony and power of Realism and Institutionalism? International lawyers might correspondingly argue that even if a distinction between liberal and nonliberal states in the legal realm is empirically verifiable, its prospective conceptual and normative benefits do not warrant significant departure from the traditional framework of sovereign equality and identity. For political scientists, the relative explanatory power of one paradigm over another is ultimately an empirical question. International lawyers should prepare to follow this debate, to complement it with their own research within the Institutionalist and Liberal frameworks, and to draw their own conclusions.

CONCLUSION: A DUAL AGENDA

However the above debate ultimately plays out, international lawyers should above all consider its significance in light of the original Realist challenge. Not one, but two powerful responses now exist within political science, responses that recognize the importance and relevance of international law under specified conditions. The prospects for genuine interdisciplinary collaboration, to the benefit of both disciplines, have never been better.

Further, although much of the debate will be conducted *between* Institutionalists and Liberals, in the end both approaches will recognize the complementarity of the other. Institutionalists will continue to believe that systemic explanations provide the most powerful and parsimonious starting point, but that explanations focusing on domestic politics and individual action will be important residual tools. Liberals, on the other hand, will claim that Liberal theories are necessary to explain the formation of state interests, but that Institutionalist theories are critical at the bargaining stage. In either case, legal adherents of both schools will find a bridge to each other, as well as to fellow-traveling political scientists.

Yet another way to envision this dual agenda is to return to my own conceptualization of how Liberal theory can be applied to international legal studies. I suggest that Liberal insights will prove most fruitful in guiding the study of various kinds of legal relations among liberal states. Much Institutionalist scholarship, on the other hand, whether conducted by international lawyers or political scientists, will prove particularly applicable to the explanation and analysis of relations between liberal and nonliberal states. The world is likely to remain heterogeneous, and brutal, for centuries yet, and the painfully accumulated store of knowledge about how to ensure at least minimal regulation of the relations between competing sovereigns will serve diplomats and decision makers for a long time to come.

These caveats notwithstanding, we are on the edge of a new fault line in international relations. The emergence of this line emphasizes the transnational ties between states that share political and economic values and institutions, states that both permit independent action and initiative by individuals and groups in domestic and transnational civil society and provide the political mechanisms to

[151] On the distinction between explanation and understanding as a means of classifying different types of international relations theories, see MARTIN HOLLIS & STEVE SMITH, EXPLAINING AND UNDERSTANDING INTERNATIONAL RELATIONS (1990). To offer a concrete example, even if it is true that individuals are the primary actors that determine the behavior of states, if our model of state behavior adequately captures the effects of individual behavior, why not preserve the fiction of states as the primary actors?

ensure representation of the resulting patterns of interest. Political, economic and, ultimately, legal relations among such states will increasingly differ in their modalities, consequences and implications from political, economic and legal relations between liberal and nonliberal states. Liberal international relations theory provides international lawyers with a conceptual apparatus to understand and analyze this phenomenon and gradually to build it into law.

Overall, international lawyers can ill afford to ignore the growing wealth of political science data on the world they seek to regulate. The measurements may be imprecise, the theories crude, but the whole offers at least the hope of a positive science of world affairs. As an adolescent discipline, international political science long rejected the insights of international law. As it grows, it rediscovers what international lawyers never forgot, but with added insights of its own. In the end, law informed by politics is the best guarantee of politics informed by law. The dual interdisciplinary agenda outlined here offers hope of reaching both goals.

[3]

Nordic Journal of International Law 65: 341–383, 1996.

Navigating the Newstream: Recent Critical Scholarship in International Law

DEBORAH Z. CASS*
Lecturer in Law. Australian National University, Canberra

1. Introduction

Generations of legal scholars have reinvented their fields by a ritual overthrowing of their predecessors[1] and one group within the current crop of international lawyers is no exception. These lawyers, who label themselves as Newstream,[2] are presently involved in a theory battle with those the new scholars label, somewhat negatively, as Mainstream.[3] This otherwise esoteric battle is interesting because it coincides with a changed perception about

* LL.B (Hons) University of Melbourne 1989, LL.M Harvard University 1995, currently S.J.D. candidate Harvard University. I would like to thank Susan Marks, David Kennedy and Gerry Simpson for their invaluable comments on earlier drafts.

[1] See e.g. the Realist school of American legal thought which was in part a project aimed at creating a new way of thinking in contradistinction to what it labeled "formalism". For a discussion of the realist critique as a response to formalism see William W. Fisher, "The Development of Modern American Legal Theory and the Judicial Interpretation of the Bill of Rights", in M. Lacey & K. Haakonssen, (Eds), *A Culture of Rights* (1991).

[2] I will use the term "Newstream" to discuss work which has been referred to variously as "New Stream" or part of a body of "New Approaches". See David Kennedy, "A New Stream of International Law Scholarship", 7 *Wis. Int L. J.* 1, (1988) [hereinafter *New Stream*] and David Kennedy & Chris Tennant, "New Approaches to International Law: A Bibliography", 35 *Harv. Int. L. J.* 417, (1994) [hereinafter *New Approaches*]. International legal scholarship which defined itself as "New Stream" first appeared around 1980: see Nigel Purvis, "Critical Legal Studies in Public International Law", 32 *Harv. Int. L. J.* 81, 89 (1991) at note 41. It has expanded considerably since then. The proportion of analyses which were so defined in 1980 was relatively small. A 1991 survey of the field noted three book length expositions and just over a dozen contributions in all: Id. At 89 and 91. Cf. In 1988 David Kennedy listed 17 scholars as pursuing "critical projects" in the field: Kennedy, *New Stream*, id., at 2. Three years later the number of analyses identified as Newstream had increased to some four hundred and fifty: Kennedy and Tennant, id., at 431–460.

[3] In this article Mainstream is intended to refer to a body of scholars who have dominated the field for the last twenty-five years. It does not indicate any homogenous category but covers a number of different theoretical approaches including realist (Schwarzenberger, Weil, Watson), classicist (Fitzmaurice), and liberal-humanitarian (Henkin, MacDougall, Falk).

the role of international law in structuring and regulating international public order. A once moribund international rule of law is assumed to have been reinvigorated by current events. The resuscitation of international law is accompanied by an optimism arising out of a perceived end to the polarized bloc politics of the late twentieth century. Actions in the Gulf and in Somalia are seen as evidence of the international community's will to collectively respond to threats to international peace and security. But that optimism is also tempered by a strange uncertainty about ordering the international plane. Besides being somewhat quelled by the experiences of Somalia and the former Yugoslavia, post Cold War confidence in international law has been replaced by a muted anxiety about its limitations. This anxiety focuses on questions which seem to have become more, rather than less, difficult to answer since the resolution of superpower politics. What is the role of the weakened nation state in the new regional arrangements of world order? How will human rights regimes overcome the chasms of cultural difference between societies? What is "culture" anyway? What is the nature of the relationship between international trade regulation and local governance? Can reconstituted units of failed federations accommodate disparate ethnic interests? It is in the service of answering these dilemmas that the new brand of legal scholarship has risen to prominence, claiming to challenge the certainties of the old. This article is about that challenge, and the attempt by the new scholars to reconceptualize the idea of what is international law.

The article is inspired by the sense that, to date, the battle between the Newstream and the Mainstream has been a rather detached, disengaged affair, and that in particular, the Mainstream has failed to respond meaningfully to Newstream critique. Instead the Newstream has been anxiously dismissed as overly theoretical or willfully obtuse.[4] Here I refine and explore some of the Newstream ideas which have invigorated the discipline and have the potential

[4] Despite the industry of Newstream writers, *supra* note 2, and the appearance of two lengthy survey articles (Purvis, *supra* note 2), book reviews (see e.g., Ian Scobbie, "Towards the Elimination of International Law: Some Radical Skepticism about Skeptical Radicalism", *Brit. Y.B. Int'l. L.* 339 (1990) frequent citation in scholarly journals by writers sharing similar concerns, and attention at international law conferences, (e.g., American Society of International Law Annual General Meeting 1994, panel on *Theoretical Perspectives on Sovereignty*, comments by Martti Koskenniemi and Karen Knop), to date, the new analyses have been largely ignored, or at least superficially treated, in recently revised publications of the traditional discipline. See e.g. a recently revised standard Casebook used in American law schools, Louis Henkin, Richard Pugh, Oscar Schachter, Hans Smit, *International Law Cases and Materials*, 3rd ed., (1993) which devotes two pages to "international law and the critical legal studies movement" id. at 48–49, four pages to "feminist perspectives" id. at 43–47, and occasionally refers to specific writers associated with Newstream such as Philip Allot, id. at 16. Other Mainstream scholars engage only very briefly with the critique in order to dismiss it. See e.g., Rosalyn Higgins, *Problems and Process: International Law and How We Use It*, (1994) esp. Ch. 1 "Nature and Function of International Law."

to create a productive dialogue between the bearers of the international tradition and its challengers.[5] I intend to show how this should lead to a gradual recasting of the field.

There is little doubt that a large body of compelling work has now been written, associated with the rubric of Newstream, and that its continued neglect by the Mainstream risks stultifying the field and prevents the development of a more nuanced and responsive international legal theory. The Newstream critique's major strength, its sense of a mission to create a new international law, risks being blunted by the lack of dialogue between the two approaches. Moreover, as pedagogical tools, the Newstream writings are invaluable because they offer plausible explanations of international law making, interpretation and application, at a point in time in which traditional understandings about law have been questioned by (post)modern insights into cultural fragmentation, the making of history and the role of language in law. The work also echoes a widespread interdisciplinary interest in language and its effect on the structure of ideas.

Despite these strengths Newstream scholars do not exploit the critique's potential because they often fail to make explicit evaluative choices. If they perceive law as simply a variable set of argumentative possibilities, these possibilities are not being used to effect change. There are problems internal to the critique as well, for example its often condescending and reductive tone, and its occasionally derivative and abstract theorizing.

I have thus positioned my own critique at the borderline in the hope that it will enable both sides to explore each others territory. Putting to one side the reality that at least some Mainstream and Newstream writers perceive their positions as antithetical, I will assume that any conversation between

[5] In addition to the quantitative impact of the work, it is having a substantive effect on academic and practitioners alike. An anecdotal survey of some international law teachers indicates that many use the writers discussed here in their teaching. International law texts now include references, albeit somewhat cursory, to these writings. Writers not formally identified with the approach use the various techniques identified above. See e.g., Patrick Thornberry in Christian Tomuschat, *The Modern Law of Self-Determination* 1993 (analyzing self-determination law as a "metalanguage" and proposing a reconstruction based on a new conception of the relationship between the State and its sub-groups). Practitioners in law firms, departments of state around the world, corporations, and non-government organizations are increasingly schooled in these methods of analysis. In some cases the experience of these practitioners is channeled back into the academic scholarship. See e.g., Ileana M. Porras, "The Rio Declaration: A New Basis for International Cooperation", in Phillippe Sands, *Greening International Law*, (1993) (arguing that the Rio Declaration represents a compromise between the interest in development of developing states and the interest of the West in environmental protection. Porras acted as government representative at the Rio Conference). The result of these developments has been to extend the effect of the work, so that it is beginning to reach into the public and private sectors, as well as the academy. Accordingly there is need to incorporate these materials more thoroughly into mainstream teaching and research.

theoretical positions is good for international law, because it generates a deeper understanding of what the discipline entails. My starting premise is that Mainstream scholars ought to pay greater heed to the transformative potential of some of the work of the Newstream, and the latter should acknowledge their continuing debt to the scholars who have preceded them, and continue to engage with that work. I will therefore set out in my paper what I believe to be the main arguments of Newstream work. By offering one translation of a sample of the recent scholarship I hope to demonstrate its richness and creativity; to provide a point of entry for dialogue between the perspectives; and to promote the use of Newstream work as a valuable source of information and analysis for Mainstream scholars.

2. Structure and Overview of Paper

The Newstream, positioning themselves in opposition to the Mainstream, have challenged the international law tradition at three levels. Section 3 of this paper is devoted to discussing the underlying conceptual challenge of Newstream work, Section 4 its methods, and Section 5 its strategies. In a concluding section, Section 6, I examine some recurring problems with the critique. Before commencing I will briefly sketch the three challenges: *conceptual, methodological*, and *strategic*.

Newstream writers are making a *conceptual* claim about Mainstream scholarship (Section 3) which has three parts. First, the Newstream regard Mainstream international law as having adopted a complacent approach toward questions of how to define culture and differences between cultures (Section 3.1). This is exemplified in the arid debates over self-determination and cultural relativism. By contrast Newstream writers claim that the way in which culture is defined determines the legal rule which ensues, and that the meaning of what is culture is thus primary to the doctrines which have evolved. Second, they contend that Mainstream international law represents itself as an account of history as progress in which the doctrine of sovereignty develops from an uncertain principle of naked power distribution to a more formal, regulable legal mechanism (Section 3.2). Newstream accounts suggests that the story is more complex and that sovereignty can be re-interpreted in the light of different readings of the historical development of international law, in a manner which would inevitably unsettle interpretations of important doctrines such as acquisition, or territorial integrity. Third, they argue that Mainstream scholars have maintained a fiction that law-making can be reduced to either custom (a reflexive process of locating and amalgamating the practice and belief of states), or agreement and the drafting of new treaties, and so have failed to sufficiently take into account contemporary theoretical insights relating to language and representation (Section 3.3). If law is constituted by language rather than simply objective behavior and belief, then its foundations are less certain and its reconstitution is not only possible but obligatory. In short, the Newstream argues that Mainstream literature relies upon an untenable set of ideas about culture, sovereignty, and law-making.

In addition to these substantive, conceptual claims the Newstream argues that the Mainstream has a limited approach to method. So the second level of challenge is *methodological* provoking Newstream writers to experiment with different analytical devices (Section 4). First, new approaches method often locates and dissects twinned conceptual oppositions underlying history, sovereignty and culture, thereby revealing the unstable and contingent nature of the law which they support (Section 4.1). Second, Newstream writings represent international actors as being engaged on a highly personal quest, thereby undermining the notional objectivity and formality of international rules (Section 4.2). The device of the quest also produces an evocative descriptive framework, a personal and personally revealing account of law, and a mechanism to explore the internal contradiction between international law's idealism and its ordinariness. Finally, Newstream work uses language in ways which emphasize the conceptual and methodological themes just noted (Section 4.3).

Third, there is a *strategic* level to the challenge (Section 5). Here Newstream scholars reinvigorate pre-existing reform strategies, in an attempt to shift the emphasis of lawmaking from one of reform to radical reconceptualization. This is accomplished by incorporating perspectives foreign to the discipline and hitherto absent, and by situating legal problems more fully in their political and cultural context (Section 5.1); by provocative rewritings of doctrinal history (Section 5.2); and by integrating political considerations into legal analysis (Section 5.3).

Finally in Section 6 I argue that while these Newstream challenges could be transformative tools of changing law their potential is largely unrealized. Section 6 extends my critique by highlighting previously identified recurring problems with the analyses, namely their lack of concretization, reductionism and tendency toward condescension.

3. The Newstream Conceptual Challenge to Mainstream International Law

This part of the essay will examine the way Newstream writings are redefining some foundational concepts of international law. The three themes I focus on are: culture, the relationship between history and sovereignty and the role of language in the constitution of legal doctrine.

3.1. *Culture*

The first conceptual theme that features strongly throughout this body of this work is a concern with what constitutes culture. This is presented by the Newstream writers as a challenge to what they perceive as international law's traditional complacency when describing different groups of people, or modes of social, political and economic organization.

Much of the Newstream scholarship begins from the premise that definitions of culture are central to the way in which international law has been constituted, and that the meanings used in Mainstream literature operate to include certain ideas and groups of people and exclude others. So for example, a first group of Newstream writers interested in culture contend that representations of indigenous people in Mainstream international law have tended to mimic the standard stereotypes. They have been depicted as backward, under-developed, or more latterly, noble and thereby excluded from the development of law.[6] Moreover, this portrayal is represented as an inevitable result

[6] See e.g., Chris Tennant "Indigenous Peoples International Institutions and the International Legal Literature from" 1945–1993, 16 *Human Rights Quarterly* 1, 7 (1994) discussing the relationship between the representation of indigenous people in international legal literature and international law's treatment of them. He argues that there is a connection between the images in the literature and international law's treatment of them. He argues that there is a connection between the images in the literature and the practices of law. Indigeneous peoples are represented in the international legal literature as either "ignoble" or noble and that both representations affect the way in which law responds to their situation. On this view, cultural (mis)representations determine law. So in the period to 1945 indigenous peoples were represented as "ignoble", located in the past, lacking and incapable of exercising political responsibility. At the same time international law emphasized strategies of technical assistance, development and assimilation, in order to bring them into the present. More recently the international legal literature has represented indigenous people as "noble", as part of a communitarian lifestyle, in harmony with the environment and detached from modernity. Accordingly current legal strategies stress "flexible concepts of self-determination and autonomy", in order to transcend the failures of modernity, Id. at 24. In both cases international processes, doctrines, and institutions are responding to representations of indigenous people and not to indigenous peoples themselves. Moreover, the different representations actually corresponded to the goals of that particular period of law. When assimilation was considered a legitimate goal of law, indigenous people were portrayed as "ignoble" and in need of civilizing; when integration lost its cachet and there was disillusionment with Western legal solutions, indigenous people were depicted as "noble" and encouraged to remain separate from Western culture. Similarly Ileana Porras, in an article on terrorism, argues that international law's definition of terrorism frequently depends upon images of Orientalism which are constructed to suit law's need to exclude this form of violence from the range of the "normal" rules: Ileana Porras, "On Terrorism: Reflections on Violence and the Outlaw", in D. Danielsen and Karen Engle Eds., *After Identity: A Reader in Law and Culture* (1995). Hence a man charged with acts of terrorism is described in the press as wearing a suit "billowing in the wind" Porras, id. 304, reminiscent of Lawrence of Arabia imagery. The depiction of terrorist actors as "other" enables their acts to be demonized as a form of violence beyond that which is "normal" and thus the ordinary rules of international law, say in relation to the laws of war, or criminal law cannot apply. The construction of cultural stereotypes determines a particular set of international rules.

of culture and so, according to the Newstream, only a concerted rewriting of Mainstream cultural depictions will lead to changes in the actual practice of law.

Not all Newstream writers confront the question of culture in the same manner. There is a marked division between those who claim that the Mainstream literature has produced a Westernized view of different cultural groups, but that this depiction can be reconstructed, and, those who argue that the foundations of international law are so saturated with partial ideas about culture, that they cannot be reconstructed.

A group representing the first viewpoint argue that international legal culture has been fashioned out of a Western set of values,[7] but ultimately they maintain that law can recognize its own subjectivity and transcend it[8] by one of two methods. International Law could become more conscious of the legal viewers' own perspective,[9] or it might apply legal rules in a manner which recognizes the particular context of the group subject to the rule.[10] In sum, according to this first group of Newstream scholars, definitions of culture, although skewed by current Mainstream work, can be reassembled in such a way so as to incorporate into law the particular practices of the exclud-

[7] See e.g., an exploration of the exclusionary power of Western cultural assumptions, on law in Rosemary Coombe, "The Properties of Culture and the Politics of Possessing Identity: Native Claims in the Cultural Appropriation Controversy", in D. Danielsen and K. Engle Eds., *After Identity: A Reader in Law and Culture* (1995). Coombe's focus is the development of new forms of legal protection for the cultural property of indigenous peoples. Cultural property protection is based on the European "art/culture system" which excludes an indigenous understanding of ownership and identity. Moreover, this criticism applies to both traditional copyright law, and to the emerging laws of cultural property protection which purport to protect group rights. So, for example, both the copyright protection accorded Picasso's use of an indigenous mask and newer forms of collective cultural protection legislation are based on the same Western concept of "possessive individualism": id. at 255. What is left out of both regulatory styles is the sense that both ownership and collective identity carry quite different and specific meanings for indigenous peoples. Ownership in an indigenous sense, for example, may include a bundle of ideas which cannot be simply directly translated into new Western forms of law. Hence she argues, the structure of Western law, steeped in cultural assumptions derived from its own art/culture system, precludes the creation of new forms of legal protection about indigenous art, ownership and identity.

[8] See, e.g., Frankenberg who argues that comparative lawyers are blinded by their own subjectivity: Gunter Frankenberg, "Critical Comparisons: Rethinking Comparative Law", 26 *Harv. Int. L. J.* (1985) 411. He claims that comparative lawyers fail to recognize that their own perspectives play a significant part in the way they view other cultures: id. at 441. Moreover given this subjectivity, comparative law actually reveals more about the culture from which the comparativist belongs, than about the legal system under investigation.

[9] Id. at 442.

[10] Coombe, *supra* note 7. Coombe's proposal to overcome this problem, is to "listen[...] to native claims in context": id. at 266. She argues that in order to develop law reflecting indigenous ways of art and culture, it will be necessary to undertake a highly specific and contextualized form of investigation into the practices of the peoples involved. Only by adopting such a localized approach will laws emerge which accommodate the concerns of indigenous peoples.

ed groups resulting in a new international law which is more contextual, comprehensive and ultimately more expressive of diverse cultures.

How effective is this form of critique? The first form argues for reconstruction. However given the underlying premise of the Newstream writers that Western social, political and economic organization dominates legal developments, it is difficult to see how law can simply transcend those limits by "listening in context."[11] The very hegemonic nature of definitions of culture will tend to work against this solution. It is unlikely, if not inconsistent, that on the one hand European culture precludes the formation of law responsive to indigenous people, and on the other to claim that if law "listens" harder, European culture can be overcome. Moreover, it is contradictory to criticize Mainstream scholars who purportedly attempt to distance themselves from their own cultural stereotyping and yet then argue that all lawyers should learn to "transcend perspective".[12] On the one hand we are entreated to "recognize we are participants of one culture and observers of another"[13] and on the other, that we can be released from the "all encompassing grip of the habit of our own truth."[14] Is it possible to recognize subjectivity and transcend it simultaneously? If one accepts the first premise, namely that as lawyers we are trapped in our own cultural vision, then it seems problematic to overcome that vision, simply by an act of will. Although there is something appealing about the possibility that knowing who we are may lead to changing what we do, it seems likely that it will take more than mere desire to achieve it.

Ultimately this first group of Newstream writers effectively exposes the role of culture in determining legal practices, but their proposals to alter it are internally contradictory. This criticism may not however be fatal in the long term. Obviously under certain conditions, and over time, concepts and ideas which are beyond law's parameters are gradually incorporated, otherwise law would remain in a form of statis. Nevertheless it would seem that in order for the argument to have real force it is first necessary for these Newstream writers to speculate as to what are those conditions and how change can occur. How can contextualized listening lead to change? In what circumstances and by what mechanisms is it likely to occur? What is the appropriate context? The claim for contextualization is, to date, too thin to support a changed practice.

[11] Id. at 266.

[12] Frankenburg, *supra* note 8 at 442. Frankenburg acknowledges that no-one can "dispose[.]" of their "cognitive history" or "baggage of assumptions", id. at 443, yet he still ultimately advocates exactly just that, the only difference being that the actor does so self-consciously.

[13] Id.

[14] Id. at 454.

While the first Newstream group advocates a redefinition of culture by either recognizing Mainstream stereotyping of cultural groups, or better contextualizing legal problem solving, or transcendence of subjectivity and other acts of will, the second group, which I now discuss, is skeptical of ever achieving these goals.[15] This second group of Newstream writers are not so sanguine about reforming the current law. For them international law does not simply rely on culture, international law *is* culture.[16] By implication, international law cannot transcend culture by recognizing group difference. It cannot undo constructed notions of culture, because the notion of culture inheres in what international law is. According to the second group of writers, the construction of culture is not only the result of human agency in creating stereotypes but results from the structures of international law, its language and its history.[17]

[15] The polarity within Newstream work reflects an irony which dogs much contemporary scholarship: at the same time that the critique of culture is strongest in some quarters, the embrace of difference is at its peak in others, even within the same project: See discussion of Arjun Appadurai, "Disjuncture and Difference in the Global Cultural Economy", 2 *Pub. Culture* (1990) 1.

[16] See, e.g., Annelise Riles discussion of the question of whether it is possible for law to ever overcome the categories of culture: Annelise Riles, "Note: Aspiration and Control: International Legal Rhetoric and the Essentialization of Culture", 106 *Harv. L. Rev.* 723 (1993) [hereinafter *Aspiration and Control*]. She argues that nineteenth century international law was built upon essentialized versions of European and non-European culture. Moreover, so dependent was law on these essentialized notions, that international law was collapsed into culture, even though it projected itself as separate and law-like. Culture as law came in two forms. In one case it manifested itself as a mechanism for ordering non-European peoples by requiring them to aspire to standards of European-ness, in order to be included within existing categories of law. Thus non-Europeans aspired to own territory in order to prove statehood, because a state without territory was like a man without clothes: id. at 733 quoting T. J. Lawrence, *International Problems and Hague Conferences* (1908). The other manifestation of culture as law was to order non-Europeans by controlling then in a "dizzying catalog of colonial topics", id. at 729, according to racial differences and political organization. Both manifestations relied on culture. In one law offers the possibility of assimilation, in the other it offers the threat of exclusion.

[17] See, e.g., Antony Anghie who shares Riles' skepticism about the conundrum of law and culture, yet whose focus is on the role of language and history: Antony Anghie, Constructing the Nation State: Colonialism and the Making of International Law (1994), (unpublished S.J.D. dissertation, Harvard University, on file with author). Anghie claims international legal doctrine has developed largely in response to colonialism. Many of the major developments in relation to acquisition of territory, sovereignty and personality, for example, are informed by, and infused with the imperatives of colonialism. He argues that the entire language of international law was based on a complex taxonomy which separated "uncivilized from civilized" in order to justify inclusion and exclusion in full membership of the international system: Id. at 6 041-054. European notions of culture, defining everything from political organizations, to sexual practices, were used to denote "civilized" and exclude all else. However in order to treat with those outside the model of civilization, international law had also to create ways that the "uncivilized" could become objects, (but not subjects) of the system. Anghie develops the notions of "calibrated recognition", id., at 6 068, to describe the process by

The second group argues that the very nature of international law as culture may preclude any possibility of modifying international law to make it more responsive to different cultures. Most importantly they argue that international law is inherently a European cultural form,[18] and that these forms continues to pervade thinking, even amongst those who attempt to deconstruct law.[19] In one example Mainstream international law is depicted as the cultural language of nineteenth century colonialism,[20] and so language, culture and the formation of laws are therefore inextricably connected. Moreover if this story of the genesis of major doctrines of international law is correct, then those same cultural considerations continue to inform law-making and its functioning. Hence inbuilt and structural cultural biases will not simply be overcome by contextualization, or transcendence of perspective. What distinguishes the second group of Newstream writers from the first then is their belief that the very structure of international law precluded, and continues to preclude any way of moving beyond these cultural categories.

While the two viewpoints are partially persuasive, they both leave unanswered the question of how international law can be loosened from the particular cultural moorings it has acquired over time and which are now represented in Mainstream literature. Can the different cultural settings present in the twentieth century inspire a different international legal language? Will the post-colonial culture engender a post-colonial law in the same way that colonial culture produced colonial law? And is it possible for any universal system of international law to incorporate competing cultural considerations? Some of these critical issues are taken up by other Newstream writers who adopt an explicitly feminist perspective.

Their response has been to focus on a specific issue and document the difficulties it raises in recasting a more culturally sensitive international law. This has been done in relation to clitoridectomy,[21] and the wearing of the veil[22] in order to demonstrate the important observation that feminist con-

which non-European groups were kept out of international law membership but sufficiently recognized, (by personality doctrine and sovereignty/property distinctions for example), so that Europeans could trade with them, make unequal treaties with them and acquire their land. "'[T]he whole edifice' of international law is constructed on a[n] initial exclusion", id., at 6 061, and disempowerment because of the conjunction of civilization and sovereignty.

[18] Riles, *Aspiration and Control, supra* note 16.

[19] See e.g. Riles' discussion of David Kennedy's and Anthony Carty's treatment of culture: Riles id. at note 81.

[20] Anghie, *supra* note 17.

[21] Karen Engle, "Female Subjects of Public International Law: Human Rights and the Exotic Other Female", 26 *New Eng. L. Rev.* 1509 (1992) [hereinafter *Female Subjects*].

[22] Lama Abu-Odeh, "Post-Colonial Feminism and the Veil: Considering the Differences", 26 *New England L. R.* 1527 (1992).

ceptions of what is (women's) culture are precarious and diffuse.[23] These studies therefore indicate that it will be even more problematic to develop an international law reflecting post-colonial culture, both where there are no clear categories of culture and where different cultural considerations, such as gender and religion, contradict and overlap.[24] While not offering any neat solutions, these Newstream writings represent an advance upon the way the debate is conducted in Mainstream literature where it tends to devolve into an irresolvable exchange about whether international law should apply universal standards or be set according to local or regional needs. The difference here is that these Newstream writers intersect and oppose gender and culture in an attempt to move the debate beyond the simple observation that when trying to construct a more inclusive international law, previously excluded cultural factors come into conflict with each other. In contrast these works attempt to

[23] Karen Engle explores and criticizes the way different feminist critiques of international human rights, identify and assimilate women's concerns: Karen Engle, "International Human Rights and Feminism: When Discourses Meet", 13 *Mich. J. of Int'l L.* 517 (1992) [hereinafter *International Human Rights*]. She categorizes feminist approaches according to how they incorporate a conception of womens' culture into human rights. A three-layered typology is produced consisting of doctrinalists, institutionalists and external critics. "Doctrinalists" work within the framework of the existing doctrine to change and improve it, id. at 522. Hence the prohibition against torture contained in various human rights instruments can be extended to a prohibition against violence in the home, through a process of reinterpretation. "Institutionalists" focus their work on the processes of law-making advocating greater participation of women ultimately affecting the production of doctrine. Those engaged in an "external critique" see international human rights law as inherently male and resistant to assimilating women's concerns into its basic framework.

[24] Drawing on the earlier typology, id., Karen Engle explores what happens when other cultural categories intersect with this range of women's cultures. Focusing on the issue of clitoridectomy, she argues that the critique which appears to be the most explicit in identifying a culture specific to women (the "external" critique) is the *least* capable of being sensitive to other non-gendered cultural contexts: Engle, *Female Subjects, supra* note 21 at 1518. The external critique fails to recognize that the issue engenders deep differences of opinion, based on ethnic culture, between women. Similarly, Lama Abu-Odeh explores the difficulties of recognizing differences between women at the same time as maintaining a skepticism toward inclusive categories of womanhood, focusing on the use of the veil by feminists in Muslim countries and Western feminism's response: Lama Abu-Odeh, *supra* note 22. She argues that it may be possible for the two seemingly opposed positions to be reconciled at the point at which the interests of the two groups intersect. This is despite contradictions between Western feminists who see the veil as a symbol of disempowerment for women, and Muslim feminists who don it as a symbol of their power to redefine its meaning. It is not the obvious point that culture and gender can clash. Instead she locates common ground upon which feminisms meet by recognizing that although the veil increases a woman's "untouchability", id., at 1530, and thus remedies a problem of sexual harassment in the street , id., at 1531, it has a "different logic" in the workplace, where it can "seriously affect the career prospects", id., at 1534, of those who wear it. Despite (significant) differences, Islamic and Western feminist attitudes to the veil, both, through different means, seek to provide opportunities for Arab women to choose their work, and lifestyle and to be free from sexual harassment. Western feminisms are portrayed as both in opposition to, and potentially in alliance with, Islamic feminisms.

problematise the issue of culture, to argue that it is no longer possible to see categories of culture, as either all the same or all different. According to this view the proposals about incorporation of difference have been superseded by a recognition that one can no longer accurately define what standard is universal or relative. Whether it be human rights standards, or indigenous art, or Coca Cola, the search for an authentically universal, or relative version of each is an idle one because, in the words of one political scientist, sameness and difference have "cannibalized" each other.[25] It is the examination of this contradiction in the Newstream writings which makes the work so provocative and worthwhile.

So far we have seen how a concern with Mainstream definitions of culture permeates much Newstream work, although it is grappled with in quite different ways. A related uncertainty within the new scholarship concerns a pronounced skepticism about ever assigning people to particular cultural groups. This problem, which pervades many of the analyses, begs the question of how to ever talk about, or generalize about a group, in order to develop legal rules. The scholarship exhibits an implicit anxiety over culture which limits and complicates the possibilities of description, of law-making, and its interpretation. One response of some Newstream writers has been to argue that, despite the instability of the concept of culture, there is something intuitively appealing about representing a group of people in terms of a particular set of common characteristics, particularly when they have defined those characteristics themselves.[26] Implicit in this argument is the view that it would be churlish and patronizing to question the self-identification of a cultural grouping such as indigenous people.

Another response has been to argue that instead of discarding cultural groupings altogether as "untenable categor[ies] of representation",[27] one needs to a reconstruct the categories of culture as they currently exist.[28] The term "perspective" is used by one writer to describe a new mode of mak-

[25] Appuradai, *supra* note 15 at 17.

[26] Maivan Clech Lam, "Making Room for Peoples at the United Nations: Thoughts Provoked by Indigenous Claims to Self-Determination", 25 *Cornell Int. L. J.* 603 (1992) arguing that indigenous peoples' participation at the Working Group on Indigenous Peoples is slowly allowing for the infiltration of indigenous concerns into international norm creation. This argument explicitly utilizes the notion of culture. Lam relies on there being in existence a recognizable, identifiable cultural category of indigeneity, just as she describes her Asian community at law school in the 1970s as an "unmistakable community" defined by "rice, fish sauce, ghost stories and anti-imperialism": id., at 604.

[27] Annelise Riles, "Disciplines and Cultures: Perspectives on International Law and the Colonial Encounter", (1994) (unpublished manuscript, on file with author) at 10 021 [hereinafter *Disciplines and Cultures*]

[28] Id.

ing and interpreting law on the basis of some method other than culture[29] and would entail accommodating the perspectives of a multiplicity of different groups, peoples and disciplinary approaches and a movement beyond its own boundaries into other fields such as anthropology. The inclusion of a wide range of perspectives would serve as a replacement for international law's singular reliance upon cultural forms, and the new perspectives would reflect against each other thus creating "a series of angles directed onto themselves"[30] giving rise to new ideas of law.[31] So having demolished culture, as defined by international law, its reconstruction might be promoted by the use of a methodology other than culture. But the danger with this version of "multi-perspectivalism" is that it must also ultimately be premised on one form of cultural, or perspectival, representation. It is not any more certain that the new perspectives would not replicate what was once referred to as culture. If the fit between law and culture is as constraining as Newstream writers have argued it is difficult to see how it can be escaped by a change in terminology.[32]

In sum Newstream work contributes to international law a sophisticated new approach to one of the basic conceptual apparatuses of the field, culture. It provides a complex rendering of definitions of culture using it to examine the inclusionary and exclusionary power of culture in doctrinal development, questions of representation of peoples, and problems of incorporating difference into law. Writers differ as to the manner in which to overcome the constraints of culture with some relying on various acts of self-will, while others argue that the nature of language, the structure of law and the problem of how to address the intersections between different categories of description make it difficult to overcome cultural definitions. On the other hand, culture may be necessary to the self-identification of peoples excluded from Mainstream processes. Ultimately no single view about culture dominates, but what emerges instead is a sometimes fraught but always provocative set

[29] Id. at 10 017.

[30] Id. at 10 035.

[31] Riles suggests that this would ultimately lead to change. "[T]he work of the discipline would be to foreground a multitude of perspectives on the perspectives that we once forced into the category of culture, and to facilitate the movement between them by representing this movement as symbolically significant": id., at 10 025.

[32] Ultimately perhaps the same criticism that was made of Frankenberg can be leveled also at Riles; how can one both be constrained by and transcend the categories of culture, or of perspective. Nevertheless Riles at least anticipates this criticism: id., at 10 033. She disassembles international law as culture in order to reassemble it, id., at 10 036, arguing in the process that the key feature to guide reconstructed perspectivalism is the increased participation of voices previously excluded from international law. In this respect, by self-consciously embracing the categories she criticizes, id., at 10 036, the analysis resembles Karen Knop's strategy, *infra*, note 129, of disassembling sovereignty and reconstructing it in a newer form taking account of the criticisms of the concept which caused it to be disassembled. While her admission lends a certain credibility to the project, it does not overcome the criticisms.

of possibilities. Culture is revealed to be both a vehicle of change and of stagnation and one the redefinition of which has much to offer to Mainstream analyses of law.

3.2. *History and Sovereignty*

The second way in which Newstream work is altering one of the conceptual bases of international law is through its redefinition of the relationship between the history of international law and the doctrine of sovereignty. Newstream scholarship maintains that Mainstream international legal history is self-servingly repetitive, excessively linear in focus, unstable, and, that it conceal interests other than the purely legal. Newstream writers therefore propose various ways in which the relationship between history and sovereignty could be reconceptualized.

A central thesis of Newstream scholarship is that international law requires rewriting because the Mainstream version constantly reiterates its own history so as to present the field as a narrative of inevitable progress and modernization.[33] And the telling of law's story corresponds to a range of other stories, conveniently buttressing each other, which are conventionally recounted about the same period of development. The organization of society from a tribal basis, to one based on communities and then on individuals; the movement from status to contract; and from religion to philosophy to law follow the same linear route. The development in law from a concern with substantive norms, to a focus on procedure; from legal rules to institutions; from naturalism to realism to pragmatism, all mirror the same Enlightenment story. By excluding stories which deviate from this format, international law is thus written to reflect the history of the Enlightenment in which law is constantly improved and refined with the progress of time.[34]

Although there is wide agreement in the new scholarship about the relationship between telling a particular history and the development of law, as with culture, Newstream writers present different versions of the Mainstream stories, and so different versions of how they could be altered. A first group

[33] See, e.g., Kennedy, *New Stream, supra* note 2 at 2.

[34] David Kennedy Lectures in International Law and Institutions, Harvard Law School, Fall 1994, [hereafter *Lectures*]. He illustrates the point by referring to a major American text which tracks a shift from a pre-modern concern with philosophy, through a classical interest in doctrine to a modern emphasis on institutions, with appropriate turning points signaled by the Peace of Westphalia in 1648, the nineteenth century rise of the nation state, and the Treaty of Versailles. See Henkin et al., *supra* note 4 at xxi–xxxi.

following the realist[35] or sociological[36] traditions, argue that international law and its history, have been constructed,[37] in such a way so that something called "law" has been made, and exists at least semi-autonomously. They are not claiming that the history which is made is fictional or fraudulent but simply that it has been made, the point being to question the Mainstream version in order to show that outcomes are chosen and not inevitable. A second group however who do not share the assumption that this process of construction has lead to the existence of a separate entity called "law". Instead (and this is discussed more fully in the next section) they contend that law may be no more than a set of argumentative practices, a form of rhetoric,[38] (although this does not necessarily make it any the less real or powerful).[39] So a concept like "the state", or "sovereignty" is actually about the relationship between something posited as law and something posited as society,[40] rather than being a thing as such.[41] If law and its history are simply structures of certain repeating practices and arguments, then these tools must be questioned and unraveled, not only revealed (as the first group advocates), in order to effect any meaningful alteration in them.

Why it is that the Newstream writers would be so keen to unsettle the conventional view of history and international law? First, they argue that an examination of sovereignty reveals that the linear, historical story is wrong, and that its acceptance has skewed our current understanding of the doctrine's meaning. Far from having progressively evolved from a nineteenth century political principle, through a positivist rule early this century[42] to a more nuanced concept today, Newstream writers argue that sovereignty has always

[35] "Realist" is used here to describe a conception of law a result of policy choices of judges. See, e.g., Karl Llewellyn, "A Realistic Jurisprudence: the Next Step", 30 *Col. L. Rev.* 431 (1930).

[36] "Sociological" is used here to describe a conception of law as a reflection of society. See, e.g., Roscoe Pound, "The Scope and Purpose of Sociological Jurisprudence", 24 *Harv. L. Rev.* 591 (1911).

[37] Philip Allot, "New International Law: the First Lecture of the Academic Year 20 -", in Warbrick (ed.), *Theory and International Law: An Introduction* (1991), 105 at 116: the "actual" is not "natural and inevitable."

[38] Kennedy, *New Stream, supra* note 2 at 9: "Law is a restatement of its imaginary relationship to society."

[39] One political science commentator claims "imagination has become an organized field of social practices,": Appadurai *supra* note 15 at 5.

[40] Kennedy, id., at 6.

[41] Id., at 44.

[42] The highpoint of positive sovereignty is conventionally represented by the holding that restrictions on sovereignty cannot be presumed: *SS Lotus Case* (*France* v. *Turkey*) (1927) PCIJ Ser A. No. 9.

been an unstable reference point.[43] For example, judicial decisions which have been traditionally interpreted as illustrative of the importance of sovereignty can equally be read as representing law's fealty to strict rules over morality.[44] Moreover the meaning of sovereignty has always been in a state of flux, particularly throughout the nineteenth and twentieth century when treatise writers used the term sovereignty to describe how large trading companies wielded power over colonial territories and inhabitants[45] and early judicial decisions implicitly rejected any absolute rule, developed subsequently, that restrictions on sovereignty could not be presumed.[46] Later treatise writers used the concept to discuss the status of the first universal international institution, the League of Nations, arguing for example, that sovereignty was not simply about territory and power, but the moral authority wielded by government over the rights of the inhabitants,[47] or that although the League lacked the critical attributes of sovereignty,[48] it nevertheless possessed a separate existence which was more than the sum of its member state parts.[49]

A second reason Newstream writers are critical of the Mainstream representation of history is that, somewhat paradoxically perhaps, they claim it inhibits lawyers confronting current problems, because they are always look-

[43] Kennedy, *Lectures*. See e.g., David Kennedy, *A New World Order: Yesterday, Today and Tomorrow* [hereafter *New World Order*], 4 Transnational Law & Contemp. Problems 329 (1994) at 350: sovereignty "means lots of things." Kennedy also argues that the critique of sovereignty itself has been a recurring one, Kennedy, *New World Order*, id., at 359, and that Newstream writers are themselves situated historically, within a "rotating critique" about sovereignty and formalism, id., at 68.

[44] *The Antelope* 23 U.S. (10 Wheaton) 66 (1825) in Deak, *International Law Cases* Vol. 1. Chief Justice John Marshall of the U.S. Supreme Court held that African slaves seized on a Portuguese ship had to be returned to their owners despite domestic abhorrence of slavery. The case is commonly understood as a landmark in the development of sovereignty, on the basis of respect for Portugal's sovereignty. Alternatively it could be seen as an example of support for the rule of law, demonstrated in the reasoning that although "public sentiment" may wish the "unnatural traffic . . . to be suppressed" this would "march somewhat in advance of strict law", id., at 3.

[45] Wheaton, *Elements of International Law* (1866) 18.

[46] *Pacquette Habana* (1900) 175 US SC Rep 677.

[47] Geoffrey Butler, "Sovereignty and the League of Nations", *Brit. Y.B. Int'l L.* (1920–21), 35. His discussion questioned any singular notion of sovereignty referring to insights from the new field of psychology, French corporations theory and recognition doctrine. According to Butler "consciousness" as much as territory created sovereignty, id., at 42. The notion that a corporation could possess "personality" suggested that such concepts were artificial constructs, id., at 36. And the emergent distinction between *de facto* and *de jure* recognition implied that there could be different types of sovereignty, id., at 35.

[48] P.E. Corbett, "What is the League of Nations?" *Brit. Y.B. Int'l L.* (1924) 119. Corbett lists criteria set out by Oppenheim: the right of legation, rights of sovereignty, the right of intervention for the protection of minorities, the capacity to hold a protectorate and to declare or peace, id., at 121.

[49] Id., 148.

ing back to past developments or anticipating an inevitably reformed future, instead of focusing upon the substantive difficulties of the present.[50] The nostalgic invocation of the past[51] thus has the added effect of suspending the doctrinal development of international law in the present.

What does the adoption of such a view signify in practical terms? To take one example, if international human rights law is perceived as constantly moving toward a more progressive state, but is instead caught in limbo between a harsh past and a utopian future, proposals to regulate the present are bound to be impeded. This prognosis can be illustrated in the ambivalence in human rights law towards the well-documented problem of violence in the home, which continues to infect most societies despite widespread condemnation. While a host of factors, such as religious belief, economic structures, and assumptions about the male right to exert power, militate against its eradication, the continued belief in the inevitability of improvements also plays a role. This optimism, often unsubstantiated by facts, blunts the impetus for change in the present by encouraging women to be satisfied that some movement is occurring and so to remain patient and passive, even if in fact conditions are worsening or remaining static rather than improving in many situations.[52] Thus current realities of continuing universal abuse are hidden if international human rights law continues to passively rely upon a history in which progress is inevitable.

A third reason for the Newstream skepticism about international law history is their claim that that the Mainstream story presumes the existence of a clear demarcation between the past, in which religion, mysticism, and universalizing ideologies reigned, and the present in which society is characterized by law, rationality and the absence of ideology.[53] Newstream critiques argue that religion, although largely unacknowledged, continues to inform inter-

[50] The field is "constantly remembering a stable origin, foreshadowing a substantive resolution, but living in an interminable procedural present": Kennedy, *New Stream, supra* note 2 at 2. The "stable origin" of Kennedy's claim would be states choosing to join together as a community of nations in order to create an international public order; the "substantive resolution" would be the promise of a fully developed set of substantive norms; and the "interminable procedural present" is represented by the burgeoning bureaucratic structure of the United Nations, its agencies, and other international law making institutions.

[51] Id., at 12.

[52] For a recent news article substantiating the view that violence in the home continues to be a widespread problem see, e.g., "More Women Killed in Pregnancy in US as Result of Beating Than All Other Diseases" P. Bone, *The Age* 24/25 Aug. 1995. For an argument claiming that economic structural adjustment policies has a disproportionately deleterious effect on women see, e.g., Marilyn Waring, "Gender and International Law: Women and the Right to Development", 12 *Australian Y.B. of Int'l L.* (1992) 177.

[53] A major casebook on international law, Henkin et al., *supra* note 4 at xxii, differentiates the past from the present by arguing that "universalist ideologies" of earlier times have been replaced by "co-existence" in the current period, id., at xxx.

national law, because it repeats in a "secular key" religion's attitude to the sacred and profane.[54] Sovereignty with its almost deified[55] status within the hierarchy of norms could be one example of the operation of this distinction, because its "sanctity" continues to operate as a barrier to the development of principles perceived as incursions on it, such as human rights protection and humanitarian intervention.

A final reason to question the Mainstream linear view of history is that it buries inequalities which lie at the very foundation of some doctrinal developments. For example it is argued that sovereignty and its associated doctrines, acquisition of territory, territorial integrity, and self-determination, arose out of, reflected and reinforced the inequities of colonialism. Anthony Anghie examines the history of colonialism and its effect on the development of sovereignty doctrine. He argues that the whole project of sovereignty was a response to colonialism. He identifies two forces which were used in the name of the colonial project to oppress colonial peoples and form the structural basis for the development of the rules of sovereignty. The first arose as a response to the Austinian challenge to international law. Typically Austin's definition of law as rules emanating from a sovereign backed by force is viewed as inimical to the idea of international law itself. However the Austinian view of law also conflicts with the characterization of indigenous social orders as non-legal. Colonial peoples who, after all, would have satisfied the criterion of sovereignty had to be distinguished. International law answered the latter part of the Austinian challenge, according to Anghie, by refocussing the discussion over the source of authority from the sovereign to society. If society was the real source of legitimacy it was a short step toward limiting the sorts of societies which could be such sources. Hence, argues Anghie, the response of international law was to utilize colonialism's definitions of civilization in order to exclude the "uncivilized" sources from operating as a legitimate source of sovereign authority. Once excluded as uncivilized, this exclusion then formed the basis of justifications for the development of international norms relating to sovereignty. There was a circular relationship then between the rejection of Austinian definitions, colonialism, and legal doctrine. Each reinforced the other.[56]

This history has continuing ramifications for international law because it has not previously been acknowledged. Newstream advocates argue that it is

[54] Kennedy, *New Stream, supra* note 2 at 17.

[55] Richard Ashley, and R. B. J. Walker, "Reading Dissidence/Writing the Discipline: Crisis and the Question of Sovereignty in International Studies", 34 *Int'l Studies Q.* (1990) 367, arguing that sovereignty has variously been reconfigured as equivalent to, *inter alia,* God, nature, citizen, nation, and history.

[56] Anghie, *supra* note 17 at 47.

imperative for international law to excavate its foundational doctrines in order to determine whether they mask disadvantages which would counter international law's claim to impartiality and fundamental equality. So, for example, adopting a Newstream approach, one could examine whether there are inbuilt restrictions upon the application of principle of permanent sovereignty over natural resources and, if there are, whether these internal limits ought to be reassessed in the light of current understandings of equality and disadvantage? Another possibility of applying the Newstream historical approach would be to ask whether the GATT "special sector" exclusions for textiles and agriculture relate to their particular historical genesis and now require readjustment?

In sum Newstream methods of analyzing history and sovereignty have been combined in imaginative ways which suggest their application could have far-reaching consequences for international law. The continuing redefinition of the relationship between history and sovereignty has been used to question the linear and progressive account of history, and the sanctity of some of law's basic principles, to uncover inequalities in doctrines, and to assist in rescuing international law from its paralysis in the face of continuing violations. The potential application of these insights in fields ranging from human rights to trade is an important project for the future. When sovereignty is no longer conceived of as natural, construction can be a liberation rather than a constraint.

3.3. *Language*

The final conceptual redefinition which Newstream introduces into international law is its focus on language as a constitutive tool of law-making. While Mainstream literature on law-making emphasizes the role of custom in the form of state practice, beliefs, and values, Newstream writers borrow from ideas associated with French post-structural theory, to argue that as law is made up of language, languages generates, rather than simply describes, legal rules.

If this view of the relationship between language and law is correct then the Mainstream approach has failed to take account of an important factor in law-making. If law is a set of arguments generated by language then it is the discussion or conversation about the arguments which creates the concepts themselves, not the actual behavior of states, their consent, or their beliefs. So Newstream lawyers refer to law to as a system of "linguistic maneuvers",[57]

[57] Edward M. Morgan, "Internalization of Customary International Law: An Historical Perspective", 12 *Yale J. Int'l Law* 63, 65 (1987).

or as a practice of argument[58] rather than a system of rules with an *a priori* existence which is subsequently reduced into language.

The second aspect of this approach to language is that it disputes the Mainstream assumption that law is different from other forms of culture. If law is simply a linguistic phenomenon made up out of language, it has much more in common with other fields such as politics, or sociology, or even drama or of visual art, and therefore its claim to being unique is weakened. And so also, the things which make up the texts of law – its instruments, its doctrines, its institutions and processes – can be interpreted as aspects of any one of those fields. So for example, war crimes trials from Nuremberg, through Eichmann to Demjanjuk, can be seen as a form of legal drama, as "retributory theater" rather than as stages in the development of legal doctrine.[59] Or a legal forum may acquire a theatrical quality. A conference on East Timor and an academic exchange to the Royal College of Madrid become scenes in a three act drama about the disillusionment of an international human rights lawyer.[60] Or a particular doctrine, such as self-determination, can be interpreted in terms of its relationship to the artistic developments in the Modernist period.[61]

However it would be a mistake to conclude that this emphasis on law as language, or artistic narrative, reduces law to semantics or renders it any the less powerful. On the contrary the Newstream scholars depict law as a set of irreconcilable binary linguistic tendencies[62] which constitute a powerful social practice[63] with very real effects. For example it is convincingly argued that the language of state sovereignty developed in such a way as to exclude colonized peoples from the benefits of sovereignty.[64] Colonized groups, although

[58] Kennedy, *Lectures*, *supra* note 34, describing statehood doctrine as being composed of a series of "argumentative tendencies".

[59] Edward Morgan, "Retributory Theater", 3 *Am. Univ. J. Int'l L. and Pol.* 1 (1988).

[60] David Kennedy, "Autumn Weekends: An Essay on Law and Everyday Life", in A. Sarat, ed., *Law and Everyday Life* 191 (1993) [hereinafter, *Autumn Weekends*].

[61] Nathaniel Berman, "Modernism, Nationalism and the Rhetoric of Reconstruction", 4 *Yale. J. of L. and the Humanities* 351 (1992). Berman aims to show how legal innovations in the inter-war period borrowed from developments in art. He argues that the principles of self-determination and minority protection fragmented sovereignty in the inter-war period in a similar way to that in which modernism fragmented representation of the body. The appearance of a principle which undermined absolute sovereignty and invested national groups with legal significance coincided with, modernism's critique of representation and its interest in primitive expressionism.

[62] Martti Koskenniemi argues convincingly that the entire structure of legal argument is based upon certain oppositions inherent in language. He shows that law can be reduced to two sets of mutually complementary "ascending" and "descending" sets of justifications. Martti Koskenniemi, *From Apology to Utopia: The Structure of International Legal Argument* (1989) [hereinafter *Apology to Utopia*].

[63] Appadurai, *supra* note 15 at 5.

[64] Anghie, *supra* note 17.

exhibiting many of the requirements of sovereignty such as group identification, territory, political organization, and an authoritative decision maker were nevertheless not "sovereign" in the sense required by international law because they were deemed "uncivilized" according to a definition of the term which excluded non-European practices. Thus the language of law in formulating a complex spectrum of types of sovereignty determined the practice of law in a manner which made it both exclusive of non-Europeans and hierarchical toward them. Non-Europeans possessed "personality" at international law which enabled them to convey land to Europeans, and to trade with them, but nothing more. The inter-dependence between legal definitions of sovereignty and the continued subjugation of the colonized peoples is evidence of the power of language and its participation in the creation of those conditions.[65] Moreover, it is evidence of the way in which the language of colonialism and international law interacted because without the language of one the other made little sense.

It is important to acknowledge however that the focus on language is not new to international legal scholarship, although the emphasis on it is. The provisional nature of the meaning of concepts such as sovereignty has long been recognized[66] as has the normative ambiguity of legal language generally.[67] But the difference between the Newstream and earlier commentators is that although the latter were aware of the inherent ambiguity of the language of law they nevertheless believed that its true meaning could be extracted by going beyond the surface meaning to find an interpretation which best fitted the purpose of the instrument.[68] The purpose could be located in ancillary texts, for example in the travaux preparotoire (itself a thing made up of language). Where these newer commentaries differ is in their claim that even looking behind the instrument, or doctrine will not reveal the true meaning of the law, because language, with all its normative ambiguities is still the constitutive tool. There is no escape from language. According to the Newstream approach, there will always be available a linguistic justification for a particular view of law that emphasizes either the need for sovereign autonomy and or the requirements of an interdependent world community. One may in

[65] "Language cannot yield to empirical reality where it would lead to collapse of the system and of language itself": id., at 6 059.

[66] See discussion of the sovereign status of the League, *supra* notes 47 & 48.

[67] Myres McDougal, *Power and Policy in Quest of Law: Essays in Honor of E. V. Rostow*, (1985) 145. [hereinafter, *Power*].

[68] Id., at 154: "[w]hen the march of events inevitably lays bare ambiguities and alternatives of interpretation. . . . rationality must require that interpretation . . . which best promotes the major purposes . . ."

certain circumstances appear more persuasive than the other, but neither is inherently or objectively correct.[69]

In Section 3, I have shown that Newstream scholarship has introduced some basic redefinitions of important conceptual relationships in international law between cultural form and legal doctrine, between history and sovereignty and between language and law. In Section 4 I turn to an examination of the methods Newstream scholarship uses in making these arguments.

4. The Methodological Challenge

Mainstream writers generally draw upon a standard range of methodological tools. Upon identifying a legal problem they classify it using a common taxonomy and common history; its textual, judicial and customary sources are discussed; the intention of the drafters or state actors is identified; as are any associated norms; and the political context or realities which constrain its interpretation. The discussion usually generates two or three possible alternatives through which the prudent scholar ordinarily divines a middle course. The objection of the Newstream to this form of analysis is that it is redundant because it simply regurgitates old problems and ultimately leads to intellectual stagnation. So in order to avoid reproducing past problems, Newstream works challenge not only the basic concepts of international law by redefining them, but also its methods. The three Newstream methods which are discussed here are the use of polarities or "doubles" to construct arguments, the personal quest device, and the focus on language.

4.1. *"Doubles"*

One Newstream strategy is to locate within international law scholarship, opposing argumentative tendencies, or, as I will call them, "doubles", in order to expose the indeterminate nature of law. Martti Koskenniemi, the best known exponent of the technique, positions international legal problems on a type of metaphorical grid in which all legal arguments veer between justifications for State behavior, or advocacy of more international regulation; between being either "apologetic" in the case of the former, or "utopian" in

[69] Hence Koskenniemi contends that "*we cannot consistently prefer either set of arguments.* Adopting a descending pattern will seem political and subjective either because it assumes the existence of a natural morality or because it creates an arbitrary distinction between States. An ascending pattern will seem political and subjective because it cannot constrain at all.... Both must be included in order to make law seem objective, that is, normative and concrete and, as such, something other than politics." Martti Koskenniemi, "The Politics of International Law", 1 *Eur. J. Int'l. L.* (1990) 4 at 45 (emphasis in original) [hereinafter *Politics*].

the case of the latter.[70] So examples of the apologetic, or "ascending" justification are arguments which emphasize state autonomy, the role of consent in law-making, and concreteness in legal interpretation. Typically, utopian or "descending" arguments will emphasize justice, normativity and community. By reducing legal argument to this simple but compelling structure, Koskeniemmi convincingly demonstrates the deficiencies of the Mainstream claim that law is founded in objective, rational, or value based choices and instead shows that it is part of a mutually reinforcing system of rhetoric.[71]

As a methodology, "doubling" is not new to international law,[72] but the technique is repeated so often in Newstream methodology, that it has become a distinguishing feature or the "voice"[73] of the approach. It serves a number of functions apart from exposing fundamental linguistic oppositions inherent in international law.[74] Doubling shows how these oppositions may combine in order to produce legal change;[75] it demonstrates how legal principles are always subject to re-interpretation because they usually contain contradictory

[70] Koskenniemi, id. Even the Newstream are caught in a puzzle in which they simultaneously criticize and embrace sovereignty: Kennedy, *New World Order, supra* note 43 at 360. The mutual dependency of the opposing forces emphasizes again how law fits together as a structure; it is not just a series of rules but a "single rhetorical fabric", Kennedy, *New Stream, supra* note 2 at 38.

[71] This mutual dependency is referred to in Kennedy's work as "double movements", Kennedy, *New Stream*, id., at 17. So, for example, the structure of sources doctrine moves between consent and non-consent, between treaty and custom, between "getting in" to custom through *opinio juris* and state practice, and "getting out" via regional custom or persistent objection are defined in this way. Or, constitutional voting mechanisms at the League of Nations referred back to the politics of establishment and forward to implementation of norms, without resolution, in the same way that sources and process doctrine "produces a practice of interminable discourse.": id., at 39.

[72] Earlier international law commentators, probably drawing on the Realist school of jurisprudence, Llewellyn, *supra* note 35, observed how doctrines "travel in opposites." Also, see e.g., McDougal, *Power, supra* note 67 at 156.

[73] Kennedy uses "voice" to refer to the style or approach encapsulated by the mainstream tradition. See, e.g., the "tragic voice of post-war public law liberalism": Kennedy, *New Stream, supra* note 2 at 2.

[74] It facilitates the Newstream arguments about the constitutive nature of language and reveals the way sets of irreconcilable oppositions in law are themselves rooted in the structure of language. Following the argument usually associated with French post-structuralism, see. e.g., Christopher Norris, *Deconstruction: Theory and Practice* (1982), that language is structured into a series of binaries, law constituted by argument must also express the same oppositions.

[75] Sometimes these binarisms are characterized as combining with each other to create a particular legal regime. Nathaniel Berman, for example, argues that self-determination law during the inter-war period combined modernism's interest in primitivism with its experimentation with form, Berman *supra* note 61. Berman illustrates his thesis by comparing the work of an artist, Picasso, with that of a legal scholar, Redslob, who wrote on nationalism. Picasso's work celebrated the period's critique of representation, and its interest in cultural expression. He fractured traditional representations of women for example and he incorporated images from "primitive" art into his work. Similarly law, described by Redslob, destabilized classic forms of concepts such as sovereignty and focused on the power of a "primitive" nationalism.

impulses;[76] and it lends support to the view that lawyers ought to look beyond the discipline, in order to avoid being paralyzed by these tensions.[77] Moreover doubling exposes international law's reliance on irreconcilable ideas;[78] illustrates the claim that Mainstream work is obsessed with procedure at the expense of achieving substantive objectives;[79] and provides one important

The period's artistic emphasis on innovation with form and with technique was translated into the legal domain in new forms such as the plebiscite and minority protection regimes, id., at 375. International law of peoples, in the inter-war period, reflected a modernist alliance of two related trends, primitivism and experimentalism, id., at 369.

[76] The doubling method impels new interpretations by providing an impetus for the release of argumentative energy. For example, Lam, *supra* note 26 at 622, examines how indigenous peoples can utilize pre-existing international law doctrine such as statehood and sovereignty to further their claim for greater participatory rights. Her primary argumentative device is to characterize statehood and sovereignty as part of a "double helix" which therefore contains "multiple inheritances" for indigenous peoples to draw upon. She relies on oppositional strands of thought which have been hidden but which are released by her analysis. Similarly, Allot describes an international law class in the twenty-first century, *supra* note 37, telling his students that society can either be like a poem and focus upon human consciousness, or it can be mechanistic like a motor car, id., at 109, and it is only the "joy of law" which will save it from the latter, id., at 113. It is the energy created by this contrast which inspires Allot's argument for a new normative vision of law in the current period.

[77] Doubling encourages writers to look outside law in order to avoid the spiral created by opposites in conflict. It encourages a questioning of law's boundaries and a dissolving of the distinctions between law and other disciplines. Newstream writers draw on anthropology, Riles, *supra* notes 16 and 27; art criticism, Berman *supra* note 61; politics, Koskenniemi, *Politics, supra* note 69; and feminism, Karen Knop, "Re/Statements: Feminism and State Sovereignty in International Law", 3 *Transnational L. & Contemporary Prob.* 293 (1993) to help resolve the law's indeterminancies. Moreover precursors of the Newstream approach use similar techniques. So, for example, Berman relies on Redslob who argues that nationalism is informed by literature and politics, Berman, *supra* note 61 at 364, 365. See also Redslob's reliance on a rich background of non-legal factors to constitute a concept which has legal status, namely nationhood. Robert Redslob, "The Problem of Nationalities", *Grotius Society*, March 2, 1931, 21. Nationalism is created as a product of various influences, including, for example, a royal family, id., at 22, "the literary and artistic patrimony", and political instruments such as the Magna Carta, id., at 23. Interdisciplinarity, both of the analyses and or their historical sources characterizes the new approaches method.

[78] Ileana Porras uses the method to examine the way the Rio Declaration on the Environment contains provisions which seeks to balance seemingly incompatible goals of development and the environment, Porras, *supra* note 5. A sovereign right to exploit resources according to the State's own development policies, an injunction that environmental standards should reflect context, and that they should not distort trade, are included alongside provisions imposing state responsibility for environmental damage, the polluter pays principle, and a requirement that States reduce unsustainable patterns of production and consumption: id., citing Rio Declaration Principles 11, 16, 2, 16, 8 respectively. Despite what Porras calls this "paradox", id., at 21, she portrays the developments as basically healthy because they are an example of inclusion of developing countries interests, which forces developed countries to modify their practices as well as enabling developing countries to contribute to law making and interpretation.

[79] A function of the doubling technique is that it concretizes the Newstream arguments about the relationship between substance and process, in three ways. First, doubling emphasizes the way process avoids substance. Koskenniemi claims that classic international law developed into

organizing device for arguments.[80] In short, the use of doubles is not only characteristic of Newstream work, but facilitates the definition of many of the conceptual challenges referred to above.

4.2. *Personal Quest*

A second challenge to Mainstream method comes in the form of the personal quest device. Mainstream methods of analysis are clearly comforted by the notion that in adopting a standard methodology, as described above, one is assured that the legal conclusions which are reached are, to an extent, objective. Newstream work implicitly questions that assumption, by adopting a different set of techniques, perhaps the most controversial of which is to personalize legal issues as part of a larger quest or journey for a better international law. The quest device serves to emphasize three features: the subjective nature of law-making, the relationship between public and private, and the search for redemption within the discipline. A well known example of a writer who uses this method is David Kennedy.

Kennedy uses the quest technique to evoke the disappointment of Newstream writers with current Mainstream lawyers who, he argues, have largely inherited a pragmatic, as opposed to normative form of analysis.[81] Non-legal

proceduralism in order to avoid the problem of resolving conflict either by using fundamental values or oppressive majoritarianism, Koskenniemi, *supra* note 62 at 128, 129. Second, it lends support to the argument that process determines substance. Kennedy claims that although state responsibility presents itself as the humble servant of substantive norms, it often supplants it, David Kennedy, *International Legal Structures* (1987) 175 [hereinafter: *Legal Structures*]. For example in the *South West Africa* cases Liberia and Ethiopia were refused standing on the basis of lack of interest. In this case South Africa's breach of the mandate on the grounds of racial discrimination was never resolved, but was nevertheless indirectly determined, id., at 125. Third, doubling facilitates the new approaches view that the move to process is seen as depleting substance. Tennant cautions against the dangers of indigenous peoples vesting energy in procedural reform because it may lead to valorizing process over substance; indigenous aspirations being "captured" and "co-opted" by participation, Tennant, *supra* note 6 at 56.

[80] So for example Riles' basic thesis is to show how a Europeanized version of culture ordered colonial societies, Riles, *supra* notes 16 & 27. But to make this argument she divides the mechanisms of order into opposed, but mutually dependent forces. Colonial peoples were ordered in one of two ways. Either they were ordered because they were controllable as categories of peoples deemed to lack civilization, or they were ordered by forcing them to aspire to be civilized. In both cases her argument aims to prove how international law ordered colonial peoples, and in both cases the organizing principle of her thesis is European culture in opposition to other cultures. Similarly Tennant, *supra* note 6, organizes his argument around two opposing standards, his aim being to contrast one legal period with another. Indigenous peoples were represented as ignoble during the period of assimilation and as noble when autonomy was the preferred strategy. Doubling is an effective tool in ordering such an argument.

[81] In a thumbnail portrait of American international lawyers in the post war era, he argues that they sacrificed a doctrinal purity for institutional pragmatism and portrays them as naive

techniques, such as a literary writing style, and the frequent use of similes and metaphors characterize the work, often as stylistic devices to repeat the theme that international law has lost its idealism and its innocence, and strayed toward realism and proceduralism. So where the emphasis is on a law of human rights which is caught between an idealistic realization of its normative framework and a realistic acceptance of its limits, Kennedy describes a human rights conference in a mood which evokes a similar equivocation and disappointment, as a "smudged Xerox affair" with a "faded agenda".[82] From the terminology we know already that the conference was held in an under-resourced field of law where the aspirations of its stated norms had a slightly soiled quality, signaling a certain weariness within the field and the inevitability or likelihood of failure[83] and passive acceptance of that failure.

The personal nature of the journey is emphasized by portraying the people involved in international law-making in an informal gossipy manner,[84] or by writing in the form of a personal narrative[85] or as a kind of social anthropology of international lawyering.[86] Again the use of the personal voice allows the Newstream writer to convey a sense of disappointment and unrequited anger about the perceived failure of Mainstream international law.

and childlike playing with toys beyond their control. There they were, "sneaking up" on sovereignty, with their enthusiasm for administration rather than rules, but their "shiny new bureaucracies failed to produce the reform which they had prophesied.": Kennedy, *New Stream, supra* note 2 at 4.

[82] Kennedy, *Autumn Weekends, supra* note 60 at 192.

[83] Metaphor is used in the same way, to repeat in stylistic mode the harsh move toward disillusionment. So in describing the way international scholarship lost its sense of direction in the post-war era, Kennedy says that its students were "invited to choose [explanations for international law] like a debutante at a smorgasbord", Kennedy, *New Stream, supra* note 2 at 4.

[84] See David Kennedy's description of the generational development of American international lawyers from the inter-war period, through the post war phase, to the present day. Kennedy describes an international law peopled by "imperialists and humanitarians", "usually Republicans", id., at 3, in the pre war era, and "Democrats eager to rebuild in the name of democracy and decolonization", id., at 4. It is a description tinged with excitement and with pathos. The inter-war characters were lawyers of "independent intellectual vision" who "rebuilt the field after the debacle of America's absence from that quintessentially progressive institution, the League of Nations", id., at 3. They are depicted as heroic if somewhat naive in ignoring the insights of realism, or the principles of the welfare state.

[85] David Kennedy often places himself at the center of a description. International scholarship is about personal discovery. It is also as much as about how individual people behave and act as a group as it is about the texts they write or write about. Friendships and companionability are important to this international law. Ideas and rules are not self generating.

[86] The same conference is described as a "site for social relations", Kennedy, *Autumn Weekends, supra* note 60 at 202, even for "flirtation", id., at 205. Much store is placed by Kennedy on the formation at the meeting of an "affinity group" id., at 204 of like minded, slightly jaded, but savvy people.

> [t]he elaborate edifice they had honored was succumbing to the erosion and fragmentation they had encouraged. Attacked from the left and right, theoretically weak, jurisprudentially behind the times, the old edifice they had so lovingly sheltered seemed hopelessly ill-equipped to the broad functions they had encouraged us to think it might perform".[87]

The voice is of the disappointed disciple who had been led to believe in international law's capacity to change the international sphere and had seen those expectations dashed[88] especially by those in the academy.[89] However it also opens the door to the Newstream to challenge its predecessors and position themselves as intellectual redeemers of the field,[90] a goal which is pursued with almost missionary zeal.[91] The reader witnesses the journey and is encouraged to identify with its success or failure.

The most distinctive feature of the quest is that it integrates the personal and public spheres, so that the twin themes of idealism and realism, of romanticism and cynicism, are repeated, eventually resolving into a sense of melancholy. So although a central theme of Kennedy's work is the tension in public international law between its potential to provide a strong, enforceable, normative framework and the actual limits of its application, he also seems engaged in a constant, perhaps therapeutic and quite public exploration of, what he calls, the "split moment"[92] between realism and idealism, best exemplified in the article about a human rights conference on the subject of East Timor.[93] This is a journey which is characterized by both romance and sexu-

[87] Kennedy, *New Stream*, *supra* note 2 at 5.

[88] The sheepish exit, id., of the ancestors seems fitting as Kennedy recounts in great detail the disaster he has inherited, berating them with their many deficiencies – theoretical, jurisprudential, political and shortsighted. What is left after this rather Oedipal outburst, is only the detritus of its former proud self, "a frail dowager, too weak to withstand sustained criticism, in need of enrichment, protection and an observant fealty," id., at 6, a group whom Spiro Agnew would justifiably label "nattering nabobs of negativism," id.

[89] In the academy all that could be offered was "an easy patois of lazy justification and arrogance for a discipline which had lost its way and kept its jobs," id. The bitterness extended to a feeling that the teachers could provide no convincing explanation for the existence of international law as law. "We were given too many reasons to believe in international law - as our teachers struggled to make good their enthusiasm after having pawned their idealism", id.

[90] Not keen to keep working in the same manner, to be a "bureaucrat, a laborer in an institutional plant that no one believed was able to respond to international racism, inequality or violence," id., the younger critics commenced on a program of reinvigoration.

[91] Their mission, their journey was to save the field of international law, to "dislodge the discipline from its stagnation in post war realism," id.

[92] Kennedy, *Autumn Weekends*, *supra* note 60 at 203.

[93] The conference, held in Portugal in 1991, concerns the legal ramifications of Indonesia's continuing presence in East Timor. The pervasive theme of the article is the conflict between activism and realism, but this theme is conveyed through the device of the author's reminiscence

ality, and by cynicism and mundaneness.[94] It is a journey in which the author indulges in self-aggrandizement;[95] adopts an ironic, almost flip tone;[96] and attempts to shock the reader with his purported amorality.[97]

At one level then the writing is cynical and self-indulgent, exhibiting, albeit consciously, all the worst traits of me-generation pop psychology narration: arrogance, self-centredness, too cleverness and mock mockery. However intertwined with the heavy and quite explicit cynicism of the style is a perhaps honest, serious, funny, vaguely optimistic but sad paen to the possibilities of human rights law. Its redemptive quality lies largely in its brutal self-scrutinization and revelation. [98] Moreover, the seriousness of its objectives,

upon his own participation in the conference and in the disillusionment which occurred there. His personal musings become the subject of the piece.

[94] Kennedy's disillusioning process of yearning for a transcendental idealistic normativity which characterized the beginnings of the East Timor conference and the cynicism and pragmatism of the Spanish nightclub, reads like the story of a failed romance. Cf. Allot's attachment to the "poetry" of international law over its mechanical qualities has a lyrical, but urgent edge to it, Allot *supra* note 37.

[95] East Timor falls away as an issue of concern or law, as does human rights or even self-determination. Instead we are left with an consciously indulgent personal dialogue, with a warts and all revelation of the author's misgivings, insecurities and conceits/vanities. Thus the author elevates himself as the subject of the work. He refers to himself in, what he himself labels, "messianic" terms: Kennedy, *Autumn Weekends, supra* note 60 at 197. At one point he is asked to provide an unscheduled interview for Portuguese television. He does so with what appears to be a general disdain for the process, for the subject of East Timor and for his audience. Subjected to questioning by a "charming reporter", he felt he "should admit that [he] had no idea what the U.S. position on Timor might be," id., at 199, but he nevertheless "wishes for a more forthcoming attitude from the State Department on Timor (don't they always disappoint)," id., at 200. He talked about the "number of crucial procedural hurdles" associated with the case and that "the case would need to be pursued diligently, but the importance of the norms involved could hardly be overstated. And so on," id. The explicit irony of the description, does not lessen its superior and condescending tone. Nowhere are the issues really aired, the whole process is treated as a sort of unpleasant but expected distraction satisfying only the subject's interest in media attention and his political detachment.

[96] Confessing to the reader that he was ignorant of the U.S. position in Timor, Kennedy asks "where were we on Indonesia these days anyway?" id., at 199. Small details are introduced in an irreverent tone. The author postpones his departure for the conference because he has "tickets for Natalie Cole" the preceding day, id., at 196, as if to heighten the disjunction between the hedonistic private and the altruistic public domains.

[97] Cogitating about whether to attend the conference, Kennedy confesses that he was motivated by reasons other than international law advocacy. He "had never been to Portugal" id., at 194, and "[a]t the very least, this sort of thing can sometimes be cashed in for political correctness points with students and colleagues," id., at 195. When Kennedy leaves the conference he flies home with a sympathetic colleague and they ruminate pretentiously over the event, creating a sort of primitive, high-altitude, concrete poetry during the flight, id., at 211–214.

[98] Kennedy's hyper-criticism of the nerdishness of others is easily matched by his own self-flagellation. As a participant in the conference, he fears that he is engaged (along with others) in a "great collective narcissism in the name of empathy," id., at 208. His overarching self-criticism contrasts with the collective self-righteousness that is a product of the conference itself.

one of which is to condemn the phenomenon of human rights conferencing as a sham, further undercuts the otherwise gratuitous flipness.[99] There is tragicomedy here. Held up by a TV journalist and having no idea what the US position was on East Timor, the author "flashed rather unhelpfully on nuclear ships and New Zealand."[100] There is no question that Timor is belittled here as just another crisis. On the other hand it is the international lawyer's fate to be somewhat dilettantish, knowing a small amount about many parts of the globe and being expected to comment intelligently on them all. The speaker's shallowness becomes a reflection of the discipline's superficiality.

In short, the personal quest device allows the writer to evoke a mood of disillusionment about international law which repeats a prominent substantive theme of the work. The personal narrative style and the emphasis on the everyday behavior of people brings the discipline to life stressing the human agency involved in its creation. The ironic, sometimes aggrandizing and shocking tone of the work highlights the melancholic conclusion of the personal voyage, and the objective nature of the law-making process is further undermined. Ultimately the continual representation of law as riven by two opposing forces of idealism and realism, heightens the dramatic possibilities of the search for a resuscitated international law.[101]

4.3. *Language*

A final aspect of Newstream methodology is its interest in the use of language. As the last section demonstrates the Newstream style of language sometimes departs from the styles used in standard Mainstream analyses. The Newstream piece may be heavy with descriptive passages, or devices such as metaphors which are more often associated with literature than law. It may be personal and gossipy. It may contain word plays and different tones shades ranging

[99] When Kennedy describes himself proposing an alternative resolution to the final conference resolution it is clear that what he is expressing represents real frustration with the ineffectiveness of international law. Instead of simply calling for action which the conference participants know will not be forthcoming, he calls on the meeting to express its sheer frustration with the hopelessness of international law's prospect of real change, id., at 210. Similarly when he refers to the Dili massacre, which occurred during the Conference, he notes how this real life incident of great magnitude barely cut in to the everyday of the conference. These are not the comments of a cynic, but of someone saddened by the disjuncture between the aims of law and its application.

[100] Id. at 199.

[101] The point of this argument, and its content, is mirrored again in the writing style. Kennedy relies on a perceived contrast between what international law should aspire to and what it had become to highlight the poignancy of the quest. In relation to the despondency of international lawyers during the Vietnam War, "either they needed a new theory of law which could account for its violation or a new theory of violation which could account for America's activity. Neither was forthcoming." Kennedy, *New Stream, supra* note 2 at 5.

from irony to pretension, from mockery to gravity. Moreover, the emphasis on language features as both a conceptual theme and a methodology. The linguistic focus reiterates the theme of the quest when it refers to the goal of the Newstream as one of "disentangle[ment]",[102] or of "translation",[103] or of trying to "describe the silences"[104]. It emphasizes the conceptual theme that law is constituted by language by the use of terms which imply structure and organization, such as "taxonomies"[105] and "map"[106] and "architectures".[107] And it sometimes translates into an open discussion of its own terminology[108] again emphasizing the self-conscious and subjective nature of the Newstream scholarship.

So in various respects Newstream work diverges from the Mainstream by introducing into international law a methodology which emphasizes doubles, is quite personal and sometimes messianic in nature, and focuses on language. The introduction of these techniques increases the transformative potential of the Newstream work by challenging the form as well as content of Mainstream analyses.

5. The Strategic Challenge

To this point the paper has identified a number of conceptual redefinitions and methods introduced by the Newstream to international law. Section 5 looks at one further defining feature of Newstream, namely its strategies. These are threefold: the incorporation of multiple perspectives into the law-making process and the contextualization of legal problems in their social, political and cultural background; the rewriting of doctrinal history; and the integration of political perspectives into legal analysis. Although not new in themselves, these strategies are applied innovatively, in a manner which reflects another difference in emphasis between Mainstream and Newstream

[102] Koskenniemi, *Apology to Utopia, supra* note 62 at xv.

[103] Anthony Carty, *The Decay of International Law* (1986).

[104] Hilary Charlesworth, Christine Chinkin & Shelley Wright, "Feminist Approaches to International Law", 85 *Am. J. Int'l. J.* 613, at 615 (1991).

[105] Anghie, *supra* note 17 at 6 051.

[106] Tennant, *supra* note 6 at 56.

[107] See, e.g., David Kennedy, "Turning to Market Democracy: A Tale of Two Architectures", 32 *Harv. Int'l. L. J.* 373 (Spring 1991).

[108] So, for example, part of Riles' critique is to write about the appropriateness of the term "perspective" to describe her methodology, or instead to use an aural metaphor such as "polyphony", Riles, *Disciplines and Cultures, supra* note 27 at 10 033. Her conclusion is irrelevant for my point, which is to show how self-consciously the writers' interest in law's language is present also in discussion of their own work. The use of words to describe law, reflects that interest in structure.

work. Mainstream work may utilize similar techniques, but its major aim is to facilitate the drafting of new instruments or affect changes in state practice, both of which seek to reform existing rules and practices. By contrast Newstream work is self-consciously concerned with affecting radical changes in international law, largely through the use of these three strategies, which shift the conventional emphasis from remoulding legal rules to one which attempts to reconceptualize their very bases. Although this latter goal is present only in nascent form in Newstream work, its trajectory is illustrated below.

5.1. *Incorporation of Multiple Perspectives and Contextualization*

As discussed earlier, Newstream work seeks to redefine the conceptual bases of international law. One strategy for achieving that goal is to incorporate into international legal analysis previously excluded perspectives, whether they be cultural, gender, race, social or political in nature. This technique, of the incorporation of multiple perspectives, is reminiscent of feminist and third world critiques, many of which advocate incorporation of perspectives beyond those usually included by Mainstream analyses[109] (are assumed to be focused on the views of Western industrialized states).

In Newstream, as with feminist and third world critiques, the function of such a strategy is inclusive. By incorporating perspectives beyond those which are ordinarily included in law-making processes, international law will gradually be cured of any inherent biases favoring a Western or an implicitly male viewpoint. So, Newstream work argues, for example, that the culture of international law could be redefined to ameliorate its biases if it were to contain within it a "multilayering" of different perspectives.[110] Comparative law, too, could be transformed by focusing on previously marginalized peoples, groups, and cultural data.[111] Moreover the incorporation of multiple perspectives functions not simply as a call for a more pluralistic international law which

[109] For a feminist version see e.g., Charlesworth, Chinkin and Wright, *supra* note 104; for a third world critique, see e.g., Mohammed Bedjaoui, *Towards a New International Economic Order* (1979).

[110] So, for example, one of Riles' objectives is to show that "culture" as currently relied upon by international law is an "untenable category of representation", Riles, *Aspiration and Control, supra* note 16 at 21, which omits the perspectives of the non-Western, non-European viewpoint. She proposes therefore that international law adopt an entirely new method, which she calls a "multilayering" of perspectives, id., at 36. In this new strategy no single perspective would dominate, in the way European view of culture does in mainstream international law.

[111] Frankenberg also advocates a form of multi-perspectivalism, even though his basic premises are quite different from Riles', Frankenberg, *supra* note 8. He is concerned with how comparative law has conducted comparisons between cultures. He derides comparative law as being a form of "tourism," id., at 412., in which the travelers/lawyers have to date been unable to distance themselves from their own assumptions about their own legal cultures; everything

would simply enlarge the field of players, [112] but as a strategy of destablizing many of the underlying premises of the field,[113] or facilitating a rethinking of the boundaries of international legal debate.[114]

But despite the intuitive appeal of the argument (and the intellectual honesty of some proponents who apply the critique to their own work[115]), the main weakness of the strategy is that incorporation remains largely speculative in nature because few concrete doctrinal or theoretical examples have, as yet, been produced by the Newstream.[116] Presumably however the consequences of such a strategy would be similar to those found in the field of political science. There, an incorporation approach suggests that the strategy will not be easily realized. A cultural practice cannot be automatically defined as

they see is referred back to their own world view or else they delude themselves in believing they can drop their cultural baggage: "[u]niversalism and relativism tend to reproduce the dichotomy between the self and other," id., at 415. In Frankenberg's view, the answer is for comparative law to adopt a new method which would enable it to move from the "ethnocentris-m" of the current approach to the "self-criticism," id., at 455., of his preferred approach. This strategy would involve adopting a "greater sensitivity to the relationship between the self and the other; recognizing that they are participant observers,", id., at 441, maintaining a skeptical attitude toward allegedly authentic interpretations and universal categories; and "focus[sing . . .] on the marginal stuff that is normally skipped for lack of relevance," id., at 443. Like Riles, Frankenberg expresses a similar optimism about the reconstructive possibilities of adopting a new strategy. However, in other important respects the analyses are quite different. First, Frankenberg claims that comparative lawyers participate in making their own culture, but are still observers in others, id., at 443. Riles implicitly rejects the idea. Her work on European colonialism emphasizes that both the categories of European and non-European culture were created according to European assumptions. Second, despite Frankenberg's skepticism about culture, there are hints in the article of a belief that with the adoption of a new strategy, comparativists will be able to ultimately discover what is authentic about cultures. So, for example, Frankenberg claims it is possible to "transcend perspective," id., at 442, as long as we recognize our participation. To Riles the idea of transcendence would be an impossibility. Ultimately Frankenberg still believes in an authentic culture, whereas Riles does not.

112 Following Marilyn Strathern, id., at 28., Riles argues that this is not a matter of merely introducing more diversity into the field. Diversity still implies, contrary to her belief, that a cohesive whole could be produced whereas Riles rejects the reformist assumptions in ideas of cohesion.

113 Riles portrays international law like a prism, in which the facets of the prism reflect upon each other and create a new international law based on a new series of angles or refractions of law, id., at 31.

114 Frankenberg is optimistic that if this new strategy was adopted comparative lawyers would therefore be more tolerant of ambiguity and be able to embrace a "multiplicity of developmental possibilities and explanations", *supra* note 8, at 454. As a result, comparative law could "imagine roads not taken, to think and explore counterfactual trajectories," id.

115 See e.g., Riles who applies the strategy to her own analysis, *Aspiration and Control, supra* note 16 at 37, acknowledging that it may lead back to the same problems it seeks to escape – perspectivalism may be a synonym for just a different form of cultural definition. To this extent, it is a courageous tactic.

116 Cf. Frankenberg, *supra* note 8 at 448-453, who discusses the effect his approach would have on the issue of abortion.

universal or relative,[117] so that the tension between universalism and relativism cannot be resolved by a simple incorporation of interests.[118] Equally, it is impossible to identify any cultural practice as entirely authentic.[119] This challenge of the basic terms of cultural theory foregrounds further significant arguments for international law, for example, that legal categories such as territorial integrity, self-determination and sovereignty are uncertain,[120] and that we therefore may need to develop a new theory of culture which more closely approximates scientific "chaos theory",[121] than does the current paradigm. As these conclusions suggest, the incorporation of multiple perspectives by

[117] Applying a form of multi-perspectivalism to political analysis, Appadurai, *supra* note 15, finds that the simple equation of universalization of culture with Americanization no longer holds sway. An example taken from Pico Iyer's work in the Philippines has a particularly eerie quality. Iyer notes that Filipinos have embraced American 1950's pop culture in a manner that is both more faithful to a Western idea of the original than the original itself ever was, and which has no connection with the conditions in which they live. Again in Riles' terms multiperspectivalism has led to unpredictable cultural combinations. A peculiarly Filipino perspective of an American past has been grafted onto the Filipino present. Thus the "hegemony of Euro-chronology "is unstable because it has created a sense of "nostalgia without memory," id., at 3.

[118] No cultural idea can sensibly be placed in either category in a world in which "sameness and difference cannibalize each other," id., at 17, bringing to an end any confidence in finding a reasonable balance between the two.

[119] Appadurai argues that it is no longer possible to rely on an authentic version of culture. In the face of the constant dislocation between the various "scapes" (see below at n. 121) of the global economy it is not possible for small groups, families, communities, to reproduce themselves. How does the Filipino mother or father working in Saudi Arabia and going home once every few years pass on the cultural meanings of being Filipino to their family? The process is likely to be either diluted by distance or strengthened by an artificial, but understandable resolve to hold on to what it means to be Filipino in the face of the fragmentation of the cultural group. "Trans-generational stability of knowledge... can no longer be assumed," id., at 17 Appadurai has shown how a multi-perspectival strategy demonstrates the instability of combining universality and relativity, and of culture itself.

[120] In the case of territory, for example, the cannibalization of sameness and difference, id., and the instability of cultural inheritance are exacerbated by "deterritorialization", id., at 11. Mass migration, caused by war and economic dislocation, as well as use of guest-workers, separates peoples from territories. Nations and states have become "one another's projects", id., at 13. So states seek to expound their sense of nationhood, even where it is fractured by gender, class or ethnic divides, national movements search for a State, id. The effect of deterritorialization is worsened by the media industry when canny entrepreneurs cash in on nationalistic desire to create new and sometimes fictional homelands, id., at 12. Thus the mythological homeland of Khalistan, id., at 13, has become implicated in the sometimes bloody and very real struggle of Sikhs to create a homeland. The pernicious effects of cultural, media, and territorial displacement are illustrated.

[121] Appadurai argues for a new "chaos theory" to explain what has happened to the once apparently stable idea of culture, Appadurai, *supra* note 102. Cultural forms are "fundamentally fractal", and that they "possess[...] no Euclidean boundaries, structures, or regularities", id., at 20. This is because, although in the past cultural intervention occurred only through warfare or religion, id., at 1, in the present it is mediated through five "scapes" of ethnicity, media, technology, finance and ideology, id., at 7. The result is that culture is increasingly subject to both homogenization and heterogenization, id., at 5. In Riles' terms then, the new perspectives

Newstream writers, although fraught, may ultimately lead to a very different international law from one in which law reform is the major strategy for change.[122]

Closely associated with the incorporation technique is the strategy of contextualizing legal problems in their particular social, political or cultural background[123] with a view to addressing the exclusion of non-Mainstream interests from international law. This is also derivative of earlier movements. Moreover in its current form it suffers from a similar deficiency, namely a lack of guidance or detail as to how it would be applied. To be effective as a strategy, the call for context ought to include a discussion of, for example, what constitutes an appropriate context, who are the legitimate decision makers and how they should be identified, otherwise it remains subject to the criticism that analyzing problems in "context" may simply introduce anoth-

are being incorporated from a variety of angles, public and private, Western and non-Western, with each incorporation and re-incorporation resulting in new "angles" and perspectives upon the existing system. So for example globalization has led to the much touted McDonaldization of culture. But even when these apparently universalized forms are transplanted into a new setting they are always modified by the indigenous culture. This has the effect of creating a global system "filled with ironies and resistances," a global "hyper-real", id., at 3. In order to better understand this potent admixture, Appadurai proposes the creation of a new theory of global cultural processes which combines both a "fractal" metaphor for shape of cultures and a "polythetic account of their overlaps and resemblances", id., at 20.

[122] For a fascinating discussion of a similar debate within the discipline of anthropology see Clifford Geertz, The Culture War, New York Review of Books, November 30 1995, 4:

> Anthropology is a conflicted discipline, perpetually in search of ways to escape its condition, perpetually failing to find them. Committed, since its beginnings, to a global view of human life - social, cultural, biological, and historical at once - it keeps falling into its parts, complaining about the fact, and trying desperately, and unsuccessfully, to project some sort of new unity to replace the unity it imagines itself once to have had, but now, through the faithlessness of present practitioners, to have mindlessly cast away.

[123] See e.g, Rosemary Coombe, *supra* note 7, who is concerned with the way the intellectual property system excludes indigenous peoples' understanding of concepts of ownership and property. She argues that "supposedly...universal principles" such as authorship operate in practice to exclude native claims and lead to "injustice", id., at 267. Both intellectual property law and cultural property law rely on a system of European art and culture. Native art either falls into the category of timelessness, and thus is considered an "authentic artifact;" or it is elevated into a "masterpiece," id., 257. Art labeled authentic is protected by the newer legal regimes of cultural protection which are based on an idea of "cultural nationalism." In such cases the group is conceived of having ownership in the property which coincides with its identity as a "collective individual," id., 261. Art considered to be a masterpiece is protected by traditional copyright law. But both protections, Coombe asserts, bear traces of a form of "possessive individualism" which does not take account of the way in which indigenous peoples actually construe their association with the works of art. The only way out of this dilemma is to "listen [. . .] to native claims "in context," id., 266.

er form of subjectivity into legal analysis.[124] The danger is that "context" functions for the Newstream as "sovereignty" does for the Mainstream. One empty and amorphous concept is substituted for another.

5.2. *Rewriting Doctrinal History*

Another maneuver is to excavate the past in order to facilitate new interpretations of doctrine for the present, a strategy also reminiscent of the third world critiques of the 1960s.[125] Of the strategies discussed so far, this is the most successful in the sense of demonstrating the transformative potential of Newstream work. Some examples include a reconfiguration of the doctrine of state sovereignty taking account of feminist concerns,[126] the rewriting of historical accounts of sovereignty and statehood to show how they might benefit the interests of indigenous peoples,[127] and a reinterpretation of a set of doctrines concerned with acquisition and personality to show that they reflect the history of colonialism.[128] Utilizing either earlier legal theories,[129]

[124] See e.g., Coombe who does not convincingly avoid the charge that indigenous peoples' interests cannot be objectively identified. Instead she retreats at the critical juncture into a rhetorical statement: that "[i]t is . . . as politically dishonest to deny the objective identity of those making culturally nationalist claims as it is to assert an internationalism that privileges the nation-building imperialist enterprises of European countries", id., at 263, 264.

[125] See, e.g., Bedjaoui, *supra* note 109, who documented the ways in which international law had disadvantaged third world interests.

[126] Knop, *supra* note 77. Knop argues that a new approach to participation in lawmaking is emerging, which undermines the traditional view of sovereignty that law is made only by state consent. Although research is still to be done, it appears that the contributions of non-sovereign groups such as NGOs, or women, or environmental groups, at international fora are becoming significant factors in the making of custom.

[127] Lam, for example, shows how indigenous peoples can utilize pre-existing histories underlying international law doctrine: Lam *supra* note 26. Earlier I noted she does this by exploring the "double helix" of sovereignty and statehood. This enables her to reveal the "multiple inheritance" of the helix so that she can "insinuate" new concepts into the "rigidities" of the law of indigenous peoples, id., *passim.*

[128] Anghie, *supra* note 17.

[129] See Karen Knop who carefully and generously crafts an enormously diverse range of materials using and re-using earlier international legal theories: Knop, *supra* note 77. She begins the process of reconfiguration by drawing upon a variety of international law and feminist sources and using them in ways probably not intended by their authors. Drawing upon Thomas Franck's claim that a right of democratic governance is emerging, id. at 301, and Fernando Teson's view that only liberal governments are deserving of the term sovereign, id., at 302, she plots the increasing trend against absolute sovereignty. (See Thomas M. Franck, "The Emerging Right to Democratic Governance", 86 *Am. J. Int'l L.* 46 (1992), and Fernando R. Teson, "The Kantian Theory of International Law", 92 *Colum. L. Rev.* (1992)). To this ingredient Knop adds the lessons of recent practice in the Balkans, showing that recognition of statehood is becoming conditional upon respect for human rights. She also draws upon the insights of the New Haven school, id., in order to argue that actors other than states contribute to the making of law. (See Myres S. McDougal et al., *Human Rights and World Public Order*

historical inconsistencies,[130] doctrinal ambiguities,[131] or law-making in the form of cases, state practice, or draft conventions,[132] these Newstream works compel a different understanding of foundational international law concepts, such as the relationship between women, indigenous peoples, colonialism and sovereignty. What is particularly ingenious about the examples mentioned is the way they draw upon existing raw materials (without having to resort to introducing excluded perspectives or contexts) sometimes deploying those

(1980)). Finally to these sources, she adds feminist arguments about equality, participation, and the breakdown of sovereignty. Here she outlines three models: the equality model proposed by Catharine MacKinnon, id., at note 40, the difference formulation of Carol Gilligan id., at note 46; and the collective autonomy response of Denise Reaume id., at note 54. In relation to participation she refers to the work of Iris Young, id., at note 54, and Isabelle Gunning, id., at 312-315 (see also Isabelle Gunning, "Modernizing Customary International Law: The Challenge of Human Rights: The Challenge of Human Rights", 31 *Va. J. Int'l. L.* 211 (1991)). And for a feminist analysis of sovereignty, Knop draws upon the work of Jean Bethke Elsthain, id., at note 126. The arguments lead ultimately to a reconstruction of the notion of sovereignty.

[130] See, e.g., Lam, *supra* note 26, identifies four "conceptual rigidities" which have traditionally militated against the rights of indigenous peoples. The first is the reliance in Westphalian theory of the nation state as the perfected form of political organization, id., at 616. This, despite evidence to the contrary in countries such as Switzerland where a federated set of cantons allowed a degree of flexibility and autonomy to the different constituent groups. Second, she argues that the idea of nationhood itself was a invention. For example, at the time of the French Revolution in 1789, it is likely that there was little sense of French nationality, id., at 613. Lam quotes figures showing that eighty years after the Revolution French language was still not spoken in approximately one-fifth of the communes. Third, there is the mechanism by which indigenous peoples were excluded from participating independently in international affairs, namely the League of Nations practice of wardship, (invented as a foil to modernist understandings of cultural identity), id., at 615. Fourth, she labels as a "conceit" the idea that some subjugation, in the form of "saltwater" domination was worse than others, id., at 616. These are the rigidities she seeks to overcome.

[131] Anghie, *supra* note 17.

[132] Lam, supra note 26, looks for any signs in the recent history which favor indigenous peoples' independent participation in international law and finds the following. The *Western Sahara Case* and the *South West Africa Cases*, facilitated recognition of a right of self-determination, id., at 618. The break-up of the former Soviet Union and former Yugoslavia were treated with "anxiety not prohibition," id., partly as a result of sympathy for national self-expression arising from the Westphalian model. Although neither instances relate directly to indigenous peoples, Lam views these developments as historical foundations for them to exploit. Moreover in 1991 the Draft Declaration on Indigenous Peoples, formulated by an expert Working Group, for the first time, included a qualified right of indigenous self-determination, id., at 620. The Working Group also provides indigenous peoples with a forum to speak and they participate in the work of a number of UN agencies. Moreover this "interface occurs across several permeable surfaces," id., Working Group members operate on behalf of the UN and yet are also professional and independent experts. They deal with NGOs and indigenous peoples groups in a manner which has "evolved through mutual criticism, accommodation and perhaps also appreciation," id. Lam has demonstrated the continuity between the history which seemed to deny indigenous people's rights and the history of acceptance. Pre-existing histories carried with them the subversion of their own rigidities.

sources in a manner probably not intended by their authors.[133] This further demonstrates the Newstream claim above that if international law is manufactured, (in the sense of being constructed rather than fraudulent) from histories made by us, it can also "be remade by us".[134]

5.3. *Integrating Politics into International Law*

Finally the Newstream advocate an international law in which political considerations are integrated in an explicit manner, another project reminiscent of realism. The political dimension is also acknowledged by mainstream scholars. The major difference is, however, that while the Mainstream writers protest that "law is politics",[135] they rarely apply that insight to their discussion of particular doctrines. Compare, for example, David Kennedy's analysis of state responsibility,[136] with that of Louis Henkin et al.[137] Kennedy looks at the political factors motivating what he terms the shift from substance to process, whereas Henkin et al focus upon the doctrine as a set of positive legal rules.

Newstream scholars argue that international law should not and cannot be separated from politics.[138] If politics were explicitly acknowledged,[139] then doctrinal biases would be disclosed. For example a purportedly neutral legal conclusion evaluating an assertion of jurisdiction over foreign nationals might be revealed to mask political considerations of national interest. [140]

[133] See, e.g., Knop *supra* note 77, who relies on arguments made by Teson. Although Teson rejects the view that under-representation of women derogates from the states representativeness, Knop argues that Teson's view about sovereign legitimacy provides the "rhetorical scaffolding", id., at 302, to support a feminist re-reading of sovereign will in which the low rates of participation by women in law-making lead to questions about the legitimacy consent.

[134] Allot, *supra* note 26 at 16.

[135] Henkin et al., *supra* note 4 at 1.

[136] Kennedy, *infra* note 146.

[137] Henkin, *supra* note 4.

[138] Koskenniemi questions the separation of international law and social life: Koskenniemi, *Apology to Utopia*, *supra* note 62 at xiii–xvi. He argues that the only way beyond the dilemma of constantly moving between community and autonomy, between concreteness and normativity, is to abandon the idea of the objectivity of law and cease what he calls the "flight from politics", *Politics, supra* note 69 at 4–7.

[139] David Kennedy argues that international law should take more explicit account of political concerns. He says the "mantra" of the renewalists should be the "politics of private law", Kennedy, *New World Order, supra* note 43 at 374, or, in another piece that international economic law fails to answer "traditional questions about the politics of international law, David Kennedy, "The International Style in Postwar Law and Policy", 194 *Utah L. Rev.* 7 (1994) 101 [hereinafter *The International Style*].

[140] See e.g., Robert Malley, Jean Manas, Crystal Nix, "Note: Constructing the State Extraterritorially: Jurisdictional Discourse, The National Interest, and Transnational Norms", 103 *Harv. L. R.* 1273 (1990) for an analysis of the doctrine of reasonableness as it relates to questions

Or analysis of the development of a particular doctrine, such as acquisition, would show it to be hamstrung by political, rather than legal, concerns.[141]

The Newstream strategy of integrating politics into law claims to expose law's silence about politics, cast doubt upon its objectivity, and facilitates the identification of underlying biases within doctrine. And it demands that international lawyers identify the politics they pursue through international law. Once the political ramifications of doctrine are revealed, the retreat into proceduralism seems no longer possible.

In Section 5 three strategies for change arising out of new approaches scholarship have been identified. Multiplicity and contextualisation address law's exclusionary power, and rewriting doctrinal history and integrating political concerns upset its constructed and discriminatory categories. To this point the approach appears to have developed the tools for changing much that it criticizes. Why then does it sometimes fail to do so?

6. Recurring Problems and Conclusion

In this conclusion I will focus on some recurring problems with Newstream analysis. I will argue that the content of the critique can be marred by, inconclusiveness, reductiveness and equivocation, and that the style suffers from a sometimes disengaged or patronizing tone.

6.1. *Inconclusiveness, Reduction and Lack of Concretization*

Newstream critiques frequently seem to pull back from the brink of affecting real change in international dialogue. For example the consequences of alter-

of jurisdiction. They show that when the United States Supreme Court engages in a balancing process to assess the "reasonableness" of allowing another state to assert jurisdiction over an American national, the Court is actually concerned with how the assertion of jurisdiction will affect American national interests, id., at 1297. Thus the political question of national interest trumps a supposedly neutral legal question. They show that reasonableness doctrine masks the political consequences of power differentials between states.

[141] See e.g., Carty, *supra* note 103 at 43–60. Carty examines how political considerations have affected the development of a particular legal doctrine. He claims that despite its apparent formality, the law of acquisition is a highly politicized concept. He demonstrates this by examining how the whole edifice of the law of acquisition is based upon Roman notions of possession of land, and a capitalist conception of commodities exchange. He argues that the influence of these two political factors foreclosed the development of self-determination and permanent sovereignty over natural resources, both of which are doctrines concerned with method of use, not exchange, id., 51–60. For another discussion of the politicized nature of acquisition doctrine with particular application to Australian Aboriginal ownership of land, see also Gerry Simpson, "Mabo, International law, Terra Nullius and the Stories of Settlement: An Unresolved Jurisprudence", 19 *Melb. Uni. L. R.* (1993) 195.

native strategies of changing international law are never fully explored,[142] arguments about what is actually wrong with international law are inconclusive,[143] or fail to speculate about the conditions which might affect a change in the Mainstream perspective.[144] Moreover the Newstream calls for the integration of politics with law is not sufficiently problematised. The call is a commendable ambition but doubts remain. There is a tendency in some Newstream work for an apparently radical critique to conclude with a facile or reductive call for a move to politics, yet the political is as contested and enigmatic as the legal. While concepts such as sovereignty are being denigrated as too incoherent to underpin the legal system, a radically pluralistic politics seems an inauspicious place to find new normative consensus.

Other Newstream scholars are internally inconsistent calling, for example, for changes in Mainstream analysis while not acknowledging that the critique must apply to Newstream analysis as well[145] while others labor under a

[142] For example, there is something dissatisfying about being left with only the conclusion that the strategy of multi-perspectivalism will lead to a "discomforting" but "instructive void," Riles, *Discipline and Cultures, supra* note 27 at 740. It is this rather vague but vaguely engaging image which is at once the most exciting and frustrating aspect of the strategy proposed. Thus despite the intuitive appeal of the analysis, the strategy as a technique to actually change the operation and description of international law, remains largely unexplained. Riles provides no definite idea of what she means by putting new perspectives together and no concrete examples of doctrinal changes which might result. While complete specificity is not required, some hypotheses about how the strategy would apply ought to have been explored. In the absence of this the consequences of this maneuver remain somewhat speculative. What would be produced by a new melange of perspectives relating to each other in new combinations and permutations? By admitting that she does not know what exactly would be produced or how these new perspectives would relate to each other, or indeed even whether they would not replicate an idea of culture, Riles withdraws from prescribing an effective application of the strategy. This last step is crucial if the incorporation of multiple perspectives strategy is to have any effect on conventional perceptions of the international. In contrast, Appadurai, *supra* note 15, is able to demonstrate not only that cultural meanings are unstable and thus must be reinterpreted with the incorporation of new perspectives, but that this process will itself lead to new instabilities. New cultural classifications will feed off each other complicating the possibility of simply improving the current system by incorporating new perspectives. American culture suffers from this defect as much as any other, and the resulting chaos is what defines culture in the late twentieth century.

[143] See e.g., Kennedy, who analyses the common intellectual history of new approaches with earlier schools but ends only with an abrupt and sketchy call for the renewalists to differentiate their critique by examining redistributive consequences and private law, Kennedy, *New World Order, supra* note 43 at 374–375. Similarly, when discussing international economic law, it is not until close to the end of the article that he explicitly states what he believes is wrong with a regime infused with the spirit of liberal trade policy, namely, that it might fail to answer political questions about how the world trading system disadvantages developing countries, or structures the debt crisis, Kennedy, *The International Style, supra* note 140 at 101, 102.

[144] See the discussion of culture and change accompanying notes 125–127.

[145] See e.g., Frankenburg, *supra* note 8, who fails to recognize the contradiction in criticizing the Mainstream for not taking account of perspective and then entreating us to trying overcome perspective.

suffocating equivocation or unwillingness to evaluate specific legal claims.[146] The reader's expectations are constantly thwarted by these retreats as the critiques seem to peter out just as they are beginning to bite and the potentially transformative moment is lost, leaving impressive descriptive analyses lacking in effect.[147]

6.2. *Equivocation, and Condescension*

Newstream work is also dogged by recurring stylistic problems which inhibit its more widespread application. The equivocatory tone of some critics leads to a voice which seems disengaged and at odds with the general call for a more involved politics.[148] There is a tendency to patronize[149] other actors making assumptions about what will be the outcome of adopting a particular strategy. A superior condescending tone is used [150] in characterizing other interna-

[146] Kennedy, e.g., argues that state responsibility process doctrine, avoids and supplants substantive outcomes but withdraws from making a normative judgments, *Legal Structures*, *supra* note 79. So the International Court's reliance on standing in the *South West Africa* Cases, to preclude considering the merits of apartheid as a breach of self-determination, is an example of the oscillation within international law between substance and process. But at the conclusion of his argument, the oscillation is described as one of the "strengths": Kennedy, id., at 191, of the discipline, leaving the reader to ponder whether a strength which had appeared to lead to injustice is a good or a bad strength. Even if Kennedy is arguing that indeterminacy opens possibilities for argument, the illustrations used seem to demonstrate that oscillation is not a positive outcome.

[147] Not all Newstream writers suffers from this deficiency. Some demonstrate why, as Riles predicts, the void might be instructive, Riles, *supra* note 16 at 740. So, for example, when Abu-Odeh locates the intersection between Islamic feminism and Western feminisms' shared concerns about equality, regardless of conflicting attitudes to the veil, she signals an enrichment of Western feminism if it better understood the complex conception of veiled sexuality in Islamic culture, Abu-Odeh, *supra* note 22 at 66. When a Toronto conference summary introduces the voices of women who have traditionally not been heard in Western feminist human rights, we begin to see what benefits multi-perspectivalism might bring, Rebecca Cook, "Women's International Human Rights: The Way Forward", 15 *Human Rights Quarterly* 230 (1993) 231–261.

[148] As one proponent comments, the method often "fails to provide answers" and that "skepticism about the material determinacy of international law seems to prevent new approaches lawyers from making normative propositions," Koskenniemi comment in Kennedy & Tennant, *supra* note 2 at 427.

[149] See, e.g., Tennant's argument, *supra* note 6, that even if participation is the goal which indigenous peoples desire, the writer assumes that it will lead to co-option. Surely if self-determination and participation have any meaning it is that the groups asserting their rights have the right to determine when and how they will utilize them. Lam is also mindful of the dangers of participation, but claims that it has led to concrete substantial goals such as realization of limited forms of self-determination: Lam *supra* note 26 at 617–618. She also notes that participation can be an end in itself.

[150] For e.g., the personal quest device of Kennedy, *Autumn Weekends, supra* note 60 at 202, while effective in some respects, also carries with it certain risks of condescension. It exposes a tendency on the part of some writers to denigrate the contributions of other participants in the

tional legal actors, and some disparage Mainstream strategies for change as ineffective without sufficient explanation. For example, it is not clear that participation has only procedural consequences,[151] or that substance is always "strong" and procedure inevitably "weak". This latter propensity to adopt a substance/procedure dichotomy in the belief that the former is strong and the latter is weak, pre-empts the reader's capacity to assess the issue. Apart from the very difficult question of whether such a content/form distinction does exist, it is a somewhat reductive way of characterizing legal practices which tells us little about the actual nature and content of the practice. Sometimes it appears to be a kind of shorthand for good and bad, rather than a useful or revealing comment upon a practice. The dangers of condescension and reductionism then, are that they trivialize, oversimplify and obscure a serious and elaborate intellectual agenda for change. These problems and others iden-

international sphere. For example, at a plenary where a "fashionable Latin American Woman ... in rather high pumps" id., suggests a reformatting of a conference resolution, Kennedy comments that:

> We all knew we should clearly distinguish the perambulatory recitation of norms and facts from the operational engagement with the everyday. Numbering would do the trick, indentation would help, id.

Portraying the woman's concerns as mere cosmetic artistry he reduces their importance and trivializes her contribution. The mocking tone permeates the entire recollection. By the time the final conference session arrives Kennedy muses on "enjoy[ing] the hilarity of voting as a bloc on one after another absurd amendment or proposal", id., at 209. The flippant tone of the description conveys a condescending attitude by the writer to the other participants. Personal and probably hurtful details are included. The constitution-drafting group is described as a "distinctly dull crew of Pedro's more earnest Portuguese acquaintances," id., at 199, and "the last refuge of the lawyer's lawyer, the nerd's nerd," id., at 201. The bitchy throwaway lines heighten the sense that unnecessary details are included at others' expense. The reader hovers endlessly between laughter and alienation.

[151] Tennant, *supra* note 6 at 50–55, is skeptical, or at least cautious, of the gains that would attend increased indigenous participation in lawmaking claiming that this participation valorizes process over the achievement of a substantial goal. He argues that the misrepresentation of indigenous peoples by international law (discussed above), led indigenous peoples to resist these images. That resistance has led them to argue for increased rights of participation in international law making processes. Tennant argues that although participation seems to be a worthwhile goal, it carries with it the danger that indigenous peoples will be co-opted by becoming part of the institutional process. "The danger lies in the shift from *substantive* political goals to the *procedural* goal of increased participation," id., at 50. The weaknesses in his argument are characteristic of new approaches work. First, it is not clear why increased participation, even characterized as a procedural rather than substantive goal, is not a desirable end in itself. In respect of other groups excluded from international law-making, the claim is often made that their increased participation will provide an opportunity to create norms which incorporate the concerns of those groups: Gunning, *supra* note 129. Second, there is some room for argument as to whether participation is simply procedural, and whether that label condemns it in any case.

tified throughout the discussion above have the ultimate effect of diminishing the influence of the new scholarship on the discipline generally.

This paper has sought to make explicit a debate within international law between two schools of thought labeled Mainstream and Newstream. It has argued that the Newstream critique has emerged as a significant body of criticism, with common themes, methods, and strategies aimed at redefining what it perceives as Mainstream forms of analysis. In disclosing some of the deficiencies and gaps of international law, Newstream work, is developing into a well crafted body of scholarship. It has dissected the way in which law constructs its own histories, is inherently indeterminate, masks distributive disadvantage, is decontextualised, and excludes a range of perspectives. As a first stage of any analysis, the critique has demonstrated its potential to renew and invigorate international legal doctrine. It is provocative and sometimes daring work.

Accurate and incisive dissection and description is critical to any project of transformation and if the point was to show that traditional legal analyses were demonstrably partial, exclusive and biased then this has been achieved. A critical descriptive and expositive function has been performed. But the Newstream works seem to aim to do more. They advocate change, contextualization, multiplicity, and politics. And it is this transformative potential of the critique that remains unrealized. In fact reading new approaches work can be a baffling experience, with frustrating results. The analyses lack concretization, and tend toward reductionism and condescension with the consequence that what is potentially transformative risks becoming rather unappealing.[152] Change is merely flagged as something which would eventuate if these techniques were adopted within the Mainstream. To paraphrase one of the its repeated themes, the critique itself remains suspended in an interminable present between the description of what has come before and the promise of what its implementation will bring.[153] So although Newstream work highlights previously untapped but important anxiety over what is culture; displays a fascination with the relationship between history and sovereignty; and a deep interest in the narrative structure of law; applies new methods and reinvigorates old strategies, creating opportunities for reading old material in new ways, to date it has led to an utterly altered vision of what international law *is* but not what international law *could be*.

[152] There is an almost poignant lack of communication between the Newstream and traditional international law. A mixture of antipathy and condescension exists between the two groups resulting in a dialogue of the deaf.

[153] David Kennedy constantly refers to an oscillation, within traditional analyses, between substance and process, Kennedy, *New Stream, supra* note 2 at 17.

Ultimately though the measure of its success may be its commitment towards enunciating another kind of international law, a commitment which is symbolized in the quest device which characterizes most of the major works.[154] Like all quests, it is characterized by a sense of sadness for what current international law has lost. Moreover what differentiates it from earlier commentators' similar journeys,[155] is the central, self-appointed, almost messianic role of the new international lawyers. Exploiting the drama of the search, the Newstream international lawyers place themselves at the center of the quest, exhibiting an almost heroic urge to save international law, and themselves, from the moral bankruptcy of indeterminate material outcomes.[156] This is the goal. But although the search and its quixotic conclusion have echoes in the modern period, the quest is all the more poignant for the post-modern realization that there can be no return either to the weak realism of the earlier phase, or to an even earlier faith in natural order. It is this melancholic view of the traditional discipline which impels the journey toward new forms of scholarship.

[154] For example, Allot is on a journey through "consciousness": Allot *supra* note 37 at 109; Koskenniemi tracks the trail of the disappointed jurists who "put their faith variably on logic and texts, history and power . . . ": but who lost their footholds; Koskenniemi, *Politics, supra* note 69 at 31, Kennedy deplores the "tragic voice of post-war public law liberalism": Kennedy, *New Stream, supra* note 2 at 2; and Carty is escaping international law's "decay", Carty, *supra* note 103.

[155] McDougal, *supra* note 67 at 156–157.

[156] Koskenniemi, *Apology to Utopia, supra* note 62, *passim.*

Part II
Is International Law, Law?

[4]

THE SCIENCE OF INTERNATIONAL LAW: ITS TASK AND METHOD

L. Oppenheim

INTRODUCTION

The first volume of this American Journal of International Law has shown *urbi et orbi* that America possesses a number of prominent international jurists who are of equal rank to those of Europe as regards learning, idealism, constructive power, and literary skill. Undoubtedly, this Journal has at once with its appearance taken up the position of a leading magazine of the science of international law. By inviting only American jurists to contribute to the first volume of this Journal the learned editor has shown to the world that America is able to foster the science of international law without being dependent upon the assistance of foreign contributors. It is my firm conviction, based upon the study of American works, that, just as the body of rules which is called "international law" shows everywhere the traces of American influence, so the science of international law will likewise soon receive new stimuli from America. I have therefore thought it fitting, although I am not an American, to draw the task and the method of this our science into discussion in this Journal. In setting to work I desire it, however, to be understood that in endeavoring to deal with this difficult and controverted subject nothing is remoter from my intention than to set up as a high priest of our science, to lay down the law of its method, and to exhaust this wide and tempting subject. I rather hope that others will likewise take up the subject and treat it in the pages of this Journal. I shall, of course, be outspoken, shall mark my standpoint, and shall try to offer clear-cut views; yet I am well aware that my standpoint and my views will have to undergo the fire of criticism: *dixi et salvavi animam meam!*

But the following pages were not exclusively written for the purpose of drawing the matter into further discussion. They are likewise intended to serve as a guide to those younger students who are desirous of working up some problem of international law. My experience with a number of such students is that they are at first frequently quite helpless for want of method. They mostly plunge into their work without a proper knowledge of the task of our science, without knowing how to make use of the assertions of authorities, and without the proper views for the valuation and appreciation of the material at hand.

I. THE SCIENCE OF INTERNATIONAL LAW NOT AN END IN ITSELF

The science of international law is just as little as any other science an end in itself; it is merely a means to certain ends outside itself. And these ends are the same as those for which international law has grown up and is still growing — primarily, peace among the nations and the governance of their intercourse by what makes for order and is right and just; secondarily, the peaceable settlement of international disputes; lastly, the establishment of legal rules for the conduct of war and for the relations between belligerents and neutrals.

Just as international law, so its science has to keep these ends always in view, and the task of the science stands in the service of these ends. But now-a-days it is impossible to say that there is only one single task to be fulfilled. There are rather a number of tasks to which our science must devote itself, if it intends to work successfully for those ends which I have defined, and these tasks are the following seven: Exposition of the existing rules of law, historical research, criticism of the existing law, preparation of codification, distinction between the old customary and the new conventional law. fostering of arbitration, and popularization of international law. I shall discuss these tasks *seriatim,* although most of them are to a certain extent connected with one another.

II. EXPOSITION OF THE EXISTING RULES OF LAW

Now, the first and chief task is the exposition of the existing recognized rules of international law. Whatever we think of the value of a recognized rule — whether we approve or condemn it, whether we want to retain, abolish, or replace it — we must first of all know whether it is really a recognized rule of law at all, and what are its commands. This task is often difficult to fulfill. The rules of the present international law are to a great extent not written rules, but based on custom. Apart from the International Prize Court agreed upon by the Second Hague Peace Conference but not yet established, there are no international courts in existence which can define these customary rules and apply them authoritatively to cases which themselves become precedents binding upon inferior courts.[1] The writers on international law, and in especial the authors of treatises, have in a sense to take the place of the judges and have to pronounce whether there is an established custom or not, whether there is a usage only in contradistinction to a custom, whether a recognized usage has now ripened into a custom, and the like. And with regard to the written rules — namely, such rules of international law as are the outcome of universal or general law-making treaties — the writers have again to take the place of the judges and have to ascertain the precise meaning of those rules with the help of interpretation. It is for this reason that text-books of international law have so much more importance for the application of the law than text-books of other branches of the law. Whereas the latter are only a means of preliminarily ascertaining the law, it being the judge who ultimately will lay it down, the former are as yet and for some time to come the only means of ultimately ascertaining what the law is. That at present many a rule is so controverted, and that the present treatises are not up to the ideal mark and frequently offer confusion instead of illumination, I do not deny. But that is just the reason why an inquiry into the task and the method of the science of international law is necessary.

III. HISTORICAL RESEARCH

However this may be, the exposition of the existing recognized rules of international law is often to a certain extent impossible

[1] Unless it be created by the Central American Peace Conference, 1907. — EDITOR.

without a knowledge of the history of the rules concerned. There is therefore an historical task for our science. Yet in spite of the vast importance of this task it has as yet hardly been undertaken; the history of international law is certainly the most neglected province of it. Apart from a few points which are dealt with in monographs, the history of international law is virgin land which awaits its cultivators. Whatever may be the merits of the histories and the historical sketches which we possess, they are in the main mere compilations. The master-historian of international law has still to come. What is particularly wanted is what the Germans call a "*Dogmengeschichte.*" We require to know of each rule of international law how it originated and developed, who first established it, and how it gradually became recognized in practice. Bearing in mind that the growth and development of international law since the seventeenth century rallied around Grotius' immortal work *De jure belli ac pacis,* the starting point of the investigation ought, of course, to be this "father" of international law. The questions to be answered are: Does Grotius know of the rule concerned? How does he justify it? Was it known before Grotius? If it was neither known before Grotius nor by Grotius himself, who was it who first formulated and established it? Has it always retained the scope which it possessed in the hands of its first professor, or had it been altered, extended, restricted? What are the causes of such alteration, extension, or restriction, if any? What are the chief events which show that it really has been authoritatively applied in practice? Has its authority always remained unshaken, or has its authority ever been assailed in theory or in practice or in both? Is it a rule which Grotius, or whoever first professed it, has abstracted from the actual practice of the states, or is it a rule which was at first asserted as the outcome of the law of nature and afterwards adopted by the practice of the states on account of its intrinsic merits for the adequate conduct of international affairs? Has it at once when it was professed become universally recognized, or had it to fight its way and thus only become recognized slowly and gradually? Was it always considered a rule of law, or does it originate from comity and has only become law lately? Is it a rule first asserted by bookwriters, or has it made its appearance during the exchange of diplomatic notes connected with the occurrence of certain events?

Of course, such a history of dogmatics can merely supply the building material which the expected master-builder will use for the purpose of a history of international law. For such history is only a branch of the history of Western civilization. All important events in the development of the state system of Europe from the last part of the Middle Ages downward to the French Revolution have had their bearing upon the development, the shaping, and the ultimate victory of international law over international anarchy, and so have all important events in the development of the state system of Europe and America since the French Revolution. And the master-historian, to whose appearance we look forward, will in especial have to bring to light the part certain states have played in the victorious development of certain rules and what were the economic, political, humanitarian, religious, and other interests which have helped to establish the present rules of international law. Thereby the factors will be laid bare which have driven the different states into the community called the "family of nations" that will in time comprise the whole of humanity. Just as out of tribal communities which were in no way connected with each other arose the state, so the family of nations arose out of the different states which were in no way connected with each other. But whereas the state is a settled institution, firmly established, and completely organized, the family of nations is still in the beginning of its development. A settled institution and firmly established it certainly is, but it entirely lacks at present any organization whatever. Such organization is, however, gradually growing into existence before our eyes. The International Prize Court created by the Second Hague Peace Conference is the first small trace of a future organization. The next step forward will be that The Hague peace conferences will meet automatically within certain periods of time, without being summoned by one of the powers. A second step forward will be the agreement on the part of the powers upon fixed rules of procedure for the future Hague peace conferences. As soon as these two steps forward are really made, the nucleus of an organization of the family of nations will be in existence, and out of this nucleus will in time grow a more and more powerful organization. What the ultimate characteristic features of this organization will be is at present impossible to foresee.

IV. CRITICISM OF THE EXISTING LAW

Next to the exposition and the history of international law comes the criticism of its rules and of its present scope. This task of the science of international law is very important and must not be neglected, if we want international law to develop progressively and to bring more and more international matters under its sway. The questions which must be answered are: Is a certain rule really just and adequate, or is it antiquated, so that it ought to be restricted, abolished, or replaced? Or is it so valuable that it ought to be extended? But if ever so much importance is attributed to the criticism of the present condition of international law, it must never be forgotten that this law is like everything else conditioned by the *milieu* of the age. It is easier to criticise than to make proposals which shall take the place of the rule which is objected to, and it is again easier to propose a new rule than to establish it in the practice of the states. If anything is dependent upon gradual historical development, it is that delicate body of rules which is called international law. The dreamer and the schemer build their castles in the air without regard to the real facts of life. The armchair politician and the moralist lay down the law without regard to the possibilities of the age. The preacher and the philosopher defend postulates which are beyond realization in practice. But the international jurist must not walk in the clouds; he must remain on the ground of what is realizable and tangible. It is better for international law to remain stationary than to fall in the hands of the impetuous and hot-headed reformer. He who knows how difficult it is to unite all the members of the family of nations for the purpose of the shortest step forward will not lend his ear and his arm to chimerical proposals.

However this may be, the task of criticism is somewhat connected with another task of the science of international law, namely, that of preparing codification. For if we find fault with an existing rule of international law, it is now-a-days only by total or partial codification that matters can be improved.

V. PREPARATION OF CODIFICATION

Now, the task of preparing codification is on its own part intimately connected with the already discussed three tasks of the science of international law, and it may be said that the task of preparing codification is nothing else but the embodiment of these three previously mentioned tasks. For there is no better way of preparing a codification of international law than, first, an accurate exposition of and a minute research into the existing rules; secondly, the bringing into view of their historical growth and development; and, thirdly, their reasonable criticism. A generation which has fulfilled these three tasks will easily be able to prepare the draft of a code of international law to be agreed upon and to be adopted by the nations in council at an international conference.

But in viewing this task of preparing codification it is necessary to emphasize that codification of international law does not necessarily involve a reconstruction of the present international order and a recasting of the whole system of international law as it at present stands. Naturally, a codification would in many points mean, not only addition to the at present recognized rules, but also repeal, alteration, and reconstruction of some of these rules. But however this may be, I do not believe that a codification ought to be or can be undertaken which would revolutionize the present international order and put the whole system of international law on a new basis. If I speak of preparation of codification as a task of our science, I have in view a codification of the body of the existing rules of international law on the basis of the at present existing international order, with such modifications and additions as are necessitated by the conditions of the age and the very fact of codification being taken in hand. If the at present recognized international law is once codified, nothing prevents reformers from making proposals which can be realized by a successive codification.

But does international law really require to be codified? Would it not be better to leave it for all the future in its uncodified condition as customary law? I do not propose to discusse here the merits of this important question; I have done it elsewhere, and it suffices to say that at least partial codification will at some future time become an absolute necessity. The practice and the views of the different states differ so much with regard to many important matters that it is only codification which can create agreement and unanimity, and thereby universally recognized rules of law. I have no doubt that the end of this the twentieth century will see at least a partial codification of international law.

Such codification will, however, never be possible unless the members of the family of nations are ready to compromise. Wherever the practice and the views of the different states are contrary to one another, no progress can be made as long as each state concerned expects the other to come round to its own views and to adopt its own practice. In some cases these different practices and views are based on vital interests of the states concerned. But in other cases no such interests are at stake, and it is therefore quite possible to come to a speedy agreement. Where vital interests are really involved no progress is possible as long as these interests are facing each other. But history teaches that interests which are vital to-day gradually lose their importance, and the time will come when a compromise is feasible and can be embodied in codification.

VI. DISTINCTION BETWEEN THE OLD CUSTOMARY AND THE NEW CONVENTIONAL LAW

This codification has in a sense already begun and is to a certain extent already a fact. The declarations of Paris and St. Petersburg; the two Geneva conventions; the Hague conventions concerning the rules of land warfare, the adaptation of the Geneva Convention to warfare on sea, and the pacific settlement of international disputes; the conventions produced by the Second Hague Peace Conference — all these law-making treaties represent in themselves codification of parts of international law. But these conventions, although they are no doubt law making, represent codification in a sense only, and not really. For either they do not create universal international law—thus, the Declaration of Paris is not signed by all the members of the family of nations — or, although they are signed by practically all the members of the family of nations, and may, therefore, be said to create universal international law, they are notifiable, and each party can cease to be a party by giving notice; thus, even the new Geneva Convention of 1906 is notifiable, although that of 1864 is not. Now I personally doubt not that these conventions will never disappear without their place being taken by others of the same kind. But the fact that they contain a clause which enables their notification must not be lost sight of by the science of international law. The reason why they contain such a clause is, I believe, that the powers did not want to bind themselves forever and for all circumstances and conditions. They want first to feel their way and see how these conventions will work in practice before they bind themselves for all the future. Now, this condition of affairs involves a very important task for the science of international law. As there is no absolute certainty that these conventions will not one day come to an end by being notified, or that one or more of the parties will not cease to be bound by them by giving notice, the science of international law must not lose sight of the customary international law, if any, at the back of these conventions, and also of such customary rules as have been abolished and abrogated by the conventions concerned. For in the case of one or more or all parties giving notice, those old customary rules would revive, and the parties concerned would then in the same way be bound by these rules as they were before they signed the conventions. For instance, if a party to the Hague convention concerning the rules of warfare on land gave notice, it would indeed not be bound in the future by such rules of the convention as were newly created by the latter, but the customary rules at the back of the convention would be binding upon such party, such as the rules that poisoned arms may not be employed, that armistices must faithfully be carried out, that prisoners of war must not be cruelly treated, and the like. These formerly customary rules have therefore not only an historical value, but they are still of practical, although latent and dormant, importance. Authors of treatises must for this reason always make it apparent that the law of these law-making conventions is a grafting-twig on the trunk of the old customary law which might one day have again to be severed from the tree.

VII. FOSTERING OF ARBITRATION

I come now to a sixth task of the science of international law. This task is connected with the fact that international law is a law not above but between states; that there is no central authority above the sovereign states which could compel them to comply with the rules of international law or to submit their differences to a juridical decision and arbitration instead of taking the law in their own hands and of resorting to reprisals or going to war. Most states are already inclined to settle differences by arbitration, provided these differences do not concern their independence, honor, or vital interests. But arbitration is as yet not obligatory for any matter, although we may in time expect a universal treaty of arbitration to be agreed upon which will make arbitration for some few matters obligatory. Now, it is a task of the science of international law to explore means and ways for bringing international differences more and more to arbitration and for defining those matters which may be made the object of obligatory arbitration. We want to know what disputes can be settled through a decision on juridical grounds, and what other matters can be settled by an arbitration which compromises between the interests at variance. And the science of international law will have to work out detailed rules of procedure for arbitration cases which come before the Permanent Court at The Hague or before other arbitration tribunals. The rules of procedure embodied in the Hague convention concerning the pacific settlement of international disputes are neither complete nor perfect. They are the result of a compromise, and they would not stand their trial if more, and specially more important, cases than hitherto were to go to the Hague Tribunal. The difficulties of the matter are created by the fact that the ideas of the different nations concerning procedure are so different. Thus, the English-American notions of what is evidence do not agree with the continental notions concerning the subject. Again, there is a deep and broad gap between the continental and the English-American ideas concerning the relations between court and counsel, the mode of examining witnesses, and the like. It will therefore not be so easy for the science of international law to construct a mode of procedure which finds approval on the part of continental as well as of English-American jurists. But the attempt must be made, although progress will naturally be only gradual and slow. It is a fact, which must not be lost sight of, that before such a mode of procedure is found as satisfies all round arbitration itself will likewise make only slow progress. It is no use having a court and stipulating arbitration for a number of cases, if the parties concerned have no confidence in the procedure before the court. What we want is not only that parties submit to arbitration, but that they have confidence in it — that they are convinced of the arbitrators' skill and ability to settle the dispute in an adequate manner. To realize this aim, we not only require learned, just, independent, and capable arbitrators, but also a mode of procedure for arbitration cases which in the eyes of the parties guarantees a just trial and an adequate consideration of their claims.

VIII. POPULARIZATION OF INTERNATIONAL LAW

There is a last task of the science of international law which must be mentioned, namely, popularization of international law. The impotence and powerlessness of international law on many occasions of the past was to a great extent due to the fact that the rules of this law were not known by the leading politicians as well as by the "man in the street." That the great majority of the lawyers of all countries knows little or nothing of international law is a point which I will not here discuss at length. This fault can easily be remedied and made good, if international law is made a part of the study of the law students and an obligatory subject of their final examination. If I speak of the task of popularizing the rules of international law, I have in my eye the body of the educated classes who are not lawyers. The science of international law must try to make the rudiments of this law known not only to politicians, journalists, and historians; these rudiments ought also to be taught in all the secondary schools, and the teachers of history are the proper persons who could best undertake to teach this fascinating subject there. Politicians are in most cases not lawyers, and in our democratic times they are recruited from all classes of society. In important international conflicts the decision in many cases ultimately rests not with the leading men, but with public opinion and the "man in the street." Public opinion with regard to international questions is at present at the mercy of the press and the agitator, and it is common knowledge that the jingo and the chauvinist frequently make use of misguided public opinion for their own ends. If the public knew something about the merits of the case concerned they would frequently look upon the matter more coolly and in a more impartial way, and it would be easier for the governments to consent to arbitration.

Of course, this task of popularization is not an easy one, but I believe that it can be fulfilled. The question is not to make everybody an international lawyer, but to make the fundamental principles and rules of international law so well known that everybody has access to them and can acquire a knowledge of them. If it is possible to teach in schools such complicated subjects as physics, chemistry, and mathematics, why should it not be possible to teach the principles of international law, for which a course of a dozen lessons would suffice? As matters stand at present, there are neither proper teachers nor proper books at hand, but I have no doubt that here as elsewhere the demand would create the supply. As I have said before, the teachers of history are the proper persons to teach international law in schools, and there is many an international lawyer of repute who would not consider it beneath his dignity to write an elementary handbook for schools, if only the schools were ready to embody international law in their curriculum.

IX. NECESSARY COOPERATION OF MANY WORKERS

I have tried to define the different tasks of the science of international law. It is obvious that they are beyond the power of a single individual. Cooperation of many is here wanted as in other fields. A man may be an excellent historical researcher, but no good as a popularizer. Another may possess that legal mind which predestines him for the analysis of intricate rules, but he may be impossible as an historical researcher. A third may be possessed of that political gift which enables him to make proposals for the improvement of the existing rules and to draft rules which, when generally accepted, would extend the scope of international law and bring such matters as are as yet outside the province of law and an object of mere political consideration within the province of law. But in spite of the fact that the body of the tasks is beyond the power of a single individual, now and then a single individual must endeavor to focus the results of his own and other people's labor in a treatise. The treatises which we possess — the present writer is allowed to say so, for he includes himself in the blame — are altogether poor in spite of the many merits they may have. Yet they can not be better than they are, for want of sufficient monographs. It is quite true that, if the author of a treatise is not a mere compiler, he does not entirely depend upon monographs, for he can embody the results of his own researches in his treatise. And where he does depend upon the monographs of others, he can throw new light on the problems and the results of the work of others by introducing his own views. But although he may be a genius in his way, he can not possibly pursue every question into its most remote corners; he must everywhere more or less build up his system of thought upon the fundaments laid by many other collaborators. And it is therefore that no one treatise alone can really embrace all the knowledge that is necessary for an international jurist. He who wants to acquire that knowledge will always be obliged to study several treatises written by authors belonging to different nationalities.

The want of monographs is altogether a want of men who can devote their time to research. When the study of international law once offers a career to candidates, matters will be different. At present there are only a few chairs in the universities and law schools whose occupants can entirely devote their labor and research to international law; special chairs of international law exist only in a minority of universities. When once every university and law school possesses at least one well-endowed chair of international law, and when the teaching and the study of this law has become an obligatory subject of the curriculum of all law schools, there will be a career open for those students who are inclined to devote their lives to research in the field of international law. We can then encourage our students to sit down and produce monographs, because these researches will not ultimately prevent their authors from gaining their livelihood, but will give them a chance of entering upon a settled career of life.

X. THE DIFFERENT SCHOOLS OF THOUGHT

Having discussed the tasks of the science of international law, we can now turn our attention to its method. Now, whereas agreement with regard to the tasks is easily realized, there is no generally recognized method of the science of international law. The three schools of the Grotians, the Naturalists, and the Positivists are still in the field, and their methods are naturally different. The Grotians keep up the distinction of Grotius between the natural and the positive international law, the former comprising such rules of international law as are supposed to be based on the law of nature, the latter embracing such rules as are based on international custom and treaties. The Naturalists maintain that no positive law is possible for the regulation of the intercourse of the sovereign states, and that therefore all so-called international law is not real law, but only a part of the so-called law of nature. The Positivists recognize only a positive international law based on custom and treaties, and deny the very existence as well of a law of nature as of a natural international law. But besides these three schools there are to be mentioned the followers of Austin in England, who define international law as a part of the so-called positive morality; it is said to be "morality" because there can not be a law between sovereign states, yet it is "positive" morality because general opinion considers it binding.

All these schools are to-day represented by prominent men whose works have contributed to the progressive development of international law itself as well as of its science. To many it would therefore seem ridiculous to take part in the fray and to join one group and fight the others. As many roads lead to Rome, so many methods lead to good results. As long as a scholar joins at all the ranks of those who till the fields of the science of international law, why should he not be welcome, to whatever school he belongs? Let us judge him, so they say, not according to his method, but according to the fruits of his labor. Now, I quite agree that every worker is welcome, to whatever school he may belong, but it is nevertheless necessary to inquire into the question, Which method is the right one? For the right method secures the best results, and it is these we are aiming at. It is on account of the disagreement as regards the right method that we disagree so much as regards certain rules of international law. Scores of controversies in our science are merely due to the difference of method applied by the authors concerned. And how could it be otherwise? Do we not start from different standpoints? Do we not apply different standards of judgment? What greater contrast can there be than between him who preaches that no real law is possible between sovereign states, and him who asserts that there is such a law created by custom or set by conventions? How can two men come to the same results, if the one abstracts the rules of international law from the actual practice of the states, and the other from what he considers to be reasonable, just, and adequate? How can international law develop progressively if one man lays bare the gaps of the existing law and asks for their filling in through an agreement of the powers, whereas according to the opinion of the other man there are no such gaps, because the law of nature provides a complete system of rules of international law? How is it possible to offer a body of firm, distinct, and clear-cut rules of law, if rules of morality and of religion, if political aspirations and chimerical schemes for a better future, are constantly mixed up with what is really law?

XI. THE LAW OF NATURE

It is for this reason that the decision as to the right method depends upon two preliminary questions: First, the question of the existence of a natural law a part of which a natural international law could be; and, secondly, the question whether there can be a law at all between sovereign states, and therefore whether international law is or is not real law. I propose at present to deal only with the first question, and I will at once emphasize that according to my opinion we are now-a-days no longer justified in teaching a law of nature and a " natural " law of nations. But do we thereby not shake the very fundament of international law as laid by Grotuis? How can we teach, what we all do, that Grotius became immortal by founding international law and the science of international law, if we deny the existence of the rock upon which Grotius thought to have built up his system? Is it not a well-known fact that Grotius founded the law of nature for the mere purpose of having an eternal and unshakable basis for the foundation of the law of nations?

My answer is that Grotius was not an infallible Pope. He was a child of his time and therefore a product of his age. Although he is rightly called the father of the law of nature as well as of the law of nations, he has created neither the one nor the other. Long before Grotius, the opinion was generally prevalent that above the positive law which had grown up by custom or by legislation there was in existence another law which had its roots in human reason and was therefore called the " law of nature." And likewise long before Grotius it was quite usual to deduce from the law of nature certain rules for the intercourse of the sovereign states. Grotius is nevertheless rightly considered the father and founder of both the law of nature and the law of nations, because he focussed the results of the works of his forerunners in his own work in such a masterly way and with such a felicitous hand that his system of the law of nature and nations pushed the work of his forerunners in the background — absolutely overshadowed it — and became the starting point for all the future works in the same field. Thus, in spite of his immortal merits, Grotius was only a child of his time and a product of his age. All of us, if we had lived in his time, would certainly have been adherents of the law of nature. At that time and age, the law of nature was a necessity. It was not a product of the fertile brain of one single individual, consciously thought out for the purpose of creating something hitherto not existing. Nothing of the kind! It was an epoch in the evolution of human reason, and it supplied one of the necessary crutches with whose help mankind walked out of the institutions of the Middle Ages into those of modern times. Three powers and systems of thought have broken the fetters in which the Middle Ages had kept Western mankind: the philosophy of pure experience, the Reformation, and the law of nature. The philosophy of experience brought freedom from scholasticism. The Reformation endeavored to lead mankind back to the original teachings of Christ. The law of nature brought social and constitutional liberty, called into existence the modern constitutional law, and laid the foundation of the law of nations.

But the law of nature has played its part. We know now-a-days that it is impossible to find a law which has its roots in human reason only and is above legislation and customary law. The innumerable systems of the professors of the law of nature neither agree in scope, nor in contents, nor in definitions, nor in the very number and contents of the rules which they profess to draw from reason. Nobody denies the right of an author to criticize the existing legal rules, to condemn the prevailing social conditions, and to construct a body of rules which, when accepted, would constitute an improvement. But such rules, although ever so much supported by reason, justice, and equity, would not be rules of law before they were either by custom or by legislation adopted for the future conduct of those concerned. Enormous as the importance and the function of the theory of law of nature has been for the past, it is for our times not only without any value whatever, but directly detrimental. It weakens the eyes of those who profess it. It prevents the proper criticism of the existing positive law. It constantly mixes up the past, the present, and the future. It offers a breach through which the deniers of the law of nations can easily come in and attack the very existence of an international law. And therefore it is that the place of the theory of the law of nature is no longer in our textbooks, law schools, and universities, but in the museums where the scientific tools are preserved with which former generations did their best to lay the foundation of our present scientific knowledge.

I know quite well that this emphatic denial of the law of nature exposes me to attacks. Most French and other Romanic and also some British and American jurists will stigmatize my standpoint as "unscientific," for they consider it inferior work to collect the "crude" real rules of international law without regard to the "higher" rules of the law of nature. And many in whom the mere sound of the term "positive" creates a shudder will, as "idealists," oppose my standpoint of "positivism." Now, to the argument that my standpoint is not scientific, I simply answer that the mere term "science" implies knowledge, and that it is a demand of science to stick to the facts, and not to hunt phantasms. And the law of nature is nothing else than a phantasm! It requires much more scientific skill to expose the real existing rules of international law, to lay bare their history and real meaning, and to criticize them in the light of reason, justice, and the requirements of the age, than to teach the rules of a law of nature in the clouds. On the other hand, to the "idealists" I have to answer that I am myself an idealist, if by that term is characterized a man who rejects the materialistic explanation of the world and believes in the eternal progress of mankind towards the good, but that my standpoint as regards the method of the science of international law has nothing to do with idealism or positivism in the philosophic meaning of those terms.

XII. THE DENIERS OF INTERNATIONAL LAW

Quite as detrimental as the theory of the law of nature is the theory of all those who deny to international law the character of real law. I have elsewhere endeavored to develop the essential characteristics of law and to show that international law bears all these essential characteristics. The mistake which is constantly made by the so-called deniers of international law is essentially one of method. They start with a wrongly conceived definition of law, and they must consequently deny the character of law to all such bodies of rules for human conduct as can not be fitted into that definition. From Hobbes down to Blackstone and Austin it is always the same wrong starting point — municipal law. They draw their definition of law in general from that of municipal law and define it as the body of rules imposed by a sovereign upon his subjects. Yet even this definition of municipal law is wrong. It contains a part but not the whole of the truth. It explains neither the existence of customary law, nor the fact that the sovereign has the legal power of imposing legal rules of conduct upon his subjects. But apart from this, I do not deny that there is an essential difference between municipal and international law. I do not maintain that international law is a law of the same power and strength as municipal law. I do not maintain that international law can undo municipal law. What I maintain is that municipal law, constitutional law, ecclesiastical law, and international law are all branches of the same tree of law in general as a body of rules for the conduct of the members of a community, which rules shall by common consent of the community be eventually enforced by external power, in contradistinction to rules of morality which by common consent of a community concerned are to be enforced by conscience only. Those who do not recognize international law as law because it does not fit their definition are like that renowned German professor of philosophy whose theories were fine but did not fit the facts, and who, when confronted with this, answered: "So much the worse for the facts!"

The question is not whether municipal courts consider international law binding upon themselves. Their attitude depends upon the fact whether the municipal law of their individual state considers international law as a body or in some parts the law of the land, or, in other words, whether the municipal law of their individual state has incorporated international law in the law of the land, as the United States of America has done. The question is rather whether the governments of the states which as a body make the family of nations consider international law binding upon themselves in their intercourse with one another. Now, nobody can deny that the governments do this, although they may on an occasion deny that a certain rule is a rule of international law, or may in a special case declare that they act by right in not carrying out a recognized rule of international law. Of course, we have as yet no decision of courts which are binding precedents. The cases which we possess as yet are either arbitration cases which are hardly connected with one another, or mostly prize court cases which are municipal cases and which, whatever their force as precedents may be for courts of the same country concerned, are not binding upon courts of other countries. But this condition of affairs will soon undergo a change. An international prize court has been established by the Second Hague Peace Conference, and a really permanent arbitration court will, I believe, be established by the Third Hague Peace Conference expected to meet in 1915. These really international courts will in time produce precedents which will possess the same degree of binding force for international law as precedents of municipal courts possess for municipal law.

It has been said that the question whether international law is real law or not, is merely a question of terminology and not worth fighting about, especially with regard to the followers of Austin, who consider international law "positive morality," and who do not deny its binding character. I would readily agree to this, if all the Austinians consented to consider this "positive morality" for all practical purposes as law, although they do not do it in theory, and if they consented to apply the rules of jurisprudence to the interpretation of the rules of international law. But that is just what they, or at least some of them, refuse to do. They rather consider international law more a body of mere principles than a body of legal rules, and they are far from consenting to these principles being applied and interpreted like other legal rules. They want to reserve to the individual governments a greater liberty of action with regard to the rules of international law than these governments would have if international law is considered real law, pure and simple. There is no doubt that these followers of Austin attribute to international law a lesser degree of binding force. And it is therefore that the question whether international law is or is not law, is ultimately not only a question of terminology but one of great and material importance. The argument that a sovereign can not be bound in the same way as a subject does not hit the point, for everybody agrees that international law is not a law above but only between the states. A rule of international law can not, without their special consent, be imposed upon the states, as a rule of municipal law can be imposed upon the subjects of a state without their special consent. But if they once consent to submit themselves to a rule of international law, states are bound by such rule to the same extent and degree as subjects are bound by rules of the municipal law of their state.

XIII. IN WHAT THE POSITIVE METHOD CONSISTS

If we exclude the law of nature and what is called "natural" international law altogether, and if we consider international law real law, the method to be applied by the science of international law can be no other than the positive method. In what this method consists and what it demands, I shall now have to demonstrate.

To put the matter in a nutshell, I can say: The positive method is that applied by the science of law in general, and it demands that whatever the aims and ends of a worker and researcher may be, he must start from the existing recognized rules of international law as they are to be found in the customary practice of the states or in law-making conventions. Authors of treatises on the municipal law of contract, tort, and real property now-a-days no longer start from the rules of a law of nature concerning these matters, but expose at once the customary or statutory rules concerning them. Why should the authors of treatises on the law of war, of neutrality, and of other parts of international law start from a law of nature, and not at once expose the customary and conventional rules concerning these subjects?

The fact that Grotius and many of his followers did start from the law of nature can not be authoritative for the method to be applied now-a-days when there are enough customary and conventional rules in existence for the construction of a fairly complete system of international law, and when we know that any rule of the so-called law of nature lacks all legal force and authority.

Now, how are the existing recognized rules of international law to be ascertained?

In so far as conventional rules are concerned, it is to a certain extent easy to find them. They are written rules. Their scope, their meaning, and their extent can in many cases be grasped at a first glance. If we only possess accurate copies of the authentic documents in which these rules are embodied, and if we are able to master the language in which these documents are drawn up, we often get at their meaning without great difficulty. But frequently they nevertheless present doubt and uncertainty enough, and then they require interpretation, a matter which I shall discuss later on (see below XVIII, pp. 349–353). However this may be, written rules never offer such great difficulties to the science of international law as rules based on custom. It is because international law is still to the greater extent based on custom that the text-books differ so much with regard to the rules they lay down as rules of international law. Many of these book rules are mere fancies, the outcome either of what the respective authors consider the law of nature, or of patriotic prejudice, or of misunderstood authority, and the like. If the method of the science of international law is to be positive, no rule must be formulated which can not be proved to be the outcome of international custom or of a law-making treaty. However great the authority of a writer may be who asserts the existence of a rule, and be it Grotius himself, the science of international law has no right to lay down the rule concerned as really existent and universally or generally recognized unless it can be ascertained that the members of the family of nations have customarily or by a law-making treaty accepted the rule. And the greatest caution is necessary in weighing the practice of the states for the purpose of ascertaining whether there is a certain custom or not. For it is possible that there is a usage only, but no custom. Of course the line between a mere usage and a ripe custom is frequently difficult to draw, for usages have a tendency to ripen into customs. And it is with regard to this matter that an ingenious text-book writer can do good work. If he has a sharp eye, if he understands how to feel the pulse of his age, if he possesses the necessary historical insight, he will be able to see that many a usage has ripened into a custom between his own time and that of his predecessors. But the greatest care must be applied to avoid the teaching of rules which either do not exist at all or not to the extent asserted by book writers. It is not the task of a writer to fill in the gaps in the existing rules of international law unless a conclusion *per analogiam* suggests itself with such force that its acceptance is obvious and absolutely necessary. Of course, the gaps must be brought into view, and the writer may offer an opinion *de lege ferenda* how to fill them in; yet there must always be clearness and distinctness between the writer's opinions *de lege ferenda* and really recognized rules of law. It is no use drawing up definitions and principles which do not agree with the facts as evidenced by the practice of the states. Wherever these facts are not clear, are uncertain, are not numerous enough to enable the researcher to see the full extent of a certain practice, definitions must be drawn up in a more or less ambiguous way, if they are at all necessary. It is a thousand times better to leave a question open than to answer it incorrectly. The science of international law can neither step into the place of legislation and of codification, nor into the place of custom. It is a fact that as regards many questions the practice of the states differs so much that either no unanimity whatever can be stated to exist, or only with regard to some points. Thus, for instance, anyone who undertakes to write about the law of blockade or contraband can only state that certain rules are universally recognized, but that as regards many questions there is a hopeless difference between the practice of the different groups of states. It shows bad manners, if not gross ignorance or bad faith, if many authors simply declare the practice of their own state as the one corresponding to the rules of international law, denouncing the other party or parties as delinquents. Thus, the abuse to which during the Russo-Japanese war the Russians were submitted on the part of several English and American writers for having sunk such neutral merchantmen carrying contraband as they were unable to bring into a port of a prize court was absolutely out of place. For although I believe that the English practice to release such vessels is a good practice, which ought to become universally recognized, there is no doubt that it is as yet not recognized, and that the practice of several states is the contrary.

Of course, an author who carefully sticks to the facts and leaves all those questions open concerning which no general or universal practice can be stated to exist will frequently be abused and blamed. The reader wants certainty and authority, and if he finds no certain opinion but a statement of divergent opinions he feels betrayed and helpless. But his good sense ought to tell him that his interests are better served by the author's honesty in stating that there is no settled practice; for by acting in this way the author makes it obvious that international law really has no generally recognized rules concerning the matter, and that it is open to a party to act independently and to select that solution of the problem concerned which is the best according to the party's own judgment.

XIV. APPRECIATION OF MUNICIPAL CASE-LAW

The divergence noted in the practice of the different states with regard to many points leads me to a very important question of method, namely, the position to be taken up by the science of international law towards cases decided by municipal courts. At a first glance there would seem for a positive method of our science no better way to gain unassailable results than by following as closely as possible such case-law. And most of the English and American international jurists think and act accordingly, and they are therefore possessed of an unappeasable case-hunger. Whenever a question turns up, they ask for a case to be thereby guided. This case-hunger is the consequence of two facts. The English common law consists entirely of case-law and has grown up from precedent to precedent, and our lawyers are therefore accustomed to seek a precedent for every new case that arises. On the other hand, customary law and judge-made law are in England and America frequently identified, and our jurists are therefore disinclined to diagnose the existence of a customary rule of law unless the courts have recognized such a rule in decided cases.

Now, I do not deny the great importance of case-law in general and of such municipal cases in particular as touch upon questions of international law. But the science of international law must be careful in the appreciation of such municipal case-law.

We have, first, not to lose sight of the fact that municipal courts can not through their decisions directly call a rule of international law into existence. It is in a sense quite correct to speak of judge-made law within the province of municipal law, for here judges are in a sense and to a certain extent makers of the law. Do they not fill in gaps of the law with new law which they find *per analogiam?* Do they not to a certain degree alter the existing law by interpreting it equitably, reasonably, and adequately? Do they not, many a time, with the help of interpretation develop a body and a system of rules out of one single principle of the law? Do they not frequently shape a rule of law to fit it to the requirements of an individual case? The municipal law shows everywhere on its body the finger-prints of the judges and other traces of their handiwork. But in spite of all this, I should not call a judge a real law-maker in the sense of a law-giver. A real law-maker is a power, like parliament, which can arbitrarily make and unmake law to any extent, according to its mere discretion, in perfect independence of any other authority in the land, and not in any way limited. Our judges, however, in shaping and making the law can never act arbitrarily like a real law-maker, can never make and unmake law according to their mere discretion. They are always bound by considerations which are far from arbitrariness, and they can shape and make the law to a certain limited extent only and in a certain limited degree only. As far as they do shape and make the law they do it with the express consent of the real law-maker in the land; they are tools in the hands of custom and legislation. They are law-shapers, law-developers, law-finders, and law-excavators, but not real law-makers and law-givers. But however this may be with regard to the municipal law of the different states, as far as international law is concerned municipal courts can not make any law or shape the existing law. Cases decided by them do indeed become precedents for the judges of the country concerned, but they are not international precedents — are not *per se* binding upon municipal courts of other countries. This is a rule without an exception, and the decisions of prize courts are not excluded from the rule. Even if it were true, what is commonly maintained in

England in consequence of a *dictum* of Lord Stowell, that the law applied by prize courts is international law, the decision of these courts, which are of course municipal courts, could *per se* never have the force of precedents outside their own country. I do not deny — having in my mind Lord Stowell's wonderful judgments — that the intrinsic value of many such decisions and the convincing arguments which accompany them had their bearing upon courts of other countries and thereby in fact made these cases precedents which are followed by the courts of all or many other countries, but in law and *per se* they are and remain precedents for the judges of their own country only. I do likewise not deny that the intrinsic value of such decisions may be the cause of the rising of general or universal customs within the family of nations which create rules of international law based upon and abstracted from such decisions, but the decisions can not by themselves and without the aid of custom or law-making treaties call those rules of international law into existence.

We have, secondly, not to lose sight of the fact that municipal courts can not through their decisions take the life out of a recognized rule of international law. The fact that municipal courts declare that a certain rule of international law can not be enforced by them, or does not exist at all, may be a precedent for the judges of the same country, but the rule itself remains thereby unshaken, provided it is a recognized rule at all. Thus, after the South African war, English courts declared that a rule of international law concerning the succession of the conqueror into the debts of the conquered state did not exist and could not be enforced in English courts. But these decisions could not take the life out of the rule concerned, if it did exist at all. If it can be proved that during the nineteenth century up to the South African war conquerors felt in duty bound to pay the public debts of the conquered, that public opinion of the world at large approved of and expected this attitude, that all authoritative writers considered this attitude necessary, the question only is, whether succession into these debts is based on a mere usage or on a custom, and whether such custom is universal or only general. It is not within the competence of municipal courts to decide these questions; it is rather a matter between the governments of the states which are members of the family of nations, and could ultimately only be decided by a court of arbitration. And however this may be, the individual creditor of the conquered state has no direct claim upon the conqueror; it is the home state of such creditor which by the right of protection over his subjects which is due to him can claim from the conqueror payment of the conquered state's debt. Municipal courts, although they might recognize the existence of the rule of international law concerned, may at the same time have to declare that they could not enforce a claim of a private individual based upon such rule, on account of the fact that they are only competent to deal with claims based upon municipal law.

After these reservations, I can define the standpoint from which the science of international law can make use of municipal case-law bearing upon questions of international law. I have already said that such case-law is of the greatest importance, for it brings into view the practice of the courts of the individual states. If this practice is everywhere the same, it may be taken for granted that a universally recognized rule of international law is at its background. If, on the other hand, this practice differs, it may be taken for granted that no universally recognized rule exists with regard to the question concerned. If, thirdly, this practice differs to such an extent only that a few courts refuse the recognition of a rule, whereas many recognize it, it may be taken for granted that there is a generally, although not universally, recognized rule in existence with regard to the question concerned. Again, if this practice differs so much that it must be taken for granted that no generally or universally recognized rule is in existence, the science of international law can examine the different decisions; can point out the relative value of the different groups; can single one out as the most adequate, reasonable, and just; can thereby foster the growth of future unanimity. It must, however, be specially emphasized that for the existence of a rule, and in especial for the recognition of a growing rule, of international law it is ultimately not the attitude of municipal courts, but that of the states themselves and their governments, which is decisive. It is quite possible that a state refuses to recognize the existence of a certain rule of international law, although a court of the land has declared that such rule does exist. And it is likewise possible that a court of the land refuses to acknowledge the existence of a certain rule which the government of the land concerned does recognize either now or hereafter. International law is a law between states, which concerns states only and exclusively; it can not *per se* concern municipal courts, but only when it has partly or totally been incorporated into the law of the land. The attitude of municipal courts can not therefore directly concern international law, although it is, as I have shown, of the greatest importance for the science of international law.

However this may be, two particularly grave sins of method are frequently committed by writers in the treatment of decisions of municipal courts.

The first is that they fall on their knees and worship the decisions of the courts of their own country, while they abuse the differing decisions of foreign courts. Look, for instance, at the position taken up by such an excellent international jurist as the late Mr. Hall with regard to the question of continuous voyage. Whereas he defends the English decisions concerning this matter, he abuses the American decisions during the civil war which extend the doctrine of continuous voyage to what I call circuitous and indirect carriage of contraband. If, on the other hand, we take a look round on the Continent we find many text-book writers who abuse both the English and the American decisions concerned! Or, to give another example, take the English and American decisions concerning enemy character. English and American writers quote them as representing universally recognized rules of international law, but the fact is that the French, the Italians, the Germans, defend opinions which are contrary to many of these decisions! The science of international law must here, as on other occasions, aim at impartiality. A writer is, of course, called upon to draw attention to the cases bearing upon international law which have arisen in the courts of his own land. But he must exercise criticism on these decisions as well as on foreign decisions. He must never abuse the latter. He ought always to bring into view the different standpoints. He ought always to be aware of it and make it quite clear to his readers when the practice of the courts of his own country differs from the practice of foreign courts.

The other grave sin of method frequently committed by writers making use of case-law is to bring case after case, with all details, without defining the principles which are the basis of the decisions given in the cases concerned. If this wrong method is applied, the writers as well as their readers can not see the wood for the trees! The right method is to abstract the principles from the decisions, and then to quote the decisions themselves as examples of the application of the principles. Of course, this is very delicate work and not to everybody's taste. It is much easier to pile case upon case and to leave it to the reader to draw the conclusions from these decisions than to find out the broad principles which are brought to light in these decisions, and to select only a certain number of typical cases as leading examples. But the science of international law can not forego this work, however difficult and painstaking it may be. Let it be said with emphasis that the collecting of cases without sifting them and without abstracting the rules they are supposed to bring into view is without any value for the science of international law, unless it is done only for the purpose of collecting material.

XV. APPRECIATION OF ARBITRATION CASES

From municipal cases I must turn the attention of the reader to arbitration cases. In appreciating the decisions of arbitration courts, writers likewise show frequently a wrong method. They take it for granted that such decisions have the force of precedents, and that the principles which are brought into view through such decisions must henceforth be recognized as settled principles of international law. Take, for example, the appreciation of the verdict in the Alabama Case. American and some English writers maintain that according to the verdict of the Geneva Court of Arbitration the three rules of Washington are settled rules of international law.

But nothing of the kind is really the case. Although England and America agreed, by the Treaty of Washington, to observe these rules between themselves, to bring them to the knowledge of other maritime powers, and to invite the latter to accede to these rules, no such communication and invitation, and therefore no accession on the part of third powers, has taken place. England and America could not communicate the three rules to other powers, because the arbitration court put a construction upon the term *due diligence* and asserted other opinions which are contested and which England could not accept. It is therefore not admissible to assert that these three rules of Washington are settled rules of international law, although it may safely be stated that these three rules became the starting point of the movement for the recognition of the rule that neutrals must prevent their subjects from building and fitting out to the order of belligerents vessels intended for warlike purposes.

Another example is the decision of Louis Napoleon as arbitrator in the case of the "*General Armstrong*." Judgment was given in favor of Portugal, because the *General Armstrong* chose to defend herself against the attack on the part of the English aggressors instead of demanding protection from the neutral Portuguese authorities. Several text-book writers assert that in consequence of this decision it is a settled rule of international law that a neutral is freed from responsibility for a violation of neutrality through a belligerent attacking enemy forces on neutral territory, in case the attacked forces, instead of trusting for protection or redress to the neutral, defend themselves against the attack. Now I do not mean to say that such or a similar rule will never be recognized; yet it is certainly not correct to maintain that it is already settled. For nothing of the kind is really the case. The only safe thing to say is that this decision has been given, and that the underlying principle might perhaps in course of time become a recognized rule of international law, although I personally have my doubts about this.

The position to be taken up by the science of international law towards decisions of courts of arbitration must at present be one of caution and reserve. Three groups of cases are to be distinguished. First, the parties may agree to bind down the arbitrators to the application of a rule or rules upon which the parties have agreed. Secondly, the arbitrators may be directed to give their decision according to recognized rules of international law. Lastly, the arbitrators may be directed to settle the dispute anyhow, which means according to their best judgment, *arbitrio boni viri.*

Now, it is obvious that decisions belonging to the first and the last group can certainly not establish and settle rules of international law, although their intrinsic value may be the starting point of a movement for the customary growth of a certain new rule. As regards decisions belonging to the second group, all depends on the rule applied by the arbitrators. If the rule is really one which is generally or universally recognized, the decision will furnish an example and proof of its validity. If the rule is not generally or universally recognized, but recognized by the practice of some states only and approved of by some authoritative writers only, the decision will help the rule to become generally or universally recognized. If the rule is one found *per analogiam* or out of considerations of equity, the decision may be the starting point of a movement for the recognition of the rule. But if the rule is based on error of judgment and ignorance, the decision is of no value whatever, and the science of international law has to put its finger into the wound and has clearly to point out that the rule applied by the arbitrators does not exist and will never become generally recognized.

Of course, matters will soon undergo a change. The permanent International Prize Court agreed upon by the Second Hague Peace Conference, which is able to revise decisions in prize cases given by municipal prize courts, will in time establish a real international prize-case law. This court will of course follow its own precedents, the different states will submit to these precedents, and the science of international law will be able to abstract the rules and principles which are at the background of these precedents. That this court will adopt many decisions given in the past by English, American, French, and Italian prize courts, I have no doubt, for the bulk of them really represents common sense and justice, and is in conformity with generally recognized rules of international law. But, on the other hand, I have likewise no doubt that it will reprobate some of these decisions.

As regards the decisions of the so-called Permanent Court of Arbitration established by the First Hague Peace Conference, matters are different. This court is not in fact a permanent court, but simply a body of individuals from which the parties select a number who are constituted as the court for a special case. As by the rules concerning these courts it is not stipulated that every successive court is bound by the decisions of his predecessors, it can and will happen that such decisions of former courts as do not recommend themselves by their intrinsic value and the force of the accompanying arguments will not be followed by their successors. But there is no doubt that the Third Hague Peace Conference will establish a really permanent court of arbitration, and the latter will of course always follow its own former decisions as precedents. What I have said with regard to the permanent International Prize Court applies therefore likewise to this future permanent court of arbitration; it will establish real international case-law, and the time will come when the science of international law will be able to bring into view judge-made international law.

XVI. APPRECIATION OF AUTHORITIES

Having discussed the appreciation due to municipal case-law and to arbitration cases, we now must approach the question, What appreciation is due to authoritative writers on international law. Here I must at once emphasize that it is quite common to make improper use of so-called authorities and to overestimate the value and importance of the mass of the literature on international law. Our English and American books go far beyond what should be done by calling everyone an "authority" who has ever written a treatise or a monograph on international law. It is right and just and helpful that a writer should enumerate the works of those before himself who wrote on the matter concerned. Yet to head such a list of literature by the term "list of authorities" is entirely wrong and misleading, unless every author of a literary production must needs be considered an "authority." But nothing of the kind is actually the case; it will always be necessary to make a distinction between writers at large and writers of authority. Now, who are the authoritative writers? They are those whose works have gained great influence; have become guides of the practice of the states, and storehouses of the opinions, usages, and customs of their generation; are expounding the existing law with accuracy, care, and ability; and are throwing side-lights on its development and improvement. Such writers of authority are of much more importance for international law than for municipal law, for in the absence of international courts and of judge-made international law writers have, as pointed out before (see above, II, pp. 314–315), a much more influential position. International law can stand just as little as municipal law the hair-splitting tyranny of the letter and the word of a legal rule. International law requires therefore, just as much as municipal law, reasonable and equitable interpretation. International law must likewise be adapted to the requirements of the circumstances and conditions of the age, and must likewise be shaped to fit the merits of the individual case. In the absence of international judges, writers have to satisfy these requirements. The teachings of authoritative writers take, therefore, within the province of international law, to a certain extent the place which judge-made law has within the province of municipal law. Assertions of authoritative writers will therefore naturally carry great weight with regard to the question whether a certain rule of international law is or is not in existence, and what is its scope, its extent, and its proper meaning. Yet ultimately it is not the authoritative assertion of a writer which decides the question, but the fact that it can be proved that the rule is really recognized and followed in practice to the extent and with the scope and meaning as asserted by the writer concerned. For even great authorities make mistakes, are influenced by their political fancies, take usages for customs, take the future for the present, confound their own opinion with what is generally recognized. The unanimous assertion of even a great number of authorities can not really make a rule of international law, if this rule is not customarily recognized in practice. Take, for instance, the rules asserted to exist by the majority of authoritative text-book writers with regard to the matter of intervention, and compare with these assertions the actual practice of the states! All these rules are mere book-rules, fancies of their authors, but not recognized rules of international law. Now, I will not deny that many rules which are now customarily recognized can be traced back to the authority of a writer or writers. Grotius and Bymkersbock and other authorities have first asserted a number of rules which the practice of the states afterwards adopted. But it is not the authority of these great men, but the practice of the states concerned, which ripened into custom and made these rules rules of international law. And times have changed considerably. It is no longer to be expected that the assertions of authoritative writers will so easily as in former ages become the starting point of a practice which ripens into custom. Times are more critical than they used to be. A fairly complete system of rules of international law has grown up. States are now-a-days more inclined than formerly to settle certain matters by law-making treaties, instead of leaving them to the mercy of the writers and the slow growth of usage and custom.

However this may be, wherever authoritative writers assert the existence of a customary rule, great care is necessary in positively verifying its existence, contents, scope, and real meaning. That it must carefully be distinguished from a mere usage, I have stated before (see above, XIII, p. 334). But even if a real custom can be diagnosed, the question is still whether it is a universal or only a general custom. Text-book writers mostly overlook that there are scores of rules which are customarily recognized, although one or more individual states refuse to recognize them. The fact is that these rules are based upon a *general* custom only, whereas others are based on a *universal* custom and are therefore recognized by every member of the family of nations. Take, for instance, the rule that fishing boats belonging to enemy subjects can not be attacked and seized by a belligerent. That this rule is based on a general custom, there is no doubt. But the custom is not universal. The fact that Great Britain has never recognized it prevented the rule from being universally recognized before the Second Hague Peace Conference. It suffices to cite this example to show what blunders are constantly being made by writers who do not see, or do not want to see, the difference between general and universal international law, who confound both, and who accuse on occasions a state of breaking a rule of international law which such state had in fact never recognized!

Just as care is necessary in the diagnosis of a customary rule asserted to exist by writers, so great caution must be exercised in the diagnosis of a *desuetudo* which makes a former customary rule of international law vanish and disappear, and in the appreciation of conventional rules which take the life out of former customary rules. Many a rule is still stated to exist by some authoritative writers which really is obsolete. On the other hand, writers sometimes teach that a rule has lost its validity, although it is still fully recognized. Take, for example, the rule that all states, whatever their size and degree of power, are equal before international law. Some writers maintain that this rule is no longer valid; that the political hegemony exercised by the great powers rests on a legal basis; that therefore states are not equal according to international law. Yet nothing of the kind is in fact the case. These writers simply confound political with legal equality. The rule of the legal equality of all full sovereign members of the family of nations will and must remain valid as long as the family of nations remains in existence, for this rule is one of the characteristics of the position of the states within the family of nations. The best proof that it is still recognized can be gained from the deliberations of the Second Hague Peace Conference where the votes of the politically most insignificant states had the same legal value as the votes of the great powers.

But however great pains a writer may take in trying to verify assertions of authorities, he will frequently not succeed, because either the material at hand is not sufficient to settle the question, or the necessary historical research is wanting, or for other reasons. He ought then to let the authorities fight their own case; he ought always to make it clear whether they are unanimous or disagree, what their arguments are, and the like. He will in particular have to investigate whether they make their assertion on the basis of the so-called law of nature, or on the basis of the observation of the actual practice of the states; and he will thereby be able to ascertain the real value of the assertion concerned. But however high his appreciation of all or of certain individual authorities may be, he must always bear the fact in his mind that authorities are not the law itself!

XVII. APPRECIATION OF LAW-MAKING TREATIES

Whereas the importance of authorities is mostly overvalued, many writers are wanting in right appreciation of law-making international treaties. They refuse to law-making treaties recognition as a source of international law. They call treaty law "contract," and recognize as international law such rules only as are the outcome of custom. There is no greater sin of method than this! If this attitude were correct, then the Declaration of Paris, the Geneva conventions, the Hague convention concerning warfare on land, and other law-making treaties were not part of international law! Yet we see that these treaties not only create new rules, but take the life out of old customary rules, or extend them, restrict them, or partly alter their contents. Here, again, it is the neglect of the distinction between general and universal international law which is at the back of this detrimental attitude. It is true, a treaty can not make universal international law unless all members of the family of nations have become parties to it, and as long and in so far as this has not been realized the law which emanates from these treaties is only general or even only particular international law. Still, law it is and remains all the same while the treaties concerned remain valid. It is quite correct that in a sense every international treaty, be it ever so insignificant, is law-making. But it is understood that if we speak of law-making treaties we do not mean international treaties in general, but treaties of a certain kind only. Treaties in general are certainly only "contract," but law-making treaties are something infinitely more than this; they are acts of the powers in council which resemble in a sense acts of parliament within the boundaries of a state. They are, so to say, international statutes passed by the powers in council for their future international conduct. They are as binding upon the powers as customary international law is, and they gain more importance every day. The Hague peace conferences are certain to become a regular institution by automatically taking place in future from time to time, without being specially summoned by one of the powers. They will gradually settle more matters of international law, and the time will come when they will deal with the codification of international law at large. Customary international law will then be pushed into the background, although it will never entirely disappear. The future of international law belongs to conventional and not to customary law. But custom will always remain at the background of international law, just as it remains at the background of statutory law within the individual states. For the power of the states in council to make international law through law-making treaties rests as much on custom as the power of a municipal parliament to pass statutes does.

XVIII. INTERPRETATION

The importance of law-making international treaties for the present and the future leads me to the discussion of another important point of method: Interpretation.

It is well known that hitherto no rules of international law are generally recognized concerning the interpretation of treaties in general. The rules of Roman law concerning interpretation as applied by Grotius and his followers are adequate rules on account of their common sense, but they are not recognized as rules of international law. The difficulties arising out of this condition of affairs are at present insurmountable, unless every case of dispute goes to arbitration. Take, for instance, the as yet unsettled controversy between America and Great Britain concerning the interpretation of the term "due diligence" in the three rules of Washington. Or take, to give another example, the meaning of the terms "cabotage" or "coasting trade" and of the "most-favored-nation" clause as applied in commercial treaties. Now, treaties in general are mostly treaties between two countries, but law-making treaties are agreements to which as a rule a great number, if not all the members of the family of nations, are parties. And the importance of these law-making treaties for international law is much greater than that of treaties in general, for the former supply daily more rules for the conduct of the states in their international affairs. It may be maintained that the whole institution of law-making treaties is to a certain extent in danger unless the science of international law succeeds in working out rules of interpretation which by becoming universally recognized enable a universally recognized construction of the treaties concerned. As yet nothing of the kind is in existence. The gap makes itself all the more felt as nearly all law-making treaties, from the Declaration of Paris down to the last Hague conventions, are the product of hasty and hurried compromises. Whereas most of the drafts of municipal statutes undergo a long process of preparation before they are laid before parliament, and are duly considered and examined before they are passed as statutes, most of the law-making international treaties which we at present possess were agreed upon at conferences without having been duly prepared a long time beforehand. The views of the different states represented at the conferences were hurriedly and superficially compromised. Terms of wide and ambiguous meaning were made use of. Gaps were intentionally left open because they could not be filled in without endangering the whole treaty concerned. Reference is made to the rules of customary international law on certain matters, although such rules are either controverted or do not exist at all. To a certain degree future conferences will have to work on the same lines, although the drafts will perhaps be prepared with greater care.

Now, how do the jurists of the different nations approach the difficulties of interpretation created by this hasty and hurried passing of law-making treaties? They do it armed with the rules of interpretation worked out by their municipal jurisprudence; possessed of those traits of mind which are peculiar to their race; imbued with their historical traditions and natural prejudices; applying their method of thought and feeling, which is different from that of other nations. Compare, for instance, the mental condition of an English jurist and that of a continental one who is called upon to interpret rules emanating from a law-making treaty. The continental jurist has gone through a course of training which has accustomed him to apply abstract rules of abstract codes; he always thinks in the abstract way, and his method of interpretation is therefore likewise abstract; he believes in principles and starts from them. The English jurist, on the other hand, has gone through a training which always makes him think in the concrete way; he starts from cases and tries to find out in what points a new case resembles the old ones; he mistrusts principles, and only believes in the characteristic traits of individual cases. If I may say so, the continental jurist endeavors to make his cases fit the legal rules, whereas the English jurist tries to make the law fit the cases. Or take a German and a French jurist called upon to interpret a law-making treaty. The German jurist, applying that exactness of method he has been brought up in, will, so to say, count, measure, and weigh the words contained in the treaty concerned; will think out the different interpretations which are possible; will select an interpretation which as far as possible agrees with the word, the letter, and the spirit of the treaty. The French jurist, on the other hand, will approach his task possessed of that *esprit* and full of that imaginative power with which his nation is gifted; he will try to find out the meaning of the rule in question by one glance; and if he detects several possible meanings, he will select the one which appeals more to his imagination, his sense of justice, and his predilection for the spirited and the ingenious.

Is it to be wondered at that under these circumstances and conditions the interpretation of certain rules of law-making treaties frequently differs among the jurists of different nations?

Now, to a certain extent these differences are and will always be insurmountable. Yet they do not, or should not, preclude the science of international law from in time producing at least certain rules of interpretation which are able to find universal recognition. What kind of rules these will be is at present impossible to say, but there can be no doubt that those few rules of interpretation upon which the jurisprudence of all civilized nations unanimously agrees will be amongst them.

However this may be, the science of international law must be on its guard to prevent the introduction — openly or surreptitiously — of such legal conceptions for the purpose of interpretation as are not common to the jurisprudence of the whole world, but are only known to the jurisprudence of one or another country. It can not therefore, to give an example, be considered admissible, although German writers do it frequently, to introduce the German conception of *Notstand,* in so far as its meaning goes beyond the meaning of the universally accepted conception of self-preservation in necessary self-defense. I will not deny that a legal conception belonging to the jurisprudence of an individual country might find its way into international jurisprudence. I should be sorry for the latter if it could not enrich itself with conceptions and ideas first arisen in the field of municipal jurisprudence. But before this can be done the conceptions and ideas concerned must be generally understood, adopted, and recognized. Therefore, if a law-making treaty should make use of such a conception there is no doubt that it has at once and *ipso facto* become naturalized. Just as technical terms of a certain language — think of the German "*Hinterland*" and "*Talweg*" — may be generally applied in international treaties and thereby become adopted by international law, so may municipal legal conceptions. Thus the English conception of "lease" has been introduced into international law by international treaties. But it can not be admissible to make use of such conceptions for the interpretation of law-making treaties, before this adoption has actually taken place.

Here, as elsewhere, much is to be expected from the International Prize Court agreed upon by the Second Hague Peace Conference and from the really permanent court of arbitration which a near future will establish. These courts will have to interpret some of the law-making treaties; they will have to work out rules of interpretation which will find general recognition. The fact that the members of these international courts will be recruited from different nations possessing different systems of law, and that these members will have to work together and will have to agree upon the interpretation of the law in question, will make these courts better fit to solve the problem than the science of international law is.

For the scholars of each nation work at this science possessed of their own bent of mind, and it is therefore not so easy for them to agree upon rules of interpretation as it is for those who do not work theoretically, but have to decide the cases as they arise in practice.

XIX. ERRORS OF JUDGMENT THROUGH POLITICAL AND OTHER BIAS

I have a last sin of method to discuss, which is frequently committed by workers in the field of the science of international law: Errors of judgment created by political, humanitarian, or other bias. Many a controversy which is ventilated at greater or shorter length owes its origin to such errors of judgment. If the positive is the right method of the science of international law, we must endeavor to get rid of bias of all kinds. Let me enumerate some examples to illustrate my proposition.

Some French writers emphatically deny that subjugation is a mode of acquiring territory. Subjugation, they say, is a mere act of force which creates only a condition of fact and not of law; to turn this condition of fact into one of law, there is required the express or tacit consent of the inhabitants of the subjugated territory. Now, I do not deny that this opinion shows humane feeling, and that perhaps the time will come when subjugation as a mode of acquisition of territory will disappear. But to teach that this opinion corresponds to the law as it stands at present is simply a gross error of judgment created by an humanitarian bias.

Again, take the Monroe Doctrine. Whereas American writers assert that the two rules emanating therefrom are recognized rules of international law, European writers assert that these two rules contain violations of international law! It would, however, seem that both assertions alike embody gross errors of judgment created by political bias. I would say to the American writers that, as they recognize the equality of all states before international law, there is no reason why there should be one law for the acquisition of territory and for intervention on the American Continent, and another law for the same acts on the remaining parts of the globe. As far as international law is concerned, European states may acquire territory and exercise intervention as much on the American Continent as anywhere else. On the other hand, I would say to the European writers, that acquisition of territory and the exercise of intervention have, besides their legal quality, a political character. Vital interests may make it necessary and therefore admissible that other powers should intervene in the case of a contemplated acquisition of territory or of a dispute between two other states. The Monroe Doctrine is an expression of the principle that the United States considers it essential that, in the interest of the balance of power and the welfare of the American Continent, European states should not acquire any more territory in America, and that she should intervene in all serious conflicts between a European and an American power. The Monroe Doctrine is therefore not of a legal but of a political character; it is the guiding star of American politics, and there is nothing whatever in it which violates rules of international law.

Or, to give a third example, take the definition of war. There are plenty of writers who consider and therefore define war as the legal remedy of self-help to obtain otherwise impossible satisfaction for a wrong sustained from another state. Thus, they make war a legal institution. But they forget that many wars have been and will be fought for mere political reasons, for which wars the same rules of international law as regards warfare apply as for wars fought in self-help. By nevertheless defining war as they do they simply commit a gross error of judgment created by a political bias. They want to restrict the making of war to cases of wrong for which a state could not otherwise obtain satisfaction, and they confound therefore war in general with such cases of war as they consider from their own standpoint justified. If we look at war as history presents it to us, we must find a definition which fits all wars, whether just or unjust. War is not an institution established by international law as a means of self-help, but a fact of life for the occurrence of which international law provides a body of rules. And as a fact of life, war is not a legal remedy of self-help, but a contention between two states for the purpose of overpowering each other. I do not mean to say that the time will never come when there will be such wars only as are fought for the purpose of getting otherwise impossible satisfaction for a wrong sustained. But this time has certainly not yet arisen, and we must needs meanwhile define war in such a way as fits the facts of life.

I could enumerate many more example of such errors of judgment, but those cited suffice to show the necessity for the science of international law to avoid them. Yet our science will not succeed in this point, unless all authors endeavor to write in a truly international and independent spirit, and unless they make an effort to keep in the background their individual ideas concerning politics, morality, humanity, and justice. We must take the facts of life as they are and the rules of international law as we find them practiced in everyday life. Nothing prevents us from applying the sharp knife of criticism, from distinguishing between what is good and bad according to our individual ideas, and from proposing improvements. But we must not confound the facts of life as they are with what they ought to be, and we must not mix up the rules of international law which are really in force with those rules which we would wish to be in force. There is no better and quicker way to the realization of international ideals than to present the facts of international life and the rules of international law as they really are. For the knowledge of the realities enables the construction of realizable ideals, in contradistinction to hopeless dreams.

XX. WORKERS TO BE IMBUED WITH IDEALISM

This distinction between the realities of life and law on the one hand, and, on the other, the ideals of the individual writer, brings me to the last word I have to say: Our method must certainly be the positive method, but it can successfully be applied only by those workers who are imbued with the idealistic outlook on life and matters. He who believes that the essential characteristic of law is the policeman who protects it is not properly fit to work at the science of international law, nor is he who has not a deep-rooted faith in the progress of the nations towards peace and civilization. International law is at present an unfinished and uncrowned system and building. He who has no faith in the possibility of accomplishing it is not wanted among us. We require men possessed of that idealism which sits down to historical research because it sees the present and the future in the past, and the past in the present and the future, although it does not confound them; which criticises the existing law for the purpose, not of pulling it to pieces, but of preparing its improvement and its codification; which believes in the good instincts of the masses and therefore helps to popularize international law in the hope of thereby improving international relations and working for the cause of peace. The science of international law has a great future to look forward to. Hundreds of hands are wanted to enable a future generation to start codification. And when this task is once achieved, hundreds of hands will again be wanted for the working up of the material supplied by codification.

No one of the present generation of international jurists will live when the codification of international law will be taken in hand. And when codification becomes an actuality, all our present books will lose their value and will go mouldy on the shelves of the libraries through not being read. But our work is nevertheless done for the future, for it must needs help to educate that future generation whose happy lot it will be to take codification in hand. Upon us and our work it depends whether, when the time for codification is ripe, there will be a generation of international jurists which is fit for the great work and which can achieve it for the benefit of mankind. The jingoes and the chauvinists of all nations may laugh at our work, and those narrow-minded people who can not see beyond their limited horizon may belittle our efforts. Ours is the faith that removes mountains, for our cause is that of humanity. The all-powerful force of the good which pushes mankind forward through the depths of history will in time unite all nations under the firm roof of a universally recognized and precisely codified law. And the words of the old prophets may after all in the end become true: "They shall beat their swords into plowshares, and their spears into pruning-hooks; nation shall not lift up sword against nation, neither shall they learn war any more" (Isaiah, ii:4).

L. OPPENHEIM.

[5]

Northwestern University Law Review

Printed in U.S.A.
Vol. 79, Nos. 5 & 6

IS INTERNATIONAL LAW REALLY "LAW"?*

*Anthony D'Amato***

Many serious students of the law react with a sort of indulgence when they encounter the term "international law," as if to say, "well, we know it isn't *really* law, but we know that international lawyers and scholars have a vested professional interest in calling it 'law.'" Or they may agree to talk about international law *as if* it were law, a sort of quasi-law or near-law. But it cannot be true law, they maintain, because it cannot be enforced: how do you enforce a rule of law against an entire nation, especially a superpower such as the United States or the Soviet Union?

I. THE "ENFORCEMENT" ARGUMENT

One intriguing answer to these serious students of the law is to attempt to persuade them that enforcement is not, after all, the hallmark of what is meant, or what should be meant, by the term "law." As Roger Fisher observed, much of what we call "law" in the domestic context is also unenforceable.[1] For example, where the defendant is the United States, such as in a case involving constitutional law, how would the winning private party enforce his or her judgment against the United States? Upon reflection, we see that the United States, whenever it loses a case (and these cases are very frequent—the myriad cases involving income taxes, social security benefits, welfare, and the like), only complies with the court's judgment because it wants to. The winning private party cannot hold a gun to the head of the United States to enforce compliance, even if there were a natural meaning to the term "head of the United States." We can go even further than Professor Fisher did: every criminal law prosecution is a case of an individual pitted against the state (or the "people" of the state). What is to stop the state from saying, "you were acquitted by the jury, but that was a travesty of justice, so we're

** Professor of Law, Northwestern University. A.B., Cornell University (1958); J.D., Harvard University (1961); Ph.D., Columbia University (1968).

1 *See* Fisher, *Bringing Law to Bear on Governments*, 74 HARV. L. REV. 1130 (1961), excerpted in B. WESTON, R. FALK & A. D'AMATO, INTERNATIONAL LAW AND WORLD ORDER 125-30 (1980). Professor Fisher has greatly elaborated on ways of improving governmental compliance with international law, and in the process, by implication, indicated how various enforcement mechanisms work against governments. *See* R. FISHER, IMPROVING COMPLIANCE WITH INTERNATIONAL LAW 39-72, 236-300 (1981).

going to imprison you anyway"? How does the defendant, in handcuffs, stop the state from going ahead? In some countries, at some times, we have heard of dictators or military regimes proceeding with the imprisonment and execution of defendants who were acquitted by their own courts. In terms of power, there is nothing to stop the United States from disregarding adverse judgments of its own courts. In this sense, therefore, a great deal of what we normally call "law" in the United States is unenforceable by private parties arrayed against the state.

It is no objection to this line of reasoning, by the way, to dismiss it as far-fetched. If one objects that the United States, in any event, routinely complies with adverse judgments of its own courts, then the international lawyer can answer that the same is true of rules of international law. As Louis Henkin put it, "almost all nations observe almost all principles of international law and almost all of their obligations almost all of the time."[2]

But a more substantial critique of Professor Fisher's analogy between cases involving the government as a party and international-law cases is that *most* domestic litigation, after all, does *not* involve the government as a party. Most cases involve one citizen against another ("citizen" including artificial persons such as corporations), and as to *those* cases the law is enforced by the full sovereign powers of the state against the losing litigant. This majority of cases, then, tends to define what we mean by "law"; it constitutes the paradigmatic instance of law. Therefore, the argument goes, the minority of cases that do involve the state or the United States as a party are, in a sense, parasitic upon the paradigmatic instance. We tend to regard this latter minority of cases as "law" only because they share certain attributes with the generality of cases. But if we look hard at this minority of cases where the government is a party, we must concede that they are not really "law" because, at bottom, they are unenforceable. They only appear to be law when looked at uncritically. In short, this line of argument *concedes* Professor Fisher's major premiss—that international-law cases are similar to domestic cases where the government is a party—but denies his minor premiss, that such cases are instances of "law." Hence, international law is no more "law" than is constitutional law or even criminal law. As John Austin stated, both constitutional and international law are merely "positive morality."[3]

---

[2] L. HENKIN, HOW NATIONS BEHAVE 47 (2d ed. 1979). This statement in a sense follows tautologically from the fact that there is an international system of legal rules. Clearly, the rules that have evolved over time are the ones that nations have found to be in their collective self-interest; this is simply a Darwinian process applied to customary international law. Professor Henkin's statement, however, while tautological, is not vacuous; after all, nations might have instead evolved into a non-rule anarchical system.

[3] J. AUSTIN, THE PROVINCE OF JURISPRUDENCE DETERMINED 127 (Hart ed. 1954). Austin, however, did not know much about classic international law; he was somewhat taken in by writers who included only treaties as international law. The term "international law" itself was after all

One might object and say that it is frivolous to exclude the vast body of constitutional law and criminal law cases from what we mean by "law." If you say that, then you see the force of Professor Fisher's argument. You are well on your way to accepting the "reality" of international law. But I have presented the skeptical argument against Professor Fisher's view because I want to be rigorous and not have to rely on an argument by analogy, which is ultimately the kind of argument that Professor Fisher has used.

Let us then consider a second line of reasoning against the proposition that enforcement is the hallmark of law. This argument is not associated with any particular writer, because it relies on early conceptions of law and also on the philosophy of law itself. If we consider what law is *not*, we soon realize that it is *not* a rationale for the application of force. It is not a system of "might makes right" in the sense that the state constantly has to compel people, at gunpoint, to behave in a certain way. If you look through a volume of cases, or even a volume of statutes or annotations, you will find that most of the matters therein concern the working-out of private arrangements in a complex society. Most of "law"concerns itself with the interpretation and enforcement of private contracts, the redress of intentional and negligent harms, rules regarding sales of goods and sales of securities, rules relating to the family and the rights of members thereof, and other such rules, norms, and cases. The rules are obeyed not out of fear of the state's power, but because the rules by and large are perceived to be right, just, or appropriate. No state could possibly compel people to obey all these rules at gunpoint; there would not be enough soldiers and policemen to hold the guns (a sort of extreme Orwellian vision of society), they would have to sleep sooner or later, and then anarchy might break out.

Even more fatal to this view of extreme enforcement is that the state would need many rules to channel the behavior of the enforcers themselves. For instance, how would all these police officials and soldiers know what rules they must enforce, and who would make sure that they enforced the rules as written? We would need another phalanx of soldiers to police the enforcers.[4] And on top of that, another layer of officials pointing the guns at the heads of the gun-pointers. The whole process would break down of its own weight. Indeed, Orwell in his novel, *1984*, avoided the question of how to coordinate and control the activities of the officials of the state he described. He simply referred to the state in the abstract as exercising monolithic power over the citi-

invented by Austin's contemporary, Jeremy Bentham, and Bentham was philosophically inimical to unwritten law. *See* J. BENTHAM, AN INTRODUCTION TO THE PRINCIPLES OF MORALS AND LEGISLATION 326 n.1 (2d ed. Oxford 1948) (1st ed. Oxford 1789).

4 The argument is elaborated and extended in A. D'AMATO, JURISPRUDENCE: A DESCRIPTIVE AND NORMATIVE ANALYSIS OF LAW 7-8, 151-53 (1984) [hereinafter cited as A. D'AMATO, JURISPRUDENCE], and in D'Amato, *Legal Uncertainty*, 71 CALIF. L. REV. 1, 39 n.78 (1983).

zenry, finessing the real problem of how to organize such a state so as to control the controllers.

If law is not, by and large, a body of rules that are enforced at gunpoint, what is an individual rule of law? Is it, as the nineteenth century positivists maintained, a command of the state that is backed by the state's enforcement power?[5] To be sure, some "laws" might be just that: a dictator issues a command for his personal indulgence or whim, and if he has sufficiently satisfied his close advisers and the military in other areas, they will probably enforce his command. But most laws will not have this characteristic. Indeed, looking at the matter more microscopically, what is it that *forces* a judge to decide the case before her on the basis of precedent and statutes? Is another judge holding a gun to her head? Does she examine whether the law will be enforced to see whether it is law? How does she know, in advance of her own decision, what will be enforced?

This point came up in the famous case of *Marbury v. Madison*,[6] familiar to generations of American law students but often misinterpreted. In that case, Chief Justice Marshall's "bottom line" was that the Supreme Court had no original jurisdiction to issue writs of mandamus. In short, there was no power to enforce that which the plaintiff demanded. If "law" were coincident with enforceability, then, since under Marshall's reasoning there was not power of enforcement in the Supreme Court because it lacked *jurisdiction*, nothing Marshall said in his opinion would have had any legal significance. To put it another way, lacking a "remedy," the plaintiff would have no "right," not even a right to get a decision from the Court on the question of "right."

But Marshall took an entirely different tack. He *began* with the question: does the plaintiff have a right? He then asked the second question: if the plaintiff has a right, does he have a remedy? And his third question was, if the plaintiff has a remedy, can the relief issue from this Court? By putting the questions in this order, Marshall did the opposite of what the positivists would require. By dealing first with the question of "right," Marshall was able to address that question wholly apart from whether there was a remedy or whether the remedy was available from the Supreme Court. As all law students know, Marshall answered his own question that there was indeed a right, and secondly, there being a right meant that the plaintiff had a remedy. By going through this reasoning, Marshall was able to establish the groundwork for his path-breaking assertion of judicial review of questions of constitutionality. He held that, in the face of a right and remedy, the congressional statute purporting to grant that remedy to the Supreme Court as a matter of original jurisdiction violated the Constitution. Marshall would

[5] *See* A. D'AMATO, JURISPRUDENCE, *supra* note 4, at 118-22 (tracing the command theory of law from Hobbes through Bentham and Austin).

[6] 5 U.S. (1 Cranch) 137 (1803).

not have been able to make his assertion of judicial review if he had begun and ended his opinion with the simple sentence, "we have no jurisdiction; case dismissed." Hence, we see that in a case where by the Court's own admission it lacked jurisdiction and the power of enforcement, nevertheless the Court was able to establish a point of fundamental substantive significance.

Marshall's persuasiveness was dependent upon a consensus at the time he wrote his opinion that there could be such a thing as a "right" without a real remedy. This was part of a larger conviction in those days that the "law" itself was not something that only works when a policeman is standing by ready to enforce it physically. Law indeed is something that is opposed to force. Right is not the same thing as might. In Continental countries, the word for "law" is, as translated, the word "right." In law, there is a fundamental element of right, of justice, dating back to Cicero's and St. Thomas' equation of "right reason" with the natural law (the latter being those reasonable rules that accommodate the peaceful affairs of persons in a society).[7]

Under this argument that we are developing, the relation of force to law, of might to right, is a contingent and not a necessary relation. We can imagine a society under law where there is no force. People obey the laws, and no one disobeys. There is no need, in this idyllic utopia, for enforcement, because there is universal willing compliance. Surely we cannot claim that such a society does not have "law." It is clear that the society is one that is under law, and that the contingent use of force is simply not necessary. To take an example closer to home, suppose that in some state of the Union there has not been a kidnaping since that state entered the Union. Would we say that the law against kidnaping in that state is not a law? Certainly no one would argue that if a law is so successful that it never needs enforcement, it is not a law. Thus, we can conclude from this hypothetical that enforcement is not intrinsic to, is not necessary to, the idea of law.

But you might object that enforcement must potentially be present, even if it is not invoked. In other words, in the state that has no kidnaping, it is nevertheless true that if someone commits this crime—or even contemplates committing it—the potential for enforcement is ever-present. It is this potential for enforcement, after all, that the positivists insist upon when they draw our attention to the necessary connection between a rule of law and its enforcement.

To take care of this objection, we may simply modify our previous

[7] "Natural law" is not something handed down from on high, nor is it the a priori speculations of "right reason." Rather, it may best be described in modern terms as those systemic rules that have survived through evolution over time as best fitting the mutual needs of a society. An example of this approach, though not in those terms, is found in J. Finnis, Natural Law and Natural Rights (1980). For a categorical historical perspective, see D'Amato, *Lon Fuller and Substantive Natural Law*, 26 Am. J. Juris. 202 (1981).

hypothetical of the idyllic utopia. Assume not only that they have never had a need to enforce their laws, but also that they have no enforcement machinery—no police, no jails, no sheriffs, no marshals. They can still have a system of laws, as complex as you please, even without the potential for enforcement.

Yet you might now object that we cannot prove something about the nature of law, an all-too-human institution, by postulating the existence of a utopia where the inhabitants never break the law. Can we modify our utopia to make it seem more realistic? Suppose occasionally someone breaks the law, but is ostracized from society. Suppose one who breaches a contract is considered a moral renegade who should not be entrusted with any further business dealings. These expressions of sharp social disapproval, and occasionally of ostracism, may work to discourage the few people who would disobey the law. They may not always work, but they may be potent enough to deter most of the people (a minority to begin with) who might consider breaking the law. Thus, our not-perfect utopia now consists of a regime where almost all of the laws are obeyed almost all of the time, where occasional disobedience is met with sharp social disapproval, and where occasionally, despite the "mechanism" of social disapproval, occasional violations of the law occur.[8] Is this not, nevertheless, a legal system?

A positivist might happen to object to this concept as follows: the idea of social disapproval, and sometimes social ostracism, is the same thing as a sanction. It constitutes a way of enforcing the law. Hence, by introducing this social-disapproval factor into the utopia, we have simply underscored the original point—that law (except in idyllic utopias which do not exist) depends upon potential enforcement.

But if that is the positivist's position, then the international lawyer should gladly concede the point. For international law recognizes that the social-disapproval factor operates as a sanction. A nation among the community of nations which violates the law, for example, by disregarding a treaty obligation, would certainly be subject to social disapproval by the other nations. In this sense, international law is really "law."

Now it is perhaps the positivist's turn to beat a hasty retreat. The positivist may now want to retract the equation of social disapproval with "sanction," for fear of including international law under the term "law." Instead, the positivist will retreat to the original position that physical or even violent enforcement is necessary to make law "law," and hence international law is not "law." We may, however, suspect that the positivist is reshaping definitions in order to *exclude* the international-law case, rather than to arrive at a general definition of law.[9] Consistent

[8] *See* M. BARKUN, LAW WITHOUT SANCTION (1968); *cf.* Reisman, *Sanctions and Enforcement*, in INTERNATIONAL LAW ESSAYS 381, 383-89 (1981) (group and community norms provide a "civic" sanction, distinguishable from a state-imposed public sanction).

[9] This is analogous to H.L.A. Hart's exclusion of international law from "mature" legal sys-

with this position, the positivist will have to argue that any legal system in which social disapproval functions as the sole sanction (for example, in a peaceful tribal society) does not have "law." "Law" is present only when, in addition to social disapproval, there is physical coercion stemming from the sovereign power of the state. But what if there is no *need* for this physical coercion? The positivist must then conclude that there is no law.

Such a position would be difficult to defend, for if there is a society where people are so law-abiding that they get along only with the social-disapproval sanction, that society manifests a rather good case of "law." It is strange to insist that, for there to be law, physical coercion must also be used even if there is no need for it.

Yet the serious student of law may not be satisfied with the preceding argument in its entirety. We want to ask what happens if the need for physical coercion should arise. In the international system, at least, we have states which occasionally break the rules of international law and which seem not to be deterred by expressions of social disapproval from the other states. This is a reality of international life. Therefore, unlike the tribal society where social disapproval may constitute an effective sanction, international society needs a physical sanction to underscore its legal rules. Otherwise, the rules will occasionally be flouted. Perhaps they will be ignored most often when the "chips are down," which is exactly when they most need to be enforced. How can we call such a system, dependent for its support on so feeble a mechanism as social approval, a "legal" system?

It is hard to discern the logic behind the preceding objection, even while it is easy to understand it. We all recognize, and regret, that rules of international law are flouted on occasion, and we are all too aware of the fact that an outraged world public opinion simply is incapable of discouraging the violation. Should our conclusion then be that the rules of international law are not "law" as we know the term, because as we know the term the "law" involves the concept of physical enforcement? Yet, even in asking this, we acknowledge that physical enforcement is not a *necessary* characteristic of law (our "utopian" examples). And we also acknowledge that, even in domestic cases, where the state is one of the parties, we cannot meaningfully speak of physical enforcement (Professor Fisher's argument). These two arguments destroy most of the logical force of our position that international law is not really law, and yet, we may cling to that position.

Some early writers on the law of nations attempted to meet the enforcement objection head-on, by asserting that rules of international law

tems, because it lacks a "rule of recognition" (Hart's equivalent of the positivist's command-backed-by-sanction). *See* H.L.A. HART, THE CONCEPT OF LAW 208-31 (1961); D'Amato, *The Neo-Positivist Concept of International Law*, 59 AM. J. INT'L L. 321 (1965) (natural-law critique of Hart).

are indeed enforced by the mechanism of war. A nation that violates the rules will be the object of a "just war" initiated precisely to punish the transgressing nation and to enforce the validity of the rules.[10] This argument today sounds like an archaic ploy, for we know enough about wars to have learned that the "transgressing" state may occasionally win if it has the physical power to do so. Physical might bears no necessary connection to international right. Interestingly, the concept of a "just war" has become, if possible, even more archaic under the collective security mechanisms of the League of Nations and its successor the United Nations. These bodies, in principle at least, are designed to stamp out acts of aggression wherever they occur. In other words, they are not set up for the purpose of enforcing international law, but simply for the purpose of enforcing international peace. It follows that if the peace is unjust, it will be enforced anyway. The United Nations seems to call for a "cease fire" in disregard of the merits of the local conflict, and it appears to be less concerned with enforcing international law than with enforcing a prohibition against the use of force no matter what the justification.

Yet there is something in the notion of a "just war" that may help us to fashion a more compelling case for the proposition that international law is really "law" than the other arguments we have examined. I will try to show in Part Three that what I will label as reciprocal-entitlement violation is a mechanism akin to the old "just war" notion that underlies a realistic enforcement mechanism for international law.

At present, we may conclude tentatively as follows:

(1) The fact that some states disobey periodically some rules of international law does not itself mean that those rules are not rules of "law," because even in domestic society some people (e.g., criminals) break the law from time to time.

(2) On the other hand, the fact that most states obey most rules of international law most of the time is not enough to call those rules "legal" because we are especially concerned with "important" cases where states may get away with violating rules of international law. If states can violate rules with impunity when it is in their national interest to do so, how can we call those rules "law"?

(3) We recognize, even though it makes us somewhat uncomfortable, that international law is more properly analogized to domestic cases where the state is a party than to domestic cases where one citizen sues another. Under this conception, we concede that our usual notions of "enforcement" are not appropriately applied to the state. But because we recognize as "law" those domestic cases involving the state as a party, we should also recognize as "law" those international controversies involving states as parties.

---

[10] *See* 2 L. OPPENHEIM, INTERNATIONAL LAW 177-79 (H. Lauterpacht 7th ed. 1952); M. WALZER, JUST AND UNJUST WARS (1977).

(4) We further concede that physical coercion is not a necessary component of "law." However, we are reluctant to conclude that it is totally unnecessary, because we have seen too many cases where a nation violates international law and gets away with it because of the lack of an effective enforcement mechanism.

(5) Hence, we are somewhat, though not totally, persuaded that international law can properly be labelled "law" for most purposes. But we may remain unconvinced, at this point, that it is *really* "law."

II. THE "VERBAL" ARGUMENT

Let us for the moment look at the question whether international law is really law from an entirely different angle. Suppose we were to read all the communications that governments officially make to one another: letters, speeches, proclamations, treaties, agreements, diplomatic initiatives, and so on. Suppose we read these with an eye toward whether the language contained in these communications refers to "law" and is "legal" language. In brief, we would be engaging in a "content analysis" of these communications to see whether what is being asserted and claimed therein can properly be called "legal."[11] We will find that, indeed, much of the content of intergovernmental communications is self-consciously grounded in legal terminology. There should be nothing surprising about this, considering the fact that lawyers typically help draft these documents and speeches. We will find, indeed, that the more important the communication the more likely it is cast in legal terms, and the more likely it is that lawyers have played a role in drafting it.

We might then want to argue that, given the reality of this legal language, it would be rather absurd to maintain that "law" is *not* involved in these intergovernmental communications. If the relevant actors call it "law," who are we to say that they are all wrong? Rather, is it not our job, as observers or scholars, to employ the terms the way the relevant actors intend those terms to be employed? Thus, the very utilization of legal language in intergovernmental communications is an argument for the proposition at least that governments resort to "law" in their attempts to influence each other; or refer to "law" in an attempt to appear to be legal and thus ward off disapproval of other states.

We might want to add to this argument the position taken by the "policy-oriented jurisprudence" of Myres McDougal and his colleagues, including Harold Lasswell, Michael Reisman, Lung-chu Chen, and others.[12] We might collect on a library shelf their voluminous works and

[11] *See* P. STONE, D. DUNPHY, M. SMITH & D. OGILVIE, THE GENERAL INQUIRER (1966); *cf.* D'Amato, *Psychological Constructs in Foreign Policy Prediction*, 11 J. CONFLICT RES. 294 (1967) (content analysis of writings of foreign policy actors to derive predictive "general constructs" of such behavior).

[12] For a good summary statement, with bibliographic references, see McDougal & Reisman,

ask, "what have they written about?" If our answer is not "law," what is it? To be sure, when we take their books down from the shelf and look into them, we begin to get an extraordinarily broad definition of "law." The concept is so broad, indeed, that we wonder if there is anything which they can properly call "non-law." They cite works from the social sciences, from the humanities, as well as works on international law and international politics. Their idea of international law is that it is a process of authoritative decision-making, but then they seem to view "authoritative" so broadly as to encompass just about any decision made by any international decisionmaker.[13] Finally, they disassociate law from enforcement. Legal rules, according to Professor McDougal, "exhaust their effective power when they guide a decision-maker to relevant factors and indicate presumptive weightings."[14]

According to the policy-oriented jurisprudence school, therefore, international law is nothing other than international communication. Under the first argument I made in this Part, the prevalence of legal language in international communication indicates that nations are talking about, and believe they are talking about, "law" in the positions they take vis-a-vis each other. Under the second McDougal-type argument, international communication itself is "law" irrespective of its being couched in legal terms. Taken together, both of these positions may convince the reader that international law is really law.

In the past, I was intrigued by the law-as-communication approach.[15] Recently, I have become uneasy with it, in part because it proves too much. *Any* international contention couched in legal language (or even, following McDougal, not couched in legal language) becomes "law." Yet surely the "law" is not everything. It does not include contradictory positions, although McDougal comes perilously close to this in his notion of the complementarity of customary prescriptions.[16] If international "law" says that nations may or may not attack one another, that the high seas are free to all and closed to all, that genocide is both permissible and prohibited, then I would conclude that there is no international "law" worth talking about on these points. (Someone who disagreed with me would probably say that the "verbal" argument I have

International Law in Policy-Oriented Perspective, in THE STRUCTURE AND PROCESS OF INTERNATIONAL LAW: ESSAYS IN LEGAL PHILOSOPHY DOCTRINE AND THEORY 103 (1983).

13 *See, e.g.*, M. MCDOUGAL, H. LASSWELL & L. CHEN, HUMAN RIGHTS AND WORLD PUBLIC ORDER 161-363 (1980).

14 M. MCDOUGAL, STUDIES IN WORLD PUBLIC ORDER 887 n.109 (1960).

15 *See, e.g.*, D'Amato, *The Relation of Theories of Jurisprudence to International Politics and Law*, 27 WASH. & LEE L. REV. 257 (1970); *cf.* D'Amato, *What "Counts" as Law?*, in LAW-MAKING IN THE GLOBAL COMMUNITY 83 (N. Onuf ed. 1982) (attempting to put the law-as-words approach in perspective).

16 For a critique, with references to Professor McDougal's writings, see A. D'AMATO, THE CONCEPT OF CUSTOM IN INTERNATIONAL LAW 220-26 (1971).

outlined in this Part compels the conclusion that there *is* international law, but that its content is incoherent.)

The other misgiving I have about the verbal argument is that scholars are, after all, not precluded from criticizing the propriety of the use of language by other persons. Even though international communications are couched in legal terms, an observer does not have to conclude that the use of those legal terms is proper. In the insurance business, contracts between insurance companies are called "treaties," even though this is not the use of the term that international lawyers recognize. An international lawyer is not precluded from criticizing the terminology of "treaties" if that criticism throws some light on what insurance companies are really doing. For example, does the use of the term "treaty" imply that rules of international law relating to treaty interpretation should be followed in disputes among insurance companies, instead of domestic contract rules? The answer is no, and thus the term "treaty" can be criticized as misleading. Similarly, we might properly criticize the resort to legal terminology in international communications if we can show that it is not really "law" that is being invoked.

We may therefore conclude this Part by saying, simply, that the prevalance of legal language in international communications *adds* to our previous conclusions that international law is properly called "law" for most purposes and in most contexts. We still, however, reserve final judgment on the question whether it is really "law."

III. The "Reciprocal Entitlements" Argument

I believe that a conclusive argument can be fashioned that international law is really law, by showing that international law is enforceable in the same way that domestic law is enforceable. Of course, I cannot make the claim that international law is always enforced. Rather, what I shall proceed to do is to take a closer look at what we mean by enforcement, and then show that it is applicable equally to the domestic and to the international legal systems.

When we examine the concept of enforcement of law, we find that law can be enforced in many ways. For example, a parent might frown upon a child who does not brush his teeth, or might express stern disapproval. This tends to "enforce" the law, although as we saw in Part I it is not a satisfactory concept when we think of enforcement.[17] For it is too easy for the child, or the nation, to decide to violate the law and pay the mild price of incurring social displeasure.

Thus, we want to narrow the concept of enforcement. Perhaps a good way to begin to narrow it is to exclude all modes of "enforcement" that are extrinsic to the legal system itself. Social disapproval, for instance, is extrinsic to the legal system as is social approval. These are

[17] *See supra* text accompanying notes 3-5.

external mechanisms for enforcing, or more accurately reinforcing, the law, but we know intuitively that they are not provided by or required by the law itself. (If the law *required* them, then you would have the regressive problem of how to force people to socially disapprove of a miscreant's behavior.)

When we look at the legal system itself, we find that it typically provides for deprivations, for disabilities. When a person disobeys the law, the law "punishes" him in some way. The possibility of punishment, in turn, is supposed to deter a rational person from violating the law in the first place.

Enforcement thus consists of some form of legally imposed sanction. A monetary fine is an example of a punishment that is not physical. Physical punishments include being deprived of your freedom, for example by being incarcerated or being forced to perform some kind of community service as part of your "sentence." In the extreme, you may be deprived of your life if convicted of a capital crime.

In this entire spectrum of legally imposed sanctions for violation of the law, we find that the law has removed one or more of your entitlements. I could use the word "rights" here—for example, your rights to life, to liberty, and to property. But the word "entitlements" is more precise, because it denotes legally recognized rights. If you claim a right that the law does not recognize (for example, a woman's claim to the right to vote before the Constitutional amendment of 1920 providing for universal suffrage), you do not have an "entitlement." Since we are talking about enforcement mechanisms intrinsic to the legal system, it is more precise to speak of entitlements than to speak of rights.

In all cases of law violation, the law responds by depriving you of one or more of your entitlements. You have a legal entitlement to liberty; you lose it if you commit a crime punishable by incarceration. You have a legal entitlement to your bank account; you lose it if you have failed to pay your taxes or if someone obtains a judgment against you and attaches it. You have an entitlement to performance under a private contract that you make with someone else; if you fail to perform your part of the bargain, a court may decide that you have forfeited your entitlement under the contract. Some of these entitlement deprivations that you suffer because you have violated the law can be effectuated against you without any need for physical enforcement. Your bank account can be taken away from you by a bookkeeping entry made in the bank pursuant to a court order. Your marriage can be legally dissolved by a court decree without your willing compliance or participation. Thus, when we think of legal enforcement, we need not imagine the use of physical force against the person of the law-violator, although, of course, in some cases physical force is appropriate. The deprivation of either your entitlement to liberty, or your entitlement to life, may result from your conviction of a major crime.

Furthermore, there would be no possibility of enforcement by entitlement deprivation if people were not assigned some entitlements in the first place. If you had no entitlements, you would obviously suffer no loss if the law deprived you of some of them. (There is no "law" in the "jungle.") However, we find in all legal systems without exception the legal recognition of certain rights of the people, which we call entitlements. At a minimum, there is recognition of life and liberty. With a set of entitlements, therefore, each person is vulnerable to removal of some of them by the law. Legal systems typically enforce their own rules by removing one or more entitlements of persons who violate the rules.

If the account I have just given of the function of entitlements in the enforcement of law is persuasive, and if it fully captures the more diffuse notion of enforcement, then we next can turn to the international legal system to see how the process of entitlements and entitlement-deprivations works to provide for the enforcement of legal rules.

Let us imagine a primitive international situation. Two nations are at war with each other, but are weary of it and are interested in the possibility of peace. The problem now is how to send a peace ambassador from one nation to the other. The war between them is so total and brutal that no one wants to be an emissary for fear of being killed by the other side. We assume that this is the first "case" of resolving the conflict between the two nations so there are no prescribed methods of establishing peace.

Perhaps nation *A* could dispatch a particularly brave person who would carry a letter saying, "don't kill the bearer of this letter, as we are attempting to set up communications with you, and we promise to give safe conduct to any person you choose to send to us who has a letter from you. Moreover, as evidence of our good faith, you can hold the bearer of this letter hostage while your emissary is en route to us." Such a letter, of course, would not guarantee that its bearer would be safe. All we know is that, in some instances, letters such as this one actually worked.[18] We don't know much about those instances where the letter was ineffective and its bearer was killed. But in those cases where the letter worked, a primitive entitlement—a limited ambassadorial immunity—between the two nations was set up.

This single entitlement, however, is precarious, for the only remedy for entitlement violation by one nation is that of a reciprocal violation by the other nation of the same entitlement. Thus, suppose nation *A* is furious with the peace terms brought by nation *B*'s emissary, and responds by killing the emissary. In effect, nation *A* has opted to resume total war. Nation *B*, it is true, can retaliate by killing the emissary it is holding, but nation *A* presumably had already taken this possibility into account and

[18] *Cf.* G. SCHWARZENBERGER, THE INDUCTIVE APPROACH TO INTERNATIONAL LAW 75-78 (1965).

decided to "sacrifice" its own emissary. The two nations have thus destroyed the only entitlement that existed between them. They revert to a lawless state of war, from which extrication will now be harder given the unfortunate experience with the emissaries. Clearly the entitlement of diplomatic immunity would have had a better chance to survive had there been a second and different entitlement between the two nations. Then a threat by one nation to destroy the diplomatic immunity could be countered by a threat to destroy the other unrelated entitlement.

Thus, stability has a better chance the more entitlements there are. It is not the purpose of this essay to discuss historically how entitlements arose among nations, or how they became more complex and differentiated. Yet we might briefly consider the perspective of a new nation (perhaps a nation that has just received its independence from a colonial power).

Our new nation receives at its birth a host of entitlements. It has not chosen nor selected any of these entitlements; instead they are, so to speak, thrust upon the new nation. The first entitlement is of fundamental importance: the entitlement of statehood, which means, in the international system, that our new nation is a geographic entity entitled to exert its own legal jurisdiction in the area within its boundaries and to claim the inviolability of those boundaries against all other states. The legal sanctity of its borders signifies that our new state is a state in a community of states, and not merely a gang of thieves subject to the untrammelled degradations of other neighboring gangs. Indeed, it appears that the very definition of a state, or nation, involves an entitlement to the sanctity of its borders. Without such boundaries, the entity is hardly a "state." Yet, the boundaries are boundaries only by virtue of their recognition by all the other states in the system.

In sum, still considering this first entitlement, our new nation depends for its very identity upon the recognition of other similar states in the community of states. I am not talking about de jure recognition; rather, all that is necessary is a sense in the international community that the new state is enclosed by international boundaries, and those boundaries, like all boundaries, are lines that differentiate the internal affairs of the state from the external affairs and cannot be crossed at will by military forces in either direction. This notion of a boundary is so fundamental that the Vienna Convention on the Law of Treaties specifically excepts boundary-establishing treaties from the normal rules of *rebus sic stantibus*,[19] and the World Court in its leading decision in the *Continental Shelf Cases* made it clear that the normal generation of customary international law cannot affect ownership of territory (in those cases, the submerged land areas) absent a showing of consent from the owner.[20]

19 Vienna Convention on the Law of Treaties, art. 62, *adopted* May 12, 1969, 8 I.L.M. 679, 702 (1969).

20 North Sea Continental Shelf (W. Ger. v. Den., W. Ger. v. Neth.), 1969 I.C.J. 3. This case has

Our new state might, therefore, look upon the international law of the sanctity of its boundaries as a gift of a valuable entitlement. But the entitlement carries with it reciprocal duties, so that it is not necessarily a gift. The entitlement provides that our new nation must respect the borders of all the other states. Suppose our new nation is very powerful militarily, and expansionist-minded; it might want to extend its boundaries at the expense of its neighboring states. In that case, the entitlement of sanctity of boundaries is, in the first instance, more of a curse than a gift. (Later on, if the new state has succeeded militarily in extending its dominion, it might then want to establish the principle of sanctity of international boundaries, so as to secure its own gains.) Obviously, we cannot know, a priori, whether a new state likes or dislikes any particular entitlement. And that is indeed the point: the new entitlements that accrue to the new state at its birth are those that the international system has imposed upon the new state. If pressed to make a judgment whether the host of entitlements as a whole are a blessing or a curse to the new nation, we would conclude that, on the whole, the system of entitlements is beneficial to the new nation. This conclusion follows from the simple observation that international entitlements did not descend from God, but rather they evolved slowly over time to serve the collective self-interest of all the states. It is unlikely, therefore, that a system of rules that serves the collective self-interest would be inimical to the individual interests of any given state. Nevertheless, it is possible that *some* of the entitlements would be contrary to the interest of our new nation. If so, there is nothing our new nation can do about it. The list of entitlements is a given; they are thrust upon our new nation without its initial consent.

At least, there is no provable manifestation of initial consent by the new nation's. But there is an inferred consent which stems from our new nation taking its position among the community of nations. By asserting the inviolability of its borders from external attack, our new nation defines itself as a state that has internationally recognized boundaries. Indeed, it is hard to think of what our new nation would be if it did not have those boundaries, and therefore the inference of its consent to statehood is very powerful. Our new nation also has the entitlement to send ambassadors to other states who want to receive them; and even before the first treaty is concluded giving those ambassadors diplomatic protection, there is an international entitlement that they have initial diplomatic immunity to proceed to other countries to negotiate such treaties. Moreover, our new nation is the beneficiary of the whole set of entitlements regarding its capacity to enter into binding treaties with other nations, and to have those treaties construed and applied according to the customary international law regarding the interpretation of treaties. Ad-

been widely misinterpreted, and thus the statement in the text has been supported by an extensive argument given elsewhere. *See* D'Amato, *The Concept of Human Rights in International Law*, 82 COLUM. L. REV. 1110, 1142-44 (1982).

ditionally, our new nation, at birth, benefits from the entitlement that all nations are free to use the high seas, to send satellites into outer space, to claim for themselves a territorial sea, an underlying continental shelf, and an exclusive economic zone. It may be that our new nation does not border upon any ocean, or if it does so border, that there is no underlying continental shelf. All the international entitlements say is that if a nation does border on an ocean it is entitled to claim an exclusive territorial sea, and if it has a continental shelf it is entitled to claim certain exclusivities with regard thereto. The full list of entitlements embraces areas such as the entitlement to protect nationals abroad, the protection of the laws of war and rules regulating the conduct of hostilities, rules regarding the exertion of extraterritorial jurisdiction, and among other topics the following: international servitudes, succession of states, international rivers, lakes, canals and straits, polar regions, rights and duties of states in outer space, nationality and status of ships, piracy, slavery, international traffic in narcotics, nationality and statelessness, rights of aliens, asylum, extradition, international communications including satellites and "jamming" of broadcasts, immunities of states and their agencies and subdivisions, protection of human rights, diplomatic and consular privileges and immunities, status and privileges of international organizations, status of armed forces on foreign territory, limits of criminal jurisdiction, enforcement of foreign judgments and commercial arbitrations, treaties (entry into force, modification, termination), pacific blockade, reprisals, arms shipments, relations between belligerants and neutrals, etc. The point of making such a list is that for our new nation, all the specific entitlements in these subject-matter categories work two ways: first, to benefit our new nation to the extent that it has any interest in claiming any specific entitlement; and second, to impose upon our new nation the duty to respect those same entitlements when they are asserted against it by other nations.

Taken as a whole, these entitlements define what it is to be a "nation" or "state" in the modern world.[21] To be sure, these are the legal definitional parameters of a nation, but a nation is admittedly a legal fiction. As a construct of international law, a nation is nothing more nor less than a bundle of entitlements, of which the most important ones define and secure its boundaries on a map, while others define its jurisdictional competency and the rights of its citizens when they travel outside its borders.

Some writers have tried to base all these competences on the "consent" of the nation.[22] They are thus compelled by their own logic to

[21] *See* D'Amato, *supra* note 20, at 1113-15.

[22] *See, e.g.*, G. Tunkin, Theory of International Law 123-33 (1974); G. Van Hoof, Rethinking the Sources of International Law 76-82 (1983). For a critique of "consent" theories, see A. D'Amato, *supra* note 16, at 187-99. Even the writers who insist upon consent will accept *tacit* consent; yet it is a short move from tacit consent to inferred consent to legally inferred

assert that a new nation is not bound by any particular rule of international law until it has consented to that rule.[23] The new nation is then in a preferred position; it can pick and choose among the rules those that it likes. This pick-and-choose position is clearly wrong as a matter of historical fact as well as logic. Historically, existing nations have never allowed new nations to pick and choose, nor have new nations asserted a *tabula rasa* position.[24] Logically, if a new nation tried to assert such a position, the reaction of the other nations might well be that the new nation's *rights* as well as its duties are up for grabs, thus placing the new nation in a perilous position vis-a-vis its boundaries and other basic legal entitlements. Perhaps some such calculus has operated to dissuade any new nation from making the claim that these writers assert.

"Consent" is an elusive notion for yet another reason. If international law is truly grounded in each nation's consent, then what is to stop a nation from withdrawing its consent at any time? Specifically, when a nation finds a particular rule of international law disadvantageous to it, it could simply withdraw consent—even up to the very moment of application of the unwanted rule. The result would be to wipe out the notion of "law." Of course, some writers, focusing on consent, claim that international law is illusory anyway.[25] That claim begs the question, for if international law is real, as I have been arguing, then "consent" does not explain its application to states. What the writers are trying to say is that consent is such a powerful explanatory mechanism that international law as a result is not real. This puts a theoretically false cart before the horse.

If one wants to insist upon finding a role for the concept of consent, it may be useful to view consent in the following way: A nation is a bundle of entitlements which define what the nation is. In choosing to exist as a nation, the nation has consented to the bundle of entitlements. However, this scholastic exercise in logic, the sort that Pascal liked to satirize, is only necessary if someone is actively worried about the concept of consent and its role in international law. The simple conclusion

---

consent, *i.e.*, that given all the other elements that constitute a norm of international law, consent ultimately is inferred. To the extent that writers espouse consent out of a notion of the sovereignty of national *will* (an insistence based on positivist theory), none of them has ever answered the following question: what happens if a state, having given its consent to a rule, wants to change its mind? Such a change of mind would appear logically to be precluded by consent theory (at least, if that theory purports to explain how nations become obligated), and yet would seem to be required by the predominance of the will.

23 *See, e.g.*, VAN HOOF, *supra* note 22, at 78. *Accord* E. ZOLLER, PEACETIME UNILATERAL REMEDIES: AN ANALYSIS OF COUNTERMEASURES 6 (1984).

24 A. D'AMATO, *supra* note 16, at 191-92.

25 *See, e.g.*, Watson, *Legal Theory, Efficacy and Validity in the Development of Human Rights Norms in International Law*, 1979 U. ILL. L.F. 609, 632-35; *cf.* Tieya, *The Third World and International Law*, in THE STRUCTURE AND PROCESS OF INTERNATIONAL LAW, *supra* note 12, at 955 (recognizing continued validity of international law, but noting chances due to emergence of Third World interests).

follows that a nation is coextensive with its international legal entitlements.

This conclusion in turn illustrates why, as a matter of its very identity, a state should act in such a manner as to preserve its entitlements. Yet, its identity as a state, its "bundle of entitlements," is dependent upon the acquiescence of all the other states in the system. Since every state has the same bundle of entitlements—otherwise there would be legal inequality among states, a proposition that has never seriously been advocated—the other states in the system have an obvious interest in acquiescing in the entitlements of any given state. In this manner, a new state starts out, as we have seen, with its full complement of entitlements.

But just as all the states in the international legal system have a collective interest in acquiescing to all the entitlements for any given state in the system, they also have an interest in preserving the entitlements per se. For ease of illustration, let us consider the previously mentioned entitlement of diplomatic immunity. All the states in the system have an interest in the preservation of this particular entitlement. The existence of this entitlement, like other entitlements, helps define what a state is and what the international legal system is. The system would be something different, perhaps diminished, if the entitlement of diplomatic immunity were undermined.

To preserve this entitlement, the states in the system collectively will allow certain actions to be taken against any given state which violates the entitlement of diplomatic immunity. Prior to 1979, it would have been difficult to come up with a single example of a state which directly violated that entitlement. In nearly every case up to 1979 in which a diplomat's life or liberty was threatened, the host state immediately took action against those persons who threatened the diplomat. If the host state itself wanted to expel the diplomat, it would arrange for the diplomat's return. But in 1979, after some radical students occupied the American Embassy in Tehran, the government of Iran took the unprecedented step of ratifying the action and holding the American diplomatic personnel hostage. This was a case of a deliberate violation of international law, the violation of the entitlement of diplomatic immunity. To allow it to go unremedied would constitute a threat to the existence of that entitlement in the international legal system.

What legal recourse did states have to prevent the erosion of such an entitlement? An obvious move would be to allow the United States to violate Iran's similar entitlement by arresting diplomatic and consular officials of Iran who were physically present in the United States at the time of the takeover of the American embassy in Iran. While this tit-for-tat strategy is generally regarded as legal under international law, it is not always a particularly effective strategy.[26] As we saw previously in

[26] For a recent, provocative explication of the tit-for-tat strategy, see R. AXELROD, THE EVOLU-

the idealized example of two states at total war, the tit-for-tat strategy would simply eliminate the incipient ambassadorial-immunity entitlement and plunge the states back into the chaos of total war. Today, under a more developed international legal system, the tit-for-tat strategy might not have as negative an outcome, but it nevertheless could operate to erode rather than to preserve the entitlement in question. For instance, if the United States had jailed all Iranian diplomatic and consular officials, such an action at least in theory could be interpreted not as an attempt to punish Iran for its initial act but rather as a recognition that Iran's act was correct and that in fact diplomats are not entitled to immunity—I say "in theory" because this example may appear to be far-fetched. But since the content of international law depends upon the recognition of what the entitlements are by all the states in the system, the action I have just hypothesized by the United States and Iran might well be interepreted as a new understanding of the entitlement of diplomatic immunity, i.e., that such immunity exists no longer. Consider the following more realistic example of the same theoretical process: nation *A* announces a territorial sea of 300 miles from its coastline; nation *B* argues that *A* has illegally infringed upon the high seas by attempting to expropriate part of it, and in retaliation, nation *B* proclaims its own 300-mile territorial sea. Despite what nation *B* said, the action it took tends to reinforce *A*'s claim. Thus, rather than challenging *A*'s claim to a 300-mile territorial sea, *B* has reinforced it. A new rule, giving coastal states a much larger area of jurisdiction over the high seas will evolve. And the old entitlement—that the high seas were open to all nations—will partly be eroded by these new claims for an extensive territorial sea. Thus, the tit-for-tat strategy, in this example, not only fails to deter the original entitlement violation but in fact reinforces it.

The United States, in fact, did not retaliate by jailing Iranian consular and diplomatic officials, although that action was considered and reported in the press.[27] Instead, the United States took steps that were also justified under international law and which constitute a more sophisti-

TION OF COOPERATION (1984). *See also* A. RAPOPORT, STRATEGY AND CONSCIENCE 48-57 (1964); A. RAPOPORT, FIGHTS, GAMES, AND DEBATES 166-79 (1960). The most complete analysis of the legality of countermeasures under international law is E. ZOLLER, *supra* note 23. However, it is not clear whether Professor Zoller confines her conclusions to countermeasures which do not violate an independent norm of international law (i.e., those which may simply violate a state's treaty commitments or other such obligations owing to a particular state). In the *Case Concerning the Air Service Agreement (U.S. v. France)*, appended to Professor Zoller's book, the Arbitral tribunal concludes:

> Under the rules of present-day international law, and unless the contrary results from special obligations arising under particular treaties, notably from mechanisms created within the framework of international organisations, each State establishes for itself its legal situation vis-a-vis other States. If a situation arises which, in one State's view, results in the violation of an international obligation by another State, the first State is entitled, within the limits set by the general rules of international law pertaining to the use of armed force, to affirm its rights through counter-measures.

Id. at 166-67.

27 *See* N.Y. Times, Dec. 13, 1979, at § A1, col. 5.

cated (though, as we shall see, perhaps more dangerous) method of enforcement. The United States "froze" approximately thirteen billion dollars of Iranian deposits in American banks and in various European banks where the United States, through American corporations, had the power to act.[28] If it were not for the initial Iranian act of holding the American diplomats hostage, the United States would be unjustified under inter-national law in violating the Iranian entitlement to the use of its own bank deposits abroad. Indeed, by freezing the Iranian assets, the United States was effectively confiscating the interest those assets would have earned.[29] This was a direct deprivation of Iranian property by the United States. Yet there was no condemnation of the American action by the international community; instead, the American action in violating a different Iranian entitlement from the one that Iran violated in the first place (diplomatic immunity) was tolerated by general silence, whereas governments from all over the world expressly condemned Iran's seizure of the American embassy. The workings of international law are rarely as explicit as scholars might like them to be, but I believe we are entitled to infer from the reaction of the community of nations that they did not perceive a threat to the shared entitlement of keeping state-owned deposits in foreign banks as a result of the American action, but rather regarded the U.S. action as a temporary infringement of an Iranian entitlement for the limited purpose of enforcing the original entitlement of diplomatic immunity.[30] Thus, the international community implicitly accepted the legality of a strategy that violates an offending nation's entitlements in order to repudiate that nation's initial offence. In the Iran-United States case, the strategy worked well, for the American diplomatic personnel were all safely returned to the United States, and the United States lifted the freeze on Iranian assets.

Of course, I am not attempting here to support my theory of a reciprocal-violation-of-a-different-entitlement by the single case of the American hostages in Tehran. The pattern is a general one and can be substantiated by numerous examples.[31] Moreover, the tit-for-a-different-tat pattern "makes sense" in a legal system that does not have a central court of compulsory jurisdiction, a world legislature, and a world police

---

28 *See* Nickel, *Battling for Iran's Frozen Billions*, FORTUNE, Dec. 15, 1980, at 117.

29 At the time the $13 billion was blocked, interest rates were approximately 15%. The assets were blocked for slightly over one year. At compound interest, this amounts to interest earned, and unpaid, of over two billion dollars. When the hostages were returned to the United States, the United States agreed to pay, in partial settlement, interest of $800 million to Iran, as reported in the New York Times. *See* N.Y. Times, Jan. 21, 1981, at § A9, col. 1.

30 Two judges out of the fifteen on the World Court felt that the blocking of Iranian assets should be set off against any reparations owing to the United States, but all fifteen members of the Court agreed that Iran's initial detention of the American diplomatic and consular personnel was unlawful. *See* United States Diplomatic and Consular Staff in Tehran (U.S. v. Iran), 1980 I.C.J. 3, 51 (Morozov, J., dissenting); *id.* at 58 (Tarazi, J., dissenting).

31 *See generally* E. ZOLLER, *supra* note 23.

force.[32] The absence of these institutions does not mean that international law isn't really law; rather, it simply means that international law is enforced in a different way.

There is a danger in relying on the enforcement of international law by allowing a retaliatory deprivation of the offending nation's entitlement. The danger is the potential escalation of entitlement violations, ultimately leading to international anarchy. In the idealized case where there was only one entitlement, its destruction put the nations back into anarchy. The same result is possible if in the modern world there is runaway destruction of many entitlements. But the fact that law can become ineffective doesn't mean that it isn't law in the first place. Some people expressed fear when President Richard Nixon faced impeachment that he might order the military to seize Congress and the Supreme Court and proclaim himself immune from any attempt to dislodge him as President. While this may not have been a very realistic fear, if such a scenario had occurred, it would mean that constitutional law had deteriorated; but it would not mean that no constitutional law existed prior to Nixon's seizure of the reins of government. Similarly, while international law could destroy itself through a runaway series of violations of entitlements, until then it polices itself by the meta-rule I have described: That it is legal to deter the violation of an entitlement by threatening a counter-violation of the same or a different entitlement. This latter enforcement action is the "physical sanction" provided by the international legal system, just as the rules regulating police, prison officials, sheriffs, etc., are its domestic legal equivalents.

IV. CONCLUSION

International law is enforced by the process I have described as re-

32 The employment of a different countermeasure raises the question of proportionality of response. International law has not evolved a specific measure of proportionality, but it is at least clear that the countermeasure cannot be wholly disproportionate to the initial delict. The *Air Service Case*, in E. ZOLLER, *supra* note 23, at 167, calls attention to the possibility of a wholly different countermeasure, and states that it should be measured in terms of quality as well as quantity in order to judge proportionality. Interestingly, the social science literature bears out the effectiveness of quantitatively non-measurable responses so long as there is an ordinal ordering of preferences. As Axelrod demonstrates, *supra* note 26, at 17-18, the payoffs of the two players need not be comparable, nor symmetric, nor measurable on an absolute scale, and there is no need to assume rationality on the part of the players. The only ordering of preferences is that a nation prefers there to be no rule violation, and prefers taking a countermeasure in the event of a rule violation rather than letting the violator get away with a rule violation. In turn, taking countermeasures, in an iterated series (which for international purposes can extend over the centuries) is a stable and robust strategy for deterring the initial delict. Nations in their interactions seem to have evolved a tit-for-tat or a tit-for-a-different-tat strategy in their numerous interactions over the centuries, and this probably accounts for the stability of international legal rules. The tit-for-a-different-tat strategy is actually codified in the Vienna Convention on the Law of Treaties, art. 60, *supra* note 19, at 701, allowing a party to suspend *any* treaty obligation or obligations if the other party commits a material breach of any of its obligations.

ciprocal-entitlement violation. The violation may be of the same entitlement or, more likely now days, of a different entitlement. But it is on the whole an effective process—as effective for the international legal system as is the enforcement of most laws in domestic systems via the state-sanctioned deprivation of one or more entitlements held by individual citizens or corporations. Occasionally people or states will break laws despite the presence of enforcement machinery, but that does not mean that there were no laws to begin with. Nor, as I have tried to argue, should we swing to the opposite side of the spectrum and say that enforcement has nothing to do with whether laws exist. We don't need to take such an extreme position with respect to international law because there is, in fact, enforcement, resulting in a stable system of international entitlements. It is impossible to understand why nations do or refrain from doing the things they do without understanding what entitlements are included in the bundle and how nations act to preserve their full complement of existing entitlements. In this sense, international law is a very realistic component of the picture that political scientists try to draw of how nations behave. The "serious students of law" who claim that international law isn't really "law" make the same mistake that some political scientists make in ignoring norms in order to be "scientific" in their "descriptions." A state cannot be described without reference to its entitlements, nor can its actions be fully understood without reference to the steps it takes to preserve those entitlements.

[6]

POSITIVISM, FUNCTIONALISM, AND INTERNATIONAL LAW

By Hans J. Morgenthau

Assistant Professor of Law and Political Science, University of Kansas City

If an event in the physical world contradicts all scientific forecasts, and thus challenges the assumptions on which the forecasts have been based, it is the natural reaction of scientific inquiry to reëxamine the foundations of the specific science and attempt to reconcile scientific findings and empirical facts. The social sciences do not react in the same way. They have an inveterate tendency to stick to their assumptions and to suffer constant defeat from experience rather than to change their assumptions in the light of contradicting facts.[1] This resistance to change is uppermost in the history of international law. All the schemes and devices by which great humanitarians and shrewd politicians endeavored to reorganize the relations between states on the basis of law, have not stood the trial of history. Instead of asking whether the devices were adequate to the problems which they were supposed to solve, it was the general attitude of the internationalists to take the appropriateness of the devices for granted and to blame the facts for the failure.[2] When the facts behave otherwise than we have predicted, they seem to say, too bad for the facts. Not unlike the sorcerers of primitive ages, they attempt to exorcise social evils by the indefatigable repetition of magic formulae. As the League of Nations was a failure, let us have another League. As the first and second Peace Conferences of the Hague did not succeed, let us have a third one. As arbitration never settled a political conflict which otherwise would have led to war, let us have more arbitration for the prevention of war. As the Disarmament Conference was a senseless waste of intellect and time, why not convoke another Disarmament Conference?

It is a strange paradox that the lay public has observed a much more sceptical and realistic, therefore scientific, attitude toward international law than the science of international law itself. The laymen were much quicker to recognize the gap between the rules of international law as represented by science, and the rules of international law as they exist in actual experience. The breakdown of the main bulk of post-World War international law has altogether destroyed public confidence in a science which, unmoved by what

[1] As to this tendency, see Lancelot Hogben, The Retreat from Reason (Conway Memorial Lecture, London, 1936); Lynd, Knowledge for What? (Princeton, 1939).

[2] See Wild, "What Is the Trouble with International Law?" Am. Pol. Sci. Rev., Vol. XXXII (1938), p. 479: "Too often in the past he has assumed the attitude that the world is out of step with his law, and too seldom has he considered the point that perhaps his science is partly to blame."

experience may show, invariably follows its preconceived pattern.[3] This breakdown implies the practical refutation of the ideas which have determined the development of international law in the last half-century. Hence, the science of international law is now confronted with the alternative of maintaining the traditional pattern of assumptions, concepts and devices in spite of the teachings of history, or of revising this pattern and trying to reconcile the science of international law and its subject-matter, that is, the rules of international law as they are actually applied.[4] The present writer has always held that only the latter way leads to theoretically correct and practically useful results. In the following paper the attempt will be made to reexamine the methodological assumptions with which the traditional science of international law starts. These assumptions are embodied in the positivist doctrine of law.

THE LEGAL PHILOSOPHY OF POSITIVISM

Positivist philosophy restricts the object of scientific knowledge to matters that can be verified by observation, and thus excludes from its domain all matters of an *a priori*, metaphysical nature.[5] Juridic positivism transfers this delimitation into the legal sphere. The juridic positivist delimits the subject-matter of his research in a dual way. On the one hand, he proposes to deal exclusively with matters legal, and for this purpose strictly separates the legal sphere from ethics and *mores* as well as psychology and sociology. Hence, his legalism. On the other hand, he restricts his attention within the legal sphere to the legal rules enacted by the state, and excludes all law whose existence cannot be traced to the statute books or the decisions of the courts. Hence, his *étatist* monism. This "positive" law the positivist accepts as it is, without passing judgment upon its ethical value or questioning its practical appropriateness. Hence, his agnosticism. The positivist

[3] Professor Quincy Wright could report in 1930 (Research in International Law since the War, p. 25): "Of the twenty jurists with whom the writer has corresponded, only two betrayed a note of pessimism at the prospects, and that in both cases was qualified."

[4] Such reëxamination is called for by many writers; see, for instance, Philip Marshall Brown, this JOURNAL, Vol. 33 (1939), p. 149; Djuvara, *Recueil des Cours de l'Académie de Droit International* (cited hereafter as Hague *Recueil*), Vol. 64 (1938), p. 485; Hudson, Proceedings of the 2nd, 3rd, and 5th Conferences of Teachers of International Law (Washington, 1925, 1928, 1933), pp. 86 *et seq.*, 72, 94, 95, respectively; MacKenzie, Proceedings of the 6th Conference of Teachers of International Law (Washington, 1938), p. 109; Friedman, "The Disintegration of European Civilization and the Future of International Law," Modern Law Review, Vol. 2 (1938), p. 213.

[5] For the characteristics of positivist philosophy, see Comte, *Discours sur l'esprit positif* (Paris, 1844), p. 41 *et seq.;* Mill, Auguste Comte and Positivism (London, 1866), p. 6 *et seq.;* see especially, the excellent article, "Positivism," by Ruggiero in Encyclopedia of the Social Sciences, Vol. 12, p. 260.

The most penetrating contemporaneous criticism of positivist science is to be found in Mortimer J. Adler, What Man Has Made of Man (New York, 1937), especially pp. 28, 87, 97, 131, 132, 158 *et seq.*, 192, 233, 238 *et seq.*

cherishes the belief that the "positive" law is a logically coherent system which virtually contains, and through a mere process of logical deduction will actually produce, all rules necessary for the decision of all possible cases. Hence, his system worship and dogmatic conceptualism.[6]

The historic importance of the positivist school of jurisprudence for the science of law was fourfold. First, positivism accepted the breakdown of the great metaphysical systems of the eighteenth and the early nineteenth centuries and the resulting decadence of metaphysical jurisprudence as an established fact. It endeavored to save the scientific character of jurisprudence by eliminating from it all metaphysical elements, thus separating it from the discredited doctrines of natural law. In the second place, positivism recognized that the subject-matter of jurisprudence was the law and nothing but the law, and that neither non-legal subjects nor non-legal considerations could have any place in it. Furthermore, legal positivism learned from the positivist movement in philosophy and the natural sciences that scientific objectivity is dependent upon an object intelligible in experience, and a method aimed at knowledge, not at evaluation. Finally, the great legal codifications of the European continental countries and the Anglo-American statutory law found in positivism a technique of interpretation and representation. This technique fulfilled its purpose satisfactorily as long as the social and political philosophy of the statutes, either directly expressed by them or indirectly derived from them by way of logical deduction, was sufficient to meet the economic and social needs as well as the political demands and ethical requirements of a given society at a given historical moment.

To be sure, this correspondence between the statutes and the standards of society has never existed completely; even under stationary conditions there will always be a marginal sphere which does not allow the mere logical subsumption of a given case under statutory law without violating the standards of society. In order to satisfy the positivist assumptions of the logical completeness of the legal order and at the same time meet the standards of society, these standards were first to be read into the statutes from

[6] For the characteristics of juridic positivism, see Finch, Hague *Recueil*, Vol. 53 (1935), p. 557, and The Sources of Modern International Law (Washington, 1937), p. 20; Oppenheim, "The Science of International Law: Its Task and Methods," this JOURNAL, Vol. 2 (1908), p. 333 *et seq.;* Bergbohm, *Staatsvertraege und Gesetze als Quellen des Voelkerrechts* (Dorpat, 1876), p. 40 *et seq.;* and *Jurisprudenz und Voelkerrecht* (Leipzig, 1892), pp. 51, 52; Kelsen, *Die philosophischen Grundlagen der Naturrechtslehre und des Rechtspositivismus* (Berlin, 1928); Pound, "Mechanical Jurisprudence," Columbia Law Rev., Vol. 8 (1908), p. 605; Morris Cohen, "The Concepts of Juridical and Scientific Law," *Politica*, Vol. 4 (1939), p. 8 *et seq.;* Ripert, "*Droit naturel et positivisme juridique*," *Annales de la Faculté de Droit d'Aix*, nouvelle série, No. 1 (Marseilles, 1918), pp. 19, 20, 32 *et seq.;* Anzilotti, *Cours de Droit International*, Vol. 1 (Paris, 1929), p. 18 *et seq.;* Waline, "*Positivisme philosophique, juridique et sociologique*," *Mélanges Carré de Malberg* (Paris, 1936), p. 519; Gény, *Science et Technique en Droit privé positif* (Paris, 1915), Vol. 2, pp. 15 *et seq.*, 31, 37, 38. A good survey is to be found in Erim, *Le Positivisme juridique et le Droit International* (Paris, 1939).

which they then appeared to have been derived by a mere logical process. Through the back door of pseudo-logical interpretation the outlawed company of natural law and extra-legal value judgments reëntered the legal system. This kind of pseudo-logical legerdemain became the predominating interpretative technique of legal positivism in the period of its decadence. In the last decades of the nineteenth century the standards of society went far away from the economic, social, political, and ethical assumptions from which the systems of statutory law had started.[7] Hence, the positivists were compelled to resort to a series of pseudo-logical makeshifts in order to maintain the fiction of "legal self-sufficiency,"[8] on which positivist jurisprudence had founded its theoretical system.

From three sides this fiction was, and still is, under attack. From the one side, sociological and realist jurisprudence, inspired partly and indirectly by the original sociological positivism of Comte, does away with the artificial barriers by which positivism has separated the legal sphere from the whole domain of the social sciences to which it actually belongs. Thus it destroys the positivist assumptions together with the positivist conclusions. From the other side, the neo-positivism of Kelsen's pure theory of law maintains the basic assumptions of positivism but undertakes to achieve the positivist ends by purifying the legal science from all material, non-legal elements, thus eliminating the subject-matter of positivist crypto-metaphysics.

Several schools of revived natural law, as well as the politico-ideological power of totalitarianism, have joined in this dual scientific attack. Totalitarianism has ostracized positivist jurisprudence as a manifestation of liberalistic decadence in Germany and Italy, where the domination of juridic thought by positivism has been at times almost undisputed, and where positivism has exerted its most far-reaching and fertile influence on the development of the legal science. Deprived of its traditional strongholds by political suppression and undermined by scientific criticism, positivism is no longer a guiding influence in modern legal thought.

POSITIVISM AND INTERNATIONAL LAW

In international law, unlike the other branches of legal science, positivism is still a determining influence. Ever since the turn of the century, internationalists have started with positivist assumptions, have followed the positivist method, and have professed adherence to the principles of positivism.[9]

[7] An excellent analysis of this development is to be found in Bonnecase's history of the French "*École de l'Exégèse,*" *La Pensée juridique française de 1804 à l'heure présente*, Vol. 1 (Bordeaux, 1933).

[8] Roscoe Pound, An Introduction to the Philosophy of Law (New Haven, 1937), p. 57.

[9] Cavaglieri could write in 1911 ("*La Conception positive de la société internationale,*" *Revue gén. dr. pub.*, Vol. 18 (1911), p. 260): "Parmi ceux qui s'adonnent aux études de droit international, il n'est aujourd'hui personne qui ne fasse pas solennellement profession d'adhérer à la nouvelle conception positive du droit. . . ." Some years later Ripert could say (*Annales, loc. cit.*, p. 18): ". . . cette génération professe un positivisme juridique absolu."

Neither the opposition of natural law,[10] nor Kelsen's neo-positivist criticism,[11] nor, finally, the rather implicit criticism of legal sociologists,[12] has been able to affect the predominance of positivist thought over the science of international law. The Permanent Court of International Justice still follows the time-honored pseudo-logical method of traditional positivism which prevailed in the jurisdiction of the domestic supreme courts at the turn of the century. The annals of this highest international tribunal record no instance where an advocate, like Brandeis in Muller *v.* Oregon,[13] dared to break through the network of positivist formulae, nor of any majority opinion which would not have clung, on a very high level of technical perfection, to the traditional pattern of positivist argumentation. When Judge Hudson looks for a realistic decision with respect to international law he has to turn to the Court of Appeals of the State of New York.[14] Compared to municipal law, international law is in a retarded stage of scientific development. As represented by its sanest elements, the science of international law still stands where the science of municipal law stood in 1910; in terms of its post-World War development, its most spectacular branches, invaded by the political ideology of Geneva, have gone back at least to the point from which positivism started in the last decades of the nineteenth century.

The collapse of the international law of Geneva, when for the first time its fictions were confronted with the full reality, meant of necessity the breakdown of the science which had been only its ideological reflection. The

[10] Professor Lauterpacht (Private Law Sources and Analogies of International Law (London, 1927), p. 27, note 5; p. 58, note 7; Oppenheim-Lauterpacht, International Law, Vol. 1 (1937, p. 100) defends the opinion that positivism no longer dominates the science of international law, but has been replaced by a new doctrine of moderate natural law. It is difficult to share this opinion. Natural law and the post-war science of international law have only this in common, that they overstep the limits of experience. However, one would do injustice to the great metaphysical systems of natural law by identifying them with the post-war science of international law. Whereas Suarez and Grotius were fully aware of the aprioristic, metaphysical character of their propositions and had good philosophical reasons for adhering to them, post-war positivism helplessly confuses reality and imagination, wish and fact, because no longer does it possess the scientific means of distinguishing between both. *Cf.*, also, Laski, The State in Theory and Practice (New York, 1935), p. 198; Wild, *loc. cit.*, p. 483 *et seq.*

[11] See, especially, *Das Problem der Souveraenitaet und die Theorie des Voelkerrechts* (1928).

[12] See, especially, Max Huber, *Die soziologischen Grundlagen des Voelkerrechts* (Berlin, 1928); Ray, Hague *Recueil*, Vol. 48 (1934), p. 631 *et seq.;* Schindler, *ibid.*, Vol. 46 (1933), p. 229 *et seq.;* Morgenthau, *La Notion du "politique" et la théorie des différends internationaux* (Paris, 1933), pp. 37 *et seq.*, 65 *et seq.*, and *La Réalité des normes, en particulier des normes du droit international* (Paris, 1934), pp. 139, 140, 215.

[13] 208 U. S. 412 (1908). An excellent appraisal of the theoretical importance of this case is to be found in Frankfurter, "Hours of Labor and Realism in Constitutional Law," Harvard Law Rev., Vol. 29 (1916), p. 353.

[14] See the reference to Cardozo's opinion in Techt *v.* Hughes, 229 N. Y. 222, 241 (1920), in Hudson, "International Law in the Twentieth Century," Cornell Law Quarterly, Vol. 10 (1925), p. 435, note 75.

post-World War science of international law shared the short-lived and delusive splendor of its political master, and now shares with him the final detection of their common sham existence as well as the resulting disrepute. The helplessness of the science of international law in the face of those dangers, its very unawareness of them, its sincere self-deception as to its scientific character, are perhaps the gravest indictments which can be brought against the scientific value of the positivist doctrine of international law.[15] The failure of the post-World War science of international law is not due to personal or accidental circumstances; it grows out of the very assumptions and methods which have led juridic positivism to defeat in the domestic field. Yet, in the international field the disastrous consequences of the genuine weakness of the positivist doctrine are doubled by the absence of the conditions which in the domestic domain made juridic positivism at least a temporary and apparent success.

Juridic positivism starts with the assumption that its subject-matter is to be found exclusively in the written law of the state. Only the rules of law, and all the rules of law which statutes and court decisions present as such, are the material with which the positivist doctrine has to deal. The criterion of the existence, that is, the validity of a legal rule, is, then, its incorporation into the written law of the state. We do not repeat here what we have said elsewhere of the scientific value of this juridic monism,[16] and consider only the results of its being applied to the rules of international law. This criterion for the validity of legal rules means, if transferred to the international field, that the only valid rules of international law are those which are revealed by the decisions of courts and international treaties duly ratified and not formally revoked. Yet this concept is at once confronted with two problems for which the positivist doctrine of international law has no solution. On the one hand, all rules embodied in written documents are not valid international law, and, on the other hand, there are valid rules of international law other than the rules embodied in written documents. The positivist formula as applied to international law is at once too narrow and too broad.[17]

[15] For criticism of post-war international law, see especially, Beckett, "International Law in England," Law Quarterly Rev., Vol. 55 (1939), pp. 261, 262, 266; Borchard, this JOURNAL, Vol. 27 (1933), p. 518, Vol. 28 (1934), p. 108; Hill, *ibid.*, Vol. 23 (1929), p. 617; John Bassett Moore, *ibid.*, Vol. 27 (1933), p. 607; the same, International Law and Some Current Illusions (New York, 1924); the same, "An Appeal to Reason," Foreign Affairs, Vol. 11 (1933), see especially pp. 548, 585; the same, "Post-War International Law," Columbia Law Rev., Vol. 27 (1927), see especially p. 412.

[16] See Morgenthau, *La Réalité des Normes*, p. 106 *et seq.*; *cf.* also, the rather analytical than critical remarks by Edwin D. Dickinson, Hague *Recueil*, Vol. 40 (1932), pp. 337, 344; Siotto-Pintor, *ibid.*, Vol. 41 (1932), pp. 265, 266; Verdross, *ibid.*, Vol. 30 (1929), p. 276.

[17] To the following discussion, see Morgenthau, "*Positivisme mal compris et théorie réaliste du Droit international,*" *Mélanges Altamira* (Madrid, 1936), p. 3 *et seq.*; see also, Affolter, "*Der Rechtspositivismus in der Rechtswissenschaft,*" *Archiv fuer oeffentliches Recht*, Vol. 12 (1896/97), pp. 40, 41.

The science of international law has not developed a criterion to distinguish, in an objective way, between *seemingly* and *actually* valid rules of international law. "One can assert that nine-tenths of the traditional doctrines of international law are not actual international law," said Professor George Jellinek as far back as 1905.[18] Declared Professor Oppenheim a few years later:

> It is also indispensable that the science should free itself from the tyranny of phrases. As things are, there is scarcely a doctrine of the law of nations which is wholly free from the tyranny of phrases. . . . Any one who is in touch with the application of international law in diplomatic practice hears from statesmen every day the complaint that books put forth fanciful doctrines instead of the actual rules of law. Now it is often not difficult to push the irrelevant to one side and to extract what is legally essential from the waste of phrase-ridden discourse. But there are entire areas in which the tyranny of phrases so turns the head that rules which absolutely never were rules of law are represented as such.[19]

"On no subject of human interest, except theology," said John Chipman Gray at about the same time, "has there been so much loose writing and nebulous speculations as on international law." [20]

If these statements were true in the first decade of the century, the development of the post-World War science of international law has only added to their significance. The Covenant of the League of Nations, for instance, is a duly ratified document which has never been repealed. But has it ever been valid international law as a whole? If not, which provisions never had the quality of valid legal rules, and which ones lost this quality in the course of the gradual collapse of the institution of Geneva? No treatise of the law of nations offers any general criterion to answer these questions, nor do the concrete answers given with reference to the actual validity of Article 16 of the Covenant reveal any such underlying objective criterion. The absolute denial of any validity, the assertion of a so-called "de facto revision," and the defense of full validity, are advanced side by side.[21] Similar problems arise with respect to the Briand-Kellogg Pact and the Peace Treaties of 1919, as well as to other political treaties, such as the Pact of the Little Entente, alliance treaties, the concepts of aggression, independence, intervention, government, and so forth.[22] They are em-

[18] *System der subjektiven oeffentlichen Rechte* (Tuebingen, 1905), p. 321; see also the even stronger criticism by Bergbohm, *Staatsvertraege*, p. 8.

[19] The Future of International Law (Oxford, 1921; first in German, 1911), pp. 58, 59; see also, The Science of International Law, pp. 315, 334.

[20] Nature and Sources of the Law (New York, 1927; first edition, 1909), p. 127.

[21] *Cf.*, for instance, Schwarzenberger, in The New Commonwealth Quarterly, Vol. 3 (1937/38), pp. 263, 360 *et seq.*; *ibid.*, Vol. 4 (1938/39), p. 60 *et seq.*; for an excellent statement of the problem, see Kunz, *id.*, p. 131, and this JOURNAL, Vol. 33 (1939), p. 33.

[22] An excellent contribution to the understanding of this problem is to be found in Baty, "The Trend of International Law," this JOURNAL, Vol. 33 (1939), p. 653 *et seq.*, and "The Abuse of Terms," *ibid.*, Vol. 30 (1936), p. 377.

bodied in written documents which were duly ratified and never invalidated. Have they ever been valid law from the beginning, and what has become of them in the years of their violation? Are they still valid? If they are not, what destroyed their validity? These are questions which the interpreter of domestic statutes, subject to a rational process of validation and invalidation, is not likely to be asked, and hence the positivist doctrine of international law, following the pattern of domestic positivism, has nothing with which to answer them.[23]

The basic assumption of juridic positivism, that its exclusive subject-matter is the written law of the state, leads legal science not only to the inclusion of alleged legal rules which no longer have or never have had legal validity, but also to the exclusion of undoubtedly valid rules of law. Positivist jurisprudence, starting with the axiom of "legal self-sufficiency," separates the law from the other normative spheres, that is, ethics and *mores*, on the one hand, and from the social sphere, comprehending the psychological, political, and economic fields, on the other hand. By doing so, positivism severs the actual relations between the law and the other branches of the normative and social sphere. It proceeds on the assumption that the law, as it really is, can be understood without the normative and social context in which it actually stands.[24] From the application of this assumption to international law there results a threefold delimitation of legal research, contrary to the exigencies of the reality, and hence a threefold misconception of what international law really is.

1. The normative sphere, comprehending the totality of rules governing a given society, is one whole with regard to the basic precepts it contains.[25]

[23] This absence of any scientific test for the validity of the rules of international law is responsible for the perplexity into which some of the foremost representatives of the international law of Geneva have fallen in recent years. Professor Scelle, who had founded a whole system of "positive" international law upon "international solidarity," "international federalism," and like "social facts," in 1937 arrives at the conclusion that there is no such thing as international law at all. "Il n'y a plus en Europe de droit des gens," he writes in the *Journal des Nations* (No. 1665, Feb. 28 and March 1, 1937). "Il n'y a plus des traités." "The conclusion seems unescapable," says Professor Zimmern ("The Decline of International Standards," International Affairs, Vol. 17 (1938), p. 12), "that positive international law, so called, has no claim to the name of law." (See also the same, The League of Nations and the Rule of Law 1918–1935 (London, 1936), p. 94.) These scholars, who never cared for such "abstract" problems as the criterion of the validity of a rule of law, now fall from one error into the other. First, they accepted the assumed validity of post-war international law without question; now, since it is obvious that the main bulk of this so-called international law never has been valid law at all, they identify this product of their imagination with the main bulk of pre-war international law, which today is as valid as it has ever been, and declare that international law simply does not exist!

[24] "Can we even understand English law without going beyond the actual rules themselves?" asks Paton in his interesting paper, "Whither Jurisprudence," *Politica*, Vol. 4 (1939), p. 16.

[25] To the following discussion, see Pound, "The Part of Philosophy in International Law," Proceedings of the 6th International Congresss of Philosophy (New York, 1927), p. 374 *et*

Although there may be in a given society particular legal rules which contradict particular ethical rules or *mores*, and *vice versa*, the main bulk of basic ideals to be realized, of ends to be achieved, and of interests to be protected, is generally the same in the different branches of a given normative order. Law, ethics, and *mores* support each other in the pursuit of these aims. Legal rules refer to ethics and *mores* for the determination of their meaning and *vice versa*.[26] The guiding influence, however, as to the ideals, ends, and interests to be pursued by the norms under which a given society lives, emanates from the ethical sphere. From it law and *mores* receive the fundamental distinctions between the good and the bad, the ends to be advanced and the ends to be opposed, the interests to be protected and the interests to be repudiated. At the base of any legal system there lies a body of principles which incorporate the guiding ideas of justice and order to be expounded by the rules of law. The intelligibility of any legal system depends upon the recognition of such a set of fundamental principles which constitute the ethical substance of the legal system, and shed their illuminating light upon each particular rule of law.

This recognition is relatively easy to perform in the domestic field, where the constitution codifies the main bulk of those fundamental principles, and a highly integrated public opinion provides supplementary moral guidance. The task is much more difficult with respect to international law. Here there is no body of such principles separate from the ordinary rules of law. Some of those principles may be only partly expressed in these rules; others may not be expressed at all, and hence have to be detected, in a dangerously uncertain procedure, in the general moral ideas underlying the international law of a certain time, a certain civilization, or even a certain nation. Yet the successful search for these principles is as essential for the scientific understanding of international law as of any legal system.

Legal positivism is unable to grant this recognition; for at its basis there is the hostility to all matters metaphysical, that is, those which cannot be ascertained by actual observation. Since non-legal rules have generally entered the horizon of the positivist jurist as metaphysical rules of natural law, the positivist is inclined to identify natural law and ethics as such, and to repudiate both as metaphysics. However, to exclude *a priori* a certain subject-matter from scientific research by calling it metaphysical, instead of impartially examining actual experience, is to blind oneself to a preconceived idea originating, not in experience, but in mere reasoning, and thus to do violence to the facts. Hence, the positivist concept of the normative sphere

seq.; Bentwich, The Religious Foundations of Internationalism (London, 1933), especially p. 262 *et seq.;* Zimmern, "International Law and Social Consciousness," Transactions of the Grotius Society, Vol. 20 (1934), p. 25 *et seq.; cf.*, particularly, the brilliant paper by Schwarzenberger, "The Rule of Law and the Disintegration of the International Society," this Journal, Vol. 33 (1939), p. 56.

[26] We have dealt with this problem in *La Réalité des Normes*, p. 155.

itself reveals a metaphysical attitude, a kind of negative metaphysics which plainly contradicts the very assumptions of a positive science.[27]

Yet positivism has never been quite able to live up to its legalistic and anti-metaphysical assumptions. The very nature of its subject-matter has compelled it time and again to violate its own assumptions and make use of fundamental principles not revealed by "positive" law. In order to give at least apparent satisfaction to these assumptions, positivism dares to make use of such principles only under the disguise of positivist concepts, and therefore develops a fictitious method which tries by pseudo-logical arguments to derive from "positive," that is, written, rules of international law something that those rules do not contain. The interminable and quite sterile discussions on the foundation of the binding force of international law are evidence of this word-juggling, since this is a problem which, as defined in the positivist terms of mutual consent and the like, is contradictory in itself, and hence insoluble within the framework of positivism. The foundation of the binding force of "positive" law can logically be found, not in this "positive" law itself, but only outside it.[28] Another example is the problem of sovereignty as defined and solved by positivism. Here again a fundamental principle which, by its very nature, cannot be derived from "positive" law, but from which "positive" law itself rather derives its meaning, is to be dealt with as if it were a rule of "positive" international law. It is for these helpless attempts to conciliate its legalistic assumptions with actual juridic experience that the positivist doctrine of international law is bound to misrepresent the reality of international law and to fail to do justice to its actual content.[29]

2. The precepts of international law need not only to be interpreted in the light of the ideals and ethico-legal principles which are at their basis. They need also to be seen within the sociological context of economic interests, social tensions, and aspirations for power, which are the motivating forces in the international field, and which give rise to the factual situations forming the raw material for regulation by international law.[30] The correctness of

[27] For this point, see Liard, *La Science positive et la métaphysique* (4th ed., Paris, 1898), pp. 38, 57, 72. See also Ruggiero, *loc. cit.*, p. 261: "Not only the extreme difficulty of maintaining itself on a level strictly positive and not exceeding the limits of experience but also the tendency . . . to identify objectivity with materiality, have often caused positivism to range over into materialism, that is, into metaphysics, in contradiction to its own premises." As to the specific legal phenomenon of "positivism ending in disregard of positive law," see Lauterpacht, in Modern Theories of Law (London, 1933), pp. 132, 133; and Morgenthau, *Positivisme mal Compris*, pp. 3, 4.

[28] Strupp, Hague *Recueil*, Vol. 47 (1934), p. 298; Brierly, The Law of Nations (London, 1936), p. 45.

[29] Brierly, The Shortcomings of International Law, p. 4 *et seq.;* Morgenthau, "The Problem of Neutrality," University of Kansas City Law Rev., Vol. VII (1939), p. 110; Wild, *loc. cit.*, p. 478 *et seq.*

[30] For this point, see Brierly, *op. cit.*, pp. 5, 16; Kenneth Colegrove, Proceedings of the 5th Conference of Teachers of International Law, p. 97; Ray, *Annales Sociologiques*, série C,

this postulate for the interpretation of municipal law is today self-evident. Nobody would ever try to interpret social legislation without reference to the conflicting social interests to be evaluated and the social relations to be settled. Nobody would ever endeavor to grasp the legal meaning of economic legislation without making economic interests and conflicts part of the reasoning. Even where the reference to the underlying economic and social forces and relations is not always explicit, as in the field of contracts, the sociological context is nevertheless always referred to by implication. It is only because of the highly typical character of the factual situations and their social and economic significance, with which everybody is familiar, and which are completely and adequately expressed in the legal rules, that the mere reference to those legal rules implies the consideration of the social and economic factors which are at their basis.

It was, historically, the most disastrous error of positivism to misunderstand completely this implicit reference to the sociological context which every legal rule contains. This error can be traced back to the tradition of the pandectists, who had in the Roman law the classical model of a highly typified legal system which expressed with perfect appropriateness the fundamental interests and relationships which can arise from the social activities of men. So perfectly was this sociological context represented in the abstractions of the Roman law, that the pandectists were only too prone to forget its very existence and to deal with those abstractions as with independent logical entities. So did the positivists, both in the municipal and international fields.[31] This methodological error was of minor importance where the legal concepts were true abstractions from the interests and relations which they were supposed to regulate. When, however, those legal rules were applied to interests and relations to which some of them referred only partly, others not at all, that methodological error was bound to have a disastrous influence upon the scientific value of positivist jurisprudence. In the domestic field, it became instrumental in distorting the legal reality and originating that positivist conceptualism with which a decadent legal science attempted to adapt the old legal rules to new economic and social needs, but at the same time maintained the fictitious assumption that the written law already contained, logically, all the rules necessary for the solution of those new problems. Thus the juridical pseudo-logic became the artificial makeshift by which a stationary law could be reconciled with a moving social reality.

In the international field, the methodological error of neglecting the socio-

---

No. 3, p. 14 *et seq.; cf.* especially, the excellent remarks by Friedman, Modern Law Review, Vol. 2 (1938), p. 194; and review, *ibid.*, p. 81.

[31] For the influence of Roman law upon international law, see Pound, *loc. cit.*, pp. 376, 377; Lauterpacht, Private Law Sources, p. 23 *et seq.;* Alvarez, *Nouvelle Conception des Études juridiques*, p. 47 *et seq.*

logical context of international law led to even worse consequences.[32] In the domestic field, the correspondence between legal concepts and sociological context was at least a temporary fact, and within this limit the negligence of the sociological context and the assumption of the "self-sufficiency" of the written law could be justified. In the most important branches of international law this correspondence has never, and could never, have existed. The sociological relationships underlying those branches of international law are characterized by their individual, non-typical nature.[33] A political situation in the international field is not likely to repeat itself, since the variety of factors of which it is composed makes for an indefinite number of possible combinations. Hence only a strictly individualized rule of law will be adequate to it. International law provides partly for such individualized rules by restricting the application of a rule to one individual case and leaving the regulation of similar future cases to new legislative efforts. Peace treaties are instances of such individualized rules of international law. In part, however, international law does maintain the form of the general, typical rule of law and depends on the interpretation of the rule to provide the flexible meaning which the ever-changing sociological context requires. All political treaties which are intent upon establishing permanent rights and duties between the contracting parties are of this kind. The same generally and typically worded text may imply quite different rules, according to the political function which it is supposed to fulfill.[34] Thus one is able, for instance, to distinguish three different periods in the history of the Treaties of Locarno.[35] Those three periods are characterized by three significant changes in the normative content of the rules, resulting from changes in the political context, although the wording of the rules remained unchanged. The Covenant of the League of Nations, as a whole, as well as particular provisions, for instance, Article 16, have been submitted to similar modifications as a result of factual sociological developments and not of legislative changes.[36]

The same phenomenon occurs not only in temporary succession, but also

[32] Reeves, Proceedings of the 2nd Conference of Teachers of International Law, pp. 72, 73.

[33] This high degree of individualization is clearly recognized by Brierly, Hague *Recueil*, Vol. 58, p. 16; Ray, *ibid.*, Vol. 48, p. 699; Schindler, *ibid.*, Vol. 46, p. 265.

[34] The same phenomenon with regard to municipal social legislation has been excellently described by Frankfurter, *loc. cit.*, pp. 369, 370: "It is now clearly enough recognized that each case presents a distinct issue; that each case must be determined by the facts relevant to it; that we are dealing, in truth, not with a question of law but the application of an undisputed formula to a constantly changing and growing variety of economic and social facts. Each case, therefore, calls for a new and distinct consideration, not only of the general facts of industry but the specific facts in regard to the employment in question and the specific exigencies which called for the specific statute."

[35] See Morgenthau, "*Théorie des Sanctions internationales*," *Revue de Droit Int. et de Lég. Comp.*, Vol. 16 (1935), p. 832.

[36] See Morgenthau, "The Resurrection of Neutrality in Europe," Am. Pol. Sci. Rev., Vol. 33 (1939), p. 473.

under contemporaneous yet different sociological conditions. The identical text of an arbitration treaty or non-aggression pact may have quite different legal meanings, according to the political situation existing between different contracting parties.[37] Even one and the same legal rule, as, for instance, Article 16 of the Covenant, lends itself to different interpretations with respect to states living under different political conditions.[38]

The positivist doctrine of international law has completely ignored this particular relationship between the rules of international law and their sociological context. Positivism transplanted schematically the highly refined positivist method of formalist and conceptualist interpretation into the domain of international law. This method developed under, and was justified by, the specific domestic conditions of a temporarily stabilized society where there was approximately no tension between law and sociological context but almost complete rationalization and representation of the sociological context within the concepts of positive law. Schematically applied to a law and a society of a distinctly different nature, this method was bound to produce entirely inadequate results. Where the experience of international law showed that an individual situation required an individual interpretation of the legal rule, the positivist method could not fail to disregard all individual aspects of the factual situation and concentrate upon the general wording of the legal rule which, by virtue of its logical self-sufficiency, was supposed to contain all elements necessary for its understanding; and to this the reference to the sociological context could contribute nothing. An arbitration treaty which submitted all conflicts between the contracting parties to international tribunals was a legal document that revealed its legal significance through its text, *i.e.*, another step towards the establishment of an international order based upon respect for law. Whether the treaty was concluded between Switzerland and Uruguay, or Denmark, Sweden, and Norway, or Great Britain and France, or Germany and Poland in 1925, 1935, or 1939—these were "political" considerations irrelevantly lying beyond the scope of positivist interpretation.[39]

3. The positivist doctrine, by recognizing as international law only the rules enforced by states, excludes from the domain of international law all rules whose validity cannot be traced to the written documents of states. On the other hand, the positivist doctrine cannot deny that such rules, like most rules of general international law, actually exist. Confronted with the embarrassing dilemma of violating its own *étatist* assumptions or of dis-

[37] Leresche, "*La Crise du Droit des Gens*," *Rev. int. Française du Droit des Gens*, Vol. 6 (1938), p. 303.

[38] See the excellent criticism by Barandon, *Das System der politischen Staatsvertraege seit 1918* (Handbuch des Voelkerrechts, Vol. 4), p. 1.

[39] See author's analysis of arbitration treaties concluded under different political circumstances, in International Jurisdiction, its Nature and its Limits (in German, 1929), p. 131 *et seq.*

regarding an obvious part of legal experience, the positivist doctrine has taken refuge in a concept which has become a veritable panacea for its theoretical troubles. We are referring to the concept of customary law, which has served for the traditional doctrine of international law as a kind of collective designation for all the rules of international law the origin of which cannot directly be traced to written sources. The insurmountable theoretical difficulties of explaining the existence of a so-called customary law have been pointed out elsewhere,[40] and this is no place to resume the discussion. It is sufficient to state that the reconciliation which the positivist doctrine is able to establish between its monist, legalistic assumptions and the existence of a so-called customary law, is merely apparent. In order to save these assumptions as well as those facts, it resorts to a series of fictions, like tacit consent, recognition, judicial admission, and so forth, which indirectly endeavor to attribute the existence of the so-called customary rules of international law to the legislative will of states.

PREFACE TO A FUNCTIONAL THEORY OF INTERNATIONAL LAW

The fundamental weakness of the positivist doctrine of international law lies in its inadequacy to international law as it really is. Unfaithful to its own assumptions, it contains at the same time more and less than the actual rules of international law, which it furthermore submits to subjective evaluation in the light of ethical and political principles of assumedly universal, yet doubtful, validity. A truly scientific theory of international law must avoid these mistakes in order to come closer to the reality. It seems to be a logical choice to call such a theory by the name of realist. There are, however, two objections to this choice. On the one hand, the increasing disrepute of the traditional doctrine of international law has led no few practitioners of this doctrine to demonstrate their closeness to the reality of international law by calling themselves "realists."[41] This misuse has deprived the term of its distinctive character in the international field. On the other hand, realism has become a collective designation for several tendencies in modern jurisprudence, all aiming at replacing, by different means, the fictitious legalism of traditional jurisprudence with a conception nearer to the realities of the law. All these tendencies have this in common: They do not regard the legal rules as definitely determined by their legislative or judicial formulation, but search for the psychological, social, political and economic forces which determine the actual content and working of legal rules and

[40] *La Réalité des Normes*, p. 89 *et seq.;* for criticism of the doctrine of customary international law, see also, Brierly, Hague *Recueil*, Vol. 58, p. 29; Ray, *ibid.*, Vol. 48, pp. 697, 698.

[41] See, for instance, Kaufmann, Hague *Recueil*, Vol. 54 (1935), pp. 319, 320; Scelle, *ibid.*, Vol. 46 (1933), p. 691; Verdross, *ibid.*, Vol. 30 (1929), p. 277; Le Fur, in *Revue de Droit International*, Vol. 17 (1936), p. 7—authors who have certainly not very much in common besides the claim of being "realists." *Cf.* also, Lundstedt who, according to Pound, *loc. cit.*, p. 145, qualifies Pound, Kelsen, and Duguit as "realists"!

which, in turn, are determined by them. In other words, their scientific goal is to formulate uniform functional relationships between those forces and the legal rules. Hence, "realist" jurisprudence is, in truth, "functional" jurisprudence.[42]

The legacy which positivism has left to the science of international law consists in the task of comprehending the international law of a given time as standing in a dual functional relationship with the social forces of this time. On the one hand, international law is the function of the civilization in which it originates, that is, of the regulative ideas laid down in the ethics and *mores* of this civilization, of the political, economic and general social forces prevailing in it, and, finally, of the specific psychological factors manifesting themselves in the individuals determining it. On the other hand, international law is a social mechanism working towards certain ends within this same civilization which, in turn, as far as determined by it, becomes a function of this same international law. By systematizing the rules of a given international law under the viewpoint of this dual functional relationship between rules and social forces, the functional theory will arrive at a real scientific understanding of the material element of the legal rules which positivism even at its best was able to describe and systematize only according to superficial legalistic viewpoints.[43]

Six important consequences for a functional theory of international law

[42] Although the doctrine developed in the text is undoubtedly of a sociological nature, we would rather prefer to avoid the term; for sociological jurisprudence, through the influence of Professor Pound's writings, is associated with the idea of "social engineering," which is, from the standpoint of the contemporaneous legal science, a very premature proposition; see, *infra* VI under.

[43] The principles of functional jurisprudence, as understood in this paper, have been admirably formulated by Llewellyn, "Legal Tradition and Social Science Method—a Realist's Critic," Essays on Research in the Social Sciences (Brookings Institution, 1931); and "Some Realism about Realism," Harvard Law Rev., Vol. 44 (1930/31), p. 1236 *et seq.* The transition from positivism to functionalism is excellently described by Pound, "Fifty Years of Jurisprudence," *ibid.*, Vol. 51 (1937/38), pp. 446, 447: "The determining impetus came from positivism and the direction was sociology, leading to functional study of legal institutions in the light of all the social sciences, and tends to consideration of the legal order as a social institution rather than exclusive consideration of the legal materials with which tribunals work in upholding that order." See also, Hudson, Cornell Law Rev., Vol. 10, p. 434. The functional viewpoint is excellently developed also by P. Alex, *Du Droit et du Positivisme* (Paris, 1876), see especially pp. 12 *et seq.*, 26 *et seq.*, 39, 118. This work, completely forgotten today, endeavors to apply the principles of a well-understood positivism to jurisprudence, and thus puts by implication the subsequent aberrations of juridic positivism in the right light. See also, the penetrating article by Felix S. Cohen, "The Problems of Functional Jurisprudence," Modern Law Review, Vol. 1 (1937/38), p. 5; and Malinowski, "The Group and the Individual in Functional Analysis," Am. Jour. of Sociology, Vol. 44 (1938/39), p. 951: "I would like to add that the science of modern jurisprudence could become inspired by anthropology in treating legal phenomena within the context of social life and in conjunction with other norms of conduct." For the philosophical background, see Kallen, "Functionalism," Encyclopedia of the Social Sciences, Vol. 6, p. 523.

can be drawn from this recognition of the functional relationship between social forces and international law.[44]

I. A functional theory of international law has to start with the recognition of the particularly intimate nature of this relationship.[45] In the domestic field, legal rules can be imposed by the group which holds the monopoly of organized physical force, that is, the officials of the state. The international sphere is characterized by the absence of such a group. International law owes its existence to identical or complementary interests of states, backed by power as a last resort, or, where such identical interests do not exist, to a mere balance of power which prevents a state from breaking these rules of international law. Where there is neither community of interests nor balance of power, there is no international law. Whereas domestic law may originate in the arbitrary will of the rule-making agencies of the state, international law is usually the result of objective social forces. When, in the international field, an arbitrary rule-making power tries to impose rules supported neither by common interests nor by a balance of power, these rules never become valid law, or gain only ephemeral existence and scant efficacy; the history of the rules embodied in the Treaty of Versailles and the Covenant of the League of Nations is a striking example of this.

It is also due to this intimate relationship between social forces and legal rules that in the international field fundamental changes of the social forces and, hence, of the legal rules, follow each other at frequent intervals and in an abrupt, often violent, manner. In the domestic field the regulative social force dominating all others is the state. It has developed not only an overwhelming power apparatus, but also highly refined mechanisms of legislative and judicial readjustment, which lead the social forces into certain channels without disrupting the legal and social continuity. Here, the state selects in authoritative decisions the social forces to be recognized by the law. It decides to what extent the existing legal rules shall yield to changing conditions, to what extent they shall resist them, and in what ways they shall try to transform them. In the international field the authoritative decision is replaced by the free interplay of political and military forces. This makes a gradual readjustment of the law to changing social conditions extremely difficult. Any fundamental change of the social forces underlying a system of international law of necessity induces the prospective beneficiaries of the change to try to bring about a corresponding change of the legal rules, whereas the beneficiaries of the legal *status quo* will resist any change of the old order. Here a competitive contest for power will determine the

[44] These consequences can be stated within the limits of this paper only in very general terms, and other consequences may be revealed through application of the principles developed in the text to special problems; see the enumeration of possible further consequences, in *Positivisme mal compris*, p. 20.

[45] This relationship is clearly recognized by Huber, *op. cit.*, p. 9 *et seq.;* Schindler, *loc. cit.*, p. 237 *et seq.;* see also, *La Réalité des Normes*, pp. 139, 140, 215.

victorious social forces, and the change of the existing legal order will be decided, not through a legal procedure provided for by this same legal order, but through a conflagration of conflicting social forces which challenge the legal order as a whole.[46]

Where such a conflict between social forces and the rules of law exists, the character and function of the whole legal order undergo a transformation. We have proposed to call this relationship by the name of "tension," and have dealt with its legal consequences elsewhere.[47]

II. This recognition of the peculiar relationship between social forces and rules of international law provides the clue for restating, in functional terms, the doctrine of the validity of international law.[48] A rule of international law does not, as positivism was prone to believe, receive its validity from its enactment into a legal instrument, as, for instance, an international treaty. There are rules of international law which are valid, although not enacted in such legal instruments, and there are rules of international law which are not valid, although enacted in such instruments. Enactment, therefore, is no objective criterion for the alleged validity of a rule of international law. A rule, be it legal, moral, or conventional, is valid when its violation is likely to be followed by an unfavorable reaction, that is, a sanction against its violator. An alleged rule, the violation of which is not followed by such a sanction, is a mere idea, a wish, a suggestion, but not a valid rule. An alleged rule of international law, against the violation of which no state reacts, and is likely to react, is proved, by this very absence of probable reaction, not to be a valid rule of international law. The gradual invalidation of the territorial provisions of the Treaty of Versailles, and of most articles of the Covenant of the League of Nations, by violation and non-intervention of sanctions against these violations, are experimental proof of the correctness of this concept of validity.[49]

How, then, are we to know beforehand when such sanctions are likely to intervene in behalf of a violated norm, and when not, and, hence, how are we

[46] This problem, which refers to the validity of international law and its dynamic aspects, should be clearly distinguished from the problem discussed *supra*, under par. 2. There we had to do with the question as to how in the international field the particular characteristics of the social context are represented in the material concepts of the legal rules.

[47] On the theory of international "tensions," see Morgenthau, International Jurisdiction, p. 59 *et seq.*; and *La Notion du "Politique,"* p. 37 *et seq.* This theory has been thoroughly discussed by Ray, *Annales sociologiques, série C*, No. 1 (1935), p. 163 *et seq.*

[48] As to the problem of the validity of international law, see Morgenthau, *La Réalité des Normes*, pp. 28 *et seq.*, 212 *et seq.* Professor Timasheff, An Introduction to the Sociology of Law (Cambridge, 1939), p. 271, calls the theory developed there an "artificial construction." However, it seems to us that the artificiality of this theory is only the reflex of the artificial character of international law itself; as to this theory of validity in general, see his remarks, *ibid.*, pp. 142, 166, 299, 300. The psychological mechanism underlying the validity of international law is well described by Baty in this JOURNAL, Vol. 33 (1939), p. 653.

[49] For the relationship between sanctions and validity, see also, "*Théorie des Sanctions Internationales,*" *loc. cit.*, pp. 474 *et seq.*, 809 *et seq.*

to say, in an objective, scientific way, which norms are valid and which are not? The consideration of the functional factor will give the answer.

1. The commonest and simplest test for the validity of an alleged rule of international law is this: State A has, in the past, requested State B to perform certain actions corresponding to the rule, whereas State B, in turn, has requested State A to perform certain actions corresponding to the same or another rule. Where these identical or complementary interests in the mutual observance of these rules did not suffice to guarantee the actual observance, both states were willing to enforce compliance with the rule by protest, reprisal, or military action. Where there was, in the past, a recognized identical or complementary interest in a certain action on the part of two or more states, together with the willingness to enforce this action, there exists the likelihood that the same sanctions for the sake of the same interests will also be performed in the future. Respect for the status of diplomatic representatives has been, in the past, an interest recognized and guaranteed with sanctions by all states; therefore, the forecast is justified that the states will follow the same course of action in the future.

The enactment of rules corresponding to such interests in international treaties may indicate the permanent nature of those interests, but this is an assumption which needs support from the facts and which can be disproved by them. Another indication of the permanence of such interests is their sublimation into moral principles, which pretend universal validity and endeavor to give certain interests of exceptional importance a justification superior to that which they could derive from the law.

2. The situation, however, is not always so simple. Three possible situations present themselves for examination. It can be that:

(a) Identical or complementary interests survive the willingness to enforce the actions corresponding to them. The provisions of the Treaties of Locarno were the function of identical and complementary interests of the contracting parties. When Germany violated these treaties by remilitarizing the Rhineland, the interests of the signatories in the demilitarization survived their willingness to enforce an attitude corresponding to their interests, and thus the respective rules of international law lost their validity.

(b) The willingness to enforce certain actions corresponding to identical or complementary interests survives the interests themselves. The provisions of the Treaty of Versailles establishing the German-Polish frontier from the outset did not correspond to the interest of both states. These provisions were observed for a period of twenty years because there existed a balance of power between both nations and their respective allies, which prevented either of them from violating the law.

(c) The interests and the willingness to enforce the actions corresponding to them disappear altogether. In this category belong the French-Russian and German-Italian military alliances, the Pact of the Little Entente, the political provisions of the Covenant of the League of Nations, and numerous provisions of the Peace Treaties of 1919.

What does the analysis of these cases show with regard to the validity of international law? In the cases (a) and (c) the rules of international law become invalid according to the functional concept of validity because no longer does there exist a likelihood of sanctions being performed, should those rules be violated. In case (b) the validity of the rules depends upon a balance of power, which may be stable for a certain time, and then suddenly become unstable, but which in our time is of a rather permanently unstable and precarious nature. All cases have this in common, that they make forecasts as to the likelihood of sanctions extremely uncertain. The enactment of the rules in international treaties is here of no avail, and, as contemporaneous examples have amply shown, is rather misleading. Their conformity with moral principles is scarcely more illuminating because of the aforesaid difficulty of ascertaining the exact moral nature of such principles.

Where the functional relationships between sociological forces and international law is in a state of transition from (1) to one of the situations under (2) the development may as well stop at an intermediate point between (1), on the one hand, and (2 a) and (c), on the other; proceed to (2 b); or, finally, come to an end at (2 a) or (c). Here, the validity of the respective rules of international law is, so to speak, in suspense, and may be as well maintained or destroyed. With respect to such rules the science of international law becomes a system of guesses, enjoying a greater or lesser chance of being proved true according to the factual development of the functional relationship between the social forces and the rules of international law.[50]

III. It follows from this analysis that there exist two obviously different types of international law, one founded upon the permanent and stable interests, the other based upon the temporary and fluctuating interests of states.[51] This differentiation is not only of fundamental importance for the understanding of the validity of international law; it leads to yet more far-reaching consequences as to the subject-matter, the methods, and the scientific character of the science of international law. One might even say that it leads to the recognition of two different sciences of international law which deal with different subject-matters, and apply, or rather ought to apply, different methods of research and systematization.

The main bulk of the concepts and principles of international law has been derived from municipal civil law. These concepts and principles have been

[50] Wharton, International Law Digest, Vol. 2 (Washington, 1881), p. 34, makes, in connection with Jones *v.* Walker, 2 Paine 688, a very interesting distinction between necessary, that is, juridic, and voluntary, that is, political validity.

[51] The classical concept of *jus necessarium* (see Morgenthau, *Positivisme mal compris*, pp. 16, 17) and Huber's distinction between territorial and extraterritorial rules (*loc. cit.*, p. 45 *et seq.*) refer to related but not identical differentiations. See also, Starke, "Monism and Dualism in the Theory of International Law," British Year Book of International Law, Vol. 17 (1936), p. 78 *et seq.*

developed within a legal system characterized by the extraordinary stability of the interests underlying it. Hence its application is, of necessity, restricted to legal systems based upon equally stable interests. In the international field such stable interests exist, for instance, with respect to diplomatic privileges, territorial jurisdiction, extradition, wide fields of maritime law, arbitral procedure, and so forth. This is the classical field of traditional international law as it has gradually developed in the practice of states since the sixteenth century. We propose to call these rules non-political international law, originating in the permanent interests of states to put their normal relations upon a stable basis by providing for predictable and enforceable conduct with respect to these relations.

But there is another type of international law which expresses, in terms of rights and duties, temporary interests ever given to change. In this category belong political agreements, especially treaties of alliance and their modern substitutes, which, under the legalistic disguise of treaties of general arbitration, consultation, or friendship, frequently pursue aims at least preparatory to close political ties. The traditional science of international law treats both types of international law alike, applying to both the concepts and methods developed in municipal civil law.[52] By doing so, it cannot but draw a completely distorted picture of those rules which belong in the category of political international law. Under such treatment, their validity appears to be firmly established, whereas it is actually always precarious; the interests which they are supposed to serve appear to be permanent and definite, whereas they are actually exposed to continuous change and are more or less uncertain; and consequently, the rights and duties established by them appear to be clearly determined, whereas they are subject actually to the most contradictory interpretations.

This writer knows of only one monograph dealing with political international law as an independent subject-matter requiring concepts and methods of its own: Rafael Erich's *Alliances and Alliance Treaties*.[53] He is aware of only a few references clearly stating the functional relationship between the political rules of international law and the underlying social factors: Judge Manley O. Hudson remarks that "if international law is to be built on solid foundations, it is no more possible to ignore the political and social phases of the prevailing international order than it is possible to ignore similar phases of the prevailing national order in the building of municipal law";[54]

[52] This problem is clearly seen by Whitehead, "An Appeal to Reason," Atlantic Monthly (March, 1939), p. 311: "Obligation, in European foreign policy, arises from the immediate situation and from duty to the future. Formal law can refer only to situations sufficiently stable." See also, Hudson, *loc. cit.*, p. 435: "Where the nineteenth century sought the vindication of natural rights, it must be our task to ascertain and evaluate interests."

[53] In German, Helsingfors, 1907.

[54] The Permanent Court of International Justice (New York, 1934), p. 567; see also p. 552 *et seq.*, and Proceedings of the 2nd Conference of Teachers of International Law, p. 40, with Fenwick, *ibid.*, p. 69, and this JOURNAL, Vol. 33 (1939), p. 107, agreeing. In the same

a similar remark in the Harvard Research in International Law reveals the same author; [55] and, finally, Professors Jessup [56] and Wild [57] urge the functional approach. There seems to be only one judicial opinion clearly pointing to the practical consequences of this relationship: Judge Anzilotti's dissenting opinion in the Austro-German Customs Union Case.[58] It remains for a functional theory of international law to develop systematically concepts and methods capable of conveying the legal characteristics, as well as the functional dependence on political factors, of political international law.

IV. As we have seen, there exist functional relationships not only between the law and the non-normative social forces, but also between the law and the other branches of the normative sphere, that is, ethics and *mores*. The latter are threefold with regard to the validity and the content of the rules of law.

As has been shown elsewhere,[59] the validity of any legal system reposes upon a fundamental norm which itself cannot be of a legal nature, but belongs of necessity to the domain of ethics and *mores*. Thus, the validity of the legal system of the United States reposes, on the one hand, upon an ethical rule enjoining upon the President, the members of Congress and of the Supreme Court to obey the Constitution, and, on the other hand, upon the *mores* keeping alive among the citizens the respect for the Constitution. When one or the other of these ethical foundations is lacking, the validity of the Constitution and of the legal system founded upon it is in a precarious state. When all are lacking, the Constitution, and with it the whole legal system, have ceased to exist as a living legal order even though they may not have been formally invalidated.

Not only does the validity of the legal system as a whole repose upon ethics and *mores*, but the validity of individual legal rules also stands frequently in a particular functional relationship with ethics and *mores*. It can be that the validity of one and the same precept, for instance, "Thou shall not kill,"

direction points the remark by McNair, Hague *Recueil*, Vol. 43 (1933), pp. 251 and 252: "Nous appartenons à l'école de ces juristes qui pensent que la science du droit international a besoin aujourd'hui des matériaux à mettre en oeuvre plus que des thèses et des monographies."

[55] Research in International Law under the Auspices of the Faculty of the Harvard Law School, this JOURNAL, Supp., Vol. 29 (1935), p. 953; see also pp. 937, 938, 947.

[56] Proceedings of the 3rd Conference of Teachers of International Law, p. 134 *et seq.*

[57] Am. Pol. Sci. Rev., *loc. cit.*

[58] As to the defectiveness of the majority decision from the functional standpoint, see Hudson, "The World Court and the Austro-German Customs Régime," American Bar Association Journal, Vol. 17 (1931), p. 793: "In our national courts, a refusal to take account of the social and political conditions to which law must be applied, has produced some of the sharpest criticism of our legal systems. . . . An international court might similarly build a law in disregard of the political factors which condition its application, but it would almost certainly lack both the appearance and the substance of reality."

[59] *La Réalité des Normes*, pp. 76 *et seq.*, 174 *et seq.*, 216 *et seq.*

reposes upon the likelihood that against its violation there will be performed sanctions pertaining to the domains of ethics and *mores*, as well as to the realm of the law. Many provisions of the Constitution, of civil and criminal law, belong to this category, and, therefore, are at the same time legal rules, ethical rules, and rules of the *mores*. It is obvious that this double or triple guaranty has an important bearing upon the observance and validity of a given precept. When such a multiple guaranty exists, that is, when ethics, *mores* and law coöperate to realize a certain order of things, there is a much greater likelihood that this order will be realized than when the law alone strives for this goal.[60]

It has already been pointed out that legal rules receive their precepts partly from ethics and *mores*. The meaning of these precepts requires explanation in the light of these other rules from which it is derived. The Constitution itself, for instance, does not reveal what "due process of law" or "freedom of contract" is; it is only by reference to the ethics and *mores* of a certain period of constitutional history that the meaning of these constitutional concepts can be determined.

The recognition, with regard to international law, of these three fundamental relationships, here hinted at rather than actually explained, calls for the discussion of a series of problems which the traditional science of international law does not even care to pose. What is, for instance, the empirical nature of the dual relationship between international law, on the one hand, and ethics and *mores* on the other? Are there ethics and *mores* of a truly international nature, or do we call by the name of "international," ethics and *mores* the precepts of which have been developed under the determining influence of the individual states and are applied to international affairs in the interest of these states? Which rules of international law belong, at the same time, to ethics and *mores*, and so have a greater chance of being observed? The meaning of which rules of international law can be only determined by reference to ethics and *mores*, and to what kind of ethics and *mores* do these rules refer?[61]

V. It follows from the preceding discussions that no branch of the traditional science of international law is more in need of reform than the doctrine of interpretation. The traditional doctrine has limited its efforts to transferring schematically the time-honored common and Roman law principles of interpretation to the international field. It has discussed the problem whether the wording of a treaty or the intentions of the parties shall be the main source of interpretation; it has gone deeply into the question whether preparatory materials may be used for purposes of interpretation; and it

[60] To this "cumulative" relationship, see *ibid.*, p. 185 *et seq.* To the following discussion see the general theoretical explanations, *ibid.*, p. 155 *et seq.;* and the remarks referring to them by Timasheff, *op. cit.*, pp. 62, 83, 84, 272, 324.

[61] The aforementioned papers by Friedman and Schwarzenberger (*supra*, notes 4, 25) are a promising beginning in this direction.

has advanced a great variety of so-called "rules of construction." Yet it has completely overlooked the fact that, due to the peculiar relationship between social forces and rules of international law, the problem of interpretation in the international field shows unique aspects for which the traditional civil law technique of interpretation is utterly inadequate.

When in the domestic field the meaning of a contract is ascertained by the usual means of interpretation, the interpretative job is done. It is generally not too difficult to perform the same task with regard to an international treaty; but then the real problem of interpretation just begins. A contract of civil law generally uses standardized language whose legal meaning is definite, or at least can be ascertained according to objective, universally recognized characteristics. An international treaty is not necessarily of the same nature. Its real meaning may be disguised with diplomatic language so that its wording is indicative only of what it does not mean. Under such circumstances, it is only from the social context that this treaty will receive its meaning. The political situation of the parties, and their intentions with respect to this situation, have to be ascertained from the viewpoint of the subject-matter of the treaty in question, for the time of the conclusion of the treaty as well as for the time of the interpretation; for, as we have seen, the legal meaning of an international treaty is ever subject to change. From this analysis one may then conclude, in a laborious and always highly uncertain manner, what might be the probable objective of the treaty and the legal meaning of the particular stipulations serving this purpose.

What, for instance, does the term "independence" in an international treaty mean? Its meaning may coincide with the accepted meaning of the term, it may be somewhat different, it may be the exact opposite, or it may have no legal meaning at all. The rules of construction will be of no avail with respect to this problem. It is only from the background of the social context and of the function the treaty is supposed to fulfill within it, that a scientific interpretation can hope, at least within certain limits, to receive a satisfactory answer. The answer will, for instance, vary according to whether the state to which the term applies is a colonial, semi-colonial, or non-colonial country; whether the treaty is concluded between two states of equal or different political power; whether or not in the last alternative, the more powerful state has imperialistic intentions with respect to the other party; whether the treaty is of a bilateral nature, pursuing a specific political aim, or is supported by the consensus of a great number of states for the sake of a general purpose common to all of them.

VI. To fulfill its task, the functional theory of international law has to take another step beyond positivism. It was the assumption of the positivist concept of science to be more scientific than any previous approach to an understanding of things. Positivist science was supposed to be free from all metaphysical elements, not asking how things ought to be and what their "real" essence might be, but seeking only uniform relations between things verifiable in experience. "*Je ne propose rien, je ne suppose rien, j'expose,*" was Comte's device. But just as Comte ended in the metaphysics of his "religion of humanity," so juridic positivism was not satisfied with knowing what the law actually was and how it worked. It was only too eager to remodel the world of the law after idealistic assumptions whose universal validity the respective authors took for granted. This tendency, variously strong in the different branches of municipal law, is uppermost in the positivist doctrine of international law. The science of international law, completely absorbed by practical problems as to what the rules of international law should be, is paying almost no attention to the psychological and sociological laws governing the actions of men in the international sphere, nor to the possible legal rules growing out of such actions. Who would dare embark upon such research would be called "impractical," and the results of his studies, if ever mentioned at all, would be qualified as "worthless." Grandiose legalistic schemes purporting to solve the ills of the world have replaced the less spectacular, painstaking search for the actual laws and the facts underlying them. This presumptuous enterprise has contributed nothing to the betterment of international relations, let alone the knowledge of what these international relations actually are. It has only shown the utter futility of all attempts to reform human conditions on the basis of idealistic assumptions without knowing the laws under which these conditions stand. As William Graham Sumner put it:

> In this view, the worst vice in political discussions is that dogmatism which takes its stand on "great principles" or assumptions, instead of standing on an exact examination of things as they are and human nature as it is. . . . The social sciences are, as yet, the stronghold of all this pernicious dogmatism; and nowhere does it do more harm than in politics. The whole method of abstract speculation on political topics is vicious. It is popular because it is easy; it is easier to imagine a new world than to learn to know this one; it is easier to embark on speculations based on a few broad assumptions than it is to study the history of states and institutions; it is easier to catch up a popular dogma than it is to analyze it to see whether it is true or not. All this leads to confusion, to the admission of phrases and platitudes, to much disputing but little gain in the prosperity of nations.[62]

"The eagerness for premature practical application . . . ," to express the same thought in the words of Vilfredo Pareto, "is ever obstructing the progress of science, along with a mania for preaching to people as to what they ought to do—an exceedingly bootless occupation—instead of finding out what they actually do." [63]

Why, then, is it that the field where the social sciences are able to work successfully is much narrower than the corresponding field of the natural

[62] "Democracy and Responsible Government," in The Challenge of Facts and Other Essays (New Haven, 1914), pp. 245, 246.

[63] The Mind and Society, Vol. 1 (New York, 1935), p. 185.

sciences? It is again Sumner who knows an answer to this question. "The reason is because the elements of any sort of problem which we do not know so far surpass in number and importance those which we do know that our solutions have far greater chance to be wrong than to be right." [64] Thus, the problem which the science of international law has to solve is clearly set. The natural sciences had to discover the laws governing nature before they could hope to dominate the natural forces, to prevent the dangers emanating from them, and to use them for human aims. In the same way, the social sciences cannot hope to master the social forces unless they know the laws which govern the social relations of men. In the natural sciences, the discovery of the infinitesimal calculus by Newton and Leibniz was bound to precede many modern technical inventions. The millennial attempts at constructing the airplane could not succeed as long as Carnot had not established his purely theoretical propositions on thermodynamics. Were it not for the theoretical efforts of Faraday, who himself did not invent anything of practical value, there would not be today any of the multiple uses of electricity for practical purposes. Had not Maxwell and Hertz, without any practical objective, carried out certain "abstruse and remote" calculations in the field of magnetism and electricity, Marconi could never have invented wireless and the radio.[65]

The science of international law, as well as the social sciences in general, are still awaiting their Newton, their Leibniz, their Faraday, their Carnot, their Maxwell, and their Hertz. To expect the contemporaneous lawyer to be an "engineer" or "technician" of the law means to expect Edison before Faraday, Wright before Carnot, Marconi before Maxwell and Hertz. And this is certainly a futile expectation. The great task which lies before the social sciences is to prepare the work of the latter so that the former can build upon it. By joining them in this endeavor the functional theory of international law will not only fulfill the task of any scientific doctrine, that is, to know what is and why it is; it will also prepare the ground for satisfying the greater ethical and political desire to improve international relations by means of the law.[66]

[64] "Speculative Legislation," *op. cit.*, p. 219.

[65] For the relationship between theory and practice in the natural sciences, see Meyerson, *La Déduction relativiste* (Paris, 1925), p. 333 *et seq.; Identité et Réalité* (Paris, 1926), pp. 36, 37; *Du Cheminement de la Pensée*, Vol. 1 (Paris, 1931), p. 3 *et seq.;* Flexner, "The Usefulness of Useless Knowledge," Harpers (October, 1939), p. 544.

[66] A highly illuminating discussion of the problem, only hinted at in the text, is to be found in Professor Hankin's paper, "Social Science and Social Action," American Sociological Rev., Vol. 4 (1939), p. 1; see also, Professor Lundberg, "Contemporary Positivism in Sociology," *ibid.*, p. 52 *et seq.* The problem is stated with intuitive insight by Lincoln Steffens in his letter of June 18, 1919, to Laura Suggett (The Letters of Lincoln Steffens (New York, 1938), Vol. 1, p. 472), picturing Wilson in Paris: "He is righteous. If only he were intelligent, scientific! But the unmoral, scientific, intellectual type is for the next generation to produce. Our part is to use the transition period to raise the questions, point away from all persons and individual guilt to the physical and economic enemies of Man."

[7]

Anarchy and the limits of cooperation: a realist critique of the newest liberal institutionalism

Joseph M. Grieco

Realism has dominated international relations theory at least since World War II.[1] For realists, international anarchy fosters competition and conflict among states and inhibits their willingness to cooperate even when they share common interests. Realist theory also argues that international institutions are unable to mitigate anarchy's constraining effects on inter-state cooperation. Realism, then, presents a pessimistic analysis of the prospects for international cooperation and of the capabilities of international institutions.[2]

For their helpful comments on this essay, I thank Louise Hodgden, Ole Holsti, Robert Jervis, Robert Keohane, Stephen Krasner, Joseph Nye, Stephen Van Evera, Kenneth Waltz, and especially John Mearsheimer. For their financial support during preparation of earlier drafts, I am grateful to the German–Marshall Fund of the United States and the Center for International Affairs at Harvard University. Of course, I remain responsible for all statements in the essay.

1. Major realist works include: E. H. Carr, *The Twenty Years Crisis, 1919–1939: An Introduction to the Study of International Relations* (London and New York: Harper Torchbooks, 1964); Hans J. Morgenthau, *Politics Among Nations: The Struggle for Power and Peace*, 5th ed. (New York: Knopf, 1973); Raymond Aron, *International Relations: A Theory of Peace and War*, trans. Richard Howard and Annette Baker Fox (Garden City, N.J.: Doubleday, 1973); Kenneth N. Waltz, *Man, the State, and War: A Theoretical Analysis* (New York: Columbia University Press, 1959); Waltz, *Theory of International Politics* (Reading, Mass.: Addison-Wesley, 1979); Robert Gilpin, *U.S. Power and the Multinational Corporation: The Political Economy of Foreign Direct Investment* (New York: Basic Books, 1975); and Gilpin, *War and Change in World Politics* (Cambridge: Cambridge University Press, 1981). This essay does not distinguish between realism and "neorealism," because on crucial issues—the meaning of international anarchy, its effects on states, and the problem of cooperation—modern realists like Waltz and Gilpin are very much in accord with classical realists like Carr, Aron, and Morgenthau. For an alternative view, see Richard Ashley, "The Poverty of Neorealism," in Robert O. Keohane, ed., *Neorealism and Its Critics* (New York: Columbia University Press, 1986), pp. 255–300.
2. Richard Rosecrance provided the insight that realism presents an essentially pessimistic view of the human condition: this is noted by Robert Gilpin, "The Richness of the Tradition of Political Realism," in Keohane, ed., *Neorealism and Its Critics*, p. 304. This pessimism in realist theory is most clearly evident in Hans J. Morgenthau, *Scientific Man vs. Power Politics* (Chicago: University of Chicago Press, 1946), especially pp. 187–203.

International Organization 42, 3, Summer 1988

The major challenger to realism has been what I shall call liberal institutionalism. Prior to the current decade, it appeared in three successive presentations—functionalist integration theory in the 1940s and early 1950s, neofunctionalist regional integration theory in the 1950s and 1960s, and interdependence theory in the 1970s.[3] All three versions rejected realism's propositions about states and its gloomy understanding of world politics. Most significantly, they argued that international institutions can help states cooperate. Thus, compared to realism, these earlier versions of liberal institutionalism offered a more hopeful prognosis for international cooperation and a more optimistic assessment of the capacity of institutions to help states achieve it.

International tensions and conflicts during the 1970s undermined liberal institutionalism and reconfirmed realism in large measure. Yet, that difficult decade did not witness a collapse of the international system, and, in the light of continuing modest levels of inter-state cooperation, a new liberal institutionalist challenge to realism came forward during the early 1980s.[4] What is distinctive about this newest liberal institutionalism is its claim that it accepts a number of core realist propositions, including, apparently, the realist argument that anarchy impedes the achievement of international cooperation. However, the core liberal arguments—that realism overemphasizes conflict and underestimates the capacities of international institutions to promote cooperation—remain firmly intact. The new liberal institutionalists basically argue that even if the realists are correct in believing that anarchy constrains the willingness of states to cooperate, states nevertheless can work together and can do so especially with the assistance of international institutions.

This point is crucial for students of international relations. If neoliberal

3. For functionalist international theory, see David Mitrany, *A Working Peace System* (Chicago: Quadrangle Press, 1966); see also Ernst B. Haas, *Beyond the Nation-State: Functionalism and International Organization* (Stanford, Calif.: Stanford University Press, 1964). On neofunctionalism, see Haas, *The Uniting of Europe: Political, Economic, and Social Forces, 1950–1957* (Stanford, Calif.: Stanford University Press, 1958); Haas, "Technology, Pluralism, and the New Europe," in Joseph S. Nye, Jr., ed., *International Regionalism* (Boston: Little, Brown, 1968), pp. 149–76; and Joseph S. Nye, Jr., "Comparing Common Markets: A Revised Neo-Functional Model," in Leon N. Lindberg and Stuart A. Scheingold, eds., *Regional Integration: Theory and Research* (Cambridge: Harvard University Press, 1971), pp. 192–231. On interdependence theory, see Richard C. Cooper, "Economic Interdependence and Foreign Policies in the 1970's," *World Politics* 24 (January 1972), pp. 158–81; Edward S. Morse, "The Transformation of Foreign Policies: Modernization, Interdependence, and Externalization," *World Politics* 22 (April 1970), pp. 371–92; and Robert O. Keohane and Joseph S. Nye, Jr., *Power and Interdependence: World Politics in Transition* (Boston: Little, Brown, 1977).

4. See Robert Axelrod, *The Evolution of Cooperation* (New York: Basic Books, 1984); Axelrod and Robert O. Keohane, "Achieving Cooperation Under Anarchy: Strategies and Institutions," *World Politics* 38 (October 1985), pp. 226–54; Keohane, *After Hegemony: Cooperation and Discord in the World Political Economy* (Princeton, N.J.: Princeton University Press, 1984); Charles Lipson, "International Cooperation in Economic and Security Affairs," *World Politics* 37 (October 1984), pp. 1–23; and Arthur Stein, "Coordination and Collaboration: Regimes in an Anarchic World," in Stephen D. Krasner, ed., *International Regimes* (Ithaca, N.Y.: Cornell University Press, 1983), pp. 115–40.

institutionalists are correct, then they have dealt realism a major blow while providing the intellectual justification for treating their own approach, and the tradition from which it emerges, as the most effective for understanding world politics.

This essay's principal argument is that, in fact, neoliberal institutionalism misconstrues the realist analysis of international anarchy and therefore it misunderstands the realist analysis of the impact of anarchy on the preferences and actions of states. Indeed, the new liberal institutionalism fails to address a major constraint on the willingness of states to cooperate which is generated by international anarchy and which is identified by realism. As a result, the new theory's optimism about international cooperation is likely to be proven wrong.

Neoliberalism's claims about cooperation are based on its belief that states are atomistic actors. It argues that states seek to maximize their individual *absolute* gains and are indifferent to the gains achieved by others. Cheating, the new theory suggests, is the greatest impediment to cooperation among rationally egoistic states, but international institutions, the new theory also suggests, can help states overcome this barrier to joint action. Realists understand that states seek absolute gains and worry about compliance. However, realists find that states are *positional*, not atomistic, in character, and therefore realists argue that, in addition to concerns about cheating, states in cooperative arrangements also worry that their partners might gain more from cooperation than they do. For realists, a state will focus both on its absolute and relative gains from cooperation, and a state that is satisfied with a partner's compliance in a joint arrangement might nevertheless exit from it because the partner is achieving relatively greater gains. Realism, then, finds that there are at least two major barriers to international cooperation: state concerns about cheating and state concerns about relative achievements of gains. Neoliberal institutionalism pays attention exclusively to the former, and is unable to identify, analyze, or account for the latter.

Realism's identification of the relative gains problem for cooperation is based on its insight that states in anarchy fear for their survival as independent actors. According to realists, states worry that today's friend may be tomorrow's enemy in war, and fear that achievements of joint gains that advantage a friend in the present might produce a more dangerous *potential* foe in the future. As a result, states must give serious attention to the gains of partners. Neoliberals fail to consider the threat of war arising from international anarchy, and this allows them to ignore the matter of relative gains and to assume that states only desire absolute gains. Yet, in doing so, they fail to identify a major source of state inhibitions about international cooperation.

In sum, I suggest that realism, its emphasis on conflict and competition notwithstanding, offers a more complete understanding of the problem of international cooperation than does its latest liberal challenger. If that is true, then realism is still the most powerful theory of international politics.

1. Realism and liberal institutionalism

Realism encompasses five propositions. First, states are the major actors in world affairs.[5] Second, the international environment severely penalizes states if they fail to protect their vital interests or if they pursue objectives beyond their means; hence, states are "sensitive to costs" and behave as unitary-rational agents.[6] Third, international anarchy is the principal force shaping the motives and actions of states.[7] Fourth, states in anarchy are preoccupied with power and security, are predisposed towards conflict and competition, and often fail to cooperate even in the face of common interests.[8] Finally, international institutions affect the prospects for cooperation only marginally.[9]

Liberal institutionalists sought to refute this realist understanding of world politics.[10] First, they rejected realism's proposition about the centrality of states.[11] For functionalists, the key new actors in world politics appeared

5. Morgenthau, *Politics Among Nations*, p. 10; see also Waltz, *Theory of International Politics*, p. 95.

6. Waltz, "Reflections on *Theory of International Politics:* A Response to My Critics," in Keohane, ed., *Neorealism and Its Critics*, p. 331.

7. Waltz, *Man, State, and War*, pp. 224–38; and Waltz, *Theory of International Politics*, pp. 79–128; Stanley Hoffmann, *The State of War: Essays in the Theory and Practice of International Politics* (New York: Praeger, 1965), pp. 27, 54–87, 129; Aron, *Peace and War*, pp. 6–10.

8. Aron, *Peace and War*, p. 5; Gilpin, "Political Realism," p. 304.

9. Waltz, *Theory of International Politics*, pp. 115–16; see also Morgenthau, *Politics Among Nations*, p. 512; and Stanley Hoffmann, "International Organization and the International System," in Leland M. Goodrich and David A. Kay, eds., *International Organization: Politics and Process* (Madison: University of Wisconsin Press, 1973), p. 50.

10. Liberal institutionalist theories may be distinguished from three other variants of liberal theory. One of these, trade liberalism, articulated by Richard Cobden and John Bright, finds that international commerce facilitates greater inter-state cooperation: for Cobden, see Arnold Wolfers and Laurence W. Martin, eds., *The Anglo-American Tradition in Foreign Affairs* (New Haven, Conn.: Yale University Press, 1956), pp. 192–205; with respect to both Cobden and Bright, see also Waltz, *Man, State, and War*, pp. 98–99, 103–7. A second variant, democratic structural liberalism, posited by Immanuel Kant and Woodrow Wilson, finds that democracies based on national self-determination are conducive to greater international cooperation. For Wilson, see Wolfers and Martin, eds., *Anglo-American Tradition*, pp. 263–79; for Kant and Wilson, see Waltz, *Man, State, and War*, pp. 101–3, 109–11, 117–19; and Michael W. Doyle, "Liberalism and World Politics," *American Political Science Review* 80 (December 1986), pp. 1151–69. Finally, a liberal transactions approach suggests that private international interactions promote international integration: see Karl Deutsch et al., *Political Community and the North Atlantic Area* (Princeton, N.J.: Princeton University Press, 1957); and Bruce Russett, *Community and Contention* (Cambridge, Mass.: MIT Press, 1963). Citing an unpublished study by Keohane, Nye recently refers to the first two variants as commercial and democratic liberalism, respectively, and suggests that the third might be termed sociological liberalism. See Joseph S. Nye, Jr., "Neorealism and Neoliberalism," *World Politics* 40 (January 1988), p. 246.

11. In a way quite different from liberal institutionalist theories, world systems analysis also challenges realism's focus on states. It suggests that they are not ultimate causes of world events but instead are themselves resultants of the development of a single world capitalist economy. See Immanuel Wallerstein, "The Rise and Future Demise of the World Capitalist System," in Wallerstein, *The Capitalist World System* (Cambridge: Cambridge University Press, 1979), pp. 1–37; and Wallerstein, *The Modern World System*, vol. 1 (New York: Academic Press, 1974).

to be specialized international agencies and their technical experts; for neofunctionalists, they were labor unions, political parties, trade associations, and supranational bureaucracies; and for the interdependence school, they were multinational corporations and transnational and transgovernmental coalitions.[12] Second, liberal institutionalists attacked the realist view that states are unitary or rational agents.[13] Authority was already decentralized within modern states, functionalists argued, and it was undergoing a similar process internationally.[14] Modern states, according to interdependence theorists, were increasingly characterized by "multiple channels of access," which, in turn, progressively enfeebled the grip on foreign policy previously held by central decision makers.[15]

Third, liberals argued that states were becoming less concerned about power and security. Internationally, nuclear weapons and mobilized national populations were rendering war prohibitively costly.[16] Moreover, increases in inter-nation economic contacts left states increasingly dependent upon one another for the attainment of such national goals as growth, full employment, and price stability.[17] Domestically, industrialization had created the present "social century": the advanced democracies (and, more slowly, socialist and developing countries) were becoming welfare states less oriented towards power and prestige and more towards economic growth and social security.[18] Thus, liberals rejected realism's fourth proposition that

12. See Mitrany, *Working Peace System*, pp. 17, 85–87, 133–34; Haas, *Beyond the Nation-State*, pp. 32–40; Haas, *Uniting of Europe*, pp. 16–31, 113–239, 283–340; Nye, "Comparing Common Markets," pp. 195–206; and Robert O. Keohane and Joseph S. Nye, Jr., "Introduction," and "Conclusion," in Keohane and Nye, eds., *Transnational Relations and World Politics* (Cambridge: Harvard University Press, 1972), pp. ix-xxix, 371–98.

13. A substantial body of literature that is not based on liberalism nevertheless shares the latter's skepticism about the unity and rationality of states. It finds that subsystemic forces, such as organizational and bureaucratic politics, small group dynamics, crisis decision-making, and individual psychology, all undermine state coherence and rationality. See Graham T. Allison, *Essence of Decision: Explaining the Cuban Missile Crisis* (Boston: Little, Brown, 1971); Irving J. Janis, *Groupthink*, 2d ed. (Boston: Houghton Mifflin, 1980); Ole R. Holsti, *Crisis Escalation War* (Montreal: McGill University Press, 1970); John D. Steinbruner, *The Cybernetic Theory of Decision* (Princeton, N.J.: Princeton University Press, 1974); Alexander L. and Juliette L. George, *Woodrow Wilson and Colonel House: A Personality Study* (New York: Dover, 1964); and Robert Jervis, *Perception and Misperception in World Politics* (Princeton, N.J.: Princeton University Press, 1976).

14. Mitrany, *Working Peace System*, pp. 54–55, 63, 69–73, 88, 134–38.

15. See Mitrany, *Working Peace System*, pp. 20, 32–38; Haas, "The New Europe," pp. 152, 155–56; Keohane and Nye, "Introduction," p. xxv, and "Conclusion," pp. 375–78; Morse, "Transformation," pp. 387–89; Cooper, "Interdependence," pp. 177, 179; and Keohane and Nye, *Power and Interdependence*, pp. 33–35, 226–29.

16. Mitrany, *Working Peace System*, p. 13; Morse, "Transformation," pp. 380–81; Keohane and Nye, *Power and Interdependence*, pp. 27–29, 228.

17. Mitrany, *Working Peace System*, pp. 131–37; Haas, "The New Europe," pp. 161–62; Cooper, "Interdependence," pp. 161–68, 173–74; Keohane and Nye, *Power and Interdependence*, pp. 26, 228.

18. See Mitrany, *Working Peace System*, pp. 41–42, 95–96, 136–37, 144–45; Haas, "The New Europe," pp. 155–58; Morse, "Transformation," pp. 383–85; and Keohane and Nye, *Power and Interdependence*, p. 227.

states are fundamentally disinclined to cooperate, finding instead that states increasingly viewed one another not as enemies, but instead as partners needed to secure greater comfort and well-being for their home publics.[19]

Finally, liberal institutionalists rejected realism's pessimism about international institutions. For functionalist theory, specialized agencies like the International Labor Organization could promote cooperation because they performed valuable tasks without frontally challenging state sovereignty.[20] For neofunctionalist theory, supranational bodies like the European Economic Community were "the appropriate regional counterpart to the national state which no longer feels capable of realizing welfare goals within its own narrow borders."[21] Finally, interdependence theory suggested that "in a world of multiple issues imperfectly linked, in which coalitions are formed transnationally and transgovernmentally, the potential role of international institutions in political bargaining is greatly increased."[22]

Postwar events, and especially those of the 1970s, appeared to support realist theory and to invalidate liberal institutionalism. States remained autonomous in setting foreign policy goals; they retained the loyalty of government officials active in "transgovernmental networks"; and they recast the terms of their relationships with such seemingly powerful transnational actors as high-technology multinational corporations.[23] Industrialized states varied in their economic performance during the 1970s in the face of similar challenges (oil shortages, recession, and inflation). Scholars linked these differences in performance to divergences, and not convergence, in their domestic political–economic structures.[24] A number of events during the 1970s and early 1980s also demonstrated that the use of force continued to be a pervasive feature of world politics: increases in East–West tensions

19. Neofunctionalists suggested that, for West European states, "the argument is no longer over the slice of the pie to go to each; it is increasingly over the means for increasing the overall size of the pastry." See Haas, "The New Europe," p. 158; see also pp. 160–62, 166–67. See also Mitrany, *Working Peace System*, pp. 92–93; Morse, "Transformation," pp. 383–85; and Cooper, "Interdependence," pp. 164–67, 170–72, 179.

20. Mitrany, *Working Peace System*, pp. 133–37, 198–211; see also Haas, *Beyond the Nation-State*.

21. Haas, "The New Europe," p. 159.

22. Keohane and Nye, *Power and Interdependence*, p. 35; see also pp. 36, 232–34, 240–42.

23. See Stephen D. Krasner, *Defending the National Interest: Raw Materials Investments and U.S. Foreign Policy* (Princeton, N.J.: Princeton University Press, 1978); Robert W. Russell, "Transgovernmental Interaction in the International Monetary System, 1960–1972," *International Organization* 27 (Autumn 1973), pp. 431–64; and Joseph M. Grieco, *Between Dependency and Autonomy: India's Experience with the International Computer Industry* (Berkeley: University of California Press, 1984).

24. See Peter J. Katzenstein, ed., *Between Power and Plenty: Foreign Economic Policies of Advanced Industrialized States* (Madison: University of Wisconsin Press, 1978); Katzenstein, *Small States in World Markets: Industrial Policy in Europe* (Ithaca, N.Y.: Cornell University Press, 1985); John Zysman, *Political Strategies for Industrial Order: State, Market, and Industry in France* (Berkeley: University of California Press, 1977); Zysman, *Governments, Markets, and Growth: Financial Systems and the Politics of Industrial Change* (Ithaca, N.Y.: Cornell University Press, 1983); and Peter Gourevitch, *Politics in Hard Times: Comparative Responses to International Economic Crises* (Ithaca, N.Y.: Cornell University Press, 1986), pp. 181–217.

and the continuation of the Soviet–American arms competition; direct and indirect military intervention and counter-intervention by the superpowers in Africa, Central America, and Southwest Asia; and the Yom Kippur and Iran–Iraq wars.[25] International institutions appeared to be unable to reshape state interests; instead, they were often embroiled in and paralyzed by East–West and North–South disputes.[26] Finally, supranationalism in West Europe was replaced by old-fashioned intergovernmental bargaining, and the advanced democracies frequently experienced serious trade and monetary conflicts and sharp discord over economic relations with the Soviet Union.[27]

And yet, international cooperation did not collapse during the 1970s as it had during the 1930s.[28] In finance, private banks and governments in developed countries worked with the International Monetary Fund to contain the international debt crisis.[29] In trade, the advanced states completed the Tokyo Round negotiations under the General Agreement on Tariffs and

25. On the continuing utility of force in the nuclear age, see Alexander L. George and Richard Smoke, *Deterrence in American Foreign Policy: Theory and Practice* (New York: Columbia University Press, 1974); Barry M. Blechman and Stephen S. Kaplan, *Force Without War: U.S. Armed Forces as a Political Instrument* (Washington, D.C.: Brookings Institution, 1978); Stephen S. Kaplan, *Diplomacy of Power: Soviet Armed Forces as a Political Instrument* (Washington, D.C.: Brookings Institution, 1981); and Richard Betts, *Nuclear Blackmail and Nuclear Balance* (Washington, D.C.: Brookings Institution, 1987).

26. East–West disputes in a specialized international agency are examined in Walter Galenson, *The International Labor Organization: An American View* (Madison: University of Wisconsin Press, 1981). North–South struggles within international institutions are discussed in Stephen D. Krasner, *Structural Conflict: The Third World Against Global Liberalism* (Berkeley: University of California Press, 1985).

27. On the problem of European integration, see Donald J. Puchala, "Domestic Politics and Regional Harmonization in the European Communities," *World Politics* 27 (July 1975), pp. 496–520; and Paul Taylor, *The Limits of European Integration* (New York: Columbia University Press, 1983). Trends towards a "new protectionism" supported realist arguments that the erosion of America's hegemonic position would produce a less open international economy. See Gilpin, *U.S. Power*, and Stephen D. Krasner, "State Power and the Structure of International Trade," *World Politics* 28 (April 1976), pp. 317–45. On trade conflicts during the 1970s, see John H. Jackson, "The Crumbling Institutions of the Liberal Trade System," *Journal of World Trade Law* 12 (March–April 1978), pp. 93–106; Bela and Carol Balassa, "Industrial Protection in the Developed Countries," *World Economy* 7 (June 1984), pp. 179–86; and Miles Kahler, "European Protectionism in Theory and Practice," *World Politics* 37 (July 1985), pp. 475–502. On monetary disputes, see Susan Strange, *International Monetary Relations of the Western World, 1959–1971*, vol. 2 of Andrew Shonfield, ed. *International Economic Relations of the Western World, 1959–1971* (Oxford: Oxford University Press for the Royal Institute of International Affairs, 1976), pp. 320–53; and Benjamin J. Cohen, "Europe's Money, America's Problems," *Foreign Policy*, No. 35 (Summer 1979), pp. 31–47. On disputes over economic ties with the Soviet Union, see Stephen Woolcock, *Western Policies on East-West Trade*, Chatham House Papers No. 15 (London: Routledge & Kegan Paul for the Royal Institute of International Affairs, 1982); and Bruce W. Jentleson, *Pipeline Politics: The Complex Political Economy of East–West Energy Trade* (Ithaca, N.Y.: Cornell University Press, 1986).

28. Stephen D. Krasner, "Preface," in Krasner, ed., *International Regimes*, p. viii.

29. See Charles Lipson, "Bankers' Dilemmas: Private Cooperation in Rescheduling Sovereign Debts," *World Politics* 38 (October 1985), pp. 200–25; also see Miles Kahler, ed., *The Politics of International Debt* (Ithaca, N.Y.: Cornell University Press, 1986).

Trade.[30] In energy, the advanced states failed to coordinate responses to the oil crises of 1973–1974 and 1979, but cooperated effectively—through the International Energy Agency—following the outbreak of the Iran–Iraq war in 1980.[31] Finally, in high technology, the European states initiated and pursued during the 1970s a host of joint projects in high technology such as Airbus Industrie, the ARIANE rocket program, and the ESPRIT information technology effort.[32] Governments had not transformed their foreign policies, and world politics were not in transition, but *states* achieved cooperation through *international institutions* even in the harsh 1970s. This set the stage for a renewed, albeit truncated, liberal challenge to realism in the 1980s.

2. The new liberal institutionalism

In contrast to earlier presentations of liberal institutionalism, the newest liberalism accepts realist arguments that states are the major actors in world affairs and are unitary–rational agents. It also claims to accept realism's emphasis on anarchy to explain state motives and actions. Robert Axelrod, for example, seeks to address this question: "Under what conditions will cooperation emerge in a world of egoists without central authority?"[33] Similarly, Axelrod and Robert Keohane observe of world politics that "there is no common government to enforce rules, and by the standards of domestic society, international institutions are weak."[34]

Yet neoliberals argue that realism is wrong to discount the possibilities for international cooperation and the capacities of international institutions. Neoliberals claim that, contrary to realism and in accordance with traditional

30. See Gilbert Winham, *International Trade and the Tokyo Round Negotiation* (Princeton, N.J.: Princeton University Press, 1986); see also Charles Lipson, "The Transformation of Trade: The Sources and Effects of Regime Change," in Krasner, ed., *International Regimes*, pp. 233–72; and Jock A. Finlayson and Mark W. Zacher, "The GATT and the Regulation of Trade Barriers: Regime Dynamics and Functions," in Krasner, ed., *International Regimes*, pp. 273–314.

31. See Robert J. Lieber, *The Oil Decade: Conflict and Cooperation in the West* (New York: Praeger, 1983); Daniel Badger and Robert Belgrave, *Oil Supply and Price: What Went Right in 1980?* (Paris: Atlantic Institute for International Affairs, May 1982); and Keohane, *After Hegemony*, pp. 217–40.

32. See Bruce L. R. Smith, "A New Technology Gap in Europe?" *SAIS Review* 6 (Winter–Spring 1986), pp. 219–36; and Walter A. McDougall, "Space-Age Europe: Gaullism, Euro-Gaullism, and the American Dilemma," *Technology and Culture* 26 (April 1985), pp. 179–203.

33. Axelrod, *Evolution of Cooperation*, p. 3; also see pp. 4, 6.

34. Axelrod and Keohane, "Achieving Cooperation," p. 226. Stein argues that his theory of international regimes "is rooted in the classic characterization of international politics as relations between sovereign entities dedicated to their own self-preservation, ultimately able to depend only upon themselves, and prepared to resort to force"; see Stein, "Coordination and Collaboration," p. 116. Lipson notes that Axelrod's ideas are important because they "obviously bear on a central issue in international relations theory: the emergence and maintenance of cooperation among sovereign, self-interested states, operating without any centralized authority"; see Lipson, "International Cooperation," p. 6.

liberal views, institutions can help states work together.[35] Thus, neoliberals argue, the prospects for international cooperation are better than realism allows.[36] These points of convergence and divergence among the three perspectives are summarized in Table 1.

Neoliberals begin with assertions of acceptance of several key realist propositions; however, they end with a rejection of realism and with claims of affirmation of the central tenets of the liberal institutionalist tradition. To develop this argument, neoliberals first observe that states in anarchy often face mixed interests and, in particular, situations which can be depicted by Prisoner's Dilemma.[37] In the game, each state prefers mutual cooperation to mutual noncooperation (CC>DD), but also successful cheating to mutual cooperation (DC>CC) and mutual defection to victimization by another's cheating (DD>CD); overall, then, DC>CC>DD>CD. In these circumstances, and in the absence of a centralized authority or some other countervailing force to bind states to their promises, each defects regardless of what it expects the other to do.

However, neoliberals stress that countervailing forces often do exist—forces that cause states to keep their promises and thus to resolve the Prisoner's Dilemma. They argue that states may pursue a strategy of tit-for-tat and cooperate on a conditional basis—that is, each adheres to its promises so long as partners do so. They also suggest that conditional cooperation is more likely to occur in Prisoner's Dilemma if the game is highly iterated, since states that interact repeatedly in either a mutually beneficial or harmful manner are likely to find that mutual cooperation is their best long-term strategy. Finally, conditional cooperation is more attractive to states if the

35. Keohane notes in *After Hegemony* (p. 9) that "I begin with Realist insights about the role of power and the effects of hegemony" but that "my central arguments draw more on the Institutionalist tradition, arguing that cooperation can under some conditions develop on the basis of complementary interests, and that institutions, broadly defined, affect the patterns of cooperation that emerge." Keohane also notes (p. 26) that "what distinguishes my argument from structural Realism is my emphasis on the effects of international institutions and practices on state behavior."

36. Keohane indicates in *After Hegemony* (pp. 14, 16) that he does not seek the wholesale rejection of realism. However, on the issue of the prospects for cooperation, like the question of international institutions, he does seek to refute realism's conclusions while employing its assumptions. He notes (p. 29) that "[s]tarting with similar premises about motivations, I seek to show that Realism's pessimism about welfare-increasing cooperation is exaggerated," and he proposes (p. 67) "to show, on the basis of their own assumptions, that the characteristic pessimism of Realism does not follow." Keohane also suggests (p. 84) that rational-choice analysis "helps us criticize, in its own terms, Realism's bleak picture of the inevitability of either hegemony or conflict." Finally, he asserts (p. 84) that rational-choice theory, "combined with sensitivity to the significance of international institutions," allows for an awareness of both the strengths and weaknesses of realism, and in so doing "[w]e can strip away some of the aura of verisimilitude that surrounds Realism and reconsider the logical and empirical foundations of its claims to our intellectual allegiance."

37. On the importance of Prisoner's Dilemma in neoliberal theory, see Axelrod, *Evolution of Cooperation*, p. 7; Keohane, *After Hegemony*, pp. 66–69; Axelrod and Keohane, "Achieving Cooperation," p. 231; Lipson, "International Cooperation," p. 2; and Stein, "Coordination and Collaboration," pp. 120–24.

TABLE 1. *Liberal institutionalism, neoliberal institutionalism, and realism: summary of major propositions*

Proposition	Liberal institutionalism	Neoliberal institutionalism	Realism
States are the only major actors in world politics	No; other actors include: —specialized international agencies —supranational authorities —interest groups —transgovernmental policy networks —transnational actors (MNCs, etc.)	Yes (but international institutions play a major role)	Yes
States are unitary–rational actors	No; state is fragmented	Yes	Yes
Anarchy is a major shaping force for state preferences and actions	No; forces such as technology, knowledge, welfare-orientation of domestic interests are also salient	Yes (apparently)	Yes
International institutions are an independent force facilitating cooperation	Yes	Yes	No
Optimistic/pessimistic about prospects for cooperation	Optimistic	Optimistic	Pessimistic

costs of verifying one another's compliance, and of sanctioning cheaters, are low compared to the benefits of joint action. Thus, conditional cooperation among states may evolve in the face of international anarchy and mixed interests through strategies of reciprocity, extended time horizons, and reduced verification and sanctioning costs.

Neoliberals find that one way states manage verification and sanctioning problems is to restrict the number of partners in a cooperative arrangement.[38] However, neoliberals place much greater emphasis on a second factor—international institutions. In particular, neoliberals argue that institutions reduce verification costs, create iterativeness, and make it easier to punish cheaters. As Keohane suggests, "in general, regimes make it more sensible to cooperate by lowering the likelihood of being double-crossed."[39] Similarly, Keohane and Axelrod assert that "international regimes do not substitute for reciprocity; rather, they reinforce and institutionalize it. Regimes incorporating the norm of reciprocity delegitimize defection and thereby make it more costly."[40] In addition, finding that "coordination conventions" are often an element of conditional cooperation in Prisoner's Dilemma, Charles Lipson suggests that "in international relations, such conventions, which are typically grounded in ongoing reciprocal exchange, range from international law to regime rules."[41] Finally, Arthur Stein argues that, just as societies "create" states to resolve collective action problems among individuals, so too "regimes in the international arena are also created to deal with the collective suboptimality that can emerge from individual [state] behavior."[42] Hegemonic power may be necessary to establish coooperation among states, neoliberals argue, but it may endure after hegemony with the aid of institutions. As Keohane concludes, "When we think about cooperation after hegemony, we need to think about institutions."[43]

3. Realism and the failure of the new liberal institutionalism

The new liberals assert that they can accept key realist views about states and anarchy and still sustain classic liberal arguments about institutions and international cooperation. Yet, in fact, realist and neoliberal perspectives on states and anarchy differ profoundly, and the former provides a more complete understanding of the problem of cooperation than the latter.

Neoliberals assume that states have only one goal in mixed-interest in-

38. See Keohane, *After Hegemony*, p. 77; Axelrod and Keohane, "Achieving Cooperation," pp. 234–38. For a demonstration, see Lipson, "Bankers' Dilemmas."
39. Keohane, *After Hegemony*, p. 97.
40. Axelrod and Keohane, "Achieving Cooperation," p. 250.
41. Lipson, "International Cooperation," p. 6.
42. Stein, "Coordination and Collaboration," p. 123.
43. Keohane, *After Hegemony*, p. 246.

teractions: to achieve the greatest possible individual gain. For example, Axelrod suggests that the key issue in selecting a "best strategy" in Prisoner's Dilemma—offered by neoliberals as a powerful model of the problem of state cooperation in the face of anarchy and mixed interests—is to determine "what strategy will yield a player the highest possible score."[44] Similarly, Lipson observes that cheating is attractive in a single play of Prisoner's Dilemma because each player believes that defecting "can maximize his own reward," and, in turning to iterated plays, Lipson retains the assumption that players seek to maximize individual payoffs over the long run.[45] Indeed, reliance upon conventional Prisoner's Dilemma to depict international relationships and upon iteration to solve the dilemma unambiguously requires neoliberalism to adhere to an individualistic payoff maximization assumption, for a player responds to an iterated conventional Prisoner's Dilemma with conditional cooperation *solely out of a desire to maximize its individual long-term total payoffs.*

Moreover, neoliberal institutionalists assume that states define their interests in strictly individualistic terms. Axelrod, for example, indicates that his objective is to show how actors "who pursue their own interests" may nevertheless work together.[46] He also notes that Prisoner's Dilemma is useful to study states in anarchy because it is assumed in the game that "the object is to do as well as possible, regardless of how well the other player does."[47] Similarly, Lipson suggests that Prisoner's Dilemma "clearly parallels the Realist conception of sovereign states in world politics" because each player in the game "is assumed to be a self-interested, self-reliant maximizer of his own utility."[48]

Finally, Keohane bases his analysis of international cooperation on the assumption that states are basically atomistic actors. He suggests that states in an anarchical context are, as microeconomic theory assumes with respect to business firms, "rational egoists." Rationality means that states possess "consistent, ordered preferences, and . . . calculate costs and benefits of alternative courses of action in order to maximize their utility in view of these preferences." In turn, he defines utility maximization atomistically; egoism, according to Keohane, "means that their [i.e., state] utility functions are independent of one another: they do not gain or lose utility simply because of the gains or losses of others."[49]

44. Axelrod, *Evolution of Cooperation*, pp. 6, 14. Stein acknowledges that he employs an absolute-gains assumption and that the latter "is very much a liberal, not mercantilist, view of self-interest; it suggests that actors focus on their own returns and compare different outcomes with an eye to maximizing their own gains." See Stein, "Coordination and Collaboration," p. 134. It is difficult to see how Stein can employ a "liberal" assumption of state interest and assert that his theory of regimes, as noted earlier in note 34, is based on the "classic [realist?] characterization" of international politics.

45. Lipson, "International Cooperation," pp. 2, 5.

46. Axelrod, *Evolution of Cooperation*, p. 9.

47. Ibid., p. 22.

48. Lipson, "International Cooperation," p. 2.

49. Keohane, *After Hegemony*, p. 27.

Neoliberalism finds that states attain greater utility—that is, a higher level of satisfaction—as they achieve higher individual payoffs. Also, in keeping with the concept of rational egoism, a utility function specified by the new theory for one state would not be "linked" to the utility functions of others. Hence, if a state enjoys utility, U, in direct proportion to its payoff, V, then the neoliberal institutionalist specification of that state's utility function would be $U = V$.[50]

Overall, "rational egoist" states care only about their own gains. They do not care whether partners achieve or do not achieve gains, or whether those gains are large or small, or whether such gains are greater or less than the gains they themselves achieve. The major constraint on their cooperation in mixed interest international situations is the problem of cheating.

And yet, realist theory rejects neoliberalism's exclusive focus on cheating. Differences in the realist and neoliberal understanding of the problem of cooperation result from a fundamental divergence in their interpretations of the basic meaning of international anarchy. Neoliberal institutionalism offers a well-established definition of anarchy, specifying that it means "the lack of common government in world politics."[51] Neoliberalism then proceeds to identify one major effect of international anarchy. Because of anarchy, according to neoliberals, individuals or states believe that no agency is available to "enforce rules," or to "enact or enforce rules of behavior," or to "force them to cooperate with each other."[52] As a result, according to neoliberal theory, "cheating and deception are endemic" in international relations.[53] Anarchy, then, means that states may wish to cooperate, but, aware that cheating is both possible and profitable, *lack a central agency to enforce promises*. Given this understanding of anarchy, neoliberal institutional theory correctly identifies the problem of cheating and then proceeds to investigate how institutions can ameliorate that particular problem.

For realists, as for neoliberals, international anarchy means the absence of a common inter-state government. Yet, according to realists, states do not believe that the lack of a common government only means that no agency can reliably enforce promises. Instead, realists stress, states recognize that, in anarchy, *there is no overarching authority to prevent others from using*

50. On payoffs and utility functions, see Anatol Rapoport, *Fights, Games and Debates* (Ann Arbor: University of Michigan Press, 1960), p. 121, and Michael Taylor, *Anarchy and Cooperation* (London: Wiley, 1976), pp. 70–74.

51. Axelrod and Keohane, "Achieving Cooperation," p. 226; see also Keohane, *After Hegemony*, p. 7; Lipson, "International Cooperation," pp. 1–2; Axelrod, *Evolution of Cooperation*, pp. 3–4; and Stein, "Coordination and Collaboration," p. 116.

52. See Axelrod and Keohane, "Achieving Cooperation," p. 226; Keohane, *After Hegemony*, p. 7; and Axelrod, *Evolution of Cooperation*, p. 6.

53. Axelrod and Keohane, "Achieving Cooperation," p. 226. Similarly, Lipson notes that while institutionalized mechanisms (such as governments) that guarantee the enforcement of contracts are available in civil society, "the absence of reliable guarantees is an essential feature of international relations and a major obstacle to concluding treaties, contracts, and agreements." The resulting problem, according to Lipson, is that "constraints on opportunism are weak." See Lipson, "International Cooperation," p. 4. Also see Keohane, *After Hegemony*, p. 93, and Stein, "Coordination and Collaboration," p. 116.

violence, or the threat of violence, to destroy or enslave them. As Kenneth Waltz suggests, in anarchy, wars can occur "because there is nothing to prevent them," and therefore "in international politics force serves, not only as the *ultima ratio*, but indeed as the first and constant one."[54] Thus, some states may sometimes be driven by greed or ambition, but anarchy and the danger of war cause all states always to be motivated in some measure by fear and distrust.[55]

Given its understanding of anarchy, realism argues that individual well-being is not the key interest of states; instead, it finds that *survival* is their core interest. Raymond Aron, for example, suggested that "politics, insofar as it concerns relations among states, seems to signify—in both ideal and objective terms—simply the survival of states confronting the potential threat created by the existence of other states."[56] Similarly, Robert Gilpin observes that individuals and groups may seek truth, beauty, and justice, but he emphasizes that "all these more noble goals will be lost unless one makes provision for one's security in the power struggle among groups."[57]

Driven by an interest in survival, states are acutely sensitive to any erosion of their relative capabilities, which are the ultimate basis for their security and independence in an anarchical, self-help international context. Thus, realists find that the major goal of states in any relationship is not to attain the highest possible individual gain or payoff. Instead, *the fundamental goal of states in any relationship is to prevent others from achieving advances in their relative capabilities*. For example, E. H. Carr suggested that "the most serious wars are fought in order to make one's own country militarily stronger or, *more often*, to prevent another from becoming militarily stronger."[58] Along the same lines, Gilpin finds that the international system "stimulates, and may compel, a state to increase its power; at the least, it necessitates that the prudent state prevent relative increases in the power of competitor states."[59] Indeed, states may even forgo increases in their absolute capabilities if doing so prevents others from achieving even greater gains. This is because, as Waltz suggests, "the first concern of states is not to maximize power but to maintain their position in the system."[60]

54. See Waltz, *Man, State, and War*, p. 232; and Waltz, *Theory of International Politics*, p. 113. Similarly, Carr suggests that war "lurks in the background of international politics just as revolution lurks in the background of domestic politics." See Carr, *Twenty Years Crisis*, p. 109. Finally, Aron observes that international relations "present one original feature which distinguishes them from all other social relations: they take place within the shadow of war." See Aron, *Peace and War*, p. 6.

55. See Gilpin, "Political Realism," pp. 304–5.

56. Aron, *Peace and War*, p. 7; also see pp. 64–65.

57. Gilpin, "Political Realism," p. 305. Similarly, Waltz indicates that "in anarchy, security is the highest end. Only if survival is assured can states safely seek such other goals as tranquility, profit, and power." See Waltz, *Theory of International Politics*, p. 126; also see pp. 91–92, and Waltz, "Reflections," p. 334.

58. Carr, *Twenty-Years Crisis*, p. 111, emphasis added.

59. Gilpin, *War and Change*, pp. 87–88.

60. Waltz, *Theory of International Politics*, p. 126; see also Waltz, "Reflections," p. 334.

States seek to prevent increases in others' relative capabilities. As a result, states always assess their performance in any relationship in terms of the performance of others.[61] Thus, I suggest that states are positional, not atomistic, in character. Most significantly, *state positionality may constrain the willingness of states to cooperate.* States fear that their partners will achieve relatively greater gains; that, as a result, the partners will surge ahead of them in relative capabilties; and, finally, that their increasingly powerful partners in the present could become all the more formidable foes at some point in the future.[62]

State positionality, then, engenders a "relative gains problem" for cooperation. That is, a state will decline to join, will leave, or will sharply limit its commitment to a cooperative arrangement if it believes that partners are achieving, or are likely to achieve, relatively greater gains. It will eschew cooperation even though participation in the arrangement was providing it, or would have provided it, with large absolute gains. Moreover, a state concerned about relative gains may decline to cooperate even if it is confident that partners will keep their commitments to a joint arrangement. Indeed, if a state believed that a proposed arrangement would provide all parties absolute gains, but would also generate gains favoring partners, then greater certainty that partners would adhere to the terms of the arrangement would only accentuate its relative gains concerns. Thus, a state worried about relative gains might respond to greater certainty that partners would keep their promises with a lower, rather than a higher, willingness to cooperate.

I must stress that realists do not argue that positionality causes all states to possess an offensively oriented desire to maximize the difference in gains arising from cooperation to their own advantage. They do not, in other words, attribute to states what Stein correctly calls a mercantilist definition of self-interest.[63] Instead, realists argue that states are more likely to concentrate on the danger that relative gains may advantage partners and thus

61. On the tendency of states to compare performance levels, see Oran Young, "International Regimes: Toward a New Theory of Institutions," *World Politics* 39 (October 1986), p. 118. Young suggests that realists assume that states are "status maximizers" and attribute to states the tendency to compare performance levels because each seeks "to attain the highest possible rank in the hierarchy of members of the international community." The present writer offers a different understanding of realism: while realism acknowledges that *some* states may be positional in the sense noted by Young, its fundamental insight is that *all* states are positional and compare performance levels because they fear that *others* may attain a higher ranking in an issue-area.

62. As Waltz suggests, "When faced with the possibility of cooperating for mutual gains, states that feel insecure must ask how the gain will be divided. They are compelled to ask not "Will both of us gain?" but "Who will gain more?" If an expected gain is to be divided, say, in the ratio of two to one, one state may use its disproportionate gain to implement a policy intended to damage or destroy the other." See Waltz, *Theory of International Politics*, p. 105.

63. Stein, "Coordination and Collaboration," p. 134.

may foster the emergence of a more powerful potential adversary.[64] Realism, then, finds that states are positional, but it also finds that state positionality is more defensive than offensive in nature.

In addition, realists find that defensive state positionality and the relative gains problem for cooperation essentially reflect the persistence of uncertainty in international relations. States are uncertain about one another's future *intentions*; thus, they pay close attention to how cooperation might affect relative *capabilities* in the future.[65] This uncertainty results from the inability of states to predict or readily to control the future leadership or interests of partners. As Robert Jervis notes, "Minds can be changed, new leaders can come to power, values can shift, new opportunities and dangers can arise."[66]

Thus, realism expects a state's utility function to incorporate *two distinct terms*. It needs to include the state's individual payoff, V, reflecting the realist view that states are motivated by absolute gains. Yet it must also include a term integrating both the state's individual payoff and the partner's payoff, W, in such a way that gaps favoring the state add to its utility while, more importantly, gaps favoring the partner detract from it. One function that depicts this realist understanding of state utility is $U = V - k\,(W - V)$, with k representing the state's coefficient of sensitivity to gaps in payoffs either to its advantage or disadvantage.[67]

64. In her review of Axelrod, Joanne Gowa cites the 1979 Waltz passage employed in note 62 and, following Taylor's terminology in *Anarchy and Cooperation* (pp. 73–74), suggests that a state may display "negative altruism." Furthermore, according to Gowa, a state "may seek to maximize a utility function that depends both on increases in its own payoffs *and* on increases in the difference between its payoffs and those of another state." See Joanne Gowa, "Anarchy, Egoism, and Third Images: *The Evolution of Cooperation* and International Relations," *International Organization* 40 (Winter 1986), p. 178. This portrays realist thinking in a manner similar to that suggested by Young and cited above in note 61. However, this understanding of state utility cannot be readily based on Waltz, for his core insight, and that of the realist tradition, is not that all states necessarily seek a balance of advantages in their favor (although some may do this) but rather that all fear that relative gains may favor and thus strengthen others. From a realist viewpoint, some states may be negative altruists, but *all* states will be "defensive positionalists." Waltz emphasizes that he does not believe that all states necessarily seek to maximize their power: see his statement cited in note 60 and see especially his "Response to My Critics," p. 334.

65. Waltz, for example, observes that "the impediments to collaboration may not lie in the character and the immediate intention of either party. Instead, the condition of insecurity—at the least, the uncertainty of each about the other's future intentions and actions—works against their cooperation." See Waltz, *Theory of International Politics*, p. 105.

66. Robert Jervis, "Cooperation Under the Security Dilemma," *World Politics* 30 (January 1978), p. 168.

67. Similar to the concept of a state "sensitivity coefficient" to gaps in jointly produced gains is the concept of a "defense coefficient" in Lewis Richardson's model of arms races. The latter serves as an index of one state's fear of another: the greater the coefficient, the stronger the state's belief that it must match increases in the other's weapons inventory with increases in its own. See Lewis F. Richardson, *Arms and Insecurity: A Mathematical Study of the Causes and Origins of War*, eds. Nicolas Rachevsky and Ernesto Trucco (Pittsburgh and Chicago: Boxwood Press and Quadrangle Books, 1960), pp. 14–15.

This realist specification of state utility can be contrasted with that inferred from neoliberal theory, namely, U = V. In both cases, the state obtains utility from the receipt of absolute payoffs. However, while neoliberal institutional theory assumes that state utility functions are independent of one another and that states are indifferent to the payoffs of others, realist theory argues that state utility functions are at least partially interdependent and that one state's utility can affect another's.[68] We may also observe that this realist-specified function does not suggest that any payoff achieved by a partner detracts from the state's utility. Rather, *only gaps in payoffs to the advantage of a partner do so.*

The coefficient for a state's sensitivity to gaps in payoffs—k—will vary, but it will always be greater than zero. In general, k will increase as a state transits from relationships in what Karl Deutsch termed a "pluralistic security community" to those approximating a state of war.[69] The level of k will be greater if a state's partner is a long-term adversary rather than a long-time ally; if the issue involves security rather than economic well-being; if the state's relative power has been on the decline rather than on the rise; if payoffs in the particular issue-area are more rather than less easily converted into capabilities within that issue-area; or if these capabilities and the influence associated with them are more rather than less readily transferred to other issue-areas.[70] Yet, given the uncertainties of international politics, a state's level of k will be greater than zero even in interactions with allies, for gaps in payoffs favoring partners will always detract from a state's utility to some degree.[71]

Faced with both problems—cheating and relative gains—states seek to ensure that partners in common endeavors comply with their promises and that their collaboration produces "balanced" or "equitable" achievements of gains. According to realists, states define balance and equity as distributions of gains that roughly maintain pre-cooperation balances of capabilities. To attain this balanced relative achievement of gains, according to Hans Morgenthau, states offer their partners "concessions"; in exchange, they expect to receive approximately equal "compensations." As an ex-

68. Robert Jervis also argues that realist theory posits at least partially interdependent state utility functions. See Jervis, "Realism, Game Theory, and Cooperation," *World Politics* 40 (April 1988), pp. 334–36.

69. A pluralistic security community, according to Deutsch and his associates, "is one in which there is real assurance that the members of that community will not fight each other physically, but will settle their disputes in some other way," and in which the members retain separate governments; the examples they provide are Canada—United States and Norway—Sweden. See Deutsch et al., *Political Community*, pp. 5–7.

70. Contextual influences on state sensitivities to gaps in gains are explored in Joseph M. Grieco, "Realist Theory and the Problem of International Cooperation: Analysis with an Amended Prisoner's Dilemma Model," *Journal of Politics* 50 (August 1988) pp. 600–24.

71. In contrast, Keohane finds that that relative gains concerns may impede cooperation only in cases in which states pursue "positional goods" such as "status"; see Keohane, *After Hegemony*, p. 54. Similarly, Lipson expects that states will be sensitive to relative gains only in security relationships; see Lipson, "International Cooperation," pp. 14–16.

ample of this balancing tendency, Morgenthau offers the particular case of "cooperation" among Prussia, Austria, and Russia in their partitions of Poland in 1772, 1793, and 1795. He indicates that in each case, "the three nations agreed to divide Polish territory in such a way that the distribution of power among themselves would be approximately the same after the partitions as it had been before."[72] For Morgenthau, state balancing of joint gains is a universal characteristic of the diplomacy of cooperation. He attributes this to the firmly grounded practice of states to balance power, and argues that "given such a system, no nation will agree to concede political advantages to another nation without the expectation, which may or may not be well founded, of receiving *proportionate* advantages in return."[73]

In sum, neoliberals find that anarchy impedes cooperation through its generation of uncertainty in states about the compliance of partners. For neoliberals, the outcome a state most fears in mixed interest situations is to be cheated. Yet, successful unilateral cheating is highly unlikely, and the more probable neoliberal "worst case" is for all states to defect and to find themselves less well off than if they had all cooperated. For neoliberal institutionalists, then, anarchy and mixed interests often cause states to suffer the opportunity costs of not achieving an outcome that is mutually more beneficial. Keohane and Axelrod argue that games like Prisoner's Dilemma, Stag Hunt, Chicken, and Deadlock illustrate how many international relationships offer both the danger that "the myopic pursuit of self-interest can be disastrous" and the prospect that "both sides can potentially benefit from cooperation—if they can only achieve it."[74]

Realists identify even greater uncertainties for states considering cooperation: which among them could achieve the greatest gains, and would imbalanced achievements of gains affect relative capabilities? In addition, a state that knows it will not be cheated still confronts another risk that is at least as formidable: perhaps a partner will achieve disproportionate gains, and, thus strengthened, might someday be a more dangerous enemy than if they had never worked together. For neoliberal theory, the problem of cooperation in anarchy is that states may fail to achieve it; in the final analysis, the worst possible outcome is a lost opportunity. For realist theory, state efforts to cooperate entail these dangers plus the much greater risk, for some states, that cooperation might someday result in lost independence or security.

Realism and neoliberal institutionalism offer markedly different views concerning the effects of international anarchy on states. These differences are summarized in Table 2. Compared to realist theory, neoliberal institutionalism understates the range of uncertainties and risks states believe they

72. Morgenthau, *Politics Among Nations*, p. 179.
73. Ibid., p. 180, emphasis added.
74. Axelrod and Keohane, "Achieving Cooperation," p. 231; see also Stein, "Coordination and Collaboration," pp. 123–24.

TABLE 2. *Anarchy, state properties, and state inhibitions about cooperation: summary of neoliberal and realist views*

Basis of Comparison	Neoliberal institutionalism	Political realism
Meaning of anarchy	No central agency is available to enforce promises	No central agency is available to enforce promises *or* to provide protection
State properties		
Core interest	To advance in utility defined individualistically	To enhance prospects for survival
Main goal	To achieve greatest possible absolute gains	To achieve greatest gains *and* smallest gap in gains favoring partners
Basic character	Atomistic ("rational egoist")	Defensively positional
Utility function	Independent: U = V	Partially interdependent: U = V − k (W − V)
State inhibitions concerning cooperation		
Range of uncertainties associated with cooperation	Partners' compliance	Compliance *and* relative achievement of gains *and* uses to which gaps favoring partners may be employed
Range of risks associated with cooperation	To be cheated and to receive a low payoff	To be cheated *or* to experience decline in relative power if others achieve greater gains
Barriers to cooperation	State concerns about partners' compliance	State concerns about partners' compliance *and* partners' relative gains

must overcome to cooperate with others. Hence, realism provides a more comprehensive theory of the problem of cooperation than does neoliberal institutionalism.

4. Conclusion

Neoliberal institutionalism is not based on realist theory; in fact, realism specifies a wider range of systemic-level constraints on cooperation than does neoliberalism. Thus, the next scholarly task is to conduct empirical tests of the two approaches. It is widely accepted—even by neoliberals—that realism has great explanatory power in national security affairs. However, international political economy would appear to be neoliberalism's preserve. Indeed, economic relationships among the advanced democracies would provide opportunities to design "crucial experiments" for the two theories.[75] That is, they would provide the opportunity to observe behavior confirming realist expectations in circumstances least likely to have generated such observations unless realism is truly potent, while at the same time they might disconfirm neoliberal claims in circumstances most likely to have produced observations validating neoliberal theory.[76]

According to neoliberal theory, two factors enhance prospects for the achievement and maintenance of political-economic cooperation among the advanced democracies. First, these states have the broadest range of common political, military, and economic interests.[77] Thus, they have the greatest hopes for large absolute gains through joint action. This should work against realism and its specification of the relative gains problem for cooperation. That is, states which have many common interests should have the fewest worries that they might become embroiled in extreme conflicts in the future and, as a result, they should have the fewest concerns about relative achievements of gains arising from their common endeavors. Neoliberal theory emphasizes another background condition: the economic arrangements of advanced democracies are "nested" in larger political-strategic alliances. Nesting, according to the theory, accentuates iterativeness and so promotes compliance.[78] This condition should also place realist theory at a disadvantage. If states are allies, they should be unconcerned that possible gaps in economic gains might advantage partners. Indeed, they should take comfort in the latter's success, for in attaining greater economic gains these partners become stronger military allies.

We can identify a number of efforts by advanced democracies to cooperate in economic issue-areas that were characterized by high common interests and nesting. In the trade field, such efforts would include the Tokyo Round codes on non-tariff barriers and efforts by the Nordic states to construct regional free-trade arrangements. In the monetary field, there are the ex-

75. A crucial experiment seeks real world observations confirming one theory's empirical expectations in circumstances most unlikely to have done so unless the theory is very powerful, while simultaneously disconfirming a competitive theory's empirical expectations in circumstances most likely to have provided such confirming observations. On the methodology of crucial experiments, see Arthur L. Stinchcombe, *Constructing Social Theories* (New York: Harcourt, Brace, 1968), pp. 20–28; and Harry Eckstein, "Case Study and Theory in Political Science," in Fred I. Greenstein and Nelson W. Polsby, eds., *Strategies of Inquiry*, vol. 7 of the *Handbook of Political Science* (Reading, Mass.: Addison-Wesley, 1975), pp. 118–20.

76. Such a crucial experiment would demonstrate realism's superiority over neoliberalism. On the other hand, if neoliberal theorists wanted to design a crucial experiment to demonstrate the superiority of their approach, they would focus not on North–North economic relations but rather on North–South relations or, better still, on East–West military interactions.

77. See Keohane, *After Hegemony*, pp. 6–7.

78. On the "nesting" of international regimes, see Keohane, *After Hegemony*, pp. 90–91; and Vinod K. Aggarwal, *Liberal Protection: The International Politics of Organized Textile Trade* (Berkeley: University of California Press, 1985).

periences of the European Community with exchange-rate coordination—the Economic and Monetary Union and the European Monetary System. Finally, in the field of high technology, one might examine European collaboration in commercial aviation (Airbus Industrie) or data processing (the Unidata computer consortium).[79] If these cooperative arrangements varied in terms of their success (and indeed such variance can be observed), and the less successful or failed arrangements were characterized not by a higher incidence of cheating but by a greater severity of relative gains problems, then one could conclude that realist theory explains variation in the success or failure of international cooperation more effectively than neoliberal institutional theory. Moreover, one could have great confidence in this assessment, for it would be based on cases which were most hospitable to neoliberalism and most hostile to realism.

However, additional tests of the two theories can and should be undertaken. For example, one might investigate realist and neoliberal expectations as to the *durability* of arrangements states prefer when they engage in joint action. Neoliberal theory argues that cheating is less likely to occur in a mixed interest situation that is iterated; hence, it suggests that "the most direct way to encourage cooperation is to make the relationship more durable."[80] If, then, two states that are interested in cooperation could choose

79. I am completing a study of the relative gains problem in the case of the Tokyo Round trade codes. Available studies suggest that the Economic and Monetary Union broke down during 1972–76 as a result of concerns by Britain, France, Ireland, and Italy that they had taken on disproportionate burdens and that West Germany was achieving disproportionate gains: see Loukas Tsoukalis, *The Politics and Economics of European Monetary Integration* (London: Allen & Unwin, 1977), p. 157. Its successor, the European Monetary System, was designed to ensure greater balance in the gains and losses among partners: see Peter Coffey, *The European Monetary System: Past, Present, and Future* (Dordrecht, Neth., and Boston: Martinus Nijhoff, 1984), pp. 21–26, 126–27. In the case of Scandinavian trade cooperation, Norway shifted from opposition during the 1950s and much of the 1960s to support at the end of the latter decade as it became less concerned about its capacity to achieve a satisfactory share of trade gains with Sweden: see Barbara Haskel, *The Scandinavian Option: Opportunities and Opportunity Costs in Postwar Scandinavian Foreign Policies* (Oslo: Universitetsforlaget, 1976), pp. 124–27. Much of the literature on the problem of regional integration among developing countries also emphasizes the importance of relative gains issues. See, for example, Lynn K. Mytelka, "The Salience of Gains in Third-World Integrative Systems," *World Politics* 25 (January 1973), pp. 236–46; W. Andrew Axline, "Underdevelopment, Dependence, and Integration: The Politics of Regionalism in the Third World," *International Organization* 31 (Winter 1977), pp. 83–105; and Constantine V. Vaitsos, "Crisis in Regional Economic Cooperation (Integration) Among Developing Countries: A Survey, "*World Development* 6 (June 1978), pp. 747–50. For case studies of the problem of relative gains in developing country regional efforts to cooperate, see Richard I. Fagan, *Central American Economic Integration: The Politics of Unequal Benefits* (Berkeley: Institute of International Studies, 1970); Lynn Krieger Mytelka, *Regional Development in a Global Economy: The Multinational Corporation, Technology, and Andean Integration* (New Haven, Conn.: Yale University Press, 1979), pp. 39–61; and Arthur Hazlewood, "The End of the East African Community," *Journal of Common Market Studies* 18 (September 1979), especially pp. 44–48 and 53–54.

80. Axelrod, *Evolution of Cooperation*, p. 129; also see Keohane, *After Hegemony*, pp. 257–59, in which he argues that there are "costs of flexibility" and that states commit themselves to regimes and thereby forgo a measure of flexibility in the future to attain cooperation in the present; and Axelrod and Keohane, "Achieving Cooperation," p. 234, in which they argue that international regimes promote cooperation because they "link the future with the present."

between two institutional arrangements that offered comparable absolute gains but that differed in their expected durability—one arrangement might, for example, have higher exit costs than the other—neoliberalism would expect the states to prefer the former over the latter, for each state could then be more confident that the other would remain in the arrangement. Realism generates a markedly different hypothesis. If two states are worried or uncertain about relative achievements of gains, then each will prefer a less durable cooperative arrangement, for each would want to be more readily able to exit from the arrangement if gaps in gains did come to favor the other.

A second pair of competing hypotheses concerns the *number of partners* states prefer to include in a cooperative arrangement. Advocates of neoliberalism find that a small number of participants facilitates verification of compliance and sanctioning of cheaters. Hence, they would predict that states with a choice would tend to prefer a smaller number of partners. Realism would offer a very different hypothesis. A state may believe that it might do better than some partners in a proposed arrangement but not as well as others. If it is uncertain about which partners would do relatively better, the state will prefer more partners, for larger numbers would enhance the likelihood that the relative achievements of gains advantaging (what turn out to be) better-positioned partners could be offset by more favorable sharings arising from interactions with (as matters develop) weaker partners.

A third pair of competing empirical statements concerns the effects of *issue linkages* on cooperation. Neoliberalism's proponents find that tightly knit linkages within and across issue-areas accentuate iterativeness and thus facilitate cooperation.[81] Realism, again, offers a very different proposition. Assume that a state believes that two issue-areas are linked, and that it believes that one element of this linkage is that changes in relative capabilities in one domain affect relative capabilities in the other. Assume also that the state believes that relative achievements of jointly produced gains in one issue-area would advantage the partner. This state would then believe that cooperation would provide additional capabilities to the partner not only in the domain in which joint action is undertaken, but also in the linked issue-area. Cooperation would therefore be unattractive to this state in direct proportion to its belief that the two issue-areas were interrelated. Thus, issue linkages may impede rather than facilitate cooperation.

These tests are likely to demonstrate that realism offers the most effective understanding of the problem of international cooperation.[82] In addition, further analysis of defensive state positionality may help pinpoint policy strategies that facilitate cooperation. If relative gains concerns do act as a

81. See Keohane, *After Hegemony*, pp. 91–92, 103–6; and Axelrod and Keohane, "Achieving Cooperation," pp. 239–43.

82. This, however, would certainly not mark the end of the liberal institutionalist challenge to realism. There are at least two related clusters of modern literature that are firmly rooted

constraint on cooperation, then we should identify methods by which states have been able to address such concerns through unilateral bargaining strategies or through the mechanisms and operations of international institutions. For example, we might investigate states' use of side-payments to mitigate the relative gains concerns of disadvantaged partners.[83] Thus, with its understanding of defensive state positionality and the relative gains problem for collaboration, realism may provide guidance to states as they seek security, independence, and mutually beneficial forms of international cooperation.

---

in the liberal institutionalist tradition, that attempt no compromise with realism, and that present an understanding of world politics markedly at odds with realist theory. The first cluster argues that international institutions embody and reinforce norms and beliefs that are held in common among states and that facilitate and guide their cooperative endeavors. The key works in this cluster include John Gerard Ruggie, "International Responses to Technology: Concepts and Trends," *International Organization* 29 (Summer 1975), pp. 557–83; Ruggie, "International Regimes, Transactions, and Change: Embedded Liberalism in the Postwar Economic Order," in Krasner, ed., *International Regimes*, pp. 195–231; Friedrich Kratochwil, "The Force of Prescriptions," *International Organization* 38 (Autumn 1984), pp. 685–708; John Gerard Ruggie and Friedrich Kratochwil, "International Organization: The State of the Art on an Art of the State," *International Organization* 40 (Autumn 1986), pp. 753–76; and Donald J. Puchala and Raymond F. Hopkins, "International Regimes: Lessons from Inductive Analysis," in Krasner, ed., *International Regimes*, pp. 61–92. The second cluster suggests that international institutions help states develop, accept, and disseminate consensual theoretical and empirical knowledge that can reinforce or introduce international norms leading to cooperation. Haas presented this argument in *Beyond the Nation State*, pp. 12–13, 47–48, 79–85; also see Haas, "Is There a Hole in the Whole? Knowledge, Technology, Interdependence and the Construction of International Regimes," *International Organization* 29 (Summer 1975), pp. 827–76; Haas, Mary Pat Williams, and Don Babai, *Scientists and World Order: The Uses of Technical Information in International Organizations* (Berkeley: University of California Press, 1977); Haas, "Why Collaborate? Issue-Linkage and International Regimes," *World Politics* 32 (April 1980), pp. 357–405; Haas, "Words Can Hurt You; Or, Who Said What to Whom About Regimes," in Krasner, ed., *International Regimes*, pp. 23–59; and Beverly Crawford and Stefanie Lenway, "Decision Modes and International Regime Change: Western Collaboration on East–West Trade," *World Politics* 37 (April 1985), pp. 375–402.

83. On the general concept of side-payments, see R. Duncan Luce and Howard Raiffa, *Games and Decisions: Introduction and Critical Survey* (New York: Wiley, 1957), pp. 168–69; and William H. Riker, *The Theory of Political Coalitions* (New Haven, Conn.: Yale University Press, 1962), pp. 34, 108–23. Deutsch and his associates determined that the capacity of advantaged regions to extend symbolic and material side-payments to disadvantaged regions was essential to national integration and amalgamation in such cases as Switzerland and Germany. See Deutsch et al., *Political Community*, p. 55. Similarly, special subsidies were provided to Italy and Ireland to attract them to the European Monetary System. See George Zis, "The European Monetary System, 1979–84: An Assessment," *Journal of Common Market Studies* 23 (September 1984), p. 58. In addition, Norway was attracted to the proposed Nordek arrangement during 1968–70 partly because Sweden offered to provide the bulk of the funds for a Nordic development bank that would be used in large measure to support Norwegian industrial projects. See Claes Wiklund, "The Zig-Zag Course of the Nordek Negotiations," *Scandinavian Political Studies* 5 (1970), p. 322; and Haskel, *Scandinavian Option*, p. 127. Finally, West Germany has sought to ameliorate U.S. concerns about relative burden-sharing in NATO through special "offset" programs aimed at reducing U.S. foreign exchange expenditures associated with its European commitment. See Gregory F. Treverton, *The "Dollar Drain" and American Forces in Germany: Managing the Political Economics of the Atlantic Alliance* (Athens, Ohio: Ohio University Press, 1978).

[8]

118 ASIL Proceedings, 1992

The View from the New Haven School of International Law

*By W. Michael Reisman**

Consider, for a moment, the sorts of professional problems encountered by the contemporary international lawyer:

*Yale Law School.

• As a member of the International Law Commission, you are charged with adapting the inherited principles of state responsibility to the political and technological environment of the twenty-first century and, as part of this task, with establishing rules for liability without fault.

• As a lawyer in the United Nations legal division, you have been asked to prepare the Secretary-General's Report on "strengthening and making more efficient within the framework and provisions of the Charter the capacity of the United Nations for preventive diplomacy, for peace-making and for peace-keeping."[1]

• As General Counsel of the National Security Council or Legal Adviser of the Department of State, you have been asked to advise the President of the United States as to whether to intercept and board, on the high seas, vessels believed to be carrying nuclear components to a Middle Eastern state.

• As a professor of international law, you want to appraise the quality of work of those who perform the tasks in the preceding examples.

The way you characterize these problems, the intellectual tools you use to research them and the information you think relevant for answering them will all be determined by your conception of law. Your conception will influence the role you assume, the method you use, the ethics you adopt and the outcome.

Like the proverbial elephant, the complex of social processes and organizations that are generally referred to as "the law" may be viewed from many different perspectives. People trained and sometimes locked into one perspective can scarcely believe there may be others, even less that they are equally authentic and that, for some or all tasks, they may be even more useful than the one with which they were indoctrinated and, as a result, with which they are comfortable. Each perspective is the basis for a legal jurisprudence.

Positivism views law from the perspective of the receiver of commands, the "political inferior."[2] From this perspective, law is a body of commands. This perspective assumes the independent moral value of obedience. The essential technical problem is properly identifying the content and meaning of the command and the circumstances and procedures for obedience to it.

An entirely different perspective, deriving from the natural law tradition, is that of the person charged with making decisions. From the perspective of the decision maker, the technical and moral problems that are confronted are not framed in terms of obedience but rather in terms of making choices that are appropriate for the relevant community.

The body of rules that serves to provide the positivist with strict commands requiring obedience does not disappear, but from the perspective of the decision maker those rules are more complex communications, conveying authoritative information about community policies of varying weights that must be assessed, in each case, and then shaped into a decision. The technical and moral problems associated with obedience recede.

Selecting the right jurisprudence for a task is critical. The New Haven School of jurisprudence is an entirely secular theory of law but it takes the perspective long associated with natural law, that of the decision maker. For New Haven, the

[1] Such a report was, in fact, requested by the Security Council on January 31, 1992. The Secretary-General is to submit the report by July 1, 1992. S/23500, 31 January 1992, at 3–4.

[2] JOHN AUSTIN, THE PROVINCE OF JURISPRUDENCE DETERMINED 1–3, 9–33 (1832). Law is a command from a political superior to a political inferior. For discussion of the relevance of this formula to the New Haven School, see W. MICHAEL REISMAN & AARON SCHREIBER, JURISPRUDENCE: UNDERSTANDING AND SHAPING LAW 270 (1987).

notion of decision extends across the range of social organization and throughout the hierarchy of power; it includes the making of law or legislation as well as its application through courts or other institutions, and it conceives of both these activities as operating at the constitutive or structural level and in all of the various value processes of a community, including the production of wealth, of enlightenment, of skill, of health and well-being, of affection, of respect and rectitude.

For the positivist, a primary jurisprudential and intellectual task is the identification of what must be obeyed. Hence the recurring concern with finding the "sources" of law. From the standpoint of the New Haven School, jurisprudence is a theory about making social choices. The primary jurisprudential and intellectual tasks are the prescription and application of policy in ways that maintain community order and, simultaneously, achieve the best possible approximation of the community's social goals. The jurisprudential tools necessary for performing these tasks must address a wide range of issues, including: (1) the way one looks at oneself; (2) the way one looks at the social process one is trying to understand and influence; and (3) the way one tries to influence it.

Clarification of Standpoint

Let's return for a moment to the proverbial elephant—the question of perspective. For any phenomenon, there are many possible standpoints, each of which affects it and how it is viewed. Clarity with regard to observational standpoint is an indispensable intellectual tool. Both the reference and content of the term "law" will vary depending on whether the standpoint is that of a member of the elite or the rank-and-file, whether the observer is a member of the system observed, is an outsider or is on the margin. Perception of the same phenomenon may vary depending on the culture, class, gender, age, or crisis-experience of the observer. Even within the legal establishment, reference and content will vary depending on whether the observer is a legislator, a judge, a prosecutor, a juror, a defense attorney, an accused or a victim. No standpoint is more authentic than another, but the scholar must be sensitive to the variations in perception that attend each perspective and must try to disengage himself or herself, select one that is appropriate to the task and carefully determine and consistently maintain it.

In all observation, the individual self-system is the ultimate instrument of perception, appraisal and choice. Because it is necessary to calibrate all instruments, a second preliminary intellectual task the New Haven School poses is one of "self-calibration" by various techniques of self-scrutiny: the person performing a decision function is urged to examine the self for latent emotional problems or neurotic tendencies, subgroup parochialism and the distortions that may arise from professional conditioning.

Focal Lenses

The New Haven School is also concerned with the way the observer looks at things, whether State Responsibility, the ability of the United Nations to perform its security functions, or the way freedom of the oceans is accommodated with security needs.

We all look at our environment and specific issues within it "through" a variety of conceptual categories. In the physical sciences, different lenses and dyes permit the observer to bring different features or properties of the same viewed object into sharper focus or greater prominence. A comparable function may be performed in the social sciences by carefully crafted conceptual categories that serve as "focal lenses."

(1) New Haven believes that a useful theory about law must avoid the temptation, so common in conventional legal method, to drastically reduce the universe of variables to a text or a few purportedly key social factors. You cannot get far with any of the problems we started with if you limit yourself to a few texts. New Haven's theory seeks to be as comprehensive as possible regarding the various factors that influence decision.

(2) In advanced, industrial and science-based civilizations, some major decisions are ongoing and incorporate, in the collection of information and the exploration of alternative possible arrangements, the efforts of many people. New Haven recognizes the demands of economy and tries to develop various techniques of selectivity, especially for rapid decision making.

(3) The notion of law as a body of rules, existing independently of decision makers and unchanged by their actions, is a necessary part of the intellectual and ideological equipment of the political inferior. It makes no sense in a jurisprudence which conceives of law as a process in which human beings try to influence the way social choices are made about the production and distribution of the things that they want, including considerations about the ways in which those decisions should be made. New Haven reserves the word "law" for processes of decision that are both consistent with the expectations of rightness held by members of a community (authoritative decisions) and effective (controlling decisions). While the particular mix of authority and control may vary widely, a conception of law as authoritative and controlling decision avoids exercises in irrelevance, whether because of absence of authority or absence of control.

(4) A commonly observed pathology of conventional legal research is its tendency to examine only words in documents. A jurisprudence concerned with understanding and influencing the way people behave must be able to study and account for what people do as well as what they say, think and feel. Deeds, as well as words, are indicators of subjectivity, so New Haven recommends a focus on both.

(5) In any group process, some decisions will be concerned with the way decisions henceforth will be taken in that setting. We reserve the term "constitutive process" to focus attention on that portion of a group's activity concerned with establishing, maintaining or changing the fundamental institutions and procedures of decision making.

A Map of Community Processes

Focal lenses address the question of *how* observers look at pertinent data. We have yet to consider *what* observers look at. Conventional legal analyses and jurisprudences that conceive of law as a body of rules look only at a limited number of texts, characterized as legal, and those social events, "facts," to which the rules direct attention. Because New Haven's goal is understanding and influencing decision in ways that will precipitate desired social outcomes, the *what* of inquiry is necessarily broader than the *what* of conventional analysis.

The New Haven School has adapted, with a number of adjustments, a scheme of cultural anthropology, in which any social process is described systematically in terms of those who engage in it (the participants), the subjective dimensions that animate them (their perspectives), the situations in which they interact, the resources upon which they draw, the ways they manipulate those resources and the aggregate outcomes of the process of interaction, which are conceived in terms of a comprehensive set of values.

The participants in any decision process include those formally endowed with decision competence, for example judges, and all those other actors who, though not endowed with formal competence, may nonetheless play important roles in influencing decisions. In international decision, the observer must examine, in addition to formal international organizations, state officials, nongovernmental organizations, pressure groups, interest groups, gangs, and individuals, who act on behalf of all other participants and on their own. I don't see how an assessment of the dangers to and assets of the international community could be realistic and useful to the Secretary-General in the second example, without this expansion of focus.

By the same token, the inventory will not be of much use if it does not take account of the ways these various actors see things. The perspectives of these actors include their specific patterns of identification and disidentification, their matter-of-fact expectations and the value demands they project. It is clear that in a complex arena such as international politics, the perspectives of the various participants actually playing a role in decision often diverge greatly in critical ways.

"Situations," as New Haven uses the term, refers generally to where decisions are made and to special properties of that "where." Conventional legal analysis generally looks to courts, secondarily examining the work of executive branches and legislatures. New Haven focuses on the range of centralized and decentralized settings in which decisions are made, their varying degree of organization and formality, the extent to which they are specialized and the extent to which they are continuous or episodic. We also examine the extent to which participants in a particular situation perceive themselves in a state of crisis—that is, a state in which critical values are deemed to be at stake.

The resources on which participants draw, their "bases of power," incorporate both effective power and symbols of authority. The New Haven School considers it appropriate for the jurist to correlate the extent, if any, to which control of power is available to support particular formulations.

In contrast to conventional legal analysis, which usually characterizes the outcome of a legal decision as a more specific statement of rule, New Haven seeks to conceive of outcomes, as do those affected by them, in terms of the confirmation and/or redistribution of the values at stake: of power, enlightenment, wealth, skill, well-being, affection, respect and rectitude.

Decision Functions

In most contemporary theories of jurisprudence, the term "decision" generally refers to a judge applying rules to a particular dispute in an organized setting. From the standpoint of a jurisprudence concerned with understanding and making choices, however, it is clear that the operation of making choices involves many more component functions. If one systematically separates out the elements of a decision, one can identify:

(1) intelligence-gathering or the collection, processing, and dissemination of information relevant to social choices;
(2) promotion or the processes by which consciousness of a discrepancy between a desirable state and one that is or is about to take place gradually leads to a demand for some type of community intervention and regulation;

(3) prescription or lawmaking, which occurs when actors, with varying degrees of authority, select and install certain preferences about policy as community law. This may be accomplished by a legislature or some other organized lawmaker; but it is usually, and, especially in international law, largely accomplished in informal and sometimes even chaotic processes whose outcomes are generally referred to as "custom."

(4) invocation or the provisional characterization of a certain action as inconsistent with a prescription or law that has been established. Invocation is often accompanied by the demand that an appropriate community institution act;

(5) application or the conventional conception of law: the organization of the facts of a dispute, the specification of a norm or norms that apply and the fashioning of a mandatory formulation. When this takes place in a court, it is called a judgment, but it also occurs in informal, unorganized situations;

(6) termination or the abrogation of existing norms and the social arrangements based upon them, the development of transitional regimes and, where appropriate or necessary, the design of compensation programs for those who have made good-faith value investments expecting the old regime to continue;

(7) appraisal, which is concerned with evaluating the aggregate performance of all decision functions in terms of community requirements.

A jurisprudential theory concerned only with obeying rules may content itself with a few of these decision functions. But a theory that wishes to understand fully the operation of law and to equip jurists to identify and influence decisions in all settings must use a more detailed concept of decision functions.

Intellectual Tasks of the Jurist

Until now, we have examined the way in which the New Haven School recommends that jurists prepare themselves for decision by clarification of observational standpoint and scrutiny of self, conscious selection of the focal lenses recommended for examining data pertinent to decision, deployment of the map of the manifold of social reality for the organization and interrelation of those data with reference to the specific decision operations through which community policy is clarified and implemented in order to influence the production and distribution of values or desired events. That production/distribution is the major concern of both politics and law in every community.

Many of these conceptual tools are used, in varying fashion, by scholars in other disciplines. Jurists are distinctive among them in that they alone undertake, explicitly, to intervene in the social process that has been examined in order to secure changes in its pattern of authoritative decision so that it will henceforth discriminate in favor of a particular party or, one hopes, in favor of the common interest. We have found it useful to develop procedures for this juridical task. The procedures relate to each of five intellectual tasks performed by all who participate in the operations or functions of decision.

(1) *Goal Clarification.* A conception of purposive behavior requires an idea of what end that behavior seeks to secure. New Haven recommends that all who perform decision functions examine the demands of particular actors in terms of their congruence with the common interest, expressed as preferred patterns of production and distribution of every value within a system of stable minimum order.

(2) *Trend Analysis.* Once a goal has been specified, it is necessary to examine the degree to which it has been achieved in past decision. This essentially historical function identifies and organizes trends in pertinent past decision in terms of the goal expressed.

124 ASIL Proceedings, 1992

(3) *Factor Analysis*. It is important to correlate past decisions with conditions that influenced them and to note whether that context of conditions has changed in a material and pertinent way.

(4) *Predictions*. What are commonly called predictions may be made by a variety of techniques, but there is no determined future. What will be is a function, in varying measure, of what actors elect to do now. Projecting different decision options and then examining the prospective aggregate value consequences of each in terms of the goals that have been clarified permits the jurist to select and, through time, to adjust particular recommendations so that they increase the probability of the eventuation of a preferred future and minimize the eventuation of a dystopian one.

(5) *Invention of Alternatives*. Each of the problems with which we commenced demands much more than a summary of the rules of the past. When, as is often the case, predictions suggest a likely discrepancy between a goal preference and a probable future, the New Haven School recommends that the jurist explicitly explore alternative arrangements to increase the probability of the eventuation of a desired future. This intellectual task is active and interventionist and engages the fundamental responsibility of the jurist and the citizen.

Conclusions

I suspect that much of the confusion and even passionate anger the New Haven School generates arises from failure to understand the perspective it adopts. Yet, one simply cannot design or amend a constitution or create new institutional arrangements in a complex community without deploying many of the conceptions and tasks that the New Haven School tries to elaborate. On the other hand, the conceptions and tools proposed by New Haven have little relevance for Austin's "political inferior." Indeed, for those who demand an ideology of strict compliance with authority, the perspective of the New Haven School seems threatening, destructive, even evil.

Bent Rosenthal[3] made the interesting observation that New Haven's methodology seems better tooled for domestic than for international legal problems; I would have thought exactly the opposite. In circumstances in which the political and power environment is relatively unstable, the ecological environment is in a process of change, there is low or soft social consensus (if any) on many critical social goals and the aggregate consequences of different decision options on minimum political order are uncertain, the perspective and some equivalent of the methodology of the New Haven School will simply be necessary. These circumstances are recurring in international politics, and may be becoming less infrequent in domestic political systems as well.

Consider again the sorts of questions with which we commenced. While some of these questions might be "resolved" by finding an appropriate rule, most thoughtful people, I submit, would incline to view these as decisions that require a wider range of considerations and intellectual tasks, including clarification of what the community goals are or should be, what the aggregate consequences of the different options available to decision makers in terms of those goals would be, whether design of a particular response or a new institutional arrangement might be required and what constraints and possibilities are provided by the effec-

[3]Bent Rosenthal, Etude de l'oeuvre de Myres Smith McDougal en matière de droit international public (1970).

tive power environment. Much of modern international law is the product of individuals performing the decision functions I reviewed. Individuals created the human rights movement and the environmental movement. New Haven is concerned with clarifying a jurisprudence for these innovators and those who wish to join them.

That is, in brief, the view from New Haven.

[9]

LEGITIMACY IN THE INTERNATIONAL SYSTEM

*By Thomas M. Franck**

INTRODUCTION

The surprising thing about international law is that nations ever obey its strictures or carry out its mandates. This observation is made not to register optimism that the half-empty glass is also half full, but to draw attention to a pregnant phenomenon: that most states observe systemic rules much of the time in their relations with other states. That they should do so is much more interesting than, say, the fact that most citizens usually obey their nation's laws, because the international system is organized in a voluntarist fashion, supported by so little coercive authority. This unenforced rule system can obligate states to profess, if not always to manifest, a significant level of day-to-day compliance even, at times, when that is not in their short-term self-interest. The element or paradox attracts our attention and challenges us to investigate it, perhaps in the hope of discovering a theory that can illuminate more generally the occurrence of voluntary normative compliance and even yield a prescription for enhancing aspects of world order.

Before going further, however, it is necessary to enter a caveat. This essay attempts a study of why states obey laws in the absence of coercion. That is not the same quest as motivates the more familiar studies that investigate the sources of normative obligation.[1] The latter properly focus on the origins of rules—in treaties, custom, decisions of tribunals, *opinio juris*, state conduct, resolutions of international organizations, and so forth—to determine which sources, qua sources, are to be taken seriously, and how seriously to take them. Our object, on the other hand, is to determine why and under what circumstances a specific rule is obeyed. To be sure, the source of every rule—its *pedigree*, in the terminology of this essay—is *one* determinant of how strong its pull to compliance is likely to be. Pedigree, however, is far from being the only indicator of how seriously the rule will be taken, particularly if the rule conflicts with a state's perceived self-interest. Thus, other indicators are also a focus of this essay insofar as they determine the capacity of rules to affect state conduct.

* Editor in Chief. The author acknowledges the generous support of the Filomen D'Agostino and Max E. Greenberg Research Fund of New York University School of Law, the very helpful advice of his colleagues Paul Chevigny, Ronald Dworkin, David W. Kennedy, David Richards, Alfred Rubin, Michael Sharpston and Roberto Unger, and the unstinting research assistance of Steven Hawkins, Laurie Oberembt and William Richter. Particular thanks are due to several colleagues on the Board of Editors, and Ag. R.-J. Dupuy of the Collège de France, who have made profoundly useful suggestions.

[1] *See especially* Schachter, *Towards a Theory of International Obligation*, 8 VA. J. INT'L L. 300 (1968).

This essay posits that, in a community organized around rules, compliance is secured—to whatever degree it *is*—at least in part by perception of a rule as legitimate by those to whom it is addressed. Their perception of legitimacy will vary in degree from rule to rule and time to time. It becomes a crucial factor, however, in the capacity of any rule to secure compliance when, as in the international system, there are no other compliance-inducing mechanisms.

Legitimacy is used here to mean that quality of a rule *which derives from a perception on the part of those to whom it is addressed that it has come into being in accordance with right process*. Right process includes the notion of valid sources but also encompasses literary, socio-anthropological and philosophical insights. The elements of right process that will be discussed below are identified as affecting decisively the degree to which any rule is perceived as legitimate.

I. Why a Quest for Legitimacy?

Why study the teleology of law? What are laws *for*? What causes obedience? Such basic questions are the meat and potatoes of jurisprudential inquiry. Any legal system worth taking seriously must address such fundamentals. J. L. Brierly has speculated that jurisprudence, nowadays, regards international law as no more than "an attorney's mantle artfully displayed on the shoulders of arbitrary power" and "a decorous name for a convenience of the chancelleries."[2] That seductive epigram captures the still-dominant Austinian positivists' widespread cynicism towards the claim that the rules of the international system can be studied jurisprudentially.[3]

International lawyers have not taken this sort of marginalization lying down. However, their counterattack has been both feeble and misdirected, concentrating primarily on efforts to prove that international law is very similar to the positive law applicable within states.[4] This strategy has not been intellectually convincing, nor can it be empirically sustained once divine and naturalist sources of law are discarded in favor of positivism.

That international "law" is not law in the positivist sense may be irrefutable but is also irrelevant. Whatever label is attached to it, the normative structure of the international system is perfectly capable of being studied with a view to generating a teleological jurisprudence. Indeed, international law is the *best* place to study some of the fundamental teleological issues that

[2] J. Brierly, The Outlook for International Law 13 (1944) (quoting Sir Alfred Zimmern).

[3] Austin believed that law was the enforced command of a sovereign to a subject. J. Austin, The Province of Jurisprudence Determined (1832); *see also* Janis, *Jeremy Bentham and the Fashioning of "International Law,"* 78 AJIL 405, 410 (1984). This Austinian view has been widely shared by critics. See, however, H. L. A. Hart, The Concept of Law, ch. 10 (1961); and Williams, *International Law and the Controversy Concerning the Word 'Law,'* 22 Brit. Y.B. Int'l L. 146 (1945).

[4] For the best recent exposition of this view, see A. D'Amato, *Is International Law Really Law?*, in International Law: Process and Prospect 1 (1987).

arise not only in the international, but also in national legal systems. This makes it odd that it is not more frequently used as a field for investigation.

Up to a point, the Austinians are empirically right. The international system of states *is* fundamentally different from any national community of persons and of corporate entities. It is not helpful to ignore those differences or to cling to the reifying notion that states are "persons" analogous to the citizens of a nation. Some of the differences are of great potential interest. In a nation, Machiavelli noted, "there cannot be good laws where there are not good arms."[5] In the international community, however, there are ample signs that rules unenforced by good arms are yet capable of obligating states and quite often even achieve habitual compliance. The Austinians, beginning with a defensible empirical observation about the difference between national laws and international rules, deduce from the difference that rules governing conduct which are not "law" in the positivist sense cannot usefully be studied as a system of community-based obligations. It is *this* deduction—not the empirical observation—which is wrong.

Indeed, it is precisely the curious paradox of obligation in the international rule system that should whet our speculative appetite, provoking the opening, not the closing, of jurisprudential inquiry. *Why should rules, unsupported by an effective structure of coercion comparable to a national police force, nevertheless elicit so much compliance, even against perceived self-interest, on the part of sovereign states?* Perhaps finding an answer to this question can help us to find a key to a better, yet realistic, world order. The answer, if there is one, may also incidentally prove useful in designing more widely obeyed, less coerced, laws for ordering the lives of our cities and states.

A series of events connected with the role of the U.S. Navy in protecting U.S.-flagged vessels in the Persian Gulf serves to illustrate the paradoxical phenomenon of uncoerced compliance in a situation where the rule conflicts with perceived self-interest. Early in 1988, the Department of Defense became aware of a ship approaching the gulf with a load of Chinese-made Silkworm missiles en route to Iran. The Department believed the successful delivery of these potent weapons would increase materially the danger to both protected and protecting U.S. ships in the region. It therefore argued for permission to intercept the delivery. The Department of State countered that such a search and seizure on the high seas, under the universally recognized rules of war and neutrality, would constitute aggressive blockade, an act tantamount to a declaration of war against Iran. In the event, the delivery ship and its cargo of missiles were allowed to pass. Deference to systemic rules had won out over tactical advantage in the internal struggle for control of U.S. policy.

Why should this have been so? In the absence of a world government and a global coercive power to enforce its laws, why did the U.S. Government, with its evident power to do as it wished, choose to "play by the rules" despite the considerable short-term strategic advantage to be gained by seizing the Silkworms before they could be delivered? Why did preeminent

[5] N. MACHIAVELLI, THE PRINCE 71 (L. de Alvarez rev. ed. 1981).

American power defer to the rules of the sanctionless system? At least part of the answer to this question, quietly given by the State Department to the Department of Defense, is that the international rules of neutrality have attained a high degree of recognized legitimacy and must not be violated lightly. Specifically, they are well understood, enjoy a long pedigree and are part of a consistent framework of rules—the *jus in bello*—governing and restraining the use of force in conflicts. To violate a set of rules of such widely recognized legitimacy, the State Department argued, would transform the U.S. posture in the gulf from that of a neutral to one of belligerency. That could end Washington's role as an honest broker seeking to promote peace negotiations. It would also undermine the carefully crafted historic "rules of the game" applicable to wars, rules that are widely perceived to be in the interest of all states.

Such explanations for deferring to a rule in preference to taking a short-term advantage are the policymaker's equivalent of the philosopher's quest for a theory of legitimacy. Washington voluntarily chose to obey a rule in the Persian Gulf conflict. Yet it does not always obey all international rules. Some rules are harder to disobey—more persuasive in their pull to compliance—than others. This is known intuitively by the legions of Americans who deliberately underreport the dutiable price of goods purchased abroad, and by the aficionados who smuggle Cuban cigars into the country behind pocket handkerchiefs, but would not otherwise commit criminal fraud. That some rules *in themselves* seem to exert more pull to compliance than others is the starting point in the search for a theory of legitimacy.

The questions raised by such examples of obedience and disobedience, however, are more interesting when examined in the context of the international than of the national community. It is the voluntariness of international compliance that heightens the mystery and lures us with the possibility of discovery. Thus, while the Austinians are right in pointing to important differences between the place of law in national society and the place of rules in the society of nations, those differences do not justify the closing of the international rule system to jurisprudential inquiry.

Indeed, such inquiry into the international system ought to be aided by the insights developed by the study of national and subnational communities. Research into the teleology of national legal systems has led the way to a recognition of the role of legitimacy, as distinct from coercion, as the key to legal order and systematic obedience. While most students of national systems, except perhaps for a few utopians such as Foucault,[6] agree with Machiavelli that governance requires *some* exercise of power by an elite supported by coercive force, few any longer believe the Austinians' claim that this necessary condition is also a sufficient one. Having reached this

[6] Foucault rejects all notions of dominance, whether embodied in theories of sovereignty (divine rule, autocracy, "public rights" and so forth) or embraced in "mechanisms of discipline," including, for example, "power that is tied to scientific knowledge." He visualizes, instead, a new form of "right," which is antidisciplinarian and divorced from concepts of sovereignty. M. FOUCAULT, POWER/KNOWLEDGE: SELECTED INTERVIEWS AND OTHER WRITINGS 106–08 (C. Gordon ed. 1980).

conclusion, most students of law, power and structure in society have sought to identify other characteristics that conduce to the rule of law. Ronald Dworkin identifies three such characteristics: *fairness*, *justice* and *integrity* (the last being a principled, more sensitive variant of consistency).[7] Jürgen Habermas emphasizes the role of discursive validation, following the tradition of Aeschylus and Aristotle.[8] Important scholarship on contract theory has demonstrated that coercion need not be an essential element in ensuring the efficacy of a contract, which is more accurately seen as self-enforcing obligation.[9] In fact, much recent work focusing on the phenomenon of obedience and obligation in national societies concerns itself primarily with noncoercive factors conducing to consensual compliance.

While some such studies have emphasized the role of strategic concepts that gain voluntary compliance by mutualizing advantage, others, beginning with the seminal work of Max Weber,[10] have emphasized the role of *legitimacy* and *legitimation*. Weber's analysis stressed process legitimacy. He hypothesized that rules tend to achieve compliance when they, themselves, comply with secondary rules about how and by whom rules are to be made and interpreted. In his view, a sovereign's command is more likely to be obeyed if the subject perceives both the rule and the ruler as legitimate. Somewhat different concepts of legitimacy have been developed by Habermas[11] and by neo-Marxist philosophers.[12] Oscar Schachter, working in the field of international normativity, has elucidated and emphasized the

[7] R. DWORKIN, LAW'S EMPIRE 176–224 (1986).

[8] According to Habermas:

> Legitimacy means that there are good arguments for a political order's claim to be recognized as right and just; a legitimate order deserves recognition. *Legitimacy means a political order's worthiness to be recognized.* This definition highlights the fact that legitimacy is a contestable validity claim; the stability of the order of domination (also) depends on its (at least) de facto recognition. Thus, historically as well as analytically, the concept is used above all in situations in which the legitimacy of an order is disputed, in which, as we say, legitimation problems arise. One side denies, the other asserts legitimacy. This is a *process* . . . .

J. HABERMAS, COMMUNICATION AND THE EVOLUTION OF SOCIETY 178–79 (T. McCarthy trans. 1979).

[9] Kronman, *Contract Law and the State of Nature*, 1 J. L., ECON. & ORG. 5 (1985).

[10] Weber postulates the validity of an order in terms of its being regarded by the obeying public "as in some way obligatory or exemplary" for its members because, at least in part, it defines "a model" which is "binding" and to which the actions of others "will in fact conform." At least in part, this legitimacy is perceived as adhering to the authority issuing an order, as opposed to the qualities of legitimacy that inhere in an order itself. This distinction between *an* order (command) and *the* order (authority) is easily overlooked but fundamental. 1 M. WEBER, ECONOMY AND SOCIETY: AN OUTLINE OF INTERPRETIVE SOCIOLOGY 31 (G. Roth & C. Wittich eds. 1968). For a critique, see Hyde, *The Concept of Legitimacy in the Sociology of Law*, 1983 WIS. L. REV. 379.

[11] "What are accepted as reasons and have the power to produce consensus . . . depends on the *level of justification* required in a given situation." J. HABERMAS, *supra* note 8, at 183.

[12] Hyde, for example, believes that the concept of legitimacy should be abandoned and replaced by investigation of "rational grounds for action." Hyde, *supra* note 10, at 380. *See also* Bos, *Friede Durch Volkerrecht—Oder Durch Volkerlegitimitat?*, 17 NEDERLANDS TIJDSCHRIFT VOOR INTERNATIONAAL RECHT 113 (1970).

role of "competence and authority" in endowing a rule with capacity to obligate.[13] All have in common, however, their emphasis on noncoercive factors as conducing to rule-compliant behavior.

It thus appears that, despite its residual Austinian propensities, national jurisprudence has quite a bit to say to the international system precisely because there is empirical evidence that, in both systems, noncoercive factors play an important part in conducing to rule/law-compliant behavior. The special value to both national and international jurisprudential inquiry of studying the international system, however, lies in its unalloyed noncoercive state. While the dependence of the international system on voluntary compliance is often (and justly) perceived as a weakness, it happens to afford a singular opportunity. Critics of efforts to study legitimacy as a noncoercive factor conducing to compliance in national legal systems have been able to argue that this factor necessarily eludes researchers because it cannot be isolated from other, authoritarian, elements compelling obedience.[14] That critique loses its force, however, in the international context. Thus, the operation of the noncoercive element, or, specifically, *legitimacy*, becomes easier to isolate and study in the interstate system than in societies of persons, where the coercive sovereign always lurks in the background.

Yet there is a stronger motivation for studying legitimacy in the international system than the academic objective of creating a bridge from national to international speculative jurisprudence. A teleology that makes legitimacy its hypothetical center envisages—for purposes of speculative inquiry—the possibility of an orderly community functioning by consent and validated obligation, rather than by coercion. This is surely the realistic approach to an international jurisprudential teleology: one that examines the objective properties of the global rule system so as to study whether and how it may advance or perfect itself in accordance with the propensities of those observable properties. That inquiry begins with the unexplained, yet evident, paradox that autonomous actors systematically engage in rule-determined conduct, not infrequently in the face of a strong countervailing desire to pursue realizable short-term gratification in violation of the rules.

Admittedly, the rule system of the community of states is far from perfected: absence of rules and disobedience continue to be important dissonant features. But it is too readily assumed that these deficiencies are attributable primarily to the lack of an Austinian sovereign with police powers. The weakness of this explanation is its failure to account for significant deviance: that many rules are obeyed much of the time. What if, instead, rule disobedience, or a rule void, were attributable—in whole or in part—not to the absence of coercive power to enforce the rules but to the perceived lack of legitimacy of the actual or proposed rules themselves and of the rule-making and rule-applying institutions of the international system? Put another way, perhaps failure to obey the rules can best be studied through a better understanding of its opposite: voluntary deference to them.

[13] Schachter, *supra* note 1, at 309.

[14] Hyde, *supra* note 10, at 411–17, 422–25.

That might be rather good news. Since the world is not about to create a global supersovereign with overriding enforcement powers, it might be encouraging to know that these are not the prerequisites of a developed, functioning international community. It would be even more helpful to know that the global system of rules could be further refined and developed, even in the absence of the Austinian factors, by augmenting the legitimacy of rules and institutions. It would spur the social imagination to realize that the creation of a global regime with enforcement power might only be the final culmination of a process capable of gradually perfecting the community, not the sine qua non for system building.

If such a noncoercive, or voluntarist, community were a reasonable goal of the study of legitimation, the resulting society of states would still not resemble the modern nation. In place of coercion, there is only the claim to compliance, based on social entitlement, which a legitimate rule makes on, and on behalf of, all members of the community. In this sense, the international community more closely resembles a membership club with house rules. Membership confers a desirable status, which is manifested when the members have internalized socially functional and status-rooted privileges and duties. Membership is reinforced by valid governance, shared experience, reciprocal gestures of deference and recognition, common rituals, mature common expectations and the successful pursuit of shared goals. Obedience to law, in contrast, at least in part is a recognition of the coercive power of the organized state.

In both the state and the voluntarist international system, obedience to commands is evidence of the existence of an organized community. The international community, however, does not closely resemble the modern state, precisely because the activist state exists to issue and enforce sovereign commands, while the more passive international community exists to legitimize, or withhold legitimacy from, institutions, rules and its members and their conduct. The legitimacy of a rule, or of a rule-making or rule-applying institution, is a function of the perception of those in the community concerned that the rule, or the institution, has come into being endowed with legitimacy: that is, in accordance with right process.

What "right process" means in practice is the subject of the remainder of this essay. Pursuing this line of inquiry, we will focus most of our attention on the legitimacy of *rules*, although attention will also have to be paid to the legitimacy of those institutions and processes through which the rules come into being. In our inquiry we will begin with the rules themselves: their literary structure, origins, internal consistency, reasonableness, utility in achieving stated ends and connection to the overall rule system, and the extent to which their origins and application comport with the international community's "rules about rules." It is the underlying hypothesis of this essay that rules, to varying degrees, contain the determining elements of their own legitimacy.

If legitimacy can be studied, it can also be deliberately nourished. There lies the practical rationale of this inquiry. Someday, perhaps, the international system will come to have law and legal institutions that mirror their domestic counterparts. But that is not now, and it is not likely to be in the foreseeable future. H. L. A. Hart put it more gently: "though it is consistent with the usage of the last 150 years to use the expression 'law' here, the absence of an international legislature, courts with compulsory jurisdiction, and centrally organized sanctions ha[s] inspired misgivings, at any rate in the breasts of legal theorists."[15] Such misgivings, however, are not a cause for despair, nor should they be the end of the road of theoretical inquiry. On the contrary, the misgivings are valid but, for that very reason, are precisely the right starting point in the search for those elements which conduce to the growth of an orderly voluntarist international community and system of rules.

Four elements—the indicators of rule legitimacy in the community of states—are identified and studied in this essay. They are *determinacy*, *symbolic validation*, *coherence* and *adherence* (to a normative hierarchy). To the extent rules exhibit these properties, they appear to exert a strong pull on states to comply with their commands. To the extent these elements are not present, rules seem to be easier to avoid by a state tempted to pursue its short-term self-interest. This is not to say that the legitimacy of a rule can be deduced solely by counting how often it is obeyed or disobeyed. While its legitimacy may exert a powerful pull on state conduct, yet other pulls may be stronger in a particular circumstance. The chance to take a quick, decisive advantage may overcome the counterpull of even a highly legitimate rule. In such circumstances, legitimacy is indicated not by obedience, but by the discomfort disobedience induces in the violator. (Student demonstrations sometimes are a sensitive indicator of such discomfort.) The variable to watch is not compliance but the strength of the compliance pull, whether or not the rule achieves actual compliance in any one case.

Each rule has an inherent pull power that is independent of the circumstances in which it is exerted, and that varies from rule to rule. This pull power is its index of legitimacy. For example, the rule that makes it improper for one state to infiltrate spies into another state in the guise of diplomats is formally acknowledged by almost every state, yet it enjoys so low a degree of legitimacy as to exert virtually no pull towards compliance.[16] As Schachter observes, "some 'laws,' though enacted properly, have so low a degree of probable compliance that they are treated as 'dead letters' and . . . some treaties, while properly concluded, are considered 'scraps of paper.' "[17] By way of contrast, we have noted, the rules pertaining to belligerency and neutrality actually exerted a very high level of pull on Washington in connection with the Silkworm missile shipment in the Persian Gulf.

The study of legitimacy thus focuses on the inherent capacity of a rule to exert pressure on states to comply. This focus on the properties of rules, of course, is not a self-sufficient account of the socialization process. How rules

[15] H. L. A. HART, *supra* note 3, at 209.

[16] Permissible activities of diplomats are set out in Article 3 of the Vienna Convention on Diplomatic Relations, Apr. 18, 1961, 23 UST 3227, TIAS No. 7502, 500 UNTS 95. Obviously, these do not include espionage.

[17] Schachter, *supra* note 1, at 311.

are made, interpreted and applied is part of a dynamic, expansive and complex set of social phenomena. That complexity can be approached, however, by beginning with the rules themselves. Those seemingly inert constructs are shaped by other, more dynamic forces and, like tree trunks and seashells, tell their own story about the winds and tides that become an experiential part of their shape and texture.

II. Determinacy and Legitimacy

What determines the degree of legitimacy of any particular rule text or rule-making process? Or, to ask the same question another way: what observable characteristics of a rule or of a rule-making institution raise or lower the probability that its commands will be perceived to obligate? It is to such questions that the remainder of this analysis is addressed. One could approach the social phenomenon of noncoerced obedience directly, through such various openings as are afforded by the study of myths, game theory or contractarian notions of social compact. Instead, these and other socializing forces will be approached indirectly, through a unifying notion of *rule legitimacy*; that is, by approaching dynamic social forces through those rules which the society chooses to obey or to regard as obligatory. It should be borne in mind, however, that the norm-centered question—what is it about the properties of a rule that conduces to voluntary compliance?—is merely the lawyer's approach to larger sociological, anthropological and political questions: what conduces to the formation of communities and what induces members of a community to live by its rules?

Let us begin by examining the literary properties of the text itself that conduce to voluntary compliance or induce a sense of obligation in those to whom the rule is addressed.

Perhaps the most self-evident of all characteristics making for legitimacy is textual *determinacy*. What is meant by this is the ability of the text to convey a clear message, to appear transparent in the sense that one can see through the language to the meaning. Obviously, rules with a readily ascertainable meaning have a better chance than those that do not to regulate the conduct of those to whom the rule is addressed or exert a compliance pull on their policymaking process. Those addressed will know precisely what is expected of them, which is a necessary first step towards compliance.

To illustrate the point, let us compare two textual formulations defining the boundary of the underwater continental shelf. The 1958 Convention places the shelf at "a depth of 200 metres or, beyond that limit, to where the depth of the superjacent waters admits of the exploitation of the natural resources of the said areas."[18] The 1982 Convention on the Law of the Sea, on the other hand, is far more detailed and specific. It defines the shelf as "the natural prolongation of . . . land territory to the outer edge of the continental margin, or to a distance of 200 nautical miles from the baselines from which the breadth of the territorial sea is measured," but takes into

[18] Convention on the Continental Shelf, Art. 1, Apr. 29, 1958, 15 UST 471, TIAS No. 5578, 499 UNTS 311.

account such specific factors as "the thickness of sedimentary rocks" and imposes an outermost limit that "shall not exceed 100 nautical miles from the 2,500 metre isobath," which, in turn, is a line connecting the points where the waters are 2,500 meters deep.[19] The 1982 standard, despite its complexity, is far more determinate than the elastic standard in the 1958 Convention, which, in a sense, established no rule at all. Back in 1958, the parties simply covered their differences and uncertainties with a formula, whose content was left in abeyance pending further work by negotiators, courts, and administrators and by the evolution of customary state practice.[20] The vagueness of the rule did permit a flexible response to further advances in technology, a benefit inherent in indeterminacy.

Indeterminacy, however, has costs. Indeterminate normative standards not only make it harder to know what conformity is expected, but also make it easier to justify noncompliance. Put conversely, the more determinate the standard, the more difficult it is to resist the pull of the rule to compliance and to justify noncompliance. Since few persons or states wish to be perceived as acting in obvious violation of a generally recognized rule of conduct, they may try to resolve the conflicts between the demands of a rule and their desire not to be fettered, by "interpreting" the rule permissively. A determinate rule is less elastic and thus less amenable to such evasive strategy than an indeterminate one.

A good example of this consequence of determinacy is afforded by the recent litigation between Nicaragua and the United States before the International Court of Justice. From the moment it became apparent that Nicaragua was preparing to sue the United States, State Department attorneys began to prepare the defense strategy. One option considered was invoking the "Connally reservation," which, as part of the U.S. acceptance of the jurisdiction of the International Court of Justice, specifically barred the Court from entertaining any case that pertains to "domestic" matters *as determined by the United States*.[21] Yet the American lawyers chose not to use this absolute defense.[22] Instead, they tried in various other ways to challenge the Court's authority. They argued that the dispute was already before the Organization of American States and the UN Security Council; that it was

[19] United Nations Convention on the Law of the Sea, Art. 76, *opened for signature* Dec. 10, 1982, UN Doc. A/CONF.62/122, *reprinted in* UNITED NATIONS, OFFICIAL TEXT OF THE UNITED NATIONS CONVENTION ON THE LAW OF THE SEA WITH ANNEXES AND INDEX, UN Sales No. E.83.V.5 (1983), 21 ILM 1261 (1982).

[20] For a legislative history and analysis of the provisions of the 1958 Convention, see Whiteman, *Conference on the Law of the Sea: Convention on the Continental Shelf*, 52 AJIL 629 (1958).

[21] 92 CONG. REC. 10,694 (1946).

[22] As I have written elsewhere:

> That the Connally Reservation did not license the United States to refuse to litigate *any* case for *any* reason whatsoever, that a "good faith" caveat was to be implied, is to be given some support by the fact that Connally was not invoked by U.S. lawyers to withdraw the Nicaraguan case from the I.C.J.'s jurisdiction.

Franck & Lehrman, *Messianism and Chauvinism in America's Commitment to Peace Through Law*, in THE INTERNATIONAL COURT OF JUSTICE AT A CROSSROADS 3, 17 (L. Damrosch ed. 1987).

not a legal dispute at all, but a political one;[23] that Nicaragua, having failed to perfect its acceptance of the Court's compulsory jurisdiction, had no right to implead the United States. The failure of the lawyers to use the Connally shield is all the more remarkable because, whereas the reservation gave the United States a self-judging escape from the Court's jurisdiction, all the other defenses left the key jurisdictional decision up to the Court, which rejected every one.[24] Had the U.S. Government simply faced the Court with a "finding" that the mining of Nicaragua's harbors was a "domestic" matter for the United States, that would have ended the litigation. Instead, the United States went on to lose, not only on the matter of jurisdiction, but also, eventually, on the merits.[25]

Why was the Connally shield rejected? The answer, surely, lies in its determinacy. Anyone reading its language would instantly understand that the reservation, while rather open-ended, nevertheless was not intended to cover such matters as the CIA's alleged mining of the harbors of a nation with which the United States was not at war. Although the term "domestic matter" is not so determinate as to bar all differences of interpretation—that, after all, is why its interpretation was reserved to the U.S. Government and not left to the Court—*no* reasonable interpretation of the concept could be stretched to cover the events in question. The U.S. legal strategists, anxious to do everything possible to stay out of court, nonetheless were unwilling to subject their client to the obloquy that would have ensued had the Connally shield been deployed. Interest gratification, convenience and advantage were sacrificed so as not to be seen as absurd.

Such foreboding of shame and ridicule is an excellent guide to determinacy. If a party seeking to justify its conduct interprets a rule in such a way as to evoke widespread derision, then the rule has determinacy. The violator's evidently tortured definition of the rule can be seen to exceed its range of plausible meanings.

Thus, while it may be true in theory, as Wittgenstein has charged, that no "course of action could be determined by a rule because every course of action can be made out to accord with the rule,"[26] some rules are less malleable, less open to manipulation, than others. Although Wittgenstein's point has merit—and has recently been wittily adumbrated by Professor Duncan Kennedy[27]—in practice, determinacy is not an illusion. No verbal formulas are entirely determinate, but some are more so than others.

[23] The United States announced that the case involved "an inherently political problem that is not appropriate for judicial resolution." Department Statement, Jan. 18, 1985, DEP'T ST. BULL., No. 2096, March 1985, at 64, 64, *reprinted in* 24 ILM 246, 246 (1985), 79 AJIL 438, 439.

[24] Military and Paramilitary Activities in and against Nicaragua (Nicar. v. U.S.), Jurisdiction and Admissibility, 1984 ICJ REP. 392 (Judgment of Nov. 26).

[25] Military and Paramilitary Activities in and against Nicaragua (Nicar. v. U.S.), Merits, 1986 ICJ REP. 14 (Judgment of June 27).

[26] L. WITTGENSTEIN, PHILOSOPHICAL INVESTIGATIONS 81, para. 201 (G. E. Anscombe trans. 1953).

[27] Kennedy, *Towards a Critical Phenomenology of Judging*, 36 J. LEGAL EDUC. 518 (1986).

The degree of determinacy of a rule directly affects the degree of its perceived legitimacy. A rule that prohibits the doing of "bad things" lacks legitimacy because it fails to communicate what is expected, except within a very small constituency in which "bad" has achieved a high degree of culturally induced specificity. To be legitimate, a rule must communicate what conduct is permitted and what conduct is out of bounds. These bookends should be close enough together to inhibit incipient violators from offering self-serving exculpatory definitions of the rule. When almost everyone scoffs at such an exculpation, the outer boundary of the rule's determinacy has been established.

There is another sense in which determinacy increases the legitimacy of a rule text. A rule of conduct that is highly transparent—its normative content exhibiting great clarity—actually *encourages* gratification deferral and rule compliance. States, in their relations with one another, frequently find themselves tempted to violate a rule of conduct in order to take advantage of a sudden opportunity. If they do not do so, but choose, instead, to obey the rule and forgo that gratification, it is likely to be because of their longer term interests in seeing a potentially useful rule reinforced. They can visualize future situations in which it will operate to their advantage. But they will only defer the attainable short-term gain if the rule is sufficiently specific to support reasonable expectations that benefit can be derived in a contingent future by strengthening the rule in the present instance.

Let us consider the case of a foreign ambassador's son who has murdered someone in Washington, D.C. He is about to be "booked" by the District police when a message arrives from the State Department demanding his release. The Secretary of State announces that the culprit is to be sent home. Hearing of this, the public understandably is outraged; members of Congress complain to the President. Patiently, the Secretary of State explains that "almost all" states "almost always" act in accordance with the universal rules of diplomatic immunity, which protect ambassadors and their immediate family from arrest and trial.[28] Although in this instance, the Secretary continues, the rule does seem to work an injustice, in general it operates to make diplomacy possible. By gratifying popular outrage and violating the rule this time, the United States would weaken the rule's future utility, its reliability in describing and predicting state behavior. Alternatively, by acting in compliance with the rule, even at some short-term cost to its self-interest, the United States will reinforce the rule text and thus its future utility in protecting U.S. diplomats and their families abroad.[29] Indeed, a study by a committee of the British House of Commons—conducted after a shot from

[28] Vienna Convention on Diplomatic Relations, *supra* note 16, Arts. 31, 37.

[29] The Department of State, on Aug. 5, 1987, submitted its views on a " 'bill to make certain members of foreign diplomatic missions and consular posts in the United States subject to the criminal jurisdiction of the United States with respect to crimes of violence.' " The Department (Ambassador Selwa Roosevelt) "could not support the proposed legislation because it would be detrimental to U.S. interests abroad." If enacted, the law "would place the United States in violation of its international obligations" and would invite more harmful reciprocal action. Contemporary Practice of the United States, 82 AJIL 106, 107 (1988). For the text of Ambassador Roosevelt's statement, see also DEP'T ST. BULL., No. 2127, October 1987, at 29.

the Libyan embassy ("People's Bureau") on April 17, 1984, killed an on-duty London policewoman—came to something very like this conclusion despite the inflamed state of public opinion.[30]

Note, however, that this thoughtful argument by the Secretary against interest gratification only makes sense if the son's immunity is seen as part of a clearly understood normative package, that other countries will refrain from arresting members of the families of U.S. ambassadors on real or trumped-up charges. Such expectations of reciprocity are important threads in the fabric of the international system; but before an expectation of reciprocity can arise, there must be some mutual understanding of what the rule covers, what events constitute "similar circumstances." If the contents of the rule are vaguely defined and fuzzy—if some countries in some instances have extended immunity to the ambassador's children while others have not, or have done so only if no capital crime is involved, or only if the child was actually working for the embassy, or have not extended immunity to second sons, or daughters or stepchildren—the impetus for gratification deferral in the instant case would diminish. The demand for the trial of the ambassador's son might then be both reasonable and irresistible. It could quite easily be defended as not violating a "real" rule. The argument could also be made that bringing the son to trial would create no more hazards for American diplomats abroad than were already posed by the vagueness of the rule. If a norm is full of loopholes, there is little incentive to impose on oneself obligations that others can evade easily.

An excellent example of this cost of indeterminacy is offered by the rules prohibiting and defining aggression that were approved in 1974 by the General Assembly after some 7 years of debate. Among the actions branded as aggression is the "sending by or on behalf of a State of armed bands, groups, irregulars or mercenaries, which carry out acts of armed force against another State." Almost in the same breath, however, the text states that nothing in the foregoing "could in any way prejudice the right to self-determination, freedom and independence . . . of peoples forcibly deprived of that right . . . ; nor the right of these peoples . . . to seek and receive support." To confuse matters further, another article declares that no "consideration of whatever nature, whether political, economic, military or otherwise, may serve as a justification for aggression"; and yet another adds that in "their interpretation and application the above provisions are interrelated and each provision should be construed in the context of the other provisions."[31] Interrelated they may be, but like a tangled skein. Do they prohibit or encourage aid by one country to an insurgent movement in

[30] H.C. Foreign Affairs Committee, First Report, The Abuse of Diplomatic Immunities and Privileges, Report with Annex; Together with the Proceedings of the Committee; Minutes of Evidence Taken on 20 June and 2 and 18 July in the Last Session of Parliament, and Appendices (1984). *See also* Higgins, *The Abuse of Diplomatic Privileges and Immunities: Recent United Kingdom Experience*, 79 AJIL 641 (1985).

[31] Definition of Aggression, GA Res. 3314, 29 UN GAOR Supp. (No. 31) at 142, UN Doc. A/9631 (1974).

another? It is not that the individual mandates and caveats are opaque, but that, seeking to reconcile irreconcilable positions, they contradict one another. Such a muddled obligation, one would expect, could have little effect on the real-world conduct of states; and one would be right.

It happens—by way of contrast—that, in international practice, the rules protecting diplomats, as codified by the Vienna Convention, have a very high degree of specificity,[32] and they are almost invariably obeyed. So, too, are the highly specific rules, in another Vienna Convention, on the making, interpreting and obligation of treaties.[33] Among other subjects covered by determinate rules that exert a strong pull to compliance and, in practice, elicit a high degree of conforming behavior by states are jurisdiction over vessels on the high seas, and in territorial waters and ports,[34] jurisdiction over aircraft,[35] copyright and trademarks,[36] and international usage of posts,[37] telegraphs, telephones[38] and radio waves.[39] There is also a high degree of determinacy in the rules governing embassy property,[40] rights of passage of naval vessels in peacetime,[41] treatment of war prisoners[42] and the duty of governments to pay compensation—even if not as to the *measure* of that compensation—for the expropriation of property belonging to aliens.[43]

[32] *See* Vienna Convention on Diplomatic Relations, *supra* note 16, Arts. 27, 28.

[33] *See* Vienna Convention on the Law of Treaties, Arts. 6, 55, *opened for signature* May 23, 1969, UNTS Regis. No. 18,232, UN Doc. A/CONF.39/27 (1969), *reprinted in* 8 ILM 679 (1969), 63 AJIL 875 (1969).

[34] United Nations Convention on the Law of the Sea, *supra* note 19.

[35] Convention on Offenses and Certain Other Acts Committed on Board Aircraft, Sept. 14, 1963, 20 UST 2941, TIAS No. 6768, 704 UNTS 219.

[36] Universal Copyright Convention, July 24, 1971, 25 UST 1341, TIAS No. 7868 (revised version of 216 UNTS 132).

[37] *See* UNIVERSAL POSTAL UNION CONST., July 10, 1964, 16 UST 1291, TIAS No. 5881, 611 UNTS 7.

[38] *See* Telegraph and Telephone Regulations, with appendices, annex, and final protocol, Apr. 11, 1973, 28 UST 3293, TIAS No. 8586.

[39] *See* International Telecommunication Convention, Oct. 25, 1973, 28 UST 2495, TIAS No. 8572.

[40] *See* Vienna Convention on Diplomatic Relations, *supra* note 16, Art. 22 (which provides for inviolability of diplomatic missions and imposes a special duty on states to protect premises of missions on their territory). *See also* Convention on the Prevention and Punishment of Crimes Against Internationally Protected Persons, Including Diplomatic Agents, Dec. 14, 1973, 28 UST 1975, TIAS No. 8532, 1035 UNTS 167 (which criminalizes violent attacks upon the official premises of internationally protected persons).

[41] The right of innocent passage was specifically provided for in Article 14 of the Geneva Convention on the Territorial Sea and Contiguous Zone, Apr. 29, 1958, 15 UST 1606, TIAS No. 5639, 516 UNTS 205, and by Article 17 of the UN Convention on the Law of the Sea of 1982, *supra* note 19.

[42] *See* Convention Relative to the Treatment of Prisoners of War, Aug. 12, 1949, 6 UST 3316, TIAS No. 3364, 75 UNTS 135. For a complete treatment of war prisoners, see N. RODLEY, THE TREATMENT OF PRISONERS UNDER INTERNATIONAL LAW (1987).

[43] As to compensation for expropriated property, there is agreement in principle, but disagreement as to the measure of compensation. *See, e.g.*, Charter of Economic Rights and Duties of States, Dec. 12, 1974, Art. 2(2)(c), GA Res. 3281, 29 UN GAOR Supp. (No. 31) at 50, UN

What is interesting about these examples is that the high degree of textual determinacy goes together with a high degree of rule-conforming state behavior. When determinacy is absent, it is unlikely that states will have compunctions about not complying with the rule. Indeed, some rules are probably written with low determinacy so that noncompliance will be easy.

A good example is the abortive effort by the United Nations to draft a code for the prevention and punishment of terrorism. In 1972, at the initiative of Secretary-General Kurt Waldheim, the General Assembly tried its hand at devising a set of rules requiring states to act in concert against what was perceived as a global problem.[44] Two years of negotiations demonstrated the difficulty of coming to a commonly acceptable definition of the activity to be prohibited.[45] The Government of Senegal, for example, proposed on behalf of the Non-Aligned Group that the prohibition should include "acts of violence and other repressive acts by colonial, racist and alien régimes against peoples struggling for liberation, for their legitimate right to self-determination, independence and other human rights and fundamental freedoms." The same group urged an exception in favor of those committing terrorist acts on behalf of "the inalienable right to self-determination and independence of all peoples under colonial and racist régimes and other forms of alien domination," in recognition of "the legitimacy of their struggle, in particular the struggle of national liberation movements."[46] The Soviet Union demanded exemption from the prohibition on terrorism for "acts committed in resisting an aggressor in territories occupied by the latter, and action by workers to secure their rights against the yoke of exploiters."[47]

Understandably, the United States and other Western countries took the position that these exculpatory caveats, if adopted, would shape a definition

Doc. A/9631 (1974). *See also* Resolution on Permanent Sovereignty over Natural Resources, GA Res. 1803, 17 UN GAOR Supp. (No. 17) at 15, UN Doc. A/5217 (1962). Article 4 of the latter states in part concerning expropriation: "In such cases the owner shall be paid appropriate compensation, in accordance with the rules in force in the State taking such measures in the exercise of its sovereignty and in accordance with international law." *But see* Resolution on Permanent Sovereignty over Natural Resources, GA Res. 3171, 28 UN GAOR Supp. (No. 30) at 52, UN Doc. A/9030 (1973). Article 3 "affirms" that "each State is entitled to determine the amount of possible compensation and the mode of payment, and that any disputes which might arise should be settled in accordance with the national legislation of each State carrying out such measures."

[44] UN Docs. A/8791 and A/8791/Add.1 (1972).

[45] *See, e.g., Ad Hoc* Committee on International Terrorism, Observations of States Submitted in Accordance with General Assembly Resolution 3034 (XXVII), UN Docs. A/AC.160/1 and Adds. 1–2 (1973).

[46] UN Doc. A/AC.160/3/Add.2, at 3 (1973).

[47] UN Doc. A/AC.160/2, at 7 (1973). However, Ambassador Oakley has reported a new Soviet "awareness that distinctions must be made between so-called liberation movements and groups whose objectives and operations are primarily directed toward producing terror, and whose targets are often unrelated to their putative 'liberation' goals." Oakley, *International Terrorism*, 65 FOREIGN AFF. 628 (1987).

of terrorism that would exacerbate, rather than ameliorate, the problem. The loopholes would be so large as to permit unimpeded passage for almost any act of violence claimed to be directed against a wicked regime. On the other hand, few governments would be willing to implement a prohibition on all politically motivated violence against every regime, no matter how repressive. Even the United States has put forward the "Reagan Doctrine,"[48] with its sophisticated distinctions that exculpate external support for "good" insurgents against "bad" regimes, while excoriating support for "bad" insurgents against "good" regimes.[49]

The Reagan Doctrine was merely the most recent restatement of the "just war" notion, evolved by Christian thinkers in the time of Emperor Constantine to reconcile their pacifist theology with imperial military needs,[50] and reinterpreted by Augustine,[51] Aquinas[52] and Grotius.[53] Each version has sought to define the circumstances in which war is permissible, against the background of a more general prohibition. These efforts appeal to common sense and human decency. As long as there is no Austinian world sovereign and centralized world police force, there will be good (defensive) wars and bad (aggressive) wars. Articles 2(4) and 51 of the United Nations Charter[54] likewise seem to bless this distinction. The problem is to distinguish good violence from bad without the benefit of a papal decision.

This problem—how to tell the sheep from the goats—operates whenever a rule tolerates exculpatory distinctions. While simple rules inherently suffer from lack of humanity, reason and texture, more complex ones tend to be hard to apply or to make exculpation too easy. Thus we have a literary conundrum. In consequence of making a simple, but irrational, rule more complex, sensible and humane, the text may become too elastic to secure compliance. For example, applying the proposed international norms known as the Reagan Doctrine, Ambassador Jeane Kirkpatrick has argued that U.S. support for the Nicaraguan contras is permissible, but Soviet and Cuban support for the Sandinistas is not, because the contras are democrats fighting a totalitarian regime while the Sandinistas are totalitarians used by

[48] See Address by Ambassador Kirkpatrick, National Press Club (May 30, 1985), which in effect gave new life to the "just war" doctrine.

[49] On this policy, see Franck, *Porfiry's Proposition: Legitimacy and Terrorism*, 20 VAND. J. TRANSNAT'L L. 195, 218 (1987). *See infra* text accompanying note 55.

[50] F. RUSSELL, THE JUST WAR IN THE MIDDLE AGES 12 (1975).

[51] *Id.* at 18–20.

[52] T. AQUINAS, SUMMA THEOLOGIAE, Question 40, Art. 1 (T. Heath trans. 1972).

[53] *See* H. GROTIUS, ON THE LAW OF WAR AND PEACE (L. Loomis trans. 1949); Edwards, *The Law of War in the Thought of Hugo Grotius*, 19 J. PUB. L. 371 (1970). Grotius expressly contemplated intervention by a third state to protect the natural law rights of the citizens of another state. *See* bk. II, ch. XXV of H. GROTIUS, *supra* (entitled "On the Causes of Undertaking War on Behalf of Others").

[54] UN CHARTER. Article 2(4) seeks to curb aggressive wars by imposing the obligation on states to refrain from the threat or use of force against the territorial integrity or political independence of any state, while Article 51 provides support for the inherent right of individual or collective self-defense in case of armed attack.

Russians and Cubans to colonize Nicaragua.[55] A rule that lends itself to that interpretation, however humane and rational its intent, is unlikely to inhibit any state from pursuing every opportunity for short-term interest gratification. It will be dismissed from serious consideration by states as they weigh their options.

Determinacy thus poses a dilemma. As defined, the term "determinacy" has been used to indicate the clarity of the message transmitted by a rule to those at whom it is directed as a command. We have argued that greater clarity conduces to compliance. Now, however, it has become apparent that "clarity" is far from identical with simplicity. For example, the UN Charter, in Articles 2(4) and 51, sets out a simple rule pertaining to the use of force. It says, in substance, that a state may not use force against another except to respond to an *actual armed attack*. This rule, on its face, seems to enjoy a high level of determinacy. And in most instances of conflict, the rule also makes sense. It is usually possible, in these days of outer space sensing devices, to provide persuasive proof of which state initiated hostilities. Even without such evidence, the answer can usually be determined by looking to see which party is winning after the first day of fighting. Nevertheless, despite its superficial clarity, the rule—under certain circumstances—does not satisfy the test of genuine determinacy: it does not send a clear message as to its meaning in such a way as to promote compliance. This is because a literal reading of the law will produce absurd obligations at the margins of its application. Thus, the rule would seem to compel a state threatened by a nuclear attack to wait until it had actually been hit ("armed attack") before being permitted to use force in self-defense.[56] The rule would also require a tiny state like Israel or Singapore to wait until after an armed attack before striking back, even though it might well have been overrun in that first offensive. In Mr. Bumble's words, "If the law supposes that, the law is a ass—a idiot." Such a rule lacks essential legitimacy, because it is easy to

[55] Address by Ambassador Kirkpatrick, *supra* note 48. The Reagan doctrine is not the only 20th-century attempt to revive the just war doctrine. The Soviet Union has long maintained that "[j]ust wars . . . are not wars of conquest but wars of liberation, waged to defend the people from foreign attack and from attempts to enslave them, or to liberate the people from capitalist slavery, or, lastly, to liberate colonies and dependent countries from the yoke of imperialism." COMMISSION OF THE CENTRAL COMMITTEE OF THE C.P.S.U., HISTORY OF THE COMMUNIST PARTY OF THE SOVIET UNION (BOLSHEVIKS) 167–68 (1939). The modern non-aligned movement has also upheld the just war doctrine, one result being the provisions of Protocol I to the Geneva Conventions. *See, e.g.*, Art. 1(4), Protocol Additional to the Geneva Conventions of 12 August 1949, and Relating to the Protection of Victims of International Armed Conflicts, *opened for signature* Dec. 12, 1977, INTERNATIONAL COMMITTEE OF THE RED CROSS, PROTOCOLS ADDITIONAL TO THE GENEVA CONVENTIONS OF 12 AUGUST 1949, at 3 (1977), *reprinted in* 16 ILM 1391 (1977). This position was dramatically put forth in a 1973 General Assembly resolution: "colonial peoples have the inherent right to struggle by all necessary means at their disposal against colonial Powers and alien domination in exercise of their right of self-determination." GA Res. 3103, 28 UN GAOR Supp. (No. 30) at 142, UN Doc. A/9030 (1973). *See also* GA Res. 2105, 20 UN GAOR Supp. (No. 14) at 3, UN Doc. A/6104 (1965). For a case study, see Dugard, *SWAPO: The Jus ad Bellum and the Jus in Bello*, 93 S. AFR. L.J. 144 (1976).

[56] *See* Franck, *Who Killed Article 2(4)?*, 64 AJIL 809, 820–22 (1970).

predict that in at least some situations no state would abide by its strictures. If a patently absurd result—a *reductio ad absurdum*—accrues from the only possible application of the evident meaning of a simple rule in circumstances requiring a more calibrated response, then it becomes evident that the rule will not be taken seriously in those circumstances, and perhaps also not in others.

If simplicity of text is an invitation to *reductio ad absurdum*, which undermines the determinacy of a rule, and if complexity imposes an elasticity that deprives it of determinate meaning, what can be said about determinacy that is not self-contradicting? There is an answer to this riddle, but it requires attention to detail and, in particular, to content. A simple, straightforward rule—"red light to port, green light to starboard"—will have a high level of determinacy if the problem to which it is addressed is widely recognized as essentially binary: that is, capable of being resolved by an objective test of compliance involving a choice between only two options. A true-false test is binary in this sense. Most traffic regulations also are of this kind. So are prohibitions on specific acts as to which there is general agreement that no exculpatory exceptions are ever admissible. One example is aerial hijacking.[57] The United States, however ruefully, has prosecuted a gunman who seized an aircraft to escape from Eastern bloc oppression,[58] because it felt obliged to discharge its obligation under the Hague Convention either to prosecute or to extradite hijackers.[59] The binary view of hijacking—it either *is* or *is not*, but no excuse will avail—is also manifest in the accord signed by the United States and Cuba in 1973,[60] and in the 1978

[57] [Tokyo] Convention on Offenses and Certain Other Acts Committed on Board Aircraft, Sept. 14, 1963, 20 UST 2941, TIAS No. 6768, 704 UNTS 219; [Hague] Convention for the Suppression of Unlawful Seizure of Aircraft, Dec. 16, 1970, 22 UST 1641, TIAS No. 7192 [hereinafter Hague Convention]; [Montreal] Convention for the Suppression of Unlawful Acts Against the Safety of Civil Aviation, Sept. 23, 1971, 24 UST 564, TIAS No. 7570.

[58] This scenario most notably occurred when an East German hijacked a Polish airliner to West Berlin. As an outgrowth of the historical and jurisdictional freak that is Berlin, the hijacker was charged with crimes under West German law but prosecuted by the United States and tried in an American court. The U.S. ambassador to West Germany appointed a New Jersey federal district judge, Herbert Stern, to preside over the trial. *See* H. STERN, JUDGMENT IN BERLIN (1984). Judge Stern, applying U.S. constitutional law, determined that the defendant was entitled to a jury trial (despite the anomaly that juries generally do not exist under German law). United States v. Tiede, 86 F.R.D. 227 (U.S. Ct. Berlin 1979). Impaneling a jury of West Berliners to judge an East German "refugee" raised the specter that the jury would refuse to convict the defendant in the American tradition of jury nullification. *See* Lowenfeld, *Hijacking, Freedom, and the "American Way,"* 83 MICH. L. REV. 1000, 1005 (1985). In other words, the jury would in effect graft a complex clause upon the linear law of the Hague Convention. In the end, the jury did acquit the defendant of hijacking but convicted him of hostage taking. H. STERN, *supra*, at 350. Judge Stern, affronted throughout the trial by the American prosecutor's stance that the Constitution was inapplicable to West Berlin and skeptical that parole (which he thought appropriate) would be granted, sentenced the hostage taker to time served (9 months) and released him from custody. *Id.* at 369–70.

[59] Hague Convention, *supra* note 57, Arts. 7, 8.

[60] Memorandum of Understanding on Hijacking of Aircraft and Vessels and Other Offenses, Feb. 15, 1973, United States–Cuba, 24 UST 737, TIAS No. 7579.

Bonn Declaration adhered to by Canada, France, Italy, Japan, the United Kingdom, the United States and the Federal Republic of Germany,[61] which imposes collective measures against states that refuse to extradite or prosecute hijackers.[62] Similarly, there appears to be near-universal belief that an objective binary test should apply to hostage taking[63] and violence against diplomats.[64] Even Islamic and Soviet authorities joined in the UN Security Council[65] to condemn the Iranian violations of U.S. diplomatic immunity in Tehran in 1979, a decision that was reaffirmed by a nearly unanimous International Court of Justice.[66] It is not difficult to visualize other narrow

[61] *International Terrorism*, DEP'T ST. BULL., No. 2018, September 1978, at 5 [hereinafter Bonn Declaration].

[62] *Id.* This language tracks Articles 7 and 9(2) of the Hague Convention, *supra* note 57. The Bonn Declaration in effect grafts an enforcement mechanism upon the norms embodied in the Hague Convention. However, imposition of sanctions under the Bonn Declaration is not premised on violation of the Hague Convention. Accordingly, sanctions might be taken against a state that had refused to sign the Hague Convention, not on the basis of the duty to prosecute or extradite (assuming, as is likely, that that is not a duty under customary international law), but on the basis that the support of international terrorism violates international law. *See* Levitt, *International Counterterrorism Cooperation: The Summit Seven and Air Terrorism*, 20 VAND. J. TRANSNAT'L L. 37 (1987). *See also* Chamberlain, *Collective Suspension of Air Services with States Which Harbour Hijackers*, 32 INT'L & COMP. L.Q. 616, 628–32 (1983); Busuttil, *The Bonn Declaration on International Terrorism: A Non-Binding International Agreement on Aircraft Hijacking*, 31 INT'L & COMP. L.Q. 474 (1982). Specifically, the Seven would (1) "take immediate action to cease all flights to that country," and (2) "initiate action to halt all incoming flights from that country or" (3) "from any country by the airlines of the country concerned." Bonn Declaration, *supra* note 61.

[63] International Convention Against the Taking of Hostages, Dec. 17, 1979, GA Res. 34/146, 34 UN GAOR Supp. (No. 46) at 245, UN Doc. A/34/46 (1979). The negotiations for the Hostages Convention reveal the opposition that a straightforward rule, even one for a compartmentalized activity, faces. Attempts at a reformulation of the Convention ranged in sophistication. Several delegations suggested the Convention should only protect "innocent" hostages. *See, e.g.*, UN Doc. A/32/39, at 38 (1977) (statement of Egypt); *id.* at 40 (statement of Guinea, using Ian Smith as an illustrative guilty hostage). The Tanzanian delegate proposed an exculpatory clause and provided an umpire: "For the purposes of the Convention, the term 'taking of hostages' shall not include any act or acts carried out in the process of national liberation against colonial rule, racist and foreign regimes, by liberation movements recognized by the United Nations or regional organizations." UN Doc. A/AC.188/L.5 (1977). The Pakistani delegate wished to condition invocation of the Hostages Convention against national liberation movements on the target state's acceptance of both the Geneva Conventions and the 1977 Protocols. UN Doc. A/C.6/34/SR.62, at 2 (1979).

[64] Convention on the Prevention and Punishment of Crimes Against Internationally Protected Persons, including Diplomatic Agents, *supra* note 40. *See also* Convention to Prevent and Punish the Acts of Terrorism Taking the Form of Crimes Against Persons and Related Extortion that Are of International Significance, Feb. 2, 1971, 27 UST 3949, TIAS No. 8413. The latter, an OAS version of the Internationally Protected Persons Convention, specifically condemns all physical attacks on diplomats, "regardless of motive" (Art. 2). This protection afforded diplomats can be analogized to the 11th-century Peace of God doctrine, which declared certain classes, especially the clergy, exempt from all violence. F. RUSSELL, *supra* note 50, at 34.

[65] SC Res. 461, 34 UN SCOR (Res. & Dec.) at 24, UN Doc. S/INF/35 (1979).

[66] United States Diplomatic and Consular Staff in Tehran (U.S. v. Iran), 1980 ICJ REP. 3 (Judgment of May 24).

categories of international offenses that could be defined without exculpatory caveats: offenses against children,[67] the use of biological[68] and chemical weapons,[69] and offenses against nonbelligerent civilians.[70]

Issues that cannot be reduced to simple binary categories invite regulation by more complex rule texts which, while avoiding the problem of *reductio ad absurdum*, suffer the costs of elasticity. A rule finely calibrated to reflect complex considerations, embodying a textured system of regulatory and exculpatory principles, may suffer legitimacy costs because it invites disputes as to its applicability in any particular case. These costs, however, can be reduced by introducing a forum in which ambiguity can be resolved case by case. Such a legitimate forum mitigates the textual elasticity of the rule by introducing process determinacy. One example is a provision in the 1982 Law of the Sea Convention that deals with the allocation of continental shelf shared by two or more riparian states. The shelf should be apportioned, the rule says, "on the basis of international law . . . in order to achieve an equitable solution."[71] The evidently nonbinary quality of this rule, the vagueness of the notion of an "equitable solution," has been redressed effectively in a series of interpretations by the International Court of Justice. The judges have noted that the treaty sets "a standard, and it is left to the States themselves, or to the courts, to endow this standard with specific content."[72] This the Court has set out to do. In a 1969 opinion, the judges had ruled that there should be some relation "between the extent of the continental shelf areas appertaining to the coastal State and the length of its coast measured in the general direction of the coastline."[73] In a 1982 case between Tunisia and Libya[74] and a 1985 dispute between Libya and Malta,[75] they gave quite specific content to an "equitable solution." In this

[67] The rights of children were recently codified in the Draft Convention on the Rights of the Child, UN Doc. E/CN.4/1986/39. In addition, these rights are treated in the Declaration of the Rights of the Child, GA Res. 1386, 14 UN GAOR Supp. (No. 16) at 19, UN Doc. A/4354 (1959); the Universal Declaration of Human Rights, GA Res. 217A (III), UN Doc. A/810, at 71 (1948), Arts. 25, 26; the International Covenant on Civil and Political Rights, GA Res. 2200, 21 UN GAOR Supp. (No. 16) at 52, UN Doc. A/6316 (1966), Arts. 6, 14, 23, 24; and the International Covenant on Economic, Social and Cultural Rights, GA Res. 2200, *id.* at 49, Arts. 10, 12. *See* Bennett, *A Critique of the Emerging Convention on the Rights of the Child*, 20 CORNELL INT'L L.J. 1 (1987).

[68] Convention on the Prohibition of the Development, Production and Stockpiling of Bacteriological (Biological) and Toxin Weapons and on Their Destruction, Apr. 12, 1972, 26 UST 583, TIAS No. 8062.

[69] Protocol for the Prohibition of the Use in War of Asphyxiating, Poisonous or Other Gases, and of Bacteriological Methods of Warfare, June 17, 1925, 26 UST 571, TIAS No. 8061, 94 LNTS 65.

[70] Convention Relative to the Protection of Civilian Persons in Time of War, Aug. 12, 1949, 6 UST 3516, TIAS No. 3365, 75 UNTS 287.

[71] United Nations Convention on the Law of the Sea, *supra* note 19, Art. 83(1).

[72] Continental Shelf (Libyan Arab Jamahiriya/Malta), 1985 ICJ REP. 13, 30–31 (Judgment of June 3).

[73] North Sea Continental Shelf (FRG/Den.; FRG/Neth.), 1969 ICJ REP. 3, 54 (Judgment of Feb. 20).

[74] *See* Continental Shelf (Tunisia/Libyan Arab Jamahiriya), 1982 ICJ REP. 18, 35 (Judgment of Feb. 24).

[75] 1985 ICJ REP. at 44.

way, the elastic rule text has gained determinacy, just as the papacy once gave content to the vague notion of "just" wars.

Process determinacy is not solely the prerogative of courts. Any institution that is seen to be acting legitimately may be used for the purpose. "Acting legitimately" means here that those it addresses perceive the forum itself as having come into being in accordance with right process. In practice, the legitimacy of a forum can be tested in the same way as that of a rule: by reference to the determinacy of its charter, its pedigree, the coherence of its mandate and its adherence to the normative institutional hierarchy of international organization. Nowadays, the UN General Assembly and Security Council, as well as organs of regional organizations, sometimes play this clarifying role. They will only succeed, however, if they are seen to be acting in accordance with their specific mandate and the general principles of fairness; that is, in a disinterested, principled fashion and not simply to gratify some short-term self-interest of a faction. Moreover, each rule-decision emanating from a legitimate forum is itself subject to the test of its perceived legitimacy: its determinacy, coherence, and so forth.

To summarize: the legitimacy of a rule is affected by its degree of determinacy. Its determinacy depends upon the clarity with which it is able to communicate its intent and to shape that intent into a specific situational command. This, in turn, can depend upon the literary structure of the rule, its ability to avoid *reductio ad absurdum* and the availability of a process for resolving ambiguities in its application.

III. Symbolic Validation and Legitimacy

As determinacy is the linguistic or literary-structural component of legitimacy, so *symbolic validation, ritual* and *pedigree* provide its cultural and anthropological dimension. As with determinacy, so here, the legitimacy of the rule—its ability to exert pull to compliance and to command voluntary obedience—is to be examined in the light of its ability to communicate. In this instance, however, what is to be communicated is not so much content as *authority*:[76] the authority of a rule, the authority of the originator of a validating communication and, at times, the authority bestowed on the recipient of the communication. The communication of authority, moreover, is symbolic rather than literal. We shall refer to these symbolically validating communications as cues.

These three concepts—symbolic validation, ritual and pedigree—are related, but not identical. The *symbolic validation* of a rule, or of a rule-making process or institution, occurs when a signal is used as a cue to elicit compliance with a command. The cue serves as a surrogate for enunciated reasons for such obedience. The singing of the national anthem, for example, is a vocal and (on public occasions) a visual signal symbolically reinforcing the citizen's relationship to the state, a relationship of rights and duties. This

[76] Schachter, *supra* note 1, at 309–11. Schachter uses the terms "competence and authority" to cover some of the same matters. In his formulation, "whether a designated requirement is to be regarded as obligatory will depend in part on whether those who have made that designation are regarded by those to whom the requirement is addressed (the target audience) as endowed with the requisite competence or authority for that role." *Id.* at 309.

compliance reinforcement need not be spelled out in the actual words of the anthem (as it is not in the commonly used stanza of the American one). The act of corporate singing itself is a sufficient cue to validate the fabric of regularized relationships that are implicated in good citizenship. We are not really singing about bombs bursting in the night air, but about free and secret elections, the marketplace of ideas, the rule of valid laws and impartial judges.

Ritual is a specialized form of symbolic validation marked by ceremonies, often—but not necessarily—mystical, that provide unenunciated reasons or cues for eliciting compliance with the commands of persons or institutions. The entry of the mace into the British House of Commons is intended to call to mind the Commons's long and successful struggle to capture control of lawmaking power from the Crown. It functions as a much more direct, literal kind of symbolic validation than the "Star-Spangled Banner." Ritual is often presented as drama, to communicate to a community its unity, its values, its uniqueness in both the exclusive and the inclusive sense.

All ritual is a form of symbolic validation, but the converse is not necessarily true. *Pedigree* is a different subset of cues that seek to enhance the compliance pull of rules or rule-making institutions by emphasizing their historical origins, their cultural or anthropological deep-rootedness. An example is the practice of "recognition." When a government recognizes a new regime, or when the United Nations admits a new state to membership, this partly symbolic act has broad significance. It endows the new entity with a range of entitlements and duties, the concomitants of sovereignty. The capacity of states, and, nowadays, perhaps also of the United Nations, to confer sovereignty and its incidents in this fashion derives not from some treaty or other specific agreement but from the ancient practice of states and groupings of states, which legitimizes the exercise of this power.[77] The time-honored recognition practices by which status is conferred symbolically include such subsets as recognition "de facto" and "de jure," recognition of states and governments, the opening of diplomatic relations, and, in the United Nations, admittance to membership and acceptance of delegates' credentials. Along similar lines, Professor Schachter has observed that a body of rules produced by the UN legislative drafting body, the International Law Commission, will be more readily accepted by the nations "after [the Commission] has devoted a long period in careful study and consideration of precedent and practice." Moreover, the authority will be greater if the product is labeled *codification*—that is, the interpolation of rules from deep-rooted evidence of state practice—"than if it were presented as a 'development' (that is, as new law),"[78] even though the Commission (as a subsidiary of the General Assembly) is equally empowered by the UN Charter to promote "the progressive development of international law and its codification."[79] The compliance pull of a rule is enhanced by a demonstrable lineage. A new rule will have greater difficulty finding compliance, and even evidence of its good sense may not fully compensate for its lack of

[77] For a discussion of the origins of recognition policy and procedure, see 1 L. OPPENHEIM, INTERNATIONAL LAW 124–52 (H. Lauterpacht 8th ed. 1955).

[78] Schachter, *supra* note 1, at 310.

[79] UN CHARTER art. 13(1)(a).

breeding. Nevertheless, a new rule may be taken more seriously if it arrives on the scene under the aegis of a particularly venerable sponsor such as a widely ratified multilateral convention, or a virtually unanimous decision of the International Court of Justice.

Symbolic validation, ritual and pedigree are part of the legitimation strategy of all communities, all compliance-inducing rule systems. A study of the legitimacy of imperial authority in ancient China observes that rituals and symbols, "by endowing authority with mystical values and legitimacy, serve not merely to reflect authority but also to recreate and reinforce it. By such means the extent to which people are persuaded to accept a given authority goes far beyond the obedience normally elicited by force."[80] Similar observations have derived from the study of Aztec legitimation strategy, which was found to employ a social tactic making extensive symbolic resources available to achieve "political socialization."[81] For example, the government made a point of distributing food to the citizenry at certain state ceremonies. Feeding as Christian sacrament is also a symbolic validation of status as members of the mystical body of Christ, of hierarchic authority structure within that community, and serves as a renewal of commitment and obligation.

"Political legitimacy," a study of ancient China notes, "can be said to adhere to a regime and its authorities when the governed are convinced that it is right and proper to obey them and to abide by their decisions."[82] This conviction was cued symbolically in Aztec society by priests who provided "supernatural sanction for legitimate state authority,"[83] rather as did the Roman Pontifex Maximus.[84] But, in many societies, ritual and pedigree will have their symbolic roots in the cultural and political, rather than the religious, experience. In a posttheistic society, ritual is not discarded; rather, politics and history are substituted for magic and myth as the compliance-inducing or status-securing cue.

For example, in Britain the rule that a parliamentary bill becomes law only after receiving the assent of the Crown[85] certainly no longer relates to the divine right of monarchs. Although the Queen's title still claims that she rules "by the grace of God," it is not widely believed either that the Queen rules or, for that matter, that there is a God, particularly one involved in

[80] H. WECHSLER, OFFERINGS OF JADE AND SILK 21 (1985).

[81] Kurtz, *Strategies of Legitimation and the Aztec State*, 23 ETHNOLOGY 301, 309 (1984).

[82] H. WECHSLER, *supra* note 80, at 10. [83] Kurtz, *supra* note 81, at 306.

[84] The Pontifex's task, originally, was to legitimate political authority by appeasing the river god Tiber over whose banks the civil authorities had built a useful, but undeniably intrusive, bridge.

[85] When presenting bills for royal assent, the Speaker of the House of Commons pays homage to the Crown with the formula: "Be it enacted by the Queen's most Excellent Majesty, by and with the advice and consent of the Lords Spiritual and Temporal, and Commons, in this present Parliament assembled, and by the authority of the same, as follows. . . ." O. PHILLIPS, A FIRST BOOK OF ENGLISH LAW 118–19 (7th ed. 1977). The Crown's right to refuse assent to bills that have properly passed through both Houses of Parliament is "practically obsolete." A. DICEY, INTRODUCTION TO THE STUDY OF THE LAW OF THE CONSTITUTION 114 (9th ed. 1939). In fact, when the Unionists posited in 1913 that the reference to assent restored a real right of veto, the theory was criticized as "obviously absurd" and was said to have troubled the king. E. RIDGES, CONSTITUTIONAL LAW 106 (8th ed. 1950).

British government. A utilitarian explanation for the survival of the historic ritual of royal assent would have to look elsewhere.

Oddly, the very obsolescence of the practice of royal assent helps keep it alive. The act of seeking the Queen's signature on legislation, even when it is clear that she has no choice but to grant it, is not meaningless. It signifies the Government's acceptance of all the accumulated encrustation of customs that define and restrict British governmental powers and practices. The Speaker of the House, for example, assures the Queen that the bill has had its customary three readings in Parliament and has passed both Houses.[86] While meaning little in itself, since the governing party usually can command the parliamentary majority necessary to do what it wants, the ritual of three readings[87] symbolizes the governing party's subordination to orderly, unhurried parliamentary procedure. In an era of relentless bureaucratic momentum, these quaint historical-political rituals provide a delay for reflection and debate between the drafting of a bill and its implementation. The result is that the rituals of three readings and monarchial assent symbolically validate, cuing public compliance and serving to certify the legitimacy of the new law.

Of course, a bad law does not become a good one for having been anointed by parliamentary ritual and having received the blessing of pedigreed authority. A citizen who believes a law to be evil probably will not be induced to think otherwise by symbolic cues. Nevertheless, when decisions to comply or defy are made by those to whom a command is addressed, such cues, with their symbolic validation of its legitimacy, may tip the scales on the side of obedience.

The three-readings ritual is the secular analogue of the church's practice of "publishing the banns" of a proposed marriage on three successive Sundays before the actual nuptials are consecrated.[88] Even in this rational era, the publication of banns also has its residual validating force, which derives not from belief in the divine, but from faith in the evolutionary history that the ritual symbolizes. Just as the House of Commons's three readings celebrate the continuity of parliamentary democracy, the publication of banns symbolizes commitment to the social status of matrimony conferred by both the church and the acquiescent congregation. Both rituals constitute a recommitment to the society's procedural rules of recognition, the "rules of

[86] When a bill is presented to the Crown for assent, it bears an endorsement signed by the Speaker of the House certifying that the provisions of the Parliament Act have been complied with. Parliament Act, 1911, 1 & 2 Geo. 5, ch. 13, §2(2), *reprinted in* SELECT STATUTES, CASES AND DOCUMENTS 350, 352 (C. Robertson ed. 1935).

[87] For a full discussion of this ritual as it applies to the enactment of both public and private bills by the House of Commons and the House of Lords, see S. A. DE SMITH, CONSTITUTIONAL AND ADMINISTRATIVE LAW 265–71 (3d ed. 1977).

[88] The calling of banns is the public and official announcement of persons who intend to marry and is meant to discover whether the parties are free to marry and whether any impediment to their lawful and valid marriage may exist. The tradition that no marriage was to be celebrated until after a triple publication of the church's banns originated in the 8th century and was extended over all Christendom by Pope Innocent III in 1215. ENCYCLOPEDIC DICTIONARY OF RELIGION 357 (1979).

the game," about which more will be said below. These *secondary* rules about rules are particularly important because they are the yardstick by which all *primary* or substantive rules and commands can be tested. The legitimacy of secondary rules is particularly dependent on the length of their pedigree. They must be difficult to change if they are to be perceived as valid and able to validate. Thus, the secondary rules, as well as the primary rules made in accordance with them, derive their legitimacy in part from the rootedness of the former deep in the history and culture of the community. For this reason, a bill that did not undergo three readings and was not presented for the assent of the Crown would undoubtedly be perceived by Britons as lacking legitimacy, not because those rituals are believed to be powerful in themselves, but because the Government's failure to perform them would be seen as a repudiation of the ancient democratic essence of the British parliamentary system, of which the rites and pedigree are still potent cues.

As we have noted, validating cues are not a modern, or a western, invention. Pedigree is a particularly universal form of symbolic validation. Most societies make some form of linguistic connection between the concepts "old" and "venerable." In the ancient Aztec state, the rulers' hereditary relation to the Toltec dynasty "was the sacred source of legitimate power and authority,"[89] supplemented by a host of "pedigree nobles."[90] So, too, in the China of 1000 B.C., where the Mandate of Heaven doctrine endowed an ancient imperial series of rulers with historically pedigreed and ritually validated power that rested on an orderly system, or line, of succession.[91]

Ritual, too, is a pandemic validator of authority. The fundamental purpose of ritual in ancient China was to create a form of procedural legitimacy that Max Weber would have understood.[92] The point is illustrated by the story of Kao-tsu (206–195 B.C.). When Kao-tsu founded the Han dynasty, he and his followers were "rough and ready fellows" and, to put them at ease, the emperor abolished the "elaborate and bothersome" *Ch'in* ritual code. Unfortunately, this made a "shambles of court audiences" as the members of his court went about "getting drunk, hurling insults at one another, and hacking up the wooden pillars of the palace with their swords. To introduce some decorum . . . , Kao-tsu was moved to appoint an erudite named Shu-sun T'ung to provide him with a court ritual consonant with his modest personal capacity for performing ceremonial." The experiment proved a great success. The ritual "served as a powerful tool for dignifying and strengthening the ruler's position and for controlling the behavior of subordinates. It emphasized the large gap between the position of emperor and that of mere bureaucrat, prevented former associates from presuming upon past friendships, and helped keep subordinates agreeably subservient."[93]

In the modern state system, ritual and other kinds of symbolic validation play much the same role as in ancient and medieval national societies, inte-

[89] Kurtz, *supra* note 81, at 306. [90] *Id.* at 308.

[91] H. WECHSLER, *supra* note 80, at 12–15.

[92] *See supra* note 10 (for Weber's perception that legitimacy in part stems from the authority issuing an order, rather than from the order itself).

[93] H. WECHSLER, *supra* note 80, at 25.

grating by inclusion and exclusion, seducing subjects into obeying rules and rulers, validating the exercise of power and generally contributing to the legitimization of the institutions and rules of the society. As a less-developed system, international society is underendowed with such symbolic validation, but what there is serves approximately the same legitimizing function as in ancient China, in the Aztec nation[94] and in modern parliamentary democracies.[95]

Despite their paucity, there are significant examples of attempts by the international system to legitimize itself through ritual and pedigree. One of the oldest and most universal was by using marriage between children of heads of state as symbolic emphasis for a practical political and social compact between nations, sometimes merely reifying the concept of a "family" of allied nations, at other times leading to—legitimizing—actual political union or federation. The practice was common not only among medieval European royal houses, but also in Asia, Africa and the precolonial Americas. For example, in Aztec Mexico, the "head of state established alliances with neighboring states through marriage. . . . Acamapichtli is reputed to have married twenty daughters of the chiefs of the clans that comprised Aztec society."[96]

One of the newest examples of symbolic international system legitimation is the creation of supranational agencies such as the United Nations Development Programme,[97] the International Bank for Reconstruction and Development[98] (the "World Bank"), the World Health Organization,[99] the Food and Agriculture Organization[100] and the United Nations International Children's Emergency Fund.[101] Their role is to distribute benefits to the deserving and the needy, either in tandem, or in competition, with the unilateral donations still given by one country to another.

The purpose of these agencies is largely and usefully instrumental. Nevertheless, the form of the organization is heavily symbolic. The World Bank, for example, could as well have been set up with only the 12 to 16 chief industrial nations as members, since they contribute almost all its working capital. Instead, the symbolic mingling of donors and recipients in the bank's governing organs and bureaucracy is intended to purge the assistance given of the aura of direct dependence between recipient and donor, a relationship in which gratitude has often been superseded by bitterness. By symbolic multilateralization, gratitude is directed to the agency, all of whose

[94] *See supra* text accompanying note 81.

[95] *See supra* text accompanying notes 86–87.

[96] Kurtz, *supra* note 81, at 308.

[97] *See* GA Res. 2029, 20 UN GAOR Supp. (No. 14) at 20, UN Doc. A/6014 (1965).

[98] Articles of Agreement of the International Bank for Reconstruction and Development, *opened for signature* Dec. 27, 1945, 60 Stat. 1440, TIAS No. 1502, 2 UNTS 134.

[99] WORLD HEALTH ORGANIZATION CONST., July 22, 1946, 62 Stat. 2679, TIAS No. 1808, 14 UNTS 186.

[100] UN FOOD AND AGRICULTURE ORGANIZATION CONST., Oct. 16, 1945, 12 UST 980, TIAS No. 4803.

[101] The United Nations International Children's Emergency Fund was founded by GA Res. 57, 1 UN GAOR (Res. pt.2) at 90, UN Doc. A/64/Add.1 (1946).

members participate, in most cases, as theoretical equals. This equality of participation is itself the symbolic representation of a confluence between sovereignty and interdependence that holds together the "community" of states.

The distribution of benefits by a global agency, with its own officials and symbols, also helps to create a sense of social solidarity—a primitive version of loyalty—between recipients (both persons and governments) and the international system (the "United Nations Family") of which the donor agency is a part, rather in the same way as did the Aztec rulers' ritual distribution of foodstuffs to subjects. This symbolic, as well as utilitarian, function of multilateral, institutionalized benevolence is familiar to anthropologists and sociologists who study the formation of national societies. In Aztec society, the "[c]onstruction and maintenance of temples and other public buildings appeased the gods, organized people's labor according to state directives and supported priests and other state functionaries."[102] The Pharaohs similarly sought to serve both personal and socializing objectives in the construction of the pyramids.[103] This concept of legitimization through the symbolism of public works has not been unknown, either, to American politicians from "Boss" Curley of Boston[104] to Nelson D. Rockefeller of New York.[105] It is also understood by the fledgling bureaucracy of the international system.

There are many other examples of ritual and other symbolic reinforcement of legitimacy in the international system. Thus, the United Nations Organization is authorized to fly its own flag, not only at headquarters, but also over regional and local offices around the world.[106] The flag has been used at the instigation of the Secretary-General to immunize such UN battle-front operations as clearing sunken ships from the Suez Canal in 1956

[102] Kurtz, *supra* note 81, at 310.

[103] Although many consider the pyramids to be solely the product of slave labor, evidence has been advanced indicating that the labor was in fact compensated. Thus, it is "probably nearer the truth [to] regard these monuments as vast public works providing economic security for a good part of the population." H. JANSON, THE HISTORY OF ART 40 (rev. ed. 1969). Erected as part of vast funerary districts, the pyramids were the scene of great religious festivities, both during and after the Pharaoh's lifetime. *Id.* at 38. At least as far as Old Kingdom pyramids are concerned, Pharaohs equipped their tombs as a "kind of shadowy replica of [their] daily environment for [their] spirit[s] . . . . [T]he Egyptian tomb was a kind of life insurance, an investment in peace of mind." *Id.* at 35.

[104] *See* J. DINNEEN, THE PURPLE SHAMROCK (1949) (which details the life of James Michael Curley, four-time mayor of Boston). *See also* E. O'CONNOR, THE LAST HURRAH (1956) (which, although fictional, is said to be based on Curley's life and career).

[105] In formulating the project for the Albany Mall, Governor Nelson Rockefeller suggested modeling New York's capitol on the palace of the Dalai Lama at Lhasa, Tibet. The revised version of the mall's plan incorporated architectural and symbolic elements from Lhasa, Washington, D.C., Brasília, Versailles, Rockefeller Center and St. Petersburg, and was meant to be "the most spectacularly beautiful seat of government anywhere in the world." Krinsky, *St. Petersburg-on-the-Hudson: The Albany Mall* (citing FORTUNE, June 1971, at 92), in M. BARASCH & L. SANDLER, ART THE APE OF NATURE 771, 778 (1981).

[106] The General Assembly adopted and authorized the use of the United Nations flag on Oct. 20, 1947. *See* GA Res. 167, 2 UN GAOR (96th plen. mtg.) at 338–39, UN Doc. A/414 (1947).

and protecting members of the Palestine Liberation Organization being evacuated from Lebanon in 1983.[107] The United Nations also issues stamps,[108] which not only are accepted for mail delivery by member states, but also generate a tidy independent income—some $8.6 million in 1986–1987.[109] Peacekeeping forces and truce observers under UN command and wearing UN symbols are stationed between hostile forces in Kashmir,[110] the Golan Heights,[111] Cyprus,[112] Lebanon[113] and Iran-Iraq.[113a] They are lightly armed, if at all, and palpably unable to defend themselves in the event of renewed hostilities; but, with their distinctive emblems, they have come to symbolize the world's interest in the continuance of an agreed truce or armistice. The blue and white helmets and arm bands also symbolize a growing body of rules applicable to peacekeeping operations, manifesting and reinforcing the authority of forces that usually are neither as numerous, nor as well armed, as those they must keep pacified. Their role is purely, but effectively, symbolic of the desire of bitter enemies—and the international community—to have respite from combat. Yet their token presence has a far more inhibitory effect on the behavior of states than can be explained by their minimal coercive power.[114] It is their perceived legitimacy, symbolically validated, that serves as their shield and usually induces more powerful forces to defer to their intangible authority.

The United Nations and its agencies also maintain headquarters and regional facilities that are accorded limited extraterritoriality and immuni-

[107] For the Secretary-General's operation to remove ships sunk in the Suez Canal during the 1956 war, see 1956 UN Y.B. 53–55; and GA Res. 1121, 11 UN GAOR Supp. (No. 17) at 61, UN Doc. A/3386 (1956). The Secretary-General also authorized, with the "support" of the Security Council, the flying of the UN flag on ships that would evacuate armed elements of the PLO from Tripoli. *See* UN Docs. S/16194, S/16195, 38 UN SCOR (Res. & Dec.) at 5–6, UN Doc. S/INF/39 (1983).

[108] The United Nations Postal Administration was established on Jan. 1, 1951. *See* GA Res. 454, 5 UN GAOR Supp. (No. 20) at 57–58, UN Doc. A/1775 (1950).

[109] The estimated 1986–1987 net revenue from the sale of postage stamps was $8,667,700. *See* Advisory Committee on Administrative and Budgetary Questions, First Report on Proposed Programme Budget for the Biennium 1986–1987, 40 UN GAOR Supp. (No. 7) at 209, UN Doc. A/40/7 (1985).

[110] The origin of the United Nations Military Observer Group in India and Pakistan (UNMOGIP) is found in a resolution of the UN Commission for India and Pakistan. *See* 3 UN SCOR Supp. (Nov. 1948) at 32, UN Doc. S/1100, para. 75 (1948). The Security Council subsequently authorized its operation. *See* SC Res. 91, para. 7, 6 UN SCOR (Res. & Dec.) at 1, 3, UN Doc. S/INF/6/Rev.1 (1951).

[111] The Security Council established the UN Disengagement Observer Force (UNDOF) for the Golan Heights on May 31, 1974. *See* SC Res. 350, 29 UN SCOR (Res. & Dec.) at 4, UN Doc. S/INF/30 (1974).

[112] The United Nations Force in Cyprus (UNFICYP) was formed by the Security Council on Mar. 4, 1964. *See* SC Res. 186, 19 UN SCOR (Res. & Dec.) at 2–4, UN Doc. S/INF/19/Rev.1 (1964).

[113] The United Nations Interim Force in Lebanon (UNIFIL) was created by the Security Council on Mar. 19, 1978. *See* SC Res. 425, 33 UN SCOR (Res. & Dec.) at 5, UN Doc. S/INF/34 (1978).

[113a] *See* Report of the Secretary-General, UN Doc. S/20093 (Aug. 7, 1988); SC Res. 619 (Aug. 9, 1988) (creating the force); GA Res. 42/233 (Aug. 17, 1988) (funding the force).

[114] For a discussion of the noncoercive role of UN peacekeeping forces, see B. URQUHART, A LIFE IN PEACE AND WAR 287–88, 342–43 (1987).

ties.[115] These have symbolic as well as practical significance. The extension of diplomatic immunity to top UN officials, privileges usually reserved for representatives of states, symbolizes the emergence of the Organization as an autonomous international actor, pedigreed in its own right. The functions and privileges of the agencies' resident representatives in various countries do not differ greatly, in practice, from those of ambassadors. Although it is not widely known, the Organization also levies an income tax[116] (staff assessment) on its employees who, with the exception of Americans, are immune from national taxation in recognition of the fact (noted by the U.S. Supreme Court in the domestic federal context[117]) that the right of states to tax federal instrumentalities must be limited because it necessarily encompasses the right to destroy.

A few more examples. Symbols of pedigree and rituals are firmly imbedded in state diplomatic practice. The titles ("ambassador extraordinary and plenipotentiary"), prerogatives and immunities of ambassadors, consuls and others functioning in a representative capacity are among the oldest of symbols and rites associated with the conduct of international relations. The sending state, by the rituals of accreditation, endows its diplomats with pedigree. They become, in time-honored tradition, a symbolic reification of the nation ("full powers" or *plenipotentiary*), a role that is ritually endorsed by the receiving state's ceremony accepting the envoy's credentials. These ceremonies, incidentally, are as old as they are elaborate and are performed with as remarkably faithful uniformity in Communist citadels as in royal palaces.[118] Once accredited and received, an ambassador *is* the embodiment of the nation. The status of ambassador, once conferred, carries with it inherent rights and duties that do not depend on the qualities of the person, or on the condition of relations between the sending and receiving states, or on the relative might of the sending state. To insult or harm this envoy, no matter how grievous the provocation, is to attack the sending state. Moreover, when an envoy, acting officially, agrees to something, the envoy's state is bound, usually even if the envoy acted without proper authorization.[119] The host state normally is entitled to rely on the word of an ambassador as if his or her state were speaking.

[115] *See* Convention on the Privileges and Immunities of the United Nations, *adopted* by the General Assembly Feb. 13, 1946, 21 UST 1418, TIAS No. 6900, 1 UNTS 1 (entered into force for the United States Apr. 29, 1970). *See also* Agreement Regarding the Headquarters of the United Nations, June 26, 1947, United States–United Nations, 61 Stat. 3416, TIAS No. 1676, 11 UNTS 11 (entered into force Nov. 21, 1947). *See further* Convention on the Privileges and Immunities of the Specialized Agencies, *approved* by the General Assembly Nov. 21, 1947, 33 UNTS 261.

[116] To rectify the inequalities it perceived in its original system of compensation, the United Nations subjected UN salaries to a tax assessed at a rate comparable to the employee's national income tax liability. GA Res. 239 (III), UN Doc. A/703, at 3 (1948), *as amended* by GA Res. 359 (IV), UN Doc. A/1949, at 1 (1949).

[117] McCulloch v. Maryland, 17 U.S. (4 Wheat.) 316, 347 (1819).

[118] *See* M. McCaffree & P. Innis, Protocol, The Complete Book of Diplomatic, Official and Social Usage 87–104 (1985).

[119] Legal Status of Eastern Greenland (Den. v. Nor.), 1933 PCIJ (ser. A/B) No. 53 (Judgment of Apr. 5).

The venerable ritual practices of diplomacy are almost universally observed, and the rules that govern diplomacy are widely recognized as imbued with a high degree of legitimacy, being both descriptive and predictive of nearly invariable state conduct and reflecting a strong sense of historically endowed obligation. When the rules are violated—as they have been by Iran and Libya in recent years[120]—the international community tends to respond by rallying around the rule, as the Security Council[121] and the International Court of Justice[122] demonstrated when the Iranian regime encouraged the occupation of the U.S. Embassy in Tehran. Violations of the elaborate rules pertaining to embassies and immunities usually lead the victim state to terminate its diplomatic relations with the offender.[123] The offended state—as Britain demonstrated after the St. James Square shooting—usually takes care not to retaliate by means that the rules do not permit.[124]

Related to the pedigreeing process of diplomatic accreditation, with its symbolic status of privileges and immunities, is the prevalent idea of sovereign immunity. That set of rules and practices has its roots in the medieval notion that the "king can do no wrong" and the monarch's claim that "I am the state." Nowadays, most governments can be sued in their own courts. Until at least the 1920s, however, nations, among themselves, generally continued to treat as sacrosanct not only foreign governments, but also all property of recognized foreign states and those activities and enterprises carried on in the foreign government's name.[125] Only in the last three

[120] For a discussion of the Iranian hostages incident, see Gross, *The Case of United States Diplomatic and Consular Staff in Tehran: Phase of Provisional Measures*, 74 AJIL 395 (1980). For an analysis of the Libyan violations, see Higgins, *supra* note 30.

[121] SC Res. 457, 34 UN SCOR (Res. & Dec.) at 24, UN Doc. S/INF/35 (1979) (adopted unanimously).

[122] *See* United States Diplomatic and Consular Staff in Tehran (U.S. v. Iran), Provisional Measures, 1979 ICJ REP. 7 (Order of Dec. 15); United States Diplomatic and Consular Staff in Tehran (U.S. v. Iran), 1980 ICJ REP. 3 (Judgment of May 24); United States Diplomatic and Consular Staff in Tehran (U.S. v. Iran), 1981 ICJ REP. 45 (Order of May 12).

[123] See, e.g., *France Breaks Iran Ties and Isolates Embassy*, N.Y. Times, July 18, 1987, at 1, col. 3, which followed the grant of sanctuary by the Iranian Embassy in Paris to a nondiplomat wanted for questioning in connection with terrorist activities.

[124] The British limited their reaction to the shooting of a policewoman from the premises of the Libyan People's Bureau to expulsion of the perpetrators and closing of the Bureau. *See* Higgins, *UK Foreign Affairs Committee Report on the Abuse of Diplomatic Immunities and Privileges: Government Response and Report*, 80 AJIL 135 (1986).

[125] In the *Steamship Pesaro* case, the U.S. Supreme Court refused to recognize the difference between ships held and used by a government for a public purpose and ships used by a government in trade. The latter "are public ships in the same sense that war ships are. We know of no international usage which regards the maintenance and advancement of the economic welfare of a people in time of peace as any less a public purpose than the maintenance and training of a naval force." Berizzi Bros. Co. v. S.S. Pesaro, 271 U.S. 562, 574 (1926). The Court expounded upon this doctrine in *The Navemar*, holding that, "[a]dmittedly a vessel of a friendly government in its possession and service is a public vessel, even though engaged in the carriage of merchandise for hire . . . ." Compania Espanola de Navigacion Maritima, S.A. v. Navemar, 303 U.S. 68, 74–76 (1938). For similar holdings in British cases, see The Jassy, 1906 P. 270; and The Gagara, 1919 P. 95.

decades have most nations begun to limit the immunity from suit of foreign governments and state commercial entities. While many nations now have restricted this status-based right of immunity by withdrawing it from purely *commercial* property and activities of foreign governments,[126] immunity continues to be granted to all officials and property engaged in *governmental* (public, or noncommercial) undertakings.[127] In practice, this means that immunity protects such officials, state property and governmental activity from legal action or, at a minimum, from the execution of a judgment against them.

Symbolically validated rules like these, precisely because they are old, or have been encrusted with quaint forms and rituals, seem easy prey to functionalist critique. They sometimes work an injustice, and they often appear anachronistic. On the other hand, a new rule, even if agreed upon, might not have the same capacity to obligate. To the extent that the legitimacy of a rule is dependent on symbolic validation, there is reason—albeit not invariably a decisive one—to leave the rule alone.

Symbols, ritual and pedigree are factors that cannot be made to order and rules endowed with them need to be husbanded. "No one makes up ritual or symbol any more than anyone makes up language," a study of ancient Chinese ritual has shown.

> Ritual and symbol arise without intention or adaptation to conscious purpose; they seem to be collective products worked out . . . over long periods of time. . . . Ironically, it appears that rituals and symbols must in some way already be regarded as "legitimate" in order for them to confer legitimacy on those who employ them.[128]

IV. Coherence and Legitimacy

Symbolic validation, like determinacy, serves to legitimize rules. But like determinacy, symbolic validation is not quite as simple a notion as it may initially appear. For example, as traditional Chinese practice makes clear, ritual invoked to enhance the capacity of a rule to compel compliance will

[126] The United States officially promulgated this policy in 1952, when the Department of State, by means of the "Tate letter," declared its adherence to the "restrictive theory" of sovereign immunity. Under this theory, immunity would be recognized with regard to sovereign or public acts (*jure imperii*) but not with respect to private acts (*jure gestionis*). Letter from Jack B. Tate, Acting Legal Adviser, Department of State, to Philip B. Perlman, Acting Attorney General, May 19, 1952, *reprinted in* 26 Dept. St. Bull. 984 (1952). For current European treatment of immunity, see the European Convention on State Immunity and Additional Protocol, 1972 ETS 74, *reprinted in* 11 ILM 470 (1972).

[127] Foreign Sovereign Immunities Act of 1976, 28 U.S.C. §§1330, 1602–1611 (1982). *See also* Higgins, *Recent Developments in the Law of Sovereign Immunity in the United Kingdom*, 71 AJIL 423 (1977). For judicial discussion of current U.S. practice and its history, see Broadbent v. Organization of Am. States, 628 F.2d 27 (D.D.C. 1980). U.S. application of the "commercial" activity concept under the doctrine of restrictive immunity is discussed in *id.* at 33–35; and the immunity accorded international organizations under the rubrics of restrictive and absolute immunity is treated in *id.* at 30–33.

[128] H. Wechsler, *supra* note 80, at 35.

only succeed if the rituals are themselves legitimate and are strictly observed. Similarly, a pedigree only confers actual rights and duties when the standards for pedigreeing are applied *coherently*. When, on the contrary, symbols, ritual and pedigree are dispensed capriciously, the desired effect of legitimization may not accrue.

Both determinacy and symbolic validation are connected to a further variable: coherence. The effect of incoherence on symbolic validation can be illustrated by reference to diplomatic practices pertaining to the ritual validation of governments and states. The most important act of pedigreeing in the international system is the deep-rooted, traditional act that endows a new government, or a new state, with symbolic status. When the endowing is done by individual governments, it is known as *recognition*.[129] The symbolic conferral of status is also performed collectively through a global organization like the United Nations when the members vote to admit a new nation to membership,[130] or when the General Assembly votes to accept the credentials of the delegates representing a new government.[131]

These two forms of validation are important because they enhance the status of the validated entity; that is, the new state or government acquires legitimacy, which, in turn, carries entitlements and obligations equal to those of other such entities. Such symbolic validation cannot alter the empirically observable reality of power disparity among states and governments, nor, properly understood, does it give off that cue. It does, however, purport to restrict what powerful states legitimately may do with their advantage over the weak. It is a cue that prompts the Soviets, however reluctantly, to do a lot of explaining when they invade Afghanistan. The pedigreed statehood of Afghanistan, together with the determinacy of the rules against intervention by one state in the internal affairs of another, then combine to render those Soviet explanations essentially unacceptable, global scorn evidencing the inelastic determinacy of the applicable rules. The practices of symbolic equality conferred by recognition also stipulate that the leader of tiny Bhutan must receive exactly the same number of volleys fired in salute as does the head of state of its huge neighbor, China. Recognition, as validation, has the effect of cuing the equal capacity of rich and poor, strong and weak, for acquiring rights and duties. It creates a presumption against all purported interpretations of existing rules—and against proposed new rules—that would make arbitrary distinctions between the rights and duties of different states or governments. Symbolic equality thus both affirms and reinforces real equality. Weaker nations, in particular, believe that ritual incantation of their symbolically validated status, at a minimum, has reduced somewhat the option of the powerful to treat the weak as tributary or

[129] For U.S. practices, see L. GALLOWAY, RECOGNIZING FOREIGN GOVERNMENTS: THE PRACTICE OF THE UNITED STATES (1978). An excellent treatment of recognition in general can be found in H. LAUTERPACHT, RECOGNITION IN INTERNATIONAL LAW (1947).

[130] J. DUGARD, RECOGNITION AND THE UNITED NATIONS (1987).

[131] See *infra* note 140 for illustrations of the converse, attempts to deny or rescind recognition by opposing delegates' credentials.

vassal states in contravention of the rights inherent in their status as states.[132]

These important benefits only accrue if the validation is effective; and it is only effective if the forms and standards have been followed.

Each kind of pedigreeing has its own rules and standards. No cue, no amount of ritual behavior, can achieve symbolic validation if its prescribed procedures are not followed or its public standards are violated. Graham Greene's "whisky priest" may have lost his faith,[133] but as long as he follows the rites, he remains an effective validator. Prescribed standards are the essential element in symbolic validation. For example, in 1948, the International Court of Justice was asked by the General Assembly to designate the test for admitting candidate states to UN membership.[134] The Court replied, essentially, by reciting the rules established by Article 4 of the UN Charter: that an applicant must be a state, peace loving, willing to accept the obligations of the Charter, able to carry them out, and willing to do so. The Court further explained that these were "not merely . . . the necessary conditions, but also . . . the conditions which suffice."[135] In other words, nations that objectively satisfy that standard are entitled to have their status validated. The standard is itself pedigreed by its inclusion in the UN Charter, the world's most inclusive multilateral treaty, and by its deep historical rootedness in analogous national recognition practices.[136]

Similarly, the legal adviser to the Secretary-General prepared a memorandum explaining the rules applicable to accepting or rejecting the credentials of a delegation when there is doubt about their validity, for example, during a civil war when there may be two adversary claimants. In such situations, too, UN members should be guided by Charter Article 4, the legal adviser said. Moreover,

> [w]here a revolutionary government presents itself as representing a State, in rivalry to an existing government, the question at issue should be which of these two governments in fact is in a position to employ the resources and direct the people of the State in fulfilment of the obligations of membership. In essence, this means an inquiry as to whether the new government exercises effective authority within the territory of the State and is habitually obeyed by the bulk of the population.[137]

[132] For example, a pledged word commits powerful as well as weak governments. There is widespread recognition by states, antedating the UN Charter, that a commitment equally obligates powerful, as weaker nations. *See* Legal Status of Eastern Greenland (Den. v. Nor.), 1933 PCIJ (ser. A/B) No. 53, at 22 (Judgment of Apr. 5).

[133] Greene shows that even though a priest may fall into a secularized life style, he retains his spiritual powers. A "whisky priest" is "a damned man putting God into the mouths of men," owing to his authority to perform communion. *See* G. GREENE, THE POWER AND THE GLORY 83 (1940).

[134] Admission of a State to the United Nations (Charter, Art. 4), 1948 ICJ REP. 57 (Advisory Opinion of May 28).

[135] *Id.* at 62, 63.

[136] *See* 1 L. OPPENHEIM, *supra* note 77, at 124–52.

[137] Letter to Trygve Lie, Mar. 8, 1950, Legal Aspects of the Problems of Representation in the United Nations, 5 UN SCOR Supp. (Jan.–May 1950) at 18, 22–23, UN Doc. S/1466 (1950).

Governments that do are eligible; those that do not are not. These standards are also rooted in venerable national recognition practices.

These standards for symbolic validation at the United Nations, like any rules, leave room for differences of interpretation in borderline cases where "willingness to carry out obligations" and "control over territory and population" are not wholly self-evident. Nevertheless, the standards have a fairly high degree of formal determinacy and are not difficult to understand, making it possible to dismiss bogus, self-serving interpretations. For example, it is surely not permissible to vote to deny membership to a new state on the ground that its president is black or that its inhabitants are poor. The standards also explain why even ardent Palestinian and Sahrawian representatives have not yet sought membership in the United Nations.

When the symbolic validation proceeds legitimately in accordance with its own prescription—when these rules are followed—it succeeds in its purpose. If validation is withheld in conformity with the same standards, the rejected candidate will be denied the hallmark of effective statehood. The legitimate refusal of governments, individually, and collectively in the United Nations, to validate the Bantustan "homelands"—which clearly do not meet the standard—has undoubtedly contributed to those pseudo-nations' failure to achieve the status of membership and equality in the international community.[138] Problems arise, however, when the standards are not applied coherently; that is, when they are applied to some but not to others equally entitled, or when the standards cease to be connected to principles of general applicability. For example, the United States Government led the fight that, for years, allowed the Nationalist regime on Taiwan, and not the Communist regime in Beijing, to occupy the Chinese seat in UN organs, on the ground that this "is a privilege and not a right."[139] The United States meant that symbolic validation could be withheld from the Beijing Government, even though it obviously met the traditional criteria, because those could be overridden by political considerations. More recently, African and Arab members of the General Assembly have led efforts to reject the credentials of the delegations from South Africa and Israel[140]

[138] The General Assembly condemned the establishment by South Africa of Bantu homelands (Bantustans) as an attempt artificially to divide the African people into "nations" according to their tribal origins, with the aim of weakening the African front in its struggle for its inalienable and just rights. GA Res. 2775E, 26 UN GAOR Supp. (No. 29) at 42, UN Doc. A/8429 (1971). The resolution passed by the resounding vote of 110 in favor, 2 opposed, with 2 abstentions. *See also* Report of the Secretary-General, UN Doc. A/8388 (1971) (transmitting consensus adopted on Sept. 13, 1971, by joint meeting of the Special Committee on *Apartheid*, the Special Committee on the Situation with regard to the Implementation of the Declaration on the Granting of Independence to Colonial Countries and Peoples, and the United Nations Council for Namibia); Dugard, *South Africa's "Independent" Homelands: An Exercise in Denationalization*, 10 DEN. J. INT'L L. & POL'Y 11 (1980) (for the development of the Bantustan policy).

[139] State Department Memorandum, *U.S. Policy on Nonrecognition of Communist China*, 39 DEP'T ST. BULL. 385 (1958).

[140] GA Res. 3207, 29 UN GAOR Supp. (No. 31) at 2, UN Doc. A/9631 (1974) (resolution on South Africa). When, in 1982, the Arab bloc decided to challenge the credentials of the

even though there is no question that these do meet the criteria for representing their respective countries. The General Assembly, with the support of the United States and a majority of Western and Third World nations, has also continued to seat the delegation of the Kampuchean regime headed by Prince Sihanouk even though it fails to control any significant part of the territory of the country it claims to represent. At least those who are responsible for the Kampuchean result have sought to justify themselves by proposing a new general rule: that a regime, even if it is in effective control, should not be rewarded for having been installed by foreign aggression.[141] That new rule may eventually acquire pedigreed legitimacy, but it has not done so as yet.

When the process of symbolic validation is abused by failure to follow its own procedural rules and standards, a divergence is likely to occur between the real world and the symbolic world, to the detriment of the status-validating processes and symbols. They may cease to be taken seriously. For example, at a time when the Chinese Communist regime was still being excluded from the United Nations, Secretary-General Dag Hammarskjöld nevertheless engaged in numerous important negotiations with Chou En-lai, Beijing's foreign minister.[142] The head of the UN Secretariat, it seems, did not feel constrained by the members' decision denying validation to the Communist authorities. Similarly, Hammarskjöld's successor, U Thant, vigorously pressed his negotiations with Hanoi during the Vietnam War,[143]

Israeli delegation, the United States announced it would boycott any UN body that excluded the Israelis and would also withhold its contribution amounting to 25% of the UN budget. T. FRANCK, NATION AGAINST NATION 217 (1985). Most recently, Oman, acting on behalf of 20 Arab states, proposed an amendment to exclude the credentials of Israel from General Assembly approval. The General Assembly voted not to act on this amendment. *Credentials Committee Reports Adopted*, UN CHRON., No. 1, February 1987, at 16. *See also* Halberstam, *Excluding Israel from the General Assembly by a Rejection of its Credentials*, 78 AJIL 179 (1984).

[141] Credentials of Representatives to the Forty-first Session of the General Assembly: First Report of the Credentials Committee, UN Doc. A/41/727, para. 12 (prov. ed. 1986).

> The representative of the United States of America stated that the credentials of the representatives of Democratic Kampuchea were in order, fulfilled the requirements of rule 27 of the rules of procedure, had already been accepted by the General Assembly in the past and should be accepted at the current session. The suggested alternative was a regime brought to power by a foreign military invasion and that was clearly not representative in any way, shape or form of the Kampuchean people.

Id.

[142] The Secretary-General conducted a series of talks with Chou En-lai "in the name of the United Nations" (*see* GA Res. 906, 9 UN GAOR Supp. (No. 21) at 56, UN Doc. A/2890 (1954)) in order to discuss the release of four U.S. fighter pilots shot down near the Yalu River between October 1952 and January 1953, while they were flying missions for the UN Command during the Korean War. See 2 PUBLIC PAPERS OF THE SECRETARIES-GENERAL OF THE UNITED NATIONS: DAG HAMMARSKJÖLD (1953–1956), at 415–59 (1972), for details of the Secretary-General's mission. *See also* T. FRANCK, *supra* note 140, at 136–37.

[143] In 1964 U Thant secretly informed President Johnson that he could arrange a meeting between the United States and North Vietnam. Believing he had secured the President's blessing, he proceeded to use his good offices to arrange a meeting in Rangoon. But when the United States failed to respond once the meeting had been agreed to by the North Vietnamese,

even though the UN political organs had never validated the nation of North Vietnam, let alone its governmental representatives.[144] The refusal to seat the South African delegates to the General Assembly likewise has not prevented Secretary-General Pérez de Cuéllar from negotiating with Pretoria over such matters as the future of illegally occupied Namibia.[145] With whom else, after all, *could* he negotiate that question?

To recapitulate: an act of recognition, the symbolic validation of a state or regime, has the capacity to bestow, symbolically, rights and duties on the recognized entity when, *but only if,* it is done in accordance with the applicable principled rules and procedures. Such pedigreed recognition, and its corporate UN equivalent, is everywhere accorded great weight. On the other hand, when the rules and standards for validation are violated, or are themselves unprincipled and capricious, then symbolic validation fails in its objective of bestowing status. Moreover, when validation is seen to be capricious, a failure to validate will do more to undermine the legitimacy of the validating process than of the state or government thus deprived of symbolic validation.

The failure of mystical ritual to do what it is invoked for is usually explained metaphysically. The excommunicate priest who elevates the host before the altar in a fraudulent Eucharist is left holding only bread and wine because his invalid orders cannot effect the miracle of transubstantiation. But failed validation can often be explained rationally. For example, the Ukraine has not been transformed into a sovereign and equal state by its membership in the United Nations. Membership held at variance with the Organization's own standards does not validate the Ukraine's statehood.[146] Similarly, when the United Nations wishes to engage in relief activities in Kampuchea, its officials do not deal with the symbolically validated government of Prince Sihanouk but, rather, with the "unrecognized" regime actually in control. The perverse use of validation, in both instances, fails to give or withhold status for reasons that are practical, rational and not in the least

Thant felt humiliated by the U.S. Government and leaked his story to the world. T. FRANCK, *supra* note 140, at 154–58.

[144] The People's Republic of China was admitted to the United Nations on Oct. 25, 1971, and Vietnam acquired membership only in 1977.

[145] For an account of how the Security Council directed Secretary-General Waldheim " 'to initiate as soon as possible contacts with all parties concerned' " so that the people of Namibia might exercise their right to self-determination and independence, see D. SOGGOT, NAMIBIA: THE VIOLENT HERITAGE 53–54 (1986).

[146] Despite the fact that the Soviet Constitution guarantees individual republics the right to secede from the Soviet Union, it was widely known that the Ukraine, like each of its sister republics, was considerably less independent than any American state and thus was otherwise ineligible for UN membership. Nonetheless, the West ultimately acceded to the Soviet request to admit two republics as UN members because it was viewed as a reasonable price to pay for Soviet participation in the United Nations. T. FRANCK, *supra* note 140, at 21. For a detailed history of the negotiations leading to the West's disposition of Stalin's initial request for membership for all 16 Soviet republics, see R. RUSSELL, A HISTORY OF THE UNITED NATIONS CHARTER 435, 533, 536–37, 539 n.49, 584, 597–98, 636 (1958).

metaphysical. If the valid procedural rules or standards are not applied, it is to be expected that no legitimacy will be conferred.

The costs to its legitimacy of applying a rule incoherently arise in three related, but different, senses. First, incoherence nullifies the flawed act of validating or withholding validation. Second, it undermines the standards, rules and processes for bestowing status or validity. Third, it derogates from the legitimacy of the institution that is charged with validating. Thus, in the UN context, when the General Assembly fails to follow the Organization's own rules, standards or procedures for accrediting delegates, it damages the claim of the whole UN system to be taken seriously as the symbolic bestower of status.

Dworkin has pointed out that coherence (he uses the term "integrity")[147] is a key factor in explaining why rules compel.[148] He observes that a rule is coherent when like cases are treated alike in application of the rule and when the rule relates in a principled fashion to other rules of the same system. Consistency requires that a rule (or, as we have noted, a ritual or standard), whatever its content, be applied uniformly in every "similar" or "applicable" instance. The opposite is what Dworkin calls "checkerboarding."[149]

There is another aspect of coherence. It encompasses the further notion that a rule, standard or validating ritual gathers force if it is seen to be connected to a network of other rules by an underlying general principle. This latter aspect of coherence merits closer examination.

Let us imagine that it has been generally agreed that the $1,010 billion debt of Third World states[150] should be retired by the borrowers' paying the lenders half the total amount owed. Both sides regard this compromise as the best deal they can get in present circumstances. The problem is one of coverage. How is the 50 percent repayment formula going to be implemented in practice? Who will repay what? Suppose it were suggested that states whose names begin with the letters *A–M* should repay their entire debt, while those whose names start with *N–Z* pay nothing. Such a rule has determinacy. Although some will fare better than others, no borrower state will be worse off with the compromise than without it. The compromise is also better for the lenders than being repaid nothing, and better for the borrowers than having to repay everything. Yet any such "checkerboard" compromise is likely to be rejected by both borrowers and lenders because of its manifest incoherence. Its incoherence makes it facially illegitimate.

To be legitimate, Dworkin points out, such a compromise must "aim to settle on some coherent principle whose influence then extends to the natural limits of its authority."[151] That means the compromise must connect what it does with some *rational principle of broader application*. The alphabetic

[147] R. DWORKIN, *supra* note 7.

[148] *Id.* at 190–92.

[149] *Id.* at 179.

[150] INTERNATIONAL BANK FOR RECONSTRUCTION AND DEVELOPMENT, WORLD DEBT TABLES, EXTERNAL DEBT OF DEVELOPING COUNTRIES, 1985–86, at xi (1986).

[151] R. DWORKIN, *supra* note 7, at 179.

compromise asserts a principle that distinguishes between countries—those which must repay and those to be forgiven—by means of a general principle that cannot be defended on any rational basis. The alphabetic compromise, like the flipping of a coin, is an admission that no rational principle can be found that will produce the desired result. Thus, the decision is left to chance: the "draw" of the alphabet. This establishes no generalizable rule, no principle to justify the basis for making a decision. It lacks coherence because it lacks nexus: both in logic and, more important, in practice. It fails to connect to a rational principle in general use. It establishes no basis for a continuing pattern of systemic interaction; it connects the particular decision to no sense of ongoing community. Even if there were other debt crises in the future, the alphabetic approach would merely become more indefensible as it lost its one vestigial merit: its randomness. Nothing in international life is ever resolved, or likely to be solved, by recourse to the alphabetic principle except seating arrangements at multinational conferences.

A coherent half-loaf compromise could be achieved by applying any one of various coherent, principled approaches. For example, debt forgiveness could be distributed on a sliding scale based on national income or on per capita productivity, the inverse of the scale of assessment used to tax UN members. Or each debtor's indebtedness could be reduced by a fixed percentage, as in a bankruptcy reorganization. Or all repayments could be stretched out in accordance with a schedule based on rise in productivity. Any of these methods of implementing the half-loaf compromise connects with a principle of distribution that commends itself rationally and has been, and will be, applied elsewhere. Coherence requires that the rule applied to a dispute about the distribution of debt relief should employ distinctions that are acceptable (or, at least, not unacceptable) in solving not only future instances of the same problem but also quite different distributive problems.

Dworkin illustrates the potency of coherence as a factor in legitimacy by asserting that a half-loaf regulation is even less acceptable than no loaf at all when it produces a checkerboard result. "Even if I thought strict liability for accidents wrong in principle," he has written, "I would prefer that manufacturers of both washing machines and automobiles be held to that standard rather than that only one of them be. I would rank the checkerboard solution not intermediate between the other two [no strict liability and universal strict liability] but third, below both, and so would many other people." Such "compromises are wrong, not merely impractical."[152] They are lacking in legitimacy.

A rule taxing only property with even-numbered addresses would be incoherent and lack legitimacy. The same rule would be perfectly coherent if odd-numbered properties, all being on the same side of each street, had received a 20-year tax abatement in return for yielding several feet of their frontal property to the city for the widening of roadways. A "selective service" lottery for induction into the armed services employs a purely random military draft, which may be justified as the fairest way to allocate a

[152] *Id.* at 182.

social burden in some circumstances. In other words, before a rule that is facially inconsistent in its application can be adjudged incoherent, it is necessary to determine not only that it applies unequally but also that no reasonable principle of general application can justify the inequality. If a rule is unequally applied, its legitimacy is placed in question. If the inequality is also unprincipled, the legitimacy of the rule—its capacity to obligate—will be severely depleted.

The idea that coherence is a key indicator of legitimacy may be illustrated further by reference to three recent developments in the international community: the emergence of a "right" to *self-determination*; the development of a notion of *state equality*, as exemplified by the voting system of the United Nations; and the entrenchment of free and nondiscriminatory terms of trade—the *most-favored-nation* system—in the General Agreement on Tariffs and Trade. Each has undergone a crisis of legitimacy occasioned by challenges to its normative coherence. Let us examine how each has attempted to meet that challenge and thus to protect its legitimacy.

The notion that national or ethnic groups are entitled to "self-determination" had its origins in the settlements made at the end of World War I. The U.S. delegation to the Versailles Peace Conference was firmly instructed to apply ethnic criteria to resolve all European territorial disputes and, to that end, President Woodrow Wilson saw to it that his team included historians, geographers and ethnologists.[153] Throughout the negotiations, Wilson insisted that settlements be based on "facts,"[154] by which he meant "racial aspects, historic antecedents, and economic and commercial elements."[155] Note, however, in passing, that this general principle need not be accepted as *just*. The legitimacy of a rule is conditioned by its coherence, but a rule may be quite coherent (in our sense of the term), as well as highly determinate and symbolically validated, and yet be thought unjust. Wilsonian self-determination, for example, may be legitimate yet work an injustice by transferring territories and resources in accordance with a general principle of ethnicity while ignoring considerations of economic well-being and the distributive claims of poor people.[156]

The Wilsonian principle achieved considerable coherence in the immediate period following World War I. Insistence on its application led to a plebiscite in Schleswig, which had been annexed by Prussia in 1864.[157] In 1920, Northern Schleswig voted to revert to Denmark, a verdict accepted by the Peace Conference.[158] The same principle governed the creation of Czechoslovakia, in accordance with the wishes of Wilson's Secretary of State Lansing, "that all branches of the Slav race should be completely freed from German and Austrian rule."[159] Similarly, the principle was used by Wilson

[153] R. S. BAKER, WOODROW WILSON AND WORLD SETTLEMENT 109 (1922).

[154] *Id.* at 187. [155] *Id.*

[156] Franck & Hawkins, *Rawls' Theory of Justice in International Context*, 10 MICH. J. INT'L L. (1988).

[157] S. WAMBAUGH, PLEBISCITES SINCE THE WORLD WAR 14 (1933).

[158] 2 A HISTORY OF THE PEACE CONFERENCE OF PARIS 205 (H. W. V. Temperley ed. 1920).

[159] 4 *id.* at 261 (1921).

to oppose efforts by France to create a buffer Rhenish Republic[160] between itself and Germany. Wilson's chief adviser, Colonel House, was scornful of the French, who "do not seem to know that to establish a Rhenish Republic against the will of the people would be contrary to the principle of self-determination."[161] The compromise accommodated some elements of both French geopolitics and American moralism. A Saar buffer was established. However, it was not to be independent but administered through the League of Nations. Although the inhabitants were not allowed to be represented in the German Reichstag, their schools, language, laws and German nationality were left untouched.[162]

The principle of self-determination was also used in drawing the boundaries of an independent Poland on incontrovertible historical and ethnic grounds.[163] Wilson succeeded in his demand that the new Polish state "should be erected" to "include the territories inhabited by indisputably Polish populations."[164] Finally, Upper Silesia was divided by the League Council in 1921 along strictly ethnic lines.[165]

The coverage, in practice, of the concept of self-determination after World War I should not be exaggerated by dwelling exclusively on these dramatic instances. The rule was extended only—and, at that, imperfectly—to the European territories of the vanquished powers. It was not applied, for example, to the dispute between Sweden and Finland over the Aaland Islands.[166] The commission of inquiry appointed to settle that problem instead declared that "the principle had not yet attained the status of a positive rule of international law."[167] On the other hand, Britain claimed to be motivated by self-determination in the partition of Ireland.[168]

After World War II, however, the self-determination principle came to be applied even more generally. The United Nations Charter for the first time expressed a general obligation of states to help enable inhabitants of all dependent non-self-governing territories to make a meaningful choice of national destiny. By joining the United Nations, its members accepted "a sacred trust" to "develop self-government, to take due account of the political aspirations of the peoples, and to assist them in the progressive development of their free political institutions."[169] Some colonial territories that previously belonged to Germany or Japan were placed under a formal

[160] THE INTIMATE PAPERS OF COLONEL HOUSE 334 (C. Seymour ed. 1928).

[161] *Id.* at 345.

[162] 2 Temperley (ed.), *supra* note 158, at 182.

[163] R. S. BAKER, *supra* note 153, at 110–11.

[164] *Id.*

[165] D. FLEMING, THE UNITED STATES AND WORLD ORGANIZATION 153 (1938).

[166] L. BUCHHEIT, SECESSION 71 (1978). [167] *Id.*

[168] Linking the issue of Ireland to self-determination, Balfour wrote: "No one can think that Ulster ought to join the South and West who thinks that the Jugo Slavs should be separated from Austria. No one can think that Ulster should be divorced from Britain who believes in self-determination." Balfour, The Irish Question, Nov. 25, 1919, PRO CAB 24/93, *quoted in* T. G. FRASER, PARTITION IN IRELAND, INDIA AND PALESTINE 27 (1984). For Lloyd George's comments, see T. G. FRASER, *id.* at 38.

[169] UN CHARTER art. 73.

trusteeship system supervised by the United Nations, which aimed "to promote . . . progressive development towards self-government or independence as may be appropriate," in accordance with "the freely expressed wishes of the peoples concerned."[170]

The principle now applied equally to all: to colonies and to Europe, to victors and to vanquished. The first article of the Charter, enumerating the Organization's "Purposes and Principles," specifies an all-embracing obligation of members to develop "friendly relations among nations based on respect for the principle of equal rights and self-determination of peoples."[171] This casts the principle in terms of universal coverage. The term "peoples," moreover, recognizes the importance of the ethnic dimension in determining *who* is entitled to invoke self-determination. No boundary separates "peoples" entitled from "peoples" not entitled. Coherence was achieved and the rule acquired powerful legitimacy.

This is not merely a matter of theory or words. Very few rules of the international system have had as dramatic an impact. Beginning with India, Burma and the Gold Coast, Britain conceded self-determination to nearly one billion persons, with France, the Netherlands, Belgium, Spain and Portugal, albeit at first reluctantly, following suit. With a host of new nations seeking validation, UN membership nearly doubled between 1960 and 1980.[172] This was achieved almost entirely by voluntary compliance in deference to a legitimate rule, rather than by coercion.

The coherence of the rule, however, did not last. Even as these dramatic events were occurring, the same principle of self-determination was being denied all of Eastern Europe. Territories largely inhabited by Latvians, Poles, Germans, Romanians, Hungarians and Slovaks were arbitrarily annexed by neighboring states, and their populations often put to flight. Somewhat later, some of the very nations of a Third World that had just benefited from the application of self-determination refused to join in censuring the Soviet Union and Warsaw Pact nations during the invasion of Hungary in 1956 and of Czechoslovakia in 1968.[173] Nor was the principle disregarded only in Europe. No sooner had India become independent than its armed forces denied self-determination to the princely state of Kashmir, which might well have been entitled to it on ethnic, religious and legal grounds.[174] So, too, neither independent Nigeria nor the Organization of African Unity felt any obligation to permit self-determination to the ethni-

[170] *Id.* art. 76(b). [171] *Id.* art. 1, para. 2.

[172] UN membership rose from 82 members at the beginning of 1960, 1959 UN Y.B. 539, to 154 by the end of 1980, 1980 UN Y.B. 1347.

[173] Saudi Arabia, Syria, Yemen, Yugoslavia, Afghanistan, Burma, Ceylon, Egypt, India, Indonesia, Iraq, Jordan, Libya and Nepal abstained from voting on a resolution condemning the 1956 Soviet invasion of Hungary. GA Res. 1004, ES-2 UN GAOR (564th plen. mtg.) at 7, 20, UN Doc. A/PV.564 (1956). Algeria, India and Pakistan abstained from voting on a Security Council resolution condemning the 1968 Soviet invasion of Czechoslovakia. 23 UN SCOR (1443d mtg.) at 28–29, UN Doc. S/PV.1443 (1968).

[174] India Independence Act, 1947, 10 & 11 Geo. 6, ch. 30.

cally and religiously distinct Ibo "nation" when it sought statehood for Biafra.[175]

Thus, the principle of self-determination began its descent into incoherence—in the sense of inconsistency of application—almost from the moment of its greatest apparent ascendance. Increasing incoherence became textually evident in 1960 with the General Assembly's adoption of the Declaration on the Granting of Independence to Colonial Countries and Peoples.[176] Drafted by the newly independent former colonies of Africa and Asia, it reiterated, on the one hand, "that all peoples have an inalienable right to complete freedom"[177] and demanded immediate implementation of this right "without any conditions or reservations in accordance with their freely expressed will and desire"[178] and regardless of "political, economic, social or educational preparedness."[179] On the other hand, the right was now to be applicable only to "territories which have not yet attained independence." The right was also offset by a new rule against any "attempt aimed at the partial or total disruption of the national unity and the territorial integrity of a country."[180]

The declaration thus revived the notion of the sanctity of existing boundaries and resistance to secession that informed the U.S. Civil War[181] and the decision in the Aaland Island case, but had briefly been disestablished by the notion of self-determination after World War I. In place of a coherent rule, there was now checkerboarding, with self-determination doctrinally sanctioned for some cases and prohibited for others. Not only has the coverage of self-determination shrunk, but also its boundaries—where it is applicable and where not—have become indistinct and incoherent. The standards for granting or withholding the right seem to lack connection to any underlying rational general principles.

This incoherence can be demonstrated by searching for applicable general principles that would justify the inconsistencies in the actual state practice since 1960. For example, Algeria was granted self-determination at the insistence of the world community, while Biafra was not. Is Algeria different from Biafra because the former is separated from France by water, while the latter is a contiguous part of the Nigerian landmass? Surely, this is not a

[175] Biafra declared its independence on May 30, 1967, but only five nations recognized its claim to independence. Neither the United Nations nor the OAU supported Biafran independence and the United Nations never even considered the issue. Nanda, *Self-Determination in International Law*, 66 AJIL 321, 326–27 (1972). *See also* 66 ASIL PROC. 58, 175 (1972).

[176] GA Res. 1514, 15 UN GAOR Supp. (No. 16) at 66, UN Doc. A/4684 (1960).

[177] *Id.*, Preamble.

[178] *Id.*, Art. 5.

[179] *Id.*, Art. 3.

[180] *Id.*, Art. 5.

[181] See, e.g., comments by President Lincoln:

> My paramount object in this struggle *is* to save the Union . . . . If I could save the Union without freeing *any* slave I would do it, and if I could save it by freeing *all* the slaves I would do it; and if I could save it by freeing some and leaving others alone I would also do that.

Letter from Abraham Lincoln to Horace Greeley, Aug. 22, 1862, *reprinted in* 5 THE COLLECTED WORKS OF ABRAHAM LINCOLN 388 (R. Basler ed. 1953).

principled distinction capable of being generalized. Many nations—the United States, the Philippines, Canada, Indonesia, India, China and the Soviet Union—have provinces or regions separated from the rest of their territory by salt water. Thus, the distance from Hawaii to Los Angeles is five times greater than that from Marseilles to Algiers. Understandably, an ultramarine principle has never been accepted in practice to define the boundaries of self-determination. No government is likely to accept a distinction that would allow the Canadian province of Prince Edward Island to enjoy the right of self-determination but not Quebec.

Other principles for making distinctions between those entitled and those not, encounter equal difficulty. A differentiation between oppressed "peoples" (entitled) and others (not entitled) has a certain moral attraction. But it is not generalizable and certainly fails to account for the actual behavior of states during the past 25 years in supporting or ignoring demands for self-determination. For example, even before their independence, the populations of Nigeria, India, Senegal and the Ivory Coast had far more say in their government than is currently enjoyed by the people of Latvia, Eritrea and the southern Sudan. Yet the international community has championed self-determination for the former, but not for the latter.

Likewise, attempts to introduce an economic variable to rationalize the "checkerboard" application of self-determination tends to be unsuccessful. It has been argued that Biafrans and other Nigerians have fared better by remaining united than they would have done had they separated.[182] But a strong case can also be made that Algeria and France would have prospered more had they remained together. And Katanga has surely suffered economically as a result of its continued union with Zaire, a denial of self-determination that was actually enforced by the United Nations.[183] The economic factor not only does not rationalize actual state practice, it is also probably bad theory. That economic considerations should or ever *will* trump political, cultural and ethnic ones is a very questionable basis for any agreed general principle.

A more defensible distinction makes self-determination applicable only to "peoples" who are treated *unequally* by government. This principle would

[182] An independent and united Nigeria was perceived to be a "model for Africa," a "key" to that continent's future stability and prosperity, because of its material wealth and rich culture. The "progressive Balkanization" of Nigeria, with its concomitant vast waste of human and social resources, was viewed with great anxiety as a tragedy for all Africa. 283 PARL. DEB. (5th ser.) 1367–76 (1967).

[183] The United Nations completely rejected the claim that Katanga was a sovereign independent nation. *See, e.g.*, SC Res. S/5002, 16 UN SCOR (Res. & Dec.) at 3, UN Doc. S/INF/16/Rev.1 (1961). The United Nations found itself at odds with Katanga. On Apr. 3, 1961, Katanga adopted a Decree on the State of Enmity with the United Nations, *reproduced in* J. GERARD-LIBOIS, KATANGA SECESSION 335–37 (R. Young trans. 1966), which, inter alia, forbade Katangans to enter into relations of any nature whatsoever with the United Nations or its agents. See also C. C. O'BRIEN, TO KATANGA AND BACK (1962), in which the author, a former representative of the United Nations in Katanga and former member of the Secretary-General's executive staff, offers a case history of UN experiences with Katanga.

explain why the inhabitants of a colony ruled by Britain or France might be entitled to self-determination, while Latvians or Biafrans were not. Even though preindependence Algeria did elect members to the French Assembly and Senate, the system of communal "colleges" then in operation gave a European vote ten times more weight than an Arab one.[184] Biafrans, by contrast, enjoyed the same rights as other Nigerians. Paradoxically, this basis for distinction may deny the right of self-determination to groups that are more oppressed than some to whom the right would accrue. Latvians, deprived of many basic freedoms, would have no right because they are treated no differently than other disempowered Soviet citizens. Thus, "peoples" of nations that treat everyone equally badly would have no right, while "peoples" treated quite well would be entitled to secede if they were not accorded quite as many rights as the most privileged of that populace.

Moreover, this theoretical basis for determining entitlement to self-determination, while coherent, and also rather congruent with prevailing state conduct, is hard to apply in practice. Once a secessionist movement is in full operation, its ethnic group is almost certain to encounter discriminatory treatment, as is demonstrated by the rise of anti-Tamil sentiment in Sri Lanka in tandem with the spread of Tamil insurrection. Secessionism and discrimination mutually reinforce one another, and it is difficult in particular instances to determine whether secessionism *caused* or *was caused by* unequal treatment.

Difficult or not, the search for a coherent general principle of coverage, or boundary, is important. If it fails, the once-dynamic right of self-determination will fall into incoherence and desuetude. As a rule of state conduct, it began to lose its power to obligate when it became a checkerboard of incoherent practice.

Coherence, in this sense, is fundamental to understanding why a rule text has sufficient legitimacy to affect the conduct of states. The power of coherence to validate derives from the phenomenon we have already identified: that the status of states is symbolically validated by admission into the community of states. It is by symbolic recognition of their membership in that community that states are confirmed in their equal capacity for rights and obligations. Coherence derives from—is the operational manifestation of—that community of rules. Dworkin, although focusing on a community of persons rather than of nations, explains *why* legitimacy is "grounded in" coherence.[185] Coherence demonstrates that states relate through more than random interactions; that they consciously accept responsibilities derived "from a more general responsibility" that is based on membership in a community. Thus, in the community of nations, each state must "treat discrete obligations that arise only under special circumstances, like the obligation to help a friend who is in great financial need, as derivative from and expressing a more general responsibility active throughout the association in different ways."[186] This concern, in principle, must be "an *equal*

[184] E. BEHR, THE ALGERIAN PROBLEM 38 (1961).
[185] R. DWORKIN, *supra* note 7, at 194. [186] *Id.* at 200.

concern for all members."[187] However, the concern is not incompatible with distinctions, so long as each distinction "fits a plausible conception of equal concern."[188] A plausible conception of equal concern is another way of describing a generalizable principle for determining the coverage of a rule-based obligation.

To take another example of such a search: the UN Charter, in Article 2, sets forth "the principle of the sovereign equality of all . . . Members." Article 27, however, provides that the five permanent members of the Security Council—Britain, China, France, the United States and the USSR—shall have a veto over substantive decisions. If states did not regard the United Nations as an aspect of a global community, this seeming contradiction would not matter. Life is full of contradiction. It only matters when a contradiction rises to the level of an incoherence that invalidates and illegitimatizes an aspect of the system of rules of a community to which the state belongs and by reference to which the state defines *its own legitimacy*. Does the contradiction between the voting procedure of the Charter and its rule of state equality invalidate the rules, the UN-based community and, thus, even the individual legitimacy of the members? To ask the question is to understand why states are reluctant to let the Charter fall into incoherence. Instead, they strive to find a reconciling "neutral principle,"[189] a rational distinction that could restore coherence and validate the "checkerboarding." The best one available is this: while all states are equal, some states, because of their special wealth and power, have greater obligations and responsibilities. Consequently, they may also be entitled to an enhanced vote in certain matters.

Unfortunately, this coherent conceptual justification for the privileges granted the "Big Five" in 1945 is not rationally defensible in 1988. In 1945, they really were the world's major powers, having vanquished the Axis and inherited the postwar leadership. Their special status had a certain plausibility, since the success of any important Security Council action would depend on their cooperation. Today, however, Britain, France and China are middle powers, and their role in the world and in the Organization has become no more important than that of some important states without the veto such as the Federal Republic of Germany, Brazil, Nigeria, India and Japan. The privilege bestowed by the rules has thus lost its rational persuasiveness as a boundary, a standard for making distinctions that connects with a rational general principle.

Apparently, this problem of incoherence, with its concomitant dangers, is recognized. While it has not been possible to amend the Charter, Britain, France and China, although casting occasional negative votes in the Council, have made it a practice not to do so except in the company of a majority, or of either the United States or the USSR.[190] In this way, they have contributed to the de facto remission of their veto power.

[187] *Id.*

[188] *Id.* at 201.

[189] For a noteworthy attempt to establish a theoretical basis for such a quest in another area of law, see Wechsler, *Toward Neutral Principles of Constitutional Law*, 73 HARV. L. REV. 1 (1959).

[190] U.S. Mission to the United Nations, List of Vetoes Cast in Public Meetings of the Security Council (Apr. 14, 1988). Only once did the People's Republic of China stand alone in its veto in

This example illustrated that coherence mandates a connectedness between various component parts of a rule or code; between several applications of a rule in various instances; and between the general principles underlying a rule's application and those implicated in other rules. The General Agreement on Tariffs and Trade of 1947[191] further illustrates these aspects of coherence. Its most basic provision is the most-favored-nation clause, which prohibits members from giving benefits to some trading partners not given to all.[192] As long as this rule is applied consistently in practice, it appears to be coherent and, thus, legitimate. In recent years, however, it has become evident that the MFN provision, if applied consistently to all nations, would undermine rather than advance GATT's underlying purpose by diminishing the trade prospects of some 50 less-developed member countries. GATT therefore adopted a Generalized System of Preferences for these special cases.[193] It allows developed states temporarily to permit preferential access to products of only some states, particularly the "least developed."[194] While GSP is inconsistent with MFN, it coheres with the underlying purpose of GATT, which is to increase trade for all nations. It thus advances the real objectives of GATT. Also, it establishes a standard for distinction between the members to whom MFN is applicable and those temporarily benefited by GSP. That standard connects coherently with boundaries commonly used in other sets of regulations to demarcate coverage. Redistributive principles such as those which underlie GSP are commonplace in the international rule system and justify distinctions that, although creating superficial inconsistencies within rules and the application of rule systems, nonetheless leave the rules coherent and legitimate. The checkerboarding, in other words, is redeemed by being seen as based on a principle that both is consistent with the real intent of the specific rule and connects with that skein of principles integrating various other rules of the international system.

To summarize: coherence, and thus legitimacy, must be understood in part as defined by factors derived from a notion of community. Rules become coherent when they are applied so as to preclude capricious checkerboarding. They preclude caprice when they are applied consistently or, if inconsistently applied, when they make distinctions based on underlying general principles that connect with an ascertainable purpose of the rules and with similar distinctions made throughout the rule system. The result-

---

the Security Council. *Id.* at 9. France has vetoed alone only twice since 1946. *Id.* at 10–11. All United Kingdom vetoes during the last 15 years have been cast with the United States. *Id.* at 12–13.

[191] General Agreement on Tariffs and Trade [hereinafter GATT], Oct. 30, 1947, 61 Stat. (5), (6), TIAS No. 1700, 55–61 UNTS.

[192] *Id.*, Art. 1(1).

[193] GATT Contracting Parties, Decision of Nov. 28, 1979, Differential and More Favorable Treatment Reciprocity and Fuller Participation of Developing Countries, GATT, BASIC INSTRUMENTS AND SELECTED DOCUMENTS, 26th Supp. 203 (1980). *See also* J. JACKSON & W. DAVEY, LEGAL PROBLEMS OF INTERNATIONAL ECONOMIC RELATIONS 1149 (2d ed. 1986).

[194] Decision of Nov. 28, 1979, *supra* note 193, paras. 1 and 6.

ant skein of underlying principles is an aspect of community, which, in turn, confirms the status of the states that constitute the community. Validated membership in the community accords equal capacity for rights and obligations derived from its legitimate rule system.

By focusing on the connections between specific rules and general underlying principles, we have emphasized the horizontal aspect of our central notion of a community of legitimate rules. However, there are vertical aspects of this community that have even more significant impact on the legitimacy of rules.

V. Adherence (to a Normative Hierarchy) and Community

Professor Hart's observation, noted above, that the international arena lacks a "legislature, courts with compulsory jurisdiction, and centrally organized sanctions" leads him to deduce "that the rules for states resemble that simple form of social structure, consisting only of primary rules of obligation, which, when we find it among societies of individuals, we are accustomed to contrast with a developed legal system."[195] Although he acknowledges that international law does have many substantive "primary" rules, such as those specific rights and duties typically enumerated in treaties or developed through customary usage, he nevertheless concludes that the system is primitive, if not illusory, because it lacks those crucial procedural "secondary" rules which permit a rule to change and adapt through legislation and the decision of courts. An even more serious disqualification of the international system, Hart alleges, is its lack of "a unifying rule of recognition specifying 'sources' of law and providing general criteria for the identification of its rules."[196] By a "unifying rule of recognition," Hart means an international equivalent of the U.S. Constitution, or the British rule of parliamentary supremacy, both of which are "ultimate" in that they test the validity of all other rules by standards that are not themselves subject to being tested by reference to any superior rule.

Hart identifies the essential elements of a developed system of rules and then concludes that they are missing at the international level. He thus finds the international community to be the approximate equivalent of a small primitive tribe that has primary rules of obligation about such matters as land and kinship, but no system of governance that allocates and regulates social roles or facilitates, by an established process, the making, changing, application and reinterpreting of these random substantive primary rules.

In effect, Hart considers the international system to be primitive because individual rules lack *adherence* to a rule hierarchy. This is a much more sophisticated critique of the international rule system than the simple Austinian one, which focuses on the absence of a system of coercion. Hart does note the lack of institutionalized coercion but puts greater critical emphasis on the failure of international rules to adhere to a hierarchic rule structure.

[195] H. L. A. Hart, *supra* note 3, at 209. [196] *Id.*

Adherence—a term Hart does not use—is used here to mean the vertical nexus between a single *primary rule of obligation* ("cross on the green; stop on the red") and a pyramid of secondary rules about how rules are made, interpreted and applied: rules, in other words, about rules. These may be labeled *secondary rules of process*. Primary rules of obligation that lack adherence to a system of secondary rules of process are mere ad hoc reciprocal arrangements. They are not necessarily incapable of obligating parties that have agreed to them. They may even connect coherently with the underlying principles of distinction found in other rules to create a horizontal skein that is an aspect of community. But the degree of legitimacy of primary rules that only cohere is less than if the same rule were also connected to a pyramid of secondary rules of process, culminating in an ultimate rule of recognition. A rule, in summary, is more likely to obligate if it is made within the procedural and institutional framework of an organized community than if it is strictly an ad hoc agreement between parties in the state of nature. The same rule is still more likely to obligate if it is made within the hierarchically structured procedural and constitutional framework of a sophisticated community rather than in a primitive community lacking such secondary rules about rules.

Hart's critique of the community of states as small and primitive is still widely accepted. Even those who think that the system is at a more sophisticated stage of development might well concede that Hart's misgivings are not wholly unjustified. The recurrence of wars, other conflicts and unremedied injustices invites the appellation "primitive."

The misgivings, however, need to be kept in perspective. Of course, there *are* lawmaking institutions in the system. One has but to visit a highly structured multinational negotiation such as the decade-long Law of the Sea Conference of the 1970s to see a kind of incipient legislature at work. The Security Council, the decision-making bodies of the World Bank and, perhaps, the UN General Assembly also somewhat resemble the cabinets and legislatures of national governments, even if they are not so highly disciplined and empowered as the British Parliament, the French National Assembly or even the U.S. Congress. Moreover, there *are* courts in the international system: not only the International Court of Justice, the European Community Court and the regional human rights tribunals, but also a very active network of quasi-judicial committees and commissions, as well as arbitral tribunals established under such auspices as the Algiers agreement ending the Iran hostage crisis.[197] Arbitrators regularly settle investment disputes under the auspices and procedures of the World Bank and the International Chamber of Commerce. Treaties and contracts create jurisdiction for these tribunals and establish rules of evidence and procedure.[198]

[197] *See* Declaration of the Government of the Democratic and Popular Republic of Algeria Concerning the Settlement of Claims by the Government of the United States of America and the Government of the Islamic Republic of Iran, DEP'T ST. BULL., No. 2047, February 1981, at 3, *reprinted in* 75 AJIL 422 (1981), 20 ILM 230 (1981).

[198] The World Bank approved the Convention on the Settlement of Investment Disputes Between States and Nationals of Other States, Mar. 18, 1965, 17 UST 1270, TIAS No. 6090,

The international system thus appears on close examination to be a more developed community than critics sometimes allege. It has an extensive network of horizontally coherent rules, rule-making institutions, and judicial and quasi-judicial bodies to apply the rules impartially. Many of the rules are sufficiently determinate for states to know what is required for compliance and most states obey them most of the time. Those that do not, tend to feel guilty and to lie about their conduct rather than defy the rules openly. The system also has means for changing, adapting and repealing rules.

Most nations, most of the time, are both rule conscious and rule abiding. Why this is so, rather than that it is so, is also relevant to an understanding of the degree to which an international community has developed in practice. This silent majority's sense of obligation derives primarily not from explicit consent to specific treaties or custom, but from *status*. Obligation is perceived to be owed *to a community of states as a necessary reciprocal incident of membership in the community.* Moreover, that community is defined by secondary rules of process as well as by primary rules of obligation: states perceive themselves to be participants in a structured process of continual interaction that is governed by secondary rules of process (sometimes called rules of recognition), of which the UN Charter is but the most obvious example. The Charter is a set of rules, but it is also about how rules are to be made by the various institutions established by the Charter and by the subsidiaries those institutions have created, such as the International Law and Human Rights Commissions.

In addition, obligation is owed not only to the rules of the game, but also *to the game itself.* This is symptomatic of a community organized by a pyramid of secondary rules at whose apex is an ultimate rule or set of rules of recognition. The ultimate rule defines the community. If the game were football, the ultimate rule of recognition would be the one justifying the statement that what is being played is not baseball or tennis, but football. Thus, when the umpire calls a "foul," the legitimacy of that judgment derives ultimately from those rules which define the activity as football rather than some other sport. In the international system, the game of nations does have its own ultimate, defining set of rules by which the validity of all subsidiary rules—secondary procedural as well as primary substantive —may be tested.

A community is sophisticated when it has such an *ultimate rule of recognition.* In the United States, France, Germany and many other countries this is in the form of a written constitution. In the United Kingdom, however, the existence of an ultimate rule of recognition must be established deductively, since there is no written law defining the community. Nevertheless, it is

575 UNTS 159, which established the International Centre for Settlement of Investment Disputes. *See* Broches, *The Convention on the Settlement of Investment Disputes: Some Observations on Jurisdiction*, 5 COLUM. J. TRANSNAT'L L. 263 (1966). For U.S. implementing legislation, see Convention on the Settlement of Investment Disputes Act of 1966, Pub. L. No. 89-532, §2, 80 Stat. 344 (codified at 22 U.S.C. §§1650, 1650a (1982)). Under certain circumstances, parties to a dispute may arbitrate in the International Chamber of Commerce Court of Arbitration.

demonstrable that parliamentary supremacy qualifies as an ultimate rule of recognition because it owes its legitimacy only to public acquiescence, or to the corporate act of social commitment sometimes metaphorically described as a social contract. Its validity, unlike all the community's other secondary and primary rules, cannot be tested by reference to any other law. No statute makes Parliament supreme, nor can any law curb that supremacy. Indeed, if an act stipulated that it could only be repealed by a two-thirds majority, Parliament could delete that two-thirds requirement by a simple majority vote.[199] The rule of parliamentary supremacy defines the legitimacy of all other laws, but its own legitimacy is undefined, and thus *ultimate*. The rule is autochthonous: one "sprung from the earth itself."

Both the British Parliament and the U.S. Constitution are repositories of ultimate power unfettered by superior authority. Both the rule of parliamentary supremacy in Britain and the rules embodied in the Constitution of the United States are ultimate secondary rules of process by which the legitimacy of all primary rules of obligation may be tested and established. A rule of ultimate recognition operates with such extraordinary power to validate a subsidiary pyramid of rules—both other secondary rules of a procedural nature and primary rules of obligation—because the ultimate rule is accepted by a community that is defined by that rule. The ultimate set of rules also defines the status of each member of the community; that is to say, each member's status derives from the recognition of membership. Rejection of the ultimate rule by the members constitutes revolution and is the only option for discarding the ultimate rule (which, in some states but not in others, may be changed—as distinct from being overthrown—but only in strict accordance with its own terms). Acquiescence, on the other hand, is demonstrated tautologically, by compliance. Ultimate rules of recognition cannot be validated by reference to any other rule. All other secondary rules of the community are inferior to, and validated by, the ultimate rule or set of rules.

It is the nature of community, therefore, both to empower authority and to circumscribe it by an ultimate rule or set of rules of recognition that exists above, and itself is not circumscribed by, the system of normative authority. Does such a notion of community exist internationally, among states? Do nations recognize an ultimate rule or set of rules of recognition or process by which the legitimacy of all other international rules and procedures can be tested, a rule not itself subject to a higher normative test of its legitimacy, a rule that simply *is*, because it is accepted as font of the community's collective self-definition?

If the international community were merely a playing field on which states engaged in various random, or opportunistic, exchanges or interac-

[199] In perhaps the most eloquent statement of Parliament's unlimited legislative authority, Sir Edward Coke has declared that its "power and jurisdiction . . . is so transcendent and absolute, that it . . . hath sovereign and uncontrollable authority in the making, confirming, enlarging, restraining, abrogating, repealing, reviving, and expounding of laws." E. COKE, FOURTH INSTITUTE 36, *quoted in* A. DICEY, INTRODUCTION TO THE STUDY OF THE CONSTITUTION 41 (9th ed. 1939).

tions, it would be easy to conclude that this was a truly primitive aggregation, a rabble, lacking the organizing structure of secondary rules of process and, of course, an ultimate secondary rule. This, rather than any absence of coercive force, would indeed justify the appellation "primitive." The international community, however, demonstrably is not like that. States—whatever their occasional rhetorical excesses—recognize that they are not sovereign. They accept that they are members of a sophisticated community with secondary rules and with what amounts to a constitution or ultimate rules of recognition. States also recognize that they derive validation from membership in this community.

The nonsovereignty of states and the existence of a set of ultimate community rules can be demonstrated by examining the way treaties operate from the perspective of those that become parties to them. It is quite wrong to think that treaties bind states *because* they have consented to them. If states were sovereign, the mere act of entering into a treaty could not "bind" them in any accurate sense. States are not bound only because they agree to be bound, in the sense in which neighbors in an apartment building might informally agree, for their mutual convenience, to turn off their television sets by 10 o'clock every evening. Those neighbors are at liberty to disregard their obligation whenever it does not suit their purpose. Nor are states obligated by treaties the way individuals are bound by a contract. In municipal law, contracts are binding because their sanctity is prescribed and enforced by the state.[200] True, most contracts operate without recourse to state sanctions, but the sanctions remain in reserve.

Treaties thus do not exactly fit either model. They are not like the free-will agreement among neighbors, which is valid only as long as it continues to suit everyone's purpose; and they are not contracts made under the authority of a sovereign and enforceable by the full authority of the state, through either compelled specific performance or an award of damages. Treaties obviously cannot be binding in the sense of being sanctioned by an Austinian sovereign; but a treaty also cannot be said to be binding only because two or more sovereign states voluntarily agree to carry it out. "Sovereign" means *unbindable*. A treaty ratified by a truly sovereign state could only *declare*, never *bind*, that state's free will. If the state were indeed sovereign, then, no matter what it had signed, it would nevertheless remain free to terminate its consent at any time, just as the sovereign British Parliament cannot legislate a law that can only be amended by a two-thirds major-

[200] While the term "contract" is susceptible of many definitions, whatever else a contract may entail, it is agreed that it is "a promise, or set of promises, for breach of which the law gives a remedy, or the performance of which the law in some way recognizes as a duty." 1 WILLISTON ON CONTRACTS §1 (3d ed. 1957); RESTATEMENT (SECOND) OF CONTRACTS §1 (1981). *See also* 1 A. CORBIN, CONTRACTS §3 (1963) (which defines a contract to include "a promise enforceable at law directly or indirectly"). In some jurisdictions, courts will routinely mandate specific performance of the promise. *See, e.g.*, Dawson, *Specific Performance in France and Germany*, 57 MICH. L. REV. 495 (1959). The Anglo-American legal system, however, prefers to impose damages at least equal to the value of the breached promise. *See, e.g.*, J. CALAMARI & J. PERILLO, THE LAW OF CONTRACTS 580–604 (1977).

ity. If states were sovereign, entering into a treaty would be nothing more than evidence of their state of mind for the time being.

Notably, states never claim this. They act, instead, as if they were bound. They believe themselves to be bound—which can only be understood as evidence of their acquiescence in something demonstrable only circumstantially: an ultimate rule of recognition. In the international community "sovereignty"—however fragile—resides in the rule, and not in the individual states of the community. States seem to be aware of this rule's autochthony. They act in professed compliance with, and reliance on, the notion that when a state signs and ratifies an accord with one or more other states, then it has an obligation, superior to its sovereign will. The obligation derives not from consent to the treaty, or its text, but from membership in a community that endows the parties to the agreement with status, including the capacity to enter into treaties.

The most recent instance of this perception of an international rule superior to the specific acquiescence of any particular state is to be found in the advisory opinion rendered by the International Court of Justice on April 26, 1988, at the request of the United Nations General Assembly.[201] At issue was a conflict between provisions of a U.S. law that required the closing of the Observer Mission of the Palestine Liberation Organization,[202] and the obligation assumed under the UN Headquarters Agreement.[203] The Court stated unequivocally that it was "the fundamental principle of international law that it prevails over domestic law,"[204] that "the provisions of municipal law cannot prevail over those of a treaty."[205] The U.S. judge (Stephen M. Schwebel) added that "a State cannot avoid its international responsibility by the enactment of domestic legislation which conflicts with its international obligations" under a treaty.[206] Unanimously, the Court accepted that clear limitation on the sovereignty of states imposed by membership in the international community.

In Hart's words, the "view that a state may impose obligations on itself by promise, agreement, or treaty is not . . . consistent with the theory that states are subject only to rules which they have thus imposed on them-

[201] GA Res. 42/229B (Mar. 2, 1988).

[202] The Observer Mission status was created by GA Res. 3237, 29 UN GAOR Supp. (No. 31) at 4, UN Doc. A/9631 (1974). The closure of the mission is required by the Anti-Terrorism Act of 1987, title X of the Foreign Relations Authorization Act, 1988 and 1989, Pub. L. No. 100-204, tit. X, §1001, 101 Stat. 1331, 1406 (codified at 22 U.S.C.A. §§5201–5203 (West Supp. 1988)).

[203] *See* Agreement Regarding the Headquarters of the United Nations, June 26, 1947, *supra* note 115.

[204] Applicability of the Obligation to Arbitrate under Section 21 of the United Nations Headquarters Agreement of 26 June 1947, 1988 ICJ REP. 12, 34, para. 57 (Advisory Opinion of Apr. 26).

[205] Greco-Bulgarian "Communities," 1930 PCIJ (ser. B) No. 17, at 32 (Advisory Opinion of July 31).

[206] 1988 ICJ REP. at 42 (Schwebel, J., sep. op.).

selves."[207] Rather, "*rules* must already exist providing that a state is bound to do whatever it undertakes by appropriate words to do."[208] This hypothetical notion itself is actually set out in the text of a global treaty defining the law of treaties,[209] a document establishing a body of secondary rules of process. Even so, the binding force of the treaty codifying the law of treaties cannot emanate from the agreement of the large majority of states that have ratified it. It must come from some ultimate, generally accepted unwritten rule of recognition that is fundamental to any real understanding of the nature of international obligation.

If there is an ultimate set of secondary rules of process that embodies an abstract sovereignty and confers legitimacy in the international community, what are its other provisions? As with the foregoing rule, *pacta sunt servanda*, the other components of an ultimate rule of recognition can only be hypothesized and demonstrated circumstantially by habitual state deference. Thus, the rule that treaties are binding is itself modified by the rule that treaties are *void ab initio* if they are against the community's basic public policy, that is, if they violate the community's ultimate (peremptory) norms.[210] A treaty to commit genocide, for example, would be invalid for this reason. A related notion that appears to qualify as part of the ultimate rule of recognition pertains to the binding obligation imposed on state conduct by global custom. There is widespread acknowledgment by states that they are obligated by international customary rules, whether or not they agree in any specific instance with the import of a rule. This was recently reiterated by the International Court of Justice in the case brought by Nicaragua against the United States, where the latter was held to be obligated by an extensive array of customary norms despite an evident desire to pursue its self-interest in a manner incongruent with those rules.[211]

There are other parts of the ultimate rule that can be deduced from the practice of states in adhering to it *as an incident of statehood* rather than as a consequence of their specific consent. For example, new states are deemed to acquire the universal rights and duties of statehood not because they have agreed but because they have joined the community.[212] Similarly, new states may "inherit" rights and duties from a "parent" state[213] not by virtue of

[207] H. L. A. HART, *supra* note 3, at 219. [208] *Id.*

[209] Vienna Convention on the Law of Treaties, *supra* note 33, Art. 26.

[210] *Id.*, Art. 53.

[211] Military and Paramilitary Activities in and against Nicaragua (Nicar. v. U.S.), Merits, 1986 ICJ REP. 14 (Judgment of June 27).

[212] It is a well-established principle that a new state to the international community is automatically bound by the rules of international conduct existing at the time of admittance. *See* 1 L. OPPENHEIM, *supra* note 77, at 17–18. Even Tunkin concedes that if it enters "without reservations into official relations with other states," a new state is bound by "principles and norms of existing international law." *See* Tunkin, *Remarks on the Juridical Nature of Customary Norms of International Law*, 49 CAL. L. REV. 419, 428 (1961).

[213] There has been wide debate over the rights and obligations a successor state can inherit from its parent. The 19th-century doctrine of universal succession maintains that all the rights and duties of the parent pass to the successor. *See* O. UDOKANG, SUCCESSION OF NEW STATES

their consent but as a concomitant of status. Successor governments, too, automatically inherit rights and obligations.[214]

One more example of a part of the ultimate rule of recognition is the previously noted notion of state equality. UN Charter Article 2(1) specifically restates this rule, and no state since Hitler's Germany has claimed anything to the contrary. All states are bound by a rule of state equality as a concomitant of their membership in the community of nations. In the words of U.S. Chief Justice John Marshall in an 1825 decision, *The Antelope*, "No principle of general law is more universally acknowledged than the perfect equality of nations."[215]

It is therefore circumstantially demonstrable that there are obligations that states acknowledge to be necessary incidents of community membership. These are not perceived to obligate because they have been accepted by the individual state but, rather, are rules in which states acquiesce as part of their own validation; that is, as an inseparable aspect of "joining" a community of states that is defined by its ultimate secondary rules of process. It is even possible to conclude that the members of the global community acknowledge—for example, each time they sign a treaty or recognize a new government—*that statehood is incompatible with sovereignty*. They acknowledge this because they must, so as to obtain and retain the advantages of belonging to an organized, sophisticated community, advantages only available if ultimate sovereignty resides in a set of rules of universal application. That is why states behave as if such rules existed and obligated.

To put the matter another way, a "community" of states exists. It has at least some important secondary rules of recognition. These rules are "associative obligations," to use Dworkin's term,[216] which fasten onto all states because of their status as validated members of the international community. Only by stretching the notion of "consent" beyond its natural limits can these specific associative obligations be said to have been assumed consensually, even though they may sometimes be restated in a treaty. Dworkin rightly points out that "associative" rules of obligation are interpretive,[217] defining what a member owes others in the community in general. Thus, the obligation to honor treaties is acquired associatively, rather than by specific consent; and it is owed generally towards all members of the community. This is universally acknowledged. It is inconceivable, for example,

---

TO INTERNATIONAL TREATIES 122–24 (1972). At the other extreme is negativist theory, which holds that a successor inherits no rights and obligations, but begins with a tabula rasa. *See* D. O'CONNELL, STATE SUCCESSION IN MUNICIPAL LAW AND INTERNATIONAL LAW 14–17 (1967). The truth lies somewhere in between, with certain rights and duties of the parent devolving upon the successor. *See* 1 L. OPPENHEIM, *supra* note 77, at 120. Hart further points to evidence that changes in a state's circumstance may automatically accord it new rights and duties, for example, when it acquires new territory giving it a coastline. H. L. A. HART, *supra* note 3, at 221.

[214] Tinoco Case (Gr. Brit. v. Costa Rica), 1 R. Int'l Arb. Awards 369 (1923), *reprinted in* 18 AJIL 147 (1924).

[215] The Antelope, 23 U.S. (10 Wheat.) 66, 122 (1825).

[216] R. DWORKIN, *supra* note 7, at 196. [217] *Id.* at 197.

that a state would announce that it would no longer be bound by treaties or custom. The obligation, moreover, cannot be extinguished by renouncing a consent that was never given, but only by extinguishing the status that is the real basis of the obligation.

According to Dworkin, a true community, as distinguished from a mere rabble, or even a system of random primary rules of obligation, is one in which the members

> accept that they are governed by common principles, not just by rules hammered out in political compromise. . . . Members of a society of principle accept that their political rights and duties are not exhausted by the particular decisions their political institutions have reached, but depend, more generally, on the scheme of principles those decisions presuppose and endorse. So each member accepts that others have rights and that he has duties flowing from that scheme . . . .

Nor are these rights and duties "conditional on his wholehearted approval of that scheme; these obligations arise from the historical fact that his community has adopted that scheme, . . . not the assumption that he would have chosen it were the choice entirely his."[218]

Moreover, the community "commands that no one be left out, that we are all in politics together for better or worse."[219] And its legitimizing requirement of rule integrity "assumes that each person is as worthy as any other, that each must be treated with equal concern according to some coherent conception of what that means."[220]

Does that accurately describe the social condition of the nations of the world in their interactive mode? The description does not assume harmony or an absence of strife. According to Dworkin, an "association of principle is not automatically a just community; its conception of equal concern may be defective."[221] What a rule community, a community of principle, does is to validate behavior in accordance with rules and applications of rules that confirm principled coherence and adherence, rather than acknowledging only the power of power. A rule community operates in conformity not only with primary rules but also with secondary ones—rules about rules—which are generated by valid legislative and adjudicative institutions. Finally, a community accepts its ultimate secondary rules of recognition not consensually, but as an inherent concomitant of membership status.

In the world of nations, each of these described conditions of a sophisticated community is observable today, even though imperfectly. This does not mean that its rules will never be disobeyed. It does mean, however, that it is usually possible to distinguish rule compliance from rule violation, and a valid rule or ruling from an invalid one. It also means that it is not necessary to await the millennium of Austinian-type world government to proceed with constructing—perfecting—a system of rules and institutions that will exhibit a powerful pull to compliance and a self-enforcing degree of legitimacy.

[218] *Id.* at 211.

[219] *Id.* at 213.

[220] *Id.* at 214.

[221] *Id.*

Part III
What is the Source of Law?

[10]

VOLUME 26, NUMBER 2, SPRING 1985

Ideals and Things: International Legal Scholarship and the Prison-house of Language

James Boyle*

INTRODUCTION

The search for a "theory" of international law, no less than the oft-repeated claims about "new directions," seems to me to be the incarnation, within the formalized language of scholarship, of a number of complex and contradictory yearnings—yearnings which are a central feature of the lives of international lawyers, scholars and activists. The strange thing about these yearnings (and it may also be sad, inevitable, or merely comical, depending on your perspective) is that the very language in which they are expressed tends both to exacerbate them and to deny us the possibility of ever dealing with them. I want to discuss these yearnings and the kinds of thinking they might lead us to engage in.

I have recently been reading the work of Alain Robbe-Grillet, a French writer who belongs to a school known as the chosists.[1] The chosists pay an inordinate amount of attention to the description of apparently unimportant household objects. This surfeit of description is supposed to bring on a sort of bittersweet melancholy. The reader contemplates the obsessive concern with the personification of the physical environment and thus becomes all the more aware of the fateful and absurd contrast between the infinite quality of human aspiration and the unrelenting indifference of a world of brute objects. Something in this idea reminds me very much of international legal scholarship.

The resemblance comes from more than the mere coexistence of lofty ideals with mundane reality. It also comes from the fact that the

* Assistant Professor, Washington College of Law, American University. Gary Peller, Peter Gabel, Richard Parker, and Roberto Unger all had a profound influence on the ideas presented in this essay. Henry Steiner was kind enough to comment on earlier versions of individual sections as they were produced. The Washington College of Law Research Fund provided financial assistance. My deepest debt of gratitude is to David Kennedy; his structuralist analysis of international law provided the spur for this focus on reification, many of the arguments developed here were originally worked out in conversation with him, and it would be hard to find the parts of this essay that do not reflect our three years of arguments about things international.

1. *See* A. ROBBE-GRILLET, POUR UN NOUVEAU ROMAIN (1963); *see also* J. STURROCK, THE FRENCH NEW NOVEL (1969).

very discourse in which we describe our experiences and hopes as lawyers and scholars is incapable of evoking (let alone exorcising) the feelings of cognitive dissonance that seem to be an occupational hazard of our profession.

Whereas the chosists spent their time describing trivial objects, international lawyers express their theoretical angst by defining international law.[2] It should be obvious that under this layer of definitionalism several very different activities are going on. Some people are trying to give a convincing account of the normative source of international law. Some are describing a normative meta-system that is supposed to give determinacy and neutrality to the everyday acts of legal interpretation within the international legal process. Others are engaged in the creation of models which, by describing how international law operates, will make it a more attractive problem-solving system to states and other international actors. Finally, some are combining all of these activities in an attempt to redefine the boundaries of the discourse in order to give more weight to the views of some particular group. All of these activities have been described as "definitions" of international law, or as attempts to answer the question "Is international law, law?" It is still true, despite Wittgenstein, that when people feel unsure as to what they should be doing they try to define the *essential elements* of their activity and thus, like medieval philsophers, to find refuge from the world in a prolonged contemplation of the word. My thesis in this article is that this fascination with definitions is not simply a "mistake." Instead I will argue that it is the manifestation of something rather more important: a pervasive reification[3] that operates on the level of everyday politics as well as in the conceptual netherworld of international legal scholarship. Here is a summary of my argument.

(1) Reification is hard to describe for two reasons. First, it is omnipresent and thus invisible. Second, when people do recognise its

---

2. For an earlier criticism see Williams, *International Law and the Controversy Concerning the World "Law"* 12 BRIT. Y.B. INT'L L. 146 (1945). Although Williams explains the linguistic fallacy inherent in the search, he does not deal with the connection that this essay tries to sketch out—that between "essentialism" and *social* reification such as sexism or role-fetishism. *See infra* note 3.

3. "Reification," in the narrow sense, is the making of a concept into a thing. In this essay I am talking about something broader and less exclusively conceptual. In this sense reification refers to the phenomena that link sexist advertisements to formalistic legal argument and then connects both of them to the debates about "what is law?". All these things rely on the *power* that can be exercised by incorporating a contentious political choice into the act of "representation"; it doesn't matter whether it is Coke commercials presenting women as "essentially" sex objects, or judicial opinions defining sovereignty as an "essential" attribute of a state, the mechanism is the same. *See*, Gabel, *Reification in Legal Reasoning*, 3 RESEARCH IN L. & SOC. 25 (1980); Peller, *The Metaphysics of American Law* (forthcoming CALIF. L. REV.); Boyle, *The Politics of Reason* (forthcoming U. PENN. L. REV.).

existence, they explain it in very different ways. Its basic form is "the conversion of an idea into a thing" but there is much more to it than that. Some people see it as being an attempt to "naturalize" the here-and-now through the claim that it is actually the universal and timeless state of affairs. Others describe it as an attempt to deny both "contingency" and choice by incorporating some political decision about a subject into the *description* of that subject. The latter form is particularly easy to recognize because it depends on claims about "essences." For example, a sexist or racist comment will habitually be couched in the form of mere description. "That's a woman for you" or "It's human nature to be acquisitive" are statements which make political decisions about the role of women and the value of social change while disguising those decisions by incorporating them into the description of "the way things are." Who can argue with "the essential nature of women" or "human nature"? But this phenomenon of "reification" is more than just an argumentative trick which happens to be used both in international legal scholarship and in defenses of the status quo. It is the key to a particular kind of social theory—one that combines the traditional scholarly concern about the theory of the state with a predilection for small-scale descriptions of the realities of social power, in the workplace and the classroom as well as in the prison and the courtroom.

(2) One way to tackle the project of creating such a social theory would be to focus on the way that reification operates to 'close' the social world, the way that it makes the most mundane workplace hierarchy seem divinely ordained. "But what does all this have to do with international legal scholarship?", one might ask. Actually, I think that it has a great deal to do with international legal scholarship, but in order to make that point I will tackle the problem from another direction.

(3) For a long time I saw the problems with international legal scholarship as being a set of separate issues: a little xenophobia here, a little formalism there, a hint of technocracy and the rule of "the best and the brightest" somewhere else. But the more that I looked at it, the more that all the problems started to seem the same. Part of this can be dismissed as "concept fatigue," but I think that there is a sense in which all of the problems can usefully be understood to be the same—they all represent the reification, the "thing-ifying," of the ideals and aspirations that drew scholars to the subject in the first place.[4] This reification happens on many different levels. I have chosen

4. The reification that I have mentioned is rarely a deliberate attempt by a scholar to obscure the political implications of her work. It is more like a general "oppression of ourselves by ourselves" in which concepts are made into things and then treated as though they *were* things

to feature its effects in two main areas; scholarship about the "nature of" international law and the source of its "binding quality" and scholarship about doctrinal interpretation, application and effectiveness. By understanding the way that reification has operated to frustrate the goals of scholars in each of these areas we will not only be able to salvage a set of scholarly projects, but also to link scholarship to our everyday attempts to act as moral beings, whether we are dealing with a workplace dispute or an anti-nuclear campaign.

I. THE "NATURE" OF INTERNATIONAL LAW: SOURCES AND OBLIGATION

It is in scholarship that deals with the "nature," or "definition," or "source" of international law, or with its "binding quality," that one finds the most obvious form of reification—the search for "essences." In our century the dominant debate in this area of scholarship has been between the purveyors of natural law and the purveyors of positivism.[5] Through the use of hypothetical examples and ingenious scholastic conceits, both have attempted to show that *they* rather than the other group have actually discovered the "essence" of law in general and international law in particular. Like all such definitionalist debates, the resulting discourse may seem to be full of sound and fury and yet to signify nothing, but there is more to it than that.

As I pointed out earlier, there are a number of very different projects being carried out under the rubric of an investigation of the "source," or the definition of international law. Some scholars are attempting to prove that treaties are more authoritative than custom,[6] or vice versa,[7] while others are attempting to argue that some new "source," such as General Assembly resolutions or the dictates of utilitarian philosophy, should be given greater prominence as a fountain-head of authoritative norms.[8] Still others are trying to retell the story of international law in order to make it appear that the things we had thought of as defeats

---

which existed prior to our invention of them. Thus my argument is closer to being a critique of idolatry than a conspiracy theory. However, one should still remember that each time we give our own creations the status of golden idols and then worship them, we are reinforcing the grip of the status quo. So there *is* a sense in which reification is paradoxically both "innocent" and profoundly supportive of the existing structures of social power.

5. *See generally* A. NUSSBAUM, A CONCISE HISTORY OF THE LAW OF NATIONS (1947).

6. *See, e.g.*, G. TUNKIN, THEORY OF INTERNATIONAL LAW (1974) (given objective differences of interest between states of differing socio-economic systems, most international law must be formed by the explicit concordance of wills made possible by treaties).

7. *See, e.g.*, H. KELSEN, PRINCIPLES OF INTERNATIONAL LAW (1952) (custom is fundamental law-creating fact that gives international law its status as law).

8. *See, e.g.*, R. HIGGINS, THE DEVELOPMENT OF INTERNATIONAL LAW THROUGH THE POLITICAL ORGANS OF THE UNITED NATIONS (1963); M. BEDJAOUI, TOWARDS A NEW INTERNATIONAL ECONOMIC ORDER: NEW CHALLENGES FOR INTERNATIONAL LAW (1979).

were actually victories. By doing so they hope to stop the so-called "realists" from burying international law before it is dead.[9] But all these projects share one attribute: they are all in one way or another engaged in showing how, and under what conditions, authority can be distinguished from power, right from might, within the international legal system. In short, they are trying to develop some conceptual way of differentiating between law and politics. Once the lawyer has such a system, she can go down her conceptual checklist and make the decision "Is this Law or Not-law?" At the same time these theorists are trying to explain (again, on a *conceptual* level) why law has normative force—what are the hidden ingredients, the analytical components that imbue law with its authoritative status?

It is not that the task of explaining or justifying the normative force of international law is *conceptually* any more difficult than the equivalent task with respect to domestic law. In fact, the problems that theorists encounter are exactly the same; the difference comes from the absence of the veil of normality, of "natural-ness," that covers the internal operations of the state, the veil that would lead us to say that "it goes without saying" that the mugger's demand for one's wallet is "essentially" different from the state's demand for income taxes.[10] Now, of all the multitude of things one might think about this quality of "authoritativeness," one of the strangest would be the belief that there was something about legal norms, some conceptual thread woven into them, that distinguished them from other phenomena and thus provided the source, or test, or surety of their authoritative nature. Nevertheless, that is the line that legal theorists have taken—and if some, like Henkin, or Tunkin, seem to have moved beyond this fascination with conceptualism, it is only because they have shifted the axis along which one asks the questions.[11]

I have already said that one would have to embrace a complicated and unlikely set of ideas in order to believe that there was some point to a search for the "essence" of law. However, in order to believe that this essence not only existed, but that it would somehow provide the key to the normative force of law—the explanation of its "authority"—one would have to jettison most of the ideas about philosophy developed since the Enlightenment.

For a start, one would have to ignore the central insight that "social constructs," such as law, do not have some pre-existing shape prior to

---

9. *See, e.g.*, L. HENKIN, HOW NATIONS BEHAVE (1979); P. JESSUP, A MODERN LAW OF NATIONS (1968).

10. *See, e.g.*, H.L.A. HART, THE CONCEPT OF LAW 79–88 (1961). Hart claims that the legal demand is perceived as more than mere force. But since the initial impulse of the discussion was to find out *why*, this does not get us very far.

11. *See infra* text accompanying notes 30–46.

human intervention. The idea of finding the essence or the real source of law distracts us from the reality that, in a very important sense, it is being created by our categories and definitions rather than being described by them. If we accept the pragmatists' insight that all definitional activity must be guided by some chosen purpose, then we must surely come to the conclusion that definitions can never be true or false but only useful or useless.[12] And if we accept that proposition, then post-medieval jurisprudence comes to resemble its scholastic ancestors fairly closely.

But there is one difference. The scholastic philosophers believed that timeless essences existed which could be uncovered by the exercise of "right reason." As I will try to demonstrate below, both the positivists and the natural law theorists relied on this notion of essences. But attacks on the essentialist approach were so common that they penetrated even the wall of anti-intellectualism surrounding lawyers and legal scholars. Consequently, the current justification for the definitional activity at the heart of international legal scholarship is not that it seeks transcendental essences, but that, being based on timeless and uncontroversial *purposes*, it provides us with a correct view of the "nature" of law. Of course, neutral, universally valid purposes seem about as likely as transcendental essences—and so they should, being basically the same thing—but the interesting thing about this strategy of confession and avoidance is that it has brought the cognitive dissonance in legal thought to the surface. On the one hand, this seems like a bad thing; scholarship appears simultaneously more irrelevant from practice and more Balkanized as these metaphysical "purposes" diverge, each claiming that it possesses the *real* fragment of the true cross.[13] On the other hand, this seems like a good thing. It brings us closer to the utopian goals that actually inspire, yet are denied by, these multifarious scholarly projects. I am going to discuss the history of this process in international legal thought about sources

12. *See* Cohen, *Transcendental Nonsense and the Functional Approach*, 35 COLUM. L. REV. 809, 835 (1935); L. WITTGENSTEIN, PHILOSPOHICAL INVESTIGATIONS 30 (G. Anscombe trans. 1958).

13. I am thinking of, for example, the different political agendas that are served by the theoretical approaches of McDougal, Tunkin, and Henkin. But this confused oscillation from essence to purpose is a more general jurisprudential phenomenon than these examples would indicate. For example, H.L.A. Hart oscillates between the realization that there are no "essences" and a series of attempts to resurrect essentialism on the basis of (supposedly uncontentious) purposes. Thus the chapter in *The Concept of Law* that deals with international law is devoted to an analysis of whether international law is "law." If one reads closely, one finds that law has been implicitly defined according to a set of purposes that are mentioned but never fully articulated, that there is no explanation of how these purposes could acquire the fundamental character that Hart imputes to them, and that the defects of this argument are compounded when the analogy is made from domestic law to international. *See* H.L.A. HART, *supra* note 10, at 1–13, 208–231.

in the hope that the critique I have outlined will allow us to conduct an investigation of the conceptual and political repression it has engendered. I will follow the argument I have laid out in this paragraph, beginning with the positivist/natural law debate, explaining the reliance that both sides put on reified essences, linking this reliance to the question "what is law," and finally describing the shift to "purposive" scholarship about sources—a shift that resurrected the same practices under different names.

The debate between positivism and natural law has dominated legal thought about the sources of international law. This definitional debate is harder to penetrate than one might expect. The main reasons for this are, first, that each side means something different by the question, "What is international law?", and second, that even when one looks *within* either camp, one finds that the question has markedly different implications in different situations. All the preconditions for a futile and circular discussion are thus present. In order to give the maximum of information about this debate in the minimum of space, I will list some of the main inquiries that are subsumed under the positivist and naturalist theories about the source of law. I will then try to show how the reification involved in the way the question was posed has limited, warped and frustrated both sets of theoretical efforts. Throughout the rest of this essay I will try to demonstrate that, at a minimum, the fact that so many people were asking so many different questions and believing that they were all the same question—"What is law?"—has stultified and trivialized the scholarly debate.

A. *Positivist Arguments*

Positivism is, or was until recently, the dominant school of jurisprudential thought in international law.[14] Confronted with the question "What is law?", positivists tended to give answers that concentrated on the institutional procedures of the state and the coercion it wielded.[15] This positivist "line" could be repeated at a number of different levels of abstraction. At the most abstract level, positivists claimed that the essence of law was that it was a command backed by a threat, or a norm stipulating a sanction—this was its imprimatur, the way that you could distinguish it from morals, religion or mere

---

14. *See* A. NUSSBAUM, *supra* note 5.

15. *See generally* H.L.A. HART, *supra* note 10; H. KELSEN, THE PURE THEORY OF LAW (1967).

habit.[16] Having set up such a reified description, positivists could then argue among themselves as to whether "international law" was really "Law". At a more concrete level, positivists claimed that the "hidden ingredient" that infused international law with normative force was some state-centered attribute such as the consent of the sovereign, rather than some more general "intangible" standard such as the sense of justice held by a nascent world-community.[17] Finally, at the most concrete level, positivists would use their definitional ideas as the basis for doctrinal arguments. But in order to do any of these three things they needed to somehow bring in the implicit purposes to which, for all their universalistic claims, their "definitions" had to appeal if they were to be convincing. This point is one of the major contradictions at the heart of classical international legal theory.[18]

In other words, my argument is that the positivists, at every level of their project, rested their claims to legitimacy on the supposedly

16. Notice that the task has already been implicitly structured by the assumption that law is to be distinguished from those things which are conceptually similar (other normative systems, or "norms" of behavior) rather than from those things that are ideologically, physically, or professionally similar. For example, what would jurisprudential scholarship look like if scholars had thought that the "obvious" task was to distinguish between law and the ideological belief that the social world is divided into a public and a private sphere; or between law and the sexist or racist prejudices that tend to support and reinforce the status quo; or between law and the acts of class violence carried out by the "invisible" hands of the market; or even to juxtapose "law-stuff" and the procedures and customs of accountants?

17. The "evolving world community" seems to be the main modern natural law idea in international law. Just as in domestic legal theory Dworkin has resurrected the idea that there are clear political rights prior to legal interpretation, so the international natural law thinkers have relied on a quasi-teleological notion that the normative consequences of some hypothetical trend towards internationalism can be both accurately identified and clearly applied. *See* R. DWORKIN, TAKING RIGHTS SERIOUSLY 81–130, 266–90 (1977). *See generally* P. JESSUP, *supra* note 9; C. JENKS, THE COMMON LAW OF MANKIND (1958).

18. For example, Hans Kelsen begins his *Principles of International Law*, *supra* note 7, with the claim that "the social phenomena called law present a characteristic in common, distinguishing them from other social phenomena of a similar kind." This characteristic is the only element "by which we are able to differentiate definitely and successfully between a legal and a moral or religious order." *Id.* at 3. This "criterion of law" is that, as a "coercive order", "[i]t provides for socially organized sanctions." *Id.* at 5. The question than becomes, "[i]s international law "law" in the true sense of the term?" *Id.* at 18. Kelsen's answer is that it is, provided that, "the forcible interference of a state in the sphere of interests of another state, [is], in principle, permitted only as a reaction against a delict, and accordingly the employment of force to any other end is forbidden . . . ." *Id.* The imprimatur of law is the application of coercive sanctions under a regime that distinguishes them from wrongful acts. The state is the body that applies these coercive sanctions against other states. One can identify legal obligations by knowing when a state has the (legal) power "to bring about a certain legal effect . . . , especially the power to apply the sanction . . . in case another individual does not fulfill his obligation." *Id.* at 8. If this seems obviously circular as well as deeply essentialist, one should remember that Kelsen thought that he had avoided these problems by postulating a "basic norm," "the hypothesis that international custom is a law-creating fact." *Id.* at 314. Kelsen thus follows all of the stages that I described as typical of an essentialist argument but, most important, he relies on the particular purpose underlying his study (the construction of a secular theory of the legal hierarchy which also separates fact and value) to confer a misplaced "universal" or "scientific" status on his ideas. *Compare* H. KELSEN, *supra* note 7, *with* L. WITTGENSTEIN, *supra* note 12.

universal character of their analysis of the international legal system.[19] Their arguments were supposed to have a fundamental quality precisely because they told us not "what is Law here and there; but what is Law; as Plato, Aristotle, Cicero and divers others have done."[20] But if, as I am claiming, the positivist analysis could only be convincing if it was actually shaped by some concrete, particular, contingent purpose, then the claims to universality cannot be taken seriously. The positivist view becomes just another way to slice up the world; but by the positivists' own standards this is not enough.

The point that I have just made may sound confusing in the abstract, but it is easy to grasp if we look at concrete examples. One of the implicit purposes to which positivism actually caters is the lawyer's need for operational definitions. If one needed to predict which pieces of paper would actually produce a formal reaction from some state organ, then the "evolving world consensus" is not going to be of much use, while a positivist's explanation of the procedural hierarchy might be. Of course this does not mean that positivism is the true definition of law. For example, one might also need to know, as a matter of practice, how far inside the Icelandic fishing limits one could get without being chased by the Icelandic coastguard, or which compensation procedures are accepted as legitimate by Third World states. What is more, we can certainly say that the answers to these questions are "the law on the subject," provided that we make clear how we are defining law and, more importantly, why we are doing so. The positivist has the same freedom, but she does not have the right to say that her definition is the "real" one. But if this is true—if all definitions are founded, implicitly or explicitly, on purpose and convention—then how can the positivist (or anyone else for that matter) use their definition of law as the basis for a claim about the essence of law, or about the normative source of law, or even as the basis for a doctrinal argument? And why did so few people notice that the arguments supporting such claims were threadbare?

I think that the answer to the last question lies in the fact that a vast number of intellectual projects are subsumed under the heading of the positivist definition of law. Even if we leave aside the ones that I mentioned earlier, such as the attempts to give more weight to General Assembly resolutions, or to utilitarian philosophy, one is still left with a staggering number of implicit purposes. Now if these purposes were shared by the reader, they could give a false patina of

19. *See* H. KELSEN, *supra* note 7, at viii, 3, 18. He contrasts the "political ideologies" of other theorists to the "scientific theory of international law," and claims to deal with "the element suited in *all regards* to form the decisive criterion for an investigation into the nature of law." *Id.* at 3 (emphasis added).

20. T. HOBBES, LEVIATHAN 311–12 (C. McPherson ed. 1968).

"correctness" to the theorist's claims of having discovered the essence of international law. Some theorists were attempting to vindicate scientistic views of knowledge and to maintain the logical positivist's dichotomy between fact and value.[21] Others were trying to establish the primacy of the national sovereign over competing centers of authority both within and outside the state. Still others, coming to an intellectual field that had been constructed around a definitionalist question (and coming to it in a historical era in which the lawyer's main task was to predict the reaction of state institutions to pieces of paper produced by other state institutions) actually thought that the positivist definition was *true* in a sense that the natural law definition was not. They did not see this quality of truthfulness as related to their historical, political or professional position, however. It was not that the positivist way of carving up the world was more useful in terms of certain functions of lawyers. Instead, it was that only positivism could accurately describe the *essence* of law.

The conceptual dogmatism I have been describing may sound unconvincing even when positivism is being applied to the standard, formalized posers of twentieth century jurisprudence. But its monomaniacal qualities become truly obvious when extended to history. Do "primitive" people fail to distinguish among the norms that govern their lives on the basis of whether the "source" of those norms was in religion, morality or the power of the state? Then that simply serves to show that they are, indeed, primitive. Since their societies have not yet "developed" a differentiated system of profane power and authority, they are obviously at an "earlier" and "lesser" stage of social development.[22] In other words, the positivist view has actually been read back into history as an indicator of some deep teleological process. And once one has this mythical teleology established in national legal systems one can then use it to "prove by analogy" almost anything one wants to about international law. How strange that this should be done by the same sort of people who, given their professional attachment to one of the drier forms of analytic philosophy, tended to react against Marxist history because of its theoretical reliance on an economic teleology.[23]

B. Natural Law: The Arguments Reversed

The main "opposition" to positivist international legal scholarship has always come from the proponents of natural law.[24] Positivists

21. *See* H. KELSEN, THE PURE THEORY OF LAW 1–3, 70–76 (1967).
22. *See* H.L.A. HART, *supra* note 10, at 89–91 ("primitive" vs. "developed" legal systems).
23. *See, e.g.*, H. KELSEN, THE COMMUNIST THEORY OF LAW (1955).
24. *See* A. D'ENTREVES, NATURAL LAW (1970).

asserted that the normative force of international law came from the fact that the sovereign had consented to it. The natural law thinkers claimed that this answer was insufficient. How could the sovereign bind itself to bind itself in the future? Why was the initial consent to law given higher normative status than some subsequent decision to renounce the applicability of international law? The natural lawyers argued that this circularity involved the positivists in an endless set of boot-strapping exercises in which they sought some higher source which could, in turn, imbue the sovereign's consent with the kind of normative force they wanted.[25] These "higher" sources generally had some kind of Latin tag, the most famous one being "pacta sunt servanda." Alternatively they relied on language of sublime generality, such as "states should act in such a way so as not to disappoint legitimate expectations." But neither Latin nor vagueness is protection against the realization that the process is endless. "Consent" must rely on a higher source if it is to bind the state to do something against its will. This higher source must rely on a still higher source and so on until one reaches something that can be called the "grundnorm," the "rule of recognition," or the "authority constituting social-legal construct," but which sounds like a definitional stop by any other name.[26]

How did the natural law theorists themselves resolve this problem of the source of legal authority? Whereas the positivists relied on state consent (validated by some mysterious normative background), the natural lawyers relied on some putative normative deep-structure which emanated from the commands of the deity, or from the dictates of right reason, or from a discoverable teleology immanent in the natural state of affairs. And this is where we get to the strange mirror images produced by the reified question at the heart of international legal theory. I say this because the natural lawyer must walk a narrow line between saying that this normative deep-structure is already clearly evidenced by the actions of states (and thus implying that whatever states do is legal) and saying that the deep-structure is *not* evidenced by what states do (and thus implying that it is hopelessly irrelevant). In order to "privilege" the particular line that she chooses, the theorist must thus give some subordinate importance to the consent and the actions of states. Thus whereas the positivists started by positing consent as the source of international law and were driven to rely on some ever-receding normative background, the natural lawyers

---

25. *Id.*

26. *See* H.L.A. HART, *supra* note 10, at 97–114 (rule of recognition); H. KELSEN, *supra* note 21, at 193–220 (*grundnorm* as transcendental-logical proposition); M. MCDOUGAL, STUDIES IN WORLD PUBLIC ORDER (1960) (constitutive processes of authoritative decision-making).

started by relying on a deep normative order and ended up depending on manifestations of consent in order to save their project from being branded as either hopeless idealism or craven apologetics.[27]

The mirror-image structure to the arguments I have just described is no accident. If you found a discipline on a question like "What is law?", your arguments are bound to be circular. They will be circular because you will have to alternate between giving precedence to your theory and giving precedence to "the facts," and you will be unable to make it seem as though your choices in this regard are necessary unless you appear to be describing something fairly close to an "essence." This sounds more complicated than it is. Suppose you have a theory about what Law *really* is. Sometimes you will have to give "precedence" to your theory by saying that it shows that something normally talked about as law (say, international law) is not *really* Law at all. At other times you will have to give precedence to the "facts" by saying that a certain feature of "legal reality" shows that your ideas are true. For example, you might say that the familiar internal division of the law into substantive and procedural rules corroborated your theory's emphasis on the difference between rules granting authority and those exercising it. But in order to defend your choice of when to give precedence to the theory and when to the "facts," you would need a meta-theory which would run into the same problem. And so on, *ad infinitum*.

Now look at the framework of the theories put forward by positivists and natural lawyers. The oscillation between state consent and normative deep-structure that I described as a set of mirror-image arguments is simply a local version of the larger problem in the structure of jurisprudential discourse. This oscillation also reappears at each of the levels of abstraction that I described within the positivist and natural law theories. In other words, when the positivists or the natural law theorists use their theory about the essence of law to make further claims about the binding nature of international law, or even to make doctrinal arguments, the same oscillation makes their claims terminally unconvincing unless the indeterminacy of the analysis is concealed by a little judicious reification.

For example, a positivist might claim that the essence of law is that it is a norm that stipulates a sanction. International law is thus dependent on the right of a state to use sanctions, including force, if its legal rights have been infringed. Since this right of self-help is

---

27. David Kennedy's work on the history of international legal scholarship demonstrates the structural contradictions that this led to in the work of the early natural lawyers. *See* D. Kennedy, International Legal Structures (1984) (unpublished manuscript available in Harvard Law School Library).

actually the basis of the binding quality of international law, it cannot be abridged by international law; the state may make a political choice to revoke it, but it can never be legally alienated. The natural law theorist might respond by saying that the essential purpose of international law is to provide a stepping-stone to a peaceful world community; that its binding force depends on the fact that it serves this trans-historically valid normative goal of "world peace through world law"; and thus, that states not only can, but should legally renounce their rights of self-help. It is not simply that positivists and natural lawyers disagree. Rather, their debates are entirely circular. One could argue from the same positivist premises with just as much logic that, *because* the sanction provided by the right of self-help is the foundation of international law, the state must *always* be able legally to renounce that right; otherwise it is not truly a state and international law is not binding on it. Or, to complete the symmetrical pattern, the natural law premises can be made to produce the argument that because the goal of international law is, in a sense, to annihilate itself by moving to a world community, the one peaceful act which a state cannot take under international law is to renounce its right to self-help. Such an act could only be "legally" accomplished in a binding way under a "higher" stage of law than international law—perhaps under "world law."

My point is not that international lawyers had bad arguments. In a sense it is the reverse: their arguments were too good. Theorists founded their discussion of sources on a definitional question. They claimed that the authoritativeness of their arguments depended on the "universal quality" of their definitions of law. Yet they could only be convincing when they covertly appealed to some "purpose," be it the operational perspective of practitioners, or the teleological perspective of internationalists. In order to maintain their arguments, they had to believe (or at least, seem to believe) that their purpose was woven into the essence of law. But once they had "reified" law in this manner (by incorporating their choice into the concept itself) they were left with arguments that were completely "flippable." As my example above may have shown, the arguments are so "essentialist" that they have been emptied of all content. In the end, both the natural law and the positivist arguments become blank assertions. One might just as well say, "Because." This fate is not particular to the theorists I have been discussing. It will always be the fate of any inquiry founded on the definition, the "essence," or the "nature" of law, or of any other phenomenon for that matter.[28]

28. In a work in progress, I am attempting to describe the way that this process affects not only traditional analytic jurisprudence, but also the philosophy of science, aesthetic theory, linguistic philosophy and "meta-mathematics".

There is another level on which reification has operated in international law—the way in which it has presented the (mainly Western) theories of natural law and positivism as being neutral perspectives on the structure of law, in contrast to the culturally and ideologically influenced theories of the Third World or the Soviet Union. Again it is the claim to be dealing with the essence of law that supports these assertions of neutrality. The positivist (or the natural law theorist) is analysing the definitional components, the *form* of international law, not propounding an ideological view of the *content* of international law. The study of such ideological views is shunted off to some poor neighbor called "the sociology of international law," or "comparative international law," and the positivist emerges with renewed authority. The self-imposed constraints on the "object" of her study reflect the fact that her "discipline" is just as chastening as its name suggests; by excluding the messy and value-laden details of these "ideological views" the theorist supposedly justifies our reliance on her analytical power. As I now move to a discussion of contemporary thought about sources, I will try to show how Western "analytic" or "formal" jurisprudes produced exactly the same kind of arguments as the contemporary "ideological" theorists they have excoriated for being partisan.

C. *Contemporary Thought About Sources*

If one looks at some of the more influential jurisprudential works at the present one might think that theorists have finally escaped from the positivist/natural law merry-go-round. In a sense that is true. The works of Henkin, McDougal, and Tunkin are not as redolent of scholasticism as those of their predecessors.[29] But I would claim that they are all dependent on the same reified form of argument, the difference simply being that they have switched the reification from essence to purpose. Instead of resting their arguments on a search for the essence of international law, they claim to be working from (or towards) some timeless purpose, a "purpose" somehow "privileged" over all other purposes. Once again this process is a lot easier to understand when one has some examples.

1. Contemporary Thought: The USSR

As always, when one has a purpose, certain things recede into the background while others become more prominent. This is particularly obvious in the writings of the Soviet Union's foremost international

29. *See supra* text accompanying notes 18–26.

legal theorist, G.I. Tunkin.[30] In Tunkin's picture, international law is founded on a socio-economic reality which changes according to the logic of the "Marxist-Leninist science of foreign relations."[31] Thus law has, incorporated within itself, a profoundly historicist element. History is not seen as some external supplement to law, a transformatory medium in which law develops. Instead, history is embedded within law; it would be meaningless to talk of "law" without specifying the historical period because "law" is simply the conceptual working out of the logic of some particular stage in world history. This historicist element provides the deep purpose of law which, in Tunkin's theory, is that it should act as a temporary method of peacekeeping and as a mode of communication between "states of differing socio-economic systems", while the world makes the inevitable transition from capitalism to socialism.[32] This deep purpose is not simply an academic conceit or a theoretical ornament. Like the essences that the positivists relied on, it actually dictates the more concrete aspects of the theory. That is to say, Tunkin uses the "historical logic of international law" as a basis for the claims he makes about the "source" of international law, for the precedence he gives to some sources rather than others, and for the doctrinal arguments he puts forward, whether general (trends within the doctrine) or specific (correct resolution of this case).

There is also a further resemblance between Tunkin and the Western jurisprudes. The positivists and natural law theorists found themselves dealing with a world which they had structured according to a tension between two concepts—state consent and some general normative background. This tension could not be resolved, but resolution was exactly what their theorizing demanded. This contradiction played itself out on each successive theoretical level, in discussions of the "nature" of law, discussions of the source of its normative authority, and in the doctrinal arguments which were based on the master theory. Compare this with Tunkin's work.

In terms of the *nature of law* Tunkin must uphold the theory that law is a reflection of the interests of the dominant class in each society. Since he describes international law as being the result of the explicit concordance of the wills of states (thus safeguarding the Soviet Union from having Western legal norms imposed on it by custom), Tunkin must explain how a capitalist ruling class and a socialist ruling class could ever have anything sufficiently in common to actually make

30. *See, e.g.*, G. TUNKIN, THEORY OF INTERNATIONAL LAW (1974) [hereinafter cited as THEORY]; Tunkin, *The Contemporary Soviet Theory of International Law*, 31 CURRENT LEGAL PROBS. 177 (1978) [hereinafter cited as *Soviet Theory*]; Tunkin, *International Law in the International System*, 147 RECUEIL DES COURS 1 (1975) [hereinafter cited as *International Law*].

31. G. TUNKIN, THEORY, *supra* note 30, at 22.

32. *See id.* at 251–52. *See also* Tunkin, *International Law*, *supra* note 30, at 20.

law.[33] When he deals with the *source of law's normative authority*, Tunkin is faced with the task of showing that international law reflects, and to some extent reinforces, the inevitable historical progression from capitalism to socialism. At the same time, however, he must argue that it also represents a set of general, external standards which can command the respect of states of differing socio-economic systems precisely because those standards are neither completely manipulable, nor tilted in favor of one side or another.[34] Finally, on the level of *doctrinal argumentation* he must distinguish between those situations to which "general international law" applies[35] (such as, the law of non-intervention: Dominican Republic 1965, Chile 1976, Grenada 1984) and those situations to which the "more specialized" rules of socialist international law apply[36] (such as, the mutual security rules of the socialist brotherhood: Hungary 1956, Czechoslovakia 1968, Afghanistan 1980).

It does not seem to be stretching a point too far to say that these contradictions, appearing at each of our three levels of concreteness, are actually the same and that, on another level of generality, they are even the same as those faced by the positivists and the natural lawyers.

2. Contemporary Thought: Behaviorism and International Law

In a number of different ways, some of the most important contemporary Western work in international legal thought seems to be based on some kind of behaviorism. By "behaviorism" I mean a theoretical approach that focuses on the behavior of states and which has a philosophical commitment to the idea that one can somehow strip behavior of the explanations given for it by the actors themselves and thus reach a more profound understanding of what is really going on. In its most extreme forms, for example in the work of B.F. Skinner,[37] behaviorism dismisses as fallacy the claim that there are actually any "internal" thought processes at all. Everything is explained as the product of stimulus and response. In international law the method has not been applied in such an extreme way. The most one could say is that scholars have been attracted by the allure of "rigor" to which the social "sciences" have long appealed. An early article by Dahl captures this perspective rather neatly. He characterizes behaviorism

33. *See* Tunkin, *International Law*, *supra* note 30, at 19; Tunkin, *Soviet Theory*, *supra* note 30, at 177; Note, *Socialist Principles of International Relations*, 65 AM. J. INT'L L. 796 (1971).

34. *See* G. TUNKIN, THEORY, *supra* note 30, at 251.

35. *See id.* at 21–24.

36. *See* Tunkin, *International Law*, *supra* note 30, at 23; THE SOVIET STATE AND LAW 264 (V. Chkhikvadze ed. 1969); *see* HAZARD, *Renewed Emphasis on Socialist International Law*, 65 AM. J. INT'L L. 142, 145 (1971) (quoting Tunkin concerning Czechoslovakia).

37. *E.g.*, B.F. SKINNER, BEYOND FREEDOM AND DIGNITY (1972).

as being based on the belief that "additional methods and approaches existed or could be developed that would help to provide political science with empirical propositions and theories of a systematic sort, tested by closer, more direct, and more rigorously controlled observation of political events."[38]

Once again international lawyers are searching for the "real" story about what is going on. Faced with an international system that we cannot even describe without taking a political position, it is tempting to "simply look at what happens" without attempting to construct a descriptive or prescriptive international theory about it. The resulting attempts to construct theory-free statements about behavior are remarkably similar to traditional scholarship about sources. Both projects rely for their "authority" on a claim to be describing an essence, which is supposed to be prior to ideological interpretation or factional polemic. Or, to put it another way, in their attempt to escape the circular arguments of positivists and natural lawyers, behaviorist legal scholars actually rely on the same reification, the same essentialism, that was the cause of the very circles they were trying to avoid.

A most interesting example of the invidious effects that the dilemma of formalism and scientism can have is that of the Yale Studies in World Public Order, the series of books and research projects produced under the aegis of Myres McDougal.[39] To reduce the study of international legal discourse to a technocratic means-end manipulation of strategically useful concepts seems unhelpful. The fact that this manipulation almost always ends up favoring the American national interest is disquieting. To claim that one can inject a universal value ("human dignity") into an avowedly means-end technique is a contradiction in terms. For this to become one of the dominant approaches to international law is a travesty.

It could be objected that I have deliberately chosen a dogmatic, scientistic example to make my point. In order to show that the contradictions I describe extend even to the non-scientistic forms of behaviorism, I will use Louis Henkin's influential work on national behavior and international law as a further example.

Henkin may seem a dubious example of a behaviorist. Admittedly, his book is called *How Nations Behave*,[40] but he explicitly points out that he sees governments as being capable of "thought," "awareness" and other "internal" qualities that seem ill-suited to a theory which, in its most extreme forms, denies the reality of "consciousness."[41] On

38. Dahl, *The Behavioral Approach in Political Science: Epitaph For a Monument to a Successful Protest*, 55 AM. POL. SCI. REV. 763, 766 (1961).
39. *See, e.g.*, M. MCDOUGAL, STUDIES IN WORLD PUBLIC ORDER (1960).
40. L. HENKIN, *supra* note 9.
41. *Id.* at 5.

the other hand, his central goal is to focus on "the influence of law on how nations behave," a subject to which jurisprudential discussion is only "incidental."[42] This sounds as though he believes that behavior can be stripped of its conflicting ideological "meanings" and analyzed from some independent standpoint. Let me say immediately that it is not so much that Henkin believes that he can provide a neutral or objective picture of what is going on, but rather that, like the legal realists, he thinks he can cut through the Gordian knots of formalist debate by presenting law as it appears in behavior. This interpretation is strengthened when one looks at the motivation for his project.

As the horrors of war fade from the minds of national elites, Henkin sees the slow decline of the old dreams of world peace through world law. How can he maintain or even expand the role of international law at a time when most people see it as an infinitely manipulable sham? Henkin's answer is that international law is actually much more important, much more influential on the day-to-day actions of states, than the old conceptual model of "hard legal rules" would have us imagine. In trying to prove that this is the case Henkin provides us with an excellent example of a major intellectual shift in conceptions about law, a shift that will be much more familiar if we compare it to its counterpart in domestic law. Richard Parker describes the domestic version of this shift, as manifested in constitutional law, in the following terms.

> The constitution of our polity—the essence of its "good order"—may be depicted, first of all, as inhering in the constitutional document or in a system of abstract doctrine of constitutional law. In that case, constitutional order is seen as transcending—disembodied from—the clash of wills and movement of passions that characterize day-to-day political life. It may then be enforced *on* political life to discipline those wills and passions. Its enforcement is necessarily a process totally divorced from politics—detached, objective, a matter of abstract legal "reason."
>
> At the other extreme, our constitutional order may be depicted as inhering not in a document or a doctrine, but in our day-to-day politics. In that case, it is seen not as transcending the political process, but as embodied in it. The political process, in turn, is seen not as threatening, but as operating spontaneously in "good order." We can count on our political system, once set up, to work well enough. Hence constitutional order need not be enforced on politics. It need hardly be enforced at all.[43]

---

42. *Id.* at x.
43. Parker, *The Past of Constitutional Theory and Its Future*, 42 OHIO ST. L.J. 223, 225 (1981).

It seems to me that Henkin's work is a striking example of the second picture of law. Like the legal realists who transformed our understanding of constitutional law, Henkin is convincing until he tries to reconcile his picture of law as enmeshed in behavior with the picture provided by the "rule of law." At that point he is faced with an impossible task. As David Kennedy has pointed out,[44] Henkin, in order to make his project succeed, must claim that law is implicated in the actions of states, so that law is what states do. But, at the same time, he must maintain some residual amount of the first picture of law—the picture that law is separate from, and critical of, state behavior. If he does not retain this residual picture of law as a set of a-political rules, then it appears that anything that states do is legal. Thus Henkin would be contradicting the body of thought that forms the implicit background to his project, the ideology of the "rule of law" with its insistence on a sharp separation between law and politics. But the second picture is in tension with the first—to explain when law is behavior and when law is imposed on behavior he would need a meta-theory . . . and so on, and so on.

My point is not simply that Henkin's argument is contradictory—David Kennedy has provided a "close reading" of Henkin's work that goes into the aporetic structure of his ideas in detail.[45] Rather, I mean to point out that, once again, the search for the "stripped-down" reality of law leads us into a morass of question-begging, circular arguments.

Henkin's work is undoubtedly more advanced than the theories it criticizes. He even disavows the intention of providing an account that is more than "impressionistic." But underneath his impressionistic project lie two contradictory pictures of what law is all about. Like Holmes in the *Lochner* opinion,[46] Henkin is trying to create a vision of dynamic law, embedded in international social life. But, also like Holmes, he carries with him another, opposite image—the image contained in the ideal of the "rule of law." In this, other, image the law is a set of external rules that must sometimes be imposed on social life so that everyday reality can be forced to live up to the utopian blueprint contained in the legal documents.

It may provide an interesting comparison to note that Holmes, unlike Henkin, confronts this problem explicitly. He tries to establish a residual category, a "supplement" to his picture of law as being enmeshed in social life. This "supplement" expresses the opposite view of law. It talks of statutes being unconstitutional if they contravene

44. Kennedy, Book Review, 21 HARV. INT'L L.J. 301 (1980).
45. *Id.*
46. Lochner v. New York, 198 U.S. 45, 74 (1905) (Holmes, J., dissenting).

"fundamental principles as they have been understood by our peoples and our law."[47] But the supplement is "dangerous" to the main project. It is the expression of a contradictory "essence"—an opposing reification. The title of the theory may be different and a focus on behavior may seem to be a far cry from the positivist obsession with hierarchies of procedural norms. Nevertheless, both theories share exactly the same underlying structure, and both must conceal their definitional groundlessness by recourse to reification.

II. DOCTRINE

I want to move straight from this discussion of the scholarship about the nature and the source of international law, to a discussion of scholarship about doctrine. I will not attempt the same kind of analysis as I gave in the last section. Instead I will give a brief impressionistic account, relying on the familiarity of the picture I paint to compensate for the absence of citations to particular examples.

What are doctrinal articles about international law like? "Mush," says the cynic. "Just as definite as a domestic law article," says the scholar. Are they both right? One standard type of doctrinal article springs out of some recent happening—for example, the invasion of Grenada. The scholar gives a useful little potted history of the conflict, discusses the applicability of various norms, and then pronounces a conclusion. Unfortunately the very next article does the same, but comes to the opposite conclusion. Another type of article starts from some norm and then proceeds to discuss the extent to which it is obeyed by states. Things often look grim. "Ah ha!," says the cynic, "this all goes to prove my point. Even scholars cannot agree on the meaning of the law, and states do not obey it anyway. International law is a sham." "Not at all," says the scholar, "people disobey domestic law all the time and lawyers would not exist if there were not differing interpretations of the law. Yet neither of these two facts causes anyone to say that domestic law is a sham. Why should they do so over international law?" Standard argument is followed by standard response. Is there life beyond this debate?

I think that there is. Just as the arguments about sources were warped and frustrated by the implicit framework within which they were conducted, so the arguments about the interpretation, and even the effect of doctrine are constructed around a set of hidden premises that create and then perpetuate the sterile debate I have just described. In other words, I am claiming that scholarship about doctrine has its own pervasive reification, a reification that is similar in form to the

47. *Id.* at 76.

one that I described in my discussion of scholarship about sources. Let me explain what I mean.

Doctrinal scholarship often appears to be an attempt to show that rules can achieve determinacy, to show that there are correct interpretations of international legal norms. My claim is that this attempt is only explicable as the objectified manifestation of a different, more contentious political project. International lawyers are not attempting to show that rules are definite, firm and predictable because they believe this exercise will be good for their health. Their aspiration is to show that international law is a legitimate system for constraining power and irrationality, and, *in their minds*, they carry the assumption that it could only be such a system if there are neutral, objective answers to legal questions. This assumption is occasionally referred to in passing, is rarely debated and is hardly ever seriously questioned. Nevertheless, it is this assumption that provides the hidden logic to the debates about international legal doctrine.

The scholars of the Western countries have modelled international law along the familiar lines of liberal state theory. Their utopian vision is that politics can somehow be constrained by (a-political) rules.[48] This vision leads them to attempt to show that language can somehow provide a neutral conduit for power. The state's consent is to something called "a rule." This rule is made up of words and the words can be interpreted in a non-political way. Thus, ideological conflict can be separated from legal argument and the nation state can logically give its obedience to the resulting "objective" structure. In doing so it is merely following the lead set by its conceptual role model, the atomistic citizen, who makes decisions according to arbitrary, subjective value-judgments. An external source of power like "the law" might seem to pose an ineradicable danger to such a citizen, or to a nation-state. It is this problem which made theorists believe that the law's normative force would depend on the possibility of objective legal interpretation, on a body of materials and a mode of reasoning which, together, could triumphantly pierce the murky subjectivity of the social world.

So far I have suggested that the debate on "whether or not international law is mush" is actually a reified place-holder for a more important aspiration, the aspiration that law can be separated from, and then enforced on, politics. If this is true and we are dealing not with a mere argument over the meaning of doctrine but with a utopian vision expressed in the arcane iconography of the law, then we can begin to understand two features of this debate that otherwise seem inexplicable. First, there is the passion with which the debate has

48. *See* R. UNGER, KNOWLEDGE AND POLITICS 80–93 (1975).

been carried on. Second, there is the marked reluctance of international lawyers to incorporate the most basic insights from legal realism, post-Wittgensteinian linguistic philosophy, or any other source of knowledge that tends to undermine the possibility of neutral legal interpretation. These phenomena seem bizarre in the extreme if taken in isolation. They become meaningful only if one sees them as a manifestation of the utopian urges that often bring people to the study of international law in the first place but which most international legal scholarship seem so incapable of expressing.

But even if scholars did want to chain power with reason (or at least with words), this is surely not an unfamiliar, let alone reprehensible, ideal. In both international affairs and in the everyday pattern of Op-Ed pieces, civics classes, and bus-stop conversations that make up "the public sphere of debate," this ideal goes under the name of the rule of law. The defense of the rule of law can be the expression of a profoundly utopian goal. It should not be confused with apologetics simply because they are so often neighbors. But the thesis of this essay is that the ideal of power constrained by reason is expressed through a discourse, the professional language of scholarship as well as the ideology of the public sphere, which actually in some cruel fashion negates it, transforms it, turns its utopia into a suburb of the place we were trying to escape.

To those not interested in the mythology of the liberal state, or in the search for world peace through world law, this matter might appear to be happily irrelevant. It is not. If there is something interesting about this critique it is that it gives us insight into the mundane actuality of power, oppression and suffering as well into the formal language in which we express our opposition to these things. My argument is that legal theorists had the same fixations on the international level as they did on the domestic level and that the method they employed to deal with those obsessions is used in almost every situation of social power. Let us start with the theoretical obsessions and work down to this mysterious method.

Most of contemporary doctrinal scholarship is founded on two basic and mutually contradictory premises. The first is that values are subjective; there can be no demonstrably correct answer to a question that involves a value judgment. The second is the claim that words have "essences," or "core meanings," that can be interpreted mechanically, or at least neutrally. The second belief is necessitated by the first, but also denied by it. This is how it happens.

There is a "legitimating story" that supports the manifestations of the liberal state which appear in legal scholarship. This story operates to justify the exercise of power. But how is power to be justified if there can be no rational defense of value judgments? There are three answers. First, the market place is defensible because it merely records the (arbitrary) choices made by millions of consumers. Second, the democratic system of government is defensible because it merely records the (arbitrary) choices made by millions of voters. Third, the legal system is justifiable because the judge only applies the words of the law to the case in hand. There is simply no value choice to justify. In order to be true to the fundamental tenet that there are no moral or political essences that would allow us to know what "the good" was, and to act upon it, liberal thinkers have had to postulate that there were essences to *words* and that these essences would allow judges to make "correct" decisions without interposing their subjectivity. When legal theorists turned their eyes to international law, in which the problems of legitimacy were more obvious, it was not surprising that they would play out their obsession with words and values all the more strongly.

I want to discuss this obsession, and the utopian goals that fueled it, at the same time as I deal with the aspirations that motivated the search for an essence of law. After describing these various utopian goals, I will make some suggestions about what "new directions" in scholarship this mode of analysis actually suggests. In the last section, I will try to describe the implications of my argument for the teaching of international law; the arena in which most of these issues have had the greatest impact.

III. UTOPIAN ASPIRATIONS IN INTERNATIONAL LEGAL SCHOLARSHIP

If we look back over the discussion of scholarship about the nature and source of international law, it seems as though all of the theorists had a single desire, a single method. Tunkin seems to share a methodology with McDougal, McDougal with Kelsen, Kelsen with Jessup, Henkin, and Hart. All of them seem to be "using" reification to establish that the thing they want us to recognise about international law is already there woven into every strand. All we have to do is to admit its presence in, and its essentiality to, international legal discourse. The same seems to be true of doctrinal scholarship. Admittedly there is less hubris involved in the claim to have identified the essential meaning of a word within a rule than there is to the claim to have identified the essence of law. Nevertheless, the substance of the claims appear remarkably similar.

Why does this "reification" seem to reappear in every new theoretical project? Are the projects really all the same? The answer to the second question is "No." The answer to the first question depends on finding out why the projects are *not* the same. To do that, we need to look to the things that I have been calling the "utopian aspirations"—the implicit political, moral, and epistemological goals that seem to motivate each project.

Reason and Enlightenment

What do international lawyers want? A car in every driveway? Tofu in every pot? For me, the goals of scholarship are easiest to understand if one sees their relationship to politics and rationality. Like all "disciplines," international law is a "rationalist" project. One feature shared by all the scholarship we have looked at, doctrinal or jurisprudential, is the belief that (if carried on according to the plan put forward by that particular author) scholarship can live up to the image of reason exemplified by the Enlightenment. Knowledge itself will be a force for progress, moral autonomy and "the good." As it happens, I hold this vision of enlightened, critical self-reflection very dear. Yet the experience on which this essay is based is that the dominant forms of discourse, the ways of conceiving of the possible and desirable that we call "reason," may be far from emancipatory. Precisely because they are the dominant forms of discourse—be "they" positivist legal theory, traditional psychoanalysis, dialectical materialism, or representational painting—they exclude, "delegitimate," or undermine other modes of thought, other ways of life.[49] We are all aware that knowledge is power, and if we are not, we have everyone from Marx to the late Michel Foucault[50] to remind us. What does this mean for the utopian goals of scholarship?

I think that the answer is something of a paradox. In attempting to pursue their own versions of the Enlightenment project, scholars incorporated the antithesis of self-critical reason into their theories. Take Kelsen as an example. Kelsen's *Pure Theory of Law*[51] and his writings on international law are based on a particular vision of reason, a utopian vision of scientific thought, free from the distortions, myths and half-truths that he saw in moral, political and religious thinking. By knowing the limits of rational thought (which basically consisted of the realm of facts) we will free ourselves from the grandiose normative mysticism of natural law thought. But if we look more closely at Kelsen's theory we see not a hyper-rational, scientific analysis of law, but a dogmatic and repetitive brand of logical positivism, long

49. I may seem to be presenting a rather heartless picture in which theorists of different schools institutionalized the Enlightenment view of truth and thus destroyed it completely, amidst utterances of self-congratulation. The self-doubt brought on by the caricatured similarity in the theorists I have described is matched only by my amazement at the reappearance of essences in each new project.

50. *See, e.g.*, M. FOUCAULT, POWER/KNOWLEDGE (C. Gordon ed. 1980).

51. H. KELSEN, *supra* note 15.

discredited. Kelsen presents himself as an enemy of dogma, myth and medieval thought, and yet he bases his whole theory on those paradigmatically medieval devices, definitions and essences.

Kelsen is not the only one to use methods that are the epistemological antithesis of the Enlightenment vision of reason in an attempt to support a purportedly "rationalist" project. The depressing merry-go-round of positivist and natural law theories which I described in the section on sources is the result of precisely this contradiction. The "authority" that a theorist supposedly gains by describing the "essence" of law is exactly the kind of armor against rational inquiry that the Enlightenment vision of reason takes as its stock villain.

Contemporary thought is not as obviously internally contradictory until one realises that the "uncontentious" purposes animating each theory are actually extremely contentious, whether we are dealing with Tunkin's attempt to plug international law into the inexorable cycle of history, or McDougal's attempt to "square the circle" by claiming that his theoretical perspective is both a neutral means-end technique and normatively loaded in the service of "human dignity." Once again, "rational" projects are mounted on the basis of the philosophical techniques which insulate political choices from criticism, whether those techniques claim the imprimatur of "nature" or of "science" (natural, social, or Marxist-Leninist—pick one).

When we move our focus to doctrinal scholarship the picture looks more or less the same. The utopian aspiration at the heart of doctrinal scholarship was the attempt to cage power (whether of the state or the citizen) with rules. But, as I pointed out in the last section, this aspiration was pursued with tools that seem incompatible to the beliefs that motivated the pursuit in the first place. Let us assume, as liberal theorists do, that values are subjective, that there are no moral essences and thus that we must depend on the "artificial reason" of the law if we wish to restrain power. Where then, do we get these miraculous powers of neutral interpretation? Ah, from the "essential" meanings of words. But wait a minute . . . .

I do not mean to argue that there is no "felt-difference" between the proceedings of the International Court of Justice and the brainstorming sessions in a political affinity-group. Nor am I forgetting the long history of lynch-mobs and pogroms (to say nothing of the bombings of abortion clinics). What I am arguing is that it was never the essential meanings of words that allowed us to do the good things we associate with the rule of law. Nor was it the essential meaning of words that caused the *Lochner* case,[52] the *Korematsu* case,[53] or any other

52. Lochner v. New York, 198 U.S. 45 (1905).

53. Korematsu v. United States, 323 U.S. 214 (1944).

decision. In all of these cases, inescapably political choices are made—some of them systemic, some substantive. The utopian aspect of these choices does not come from any a-political process of neutral reason, but from the struggles and ideals of courageous men and women.

If as a last resort you wish to argue that it is a good thing to maintain the myth of the neutral rule of law (while privately acknowledging its emptiness), I would remind you that those who rely for their defense on myths are always misdirected and often disappointed. Besides, does it not seem a trifle Kafka-esque to be promoting myths we acknowledge to be false. all in the name of "enlightened reason?"

IV. "WHAT IS TO BE DONE?"

It would be fairly ironic if, at the end of a long essay about the perils of reification and the dangers of "the real level of what is going on," I was to provide a description of the "essence of good international law teaching and scholarship." Nevertheless, it would be craven, as well as unsatisfying, to finish a critique and not offer something in the way of a utopian proposal of my own. The suggestions that follow have their roots in the criticism of reification, but of course they are not logically derived from it.

Throughout this essay I have talked about the "utopian aims" of scholarship and of the ways that those aims are distorted or frustrated by the "language" in which they are expressed. But I have also fudged the question of what those utopian aims are; I only deal with their "manifestation" in scholarship about sources, doctrine and so on. I want to now make some implausible and "personal" claims about utopian thinking in international law.

The thing that first attracted me to international law was the lure of internationalism. There was a hefty dose of an adolescent desire to be truly cosmopolitan, there was some connection to my membership in the Campaign for Nuclear Disarmament, and there was the burgeoning outrage against war, famine and pestilence that we condescendingly refer to as "youthful idealism." If you had asked me then whether these ideas were connected to my other political views I might have given a confused answer about monopoly capitalism, or the Judeo-Christian ethic, but in reality I would not have made a connection between, say, my opposition to the sexist Student Union at my university and my belief in world peace through world law.

Things at present look a bit different. As this essay no doubt demonstrates, I now spend a lot of time thinking about reification—the way we turn other people, or social systems, or institutional hierarchies into objects which we then confront as disempowered observers. And a sense of outrage at this "objectification"—this fateful separation from "the Other," who is seen as "a woman," or "a Professor" or "a foreigner," or "a famine victim"—seems to me to be the general purpose fuel for a commitment to internationalism as well as to the demonstrations outside an all-male pub. Which is all very nice, but so what?

This essay is part of a symposium on new directions in international legal scholarship—a fairly abstruse subject, and one that does not seem likely to be connected to the intimate realities of our lives as lawyers, let alone those of the rest of the world's population, people who appear in our texts as populations to convince, victims of war, subjects of human rights violations, or, at best, as part of a "growing world consensus." I alluded to this disjunction—between the intensity of our aspirations and their impact on everyday life—in my comparison of international legal scholarship to the works of the chosist novelists. Is this the end of the story?

I think not. It is precisely because the utopian aims of international lawyers do express a hostility to the division of the world into Self and Other, North and South, Commie and Plutocrat, that their writing is still compelling even when it is covered over with medieval preoccupations about the "nature" of law. It is for the same reason that the disjunction between the world of international law as it is taught and written about, and the political and moral dilemmas of everyday life, that this disjunction is neither irrevocable nor completely disabling. As I have just argued, there is a plausible way of connecting these two arenas—of seeing internationalism as being inextricably intertwined with an opposition to sexism, racism and the calcification of authority. If we tried to concentrate on this connection and the general opposition to *social* as well as to *conceptual* reification that it suggests, what would our "new directions" look like?

For one thing, it would be hard to maintain the same kind of separation between "big" politics and "small" politics. This is not just a matter of realizing every day that there are things wrong with having a classroom structure in which "a professor" stands on a dais at the front of room and tells the people who are sitting down that they must always question authority and take the underdog's position. It is not just a matter of understanding that the teacher who is "Mr. Human Rights" may be dictatorial in the extreme in the classroom, or that the workplace hierarchies of "good" non-governmental organisations may mirror in microcosm the authoritarian politics of governments they condemn.

It more than understanding these things because it depends on a grasp of *how* they happen—the way that (public) politics is roped off from (private) work-life and thus the way that the fatal political paralysis induced by law school is amplified when we come to international politics. If I conceive of state politics as the only real politics, then I am unlikely to be able to conceive of being an effective political actor and doubly unlikely to be able to imagine myself as an effective actor in international political issues. So the University will go on investing in South Africa, and when I don't do anything about *that* it will be all the easier to explain the advantages of Krugerrands to my clients ten years hence, and still think I am an internationalist. After all, it's international law, isn't it?

What follows is an attempt to describe some of the other implications of this focus on both conceptual and social reification. I have chosen to deal with some of the areas that I criticised earlier (scholarship about sources and doctrine), but also to deal with the question of how one might teach using the kind of approach I outlined.

A. *Scholarship and Teaching About Sources*

It may seem bizarre to resurrect this category of scholarship. Surely it was the worst offender when it came to essentialism? Actually, in my own teaching, I have found that it was extremely important to start with a history and critique of the jurisprudence of international law. Otherwise students had the feeling that we were either trying to trick them into accepting a mass of formalistic premises (the same kind of premises they were so used to dissecting in their other first-year classes), or trying to make them believe that people could get excited about a set of definitional formulations that were obviously meaningless. I think of all the case-books that start with the *Lotus* case. Students who have carefully worked their way through the court's reasoning as to how international law is compatible with sovereignty are apt to drop international law straight away. Since the court starts out by trying to explain conceptually how it is that states can be bound when they do not want to be bound, it can hardly solve the problem by claiming that, because of their prior consent, they actually *do* want to be bound. It's just like saying that the small print in the contract represents the will of the parties. It may be an argument that convinces a judge, but it is not an answer to the question "under a will theory, how can this person be obligated to perform terms she did not know about?" In fact it is simply a restatement of the question. How many international law courses never get beyond the stage of restating the questions?

Instead of doing it that way, I introduce the court's heroic attempts to "answer the unanswerable" in terms of the utopian aims that motivated their project and the structural contradictions that made it impossible for them to complete it successfully. It is my perception at least, that rather than getting confused and angry at the circularity of the court's reasoning, the students come to see it as their first exposure to the legal version of a laudable internationalist aim.

I carry on using this general method as we deal with the ideas behind positivist, natural law, and behaviorist thinking. At the same time I try to introduce the class to some of the approaches to international law developed by scholars from the Third World and the USSR. My main aim here is to avoid the uncritical view that I described earlier. If the student decides that, say, Tunkin's ideas are both deeply apologetic and politically objectionable, that is fine. What I want to avoid is the belief that these "outsider's" views are somehow qualitatively distinct from the "real, neutral legal theory" produced by Western scholars. A modest enough little piece of relativism, but one that is more honoured in throwaway introductory lectures than in practice, as far as I can see.

B. *Doctrinal Scholarship and Teaching*

In terms of doctrinal scholarship, I think that we should pursue two apparently contradictory strategies. First, there is the possibility of developing a structuralist account of legal doctrine. Second there is the possibility of using the highly contextualized, politicized knowledge produced by working in clinical programs with international agencies and non-governmental organizations.

1. Structuralism and Doctrine

David Kennedy seems to have provided the best model for the structuralist part of the project.[54] A structuralist account takes the approach, familiar to the legal realists, of dealing with "binary oppositions," pairs of contradictory principles or premises about social life. It differs from the legal realist method in that it tries to explain all of the doctrine, or the legal arguments in a particular area, as being a product of the most basic of these tensions.

Kennedy's own work has focused on the conflict between the co-operative, communal, socialized aspect of international sovereignty, and the atomistic, individualized, and independent aspect. By using this familiar opposition, he tries to show how *all* of the rules, sub-rules and even the arguments by which they are manipulated, can be developed if one simply postulates an unconscious desire to "mediate the contradiction." By "mediating the contradiction" he means the attempt to make it seem as though the two aspects are actually perfectly compatible and thus that the doctrinal edifice has a suffi-

---

54. *See* Kennedy, *supra* note 27.

ciently coherent and logical structure to maintain its qualitative distinction from all that messy political and ideological conflict.

My favorite example of mediation is a theological one. If I believe that given the existence of a benevolent deity, virtue should be rewarded, but have the experience that wickedness is actually rewarded, I must develop a mediating structure to cover up the conflict between these two beliefs. A common mediator of this particular opposition is "God moves in mysterious ways"—asserting that some deep divine plan is actually going on underneath the (apparently) successful venality all around me. But this raises new problems. If God moves in mysterious ways, how can I ever know Her will with sufficient certainty to act on it as a good person myself? A new mediator must be deployed—common examples include direct, or textual revelation, preselection, or a sense of "reason" tilted toward the divine plan. But each of these . . . . And so on and so on.

If we look at international law this way, what happens? The focus on the generation of mediators for a set of recurring contradictions seems to capture something about the experience of "making a good legal argument." At the same time it becomes obvious that there is a Sisyphean quality to all of this. Why are we trying so hard to cover up these contradictions? Why does it seem as though law has this inner dynamic towards determinacy, this compulsion to make it look as though we are dealing with a "closed system?" One possible answer is the argument raised by my discussion of scholarship about sources and doctrine. The dominant background conception of "reason," self-interest and politics—and the utopian vision of power constrained by rules that is generated within that conception—seem to *require* a set of a-political rules. Since the mark of a neutral set of rules is their ability to provide one logically correct answer to each case, both the compulsive denial of contradiction and the doctrinal structure that this denial "generates" can be seen as products of the initial reification—the attempt to define "what law is," in order to separate it conceptually from morals and political argument.

Theoretically speaking this is all very tidy, but what use is it to teachers, students or practitioners? One of the exciting things about this kind of scholarship is that it lays out both doctrine and the arguments used to manipulate doctrine in a way that is almost reminiscent of classical legal thought, and yet it does so without the same tendency to turn what is into "what should be." In other words, structuralist legal theory has the analytical power of the great formalistic doctrinal edifices without the same commitment to apologetic politics.

What this means, I think, is that we can teach a large amount of doctrine and a large number of analytical techniques quickly, but because this method lays out doctrine in structural terms, we will not be concentrating on the trees to the exclusion of the forest. More importantly, we can give the student a perspective on doctrine that is neither formalistic, nor apologetic. Because the rules and the arguments used to manipulate them are presented as attempts to cover up a set of contradictions, the student does not get the misleading sense that these are the "right answers." What is more, there is no reason why this method should be confined to the (now-decaying) doctrinal structure established by the Western colonial powers. It is quite capable of being turned on the theoretical constructions produced by the USSR and the Third World.

2. Clinical Internationalism

I argued earlier that it was important to see the connection between internationalism and a general opposition to reification in social and intellectual life. I also claimed that this was necessary if we did not wish to become politically disempowered by a constraining vision of politics—"the only good politics is 'big' politics and I can't do anything to influence 'big' politics." One of the implications that I draw from this argument is that it is extremely important to show students that political activity with very real consequences can go on far away from the world of Kondratieff cycles, or trans- versus inter- nationalism. International clinical programs seem to provide the ideal method to accomplish this and at the same time to escape from the constraining world of formalistic international doctrinal scholarship.

Here we have some models to copy from, and some mistakes to avoid. The revolt against formalism in domestic law was connected with the idea that there were other methods to teach students than by relying on the antiseptic words of appellate opinions. This is the obvious connection between theory and practice, clinic and jurisprudence. The mistakes are also obvious. Clinical programs started out as being both politically and pedagogically threatening to the ideology of law schools. Gradually they have been assimilated; the ideals of "justice for all" and legal services for poor people have been traded in for video recorders and simulation classes. This is a mistake that international clinical programs in economic development or human rights should not make.

CONCLUSION

At the beginning of this essay I mentioned the chosists—those who sought to throw the universal quality of human aspiration into sharp relief by counterposing it against lengthy descriptions of objects. I said that international legal thought was similar to chosism, and in the body of the essay I have tried to show both why and how this could be the case. Theorists got their "authority" by being essentialist—by claiming they were dealing with the essence of law, or the "true" source of international obligations, or the "real" meaning of a doctrinal rule. I am going to assert blankly that they often wanted this authority for profoundly utopian reasons—internationalism, world peace through world law, enlightened international dialogue. Yet the fetishism of essences, the belief that this is how one showed oneself to be correct, actually subverts the commitment to enlightened rationality and replaces it with reified ideas, thus ruling out the possibility of real discussion.

So as we read international legal scholarship we might think that it is very like chosist writing—an ironic contrast between high aspiration and mundane description. The crucial difference is that scholars don't seem to *intend* the irony. They think that they are merely describing something—whether that "something" is a rule, or an obligation, or the source of law—when in fact they are putting forward a profoundly political set of arguments. For me it is this, the political effect of reification, that makes the critique put forward in these pages more than an academic exercise. There is something demeaning, something evil, about blindly obeying the imagined "dictates" of some social construct, whether it is the portrayal of women as sex objects, the ethnocentric circularity of positivist legal arguments, or the restrictive set of roles for "partner and associate," "child and parent." And this evil is precisely the one addressed by the critique of reification, or idolatry, or objectification. So what is one to do?

Part of the answer consists of presenting the structure of doctrine and the interplay of the arguments without pretending that they are the "real" level of what is going on. Part of the answer consists in trying to explain why all of the international legal scholars did what they did. It turns out, for example, that the international legal arguments of the USSR are a lot easier to understand if you can discern the mirror-image pattern of arguments that we found in Tunkin and Henkin, as well as in positivism and natural law. Part of the answer consists of thinking up methods of getting ourselves away from the objectified fantasy world of state sovereignty, and towards the actual human beings whose lives our abstractions affect—this means more international clinical programs, but is also means teaching and learning our subject by using poems and pictures as well as treaties and *travaux preparatoires*. Finally, and this seems to be the most important point, part of the answer consists in realizing that one should not divide one's life into tiny, discrete worlds—the struggle against racism and sexism and class-violence in one box, relationships with one's co-workers in another, the production of scholarly utopias in still another.

If one does this, one is simply recreating, in the social world, the kind of mirror-image contradictions that we saw in the conceptual structure of international law.

While I was writing this essay, I was looking for the best examples of attacks on reification; I hate to say this, but it ended up that my two favorites involved Marx[55] and God.[56] If one thing links Marx with the God of the Old Testament it is that both of them seemed to get fairly angry when people not only gave up their ability to choose, but gave it up to the very objects—be they industrial goods or the golden calf—that they had just created. International lawyers are making the same mistake. And that is something that even the chosists could understand.

55. *See* Marx, *Estranged Labour* (from *The Economic and Philosophical Manuscripts of 1844*) and *The Fetishism of Commodities and the Secret Thereof* (from *Capital*), in THE MARX-ENGELS READER 53–67, 215–25 (R. Tucker ed. 1972).

56. *See Exodus* 32:1–35, 34:17.

Part IV
Who are the Primary Actors?

[11]

Professor Harold Hongju Koh*

Transnational Legal Process

TABLE OF CONTENTS

I. INTRODUCTION

It is with a sense of homecoming that I deliver this lecture bearing the name of Dean Roscoe Pound, a legendary figure in my own home. My late father, Dr. Kwang Lim Koh, an international law professor from Korea, came to Harvard Law School in the early 1950s to pursue his graduate education. Each morning at 5:00 a.m., he would rise and walk through the dark streets of Cambridge to his carrel deep in the

* Gerard C. and Bernice Latrobe Smith Professor of International Law and Director, Orville H. Schell, Jr., Center for International Human Rights, Yale University. The following is a lightly edited and footnoted version of the *1994 Roscoe Pound Lecture*, delivered on October 28, 1994 at the University of Nebraska College of Law. An earlier version was presented as the inaugural lecture for the Gerard C. and Bernice Latrobe Smith Professorship of International Law at Yale Law School. This essay sketches the argument underlying a forthcoming book, tentatively entitled *Why Nations Obey: A Theory of Compliance With International Law*. It should be disclosed that the author participated in several of the cases discussed here as an attorney. *See* United States v. Alvarez-Machain, 504 U.S. 655 (1992)(counsel for amicus curiae); Sale v. Haitian Centers Council, 509 U.S. 155 (1993) and 823 F. Supp. 1028 (E.D.N.Y. 1993)(Counsel of Record for Haitian refugees); Cuban-American Bar Ass'n v. Christopher, 43 F.3d 1413 (11th Cir. 1995)(Of Counsel to Cuban plaintiffs).

bowels of Langdell Hall, where invariably, he would find just one other person stirring: Harvard's eighty year-old former Dean, Roscoe Pound, wearing his visor and working on his five-volume treatise on jurisprudence.

Not until many years later, when I was myself studying at Harvard Law School, did I learn about Roscoe Pound as a legal scholar. Late one night, while reading about the revolt against formalism led by the father of sociological jurisprudence,[1] I wandered through Harvard's Law Library in search of Dean Pound's assembled works. I was startled to find an entire bookshelf in the Langdell stacks devoted to Pound's writings on domestic legal theory, but only three short pamphlets on international legal theory.[2]

The image of a crowded bookshelf of domestic legal theory alongside near-empty shelves on international legal theory has haunted me ever since. Throughout my career, I have sought to understand this puzzling void in international legal scholarship. To many domestic legal scholars, the reason seems self-evident: they consider the very term "International Legal Scholarship" to be a complex oxymoron, like the "Holy Roman Empire" or the "New York Giants."[3] Most domestic legal scholars tend to view international legal scholarship the same way. "If it's international," they say, "there can be no law involved. If it's international law, there can be no scholarship involved." They believe that when it comes to international legal scholarship—like Gertrude Stein's Oakland—there is "no there, there." To the extent that international law professors write articles, domestic scholars consider them at worst, irrelevant, and at best, thick description. In their view, international legal scholars have few ideas, and those they have do not really matter.

In this lecture, I argue that this notion is wrong. There *is* such a thing as international legal scholarship. Committing it and being committed to it are worthwhile activities. International legal scholars

1. *See generally* DAVID WIGDOR, ROSCOE POUND (1974); PAUL L. SAYRE, THE LIFE OF ROSCOE POUND (1948).

2. One, a lecture Roscoe Pound gave in Leiden in 1922, was entitled *The Philosophical Theories on International Law*; the second was an address Pound gave at the Congress of International Law held at Harvard in 1926; and the third, Roscoe Pound, *Philosophical Theory and International Law*, 1 BIBLIOTHECA VISSERIANA 73 (1932), is quoted in note 31, *infra*.

3. A complex oxymoron—like the Holy Roman Empire (which was neither Holy, Roman, nor an Empire) or the New York Giants (which are neither New, from New York, or Giants)—may be distinguished from the more familiar simple oxymoron, such as "jumbo shrimp" or "working vacation." Other complex oxymorons of which I have been reliably informed include the Uniform Code of Military Justice, the Chicago School of Law, and the Union of Soviet Socialist Republics.

do have an idea that has power, and that idea is *Transnational Legal Process*.[4]

Transnational legal process provides the key, in my view, to understanding the critical issue of compliance with international law. Some years ago, in an oft-quoted phrase from his book *How Nations Behave*, Professor Louis Henkin asserted that "almost all nations observe almost all principles of international law and almost all of their obligations almost all of the time."[5] But Henkin's hedged description of how nations behave leaves a critical question unanswered: namely, *why* do nation-states and other transnational actors obey international law, and why do they sometimes disobey it? That question—why nations obey—centrally challenges scholars of both international law and international relations. It vexes all the subjects that I teach, from international business transactions to international trade, from international organizations and the law of United States foreign policy to international human rights. For the last few years, it has also taxed my students in Yale Law School's Allard K. Lowenstein International Human Rights Clinic, as we have engaged in "transnational public law litigation" against a variety of foreign and United States government officials on behalf of victims of human rights abuses.[6]

These claims raise three obvious questions. First, what is transnational legal process? Second, where did it come from? Third, how does it help explain why nations obey? In addressing these questions, I will argue that transnational legal process has been the dominant mode of international legal scholarship for the last few decades. I make the bolder claim that it not only lies at the heart of what international legal scholarship is about, but also at the heart of what international law scholarship should be about in the years ahead.

II. WHAT IS TRANSNATIONAL LEGAL PROCESS?

What, to begin with, is transnational legal process? Transnational legal process describes the theory and practice of how public and private actors—nation-states, international organizations, multinational enterprises, non-governmental organizations, and private individuals—interact in a variety of public and private, domestic and interna-

4. I have previously sketched some of these ideas in Harold Hongju Koh, *The "Haiti Paradigm" in United States Human Rights Policy*, 103 YALE L.J. 2391, 2405-09 (1994); Harold Hongju Koh, *Refugees, the Courts and the New World Order*, 1994 UTAH L. REV. 999; and Harold Hongju Koh, *Transnational Public Law Litigation*, 100 YALE L.J. 2347, 2398-2402 (1991)(discussing "The New International Legal Process").

5. LOUIS HENKIN, HOW NATIONS BEHAVE 47 (2d ed. 1979). *See also* Abram Chayes & Antonia Chayes, *On Compliance*, 47 INT'L ORG. 175, 195 n.64 (1993).

6. *See generally* Koh, *Haiti Paradigm, supra* note 4, at 2391 (1994); Koh, *Transnational Public Law Litigation, supra* note 4, at 2347 (describing the litigation strategy underlying these cases).

tional fora to make, interpret, enforce, and ultimately, internalize rules of transnational law.

Transnational legal process has four distinctive features. First, it is *nontraditional*: it breaks down two traditional dichotomies that have historically dominated the study of international law: between domestic and international, public and private. Second, it is *nonstatist*: the actors in this process are not just, or even primarily, nation-states, but include nonstate actors as well. Third, transnational legal process is *dynamic*, not static. Transnational law transforms, mutates, and percolates up and down, from the public to the private, from the domestic to the international level and back down again. Fourth and finally, it is *normative*. From this process of interaction, new rules of law emerge, which are interpreted, internalized, and enforced, thus beginning the process all over again. Thus, the concept embraces not just the descriptive workings of a process, but the *normativity* of that process. It focuses not simply upon how international interaction among transnational actors shapes law, but also on how law shapes and guides future interactions: in short, how law influences why nations obey.

To see these four features, consider the case of a California engineering firm called Dames & Moore.[7] In the late 1960s, the firm signed a contract to conduct a nuclear power plant site study. By most measures such a contract would constitute the classic "private domestic business deal," except that it was struck not with Pacific Gas and Electric, but with the Atomic Energy Organization of Iran. Moreover, this agreement was negotiated against a "public" backdrop not just of Iranian and United States domestic law, but of numerous bilateral and multilateral treaty commitments between the Iranian and United States governments. In 1979, a cataclysmic public event—the ouster of the Shah, his flight to the United States, and the seizure of 52 American hostages—triggered a surge of emergency host and home-country regulations that dramatically affected these preexisting "private" deals.[8] The Atomic Energy Organization cancelled the contract, leading Dames & Moore to sue Iran and its instrumentalities in United States district court. When the court vacated Dames & Moore's judicial attachment of Iranian bank property based on the January 1981 executive orders implementing the United States-Iran executive agreement that freed the hostages, Dames & Moore filed a

7. *See* Dames & Moore v. Regan, 453 U.S. 654 (1981).

8. These regulations took the form of Iranian expropriatory actions and retaliatory United States government sanctions, including a trade embargo, an extraterritorial assets freeze, and, ultimately, an executive agreement that nullified judicial attachments on frozen Iranian assets, suspended private claims against Iran, and transferred them to arbitration before the newly created Iran-United States Claims Tribunal.

new district court complaint against the United States, seeking to enjoin enforcement of those executive orders. That suit ultimately resulted in a historic loss in the United States Supreme Court a few months later. As a last resort, Dames & Moore proceeded to the Iran-United States Claims Tribunal, which excluded it from the Tribunal's jurisdiction, citing to an Iranian forum-selection clause in its original contract.[9]

The Iranian Hostages crisis illustrates each of the features of transnational legal process mentioned above. First, it does not fit traditional categories. It cannot be neatly cabined within "domestic law"—traditionally thought to govern conduct within borders—or "international" law, which has been thought to govern conduct across borders. Nor can it be characterized as "public" international law—the law among nation-states, which encompasses what nations do to or with each other[10]—or "private" international law, classically thought of as cross-border law among nonstate actors. Second, the process was dynamic, not static. An ostensibly "private business deal" entered between a United States multinational and a developing-country government dissolved into a domestic legal dispute, then percolated upward into a public international dispute, which was ultimately resolved by sovereign governments by an agreement based on public international and domestic public law in a manner that triggered both domestic constitutional claims by a multinational corporation against its own government in its own domestic courts and international expropriation and breach of contract claims against a foreign government in a newly-minted international forum.[11]

Third, the key actors in this process were not just nation-states, but also the International Monetary Fund, various multinational enterprises (particularly the large banks who participated in freezing and transferring the assets), and the individual hostages whose human rights were at stake. Fourth and finally, the interaction

9. *See* Dames & Moore v. Iran, Award No. 97-54-3, Dec. 20, 1983, Iranian Assets Lit. Rep. 7,727 (Jan. 13, 1984); Dissenting Opinion of Judge Mosk, Dec. 21, 1983, Iranian Assets Lit. Rep. at 7,738 (Jan. 13, 1984).

10. *E.g.*, making war and peace; forming international agreements; allocating rights to air, sea, and space; state responsibility; international organizations; and such topics as jurisdiction, immunities, and diplomatic relations.

11. For a similar process of mutation, witness transnational contract law, which began as customary international law—the law merchant or *lex mercatoria*—but transformed into English common law when England became the world's leading commercial power. Upon the founding of the United States, that English common law migrated to the United States as federal general common law. *See* Swift v. Tyson, 41 U.S. (16 Pet.) 1 (1842). Such contract law then became the subject of state codification in the Uniform Commercial Code until, in 1988, the United States became a party to the U.N. Convention for Contracts for the International Sale of Goods, an act that re-elevated transnational contract questions to positive international treaty law.

among these transnational players was what Robert Cover calls "jurisgenerative."[12] It not only generated law—the domestic private law of letters of credit, the domestic public law of executive power, the international private law of dispute-resolution, and the public international law of diplomatic relations law—but generated new interpretations of those rules and internalized them into domestic law that now guides and channels those actors' future conduct.

III. THE EVOLUTION OF TRANSNATIONAL LEGAL PROCESS

A. The Evolution of Legal Process Scholarship

If this is what transnational legal process is, where did it come from? Of course, the concept of transnational law is decades old; the phrase was coined by Phillip Jessup in his Storrs Lectures at Yale in 1956. Similarly, the concept of International Legal *Process*—studying law's role in the process of policy decisions in the international realms—was pioneered in a casebook developed by Abram Chayes, Tom Ehrlich, and Andreas Lowenfeld in 1968. Process inquiries also run through the work of Myres McDougal, Harold Lasswell, and Michael Reisman at Yale Law School on the world constitutive process of authoritative decision.[13] Finally, the idea of Transnational Legal Problems—a category that mixes public and private, domestic and international, and embraces international human rights, international business transactions, and the law of U.S. foreign policy—was first captured by Harvard professors Henry Steiner and Detlev Vagts in a casebook that in turn grew out of a 1960 casebook on the Law of International Transactions and Relations authored by Milton Katz and then-Professor Kingman Brewster.[14]

It is precisely because this idea is not new, that it has been overlooked. Precisely because it has been latent and inchoate, it has not been recognized, accepted, or specifically developed as a way of understanding and affecting the world. To make this case, let me take you briskly through two types of intellectual history: the history of scholarly discourse *within* international law in this century and the history of scholarly discourse *between* international law and its companion discipline of international relations.

12. Robert M. Cover, *The Supreme Court, 1982 Term—Foreword, Nomos and Narrative*, 97 HARV. L. REV. 4 (1983).
13. *See, e.g.*, HAROLD D. LASSWELL & MYRES S. MCDOUGAL, JURISPRUDENCE FOR A FREE SOCIETY: STUDIES IN LAW SCIENCE AND POLICY (1992); MYRES S. MCDOUGAL & W. MICHAEL REISMAN, INTERNATIONAL LAW IN COMPARATIVE PERSPECTIVE (1981); W. MICHAEL REISMAN & ANDREW WILLARD, INTERNATIONAL INCIDENTS (1988).
14. H. STEINER ET AL., TRANSNATIONAL LEGAL PROBLEMS (4th ed. 1994); MILTON KATZ & KINGMAN BREWSTER, INTERNATIONAL TRANSACTIONS AND RELATIONS: CASES AND MATERIALS (1960).

Within the American legal academy, we are all familiar with the evolution of domestic legal scholarship from Christopher Columbus Langdell to Catherine MacKinnon. In this century alone, we have moved through a series of well-charted intellectual eras. This history began with Langdell's Legal Formalism—the case method and the notion of law as a science—followed by the attack on Formalism by the Legal Realists of the twenties and thirties.[15] Realism itself triggered two principal responses, designed to curb its perceived indeterminacy: the codification movement, represented by the American Law Institute's Restatements, the Uniform Commercial Code, and what Guido Calabresi has called the "age of statutorification;"[16]and the Legal Process movement of Hart and Sacks[17] and Hart and Wechsler[18], which focused on the study of legal institutions, "reasoned elaboration," neutral principles, and the optimism—fed by Robert Dahl's school of political science—that rational but orderly policy change could be achieved through a pluralistic political process.

In the 1960s, we saw a three-part response to the Legal Process movement: first, the rights movement—the due process[19] and equal protection revolutions[20] led by the work of the Warren Court; second, poverty law, heralded by the rise of clinical studies, poverty and entitlements law, and Charles Reich's *The New Property*;[21] and third, the Law And Movement, which brought to American law faculties economists, sociologists, anthropologists, psychiatrists, doctors, and others. In the 1970s, when I went to law school, each of these strands continued and broadened. Legal process continued in the work of constitutional scholars like John Hart Ely and Jesse Choper. The rights movement—carried forward on the academic front by Laurence Tribe[22] and Ronald Dworkin[23] and on the activist side by such groups as the NAACP Legal Defense Fund, Planned Parenthood, NOW, and the ACLU—shifted focus from the activist trends of the Warren Court

15. Ironically, Roscoe Pound's own work on sociological jurisprudence, which attacked this "mechanical jurisprudence," helped give birth to the very school with which he ultimately went to war: the legal realists, like Karl Llewelyn, William O. Douglas, Thurman Arnold, Jerome Frank, Leon Green, and Underhill Moore, many of whom found their home, not at Pound's Harvard, but at Yale and Columbia Law Schools.

16. Guido Calabresi, A Common Law for the Age of Statutes (1982).

17. Henry M. Hart & Albert M. Sacks, The Legal Process (1995).

18. Henry M. Hart & Herbert Wechsler, The Federal Courts and the Federal System (1953); Herbert Wechsler, *Toward Neutral Principles in Constitutional Law*, 73 Harv. L. Rev. 1 (1959).

19. On the criminal side, see, e.g., Miranda v. Arizona, 384 U.S. 436 (1966), and the civil side, see, e.g., Goldberg v. Kelly, 397 U.S. 254 (1970).

20. *See, e.g.*, Brown v. Board of Educ., 347 U.S. 483 (1954).

21. Charles A. Reich, *The New Property*, 73 Yale L.J. 733 (1964).

22. Laurence H. Tribe, American Constitutional Law (1978).

23. Ronald Dworkin, Taking Rights Seriously (1977).

to the counter-revolutionary tendencies of the Burger Court.[24] Poverty law and clinical education continued to fight for status within American law schools. The Law And movement, now dominated by Law and Economics, bifurcated into a hard, conservative strand based at Chicago and led by now-Judge Richard Posner[25] and a somewhat more liberal camp centered at Yale,[26] with the Law And Society movement maintaining footholds in Wisconsin and elsewhere.[27]

The 80's and 90's have witnessed what George Priest has called the "new scientism" in legal scholarship: the continuing strength of the Law and Economics movement, the emergence of rational choice and organizational theory,[28] and new critical schools of thought and methodology—critical feminist, race, and legal studies, law and literature, and postmodernism. Yet through these years, a group of progressive legal scholars kept the Legal Process movement alive by informing it with a rights tradition.[29] They saw the law's legitimacy as resting not just on process but also on its normative content. They viewed lawmaking as not merely the rubberstamping of a pluralistic political process, but as a process of value-creation in which courts, agencies, and the people engage in a process of democratic dialogue. In the last few years, these thinkers have spawned a third generation of public law scholars—calling themselves the "new public law movement"[30]—who

24. *See, e.g.*, V. BLASI, THE BURGER COURT: THE COUNTER-REVOLUTION THAT WASN'T (1979).
25. *See, e.g.*, RICHARD A. POSNER, ECONOMIC ANALYSIS OF LAW (1st ed. 1973).
26. *See, e.g.*, GUIDO CALABRESI, THE COSTS OF ACCIDENTS: A LEGAL AND ECONOMIC ANALYSIS (1970).
27. *See, e.g.*, the extensive writings in the *Law & Society Review*, now more than thirty years old; David Trubek, *Back to the Future: The Short, Happy Life of the Law and Society Movement*, 18 FLA. ST. U. L. REV. 1 (1990).
28. See, for example, *The Journal of Law, Economics, & Organization*, now more than eleven years old.
29. *See, e.g.*, BRUCE ACKERMAN, WE THE PEOPLE: FOUNDATIONS (1991)(work on constitutional moments); ROBERT BURT, THE CONSTITUTION IN CONFLICT (1992); CALABRESI, *supra* note 16; ROBERT COVER ET AL., PROCEDURE (1989); JOHN HART ELY, DEMOCRACY AND DISTRUST: A THEORY OF JUDICIAL REVIEW (1980); JERRY MASHAW, DUE PROCESS IN THE ADMINISTRATIVE STATE (1985); Abram Chayes, *The Role of the Judge in Public Law Litigation*, 89 HARV. L. REV. 1281 (1976); Robert Cover & T. Alexander Aleinikoff, *Dialectical Federalism: Habeas Corpus and the Courts*, 86 YALE L.J. 1035 (1977); Owen Fiss, *The Supreme Court, 1978 Term—Foreword: The Forms of Justice*, 93 Harv. L. Rev. 1 (1979)(work on procedure). Some of Laurence Tribe's work on American Constitutional Law also partakes of this tradition. *See, e.g.*, Laurence Tribe, *Structural Due Process*, 10 HARV. C.R.-C.L. L. REV. 269 (1975)(positing active role for courts in policing structures through which policies are formed and applied).
30. *See generally* William N. Eskridge, Jr. & Phillip P. Frickey, *Introduction* to HENRY M. HART, JR. & ALBERT M. SACKS, THE LEGAL PROCESS cxxv-cxxxiv (1994) (reviewing recent literature); William N. Eskridge, Jr. & Phillip P. Frickey, *The Supreme Court, 1993 Term, Foreword: Law As Equilibrium*, 108 HARV. L. REV. 1 (1994); William N. Eskridge, Jr. & Gary Peller, *The New Public Law Movement: Moderation as a Postmodern Cultural Form*, 89 MICH. L. REV. 707 (1990). For

have tried to couple the normativity of process with interdisciplinary understandings of how law is made in writings about legislation, statutory interpretation, civic republicanism, and the like.

From the perspective of international law, what is most striking about this recitation of intellectual history is the blind assumption that during these eras, international law scholarship has just been sitting there, caught in a time warp of obscure Latin terminology: *pacta sunt servanda, rebus sic stantibus, jus ad bello, jus in bello.* In fact, international legal scholarship has moved through precisely the same stages of intellectual development as domestic legal scholarship, from rule formalism to new scientism. Again, the story begins with the transition from Formalism—typified by the classical study of international law as a science at the Hague Academy of International Law—to Legal Realism, captured in the policy science work of Myres McDougal and Harold Lasswell.[31] As in the domestic realm, two principal responses to Legal Realism emerged: the codification movement, represented by the Harvard Research on International Law, the International Law Commission's drafting activities, the American Law Institute's Restatements of Foreign Relations Law, and the international legal process work of Abram Chayes, Thomas Ehrlich, and Andreas Lowenfeld (which like Hart and Sacks, posited that legal issues mainly arise not before courts, but in the process of making policy decisions, with lawyers playing a more important role than judges, and consent playing a greater role than command).[32]

The 60's and 70's witnessed the same reactions to Legal Process: the rise of the international human rights movement in the work of Louis Henkin, Myres McDougal, Louis Sohn, and Tom Buergenthal;

other examples, see WILLIAM N. ESKRIDGE, JR., DYNAMIC STATUTORY INTERPRETATION (1994); Philip P. Frickey, *Congressional Intent, Practical Reasoning, and the Dynamic Nature of Federal Indian Law,* 78 Cal L. REV. 1137 (1990); T. Alexander Aleinikoff, *Updating Statutory Interpretation,* 87 MICH. L. REV. 20 (1988); Daniel Farber, *Statutory Interpretation and Legislative Supremacy,* 78 GEO. L.J. 281 (1989); Cass Sunstein, *Interpreting Statues in the Regulatory State,* 103 HARV. L. REV. 405 (1989).

31. *See, e.g.,* LASSWELL & MCDOUGAL, *supra* note 13; MYRES S. MCDOUGAL, INTERNATINAL LAW, POWER, AND POLICY: A CONTEMPORARY CONCEPTION (1954); MCDOUGAL & REISMAN, *supra* note 13; REISMAN & WILLARD, *supra* note 13. In important ways, McDougal and Lasswell's view of law as a social, not a natural science, picked up on notions of sociological jurisprudence first developed by Dean Roscoe Pound. *See, e.g.,* MCDOUGAL, *supra* at 137 (quoting Roscoe Pound, *Philosophical Theory and International Law,* 1 BIBLIOTHECA VISSERIANA 73, 89 (1932)(demanding "a functional critique of international law in terms of social ends, not an analytical critique in terms of itself, and above all that shall conceive of the legal order as a process and not as a condition.")). In other work, I am exploring the role of Myres McDougal's Legal Realism as the critical link between the domestic and international worlds of legal scholarship.

32. ABRAM CHAYES ET AL., INTERNATIONAL LEGAL PROCESS: MATERIALS FOR AN INTRODUCTORY COURSE (1968).

international poverty law, as focused on the subject of law and development;[33] and a truncated version of the Law And movement, with Law and Economics, for example, making some headway in studies of the GATT[34] and Law and Society in the study of customary international norms.

Not surprisingly, in the 1980s and 90's a new scientism came to international legal scholarship as well, with the arrival of high-tech economics in international trade law,[35] the introduction of rational choice theory to the study of arms control and trade,[36] and a number of critical schools coming to grips with contemporary issues. Thus, critical feminist theory now confronts notions of sovereignty and violence against women in Bosnia,[37] postmodernism tackles problems of ethnic nationalism,[38] and critical race theory examines the rights of indigenous minorities.[39] Law and economics, critical legal studies,[40] postmodernism and feminism have each developed theoretical analogues and counterparts in international legal scholarship. But these new theoretical schools of international legal scholarship, which grew largely out of a resurgence of theory in domestic American legal scholarship, have been the doughnut and not the hole, the periphery and

33. *See, e.g.*, David M. Trubek & Marc Galanter, *The Scholars in Self-Estrangement: Some Reflections on the Crisis in Law and Development Studies in the United States*, 4 WISC. L. REV. 1062 (1974); David M. Trubek, *Toward a Social Theory of Law: An Essay on the Study of Law and Development*, 82 YALE L.J. 1 (1972).

34. *See, e.g.*, KENNETH W. DAM, THE GATT—LAW AND INTERNATIONAL ECONOMIC ORGANIZATION 214-21, 274-95 (1970); Warren F. Schwartz & Eugene W. Harper, Jr., *The Regulation of Subsidies Affecting International Trade*, 70 MICH. L. REV. 831 (1972).

35. *See, e.g.*, Alan O. Sykes, *Countervailing Duty Law: An Economic Perspective*, 89 COLUM. L. REV. 199 (1989).

36. For recent scholarship espousing this "rationalistic" view of international law in trade and arms control law, see, for example, Kenneth W. Abbott, *The Trading Nation's Dilemma: The Functions of the Law of International Trade*, 26 HARV. INT'L L.J. 501 (1985); Kenneth W. Abbott, *'Trust But Verify': The Production of Information in Arms Control Treaties and Other International Agreements*, 26 CORNELL INT'L L.J. 1 (1993).

37. *See, e.g.*, CATHARINE MACKINNON, CRIMES OF WAR, CRIMES OF PEACE: ON HUMAN RIGHTS 83 (Stephen Shute & Susan Hurley eds., 1993); Hilary Charlesworth et al., *Feminist Approaches to International Law*, 85 AM. J. INT'L L. 613 (1991); Hilary Charlesworth & Christine Chinkin, *The Gender of Jus Cogens*, 15 HUMAN RTS. Q. 63 (1993); Karen Engle, *International Human Rights and Feminism: When Discourses Meet*, 13 MICH. J. INT'L L. 517 (1992).

38. *See, e.g.*, Nathaniel Berman, *"But the Alternative is Despair": Nationalism and the Modernist Renewal of International Law*, 106 HARV. L. REV. 1792 (1993).

39. *Cf.* Chris Tennant, *Indigenous Peoples, International Institutions, and the International Legal Literature from 1945-1993*, 16 HUMAN RIGHTS Q. 1 (1994).

40. *See, e.g.*, MARTTI KOSKENNIEMI, FROM APOLOGY TO UTOPIA: THE STRUCTURE OF INTERNATIONAL LEGAL ARGUMENT (1989); David Kennedy, *A New Stream of International Law Scholarship*, 7 WIS. INT'L L.J. 1 (1988); Nigel Purvis, *Critical Legal Studies in Public International Law*, 32 HARV. INT'L L.J. 81 (1991).

not the center. What the center has been, I will defer for the moment, but let me leave one hint: transnational legal process.

B. The Evolution of International Scholarship

So much for the scholarly discourse within international law. What about the discourse between international law and its sister disciplines, particularly International Relations theory? Here the picture was substantially clouded by the Cold War.

The years immediately following World War II represented the heyday of international law: the rise of the United Nations and international organizations, both political and economic, the international human rights movement, and the notion that international lawyers could be both the architects and executors of a new world order under law. In the main, those who designed the postwar international system were lawyers who believed in the rule of law, not power, in international affairs and in the willingness of states to cooperate within international institutional and constitutional frameworks.

But as the Cold War set in and reality intruded, the fields of international law and international relations became oddly estranged. Although the two disciplines covered much of the same territory, they evolved independently of one another, pursuing different analytic missions and reaching different conclusions about the function and influence of law. International lawyers and international relations theorists adopted an odd division of labor regarding the intellectual projects that they would pursue. International lawyers began to perform three kinds of tasks: first, *description* of the law through analysis of customary law and treaties; second, *application* of the law to particular cases, *e.g.*, evaluating the lawfulness of particular instances of state conduct; and third, modest *prescription* about what the rule of law should be, particularly in certain growth areas, such as international human rights.

At the same time, international lawyers tended to avoid two other tasks: causal explanation and prediction. Thus, Louis Henkin's famous book carries the descriptive title *How Nations Behave*, attempting precious little causal or predictive analysis of why nations obey, what kinds of law will emerge in certain issue areas, and under what circumstances international law will or will not be obeyed. Yet, it was precisely these questions upon which international relations theorists—particularly in the area of political science—began to focus, in part because they thought of themselves as scientists, engaged in a value-free, nonprescriptive inquiry into causal explanation.

By the early 1980s, the schism between the two disciplines was nearly complete. International lawyers tended to find the glass half full, typified by Henkin's famous phrase, "almost all nations observe almost all principles of international law and almost all of their obligations almost all of the time."[41] International relations theorists, by contrast, (particularly the realists) found such legalism naive and utopian, and tended toward the opposite conclusions: that international law always fails in the big case; that international law cannot be enforced; and that when power and law come into conflict in international affairs, politics is the phenomenon and law is the epiphenomenon. Law, they concluded, has no independent, driving force in international affairs. Law is simply a mask for power, and in the end power prevails. The irony, of course, is that much the same conclusion was reached in law not by the right wingers but by the left-wing critical legal studies scholars, and so in the international realm, the political realists and the critical legal theorists made strange bedfellows.

But notice that the realists regularly made four simplifying assumptions to support their findings: first, that international affairs are a state of anarchy; second, that states are the principal actors in international affairs; third, that states act rationally in deciding whether to engage in cooperation or conflict with other states in the system; and fourth, that the principal interest of rational states is in seeking and maintaining power and security.

Each of these four core assumptions is demonstrably false, particularly in the realm of international economic law. In the modern global economy, the idea that the principal interest of rational states is in seeking and maintaining power and security is falsified by the growing importance and interdependence of economic transactions. Superpowers such as Japan or the European Community have achieved economic prosperity in good part because of their success in externalizing security concerns to other nations. Similarly, the notion that states are the principal actors in international affairs cannot hold sway in a world where nonstate actors—*e.g.*, banks, multinational enterprises, the Paris and London Clubs—dwarf the power of microstates (like Haiti and Burundi) in a system of international commercial transactions that operates largely without governmental intervention. Third, domestic political science learning about bureaucratic politics long ago undercut the fiction that states act rationally in deciding whether and how to engage other states in the global trading system. No one seriously believes that the omnibus trade bill that implemented the Uruguay Round, for example, was the product of a single, rational guiding intelligence. Fourth, as liberal neoinstitutionalists like Robert Keohane recognized years ago, the notion that international affairs are a state of anarchy must address the puzzling persistence of interstate cooperation, and growth of formal

41. Henkin, supra note 5, at 47.

and informal, public and nonpublic, mechanisms to promote the evolution of norms to further that cooperation.[42]

I have challenged each of these four notions in the realm of international economic law. But in other global issue areas, such as international human rights and environmental law, it is equally true that power and security are not the only concerns, that states are not the only important actors, that states do not behave rationally, and that international relations are not in a state of anarchy.[43] The fact that burglaries still occur in Nebraska does not demonstrate a state of anarchy, nor does it prove that laws against burglary have no force and effect. Similarly, the World Trade Center and Oklahoma City bombings do not disprove the existence of international norms against terrorism, multilateral treaties against terrorism, or international regimes to battle terrorism.[44] Nor do defaults on sovereign debt or the persistence of environmental degradation disprove the vast web of global norms, principles, and decisionmaking procedures designed to

42. *See, e.g.*, ROBERT O. KEOHANE, JR., AFTER HEGEMONY: COOPERATION AND DISCORD IN THE WORLD POLITICAL ECONOMY (1984). In the 1970s this more optimistic, "rationalistic" picture of why nations cooperate began to center on what some call "liberal institutionalism": functionalism, regionalism, and interdependence theory. *See* JOSEPH GRIECO, COOPERATION AMONG NATIONS: EUROPE, AMERICA, AND NON-TARIFF BARRIERS TO TRADE 27 (1990). But the resurgence of international tensions and bipolar conflicts during the later years of that decade undermined these early efforts and appeared to reinforce core realist assumptions. In the 1980s, the demonstrable continuation of interstate cooperation fostered a new, highly influential strand of liberal institutionalism focused upon "regime theory." A regime, as defined by political scientist Stephen Krasner, is a set of "implicit or explicit principles, norms, rules, and decision-making procedures around which actors' expectations converge in a given area of international relations." STEPHEN KRASNER ED., INTERNATIONAL REGIMES 2 (1983). Although the precise boundaries of the regime concept remain indistinct, the core notion is that institutional, governmental, and private participants in a given issue area will develop a set of governing arrangements, along with a set of ideologies and expectations, that both restrain the participants and provide means for achieving their common aims. Thus, for example, regime theory notes that international debt questions are not settled entirely within the confines of an international organization like the International Monetary Fund, but rather, within the broader "debt regime," a set of arrangements in which intergovernmental organizations, national governments, private and public debtors and creditors, and informal arrangements like the London and Paris Clubs all participate. Regime theorists further recognize that the phenomenon ultimately to be studied is not the functioning of international organizations *per se—e.g.*, the United Nations—but the broader phenomenon of *international cooperation—e.g.*, the regime of "international peacekeeping"—as it transpires both within and without institutional settings.

43. When political scientists tell me, "international relations are in a state of anarchy," I usually answer, "I'm from Yale Law School. I know from anarchy, and this is not it."

44. *See generally* Harold Hongju Koh, *Civil Remedies for Uncivil Wrongs: Combatting Terrorism through Transnational Public Law Litigation*, 22 TEX. INT'L L.J. 169 (1987)(describing these regimes).

guard against such transnational events. So, in the end, I find myself sounding like Louis Henkin, arguing that the glass is half full and that "almost all nations observe almost all principles of international law almost all of the time." Just because the 55 mph speed limit is not strictly enforced does not mean that that law lacks all power. When the speed limit is 55, people tend to drive 65, not 85. The law may be underenforced, it may be imperfectly enforced, but it *is* enforced, not by a simple domestic process of legislation, adjudication, and executive action, but by a process of complex enforcement that transpires in a variety of public and private fora, under a variety of domestic and international laws, triggered by a variety of governmental and non-governmental actors. In short, international law is enforced by a *transnational legal process*, which is triggered not just by the United States and Russia, but also by the Security Council, the GATT, Exxon, Greenpeace, the Paris Club, Amnesty International, and the Lowenstein International Human Rights Clinic at Yale Law School.

IV. WHY NATIONS OBEY

What about the claim that international law is epiphenomenal, and plays no driving role in international affairs? One can believe this claim only if you are not willing to look closely and carefully enough at the process by which law intersects with power in international affairs. Take three examples, from the areas of arms control, international criminal law, and international human rights.

A. When Nations Have Obeyed

Take first the story of the ABM Treaty Debate.[45] In October 1985, the Reagan Administration proposed the Strategic Defense Initiative (SDI), popularly called "Star Wars," which amounted to an antiballistic missile system for American territorial defense. Unfortunately, in 1972, the United States and the USSR had signed a bilateral treaty—the Anti-Ballistic Missile Treaty—that expressly banned the development of space-based systems for the territorial defense of our country.[46] To skirt the plain language of the Treaty, the Reagan Administration proposed to "reinterpret" the ABM Treaty to permit Star Wars, *i.e.*, to amend it without the consent of either the Senate or our treaty partner. That decision triggered an eight-year battle in which numerous present and former government officials, including six former Secretaries of Defense and numerous key Senators (princi-

45. This history is reviewed in Harold Hongju Koh, *The Treaty Power*, 43 U. Miami L. Rev. 106 (1988).
46. Abram Chayes & Antonia Chayes, *Testing and Development of "Exotic" Systems under the ABM Treaty: The Great Reinterpretation Caper*, 99 Harv. L. Rev. 1956 (1986).

pally Sam Nunn), rallied in support of the original interpretation of the treaty.[47]

The ABM controversy never reached any court, but raged in many forums: Senate hearings, debates over other arms control treaties, law review articles, and op-ed columns. In the end, Congress withheld appropriations from SDI tests that did not conform with the treaty; the Senate reported the ABM Treaty Interpretation Resolution, which reaffirmed its original understanding of the treaty; and in 1988, the Senate attached a condition to the Intermediate-Range Missile Treaty (INF treaty), which specified that the U.S. shall interpret the treaty in accordance with the understanding shared by the President and the Senate at the time of advice and consent.[48] In response, the Reagan and Bush Administrations still claimed that their broad reinterpretation was "legally correct," but announced that they would comply with the original understanding as a matter of "policy." In 1993, the episode ended, when President Clinton repudiated the unilateral Reagan reinterpretation and announced that his administration would abide by the original ABM treaty interpretation.

None of this legal dispute reached any court. Indeed, had one stopped tracing the process of the dispute in 1987, one might have concluded that the United States had breached the treaty and gotten away with it. But in the end, the ABM Treaty Reinterpretation Debate is a story of how a powerful nation, the United States, returned to compliance with international law.

Much the same lesson applies to the saga of extraterritorial kidnapping played out in *United States v. Alvarez-Machain*.[49] In that case, the Supreme Court held that a Mexican accused's forced abduction by U.S. agents from Mexican territory, without resort to an existing bilateral extradition treaty, did not divest U.S. courts of criminal jurisdiction to try that defendant.[50] But the Supreme Court's decision did not end the story. *Alvarez-Machain* sparked intense media criticism and protests from political leaders in Mexico, Canada, Europe, and the Caribbean.[51] The decision triggered congressional

47. A key role in the fight against the ABM treaty reinterpretation was played by Gerard C. Smith, the chief American negotiator at SALT I and one of the principal negotiators of the ABM Treaty. Smith chaired the Board of an important nongovernmental organization, the Arms Control Association, and a grassroots organization, the National Committee to Save the ABM Treaty. He is the namesake of the professorship I now hold.

48. See HAROLD HONGJU KOH, THE NATIONAL SECURITY CONSTITUTION: SHARING POWER AFTER THE IRAN-CONTRA AFFAIR 43 (1990).

49. 504 U.S. 655 (1992).

50. In dissent, Justice Stevens argued that "most courts throughout the civilized world . . . will be deeply disturbed by the 'monstrous' decision the Court announces today." *Id.* at 687 (Stevens, J., dissenting)(citations omitted).

51. *See* Jonathan A. Bush, *How Did We Get Here? Foreign Abduction After* Alvarez-Machain, 45 STAN. L. REV. 939, 941-42 & nn.11-15 (1993).

hearings,[52] proposals for remedial legislation, and an internal Justice Department review of the policy of transborder kidnapping.[53] The Permanent Council of the Organization of American States requested a legal opinion regarding the international legality of the Supreme Court's decision from the Inter-American Juridical Committee, which concluded that "the decision is contrary to the rules of international law."[54] Later that year, an exasperated district judge acquitted Alvarez-Machain of criminal charges,[55] and Alvarez promptly filed a civil action in federal court against the U.S. officials who ordered his kidnapping.[56] Finally, in June 1993, amid the North American Free Trade negotiations, Secretary of State Warren Christopher announced that the United States and Mexico had agreed to amend the U.S.-Mexico Extradition Treaty to prohibit transborder kidnappings. Thus, once again, the United States reluctantly obeyed.[57]

My final example is a case I know too well: the extraterritorial return of Haitian and Cuban refugees. Beginning in the spring of 1992, the Bush Administration began to intercept and directly return Haitians fleeing Haiti on the high seas, in apparent violation of past governmental precedents[58] and the "*nonrefoulement*" requirement of

52. *See Kidnapping Suspects Abroad: Hearings Before the Subcomm. on Civil and Constitutional Rights of the House Comm. on the Judiciary*, 102d Cong., 2d Sess. 82 (1992).
53. *See* Paul Hoffman, *U.S. Must Not Kidnap Suspects Abroad*, NEWSDAY, Dec. 2, 1993, at 114 (noting legislation introduced by Senator Moynihan and internal Justice Department review ordered by Attorney General Reno in response to decision).
54. Organization of American States, Permanent Council, *Legal Opinion on the Decision of the Supreme Court of the United States*, 4 CRIM. L. F. 119, 124 (1993). The United Nations Working Group on Arbitrary Detention further determined that Alvarez had been arbitrarily detained in violation of international law.
55. Seth Mydans, *Judge Clears Mexican in Agent's Killing*, N.Y. TIMES, Dec. 15, 1992, at A20.
56. Alvarez-Machain v. United States, No. CV 93-4072 JGD (JHx)(C.D. Cal. 1994).
57. *U.S. Curbs Its Agents in Mexico*, NEW HAVEN REG. (June 22, 1993), at 20.
58. Various contemporaneous government documents and instruments implementing the interdiction program confirmed that the *nonrefoulement* obligation applied even on the high seas. President Reagan's first Executive Order on interdicting Haitians stated that in order to ensure "the strict observance of our international obligations concerning those who genuinely flee persecution in their homeland," "that no person who is a refugee will be returned without his consent." Executive Order No. 12,324, 46 Fed. Reg. 48109, 48109 (1981). INS Guidelines issued to implement the 1981 Executive Order further mandated that INS personnel be constantly watchful "for any indication (including bare claims) that a person or persons on board the interdicted vessel may qualify as refugees under the United Nations Convention and Protocol." INS Role In and Guidelines For Interdiction at Sea, October 6, 1981 (emphasis added), quoted in Brief for Respondents at 31, Sale v. Haitian Centers Council, 509 U.S. 155 (1993). Finally, two opinions from the Justice Department's Office of Legal Counsel reaffirmed the point. *See* Proposed Interdiction of Haitian Flag Vessels, 5 Op. Off. Legal Counsel 242, 248 (1981)(reasoning that interdicted Haitians "who claim that they

Article 33 of the 1951 U.N. Refugee Convention Relating to the Status of Refugees.[59] An ad hoc coalition of human rights lawyers, including Yale's Lowenstein International Human Rights Clinic, challenged that policy unsuccessfully at the Supreme Court against the Clinton Administration, which surprised everyone by maintaining the Bush direct return policy upon taking office.[60] Thus, as of June 1993, it appeared that two American presidents had violated a core international human rights norm with impunity.

But once again, the Supreme Court's decision was not the last word on the legality of the interdiction policy under *international*, as opposed to domestic, law. The U.N. High Commissioner on Refugees, whose support the Clinton Administration required elsewhere in the world, loudly protested the Supreme Court's ruling.[61] Other human rights groups began pressing arguments similar to those urged by the *HCC* plaintiffs as a basis for challenging the U.S. government's policy before the Inter-American Commission on Human Rights.[62]

---

will be persecuted . . . must be given an opportunity to substantiate their claims."); Memorandum from Larry L. Simms, Deputy Assistant Att'y Gen., Off. of Legal Counsel, to the Assoc. Att'y Gen. (Aug. 5, 1981)("Those who claim to be refugees must be given a chance to substantiate their claims [under Article 33]."), quoted in Joint Appendix at 222, Sale v. Haitian Centers Council, 509 U.S. 155 (1993).

59. 19 U.S.T. 6259, 189 U.N.T.S. 150, done July 28, 1951 ("[n]o Contracting State shall expel or return ("*refouler*") a refugee *in any manner whatsoever* to the frontiers of territories where his life or freedom would be threatened on account of his . . . political opinion.") (emphasis added). The United States became a party to the Refugee Convention when it acceded to the United Nations Protocol Relating to the Status of Refugees, Jan. 31, 1967, 19 U.S.T. 6223, T.I.A.S. 6577. For an account of this history, see Koh, *The Haiti Paradigm, supra* note 4.

60. *See* Sale v. Haitian Centers Council, 509 U.S. 155 (1993). Justice Stevens' opinion for the Court held that the *nonrefoulement* obligations of neither INA § 243(h) nor Article 33 of the Refugee Convention applied to Haitians apprehended on the high seas, thereby articulating a domestic rule of "territorial *nonrefoulement.*" Another wing of the litigation, however, won the release of more than 300 Haitians being held on Guantanamo, who had established prima facie claims of political asylum. Haitian Centers Council v. Sale, 823 F. Supp. 1028 (E.D.N.Y. 1993).

61. *See U.N. High Commissioner for Refugees Responds to U.S. Supreme Court Decision in* Sale v. Haitian Centers Council, 32 I.L.M. 1215 (1993)("[T]he obligation not to return refugees to persecution arises irrespective of whether governments are acting within or outside their borders. . . . UNHCR considers the Court's decision a setback to modern international refugee law. . . .").

62. The Inter-American Commission on Human Rights considered a petition brought by the Center for Human Rights and Constitutional Law which challenged the Haitian interdiction program as a violation of the American Declaration of the Rights and Duties of Man and the American Convention on Human Rights, OAS Treaty No. 36. In March 1993, the Commission issued an interim Resolution adopting Provisional Measures, "[c]alling upon the United States Government to review as a matter of urgency its practice of stopping on the seas vessels destined for the USA with Haitians and returning them to Haiti without affording them an opportunity to establish whether they qualify as refugees," and noting that the U.S. policy prevents the exercise by the Haitians of the right to seek refuge. *See*

As the Clinton Administration maintained its policy of direct return, domestic political pressure began to build. The African-American community began drawing attention to the gross inconsistency of the Haitian policy with our international obligations and the discriminatory treatment of Haitians *vis-à-vis* Cubans and other immigrant groups. TransAfrica leader Randall Robinson undertook a hunger strike to publicize the Haitians' plight, personalizing the issue and becoming a focal point for media attention. The African-American community magnified its voice through the forty-member Congressional Black Caucus (CBC), which in March 1994 sent President Clinton a letter announcing that "The United States' Haiti policy must be scrapped."[63]

In May 1994, President Clinton finally conceded that his Haitian policy had failed. He abandoned his direct return policy, and shifted to a new policy of "safe haven" for Haitian refugees, pending Aristide's return.[64] In the summer of 1994, tens of thousands of Cuban refugees began fleeing again on the high seas and were detained in Guantanamo camps, and after extensive new litigation, were ultimately released into the United States.[65] Although the new "safe haven" policy itself proved fraught with problems under international human rights law,[66] amid the post-mortems on the Haitian crisis a salient fact got lost: that after several years of counterproductive noncompliance with the global norm against extraterritorial *refoulement* of refugees, at least for a time, the United States came back into compliance with that norm.

Case No. 10.675, discussed in *Petitioners Release Resolution of the Inter-American Commission on Human Rights concerning U.S. Program of Haitian Refugee Interdiction*, 32 I.L.M. 1215 (1993). In the spring of 1995, the Commission issued an interim order against the United States.

63. Peter J. Boyer, *The Rise of Kweisi Mfume*, NEW YORKER, Aug. 1, 1994, at 34.

64. *Id.* at 34. Other personnel changes, for example, the appointment of Strobe Talbott as Deputy Secretary of State, also apparently played a role in promoting reconsideration of the direct return policy. Initially, Clinton announced that he would shift to a new policy of subjecting fleeing Haitian boat people to full-fledged refugee interviews aboard United States Navy ships docked in the harbor at Kingston, Jamaica. But the policy change, coupled with favorable weather and new desperation in Haiti, coincided with a refugee outflow of more than 15,000 refugees that quickly swamped the capacity of the Jamaican processing facility. Thus, in July 1994, the Administration switched course again and announced that henceforth, all fleeing refugees would be given "safe haven" in various offshore camps, most prominently in Panama, Honduras, and various Caribbean countries.

65. The legality of the safe-haven policy was ultimately sustained by the Eleventh Circuit in *Cuban-American Bar Ass'n v. Christopher*, 43 F.3d 1413 (11th Cir. 1995).

66. *See generally* Harold Hongju Koh, *America's Offshore Refugee Camps*, 29 RICHMOND L. REV. 139, 164-73 (Allen Chair 1994)(arguing that the policy of temporary safe haven on Guantanamo crossed the line into illegal arbitrary detention).

The larger point is that on such matters, decisions of the U.S. Supreme Court are neither final nor infallible. Such domestic decisions no longer represent final stops, only way stations, in a transnational legal process of "complex enforcement," triggered here by transnational public-law litigation.[67] Even resisting nations cannot insulate themselves forever from complying with international law if they regularly participate, as all nations must, in transnational legal interactions. Thus, in the same way that the United States finally abided by the ABM Treaty, the Soviet Union finally conceded that its invasion of Afghanistan was illegal. Through a complex process of rational self-interest and norm internalization—at times spurred by transnational litigation—international legal norms seep into, are internalized, and become entrenched in domestic legal and political processes. In this way, the "normativity of transnational legal process" helps drive how national governments conduct their international relations.

B. Explaining Why Nations Obey

In recent years, international legal scholars have begun to offer two different accounts of why nations obey international law: one based on *interest*, the other based on *identity*. While both theories provide useful insights, neither fully accounts for the importance of *interaction* within the transnational legal process and domestic *internalization* of international norms as determinants of why nations obey.

1. Interest

The "interest" story is familiar and straightforward. Nation-states obey international law when it serves their short or long-term self-interest to do so. As contemporary international relations theorists have long recognized, nations are not exclusively preoccupied with maximizing their power vis-à-vis one another in zero-sum games. Rather, they employ *cooperative* strategies to pursue a more complex and multi-faceted long-run national interest, in which compliance with negotiated norms serves as a winning strategy in a reiterated

67. European human rights litigants have long understood, for example, that adverse national court decisions may be "appealed" to and even "reversed" by the European Court of Human Rights. *See, e.g.*, the European Court's decision in the *Sunday Times* case, 30 Eur. Ct. H. R. [ser.A], Judgment of April 26, 1979, ser. A., no. 30. In that case the British Attorney General sought and won an injunction restraining a British newspaper from publishing a story about thalidomide children. At various stages, eight (of eleven) English judges ruled against the newspaper, but in the end both the European Commission and the European Court ruled in favor of the *Times,* and required the British government to pay more than 22,000 pounds. For a description of the *Sunday Times* litigation, see Mark Janis, An Introduction to International Law 263-64 (2d ed. 1993).

"prisoner's dilemma" game. Game theory predicts that states, as rational, self-interested actors, will pursue a variety of strategies to achieve both short- and long-term gains, depending on the relative costs and benefits of competition, cooperation, or "defection" from a cooperative scheme. Thus, even when competition or defection provides a short-term advantage, patterns of cooperation may nevertheless emerge from anarchy because "the logic of collective action" convinces self-interested states that cooperation better serves their longer-term interests.[68]

Under this account, governmental and private participants in a given issue area will develop a set of governing arrangements—called "regimes"—along with a set of ideologies and expectations, that both restrain the participants and provide means for achieving their common aims. Within these regimes, there is conceptual space for international law: law plays a critical role both in stabilizing the expectations and in reinforcing the restraints that regimes seek to foster. Among rational states, legal rules promote compliance with regime norms by reducing transaction costs, providing channels for dispute-settlement, triggering retaliatory actions, signaling states when negative responses by other states may ensue, and requiring states to furnish information that will highlight defections on their own part.

Recently, a number of international legal scholars, most prominently Kenneth Abbott, have usefully espoused this "rationalistic" view of international law in trade and arms control law.[69] At this basic level, international lawyers and international relations theorists now agree that law forms a crucial part of the background against which the complex web of interactions among self-interested nations transpires.[70] Not surprisingly, Abbott's chosen issue areas are ones

68. *See, e.g.*, Robert Axelrod, The Evolution of Cooperation (1984); Robert O. Keohane, After Hegemony: Cooperation and Discord in the World Political Economy (1984); Mancur Olson, The Logic of Collective Action (1971); Robert O. Keohane, *International Institutions: Two Approaches*, 32 Int'l Stud. Q. 379 (1988); International Regimes (Stephen D. Krasner ed. 1983).

69. *See, e.g.*, Kenneth W. Abbott, *Modern International Relations Theory: A Prospectus for International Lawyers*, 14 Yale J. Int'l L. 335 (1989); Kenneth W. Abbott, *The Trading Nation's Dilemma: The Functions of the Law of International Trade*, 26 Harv. Int'l L.J. 501 (1985); Kenneth W. Abbott, *'Trust But Verify': The Production of Information in Arms Control Treaties and Other International Agreements*, 26 Cornell Int'l L.J. 1 (1993).

70. Yet whether by training or habit, international relations theorists still rarely speak of "law," even while subjects on which they train their sights—compliance, commitments, rules, norms, decisionmaking processes, institutions, and regimes—are increasingly the traditional grist for international law inquiry. "Regime theorists find it hard to say the 'L-word' but 'principles, norms, rules, and decision-making procedures' are what international law is all about . . . ." Chayes & Chayes, *On Compliance*, *supra* note 5, at 195 n.64.

where nation-states remain the primary players and traditional realist assumptions still largely prevail. But rationalistic, state-centered theories work far less well, for example, in such areas as human rights, debt restructuring, or international commercial transactions, where nonstate actors abound, pursue multiple goals in complex nonzero-sum games, and interact repeatedly within formal institutional settings nested within broader informal regimes.

Abbott concedes that nonstate actors are critical players in the transnational legal process but deliberately chooses not to focus on them. Nor, because he operates at Kenneth Waltz's "third image"[71]—the systemic level—does he have much of a domestic politics story to tell. In Abbott's view, international law regulates behavior by changing national incentives, but does not fundamentally affect state interests. The process he studies is the dynamic interaction among exogenously constituted actors. Abbott sees norms as reducing transactions costs, and explains the evolution of norms, much like Robert Axelrod,[72] as ultimately driven by considerations of long-run self-interest, not through a process of national identity-formation.

2. *Identity*

A second explanation for compliance rests not on interest, but identity. In a string of writings drawing upon emerging "liberal international relations theory,"[73] Anne-Marie Slaughter has argued that the determinative factor for whether nations interact in a "zone of law" or a "zone of politics" is whether or not the state can be characterized as "liberal" in identity.[74] In place of Abbott's model of the rational state actor, Slaughter offers the liberal state, defined as a state like the United States, with "some form of representative government secured by the separation of powers, constitutional guarantees of civil and political rights, juridical equality, and a functioning judicial system dedicated to the rule of law."[75] Flipping the now-familiar political science maxim that "democracies don't fight one another,"[76] Slaughter

71. KENNETH WALTZ; MAN, THE STATE, AND WAR (1959).
72 ROBERT AXELROD, THE EVOLUTION OF COOPERATION (1984).
73. *See, e.g.*, Andrew Moravcsik, Liberalism and International Relations Theory (Center for International Affairs, Harvard University, Working Paper No. 92-6, 1992).
74. *See, e.g.*, Anne-Marie Slaughter Burley, *International Law and International Relations Theory: A Dual Agenda*, 87 AM. J. INT'L L. 205 (1993).
75. Anne-Marie Slaughter, *International Law in a World of Liberal States*, 6 EUROPEAN J. INT'L L. 503, 509 (1995). "Non-liberal" states, by contrast, are those that have "neither a representative government nor a market economy." *Id.* at 529 n.57.
76. BRUCE RUSSETT, GRASPING THE DEMOCRATIC PEACE: PRINCIPLES FOR A POST-COLD WAR WORLD 11-23 (1993); Michael Doyle, *Kant, Liberal Legacies, and Foreign Affairs*, 12 PHIL. & PUB. AFF. 205, 207-08 (1983).

posits, in effect, that liberal democracies are more likely to *do law* with one another. Under this view, legal relations among liberal states do and should differ from relations between liberal and illiberal states: the former transpire in a "zone of law," the latter in a "zone of politics beyond law."[77]

Unlike the rationalistic account, identity theory at least focuses upon both nonstate actors and domestic politics. In its current version, Slaughter's account assumes:

> that the primary actors in the international system are individuals and groups acting in domestic and transnational civil society. Thus where Realists look for concentrations of state power, Liberals focus on the ways in which interdependence encourages and allows individuals and groups to exert different pressures on national governments.[78]

Nor does liberal theory exclude considerations of transnational legal process.[79]

But what this essentialist analysis misses is that a state's identity is neither exogenously nor permanently given. Like national interests, national identities are not givens, but rather, socially constructed products of learning, knowledge, cultural practices, and ideology.[80] Nations like Argentina, Chile, Czechoslovakia, and Peru are neither permanently liberal nor illiberal, but make transitions back and forth from dictatorship to democracy, prodded by norms and regimes of international law. A central question facing Haiti, for example, is whether adherence to the rule of international law will help or inhibit its efforts to rebuild its civil society. Thus, identity analysis leaves unanswered a critical question: to what extent does law itself help *constitute the identity* of a state as one that obeys international law, and hence, as "liberal" or not?

Slaughter's claim that compliance with transnational law marks law among liberal states has a troubling flipside: the notion that nonliberal states somehow participate in transnational process within a

77. *See, e.g.*, Slaughter Burley, *Law Among Liberal States: Liberal Internationalism and the Act of State Doctrine*, 92 Colum. L. Rev. 1907, 1920 (1992)(calling "Transnational Relations Among Liberal and Nonliberal States" "The 'Zone of Politics' Beyond Law").

78. Slaughter, *supra* note 75, at 508.

79. To the contrary, according to Slaughter, "Liberals assume that the 'State' interacts with these [nonstate] actors in a complex process of both representation and regulation," which yields state preferences. Slaughter, *supra* note 75, at 508.

80. *See* Keohane, *supra* note 68, at 389-92 (referring to the "cognitivist" or "reflective" models of institutional behavior found in the work of Hayward Alker, Richard Ashley, Friedrich Kratochwil, John Ruggie, and Alex Wendt); Peter Katzenstein, *Norms and National Security: The Japanese Police and Military as Agents of Non-Violence*, unpublished manuscript presented at Yale Law and International Politics Seminar, April 4, 1994, at 21 ("Norms condition interests, and interests affect norms.")

zone of politics, not law.[81] Strictly understood, this claim denies the universalism of international law and implicitly condones the confinement of nonliberal states to a realist world of power politics. To the extent that identity theory suggests that nations who do not share *political* cultures are not obliged to deal with one another within the terms of universal law, the claim becomes uncomfortably reminiscent of the "cultural relativism" debate in international human rights law. And if the suggestion is that somehow *only* liberal states do law with one another, the claim is empirically falsifiable. In such areas as international commercial law—the execution of transborder letters of credit, for example—states regularly abide by international rules without regard to whether or not they are representative democracies or have market economies.[82]

3. *Interaction and Internalization*

Neither interest nor identity theory fully account for the normativity of transnational legal process. Participation in the transnational legal process helps constitute the identity of a state as one that obeys the law, but what is critical is the *interaction*, not the label that purports to identify a state as liberal or not.[83] In part, actors obey international law as a result of repeated interaction with other governmental and nongovernmental actors in the international system. A state's violation of international law creates inevitable frictions and contradictions that hinder its ongoing participation within the transnational legal process. As the *Alvarez-Machain* incident showed, when the U.S. engaged in governmental kidnapping of Mexican citizens, for example, that activity impaired its ability to negotiate the North American Free Trade Agreement with the Mexican government. When a developing nation defaults on a sovereign debt, that activity impairs its ability to secure new lending. When the United States denies the jurisdiction of the International Court of Justice in a suit in which it is a defendant, that decision impairs its ability to in-

81. *See, e.g.*, Slaughter, *supra* note 77, at 1920 (calling "Transnational Relations Among Liberal and Nonliberal States" "The 'Zone of Politics' Beyond Law). Slaughter sometimes seems to suggest that domestic courts have an expanded role to play in sustaining international order—but only among certain states—and that legal order can be established transnationally, but based only on the common values and institutions shared by liberal states. *Id. See also* Slaughter, *supra* note 75, at 504 (thought experiment).

82 F. Dely, International Business Law and Lex Mercatoria (1992).

83. Slaughter's most recent work recognizes this by deemphasizing the liberal/illiberal label and emphasizing two transnational legal process elements: the density of transnational transaction and transgovernmental communication among transnational actors. Slaughter, *supra* note 75, at 522-28. As I argue in the text, these aspects of transnational legal process, and not the "liberal" label, explain the phenomenon of compliance with transnational law.

voke the Court's jurisdiction as a plaintiff.[84] Thus, a nation's leaders may shift over time from a policy of violation of international law to one of compliance to avoid such frictions in its continuing interactions.

As transnational actors interact, they create patterns of behavior and generate norms of external conduct which they in turn internalize. Law-abiding states *internalize* international law by incorporating it into their domestic legal and political structures, through executive action, legislation, and judicial decisions which take account of and incorporate international norms.[85] Nations also react to other states' reputations as law-abiding or not. Legal ideologies prevail among domestic decision-makers such that they are affected by perceptions that their actions are unlawful, or that domestic opponents or other nations in the global regime will so categorize them. Moreover, domestic decision-making becomes "enmeshed" with international legal norms, as institutional arrangements for the making and maintenance of an international commmitment become entrenched in domestic legal and political processes.[86] It is through this repeated process of interaction and internalization that international law acquires its "stickiness," that nation-states acquire their identity, and that nations define promoting the rule of international law as part of their national self-interest.

The example of the 55 mph speed limit used above helps make the point. After the oil crisis of 1974, why did American drivers start driving slower on the highways? Perhaps in part because individual drivers recalculated their self-interest, and determined that it was rational to drive slower because of safety reasons or to save gas. It may in part have been because many citizens view themselves as law-abiding, and complied with the law because of their sense of self-identity. But other factors were also undoubtedly at work. Those who drove repeatedly—*e.g. interacted* within the process—encountered highway patrols and other enforcement mechanisms. Complying vehicles blocked lanes and made it harder to speed. Federal standards crept down and became incorporated into state laws. Authorities exhorted drivers, using threats, tickets and appeals to patriotism, to in-

84. *See, e.g.*, Nicaragua's suit against the United States, Military and Paramilitary Activities (Nicar. v. U.S.), 1986 I.C.J. Rep. 14 (June 27).
85. One prime example is the refugee area and the international law norm of *nonrefoulement*. Not only is that norm embodied in the 1951 Refugee Convention, it has been internalized in the 1981 U.S.-Haiti Agreement and § 243(h) of the Immigration and Nationality Act. The *Haitian Centers Council* litigation can thus be understood as an unsuccessful attempt by private litigants to convince the Supreme Court to internalize the norm of *extraterritorial nonrefoulement* as United States domestic law.
86. *See* Robert O. Keohane, *Compliance with International Commitments: Politics within a Framework of Law*, *in International Law and International Relations Theory: Building Bridges*, American Society of International Law, Proceedings of the 86th Annual Meeting 167 (1992)(describing concept of "enmeshment").

ternalize the new norm. Drivers in many jurisdictions came to view noncompliance as costly while viewing the new rule itself as legitimate and generally fair. Was the new law enforced? Most would agree that it was underenforced, that it was enforced through a complex enforcement process, but few would deny that the law mattered. As an independent variable, the law affected conduct. Interaction and internalization (which together comprise the normativity of the process) provided a critical link between the explanatory variable of interest, on the one hand, and identity on the other. In the same way, as nations participate in transnational legal process, through a complex combination of rational self-interest, transnational interaction, norm-internalization, and identity-formation, international law becomes a factor driving their international relations.

To summarize, the critical idea is the normativity of transnational legal process. To survive in an interdependent world, even the most isolated states—North Korea, Libya, Iraq, Cuba—must eventually interact with other nations. Even rogue states cannot insulate themselves forever from complying with international law if they wish to participate in a transnational economic or political process. Once nations begin to interact, a complex process occurs, whereby international legal norms seep into, are internalized, and become embedded in domestic legal and political processes.

In some cases, of course, instead of returning to compliance, the noncomplying state seeks actively to promote its departure from international norms as the new governing international rule.[87] In the same way as a river that has overflowed its banks may either recede or carve a new path, the noncomplying government may try to argue internationally—as the United States did in the ABM Treaty Debate and before its own Supreme Court in the *Alvarez-Machain* and *Haitian* cases—that the contested norm it is violating should be reinterpreted so as to avoid any claim of violation. Yet such arguments, when made, do not settle the question of international legality. Instead, they stimulate another round of transnational legal interaction, in which the integrity of the revised norm can be challenged and tested by other nations and nongovernmental actors. The transnational legal process of institutional dialogue begins again, starting with a debate over whether to amend or reinterpret the norm in light of the new circumstances.[88]

87. *See, e.g.*, Ted L. Stein, *The Approach of the Different Drummer: The Principle of the Persistent Objector in International Law*, 26 HARV. INT'L L.J. (1985).

88. An analogous process has occurred in the United States with regard to the death penalty, whereby individual states have progressively taken narrower views of what constitutes cruel and unusual punishment, thereby prompting Supreme Court reconsideration of the Eighth Amendment rule. *See, e.g.*, Stanford v. Kentucky, 492 U.S. 361 (1989).

V. CONCLUSION

If one accepts a theory of transnational legal process, what conclusions follow? Let me quickly suggest four.

First, like postwar international relations theories, a theory of transnational legal process has both predictive capacity[89] and explanatory power regarding questions of causation. It predicts that nations will come into compliance with international norms if transnational legal processes are aggressively triggered by other transnational actors in a way that forces interaction in forums capable of generating norms, followed by norm-internalization. This process of interaction and internalization in turn leads a national government to engage in new modes of interest-recognition and identity-formation in a way that eventually leads the nation-state back into compliance.[90]

Second, this is a theory that well serves our comparative advantage as lawyers. Unlike political scientists, lawyers specialize in the close reading of texts, examining the social impact of procedural rules, understanding the power of norms in civil society, and designing public policy against a backdrop of law. A lens of transnational legal process calls upon lawyers to exercise all of their interdisciplinary tools, without asking them to forsake their traditional lawyerly skills.[91]

Third, the theory suggests the value and the imperative of clinical work in international law. Transnational legal process forces states to become more law-abiding by incorporating international law into their

89. "This reasoning," I argued shortly before the Clinton Administration's 1994 policy change regarding Haitian refugees, "predicts that in time, the United States will comply with the norm of 'extraterritorial nonrefoulement.'" *See* Koh, *Haiti Paradigm*, *supra* note 4, at 2408.

90. By this reasoning, North Korea and Libya will eventually permit international inspections of their nuclear facilities, Guatemala will acknowledge its extrajudicial killings, Japan will acknowledge the illegality of its unilateral trade actions and its wartime treatment of Korean comfort women, and the United States will eventually comport with norms against arbitrary detention with respect to its offshore refugee detention policy. *See* Koh, *America's Offshore Refugee Camps*, *supra* note 66. For an effort to trace how American domestic political processes took account of and incorporated the international norm against *refoulement* with respect to Haitian refugees, substituting in its place a rule of temporary safe haven, see Koh, *Refugees, the Courts, and the New World Order*, *supra* note 4, at 999.

91. Political scientists may say, for example, that they saw no effect of law upon the resolution of the ABM treaty debate, the extraterritorial kidnapping affair, or the Haitian refugee crisis discussed in text. But to me, these are simply matters of not looking closely enough, of failing to trace the process of compliance. A scientist passing a magnet over a chemical solution may change all of the ions from positive to negative, without affecting any change visible to the uninformed observer. In the same way, lawyers tracing transnational legal process can trace in ways that political scientists often miss the minute modes by which law affects the incentives of political actors, thereby changing the receptivity of those actors to compliance with legal rules.

domestic legal and political structures. When such a state violates international law, that violation creates frictions and contradictions that disrupt its ongoing participation in the transnational legal process.[92] Transnational public law litigation brought by nongovernmental organizations is designed precisely to provoke judicial action that will create such frictions, thereby helping shape the normative direction of governmental policies.

If this is so, nongovernmental organizations are not just observers of, but important players in, transnational legal process. Their actions influence the process and their inaction ratifies its outcomes. It is sometimes said that someone who, by acquiring medical training, comes to understand the human body acquires as well a moral duty not just to observe disease, but to try to cure it. In the same way, I would argue, a lawyer who acquires knowledge of the body *politic* acquires a duty not simply to observe transnational legal process, but to try to influence it. To use H. Ross Perot's blunt words, if a lawyer really cares about international human rights, "you can't just talk about it, you've got to do it."

Fourth and finally, transnational legal process fills the hole in the doughnut of international legal scholarship. What I have suggested is that what mainstream scholars in international law have been doing these last forty years has not been simply thick description, but examination of the complexity and normativity of transnational legal process. Like the new public law scholars in the domestic realm, the transnational legal process scholars of my generation are focused on the normativity of process, sensitive to practice, and alive to interdisciplinary theory. Even a cursory examination of most journals of international law over the last few decades reveals that most international legal scholars have been pursuing not law and economics, postmodernism, or critical theories, but applied studies in transnational legal process.[93] In Moliere's famous words, "Good heavens, for more than forty years I've been speaking prose without knowing it."[94] In the same way, for more than forty years, international legal scholars have been studying transnational legal process without knowing it. In the end, fathoming international law's role in the post-Cold War era means participating, influencing, and ultimately enforcing transnational legal process: the key to understanding why nations obey.

---

92. *See, e.g.*, KOH, THE NATIONAL SECURITY CONSTITUTION, *supra* note 48, at 155 ("Because the United States is a party to a network of closely interconnected treaties, unilateral administration decisions to break or bend one treaty have forced it into vicious cycles of treaty violation.").

93. *See, e.g.*, CHAYES, *supra* note 32; HENKIN, supra note 5; REISMAN & WILLARD, *supra* note 13.

94. MOLIERE, THE BOURGEOIS GENTLEMAN (1670).

[12]

VOLUME 32, NUMBER 2, SPRING 1991

The Future of Statehood

Martti Koskenniemi*

Confronted by recent events, many international lawyers argue that the basis of international law in sovereign statehood is withering away. The legal order as a system of contractual obligations between independent states declared at Westphalia—the law of nations—is being replaced by an as yet unarticulated "new world order." But the unanimous legal rhetoric surrounding the Gulf Crisis (and hence much of public discourse) belies any such assertion of a change in the foundations of international law. The relative ease with which most states supported violent action to defend Kuwait's statehood reaffirms the continuing vitality of statehood as the ultimate value of the international legal system. Indeed, the legal argument still depends on the *formal* and universalizeable character of Kuwait's statehood and not the *substantive*, particular quality of that statehood in the circumstances of the Gulf.

Despite this ratification of the principle of statehood, certain substantive values in contemporary international law pose real challenges to the legitimacy of statehood as a basis for international order. In this essay I shall examine these challenges to statehood, and to what extent they might or should contribute to the emergence of what some have called a "*new* world order." I shall argue that as long as there is no wide agreement on what constitutes the good life, the formality of statehood remains the best guarantee we have against the conquest of modernism's liberal aspect by modernism's authoritarian impulse.

I. HUMAN RIGHTS AND STATEHOOD

An international law of sovereign equality has always contained the unfortunate implication of providing legitimacy for the national repression of citizens, or at least impunity for tyrants. The emergence of a body of human rights law may seem to be "competing—if not at loggerheads—with the traditional principles of respect for sovereign equality of States and of non-interference . . . ."[1] The 1966 U.N.

* Counsellor for the Ministry of Foreign Affairs of Finland. The opinions expressed in this essay are solely those of the author.

1. ANTONIO CASSESE, INTERNATIONAL LAW IN A DIVIDED WORLD 148 (1986).

Covenants on Economic, Social and Cultural Rights[2] and on Civil and Political Rights[3] have affirmed that states have international obligations to their citizens. Along with the more recent instruments on the prevention of racial and sexual discrimination and torture, and on the establishment of rights for children and migrant workers, these covenants have also instituted a universally applicable system of international inspection and supervision. The practical effects of such international standards may still be rather small, but their existence means that a state may not claim that mere statehood justifies any internal activities.[4]

During the 1970's and 1980's, many U.N. policies, such as developmental and peace programs, were characterized as a right of the policies' beneficiaries.[5] This practice may have somewhat obscured the meaning of human rights as legally cognizable claims by an individual or a community against the state. Developments in Eastern Europe, however, have again focused global attention on the right to be free from state interference. In essence, "[l]iberation in these countries means curtailing the power of the state and its bureaucracy."[6] Similarly, the "Charter of Paris for a New Europe," adopted at the Summit Meeting of Heads of State or Government of States participating in the Conference on Security and Cooperation in Europe (CSCE), begins with a section entitled "Human Rights, Democracy and the Rule of Law":

> Human rights and fundamental freedoms are the birthright of all human beings, are inalienable and are guaranteed by law. Their protection and promotion is the first responsibility of government. Respect for them is an essential safeguard against an over-mighty State.[7]

Forums like the CSCE, the Council of Europe, and the U.N. Human Rights Commission are developing and strengthening mechanisms to curtail state power. Such developments may even have supported

2. International Covenant on Economic, Social and Cultural Rights, Dec. 16, 1966, 993 U.N.T.S. 3.

3. International Covenant on Civil and Political Rights, Dec. 19, 1966, 999 U.N.T.S. 171.

4. For a review, see UNITED NATIONS, UNITED NATIONS ACTION IN THE FIELD OF HUMAN RIGHTS (1983). In addition, see Philip Alston's very useful assessment of the work of the "treaty bodies," 44 U.N. GAOR Annex (Agenda Item 109), U.N. Doc. A/44/668 (1989).

5. *See, e.g.*, Declaration on the Right of Peoples to Peace, G.A. Res. 39/11, 39 U.N. GAOR Supp. (No. 51) at 22, U.N. Doc. A/39/51 (1984); Declaration on the Right to Development, G.A. Res. 41/128, 41 U.N. GAOR Supp. (No. 53) at 186, U.N. Doc. A/41/53 (1986).

6. Andras Sajo, *New Legalism in East Central Europe: Law as an Instrument of Social Transformation*, 17 J. OF LAW & SOC'Y 329, 330 (1990).

7. 45 U.N. GAOR Annex at 4–5, U.N. Doc. A/45/859 (1990).

claims regarding the customary character of certain core restraints on the power of states.[8]

The protection of human rights, however, cannot form a meaningful basis for social order. If we are to define our polity in terms of human rights, we must ascertain the number and content of such rights. If our polity is to be orderly, these rights must form a harmonious whole. Rights discourse, insofar as it is carried to the level of political theory, consequently rests on two naturalistic assumptions: knowability and harmony. Sad experience reveals that neither assumption can be sustained in a manner sufficiently compelling for the conduct of politics.

Much of rights discourse is no more than the transformation of substantive political goals into human rights language, perhaps most evident in the perennial argument about whether economic and social rights and, *a fortiori*, the so-called third generation or solidarity rights are "real" human rights. But even in the core area of personal freedom and inviolability, agreement reigns only on the general formulation of some rights, such as the right to life, the prevention of torture, and the right to a fair trial. The appearance of consensus is soon dispelled by interpretative controversy: Does the right to life preclude capital punishment? Is solitary confinement "torture"? Is trial by politically elected bureaucrats "fair"? The indeterminacy of human rights language may not be any greater than the indeterminacy of legal rules and principles in general. But the omnipresent debate over rights highlights the fact that such rights cannot *replace* the institutions that are needed to enumerate and interpret them. Rights discourse cannot form a polity because it relies on (conceptually independent) political institutions to define rights. We do not know our rights; we create them through our political processes.

Rights—legally cognizable powers—are scarce resources and are more often than not mutually exclusive. For example, political rights may be achieved only at the cost of economic sustainability, just as free speech overlaps with the right of privacy. Regardless of how we enumerate and construe human rights, we cannot avoid these conflicts. The assumption that human rights exist in some pre-established harmony may only be held with a prior commitment to the kind of naturalism that not only defines rights as coterminous with each other, but in doing so, also provides an inherently authoritarian standpoint towards existing conflict.[9]

Insofar as we do not understand political controversy between the substance and the delimitation of a human right as requiring the

8. *Cf.* THEODOR MERON, HUMAN RIGHTS AND HUMANITARIAN NORMS AS CUSTOMARY LAW (1989).

9. *Cf.* SIR ISAIAH BERLIN, *Two Concepts of Liberty*, in FOUR ESSAYS ON LIBERTY (1969).

determination of the right's essence, that is, insofar as naturalism is not an option for the resolution of political conflict, we can only conclude that as a set of social norms, human rights owe their existence and meaning to decision-making processes. There is no reason to construe those processes in such a way that one political position would be permanently privileged. Thus, something very much like the (ideal) liberal state, which aims to maintain the integrity of the decision-making process, may be a precondition for the proper administration of human rights.

II. NATIONALISM AND STATEHOOD

Recent European events may have detached the concept of self-determination from its former, almost exclusively anti-colonial connotation. Some have claimed that national self-determination is "the most important basic ideological principle of the 1990's."[10] Nationhood may now justify both the abolishment of states, as in German unification and calls for an "Arab nation," as well as breaking states apart, as in the cases of Czechoslovakia, Yugoslavia, and the Soviet Union. The recognition of "Palestine" as a state for the purposes of the United Nations may bear an element of fiction, but there is no fiction in the law's clear provision for a future Palestinian state.

Nationhood, however, cannot determine statehood because "nation" is equally a political construct. Popular "proto-nationalistic" affiliations based on language, ethnicity, religion, or history are not sufficient to establish a nation, although they may significantly contribute to its self-definition.[11] Such affiliations, from which the nation allegedly can be derived, are meant to ground the institution of the nation in the human condition, but in fact encompass a wide variety of political arrangements. While the Finnish language may indeed be relevant to Finnish nationalism, this can hardly be the case for English. Indian nationhood is capable of accommodating the widest variety of linguistic groupings, while some multiethnic nations like the United States may establish part of their national identity precisely on the elimination of such variety. No "natural" affinity organizes people into discrete groups among which power may be distributed. What may have been President Wilson's vision—an international system of natural national communities—has proved a mirage. The definition of a nation remains a matter of political struggle, which in each case enlists support by invoking popular feelings of affinity, and which may even create the social phenomena to be shared, such as a vernacular lan-

10. László Lengyel, *Europe Through Hungarian Eyes*, 66 INT'L AFF. 291, 291 (1990).
11. *See* ERIC J. HOBSBAWM, NATIONS AND NATIONALISM SINCE 1780, 46–79 (1990).

guage.[12] In many cases, statehood, or the will to statehood, is prior to nationalism; in all cases, statehood, like other institutions and affinities, is a matter of contest rather that reception.

Calls for national self-determination will continue to be used in the traditional way—to reinforce the mass appeal of political movements. Wilson used it to oppose Bolshevism, and today Walesa uses it for essentially the same reason. Both socialists and religious fundamentalists have found and will continue to find use for it. But inasmuch as we lack the naturalist knowledge about the "correct" principle of communal identification, the law will have to remain selective: our attitude towards particular nationalisms will continue to depend on our evaluation of the substance of the types of communal life advanced by their alternatives.

III. WORLD ORDER AND STATEHOOD

Modernity appears "inherently globalising."[13] Many forms of contemporary culture, such as architecture, food, popular life style, and fashion, have become ubiquitous. At the same time, there has been a qualitative change in the conditions of political life in the latter part of the twentieth century. Michael Donelan notes:

> In the past, each country had separate fundamental problems; the present problems face all men in all countries; they are common problems . . . . The problems and their solutions . . . are beyond the capacity of 150 separate states. The old political organisation of the world corresponds no longer to the technological abilities and appetites of modern man and the consequent dangers.[14]

Yet this is old news to international lawyers, who presume an international polity, the laws of which they practice. Against this background, international lawyers have worried about the persistent étatism of the international polity, and consequently of international law.

Two kinds of criticism of statehood have been common, a moral and a sociological criticism. Moral critics have argued that the very notion of sovereign statehood strengthens the national egoism that has been responsible for so many of the cataclysms of the present century. From this perspective, we should replace self-interested behavior with behavior that conforms to global conceptions of justice. Today, this rhetoric is heard in reference to achieving a more equitable economic

12. *Id.* at 112–19.
13. ANTHONY GIDDENS, THE CONSEQUENCES OF MODERNITY 63 (1990).
14. Michael Donelan, *A Community of Mankind*, in THE COMMUNITY OF STATES 140, 142 (James Mayall ed. 1982). *See generally* EVAN LUARD, THE GLOBALIZATION OF POLITICS (1990).

distribution among states, but the beliefs are equally expressed by those advocating a general turn from hard and fast rules to flexible standards of reasonableness and international equity.

By contrast, sociological critics stress the factual interdependence that has made "sovereignty" a tenuous fiction. Global capitalism has marginalized the role of national governments to adjusting the national economy to cyclical economic fluxes of essentially global character.[15] Similarly, "natural processes do not stop at human frontiers, but can be controlled only through the free cooperation of people and governments from many (if not all) countries and states."[16] The efforts of individual states may also be insufficient to tackle such problems as AIDS, international terrorism, drug trafficking, and the control of transnational commercial business.

It is unclear, however, what force either of these criticisms have. If they are intended to imply more than the truism that states should cooperate to solve important problems, they tend toward a vantage point—a set of rules or institutions—somewhere outside state policy which should determine the course of action to be taken.

Replacing the *raison d'état* with global justice would transform public international law into a set of instrumental rules which attempt to realize the pre-existing global ideal. Such an ideal, of course, remains vulnerable to the Enlightenment suspicion of substantive notions of universal justice. The liberal version of the Rule of Law—the establishment of formal procedures as the basis of legality—was constructed in order to *avoid* having to rely on unverifiable, and consequently manipulable, notions of a contextless, natural Good. Today, the ascertainment of universal values remains a search for compromise between conflicting value systems. In this political struggle something like a formal, procedural state system helps to prevent adherents to opposing values from resorting to corporal violence. Understandably, calls for world order tend to concentrate more on the creation of global institutions and procedures than the distillation of global values.

A procedural approach is further buttressed by the sociological criticism that argues for the establishment of functional institutions to manage global affairs. For example, the Hague declaration on global action concerning the environment, signed in 1989 by high representatives of twenty-four countries, culminates in suggesting the creation of a "new institutional authority" and the enhancement of the role of the International Court of Justice.[17] In addition, the development of

15. *See generally* IMMANUEL WALLERSTEIN, THE POLITICS OF THE WORLD-ECONOMY: THE STATES, THE MOVEMENTS, AND THE CIVILIZATIONS (1984).

16. STEPHEN E. TOULMIN, COSMOPOLIS: THE HIDDEN AGENDA OF MODERNITY 205 (1990).

17. Hague Declaration on the Environment, 28 I.L.M. 1308 (1989).

international environmental law has led to suggestions for improving the procedural mechanisms of prior notification, consultation, and the establishment of "regimes," instead of substantive standards for environmental quality.[18] The U.N. Convention on the Law of the Sea—a world order instrument par excellence—created a massive procedural framework to govern the oceans. By dividing competences and jurisdiction, as well as creating institutions for cooperation, the Convention avoids taking a stand on difficult questions regarding the permissible uses of the oceans, and defers decision on those uses to the mechanisms established.[19]

The realists have been correct to point out that instead of the enforcement of a pre-existing harmony of interests, the task of such institutions consists of the establishment and arrangement of priorities.[20] The official ideology of the U.N. Conference on Environment and Development (UNCED) compels diplomats to speak of environmental and developmental goals as if there were no essential conflict between them, by defining one in terms of the other. Poverty is pollution; environmental quality is an aspect of the standard of living. Such harmony is soon dispelled when concrete action is debated. Agreements on institutions and procedures for decision-making may postpone and partially veil conflict, but they cannot eradicate it. Action remains a matter of compromise and adjustment by the participating states, but within global institutions. All the talk about a world economy or global interdependence is not likely to prevent the emergence of protectionism as a result of the failure of GATT negotiators to agree. A more communal world is not so much a matter of the universal acceptance of some sociological "facts" as it is of sharing values. Since any conceivable consensus of values will include the redistribution of wealth, such consensus will not be easily attained.

Sociologists have argued that the globalization of popular culture is essentially the proliferation of simulacra of once true, authentic artifacts that conveyed a sense of, and ultimately helped constitute, community.[21] Contemporary culture, by contrast, focuses on symbols and values that have been disembedded from the conditions of life as we experience them. Thus distanced from the particular contexts in which audiences inevitably stand, our simulacra are incapable of compelling the level of altruism required by redistributory management.

---

18. For a recent example, see *Conclusions of the Siena Forum on International Law of the Environment*, 45 U.N. GAOR Annex (Agenda Items 79, 80, 81, 138), U.N. Doc. A/45/666 (1990).

19. *Cf.* Philip Allott, *Power Sharing in the Law of the Sea*, 77 AM. J. INT'L L. 1 (1983).

20. *Cf.* EDWARD H. CARR, THE TWENTY YEARS' CRISIS 1919 - 1939 (1939).

21. For a discussion of "simulacrum," see JEAN BAUDRILLARD, *Simulacra and Simulations*, in SELECTED WRITINGS 166 (1988).

In sum, our rhetoric—mere simulacra but the vessels of our meanings nonetheless—is not powerful enough to realize our express commitments.

Shared vocabulary does not necessarily entail unity of purpose. Rather, it exists in order to allow states to address one another. One international lawyer has observed that during his long career, international law has functioned as such "a universal juridical language" that there was "never any difficulty in recognizing the structure and meaning of a colleague's legal argument."[22] The global rhetoric of diplomats—"only one earth"—implies an acknowledgment that the environment must be discussed, but without making any deep commitment to change. The mythical harmony of interests, including environmental interests, remains an insufficient justification for action. As we have recently discovered, states may be unanimous in their wish to establish a "Decade of International Law" and remain at the same time completely divided in determining what sorts of substance should be enhanced by it.[23]

IV. THEORIZING THE CHALLENGES

The values of the international system as expressed in public international law are those of liberal individualism transposed to the inter-state level. The system denies the existence of an external standard of judgment that is valid regardless of whether it is held by states themselves. Its law, Louis Henkin observed recently, "is designed to further each state's realization of its own notion of the Good."[24] The "system" exists only in the formal sense of a shared vocabulary and a set of institutional practices that states use for cooperation or conflict. It is an artificial creation, a contrived synthesis of power and ideas. In short, it is not an organism that embodies some autonomous ideal of authentic communal life.

This is the understanding of the present state system shared and challenged by each of the discourses discussed above: human rights, nationalism, and world order. Each posits an ideal of *authenticity* outside the system that contrasts with the formal and artificial character of statehood. These ideals, however, cannot be sustained within liberal political rhetoric. To the contrary, their enforcement might

22. Robert Y. Jennings, *An International Lawyer Takes Stock*, 39 INT'L & COMP. LAW Q. 513, 526–27 (1990).

23. The first two-year program of the Decade is a procedural call for studies and suggestions on the peaceful settlement of disputes and for the support of the teaching, study, and wider dissemination of international law. *See* G.A. Res. 45/40, 45 U.N. GAOR Annex at 654, U.N. Doc. A/45/733 (1990).

24. Louis Henkin, *Law and Politics in International Relations*, 44 J. INT'L AFF. 183, 186 (1990).

appear as precisely the kind of authoritarianism against which the state system was created.

Human rights discourse builds on the psychological assumption of an authentic self and a normative rejoinder regarding the character of communal life as an instrument for the realization of the self's authentic potential. As we have seen, the difficulty with this assumption is the absence of agreement about the content of that authenticity, that is, what should actually be held to be inalienable "human" rights. Perhaps our lack of consensus is more than ignorance about our true natures. Perhaps no authentic self exists. Instead of a socially circumscribed instantiation of human nature, personhood itself is likely to be a social construct. But if the self is more like a bottomless pit than a set of determinate potentials, any rigorous effort to ground society on personal self-realization would do away with normativity altogether. Under these circumstances, a demand for self-fulfillment and its corollary, a general presumption against restricting liberty, accompanied by an absence of faith in a natural law—a set of natural constraints on liberty—argues for Leviathan. A generalized call for unmitigated, compulsive egoism is bound to make social life impossible, and thereby justify an authoritarian reaction for the purpose of restoring order and protecting everyone's "real interests."

A social construct such as a "nation," accompanied by the official ideology which denies its social background and claims to exemplify an ideal of authentic communal life, is a powerful political weapon. I may find sympathy for it in its irredentist form, and I may, for example, applaud Baltic nationalism in the face of Soviet tanks. But its étatist version tends to become a justification for expulsion, massacre, and fascism. Just as human rights are a beneficial, if not necessary, aspect of communal life, nationalism may be, too, when used for the correct political causes.

We also have little reason to be confident that some subject-matters—such as peace, economy, and the environment—are authentically global and must be dealt with by globally uniform solutions. The types of social life constituting or advancing "true peace," "a stable economy," or "a healthy environment" are determined with reference to political values. The increasing recourse to justice, equity, and general principles by international lawyers resembles the turn in national societies away from the *Rechtstaat* into a more contextually responsive social order. Thus, the paradox emerges in that universalizing, although still indeterminate, rhetoric in fact contextualizes the law. As flexible standards tend to increase the power of the institutions which intend to apply them, the *dédoublement fonctionnelle* guarantees that states remain in control.

Calls for both localizing and globalizing authenticity reflect what some have called a turn to post-modernity in contemporary political culture.[25] Disappointed with modernism's cold rationalism and the incapability of democratic politics to attain the good life, people look elsewhere: to ideals of (lost) authenticity, assimilation into some given ideal, a true self, a natural affinity within the nation, and a natural just order for the world. But suggested notions of authenticity, when applied to particular areas of politics, have turned out to reflect only partial, more controversial aspects of social life. To become acceptable, such notions have been transformed from the carriers of authentic substance into simulacra, vessels that labor under the constraint that their practical significance will be measured in conclusive acts of institutional definition and application that reinforce the centrality of statehood in the exercise of power.

By establishing and consenting to human rights limitations on their own sovereignty, states actually define, delimit, and contain those rights, thereby domesticating their use and affirming the authority of the state as the source from which such rights spring. Nationalism tends to work in a similar fashion, not only as a substantive aspiration threatening statehood but also as a remarkable instrument supporting statehood. If the revolution in Eastern Europe is now followed by frustration, this may reflect a mass realization that the revolution failed to provide a compelling sense of authenticity to society. Thus, one set of state apparatuses was replaced by another, sturdier ideology in 1989.

The most universally acclaimed principles of international law continue to be those of sovereignty, self-determination, territorial integrity, non-intervention, and consent, each of which is a reaffirmation of statehood as the law's creative center. "Universalist" projects like the New International Economic Order tend to show at their core the enhancement of national independence and self-determination in economic matters. Despite the rhetoric of "common heritage" in the U.N. Convention on the Law of the Sea, the Convention legitimized a system whereby forty percent of the oceans' surface was brought under national control. Using procedure, internationalism reaffirms statehood while at the same time, shared statehood provides the basis of procedural internationalism. To this point, Guyora Binder has noted that "[t]he discourse of international law contains contradictory propositions because it is carried on in the context of a culture profoundly ambivalent about the legitimacy of international institutions."[26]

There is little doubt that the direct applicability of European Community law is *sui generis* and constitutes an important encroachment

25. *Cf.* David Harvey, The Condition of Postmodernity 299–307 (1989); Toulmin, *supra* note 16, at 205–09.

26. Guyora Binder, Treaty Conflict and Political Contradiction: The Dialectic of Duplicity 120 (1988).

on the freedom of action by Member States, which will be further reduced by the completion of the internal market at the end of 1992. Whether this challenges the statehood of Member States, however, is another matter. Plans for a European political union remain relatively ambiguous and prospective.[27] The Single European Act of 1986[28] establishes an essentially consultative machinery for the coordination of the external policy of the Member States. Their distinct identities seem to be confirmed internally by their role in the Community's decision-making process and confirmed externally by their coordinated foreign policies. Still, even if the union were to emerge in its maximalist form, that event would likely signify no more than the creation of a new state—the United States of Europe—rather than any derogation from the principle of statehood as such.

Statehood survives and should continue to survive for the foreseeable future because its formal-bureaucratic rationality provides a safeguard against the totalitarianism inherent in a commitment to substantive values, which forces those values on people not sharing them. Indeed, it may be that the failure of established political parties to offer authentic political alternatives will only leave us with the choice either of accepting the rule of the market or of buttressing the sort of bureaucratic policy-making by state organs that we have witnessed in Western Europe during the past few years.[29]

V. THE LIMITS OF STATEHOOD

These reflections and the practical validity of the relativism they imply do not require an unreserved commitment to statehood as the ideal, or even ultimate, matrix for organizing thought and action in international life. Statehood remains a second best—defensible but only to the extent that there can be no general agreement about the authentic purpose of social life. Whether or not the state is an institution worthy of protection by international law depends on the extent to which its legal order translates local political conflict into reasoned compromise. Too easily, as A.V. Lowe has stated, "[w]hat begins as an attempt to guarantee freedom from foreign oppression is perverted into a veil to be drawn over domestic oppression."[30] But statehood has its reasons—it is not a naturalist *deus ex machina*. If and when

27. *Cf.* Report of the European Council meeting of 25–26 June 1990, Bull. EC 6-1990 at 15–17.

28. Single European Act, Bull. EC Suppl. 2/86.

29. *Cf.* GIANFRANCO POGGI, THE STATE: ITS NATURE, DEVELOPMENT AND PROSPECTS 129–41 (1990).

30. A.V. Lowe, *Peace without Justice: Reconsidering the Law on the Use of Force*, in PERESTROIKA AND INTERNATIONAL LAW 281, 284 (William E. Butler ed. 1990).

those reasons do not exist, statehood can claim no particular protection.

There is another important reason why statehood alone is an insufficient basis for international law. The status of statehood can be associated with various sets of rights and duties. It carries no given, determinate, normative implications. Much has been written about the apparent puzzle that statehood is a quality enjoyed both by states that have entered into extensive integration obligations, as well as by states living in hermetic isolation.[31] In other words, we cannot deduce the extent of a state's freedom of action from the mere fact of its statehood. Sovereignty is, as the Permanent Court of International Justice noted in 1923, an "essentially relative question"—dependent on whatever law there is to curtail it.[32]

Any international conflict juxtaposes the freedom of action of two or more states. All conflict resolution involves boundary determination, or the delimitation of one sovereign's freedom of action against that of another. We cannot look for justification in statehood because our task consists precisely of giving statehood some normative sense. To decide boundary disputes without violating sovereign equality, we are limited to criteria that are hierarchically more important than statehood to provide a justification for drawing its limit in some particular way.

This is perhaps most vividly illustrated in conflicts over territory or natural resources. In such cases, the disputing states unilaterally devise an interpretation of their statehood that covers the desired assets. Because statehood implies no particular extent of the state's sphere of freedom, such cases cannot be understood as simply giving effect to a limit that is somehow "already" there. As the practice of the International Court of Justice has shown, such disputes require the construction of an "equitable" solution rather than the determination of any rights and duties existing *ex ante*.[33]

In a similar fashion, environmental pollution typically opposes the sovereignty of the source state with the sovereignty of the target state. From the former's perspective, the conflict concerns its right to engage in economically beneficial activities within its own borders. The latter sees the issue in terms of its right to territorial integrity and inviolability. Both states are capable of describing their statehood in such a fashion as to contain their preferred norm. If statehood does not have any determined limit, and if no rule is determining, then we can only

31. *See, e.g.*, ALAN JAMES, SOVEREIGN STATEHOOD (1986).

32. Nationality Decrees in Tunis and Morocco, (advisory opinion) 1923 P.C.I.J. (ser. B) No. 4, at 24.

33. *See* North Sea Continental Shelf Cases (W.Ger. v. Den./W.Ger. v. Neth.), 1969 I.C.J. 22, and compare with Continental Shelf (Tunisia v. Libyan Arab Jamahiriya), 1982 I.C.J. 59.

construct a decision in the light of whatever contextually applicable criteria we might find. We seem compelled to insist on contextuality so as not to imply that we impose some generally applicable scheme of the good life which we either cannot defend without going beyond our own legal rhetoric or which remains so general as to be useless.

The adjudications of the permissible limits of extraterritorial jurisdiction and of the conditions for permissible intervention are structurally identical. In each, two freedoms of action and two unilateral views about the permissible extent of such freedoms counter each other. No defining rules exist that can be applied "automatically." It is consequently unsurprising that both doctrine and practice resort to contextualizing formulae such as "balance of interests," "reasonableness," "proportionality," and the like. In deciding such cases, reference to statehood entails a *non-sequitur*. Each state's statehood is at issue, and each possesses a *prima facie* plausible conception of it. The construction of rights and duties—giving substance to statehood—remains a matter of political adjustment, and of finding a contextual equilibrium in particular circumstances.[34]

It is possible that the growing uncertainty about authenticity and truth in late modern experience finds a parallel in lawyers' anxiety about the omnipresent indeterminacy of legal concepts (such as the state) and rules (such as non-intervention). The result, whatever the cause, has either been a doctrinal and practical turn towards equally indeterminate, less pretentious and more responsive notions of reasonableness, balance, and justice,[35] or a complete rejection of normativity and a reexamination of the workings of international law's conceptual structures.[36]

VI. FORM OR SUBSTANCE?

The preoccupation of international lawyers with change in the international system may be connected with the more general turn in contemporary thought and experience from bureaucratic formalism to substantive ideals of communal life. Just as the responsiveness of the strictly formal *Rechtsstaat* to these ideals appears inadequate, the extreme rationalism of the Westphalian system may also seem responsible for such unacceptable consequences as economic disparity and the permanent threat of nuclear war.

---

34. *Cf.* MARTTI KOSKENNIEMI, FROM APOLOGY TO UTOPIA, THE STRUCTURE OF INTERNATIONAL LEGAL ARGUMENT 220–36, 410–21, 431–57 (1989).

35. For the doctrinal turn, see THOMAS M. FRANCK, THE POWER OF LEGITIMACY AMONG NATIONS (1990); ANTHONY CARTY, THE DECAY OF INTERNATIONAL LAW? (1986).

36. DAVID KENNEDY, INTERNATIONAL LEGAL STRUCTURES (1986).

Despite the dismantling of both intermediate-range nuclear weapons and the Berlin Wall, the romantic ideal of a "new world order" based on substantive values that transcend statehood may not have come much closer to realization. People still disagree about the political good. In normal circumstances, states still provide the means to direct substantive disagreement into institutionalized debate. When such disagreement extends beyond the state, it is soon formalized into regular diplomatic intercourse.

At the time that I wrote this, war had begun in the Gulf, and the Soviet Union had increased military pressure on the Baltic republics. Both crises involved statehood: the former involved an attempt to restore it, the latter an effort to preserve the boundaries claimed by one state and to prevent the creation of a new state. In these cases, statehood no longer performs its formalizing function of channeling political debate into institutions. As the Marxist critique once claimed, form has become a camouflage for substance. Statehood has become a pretense for enforcing politics. Attempts to discuss these situations as if they only manifested a formal-legal difficulty about "right to statehood" sound increasingly hollow. Inasmuch as statehood, too, has its substantive reasons, it is difficult to see how international lawyers could discuss these two cases without invoking *those* substances. This, of course, creates difficulties for an agnostic legal rhetoric, denying its reliance on any particular substance. Nonetheless, it challenges international lawyers to formulate and agree upon some very basic ideals of communal life, however tentative. Without this, it is hard to see how we might feel justified in looking beyond today's crises with any confidence in a shared future.

Part V
Is International Law Neutral?

[13]

The Politics of International Law

Martti Koskenniemi *

I. The Flight from Politics

It may be a matter of some controversy among historians as to when one should date the beginning of the modern states-system.[1] Less open to debate, however, is that somehow the idea of such a system is historically as well as conceptually linked with that of an international Rule of Law. In a system whose units are assumed to serve no higher purpose than their own interests and which assumes the perfect equality of those interests, the Rule of Law seems indeed the sole thinkable principle of organization – short of the *bellum omnium*. Since the publication of Emmerich de Vattel's *Droit des gens ou principes de la loi naturelle appliquées à la conduite et aux affaires des nations et des souverains* (1758), jurists have written about international matters by assuming that the liberal principles of the Enlightenment and their logical corollary, the Rule of Law, could be extended to apply in the organization of international society just as they had been used in the domestic one.[2]

Notwithstanding the historical difficulty with dates and origins, the connexion between the Rule of law and the principles of the Enlightenment appear evident. Of

* Permanent Mission of Finland to the United Nations.

1 For example, A.F. von der Heydte: *Geburtstunde des souveränen Staates* (1952) suggests the turn of the 14th century, 41-43, while F.H. Hinsley: *Power and the Pursuit of Peace.*(1962), 153, argues that one cannot properly speak of a states-system until the 18th century.

2 The analogy is explicit in J.J. Rousseau: *The Social Contract* (trans. & introd. by Maurice Cranston) (1986) Bk.I Ch. 7 at 63; J. Locke, *Two Treatises on Government* (intr. by W.S. Carpenter) (1984) Second Treatise, sect. 183 at 211. For commentary, see, e.g., P. Vinogradoff, *Historical Types of International Law* (1920), 55-57; E.D. Dickinson, *The Equality of States in International Law* (1920), 29-31, 49-50, 97-98, 111-113. See also M. Walzer, *Just and Unjust Wars* (1980), 58-63; C.L. Beitz, *Political Theory and International Relations* (1979) 74. For useful analysis of the effect of the analogy to the conception of a state's (territorial) rights, see A. Carty, *The Decay of International Law?* (1986) 44-46, 55-56.

the latter, none seems more important than that of the subjectivity of value.[3] Hobbes writes:

> For one calleth wisdom what another calleth fear and one cruelty what another justice; and prodigality what another magnanimity... And therefrom such names can never be ground for any ratiocination.[4]

However much later liberals may have disliked Hobbes' substantive conclusions or his political realism, the one thing which unites them with Hobbes is their criticism of relying upon natural principles to justify political authority. Appealing to principles which would pre-exist man and be discoverable only through faith or *recta ratio* was to appeal to abstract and unverifiable maximums which only camouflaged the subjective preferences of the speaker. It was premised on utopian ideals which were constantly used as apologies for tyranny.

From the simple denial of the existence of principles of natural justice – or at least of our capacity to know them – follow the three liberal principles of social organization: freedom, equality and the Rule of Law. If man is not born to a world of pre-existing norms, then he is born free; if there are no antecedent principles establishing the relative worths of individuals, the individuals must be assumed equal. And finally, freedom and equality are guaranteed only if social constraint is governed by public, verifiable and determining rules: "A free people obey but it does not serve; it has magistrates but not masters; it obeys nothing but the laws, and thanks to the force of laws, it does not obey men."[5]

The fight for an international Rule of Law is a fight against politics, understood as a matter of furthering subjective desires and leading into an international anarchy. Though some measure of politics is inevitable, it should be constrained by non-political rules: "...the health of the political realm is maintained by conscientious objection to the political."[6]

The diplomatic history of the 19th century is a history of such a fight. Since the Vienna Congress of 1814-15 and the defeat of Napoleon, the relations between European powers were no longer built on one power's search for primacy but on a general pursuit of the maintenance of the balance of power, guaranteed by complicated legal procedures and alliances.[7] As contemporaries increasingly saw Europe as a "system" of independent and equal political communities (instead of a *respublica*

3 My discussion of this principle is influenced by R.M. Unger, *Knowledge and Politics* (1975) 76-81, and A. MacIntyre, After Virtue; A Study in Moral Theory (2nd ed.) (1985) 6-35.

4 T. Hobbes, *Leviathan* (ed. & intr. by C.B. Macpherson) (1982) Ch. 4, at 109-110.

5 J.J. Rousseau, *Œuvres complètes*, Pléiade (Vol. III sect. 841-2) quoted by Cranston (Introduction to J.J. Rousseau, *The Social Contract*, *supra* note 2, at 32).

6 Wight, 'Western Values in International Relations', in Butterfield, Wight, *Diplomatic Investigations; Essays in the Theory of International Politics* (1966) 122.

7 See, e.g., F.H. Hinsley, *supra* note 1, at 186-271.

Christiana) they began to assume that the governing principles needed to become neutral and objective – that is, legal.

The legal scholarship of the 19th century interpreted and systematized diplomatic practice into legal rules. It assumed that the behavior of European states was determined and explicable by reference to a body of (European) public law. The plausibility of this assumption relied on the procedural character of that law. Containing mainly rules concerning diplomatic and consular contacts, procedures for attaining statehood, territory or neutral status, it did not severely restrict the ends which European sovereigns attempted to pursue. In particular, it renounced theories of the just war: war became now one political procedure among others.[8] Though the professional lawyers of the 19th century did speak about justice in the conduct of the sovereigns' affairs, they no longer thought of justice as material principles. Woolsey put the matter adroitly:

> By justice, however, we intend not justice objective, but as it appears to the party concerned or, at least, as it is claimed to exist. From the independence of nations it results that each has a right to hold and make good its own view of right in its own affairs.[9]

Though 20th-century lawyers have not looked too kindly upon the scholarship of the preceding century, they never rejected the ideal of the Rule of Law. On the contrary, the reconstructive scholarship which emerged first from the catastrophe of the First World War and then in the 1950s and 1960s accused the pre-war doctrines of *not going far enough* to uphold the Rule of Law. Wherever attempts by jurists to construct a solid framework of public law had faltered, it had done so not because of some defect in the liberal assumptions behind this project but because jurists had deviated from them.

The vision of a Rule of Law between states (which re-emerged most recently in United Nations General Assembly Resolution 44/23 [15 November 1989] declaring the period 1990-1999 as the "United Nations Decade of International Law") is yet another reformulation of the liberal impulse to escape politics. So strong is the grip of this vision that the representative of the Soviet Union at the same session of the General Assembly explained that in his view to restructure the basis of international relations there was a need to "arrive at a comprehensive international strategy for establishing the primacy of law in relations between states."[10]

Throughout the present century, reconstructive doctrines have claimed that what merits criticism is the corruption of the Rule of Law either in the narrow chauvin-

8 See, e.g., H. Wheaton, *Elements of International Law* (Text of 1866 with Notes, Carnegie Endowment, Classics of International Law, No. 19) (1936) 313-4.

9 T.D. Woolsey, *Introduction to the Study of International Law; Designed as an Aid in Teaching, and in Historical Studies* (5th ed.) (1879) 183.

10 'Memorandum: On Enhancing the Role of International Law', UN Doc.A/44/585 (2 October 1989).

ism of diplomats or the speculative utopias of an academic elite. If only the Rule of Law can be fortified to exclude these contrasting distortions, then at least the jurist's part in the construction of a just world order has been adequately executed.

In this article, however, I shall extend the criticism of the liberal idea of the *Rechtstaat*, a commonplace in late modern western society,[11] into its international counterpart. I shall attempt to show that our inherited ideal of a World Order based on the Rule of Law thinly hides from sight the fact that social conflict must still be solved by political means and that even though there may exist a common legal rhetoric among international lawyers, that rhetoric must, *for reasons internal to the ideal itself*, rely on essentially contested – political – principles to justify outcomes to international disputes.[12]

II. The Content of the Rule of Law: Concreteness and Normativity

Organizing society through legal rules is premised on the assumption that these rules are objective in some sense that political ideas, views, or preferences are not. To show that international law is objective – that is, independent from international politics – the legal mind fights a battle on two fronts. On the one hand, it aims to ensure the *concreteness* of the law by distancing it from theories of natural justice. On the other hand, it aims to guarantee the *normativity* of the law by creating distance between it and actual state behaviour, will, or interest. Law enjoys independence from politics only if both of these conditions are simultaneously present.

The requirement of concreteness results from the liberal principle of the subjectivity of value. To avoid political subjectivism and illegitimate constraint,[13] we must base law on something concrete – on the actual (verifiable) behaviour, will and interest of the members of society-states. The modern view is a *social conception of law*.[14] For it, law is not a natural but an artificial creation, a reflexion of social circumstances.

11 For the ensuing text, particularly relevant are criticisms stressing the *internal* tensions of liberal theory. See generally Unger, *supra* note 3, at 63-103 and, e.g., A. Levine, *Liberal democracy; A Critique of its Theory* (1981) 16-32; Fishkin, 'Liberal Theory and the Problem of Justification', *NOMOS* XXVIII at 207-231.

12 This article is a condensed version of some of the themes in M. Koskenniemi, *From Apology to Utopia; the Structure of International Legal Argument* (1989).

13 For a typical argument stressing the political character of natural law, see, e.g., S. Sur, *L'interprétation en droit international public* (1974) 25-32 or J.H.W. Verzijl, *International Law in Historical Perspective* (Vol. I) (1968) 391-3.

14 'C'est à une conception fonctionnelle de pouvoir, à une conception sociale du droit que s'attache notre enseignement', De Visscher, 'Cours général de principes de droit international public', 86 *RCDI* (1954) 451.

According to the requirement of normativity, law should be applied regardless of the political preferences of legal subjects. In particular, it should be applicable even against a state which opposes its application to itself. As international lawyers have had the occasion to point out, legal rules whose content or application depends on the will of the legal subject for whom they are valid are not proper legal rules at all but apologies for the legal subject's political interest.[15]

Stated in such a fashion, I believe that the requirements of legal objectivity *vis-à-vis* political subjectivity are met. For if the law could be verified or justified only by reference to somebody's views on what the law *should* be like (i.e. theories of justice), it would coincide with their political opinions. Similarly, if we could apply the law against those states which accept it, then it would coincide with those states' political views.

This argumentative structure, however, which forces jurists to prove that their law is valid because concrete and normative in the above sense, both creates and destroys itself. For it is impossible to prove that a rule, principle or doctrine (in short, an argument) is both concrete and normative simultaneously. The two requirements *cancel each other.* An argument about concreteness is an argument about the closeness of a particular rule, principle or doctrine to state practice. But the closer to state practice an argument is, the less normative and the more political it seems. The more it seems just another apology for existing power. An argument about normativity, on the other hand, is an argument which intends to demonstrate the rule's distance from state will and practice. The more normative a rule, the more political it seems because the less it is possible to argue it by reference to social context. It seems utopian and – like theories of natural justice – manipulable at will.

The dynamics of international legal argument are provided by the constant effort of lawyers to show that their law is either concrete or normative and their becoming thus vulnerable to the charge that such law is in fact political because apologist or utopian. Different doctrinal and practical controversies turn on transformations of this dilemma. It lies behind such dichotomies as "positivism"/"naturalism", "consent"/"justice", "autonomy"/"community", "process"/"rule", etc., and explains why these and other oppositions keep recurring and do not seem soluble in a permanent way. They recur because it seems possible to defend one's legal argument only by showing either its closeness to, or its distance from, state practice. They seem insoluble because both argumentative strategies are vulnerable to what appear like valid criticisms, compelled by the system itself.[16]

This provides an argumentative structure which is capable of providing a valid criticism of each substantive position but which itself cannot justify any. The fact

15 See, e.g., H. Lauterpacht, *The Function of Law in the International Community* (1933) 189 and *passim*.

16 For an alternative but similar type of exposition, see D. Kennedy, *International Legal Structure* (1987)

that positions are constantly taken and solutions justified by lawyers, demonstrates that the structure does not possess the kind of distance from politics for which the Rule of Law once seemed necessary. It seems possible to adopt a position only by a political choice: a choice which must ultimately defend itself in terms of a conception of justice.

III. Doctrinal Structures

Two criticisms are often advanced against international law. One group of critics has accused international law of being too political in the sense of being too dependent on states' political power. Another group has argued that the law is too political because founded on speculative utopias. The standard point about the non-existence of legislative machineries, compulsory adjudication and enforcement procedures captures both criticisms. From one perspective, this criticism highlights the infinite flexibility of international law, its character as a manipulable facade for power politics. From another perspective, the criticism stresses the moralistic character of international law, its distance from the realities of power politics. According to the former criticism, international law is too *apologetic* to be taken seriously in the construction of international order. According to the latter, it is too *utopian* to the identical effect.

International lawyers have had difficulty answering these criticisms. The more reconstructive doctrines have attempted to prove the normativity of the law, its autonomy from politics, the more they have become vulnerable to the charge of utopianism. The more they have insisted on the close connexion between international law and state behaviour, the less normative their doctrines have appeared. Let me outline the four positions which modern international lawyers have taken to prove the relevance of their norms and doctrines. These are mutually exclusive and logically exhaustive positions and account for a full explanation of the possibilities of doctrinal argument.

Many of the doctrines which emerged from the ashes of legal scholarship at the close of the First World War explained the failure of pre-war international doctrines by reference to their apologist character. Particular objects of criticism were "absolutist" doctrines of sovereignty, expressed in particular in the *Selbstverpflichtunglehre*, doctrines stressing the legal significance of the balance of power or delimiting the legal functions to matters which were unrelated to questions of "honour" or "vital interest." Writings by Hersch Lauterpacht, Alfred Verdross and Hans Kelsen among others, created an extremely influential interpretation of the mistakes of pre-war doctrines.[17] By associating the failure of those doctrines with their excessive

[17] Lauterpacht, *supra* note 15; A. Verdross, *Die Verfassung der Völkerrechtsgemeinschaft* (1926); H. Kelsen, *Das Problem der Souveränität und die Theorie des Völkerrechts* (1920).

closeness to state policy and national interest and by advocating the autonomy of international legal rules, these jurists led the way to the establishment of what could be called a *rule approach* to international law, stressing the law's normativity, its capacity to oppose state policy as the key to its constraining relevance.

This approach insists on an objective, formal test of pedigree (sources) which will tell which standards qualify as legal rules and which do not. If a rule meets this test, then it is binding. Though there is disagreement between rule approach lawyers over what constitutes the proper test, there is no dispute about its importance. The distinctions between hard and soft law, rules and principles, regular norms and *jus cogens*, for instance, are suspect: these only betray political distinctions with which the lawyer should not be too concerned.[18] Two well-known criticisms have been directed against the rule approach. First, it has remained unable to exclude the influence of political considerations from its assumed tests of pedigree. To concede that rules are sometimes hard to find while their content remains, to adopt H.L.A. Hart's expression "relatively indeterminate"[19] is to undermine the autonomy which the rule approach stressed. Second, the very desire for autonomy seems suspect. A pure theory of law, the assumption of a *Völkerrechtsgemeinschaft* or the ideal of the wholeness of law – a central assumption in most rule approach writing[20] – may only betray forms of irrelevant doctrinal utopianism. They achieve logical consistency at the cost of applicability in the real world of state practice.

The second major position in contemporary scholarship uses these criticisms to establish itself. A major continental interpretation of the mistakes of 19th-century lawyers and diplomats explains them as a result of naive utopianism: an unwarranted belief in the viability of the Congress system, with its ideas of legality and collective intervention. It failed because it had not been able to keep up with the politics of emergent nationalism and the increasing pace of social and technological change. Lawyers such as Nicolas Politis or Georges Scelle stressed the need to link international law much more closely to the social – even biological – necessities of international life.[21] Roscoe Pound's programmatic writings laid the basis for the contemporary formulation of this approach by criticizing the attempt to think of inter-

18 This approach is best illustrated in G. Schwarzenberger, *The Inductive Approach to International Law* (1965). Many of its points are forcefully made in Weil, 'Towards Relative Normativity in International Law', 77 *AJIL* (1983) 413-442. For further references on this and the other approaches, see Koskenniemi, *supra* note 12, at 154-186.

19 H.L.A. Hart, *The Concept of Law* (1961) 132.

20 See, e.g., Lauterpacht, 'Some Observations on the Prohibition of "Non Liquet" and the Completeness of Law', *Symbolae Verzijl* (1958) 196-221 and the "realist" criticism by Stone, 'Non-Liquet and the Function of Law in the International Community', XXV *BYUL* (1959) 124-161.

21 G. Scelle, *Précis de droit des gens. Principes et systématique I-II* (1932, 1936); N. Politis, *Les nouvelles tendances du droit international* (1927).

national law in terms of abstract rules. It was, rather, to be thought of "in terms of social ends."[22]

According to this approach – the *policy approach* – international law can only be relevant if it is firmly based in the social context of international policy. Rules are only trends of past decision which may or may not correspond to social necessities. "Binding force" is a juristic illusion. Standards are, in fact more or less effective and it is their effectiveness – their capacity to further social goals – which is the relevant question, not their formal "validity."[23]

But this approach is just as vulnerable to well-founded criticisms as the rule approach. By emphasizing the law's concreteness, it will ultimately do away with its constraining force altogether. If law is only what is effective, then by definition, it becomes an apology for the interests of the powerful. If, as Myres McDougal does, this consequence is avoided by postulating some "goal values" whose legal importance is independent of considerations of effectiveness, then the (reformed) policy approach becomes vulnerable to criticisms which it originally voiced against the rule approach. In particular, it appears to assume an illegitimate naturalism which – as critics stressing the liberal principle of the subjectivity of value have noted – is in constant danger of becoming just an apology of some states' policies.[24]

The rule and the policy approaches are two contrasting ways of trying to establish the relevance of international law in the face of what appear as well-founded criticisms The former does this by stressing the law's normativity, but fails to be convincing because it lacks concreteness. The latter builds upon the concreteness of international law, but loses the normativity, the binding force of its law. It is hardly surprising, then, that some lawyers have occupied the two remaining positions: they have either assumed that international law can neither be seen as normatively controlling nor widely applied in practice (the sceptical position), or have continued writing as if both the law's binding force as well as its correspondence with developments in international practice were a matter of course (idealist position). The former ends in cynicism, the latter in contradiction.[25]

The late modern mainstream often situates itself between the rule and the policy approaches. In Richard Falk's words, the task of an adequate doctrine is to establish:

22 Pound, 'Philosophical Theory and International Law', I *Bibliotheca Visseiana* (1923) 1-90.

23 The contemporary formulation of this approach is perhaps clearest in McDougal, 'International Law, Power and Policy: A Contemporary Perspective', 82 *RCDI* (1953) 133-259. For useful analysis, see B. Rosenthal, *L'étude de l'œuvre de Myres Smith McDougal en matière du droit international public* (1970).

24 For such criticisms, see, e.g., Allott, 'Language, Method and the Nature of International Law', 45 *BYIL* (1971) 123-125; Boyle, 'Ideals and Things: International Legal Scholarship and the Prison-House of Language', 26 *Harvard Journal Int'l Law* (1985) 349, and Fitzmaurice, 'vae Victis or Woe to the Negotiators!', 65 *AJIL* (1971) 370-373.

25 For references, see Koskenniemi, *supra* note 12, at 167-170, 178-186.

> [a]n intermediate position, one that maintains the distinctiveness of the legal order while managing to be responsive to the extralegal setting of politics, history and morality.[26]

But such a movement towards pragmatic eclecticism seems self-defeating. There is no space between the four positions, rule approach, policy approach, scepticism and idealism. Middle-of-the-road doctrines may seem credible only insofar as their arguments, doctrines or norms are not contested. But as soon as disagreement emerges, such doctrines, too, must defend their positions either by showing their autonomous binding force, or by demonstrating their close relationship with what states actually do. At this point, they become vulnerable to the charge of being either utopian or apologist.

The result is a curiously incoherent doctrinal structure in which each position is *ad hoc* and therefore survives only. Mainstream doctrine retreats into general statements about the need to "combine" concreteness and normativity, realism and idealism, which bear no consequence to its normative conclusion. It then advances, emphasizing the contextuality of each solution – thus undermining its own emphasis on the general and impartial character of its system.

A doctrine's own contradictions force it into an impoverished and unreflective pragmatism. On the one hand, the "idealist" illusion is preserved that law can and does play a role in the organization of social life among states. On the other, the "realist" criticisms have been accepted and the law is seen as distinctly secondary to power and politics. Modern doctrine, as Philip Allott has shown, uses a mixture of positivistic and naturalistic, consensualistic and non-consensualistic, teleological, practical, political, logical and factual arguments in happy confusion, unaware of its internal contradictions.[27] The style survives because we recognize in it the liberal doctrine within which we have been accustomed to press our political arguments.

A final point is in order. Both of the main positions reviewed, as well as their combinations, remain distinctly modern. Each refuses to develop its concept of law in terms of some material theory of justice. Each assumes that law is an artificial, human creation which comes about through social processes and that an adequate concept of law is one which provides a reliable description of those processes. Moreover, each bases its claim to superiority *vis-à-vis* the other on that very description. The point at which they diverge is their theory on how to interpret those processes, how to understand what goes on in social life in terms of law-creation and law-application.

The difficulty in choosing between a rule and a policy approach is the difficulty of defending the set of criteria which these put forward to disentangle "law" from other aspects of state behaviour. For the rule approach lawyer, the relevant criteria

26 Falk, 'The Interplay of Westphalia and Charter Conceptions of the International Legal Order' in R. Falk, Black (eds.), *The Future of the International Legal Order* (Vol. I) (1969) 34-35.

27 Allott, *supra* note 24, at 100-105, 113.

are provided by his theory of sources. For the policy approach, the corresponding criteria are provided by his theory of "base-values", authority or some constellation of national or global interest and need. Because it is these criteria which claim to provide the correct description of social processes, they cannot be defended without circularity in terms of social processes themselves.[28] To decide on the better approach, one would have to base oneself on some non-descriptive (non-social) theory about significance or about the relative justice of the types of law rendered by the two – or any alternative – matrices.[29] Such a decision would, under the social conception of law and the principle of the subjectivity of value, be one which would seem to have no claim for objective correctness at all. It would be a political decision.

IV. Substantive Structures

It is possible to depict the tension between the demands for normativity and concreteness in two contrasting methods of explaining the origin of the law's substance. From the perspective of concreteness, this substance comes about as a consequence of the fact of sovereignty of the state. One aspect of sovereignty is the liberty to "legislate" international norms which bind oneself. Wherever particular norms have not been thus established, the metaprinciple of sovereign liberty – the "Lotus principle" – remains valid.

It is equally possible to understand the law as a consequence of the functioning of normative criteria for law-emergence. From the perspective of normativity, there must be assumed criteria – "sources" – which allow us to distinguish between the fact of the existence and behaviour of certain centres of power (states) and the law. In this sense, all international legal substance is dependent on the content of those criteria. These explanations seem radically conflicting and appear to provide exhaustive but incompatible methods for elucidating the origin and character of international law. Indeed, much of the dispute between "idealists" and "realists", or the rule and policy approaches, seems captured in this contrast, reflected also in the organization of the substance of standard textbooks. One style consists of preceding the law's substance with an analysis of the character of statehood and that of the international order – the "political foundations." Another starts out by listing the sources of international law and lets the law's substance follow therefrom.

28 The point about conceptual matrices, scientific theories, "paradigms", interests of knowledge or prejudices, if not strictly determining what we can know of the social world at least significantly influencing our perception, is a common theme in much modern epistemology. See further Koskenniemi, *supra* note 12, at 466-471.

29 On choosing significant features for description, see, e.g., J. Finnis, *Natural Law and Natural Rights* (1980) 3, 9-18. See also MacIntyre, 'The Indispensability of Political Theory', in Miller, Siedentop, *The Nature of Political Theory* (1983) 19-33.

Despite their initially contrasting outlook, both "methods" rely on each other. "Realist" doctrines use criteria to distinguish between law and coercion which fall short of a doctrine of sources only by not bearing that name. "Idealist" programmes look at state practice to defend the relevance of their sources and to verify the content of the law they support.[30] The fact that the available outlooks provide identical substantive systems and both remain vulnerable to well-rehearsed arguments further explains the late modern turn to doctrinal pragmatism.

In the practice of international dispute resolution the lack of a satisfactory explanation for the origin of legal rules has led lawyers to abandon seeking justification for solving interpretative controversies from any of the suggested explanations. Behind ritualistic references to well-known rules and principles of international law (the content of which remains a constant object of dispute), legal practice has increasingly resorted to solving disputes by a contextual criterion – an effort towards an equitable balance. Though this has seemed to work well, the question arises as to whether such practice can be adequately explained in terms of the Rule of Law.

A. Sovereignty

There is a body of doctrine which addresses itself to the questions: what are the character and normative consequences of statehood? It deals with such themes as the acquisition and loss of statehood, the justification and extent (limits) of territorial sovereignty, the rights of states, the delimitation of competing jurisdictions, etc. The rhetorical importance of this doctrine has varied, but its urgency within the liberal doctrine remains unchallenged. In some ways, sovereignty doctrine plays a role analogous to that played by individual liberty in legitimation discourse. It explains a critical character of legal subjects and sets down basic conditions within which the relations between legal subjects must be organized.

The character and consequences of sovereign statehood might, however, be explained from different perspectives. One explanation holds sovereignty as basic in the sense that it is simply imposed upon the law by the world of facts. Sovereignty and together with it a set of territorial rights and duties are something external to the law, something the law must recognize but which it cannot control. I shall call this the "pure fact view."[31] Another explanation holds sovereignty and everything associated with it as one part of the law's substance, determined and constantly determinable within the legal system, just like any other norms. This might be called the "legal" view.[32]

30 Compare also Kennedy, *supra* note 16.

31 G. Jellinek, *Allgemeine Staatslehre* (3. Aufl.) (1925) 337, 364-367 and, e.g., Korowicz, 'Some Present Problems of Sovereignty', 112 *RCDI* (1961) 102.

32 See, e.g., Verdross, *supra* note 17, at 35 and, e.g., Rousseau, 'Principes de droit international public', 93 *RCDI* (1958) 394.

Normative argument within the different realism of sovereignty doctrine uses the contrast between these explanations to constitute itself. One party argues in terms of pure facts (of effectiveness, for example) while the other makes its point by reference to a criterion external to facts (general recognition, for example). But neither position is sustainable alone. Relying on the pure fact of power is apologist.[33] Relying on a criterion independent of effectiveness is both abstract and question-begging.[34] It is question-begging as it merely raises the further question about whose interpretation of the criterion or its application should be given precedence. A defendable argument seems compelled to make both points: it must assume that sovereign rights are somehow matters of pure fact as well as of some criterion external to those facts themselves.

The development of the positions of Norway and Denmark during the *Eastern Greenland* case (1933) illustrates this. Originally, Norway based its rights to the disputed territory on its effective occupation. Relying on the views of other states would have violated Norway's sovereign equality. Denmark based its own claim on general recognition and challenged Norwegian title on the absence of such recognition. As the title was to be valid *erga omnes*, it could not be dependent on Norway's acts. In their subsequent arguments both states replied assuming their adversary's first position: Norway argued that its occupation was sanctioned by a generally recognized rule which based title on occupation. Denmark aimed to show that Norway in fact could not have occupied the territory because it had already been effectively occupied by Denmark.[35]

Neither claim could be preferred by simply preferring the "pure fact" or the "criterion" of general recognition because both states argued both points. Consequently, the Court affirmed both argumentative tracks. To support its view that Denmark had sovereignty it argued from Danish occupation as well as general recognition and denied both in respect of Norway.[36] To reach this conclusion, the Court had to make interpretations about the facts (effective occupation) as well as the law (the extent of general recognition) which, however, were external to the applicable facts and the law and which were difficult to justify against Norway's conflicting sovereign interpretation of them. The crucial point in the judgement was the Court's discussion of the famous "Ihlen declaration", which allowed the Court to protect Norwegian sovereignty by denying its possession in reference to the construction according to which Norway itself had already "recognized" Danish sovereignty in Eastern Greenland.[37]

33 See, e.g., H. Lauterpacht, *International Law* (Vol. I) (1979) 341-344.

34 See, e.g., *Island of Palmas* case, II *UNRIAA* at 839, 843-846.

35 These points are belaboured at length in the written proceedings. See PCIJ, *Eastern Greenland* case, Ser.C.62 and C.63 and the parties' oral arguments, C.66. For more detailed analysis, see Koskenniemi, *supra* note 12, at 251-253.

36 PCIJ, *Eastern Greenland* case, Ser.A.53 at 45-62

37 *Id.* at 64-74.

The same structure can be detected in all territorial disputes. In each, the "pure fact" and "legal" approaches dissolve into each other in a way which makes it impossible for the court or tribunal to solve the case by merely choosing one over the other. There are two difficulties. First, the need to make both points loses the initial sense of both: the pure fact view was premised on the assumption that the law follows from what facts say. The legal view assumed that the sense of facts was to be determined by rules. In argument, both points claim to defer, or *overrule* each other. To assume that they could be valid (determining) simultaneously makes both meaningless. Second, that the "pure fact" and the "legal" approaches show themselves indeterminate compels the decision-maker to look closer into the relevant "facts" and the relevant "legal" criterion. Decisions turn on contextual interpretations about the facts and the law – interpretations which, by definition, can no longer be justified by reference to those facts or criteria themselves.

Late modern practice of solving sovereignty disputes pays hardly more than lip-service to the traditional bases of territorial entitlement. Deciding such questions is now thought of in terms of trying to establish the most equitable solution.[38] The point is that the various interpretations and pragmatic considerations, as well as the final appreciation of the equity of the proposed solution, cannot be justified by reference to legal rules. On the contrary, recourse to the kind of justice involved in such appreciation can only mean, from the perspective of the Rule of Law, capitulation to arbitrariness or undermining the principle of the subjectivity of value, required in the pursuit of a Rule of Law. Let me take another example. It was often argued that the existence of states is a "matter of fact" and that "recognition" was only "declaratory" and not "constitutive" of statehood. If states were created by an external act of recognition, this would introduce for existing states a political right to decide which entities shall enjoy the status of legal subjects. This conflicts with the principles of self-determination and equality – both following from the rejection of a natural law.[39]

Yet, even such an apparently realistic and democratic view needed to assume the existence of some kind of pre-existing criteria whereby it could be ascertained whether statehood was present in some entity or not. The problem was never really that anyone would have seriously contested that the emergence of states was a factual, sociological process. The problem was – and remains – that people view the normative consequences of social process through different criteria and arrive at irreconcilable conclusions even when using the same criteria.

There is, though, a measure of common agreement on a matter as important as statehood. But it has very little to do with factual power or effectiveness. Rhodesia,

38 See ICJ, *Burkina Faso – Mali Frontier* case, Reports (1986) 567-568 (para. 28) and *infra* note 47.

39 The classic remains Ti-Chiang Chen, *The International Law of Recognition* (1951). See also Kato, 'Recognition in International Law; Some Thoughts on Traditional Theory, Attitudes of and Practice by African States', 10 *IJIL* (1970) 299-323.

Transkei and Taiwan were never regarded as states, whereas Tuvalu and Monaco were. But to explain these "anomalies" – as well as other apparently puzzling cases of statehood – simply by reference to the "constitutive" view is equally unsatisfactory. The original objections against the imperialistic character of this theory remain valid. Lauterpacht's middle-of-the-road position about a *duty* to recognize when the legal criteria have been fulfilled remains question-begging:[40] if a state refuses to recognize an entity because it says that this fulfilled the relevant criteria, there is little point to insist upon the existence of the duty. The matter turns on the interpretation of either the factual circumstances or the content of the relevant norm. The real problem is that it is impossible, within liberal premises, to overrule any participant interpretation in a legitimate fashion. Under those premises norms are "auto-interpretative" and each state must be presumed to have the liberty to interpret the sense of factual events around it.[41]

These anomalies of statehood as well as the resurgence of the time-honoured practice of non-recognition after the *Namibia* Opinion (1971) suggest that the attainment of statehood territorial title – at least if the matter is of some importance – has a relationship to what is decided externally.[42] But they also show that to believe that such decision can be understood as "following a rule" requires either a rule or an imagination so flexible that neither the legal nor the pure fact view can take much credit in trying to establish itself upon it.

If the presence of the quality of sovereignty in some entity is difficult to explain in terms of pure facts or legal rules, it is even more trying to do this in respect of the consequences of sovereignty. That the boundaries of domestic jurisdiction are shifting, and that "sovereignty" has seemed compatible with a state's hermetic isolation as well as extensive integration, indicates that whatever rights or liberties this quality may entail is, as the Permanent Court of International Justice observed, a "relative matter" – dependent on the content of the state's obligations at any given time.[43] In other words nothing determinate follows from sovereignty as a matter of "pure fact" – on the contrary, the content of sovereignty seems determinable only once we know what obligations the state has.

Lawyers adopting the "legal view" sometimes believe that the above conclusion fully vindicates their position. "Sovereignty" is not a matter outside but within the law, a convenient shorthand for the rights, liberties and competences which the law has allocated to the state – and which can be retrieved at any time.[44] To solve a

40 H. Lauterpacht, *Recognition in International Law* (1948).

41 For a useful restatement of this (liberal) point, see Bin Cheng, Custom, 'The Future of General State Practice in a Divided World', in Macdonald, Johnston (eds.) *The Structure and Process of International Law*, at 513, 519-523.

42 ICJ, *Namibia* case, Reports (1971) 51, 54 (paras. 112, 117, 119).

43 PCIJ, *Nationality Decrees* case Ser.B.4. at 24.

44 Schwarzenberger, 'The Forms of Sovereignty', 10 *CLP* (1957) 284; Hart, *supra* note 19, at 218.

sovereignty dispute it suffices only to look at the body of legal rules, and see if the state has the capacity which it claims by a legislative allocation.

The problem with such a conclusion, however, is that on most areas of state conduct no definite legislative act can be found which would establish the state's competence to act in some particular way. Moreover, and here is another paradox, the most important rules of general application seem to be precisely those rules which lay down the right of exclusive jurisdiction, self-determination, non-intervention and – sovereignty. It is not only that if sovereignty were reduced to a non-normative abstraction, then international law would appear as a huge *lacuna*, we would also lack a connected explanation, an interpretative principle to solve differences of opinion about the content or application of the few particular rules which we could then discern.

In most areas of non-treaty-related state conduct, specific obligations are, or can be, plausibly made to seem either ambiguous or lacking. In such case, the state's sovereignty – its initial liberty – will re-emerge as a normative principle in its own right: in the absence of clear prohibitions, the state must be assumed free. This principle – the *Lotus* principle[45] – is not only a convenient rule of thumb. It encapsulates the assumption that the mere fact of statehood has a normative sense (right of self-determination) and that in the absence of unambiguous legislative prohibitions any attempt to overrule the liberty inherent in statehood can only appear as illegitimate constraint.

The difficulty with the *Lotus* principle is twofold. First, all the rules and principles are more or less indeterminate in their content. If the mere fact of the existence of differing interpretations were sufficient to trigger the presumption of liberty, then the binding force of most rules would seem an illusion. The even more important difficulty is useless if the case involves a *conflict* of liberties. But if it is assumed – as is inevitable if the idea of a material natural law is discarded – that the liberties of one state are delimited by those of another, then any dispute about the rights or obligations of two or more states can be conceptualized in terms of a conflict of their liberties and, consequently, would not seem soluble by simply preferring "liberty" – because we would not know which state's liberty to prefer.

At that point, legal practice breaks from the argumentative cycle by recourse to equity – an undifferentiated sense of justice.

Continental shelf disputes are one example. The International Court of Justice (ICJ), as is well-known, started out with the assumption that the entitlement to continental shelf was a matter of giving effect to the coastal state's *ab initio* and *ipso facto* right. It was not a matter of "abstract justice" but of (objective) fact.[46] But this view has proved unhelpful. Which facts are relevant – the decisive problem – is decided by the Court *ad hoc* and it is not inscribed in some transcendental code *ex*

45 PCIJ, *Lotus* case, Ser. A.10 at 30. See further Koskenniemi, *supra* note 12, at 220-223.

46 ICJ, *North Sea Continental Shelf* cases, Reports (1969) 22-23 (paras. 19-20).

ante. Later delimitations have even ceased paying lip-service to the *ipso facto/ab initio* theory and seen "arriving at an equitable result" as its prosper task.[47] The history of the argument in continental shelf cases is the history of the Court first noting the lack, or at least the ambiguity of the relevant rule, it then making appeal to a pure fact (*ipso facto*) view; then abandoning that view (because no "fact" can be normative without an anterior criterion) in favour of a legal view (equity *infra legem*[48] as the correct rule) and the whole cycle ending in the content of that rule being dispersed into justice – a justice which can, under the principle of subjective value and the Rule of Law, only be seen as arbitrary.[49]

Transboundary pollution, to take another example, involves the juxtaposition of the freedoms of the source-state and the target-state: on the one hand, there is the former's sovereign right to exploit its natural resources in accordance with its own environmental policies; on the other hand, there is the victim's sole right to decide what acts shall take place in its territories.[50] The former's liberty to pursue economically beneficial uses of its territory is contrasted with the latter's liberty to enjoy a pure environment. The conflict is insoluble by simply preferring "liberty", or some right inscribed in the very notion of sovereignty. Balancing seems inevitable in order to reach a decision.[51]

A similar structure manifests itself everywhere within sovereignty doctrine. While sovereignty immunity is usually stated either in terms of the (pure fact of) sovereignty or a systematic necessity for international communication, legal practice tends to construct the foreign sovereign's exemption from local jurisdiction by balancing the two sovereigns' interests *vis-à-vis* each other.[52] The same seems true in cases dealing with the determination of the allowable reach of a state's extraterritorial jurisdiction.[53] The law on uses of international watercourses[54] and fishery re-

47 ICJ, *Tunisia-Libya Continental Shelf* case, Reports (1982) 59 (para. 70); *Gulf of Maine* case, Reports (1984) 312 (para. 155); *Libya-Malta Continental Shelf* case, Reports (1985) 38-39 (para. 49). See further Koskenniemi, *supra* note 12, at 223-232.

48 ICJ, *North Sea Continental Shelf* cases, Reports (1969) 20-22 (paras. 15-20).

49 For this criticism, see, e.g., Gros, *diss.op.* ICJ, *Tunisia-Libya Continental Shelf* case, Reports (1982) 151-156 and *Gulf of Maine* case, Reports (1984) 378-380.

50 See Principle 21, UN Conference on the Human Environment, Stockholm 5-16 June 1972, UN Doc. A/CONF.48/14.

51 See, e.g., Koskenniemi, 'International Pollution in the System of International Law', 17 *Oikeustiede-Jurisprudentia* (1984) 152-164; Lammers, "Balancing the Equities" International Environmental Law', *RCDI Coll.* (1984) 153-165.

52 Crawford, 'International Law and Foreign Sovereigns, Distinguishing Immune Transactions', 54 *BYIL* (1983) 114-118.

53 Meng, 'Völkerrechtliche Zulässigkeit und Grenzen der wirtschaftsverwaltungsrechtlichen Hoheitsakte mit Auslandswirkung', 44 *ZaOeRV* (1984) 675-783; Lowe, 'The Problem of Extraterritorial Jurisdiction: Economic Sovereignty and the Search for a Solution', 34 *ICLQ* (1985) 730.

54 Schwebel, 'Third Report on the Non-Navigational Uses of International Watercourses', *YILC* (1982/II/1) 75-100.

sources,[55] as well as conflicts concerning foreign investment between the home state and the host state,[56] entails the drawing of a boundary between the two sovereigns, a determination of the extent of their sovereign liberty. In the absence of any determinate rules, and being unable to prefer one sovereign over another, legal practice has turned to equity in order to justify the delimitation of the two sovereignties *vis-à-vis* each other.

The substance of the law under sovereignty doctrines has dispersed into a generalized call for equitable solutions or "balancing" whenever conflicts arise. Standard academic justifications of state rights, either as a consequence of the pure fact of statehood or as laid down in legislative enactments, have no application. Nor can they have application because neither "facts" nor "rules" are self-evident in the way Enlightenment lawyers once believed. The facts which are assumed to establish title do not appear "automatically" but are the result of choosing a criterion from which facts may be invested with normative significance.[57] But rules, too, are always subject to interpretation. In order to link itself to something tangible, interpretation should refer back to some kind of facts. To establish the sense of facts, we must take the perspective of a rule; to decide interpretative controversies about the rule, we must – under the social conception – look at facts. Hence the late modern silence about theoretical justifications and the leap to *ad hoc* compromise.

B. Sources

Despite its original emphasis on actual power, the doctrine of sovereignty seemed unworkable because of the abstract and arbitrary way in which its normative content was determined. It is possible to make a fresh start and imagine that international law might just as well be described not as consequence of statehood but through a set of normative criteria – sources – for law-creation and identification.

Not surprisingly, sources doctrine is riddled with dualisms which express in different ways the conflicting pull of the demands for concreteness and normativity. The very doctrine is often understood from two perspectives: as a description of the social processes whereby states create law (concreteness) and as a methodology for verifying the law's content independently of political opinions (normativity). By integrating both explanations, sources doctrine can maintain its apparent objectivity. On the one hand, something would not be law merely as a result of its content but as a result of a social process. On the other hand, the existence of sources as a con-

55 *Fisheries Jurisdiction* cases, ICJ Reports (1974) 30 (paras. 69-70).

56 *The LIAMCO Award*, 20 ILM (1981) 76-77 (paras. 150-151).

57 "In the realm of law there is no fact in itself, no immediately evident fact; there are only facts ascertained by the competent authorities in a procedure determined by law." H. Kelsen, *Principles of International Law* (ed. & rev. by R.M. Tucker) (1966) 388.

straining methodology creates the needed distance between it and whatever states might will at any one moment.

Though there is no major disagreement among international lawyers about the correct enumeration of sources (treaties, custom, general principles), the rhetorical force of sources ("binding force") is explained from contrasting perspectives. Their importance is sometimes linked with their capacity to reflect state will (consensualism). At other times, such binding force is linked with the relationship of sources arguments with what is "just", "reasonable", "in accordance with good faith", or some other non-consensual metaphor.

Standard disputes about the content or application of international legal norms use the contradiction between consent and justice based explanations. One party argues in terms of consent, the other in terms of what is just (reasonable, etc.). But neither argument is fully justifiable alone. A purely consensual argument cannot ultimately justify the application of a norm against non-consenting states (apologism). An argument relying only on a notion of justice violates the principle of the subjectivity of value (utopianism). Therefore, they must rely on each other. Arguments about consent must explain the relevance and content of consent in terms of what seems just. Arguments about justice must demonstrate their correctness by reference to what states have consented to. Because these movements (consent to justice; justice to consent) make the originally opposing positions look the same, no solution can be made by simply choosing one. A solution now seems possible only by either deciding what is it that states "really" will or what the content of justice "really" is. Neither question, however, is answerable on the premises of the Rule of Law.[58]

For the modern lawyer, it is very difficult to envisage, let alone to justify, a law which would divorce itself from what states think or will to be the law. The apparent necessity of consensualism seems grounded in the very criticism of natural norms as superstition. Yet, the criticisms against full consensualism – its logical circularity, its distance from experience, its inherent apologism – are well-known.[59] Consensualism cannot justify the application of a norm against a state which opposes such application unless it creates distance between the norm and the relevant state's momentary will. It has been explained, for example, that though law emerges from consent, it does not need every state's consent all the time, that a general agreement, a *volonté générale* of a *Vereinbarung* is sufficient to apply the norm.[60]

But these explanations violate the principle of sovereign equality – they fail to explain why a state should be bound by what another state wills. This can, of course, be explained from some concept of social necessity. But in such case we have already moved away from pure consensualism and face the difficulty of explain-

58 See also Kennedy, *supra* note 16, at 11-107.

59 Koskenniemi, *supra* note 12, at 270-273.

60 For the classic, see H. Triepel, *Völkerrecht und Landesrecht* (1899) 27, 51-53.

ing the legal status of the assumed necessity and why it should support one norm instead of another.

A more common strategy is to explain that the state has originally consented (by means of recognition, acquiescence, by not protesting or by "tacitly" agreeing) although it now denies it has. Such an argument is extremely important in liberal legitimation discourse. It allows defending social constraint in a consensual fashion while allowing the application of constraint against a state which denies it consent.[61] But even this argument fails to be convincing because it must ultimately explain itself either in a fully consensual or fully non-consensual way and thereby become vulnerable to the objections about apologism or utopianism.

Why should a state be bound by an argument according to which it has consented, albeit "tacitly"? If the reason is stated in terms of respecting its own consent, then we have to explain why we can know better than the state itself what it has consented to. Even consensualists usually concede that such knowledge is not open to external observers. But even if it were possible to "know better", such an argument is not really defensible within the premises of the Rule of Law. It contains the unpleasant implication that we could no longer rely on the expressed will of the legal subject. It would lose the principal justification behind democratic legislation and justify the establishment of a Leviathan – the one who knows best what everyone "really" wills. It is a strategy for introducing authoritarian opinions in democratic disguise.

Tacit consent theorists usually explain that the question is not of "real" but of "presumed" will. But what then allows the application of the presumption against a state denying that it had ever consented to anything like it? At this point the tacit consent lawyer must move from consensualism to non-consensualism. Tacit consent – or the presumption of consent – binds because it is "just" or in accordance with reasonableness or good faith, or it protects legitimate expectations or the like.[62] Now the difficulty lies in defending the assumed non-consensual position. But under the principle of subjective value, "justice" cannot be discussed in a non-arbitrary way.[63] Were this otherwise, the Rule of Law would be pointless if not harmful. One might, of course, say that a notion of reasonableness is justified because the state in question has itself accepted it. But this defence will re-emerge the problem of how it is possible to oppose a consensual justification against a state denying its validity. And so on, *ad infinitum.*

61 See, e.g., the argument in A. Bleckmann, *Grundprobleme und Methoden des Völkerrechts* (1982) 81, 184-189. On the tacit consent construction generally, see Koskenniemi, *supra* note 12, at 284-291.

62 See, e.g., J.P. Müller, *Vertrauenschutz im Völkerrecht* (1970); A. Martin, *L'estoppel en droit international public* (1979).

63 "[l]e principe de bonne foi est un principe moral et rien de plus." E. Zoller, *La bonne foi en droit international public* (1977) 345.

In the *Gulf of Maine* case (1984), Canada argued that the United States was bound to a certain line of delimitation as it had not protested against its *de facto* use. Relying on absence of protest reflected, Canada explained, on the one hand, U.S. consent to be bound and, on the other hand, gave expression to good faith and equity. It argued in terms of consent as well as justice. The Chamber of the Court accepted both explanations. It started out with the latter, non-consensual one. What is common to acquiescence and estoppel is that: "... both follow from the fundamental principle of good faith and equity."[64]

Had it followed this understanding, it should, because not *all* silence creates norms, have had to enter a discussion of whether or not the conditions of good faith or equity were present to bind the United States now. But there was no such discussion. This is understandable, as arguing from non-consensual justice seems so subjective. Instead, it moved to a consensual understanding of relying on absence of protest and went on to discuss whether the "Hoffmann letter" was evidence of United States acceptance of the Canadian equidistance. It was not: "... facts invoked by Canada do not warrant the conclusion that the U.S. Government thereby recognized the median line..."[65]

In other words, the United States was not bound because there was no subjective intent to be (regardless of considerations of good faith or equity). How did the Court arrive at this conclusion? This would have been apologist and a violation of Canadian sovereignty. The Chamber's conclusion did not concerns lack of "real" intent but rather of "constructive" U.S. intent. On what principles was that construction based? Mainly on inconsistency in the facts and on the low governmental status of the authorities involved.[66] But what justified this choice of relevant facts and their ensuing interpretation? What made the Court's construction better than the Canadian one? The argument stops here. The principles of construction were left undiscussed.

In theory, the Chamber could have used two principles of construction: 1) a construction is justified if it corresponds to intent; 2) a construction is justified if it reflects non-consensual justice. These are exclusive justifications. But neither was open to the Chamber. The former was excluded by the previous argument which ruled out the possibility of knowing real U.S. intent and using it against Canada. The latter was excluded because it would have involved arguing in a fully non-consensual way against Canadian non-consensual justifications. This would have assumed the correctness of an objective justice and would have conflicted with the Chamber's previous refusal to think of acquiescence-estoppel in a fully non-consensual way. The Chamber simply took another interpretation of U.S. conduct than Canada. Why it was better was not discussed as it could not have been discussed. The decision was, on its own premises, undetermined by legal argument.

64 *Gulf of Maine* case, ICJ Reports (1984) 305 (para. 130).

65 *Id.* at 307 (para. 138).

66 *Id.*

An identical argumentative structure is present in treaty interpretation. Particular interpretations are traced back either to party will or to some idea of good faith, reasonableness, etc.[67] Because "real" party will cannot be identified and justifiably opposed to a party denying such intent, and because the content of what is a "just" interpretation cannot be determined in a legal way, late modern doctrines usually concede the aesthetic, impressionistic character of the interpretative process.[68] Controversial points about party will clash against equally controversial points about the justice of particular interpretations.

In the *case Concerning the Interpretation of the Algerian Declarations of 19 January 1981*, the Iran-United States Claims Tribunal was to decide whether Article II of the Claims Settlement Declaration included a right for Iran to press claims against United States' nationals. The majority held that it could not be so interpreted. A "clear formulation" of that Article excluded Iranian claims from the Tribunal's jurisdiction. This clear formulation had authority because it was clearest evidence of Party consent.[69] The minority argued that a literal construction failed to give effect to the settlement's reciprocal character. According to the minority, reciprocity had been the very basis on which Iran had entered the agreement. By excluding reciprocity, the majority had violated Iranian consent and unjustifiably preferred the justice of literality to the justice of reciprocity.[70] Both sides invoke consent and justice but are unable to address each others' views directly. Neither side argues on the basis of "real consent." But while the majority sees consent manifested in the text, the minority sees consent in reciprocity. Both sides say their interpretative principle is better as it better reflects consent. But deciding the dispute on these arguments would require a means of knowing consent independently of its manifestations – a possibility excluded as reference was made to manifestations because of the assumption that real consent could not be known. Moreover, neither can the two sides argue that their justice – the justice of literality or the justice of reciprocity – is better without arguing from a theory of justice which seems indefensible under the Rule of Law. Ultimately, both interpretations are unargued. A doctrine which excludes arguments from "knowing better" and natural justice has no means to decide on the superiority of conflicting interpretations.

Attempts to explain why states should be bound by unilateral declarations meet with similar problems. In the first place, as the ICJ observed in the *Nuclear Tests* case (1974) such statements might be held binding "(w)hen it is the intention of the state making the declaration that it should become bound according to its terms."[71] However, their binding force cannot be *fully* consensual because then the state could

67 For this contrast generally, see, e.g., Zoller, *supra* note 63, at 205-244.

68 Sur, *supra* note 13. See also McDougal, *supra* note 23 at 149-157.

69 Iran – United States Claims Tribunal, 'Interpretation of the Algerian Declaration of 19th January 1981', 62 ILR (1982) 599-600.

70 *Id.* at 603-606.

71 *Nuclear Tests* cases, ICJ Reports (1974) 267 (para. 43).

be freed simply by a further act of will. Therefore, the Court also noted that "(o)ne of the principles governing the creation and performance of legal obligations ... is the principle of good faith... Thus interested states may take cognizance of unilateral declarations and place confidence in them, and are entitled to require that the obligation thus created be respected."[72] Now the declaring state is bound regardless of its will, by the simple fact of the statement and others' reliance.

The necessity of making both arguments seems evident. The Court's first – consensual – argument justified holding the France bound by its statements. But it was also threatening because it implied that France could modify or terminate this obligation at will. This would violate the wills and sovereignty of the Applicants (Australia and New Zealand). The second – non-consensual – argument about good faith and legitimate expectations was needed to protect the latter. The decision was consensualist and non-consensualist at the same time. It allowed basing the applicable norm on protecting the sovereignty of each state involved. Simultaneously, it seemed to give effect to what justice seemed to require.

But the decision remains also vulnerable from each perspective. How could the Court base its norm on French consent in face of French denial of such consent? It leaves unexplained how it can protect the Applicants' reliance, as they denied having relied. And it leaves unexplained its theory of justice which says that these statements and actions in these circumstances bind because that is in accordance with good faith.

The structure, importance and weaknesses of tacit consent is nowhere more visible that in the orthodox argument about customary international law.

According to this argument, binding custom exists if there is a material practice of states to that effect and that practice is motivated by the belief that it is obligatory. This "two-element theory" gives expression to the principle of liberal sociology for which the meaning – law or not law – of social action lies neither in its external appearance nor in what someone thinks about but is a combination of the two: an external (material) and an internal (psychological) element.[73] The function of the former element is to ensure that custom can be ascertained without having to rely on states' momentary, political views. The point of the latter is to distinguish custom from coercion.

The problem with the two-element theory is that neither element can be identified independently of the other. Hence, they cannot be used to prevent the appearance of Mr. Hyde in each other.

Modern lawyers have rejected fully materialistic explanations of custom as apologist, incapable of distinguishing between factual constraint and law. If the possibil-

72 *Id.* at 268 (para. 46).

73 See Hart, *supra* note 19, at 91. For discussion, see Koskenniemi, 'The Normative Force of Habit; International Custom and Social Theory', 1 *Finnish Yearbook of International Law* (forthcoming).

ity is excluded that this distinction can be made by the justice of the relevant behaviour, then it can only be made by reference to the psychological element, the *opinio juris*. But, as many students of the ICJ jurisprudence have shown, there are no independently applicable criteria for ascertaining the presence of the *opinio juris*. The ICJ has simply inferred its presence or absence from the extent and intensity of the material practice it has studied.[74] Moreover, it does not even seem possible to assume the existence of such criteria and that the *opinio* thus received could be opposed to a non-consenting state. That would be an argument about knowing better. In other words, though it seems possible to distinguish "custom" from what is actually effective only by recourse to what states believe, such beliefs do not seem capable of identification regardless of what is actually effective.

One might try to avoid the above circularity by assuming that some types of behaviour are by their character – "intrinsically" – such as to generate (or not to generate) normative custom. But attempts to single out lists of such types have been unsuccessful. A "flexible" concept of material practice has emerged: any act or statement may count as custom-generating practice if only the states wish so.[75] (Indeed, any other conclusion would manifest an illegitimate naturalism and violate the principles of liberal sociology: it would fail to have regard to the "internal aspect"). Using this criterion (what it is that states wish), however, would assume that we can know the *opinio* independently of the act in which it is expressed. But this possibility was already excluded by our previous argument about the need to look at material practice in the first place. Indeed, were it so that we could know state intentions regardless of what states do, the whole two-element theory would become unnecessary: we could simply apply those intentions. Custom would coalesce with (informal) agreement. (In which case, of course, we would face the difficulty of having to interpret the content embedded in any such agreement by further reference to the parties' "real" wills or to some notion of justice, as explained above).

Customary law doctrine remains indeterminate because it is circular. It assumes behaviour to be evidence of states' intentions (*opinio juris*) and the latter to be evidence of what behaviour is relevant as custom. To avoid apologism (relying on the state's present will), it looks at the psychological element from the perspective of the material; to avoid utopianism (making the distinction between binding and non-binding usages by reference to what is just), it looks at the material element from the perspective of the psychological. It can occupy neither position in a permanent way without becoming vulnerable to criticism compelled by the other. The very as-

74 See, e.g., M. Sørensen, *Les sources du droit international* (1946) 108-111; Virally, 'The Sources of International Law', in Sørensen (ed.), *Manual of Public International Law* (1968) 134-135; H. Günther, *Zur Entstehung von Völkergewohnheitsrecht* (1970) 70. See further, Koskenniemi, *supra* note 12, at 380-381.

75 See, e.g., Ferrari-Bravo, 'La coutume internationale dans la pratique des Etats', 192 *RCDI* (1985) 243, 261 and Koskenniemi, *supra* note 12, at 383-384.

sumptions behind customary international law provide the mechanism for its self-destruction.

For late modern international practice the standard theory is increasingly a camouflage for what is really an attempt to understand custom in terms of a bilateralized equity. The ICJ, for instance, has always been somewhat ambiguous as to the character of the rules of non-written law which it has discerned. The Court's argument about the relevant custom in the *Anglo-Norwegian Fisheries* (1951) as well as *Fisheries Jurisdiction* (1974) cases already looked upon the matter more in terms of the relevant interest at stake than trying to find some general rule to "apply."[76] The several maritime boundary cases further extended this move. The judgement in the *U.S. Military and Paramilitary Activities* case (1986) did not even seriously attempt to justify its four customary rules – non-use of force, non-intervention, respect for sovereignty and especially the relevant humanitarian rules – in terms of material practice and the *opinio juris.*[77]

Many have been dissatisfied with the modern strategy of arguing every imaginable non-written standard as "custom." Sir Robert Jennings, among others, has noted that what we tend to call custom: "is not only not customary law: it does not even faintly resemble a customary law."[78] But if a non-written standard is not arguable in terms of material practices or beliefs relating to such practices then it can only exist as natural law – being defensible only by reference to the political importance of its content. In fact, much ICJ practice in the relevant respect remains *ex cathedra*: the Court has "instituted a system of decision-making in which the conclusion reached is determined by the application of rules largely treated as self-evident."[79] To be sure, often there is *consensus* on such rules, for instance, on the "elementary considerations of humanity" invoked by the Court in the *Corfu Channel* case (1949). But the problem is clearly less to explain why people who agree are bound than why also those should be who do not and how one should argue if interpretative controversies arise.

V. The Politics of International Law

The idea of an international Rule of Law has been a credible one because to strive for it implies no commitment regarding the content of the norms thereby established or the character of the society advanced. It was possible for 19th-century European

76 *Anglo-Norwegian* case, ICJ Reports (1951) 133; *Fisheries Jurisdiction* cases, Reports (1974) 30-33 (paras. 69-79).

77 *US Military and Paramilitary Activities* case, ICJ Reports (1986) 97-115 (paras. 183-220).

78 Jennings, 'The Identification of International Law', in Cheng (ed.), *International Law, Teaching and Practice* (1982) 5.

79 Kearney, 'Sources of Law and the International Court of Justice', in Gross (ed.), *The Future of the International Court of Justice* (Vol. I) (1976) 653.

powers to start thinking of their relationships in terms of legal rules because they formalized inter-sovereign relationships and no sovereign needed to feel that his substantive policies were excluded by them it. It was possible for the UN General Assembly to accept by consensus the Declaration on the "Decade for International Law" for precisely those same reasons. This is strikingly highlighted by the fact that the Decade contained no substantive programme. The declaration merely calls for the promotion of respect for the principles of international law and the peaceful settlement of disputes and for the encouragement of the development and dissemination of international law. For what purpose the law was to be put or what kinds of rules it should promote is not addressed by it.

Modern international law is an elaborate framework for deferring substantive resolution elsewhere: into further procedure, interpretation, equity, context, and so on. The 1982 Law of the Sea Convention is the typical example: in place of a list of do's and dont's it establishes a framework for delimiting sovereign powers and allocating jurisdictions – assuming that the substantive problems of the uses of the sea can be best dealt with through allocating decision-power elsewhere, into context and usually by reference to "equitable principles."[80] The success of international law depends on this formality; this refusal to set down determining rules or ready-made resolutions to future conflict. Though there is a distinctly legal "process" – and in this sense a relatively autonomous and coherent system which can be abstracted in academic treatises – there are no determining legal standards. Let me explain this somewhat schematically.

The Rule of Law constitutes an attempt to provide communal life without giving up individual autonomy. Communal life is, of course, needed to check individualism from leading either into anarchy or tyranny. Individualism is needed because otherwise it would remain objectionable for those who feel that the kind of community provided by it does not meet their political criteria. From their perspective, the law's communitarian pretensions would turn out as totalitarian apologies.[81]

The law aims to fulfil its double task by becoming formal: by endorsing neither particular communitarian ideals nor particular sovereign policies. Or, conversely, an acceptable legal rule, argument or doctrine is one which can explain itself both from the perspective of enhancing community (because it would otherwise seem apologist) as well as safeguarding sovereignty (because its implications would otherwise remain totalitarian). The problem is that as soon as any of these justifications are advanced to support *some particular kind of communal existence or some determined limit for sovereign autonomy*, they are vulnerable from an opposing substantive perspective. So, while an advocate justifies his preferred substantive outcome by its capacity to support community, it becomes simultaneously possible for his coun-

80 See generally, Allott, 'Power Sharing in the Law of the Sea', 77 *AJIL* (1983) 1-30; Kennedy, *supra* note 16, at 201-245.

81 See further the seminal article by Kennedy, 'The Structure of Blackstone's Commentaries', 18 *Buffalo L.R.* (1979) 205.

terpart – not sharing the same communal ideal – to challenge the very justification as totalitarian. Correspondingly, a rule, principle or solution justified by resource to the way it protects sovereignty may – for someone drawing the limits of "sovereignty" differently – be objected as furthering egoism and anarchy.

Take the case of transfrontier pollution. Noxious fumes flow from state A into the territory of state B. State A refers to its "sovereign right to use its natural resources in accordance with its national policies." State B argues that A has to put a stop to the pollution. It interprets A's position to be an egoistic one while it makes its own argument seem communitarian. It might refer to a norm of "non-harmful use of territory", for example, and justify this by reference to analogies from rule concerning international rivers and natural resources as well as precedents and General Assembly resolutions.[82]

State A can now retort by saying that norms cannot be opposed to it in such a totalitarian fashion. A is bound only by norms which it has accepted. It has never accepted the analogies drawn by B. This would force B either to argue that its preferred norm binds irrespective of acceptance – in which case it stands to lose as its argument would seem utopian – or to change ground so as to make its position seem protective of sovereignty as well. State B might now argue that the pollution violates its own freedom and constitutes an interference in its internal affairs as Australia did in the *Nuclear Tests* case.[83] B's position would now seem both communitarian (in respect to A) and individualistic (in respect to B itself).

To counter this last argument by B, A needs to make a communitarian point. It may argue that there is a norm about friendly neighbourliness, for example such as that observed in the *Lake Lanoux* case (1957), which requires that states tolerate minor inconveniences which result from legitimate uses of neighbouring states' territories.[84] B cannot demand complete territorial integrity. A's position is now both individualistic (in respect of A itself) and communitarian (in respect of B).

The argument could be continued. Both parties could support the communitarian strand in their positions by referring to equity, general principles and the like, to deny the autonomy (egoism) of the other. And they could support the sovereignty-based arguments by further emphasis on their independence, consent, territorial integrity, self-determination, etc. to counter their adversary's communitarian (totalitarian) arguments. As a result, the case cannot be decided by simply preferring autonomy to community or vice-versa. Both arguments support both positions. The case cannot be solved by reference to any of the available concepts (sovereignty, non-harmful use of territory, territorial integrity, independence, good neighbourliness, equity, etc.) as each of the concepts may be so construed as to support either

82 For both arguments, see Principle 21 of the Stockholm Declaration, *supra* note 50 and further Koskenniemi, *supra* note 51, at 100-103.

83 *Nuclear Tests* cases, ICJ Pleadings I at 14.

84 *Lake Lanoux* case, XII UNRIAA at 316.

one of the claims. And the constructions have no *legally* determined preference. A court could say that one of the positions is better as a matter of equity, for example. Or it might attempt to "balance" the claims. But in justifying its conception of what is equitable, the court will have to assume a theory of justice – a theory, however, which it cannot justify by further reference to the legal concepts themselves.

Another example concerns the relations between a foreign investor and the host state. The view which emphasizes individualism, separation and consent may be put forward to support the host state's sovereignty – its right to nationalize the corporation without "full, prompt and adequate" compensation. But the same position can equally well be derived from communitarian points about justice, equality or solidarity or the binding character of the new international economic order, for example.[85] The home state's case may be argued in a similar way, by laying emphasis on that state's freedom, individuality and consent – as expressed in the acquired rights doctrine – or the non-consensually binding character of the *pacta sunt servanda* norm, good faith or other convenient conceptions of justice. To make a choice, the problem-solver should simply have to prefer one of the sovereignties – in which case sovereign equality is overruled – or it should use another theory of justice (or equity) which it cannot, however, justify by reference to the Rule of Law.[86]

The relationship between the principles of self-determination and territorial integrity, both having been enshrined in countless UN General Assembly Resolutions has remained a puzzle.[87] The problem, as we now can understand it, is that neither of the conflicting principles can be preferred because they are ultimately the same. When a people call for territorial integrity, they call for respect for their identity as a self-determining entity and vice-versa. In order to solve the conflict, one should need an external principle about which types of human association entail this respect and which do not. And this seems to involve arguing on the basis of contested, political views about the type of organization the law should materially aim at.

The formality of international law makes it possible for each state to read its substantive conception of world society as well as its view of the extent of sovereign freedom into legal concepts and categories. This is no externally introduced distortion in the law. It is a necessary consequence of a view which holds that there is no naturally existing "good life", no limit to sovereign freedom which would exist by force of some historical necessity. If this kind of naturalism is rejected – and since the Enlightenment, everybody has had good reason to reject it –

85 Both justifications for this right may be read, for example, from the Charter of Economic Rights and Duties of States, UNGA Res. 3281 (XXIX) (12 December 1974).

86 "A solution therefore should recognize the home state's and the host state's sovereign right to the investment concerned and should endeavour to find an equitable balance between them," Seidl-Hohenveldem, 'International Economic Law. General Course on Public International Law', 198 *RCDI* (1986) 54.

87 See UNGA Res. 1514 (XV) 14 December 1960; 2625 (XXV) 24 October 1970 and comments, e.g., in M. Pomerance, *Self-Determination in Law and Practice; the New Doctrine in the United Nations*, 43-47 and *passim*.

then to impose any substantive conception of communal life or limits of sovereignty can appear only as illegitimate constraint – preferring one state's politics to those of another.

It is impossible to make substantive decisions within the law which would imply no political choice. The late modern turn to equity in the different realms of international law is, in this sense, a healthy admission of something that is anyway there: in the end, legitimizing or criticizing state behaviour is not a matter of applying formally neutral rules but depends on what one regards as politically right, or just.

Conclusion

Theorists of the present often explain our post-modern condition as a result of a tragedy of losses. For international lawyers, the Enlightenment signified loss of faith in a natural order among peoples, nations and sovereigns. To contain political subjectivism, 19th and 20th-century jurists put their faith variably on logic and texts, history and power to find a secure, objective foothold. Each attempt led to disappointment. One's use of logic depended on what political axioms were inserted as the premises. Texts, facts and history were capable of being interpreted in the most varied ways. In making his interpretations the jurist was always forced to rely on conceptual matrices which could no longer be defended by the texts, facts or histories to which they provided meaning. They were – and are – arenas of political struggle.

But the way back to Victoria's or Suarez' unquestioning faith is not open to us. We cannot simply start assuming that politics – justice and equity – could be discussed so that in the end everyone should agree. This teaches us a lesson. Because the world – including lawyers views about it – is conflictual, any grand design for a "world order" will always remain suspect. Any legal rule, principle or world order project will only seem acceptable when stated in an abstract and formal fashion. When it is applied, it will have overruled some interpretation, some collective experience and appear apologist.

Social theorists have documented a recent modern turn in national societies away from the *Rechtstaat* into a society in which social conflict is increasingly met with flexible, contextually determined standards and compromises.[88] The turn away from general principles and formal rules into contextually determined equity may reflect a similar turn in the development of international legal thought and practice. There is every reason to take this turn seriously – though this may mean that lawyers have to re-think their professional self-image. For issues of contextual justice cannot be

88 See, e.g., R.M. Unger, *Law in Modern Society. Toward a Criticism of Social Theory* (1976); T. O'Hagan, *The End of Law?* (1984).

solved by the application of ready-made rules or principles. Their solution requires venturing into fields such as politics, social and economic casuistry which were formally delimited beyond the point at which legal argument was supposed to stop in order to remain "legal." To be sure, we shall remain uncertain. Resolutions based on political acceptability cannot be made with the kind of certainty post-Enlightenment lawyers once hoped to attain. And yet, it is only by their remaining so which will prevent their use as apologies for tyranny.

[14]

Re/Statements: Feminism and State Sovereignty in International Law †

*Karen Knop**

† Portions of this Article expand on ideas contained in Karen Knop, *Why Rethinking the Sovereign State is Important for Women's International Human Rights Law*, *in* HUMAN RIGHTS OF WOMEN: NATIONAL AND INTERNATIONAL PERSPECTIVES (Rebecca J. Cook ed., forthcoming 1994) (on file with author).

* Faculty of Law, University of Toronto. I am grateful to Hilary Charlesworth, Christine Chinkin, John Claydon, Rebecca Cook, Ralph Glass, and Mayo Moran for their insightful and supportive comments on earlier work. Jo Anne Frenschkowski provided wonderful last-minute research assistance. My thanks also go to the International Law Society and Women and the Law, Queen's University for giving me the opportunity to present a first version of the Article.

I. INTRODUCTION

International law does not yield easily to feminist legal methods.[1] If international law aspires to regulate the use of force, to prohibit wars capable of devastating countless women's lives, it does so at a level of abstraction that is difficult to relate to women's experiences.[2]

Feminist approaches to international law may be understood as seeking to personalize and personify its normative constructs. They draw attention to the male environment in which international legal principles are created and applied: the predominantly male elites who formulate policy in foreign ministries, debate in international fora, draft treaties and declarations, sit on international and regional courts, and make up the supervisory bodies for key international human rights treaties.[3] Seen through women's eyes, the landscape to which international law applies assumes quite different–and disturbing–contours, women standing out from men in sharp relief. Feminist scholars in international law have written, for example, on the brutality of mass rape in wartime,[4] and on the complex symbolic appropriation of the female image and ultimate political sacrifice of women's aspirations in a people's struggle for self-determination.[5]

---

1. *See generally* Katherine T. Bartlett, *Feminist Legal Methods*, 103 HARV. L. REV. 829 (1990); Carrie Menkel-Meadow, *Mainstreaming Feminist Legal Theory*, 23 PAC. L.J. 1493 (1992); Ann C. Scales, *The Emergence of Feminist Jurisprudence: An Essay*, 95 YALE L.J. 1373 (1986).

2. *See* Hilary Charlesworth, *Alienating Oscar*, *in* RECONCEIVING REALITY: WOMEN AND INTERNATIONAL LAW (Dorinda G. Dallmeyer ed., forthcoming 1993) (Am. Soc'y Int'l L. Series Studies in Transnat'l Legal Pol'y No. 25) (manuscript at 1, on file with author) [hereinafter RECONCEIVING REALITY].

3. Hilary Charlesworth et al., *Feminist Approaches to International Law*, 85 AM. J. INT'L L. 613, 621-25 (1991); Christine Chinkin, *Peace and Force in International Law*, *in* RECONCEIVING REALITY, *supra* note 2 (manuscript at 12-13, on file with author)

4. Donna E. Arzt, Genocidal Rape in Bosnia-Hercegovina and Croatia and the Role of International Law, Paper presented at Rape as Genocide in Bosnia-Hercegovina and Croatia: A Symposium on War Crimes, Rights, and International Law, Syracuse University College of Law (Apr. 1993) (unpublished manuscript, on file with author); Chinkin, *supra* note 3, at 14-18; Catharine A. MacKinnon, *Crimes of War, Crimes of Peace*, *in* ON HUMAN RIGHTS (forthcoming 1994) (on file with author).

5. Charlesworth et al., *supra* note 3, at 642-43; Christine Chinkin, *A Gendered Perspective to the International Use of Force*, 12 AUSTL. Y.B. INT'L L. 279 (1992); Judith Gardam, *A Feminist Analysis of Certain Aspects of International Humanitarian Law*, 12 AUSTL. Y.B. INT'L L. 265, 268-78 (1992). From a non-legal perspective, see, e.g., KUMARI JAYWARDENA, FEMINISM AND NATIONALISM IN THE THIRD WORLD (1986); R. Radhakrishnan, *Nationalism, Gender, and the Narrative of Identity*, *in* NATIONALISMS AND SEXUALITIES 77 (Andrew Parker et al. eds., 1992); Samita Sen, *Motherhood and*

Based on the analogy between the individual in liberal society and the sovereign State, some feminist thinkers argue that as between individuals, an ethic of care should apply to relations between States.[6] Using the same analogy to analyze the jurisdiction of international law, others show that like the distinction between the public and private spheres in liberal thought, the international legal principle of nonintervention in the internal affairs of States leaves women vulnerable to discrimination and abuse.[7]

If the personification of the State exposes international legal norms as male, the acceptance of the sovereign State, sovereign self[8] equation paradoxically denies the individual and collective identity of women within and across States. In an international society peopled by States, women are analytically invisible because they belong to the State's sphere of personal autonomy. This mode of feminist analysis implicitly resurrects the older idea of international law as governing relations between sovereign States, leaving unexplored contemporary international legal methodologies that encompass other participants, interactions, and trends.

State sovereignty is an ambivalent concept in international law and the international legal imagination–at once brute fact of power and central metaphor of normativity, obstacle to paradisical future worlds and means of their realization, barrier to transparent global relations between individuals and groups and essential sanctuary for them.[9] This Article argues that women should seek to become

---

Mothercraft: Gender and Nationalism in Bengal, 5 GENDER & HIST. 231 (1993).

6. Isabelle R. Gunning, *Modernizing Customary International Law: The Challenge of Human Rights*, 31 VA. J. INT'L L. 211 (1991); Robert O. Keohane, *International Relations Theory: Contributions of a Feminist Standpoint*, *in* GENDER AND INTERNATIONAL RELATIONS 41 (Rebecca Grant & Kathleen Newland eds., 1991); Moira L. McConnell, Making Sense: International Law and its Developing Ethos of Care: "The Sound of One Hand Clapping" (Oct. 1991) (unpublished manuscript, on file with author).

7. On this public/private distinction, see Charlesworth et al., *supra* note 3, at 625; Hilary Charlesworth, *The Public/Private Distinction and the Right to Development in International Law*, 12 AUSTL. Y.B. INT'L L. 190, 194 (1992); Riane Eisler, *Human Rights: Toward an Integrated Theory for Action*, 9 HUM. RTS. Q. 287, 289-91 (1987); Jean Bethke Elshtain, *Sovereign God, Sovereign State, Sovereign Self*, 66 NOTRE DAME L. REV. 1355, 1370-73 (1991); Karen Engle, 86 AM. SOC'Y INT'L L. PROC. 253 (1992); Shelley Wright, *Economic Rights, Social Justice and the State: A Feminist Reappraisal*, *in* RECONCEIVING REALITY, *supra* note 2 (manuscript at 11-15, 19-20, on file with author).

8. The phrase is that of Jean Bethke Elshtain. *See* Elshtain, *supra* note 7.

9. *See* Engle, *supra* note 7; Karen Engle, *After the Collapse of the Public/Private Distinction: Strategizing Women's Rights*, *in* RECONCEIVING REALITY, *supra* note 2 (manuscript on file with author); David Kennedy, *Some Reflections on "The Role of Sovereignty in the New International Order,"* *in* STATE SOVEREIGNTY: THE CHALLENGE

conscious of their own assumptions about State sovereignty, to understand its potential as a strategy of empowerment, and to examine critically the ways in which State sovereignty sets the functional and allegorical parameters. of international law.[10]

The argument is developed by addressing two interrelated questions simultaneously. A first, concrete question is how to increase women's participation in the process of international law-making: the "hard" law of international treaty and custom, as well as other "softer" forms of international law. The implications of feminist theory for alternative conceptions of sovereignty is the second, abstract question explored here. In some cases, one question necessarily involves the other. Some strategies for ensuring women's direct participation in creating international law may require a reevaluation of the sovereign State as the exclusive representative of its population in the international sphere, whereas others can draw on arguments that are part of ongoing debates in international legal scholarship. Conversely, some feminist visions of a world order beyond State sovereignty may have radical implications for women's participation in international law-making, while others may seek to transcend the destructive logic of the nation-state by using insights from feminist theory to analyze national and ethnic claims to sovereign statehood and therefore may affect women only indirectly.

These two intertwined questions organize the analysis of three different aspects of State sovereignty, corresponding to Parts II, III, and IV of the Article: statism, the centrality of the State in international law, and the sovereign State as a bounded, unified self.

By statism, I mean the view of international law that regards State sovereignty as a function of political power, rather than justice; as the acknowledgement of political control by a government over a people and territory, rather than the judgment that a government justly represents the people. Part II looks at the much-debated

---

OF A CHANGING WORLD: "NEW APPROACHES AND THINKING ON INTERNATIONAL LAW" 237 (proceedings of the 21st Annual Conference of the Canadian Council on International Law at Ottawa, Oct. 1992) [hereinafter STATE SOVEREIGNTY].

10. Although scholars in the field of international relations have begun to examine the sovereign State through the lens of gender, those in international law have been slower to explore this central concept of international law. *See generally* GENDERED STATES: FEMINIST (RE)VISIONS OF INTERNATIONAL RELATIONS THEORY (V. Spike Peterson ed., 1992) [hereinafter GENDERED STATES]. For the argument that women should "work to change the heartland of international law," in particular the notions of statehood and sovereignty, see Charlesworth, *supra* note 2, at 6-8. *See also* Celina Romany, *State Responsibility Goes Private: A Feminist Critique of the Public/Private Distinction in International Human Rights Law*, *in* HUMAN RIGHTS OF WOMEN: NATIONAL AND INTERNATIONAL PERSPECTIVES (Rebecca J. Cook ed., forthcoming 1994) (manuscript at 8, on file with author) [hereinafter HUMAN RIGHTS OF WOMEN].

demise of statism and revival of liberalism in international legal discourse, and the arguments for women's increased participation in international law through the State that might flow from this rhetorical development.

Related to statism, the centrality of the sovereign State reflects the understanding that despite the growing cast of characters on the international scene, the State continues to be the only actor in international law that really matters, that is, the actor that plays the decisive role in making, interpreting, and enforcing international law. Part III explores the growing role of non-State actors in the creation of international law and the strategic implications for the creative and effective contribution of gender-conscious groups outside the State to international law.

In Part IV, the metaphor of the sovereign State as a bounded, unified self returns us to the problematic equation of State sovereignty with individual autonomy. Section A shows that the acceptance of this analogy in most feminist international legal scholarship prevents it from going beyond a contradictory understanding of State sovereignty and obscures the ways in which feminists might reimagine sovereignty. Section B introduces a number of alternative approaches to sovereignty that break apart the sovereign State into either the functions or the individuals and groups of which it is composed. Some of these approaches reconfigure participation in international law-making so as to permit the direct participation of non-State groups through the recognition of limited or overlapping sovereignty. Section B suggests how these approaches might interact with certain emerging strands of feminist theory and might ground women's direct participation in international law, instead of or in addition to State participation.

Rather than preferring a single approach, the Article develops a series of gendered perspectives on State sovereignty. The diversity of women's experiences with the internal aspects of State sovereignty[11] suggests that a single strategy or theory concerning its external aspect may be neither possible nor desirable. Moreover, women's identities are multifaceted[12] and on certain issues they may choose to

11. In TOWARD A FEMINIST THEORY OF THE STATE, Catharine MacKinnon writes, "Feminism has no theory of the state." CATHARINE A. MACKINNON, TOWARD A FEMINIST THEORY OF THE STATE 157 (1989). Nor, despite the promise of the book's title, is MacKinnon successful in developing one. *See* Drucilla Cornell, *Sexual Difference, the Feminine, and Equivalency: A Critique of MacKinnon's TOWARD A FEMINIST THEORY OF THE STATE*, 100 YALE L.J. 2247 (1991) (book review); Denise G. Réaume, *The Social Construction of Women and the Possibility of Change: Unmodified Feminism Revisited*, 5 CAN. J. WOMEN & L. 463 (1992) (book review).

12. *See, e.g.*, ELIZABETH V. SPELMAN, INESSENTIAL WOMAN: PROBLEMS OF EXCLUSION IN FEMINIST THOUGHT 133-59 (1988).

participate in international law in ways that reflect their identity as part of an ethinic, linguistic, or religious group, rather than the united front of gender.

II. STATISM

Part II offers a series of examples drawn from recent international legal practice and theory that suggest a trend away from the rhetoric of statism toward some form of liberal agenda.[13] From the ashes of an ideologically divided system has emerged a new willingness to condition the international status of the State on its respect for human rights, in particular the political rights central to notions of classical liberal democracy.[14] If the accepted definition of statehood[15] revolves around effective government,[16] the policies and scholarly arguments outlined in Part II amount to a reinterpretation of this requirement as democratic government. While no example goes so far as to alter the definition itself, they strike at the actualization of statehood in the international sphere by making democratic government a criterion for recognition of the State,[17] for protection of its territorial integrity, or for its full participation in relations between States.

Having made the rather contentious case for a trend away from statism, Part II then indicates how the trend might be used to ground arguments for women's increased participation and representation in the law-making process, both domestic and international. If the status of the State in international law rests on its respect for the right of participation in democratic governance, then it is open to women to insist, drawing on arguments developed in feminist critiques of domestic law, that the right be interpreted in ways that truly afford women equal representation in government.

---

13. On the liberal agenda in international law and international relations, see generally Anne-Marie Slaughter Burley, *International Law and International Relations Theory: A Dual Agenda*, 87 AM. J. INT'L L. 205, 226-38 (1993).

14. The international legal documents and literature discussed in Part II tend either to use the notions of representative, democratic, and liberal government interchangeably or to refer simultaneously to democracy and human rights.

15. For the best-known formulation, see the Convention on Rights and Duties of States, Dec. 26, 1933, art. 1, 49 Stat. 3097, 165 L.N.T.S. 19.

16. JAMES CRAWFORD, THE CREATION OF STATES 42 (1979).

17. *But see* Karen Knop, *The "Righting" of Recognition: Recognition of States in Eastern Europe and the Soviet Union*, *in* STATE SOVEREIGNTY, *supra* note 9, at 36, 36-43 (demonstrating the impossibility of determining whether the criteria for statehood are identical to the criteria for recognition of States or whether the two concepts, statehood and recognition, are separable).

The recent American and European Community guidelines on recognition of new States in Eastern Europe and the Soviet Union provide a first example. These guidelines condition recognition on respect for democracy and human rights. The five principles intended to govern American recognition of the Soviet and Yugoslav republics, as summarized by Deputy Assistant Secretary of State Johnson in October 1991, include:

> –Support for democracy and the rule of law, emphasizing the key role of elections in the democratic process;
> –Safeguarding of human rights, based on full respect for the individual and including equal treatment of minorities; and
> –Respect for international law and obligations, especially adherence to the Helsinki Final Act and the Charter of Paris.[18]

The E.C. Guidelines on the Recognition of New States in Eastern Europe and in the Soviet Union, adopted on December 16, 1991, require, among other things:

> –respect for the provisions of the Charter of the United Nations and the commitments subscribed to in the Final Act of Helsinki and in the Charter of Paris, especially with regard to the rule of law, democracy and human rights;
> –guarantees for the rights of ethnic and national groups and minorities in accordance with the commitments subscribed to in the framework of the CSCE;[19]

An E.C. statement on recognition of the Yugoslav republics, adopted the same day as the more general Guidelines, reiterates the Community's concern for human rights in war-torn Yugoslavia. That statement provides that Yugoslav republics wishing to be recognized as independent States were by December 23, 1991 to state, among other things, whether:

> –they accept the commitments contained in the above mentioned guidelines;

18. *Yugoslavia: Trying to End the Violence*, FOREIGN POL'Y BULL., Nov.-Dec. 1991, at 39, 42 (testimony of Ralph Johnson, Deputy Assistant Secretary of State for European and Canadian Affairs, Oct. 17, 1991). *See also The New Situation in the Soviet Union and the Republics*, FOREIGN POL'Y BULL., Sept.-Oct. 1991, at 39, 44 (statement of Robert B. Zoellick, Under Secretary of State for Economic and Agricultural Affairs and Counselor, Oct. 2, 1991).

19. Declaration on the Guidelines on the Recognition of New States in Eastern Europe and in the Soviet Union, 31 I.L.M. 1486, 1487 (1992).

> –they accept the provisions laid down in the draft Convention–especially those in Chapter II on human rights and rights of national or other ethnic groups–under consideration by the Conference on Yugoslavia;[20]

Although it was the rights of ethnic minorities that came under particular scrutiny in the application of the guidelines,[21] the criteria for recognition listed by both the United States and the European Community are broad enough to encompass respect for both women's right to participate equally in the democratic process and women's rights more generally.

A second example of the move away from statism is the recent international legal literature that seeks to establish a basis in international law for a right to democratic governance *and* to condition statehood, in some way, on this right. I include two related schools of thought in this literature. The work of the first, older school is part of a larger debate on the meaning of self-determination in post-colonial international law. These scholars, who include Antonio Cassese[22] and Allan Rosas,[23] associate the right of internal self-determination with the right to representative democracy. A number of them condition statehood on the right to representative democracy in the negative sense that the territorial integrity of a State without representative government (where *internal* self-determination has not been realized) is not protected by international law against secessionist demands (the exercise of *external* self-determination) by the unrepresented group.[24]

The second, newer school of thought is represented most

20. Declaration on Yugoslavia, 31 I.L.M. 1485, 1486 (1992).

21. *See* Opinions 4-7, 31 I.L.M. 1501-17 (1992) (Arbitration Commission established by the European Community within the framework of the Conference on Yugoslavia).

22. Antonio Cassese, *The Self-Determination of Peoples*, *in* THE INTERNATIONAL BILL OF RIGHTS: THE COVENANT ON CIVIL AND POLITICAL RIGHTS 92, 96-98, 101-102, 106 (Louis Henkin ed., 1981); Antonio Cassese, *The Helsinki Declaration and Self-Determination*, *in* HUMAN RIGHTS, INTERNATIONAL LAW AND THE HELSINKI ACCORD 83, 100, 102-03 (Thomas Buergenthal ed., 1977) [hereinafter Cassese, *Helsinki Declaration*].

23. Allan Rosas, *Internal Self-Determination*, *in* MODERN LAW OF SELF-DETERMINATION 225 (Christian Tomuschat ed., forthcoming 1993) (on file with author); Allan Rosas, *Democracy and Human Rights*, *in* HUMAN RIGHTS IN A CHANGING EAST-WEST PERSPECTIVE 17, 31-33 (Allan Rosas & Jan Helgesen eds., 1990). *See also, e.g.*, Asbjørn Eide, *Possible Ways and Means of Facilitating the Peaceful and Constructive Solution of Problems Involving Minorities*, ¶ 165, U.N. Doc. E/CN.4/Sub.2/1992/37 (1992).

24. Cassese, *Helsinki Declaration*, *supra* note 22, at 90-92, 104; Erica-Irene A. Daes, *Explanatory Note Concerning the Draft Declaration on the Rights of Indigenous Peoples*, ¶¶ 20-23, U.N. Doc. E/CN.4/Sub.2/1993/26/Add.1 (1993); Eide, *supra* note 23.

prominently by Thomas Franck, whose article *The Emerging Right to Democratic Governance*[25] set the parameters for the scholarly debate[26] on whether democratic government has become the acid test of legitimacy[27] in the international system. This school seeks to craft a right to democratic governance from existing rights of different lineages, the most venerable of which is the right of self-determination. Although Franck focuses on establishing the existence–or, at least, the emergence–of the right, he anticipates that "the legitimacy of each government someday will be measured definitively by international rules and processes."[28] Rather than being isolated as a criterion for the recognition of statehood alone, democracy will be promoted and protected by the entire fabric of collective international processes.[29]

---

25. Thomas M. Franck, *The Emerging Right to Democratic Governance*, 86 AM. J. INT'L L. 46 (1992). *See also* Gregory H. Fox, *The Right to Political Participation in International Law*, 17 YALE J. INT'L L. 539 (1992); Morton H. Halperin, *Guaranteeing Democracy*, 91 FOREIGN POL'Y 105 (1993); Dinah Shelton, *Representative Democracy and Human Rights in the Western Hemisphere*, 12 HUM. RTS. L.J. 353 (1991); Henry J. Steiner, *Political Participation as a Human Right*, 1 HARV. HUM. RTS. Y.B. 77 (1988).

26. Panel Discussion, *National Sovereignty Revisited: Perspectives on the Emerging Norm of Democracy in International Law*, 86 AM. SOC'Y INT'L L. PROC. 249 (1992); Panel Discussion, *Democracy and Legitimacy–Is There an Emerging Duty to Ensure a Democratic Government in General and Regional Customary International Law?*, *in* CONTEMPORARY INTERNATIONAL LAW ISSUES: SHARING PAN-EUROPEAN AND AMERICAN PERSPECTIVES 126 (1992) (proceedings of a conference jointly sponsored by the American Society of International Law & Nederlandse Vereniging Voor Internationaal Recht at the Hague, June 1991) [hereinafter CONTEMPORARY INTERNATIONAL LAW ISSUES].

27. Franck uses the term "legitimacy" in two different senses: to refer to the property of a given international legal norm, in this case the right to democratic governance, and to describe a State or government that complies with this right. I intend it here in the latter sense.

28. Franck, *supra* note 25, at 50.

29. *Id.* at 46. *See also* W. Michael Reisman, *Sovereignty and Human Rights in Contemporary International Law*, 84 AM. J. INT'L L. 866 *passim* (1990). (Modern international law has redefined State sovereignty as popular sovereignty, working qualitative changes in virtually every component of the system.). Authors differ, however, as to what international processes might give effect to the right to democratic governance. *Compare id.* at 869-72 (If sovereignty is understood as the sovereignty of the people, then cross-border military actions aimed at displacing a usurper and emplacing the people who were elected in elections endorsed by international monitors as free and fair is not necessarily a violation of sovereignty.) *with* the panel discussions in 86 AM. SOC'Y INT'L L. PROC., *supra* note 26, at 267 (The wave of democratization will ebb, depriving intervention of its normative justification; the emphasis is not on intervention, but on the design of international institutions to preserve this wave.) *and* CONTEMPORARY INTERNATIONAL LAW ISSUES, *supra* note 26, at 133, 135-36, 139-40 (The duty to "promote" democratic government does not extend to "ensuring" it.).

A final example of anti-statism is drawn from Fernando Tesón's work on the morality of international law.[30] Unlike the two previous examples, this example does not concern positive international law, but is part of the theory of international law that Tesón develops from the philosophy of Immanuel Kant. At the same time, the previous examples may be seen as instantiating the philosophical premises adopted by Tesón.

According to Tesón's Kantian theory of international law, only a State that respects human rights and the principle of democratic representation is legitimate and therefore entitled to represent its citizens internationally.[31] For Tesón, while an illegitimate State should retain some rights, it should not benefit from the rights conferred by membership in the alliance of legitimate, that is, liberal democratic, States.[32] He recommends, for instance, that the U.N. Charter be amended so as to require that only democratic governments that respect human rights be allowed to represent members and that only democratic States be accepted as new members.[33]

For women, the significance of the above examples lies in their rejection of the statist model of the international system, which is indifferent to the type of domestic regime and the relationship between state and society. In its place, these examples premise the State's international recognition or legitimacy on its status as a representative democracy. The treatment of representative democracy in these examples does not explicitly take account of gender; indeed the references contained in much of the literature to such thinkers as Hume, Locke,[34] and Kant[35] suggest that these authors see the universality of the right to participate in the democratic process as obviating the need to consider gender separately. Nevertheless, the rhetorical scaffolding has been put in place and women can now use it to construct the argument that a State's international status should be conditional on other, gender-

30. Fernando R. Tesón, *The Kantian Theory of International Law*, 92 COLUM. L. REV. 53 (1992).

31. *Id.* at 69-70. The distinction between liberal and nonliberal States is fundamental to liberal analyses of international law and international relations. *See, e.g.* Burley, *supra* note 13, at 229-30, 232, 236-38.

32. Tesón, *supra* note 30, at 89.

33. *Id.* at 100. *Cf.* Fox, *supra* note 25, at 597-606 (The United Nations should use the recommendations of U.N. election monitors as a basis for seating delegates.).

34. Franck, *supra* note 25, at 49.

35. Tesón, *supra* note 30; Franck, *supra* note 25, at 88. *See* R.B.J. Walker, *Gender and Critique in the Theory of International Relations*, *in* GENDERED STATES, *supra* note 10, at 179, 194 ("a new celebration of Kantian republicanism").

conscious ideas of representation and democracy.[36]

It is an indisputable fact that women are conspicuously few at the highest echelons both of national foreign service[37] and of international organizations.[38] Even at lower levels of diplomacy, it is not unusual for a female diplomat to find herself the only woman amid a group of somber-suited male diplomats. Classical liberal theorists of international law would argue that, at least in the case of national diplomatic corps and national political delegations, this situation does not constitute under-representation so long as it is the result of formally equal opportunities for political participation afforded men and women. Feminist jurisprudence suggests three main types of response to the argument that formal equality is sufficient to ensure adequate representation of women at all levels of decision-making: an equality response, a difference response, and, more tentatively, a collective autonomy response. Although the first two types have become standard critiques of domestic law, they have yet to be applied to international legal theory.[39]

---

36. *See* Donald M. McRae, Notes for Presentation to Department of Justice Seminar 22 (Sept. 14, 1992) (on file with author).

Such an argument need not lead toward greater internationalization and away from strong national authorities. Mona Harrington, writing in international relations, argues for a feminist liberal State, whose process of government would give particular weight to the voices of subordinated groups. Since she conceives of the primary international task of a feminist liberal State to be the safeguarding of the priorities set domestically though this process, the result would be a system of inward-looking States. Mona Harrington, *What Exactly Is Wrong with the Liberal State as an Agent of Change?*, *in* GENDERED STATES, *supra* note 10, at 64, 74-76.

37. *See* sources cited *supra* note 3. *See also Report of the Secretary-General, Equality: Equality in Political Participation and Decision-Making*, ¶ 53, U.N. Doc. E/CN.6/1990/2 (1989), *supplemented by* U.N. Doc. E/CN.6/1990/2/Corr.1 (1989) [hereinafter *Equality in Political Participation*]. On the U.S. Department of State, see NANCY E. MCGLEN & MEREDITH REID SARKEES, WOMEN IN FOREIGN POLICY: THE INSIDERS 75-77 (1993).

38. *See* sources cited *supra* note 3. *See also Report of the Secretary-General, Peace: Women and the Peace Process*, ¶¶ 74-81, U.N. Doc. E/CN.6/1993/4 (1992) [hereinafter *Women and the Peace Process*]; *Report of the Secretary-General, Peace: Equal Participation in All Efforts to Promote International Cooperation, Peace and Disarmament*, ¶¶ 26-27, U.N. Doc. E/CN.6/1992/10 (1991) [hereinafter *Equal Participation*]; *Equality in Political Participation*, *supra* note 37, ¶¶ 49-56.

39. While feminist critiques may not yet have entered international legal theory, they implicitly inform a series of U.N. reports on women's unequal participation at all levels of political decision-making. *See Women and the Peace Process*, *supra* note 38; *Equal Participation*, *supra* note 38 (including as annex Draft Platform Recommended by the Expert Group on the Role of Women in Public Life); U.N. OFFICE AT VIENNA CENTRE FOR SOCIAL DEVELOPMENT AND HUMANITARIAN AFFAIRS, WOMEN IN POLITICS AND DECISION-MAKING IN THE LATE TWENTIETH CENTURY: A UNITED NATIONS STUDY (1992), based on *Equality in Political Participation*, *supra* note 37; *Report of the Secretary-General, Peace: Full Participation of Women in the Construction of their*

The equality response is to say that even if institutions and practices do not overtly discriminate against women, they effectively exclude or inhibit women's participation by adopting a male norm as the standard by which eligibility or behavior is judged.[40] Equality can be achieved only through rules that take account of the different needs and characteristics of women.[41] Three examples[42] serve to illustrate the application of feminist equality theory to representation in international law-making, where law is made not only through the formalized negotiation process leading to the conclusion of an international treaty and momentous diplomatic incidents contributing to the creation of a rule of customary international law, but also through the ritualized minutiae of statements, telegrams, political declarations, and other diplomatic acts. First, the questions on foreign service entrance examinations may be biased in favor of male applicants, as was found to be the case in the United States, where a federal district court required the State Department to revise its entrance examinations.[43] Second, many aspects of the diplomatic

---

Countries and in the Creation of Just Social and Political Systems, U.N. Doc. E/CN.6/1989/7 (1989).

40. CATHARINE A. MACKINNON, FEMINISM UNMODIFIED: DISCOURSES ON LIFE AND LAW 32-45 (1987); MARTHA MINOW, MAKING ALL THE DIFFERENCE: INCLUSION, EXCLUSION, AND AMERICAN LAW 49-78 (1990). For a discussion of equality by MacKinnon in the context of international human rights law, see MacKinnon, *supra* note 4; Catharine A. MacKinnon, *On Torture: A Feminist Perspective on Human Rights, in* HUMAN RIGHTS IN THE TWENTY-FIRST CENTURY: A GLOBAL CHALLENGE 21 (Kathleen E. Mahoney & Paul Mahoney eds., 1993).

41. Christine A. Littleton, *Equality Across Difference: A Place for Rights Discourse?*, 3 WIS. WOMEN'S L.J. 189 (1987).

42. The U.N. report on equality in political participation and decision-making contains a list of constraints on women's participation at senior levels of the civil service generally, as well as strategies for change. *Equality in Political Participation*, *supra* note 37, ¶¶ 46-47. For the argument that the culture and gender ethos of the U.S. Department of State and the Department of Defense–currently the two major players in American foreign policy decision-making–have restricted and continue to restrict women's ability to participate fully in the process, see MCGLEN & SARKEES, *supra* note 37, at 60-129.

43. The U.S. Department of State cancelled its Foreign Service Exam for 1989 following a court decision that the test discriminated against women because roughly twice as many men as women passed its mandatory general background section. Judith Havemann, *State Dept. Acknowledges Sex Bias*; *Women Hindered in Foreign Service*, WASH. POST, Apr. 20, 1989, at A1. A U.S. district court required the State Department to throw out the scores on the general background section of the exam for 1985, 1986, and 1987, and to re-rank the candidates for hiring. Palmer v. Shultz, No.76-1439 (D.D.C. Jan. 19, 1989) (order), *modified* Palmer v. Baker, No. 76-1439 (D.D.C. Mar. 22, 1989) (order). The challenge to the Foreign Service Exam was originally part of a suit brought in 1976 by Foreign Service officer Alison Palmer alleging that numerous practices of the State Department, including hiring, promotion, and

life-style assume the model of the male diplomat whose wife either does not work outside the home or is willing to give up her own work to accompany her husband on his far-flung postings and missions, and to act as his hostess for a variety of diplomatic functions.[44] Female diplomats are more limited in their choice of postings; in addition to certain traditional societies where women representing their State would encounter tremendous official resistance, women–and increasingly men–are restricted by the need to consider where their spouse will be able to practice his or her profession.[45] A feminist theory of equality would require that female diplomats' different needs and characteristics be reflected in formulating transfer policies, categorizing posts as "hardship," or ranking posts for the purpose of career advancement. Finally, the negotiating style of women, who are late-comers to the table, tends to be measured against the demeanor and strategies already established as the norm by male negotiators, little consideration being given to whether other approaches to negotiation might be equally effective.

Gender-sensitive change to the foreign service may include some form of temporary affirmative action for women as a way to accelerate systemic and attitudinal change. Alternatively, the case can be made that equal representation of women in international law-making should be guaranteed permanently, whether for all aspects of foreign relations or only those of particular relevance to women. Permanent equal representation may be justified on either a difference response or a collective autonomy response to formal equality.

The difference response is that men's experiences, interests, and ways of reasoning are so different from those of women[46] that male

---

performance evaluation, discriminated against women. For a discussion of the Palmer case and its impact on State Department practice, see McGLEN & SARKEES, *supra* note 37, at 63-65, 82-84, 90-91, 114-21. In a recent development, a group of female Foreign Service officers filed a motion in June 1993 seeking a five-year extension of an order that came out of the Palmer case. *Women Foreign Service Officers Sue State*, CHRISTIAN SCI. MONITOR, June 21, 1993, at A4.

44. *See* CYNTHIA ENLOE, BANANAS, BEACHES AND BASES: MAKING FEMINIST SENSE OF INTERNATIONAL POLITICS 95-114 (1989).

45. *See generally id.* at 114-23.

46. *E.g.*, CAROL GILLIGAN, IN A DIFFERENT VOICE: PSYCHOLOGICAL THEORY AND WOMEN'S DEVELOPMENT (1982). A U.N. report on equal participation in all efforts to promote international cooperation, peace, and disarmament argues that women and men differ in their priorities, attitudes, behavior, and political style. *Equal Participation*, *supra* note 38, ¶¶ 36-56; Draft Platform Recommended by the Expert Group on the Role of Women in Public Life, *in id.* at annex, ¶¶ 12-20. Data from public opinion surveys of average citizens conducted in the United States, for instance, point to a "gender gap" in foreign policy beliefs. McGLEN & SARKEES, *supra* note 37, at 189-94.

The objection is sometimes raised that nevertheless, the policies of women in office

voices can never speak for female voices. This response takes a weak and a strong form. According to the weak form, women's voices should be equally represented because all voices should be represented and women are half of humankind. A strong form is rooted in the idea that women's experience is ethically superior and can therefore provide a standard for judging the world.[47] One of the central dilemmas for feminist legal theory, however, is why women's experience should be recognized and valued in this special way: what is women's experience anyway, and why should it count for more than other people's experience?[48]

A collective autonomy response might be derived from the justification outlined by Denise Réaume for parallel institutional structures for ethnic and cultural groups.[49] Réaume suggests that separate representation may be based on an argument for collective autonomy, which she constructs as analogous to the standard arguments for individual autonomy, namely, that in part "at least in respect of some issues, value lies in being chosen by the individual" and in part "it is better to choose one's own life plan, even if one chooses unwisely, than to have a better plan thrust upon one."[50] On both a difference response and a collective autonomy response, the relevant unit is women as a group. On the collective autonomy response, however, women should be able to decide at least certain international issues not because they will decide them better than or even differently from men, but because they as a group, for the reasons Réaume outlines, should be able to make the decisions that

do not differ significantly from those of their male counterparts. Studies on the foreign policy preferences of decision-making elites in the United States, including studies focused exclusively on the views of the elite actually responsible for U.S. foreign policy, tend to support this objection. *Id.* at 194-215, 283-84. However, U.N. reports cite research to show that this will hold true until a "critical mass" of women, at least 30% representation, is reached, which is currently the case only in a handful of countries. *Equal Participation*, *supra* note 38, ¶¶ 10-11, 38-40; WOMEN IN POLITICS AND DECISION-MAKING IN THE LATE TWENTIETH CENTURY, *supra* note 39, at 107-08.

Researchers studying the Norwegian experience, where a critical mass has been achieved, maintain that beyond the problem of critical mass lies the problem of collective action within and across political parties. HEGE SKJEIE, THE FEMINIZATION OF POWER: NORWAY'S POLITICAL EXPERIMENT (1986-) 64-75, 77-79 (Institute for Social Research, Oslo, Report 88:8, 1988).

47. For an overview of the debate both among women activists and among feminist theorists on equality versus difference as a justification for women's inclusion in the foreign policy process, see MCGLEN & SARKEES, *supra* note 37, at 3-10.

48. *See* Deborah L. Rhode, *Feminist Critical Theories*, *in* FEMINIST JURISPRUDENCE 594, 597-99 (Patricia Smith ed., 1993).

49. Denise G. Réaume, *Moral and Legal Responses to the Multi-Cultural, Multi-Ethnic State*, 15 RECHTSTHEORIE 251, 255 (1993).

50. *Id.*

affect their lives. While equal representation of women in diplomacy is admittedly less assurance of collective autonomy than the separate institutional structures Réaume discusses, I submit that they may be justified in the same way.

As the case of the International Labour Organisation suggests, however, how representation reconciles a feminist approach with the purposes of a particular international organization may not be easily resolved. Article 3 of the ILO Constitution reads in part:

> (1) The meetings of the General Conference of representatives of the Members shall be held... at least once in every year. It shall be composed of four representatives of each of the Members, of whom two shall be *Government* delegates and the two others shall be delegates representing respectively the *employers* and the *workpeople* of each of the Members.
> (2) Each delegate may be accompanied by advisers, who shall not exceed two in number for each item on the agenda of the meeting. *When questions specially affecting women are to be considered by the Conference, one at least of the advisers should be a woman.*
> ...
> (6) Advisers shall not speak except on a request made by the delegate whom they accompany and by the special authorisation of the President of the Conference, and may not vote.[51]

The annual Manual for the Conference expands as follows:

> The questions considered at the ILC and other ILO meetings nowadays are of equal relevance to women and men...as early as 1975, at its 60th Session, the Conference asked in a resolution that women be appointed to delegations on the same basis and by the same standards as men.[52]

Should women strive to be equally represented within each of the three groups (government, employers, and workpeople) that compose the member-State delegations to the International Labour Conference, or should the tripartite composition of the member-State delegations be changed to quadripartite for some or all agenda items

51. INTERNATIONAL LABOUR OFFICE, CONSTITUTION OF THE INTERNATIONAL LABOUR ORGANISATION AND STANDING ORDERS OF THE INTERNATIONAL LABOUR CONFERENCE (May 1989) (emphasis added).

52. *Quoted in* HILKKA PIETILÄ & INGRID EIDE, UNITED NATIONS AND THE ADVANCEMENT OF WOMEN: THE ROLE OF THE NORDIC COUNTRIES TO PROMOTE EFFORTS BY THE U.N. SYSTEM FOR THE ADVANCEMENT OF WOMEN annex 3, at 2 (Nordic U.N. Project Report 16:1990, 1990).

by adding representatives of women to the representatives of government, employers, and workpeople? This question engages the ongoing Marxist-feminist debate on the relative importance of class and gender.[53]

III. CENTRALITY OF THE STATE

> Is there, then, in international politics something like an international civil society that repoliticizes public life outside or at the margins of these official state activities? I think there is, and that investigation of marginal international economic networks, the international peace movement, international people-to-people organizations of material and cultural solidarity, and international movements of women, people of color, and other groups can reveal a promising underside to the future of international relations.
>
> Iris Marion Young[54]

In exploring how her discussion of social justice in Western welfare capitalist societies might be extended to international politics, political philosopher Iris Young speculates on the existence of an international civil society. Part III argues that as she surmises, this civic space is becoming increasingly important in the doing and thinking of international law. It argues further that for women to realize fully this "promising underside to the future of international relations," they not only must take an active part in international civil society, but also must develop a theoretical justification for enlarging its role in the creation of international law.

Whereas the arguments presented in Part II were premised on women working through the State, Part III suggests that by rejecting the centrality of the State, women can work through the non-State groups and networks that make up international civil society to influence the development, interpretation, and implementation of international law by States.

Why might it be important for women to reject–or, at least, not to assume–the centrality of the State? Perhaps the most obvious reason is that women's interests and concerns are not defined exclusively, or in many cases even significantly, by State borders; they are shaped by gender, sexuality, culture, and other factors. The fact of

53. For an overview of the debate, see MARIANNE HESTER, LEWD WOMEN AND WICKED WITCHES: A STUDY OF THE DYNAMICS OF MALE DOMINATION 8-57 (1992).

54. IRIS M. YOUNG, JUSTICE AND THE POLITICS OF DIFFERENCE 259 (1990).

common citizenship does not mean that women and men of the same State think similarly or are affected similarly by international issues on which their State takes a position. At the same time, women may feel themselves members of a group based on gender, or gender in combination with factors such as religion or ethnicity, that extends beyond their State. So long as States are the primary international actors, however, women's voices can be heard only through the medium of the State, and alliances between groups of women in different States are dependent on alliances between their respective States.[55]

Richard Falk hypothesizes the development of an "international civil society" within which groups would form to take normative initiatives without state authorization, as exemplified by the MacBride Commission to assess Israel's conduct in the 1982 Lebanon War and the Permanent People's Tribunal established by the 1976 Algiers Declaration of the Rights of Peoples.[56] Another such initiative, not cited by Falk, was the 1976 International Tribunal on Crimes Against Women, a non-governmental tribunal that heard women from many different States testify about their experiences of oppression and violence.[57]

Within the international civil society that Falk describes, women's initiatives may take a variety of forms.[58] Radical,

---

55. *Cf.* Gunning, *supra* note 6, at 229-30 ("[T]he Women in Development movement represented the interests of its constituent group in a way that was different from how the members' respective states would.").

56. Richard Falk, *The Rights of Peoples (In Particular Indigenous Peoples), in* THE RIGHTS OF PEOPLES 17, 27-31 (James Crawford ed., 1988). *See also* Richard Falk, *Keeping Nuremberg Alive, in* INTERNATIONAL LAW: A CONTEMPORARY PERSPECTIVE 494 (Richard Falk et al. eds., 1985). *Cf.* Douglas M. Johnston, *Functionalism in the Theory of International Law*, 26 CAN. Y.B. INT'L L. 3, 29 n.91 (1988) (A pragmatic alternative to making individuals and groups limited subjects of international law would be "the design and organization of new, non-statist forums or arenas, where these other interests can be represented outside the framework of the United Nations.").

57. CRIMES AGAINST WOMEN: PROCEEDINGS OF THE INTERNATIONAL TRIBUNAL (Diana E.H. Russell & Nicole Van de Ven eds., 1984); Chinkin, *supra* note 5, at 292 (As an initiative by civil society, the International Tribunal on Crimes Against Women ranks with examples given by Falk). On the Global Tribunal on Violations of Women's Human Rights held at the 1993 World Conference on Human Rights in Vienna, see Biographies of Women Testifying at the Global Tribunal on Violations of Women's Human Rights (Women's Human Rights,Vienna No. 9, June 15, 1993) (on file with author); Report of the Global Tribunal on Violations of Women's Human Rights (submitted to the World Conference on Human Rights, Vienna, June 14-25, 1993) (on file with author); Women's Tribunal Judges Issue Recommendations to United Nations (Women's Human Rights,Vienna No. 16, June 17, 1993) (on file with author).

58. One of the richest traditions of women's participation in international civil society is the women's peace movement. For a historical overview, see, e.g., *Women and the*

deliberately marginal actions aim at dislodging the most fundamental preconceptions of international law, while the more mainstream lobbying efforts of women's non-governmental organizations are adapted to the framework of international and regional organizations, for example, their lobbying of the U.N. Committee on the Elimination of Discrimination Against Women.[59] Although these initiatives typically have a greater impact on the development of "soft" law, such as U.N. resolutions and Conference on Security and Cooperation in Europe (CSCE) documents, they are also capable of influencing the creation of "hard" law, that is, treaty and custom.

There are signs that non-governmental organizations (NGOs) may assume greater importance in the post-Cold War international legal order. The CSCE process illustrates the passage of NGOs from pawns in a game of ideological standoff between the Western States and the Soviet bloc to sought-after participants in a political process now confronted with the fault-lines of ethnic conflict and economic disparity.[60] The growing receptiveness to NGO participation in the process has translated into CSCE provisions that allow NGOs to move from the corridors into the sessions. At the three recent Human Dimension Seminars, on tolerance, migration, and national minorities respectively, not only did NGOs have access to all plenary sessions and discussion groups, but they had the same standing to make oral contributions as the government delegations.[61] In his final report on the realization of economic, social, and cultural rights, U.N. Special Rapporteur Danilo Türk recommends not only that NGOs act as conduits for information, but that international NGOs be encouraged to submit "detailed analyses of the degree to which economic, social and cultural rights are realized in different settings," including their insights into the problems for the

---

Peace Process, *supra* note 38, ¶¶ 6-40.

59. For the ways in which non-governmental organizations concerned with women's rights can interact with the Committee on the Elimination of Discrimination Against Women, see Arvonne Fraser & Miranda Kazantsis, CEDAW No. 11 at 23-27 (Int'l Women's Rights Action Watch, 1992).

60. Rachel J. Brett, *NGOs and the Human Dimension of the CSCE*, 1 (No. 1) CSCE OFF. DEMOCRATIC INSTITUTIONS & HUM. RTS. BULL. 1, 2-5 (1992-93).

61. *Id.* at 4. *See* Helsinki Decisions, ch. IV, § 15; ch. VI, § 18 (1992). For a summary of recommendations for increased NGO participation in many of the CSCE mechanisms made at the most recent of the three CSCE Human Dimension Seminars, see the unofficial Moderator's Report from Discussion Group 1, *Case Studies on National Minorities Issues: Positive Results*, 1 (No. 3) CSCE OFF. DEMOCRATIC INSTITUTIONS & HUM. RTS. BULL. 28, 32 (1993).

realization of these rights and the root causes of these problems.[62] According to Elizabeth Dowdeswell, U.N. Undersecretary-General and Executive Director of UNEP and Habitat, the process of formally involving interested non-governmental groups in the preparation for a U.N. conference and in the conference itself, illustrated by the 1992 Earth Summit in Rio de Janeiro, is becoming entrenched in the U.N. system.[63]

The even greater degree of official involvement of NGOs in the 1993 World Conference on Human Rights in Vienna bears out Dowdeswell's prediction. At the same time, the NGO experience at the World Conference underlines the perils of NGOs becoming too "inside" to produce a strong alternative document while remaining too "outside" to influence the official document drafted by governments.[64] The agenda for the parallel NGO conference was altered when it diverged from the guidelines for discussion set by the government conference,[65] while NGOs were excluded from the drafting of the final document.[66]

If NGOs are seen as a chance for women's voices to be heard unmediated by States, then it is necessary to develop an international legal basis, independent of the consent of States, for NGO participation in the creation of international law. In an article on modernizing customary international law, Isabelle Gunning argues that to regard the actions of certain NGOs as contributing directly to the formation of customary international law would do no more than reflect the contemporary dynamic of its formation.[67] The work of Hilary Charlesworth,[68] Christine Chinkin,[69] and Donald McRae[70] also raises the possibility of a greater role for NGOs in the creation of international law, but appears to frame it as part of a more fundamental feminist reconceptualization of how international law functions. Whereas Gunning addresses how to formalize the influence that certain well-established NGOs already exert on the

62. Danilo Türk, *The Realization of Economic, Social and Cultural Rights*, ¶ 244, U.N. Doc. E/CN.4/Sub.2/16 (1992).

63. James Rusk, *Top UN Post Was a Shocker*, GLOBE & MAIL, Apr. 21, 1993, at A3.

64. I am grateful to Professor Craig Scott for sharing his impressions of the Conference with me. Interview with Craig Scott, Academic Advisor to the Canadian Delegation to the 1993 World Conference on Human Rights (July 16, 1993).

65. *Id.*

66. Alan Riding, *China Wins on Ejecting Unofficial Rights Groups at Vienna Meeting*, N.Y. TIMES, June 17, 1993, at A6.

67. Gunning, *supra* note 6, at 220-22, 227-34.

68. Charlesworth, *supra* note 2, at 7.

69. Chinkin, *supra* note 5, at 293.

70. McRae, *supra* note 36, at 23.

creation of custom, Charlesworth, Chinkin, and McRae seem to contemplate a restructuring of participation that would not just recognize the power that some women's NGOs now have, but would actually give power to women's NGOs more widely.

Gunning's article is instructive because it is, to my knowledge, the only work of international law to develop an alternative account of participation in international law-making grounded in feminist theory. Through the following discussion of her argument, I also seek to bring out some of the different types of arguments that might be made for more inclusive structures of participation.

Gunning's reasoning proceeds from what international relations actually are–when seen from a perspective that incorporates not only masculine, but also feminist and Afrocentric ways of seeing.[71] She maintains that the traditional view of international relations as a Hobbesian war of all against all focuses only on the conflictual behavior of states, ignoring the cooperative behavior observable for centuries in military and economic alliances. In this Hobbesian world, the power sought by States is defined as control over others. Gunning characterizes the conflictual account of international relations as male because its assumptions about State behavior reflect the masculine view of the individual as separate.[72] Feminist and Afrocentric views of the individual as connected to others by relationships and community, Gunning indicates, would produce a different account of international relations, one capable of explaining cooperative behavior between States.[73] From a feminist perspective, power among States would be understood in Hannah Arendt's terms of action in concert,[74] rather than in the traditional

---

71. Gunning, *supra* note 6, at 215-21.

72. *Id.* at 217. Mona Harrington argues on the basis of the American experience that psychologically, political fixation on boundedness is related not only to anxiety about masculinity, but also to a material condition of insecurity. Harrington, *supra* note 36, at 69-72. Moreover, she insists that philosophically, atomism in selves/States is characteristic only of the contractarian tradition in liberalism. *Id.* at 72-73. *See also* CHARLES TAYLOR, *Atomism, in* 2 PHILOSOPHY AND THE HUMAN SCIENCES: PHILOSOPHICAL PAPERS 187 (1985).

73. Gunning aims here to provide an alternative account of *how* States reason. Recently-developed regime theories of international relations also seek to explain and predict cooperative behavior in the State system. Most regime theories, however, differ from Gunning's analysis in that they offer an alternative account of *the environment* in which States reason. Gunning, *supra* note 6, at 216-17.

74. *Id.* at 218. *See* HANNAH ARENDT, ON VIOLENCE 44 (1969) ("*Power* corresponds to the human ability not just to act but to act in concert. Power is never the property of an individual; it belongs to a group and remains in existence only so long as the group keeps together."). *See also* HANNAH ARENDT, THE HUMAN CONDITION 200-05, 244-45 (1958). For other specialists in international relations and international political theory who see Arendt's definition of power as representing a feminist paradigm shift in

terms of control over others.

The point might be made here that Hannah Arendt's definition of power *as such* is not feminist. While her definition of power as action in concert may highlight the cooperative behavior of States suggestive of a feminist ethic of care, it does not carry with it that ethic. Arendt's project was to separate power from violence. Her definition of power has a democratic dimension, but at its most extreme, All against One, as she puts it, it is potentially oppressive of minorities.[75] Moreover, power is not justified in terms of aims; in Arendt's view, power is an "end in itself" because the power structure precedes and outlasts any aim that it might be used to pursue.[76] Finally, if "power needs no justification, being inherent in the very existence of political communities," it does need legitimacy, which is traceable to the initial getting together.[77]

For Gunning, Arendt's conception of power acts as the bridge between what international relations really are, if seen from a more complex perspective, and who the actors that create international law should be. Once we regard power as action in concert, she argues, then there is no reason not to accord significant instances of concerted action other than State action the ability to help create law: "non-national entities which marshal broad support may have the right to participate in the creation of custom,"[78] and, later on, "[i]f power, and hence sovereignty, is understood as the ability to effect action through cooperation as well as coercion, then the actions of NGOs have a clear role to play in international law, even before their efforts result in a state 'act.' "[79]

This step in Gunning's argument is difficult to follow because it reflects only indirectly that international law and international relations are different types of enquiries.[80] As she herself points out, the assumption that only State actions contribute to the formation of customary international law is traditionally justified in terms of consent: States are bound by international law because they consent to be bound by signing treaties or by acting consistently out of a sense

---

international politics, see, e.g., Jean Bethke Elshtain, *Reflections on War and Political Discourse: Realism, Just War, and Feminism in a Nuclear Age*, *in* JUST WAR THEORY 260, 272-76 (Jean Bethke Elshtain ed., 1992); Keohane, *supra* note 6, at 42-44; J. Ann Tickner, *Hans Morgenthau's Principles of Political Realism: A Feminist Reformulation*, *in* GENDER AND INTERNATIONAL RELATIONS, *supra* note 6, at 27, 33.

75. ARENDT, ON VIOLENCE, *supra* note 74, at 42.

76. *Id.* at 51.

77. *Id.* at 52.

78. Gunning, *supra* note 6, at 220-21.

79. *Id.* at 227-28.

80. *See* Oran R. Young, 86 AM. SOC'Y INT'L L. PROC. 172, 174-75 (1992).

of obligation so as to give rise to a custom.[81] Gunning's argument for changing this assumption does not engage this justification, but derives instead from a new understanding of power. Showing us something about power, however, does not show us why we should change the way we think about law. Proving that the National Rifle Association is a powerful lobby in the United States would not convince us that the NRA should be given a direct voice in the legislative process as a normative rather than a pragmatic matter. By showing us that States are not autonomous, she has not demonstrated that we should no longer regard their consent as foundational to international law.

To establish a greater role for NGOs in the formation of international custom, Gunning may make one of three arguments: a consent argument in positive international law, an internal critique of consent in international law, or an external, feminist critique. According to the first of these arguments, some NGOs have the right to participate in the formation of custom because it can be shown that States have consented, either directly or indirectly, to their participation. This reasoning reduces the feminist reconceptualization of power from the basis for modernizing customary international law to the inspiration for a classical doctrinal argument rooted in the consent of States.

An internal critique of consent in international law engages the premise that the consent of States is basic to international law because power is concentrated in States. If developments in international relations theory reveal power to be distributed differently, then States may no longer be the only entities whose consent is fundamental to international law. This reasoning suggests that if an NGO wields sufficient power, its actions should count toward the formation of customary international law.

While Gunning's justification for the role of NGOs in the creation of custom appears to be an internal critique of consent, much of her argument may also be seen as consistent with a consent argument in positive international law. The same is true of her earlier argument that the actions of international organizations, such as U.N. General Assembly resolutions, should contribute to the formation of international custom because they represent the collective actions of States.[82] While these actions may be analyzed as actions in concert, they may also be regarded as consensual behavior. Even Gunning's example of the International Labour

81. Gunning, *supra* note 6, at 215. Lest the criticism be made that I am giving consent-based theories of international law too much credit, I stress that the treatment of consent below reflects its embeddedness in the structure of Gunning's argument and not necessarily my own understanding of international law.

82. *Id.* at 221, 222-27.

Organisation as a forum in which both State and non-State actors participate may also be taken as an instance where States consented by treaty to a system of tripartite State delegations involving non-State actors.[83]

In certain places, moreover, Gunning's argument does not follow automatically from an internal critique of consent. She suggests that only NGOs which satisfy criteria akin to the U.N. Economic and Social Council (ECOSOC) criteria for consultative status should have the right to participate.[84] The ECOSOC criteria require the organization, among other things, to have aims that conform to the goals of the U.N. Charter, have an international character or express views of "major sections," and have a democratically elected constitution and essentially democratic procedure for making policy decisions.[85] Whereas some of the ECOSOC criteria follow from an internal critique as a convenient formulation of Gunning's alternative, feminist definition of power, that is, power measured as the ability to act in concert, others do not. Adherence to the values of the U.N. Charter, for instance, does not relate to the ability to act in concert, and the justification for this criterion is not made explicit in Gunning's commentary:

> The requirement that the organizations be committed to the goals and aims of the U.N. Charter would also be an attempt to exclude those organizations the primary goals of which might put them at odds with the core values embodied in the U.N. Charter.[86]

It is therefore necessary, I suggest, to place at least this criterion on some other basis, such as consent or natural rights.

Whether Gunning relies on a consent argument or an internal critique of consent in international law, her modernized view of customary international law, by definition, does not question either the idea of consent or the underlying distribution of power in the international system. This type of external critique is developed more generally by Shelley Wright. Wright argues, for example, that real inequalities in relationships between States are masked by the assumption common to customary and treaty law that States contract with one another as independent actors operating on an equal basis.[87] A consent argument or an internal critique of consent in international law benefits only those NGOs that are already part

83. *Id.* at 232-33.

84. *Id.* at 230.

85. *Id.* at 231.

86. *Id.* at 231-32.

87. Wright, *supra* note 7, at 13-14.

of the world power structures. To justify giving a voice to women's NGOs which may lack even the possibility to organize on a wide scale and act globally, due to oppressive or discriminatory regimes or insufficient resources, it would seem necessary to develop a more radical critique of participation in the creation of international law.

Ultimately, international civil society is a creature both liberated and enslaved by its marginality. Its existence at the edges of the system of States frees this mix of non-governmental organizations, unofficial groups of experts, and other initiatives from the narrow confines of self-interest that often dictate the position of States, and enables it to be more responsive to women's aspirations and more creative in developing proposals for change.[88] From the perspective of some Western feminists, the fluid and unconstricted nature of emerging international civil society may make it the optimal site for the cross-cultural feminist coalition politics advocated by Anne Marie Goetz[89] that "struggles to eliminate the elements of centre, unity and totality that organize structures into hierarchical oppositions" and "allows for the fact that women experience simultaneously many oppressions and must engage in a multitude of struggles that conflict and supplement each other."[90] Working outside the conclave of sovereign States in international law also corresponds to the domestic experience of some non-Western feminists that the state is neither a possible nor an appropriate arena for change.[91]

Despite the transformative potential of dancing in the normative margins of international law, gender-conscious groups in international civil society must contend with the fact that these margins are defined by the mainstream fora. That is, NGO participation in international and regional organizations must shape itself to the organizational structure and the contours of the issue as defined by the organization. Contrast, for instance, the growing opportunities for NGO involvement in the CSCE process with the argument of Finnish diplomat Anja-Riitta Ketokoski that women activists should not concentrate their efforts and hopes on the CSCE because it "may be *by its nature* the least women-friendly

88. *Cf.* Karen Engle, *International Human Rights and Feminism: When Discourses Meet*, 13 MICH. J. INT'L L. 517, 519-20 (1992) (International human rights law has been developed largely through challenges from the margins).

89. Anne Marie Goetz, *Feminism and the Claim to Know: Contradictions in Feminist Approaches to Women in Development*, *in* GENDER AND INTERNATIONAL RELATIONS, *supra* note 6, at 133, 149-53.

90. *Id.* at 151-52.

91. *See, e.g.*, Radhika Coomaraswamy, *To Bellow Like a Cow: Women, Ethnicity and the Discourse of Rights*, *in* HUMAN RIGHTS OF WOMEN, *supra* note 10 (manuscript at 10-12, on file with author).

organisational environment European women could choose."[92] While the conceptual framework of the CSCE does connect security issues with human rights issues, Ketokoski charges the CSCE with defining security too narrowly as military security. Instead, a feminist definition of security might reflect the interdependence of military, economic, and environmental security.[93]

As mainstream NGO participation shapes itself to the organizational and conceptual margins set by key international and regional fora, it risks creating a second margin that closely parallels the first. The 1993 World Conference on Human Rights may be seen as an instance of this double margin. There was a tendency for the NGO conference, held at the same time and in the same building as the government conference, to replicate the structure of representation and treatment of issues of the main conference. Reacting against the gravitational pull of the main conference, some NGOs insisted that a representative NGO committee not just correspond to geopolitical groupings similar to the coalitions formed in the main conference, but also reflect other overlapping forms of identification such as gender and ethnicity.[94]

More generally, the dark side of unregulated international civil society is its tendency to replicate the imbalance of political and economic power that characterizes the system of States,[95] an imbalance apparent in relations between First World and Third World NGOs.[96] In addition, international civil society is not constituted exclusively by non-State actors seeking to hold States morally accountable; it also includes powerful multinational

92. Anja-Riitta Ketokoski, Toward a More Effective Application of Women's Rights in the European System 7, Paper presented at the Consultation on Women's International Human Rights, Toronto, Canada (Sept. 2, 1992) (unpublished manuscript, on file with author) (emphasis added). Very few women's NGOs took part in the three recent CSCE Human Dimension Seminars. In the Seminar on Tolerance, one of 17 NGOs, the Lambda Group, was concerned with lesbian and gay issues; in the Seminar on Migration, the Women's International League for Peace and Freedom was the only women's NGO of the 27 participating NGOs; and in the Seminar on National Minorities, none of the 40 NGOs could be considered a women's NGO. (Lists of NGO Participants on file with author).

93. *See, e.g.*, Tickner, *supra* note 74, at 34; *Women and the Peace Process*, *supra* note 38, ¶¶ 13-18, 35-36.

94. This account of the Conference was suggested to me by Professor Craig Scott. Interview with Craig Scott, Academic Advisor to the Canadian Delegation to the 1992 World Conference on Human Rights (July 16, 1993).

95. Abdullahi Ahmed An-Na'im, Discussion at the Consultation on Women's International Human Rights, Toronto, Canada (Sept. 1, 1992).

96. For Third World criticisms of First World NGOs, see HENRY J. STEINER, DIVERSE PARTNERS: NON-GOVERNMENTAL ORGANIZATIONS IN THE HUMAN RIGHTS MOVEMENT 22-28, 61-64 (Report of Retreat of Human Rights Activists, 1991).

corporations motivated by economic self-interest. As part of her suggestion that women rethink their obsession with becoming insiders in international law, Karen Engle reminds us that "some, particularly some who have a lot of power, see being outside the grip of public international law as positive and liberating."[97] While Engle's point is presumably that women can take advantage of being outside the scope of international law, it indirectly acknowledges that their ability to do so may be a function of power. Those "who have a lot of power" prefer the relative freedom of international civil society precisely because they "have a lot of power."

In the final analysis, the participation of international civil society in the development of international norms is thrown back on the hope that some form of meaningful public debate is possible under the conditions of the late twentieth century international order.[98]

IV. THE STATE AS BOUNDED, UNIFIED SELF

The recognition of the essential identity of States and individuals is one of the enduring features of the Grotian tradition in international law.[99] Largely because of this analogy, international law has been enriched and advanced by Roman and other private

97. Engle, *supra* note 9, at 10.

98. *See* J.A. Carty, *Changing Models of the International System*, *in* PERESTROIKA AND INTERNATIONAL LAW 13 (William E. Butler ed., 1990). Carty summarizes the challenge as follows:

> [P]ower is now transferred to groupings, whether public or private, whose interests are reflected in attitudes, and which use publicity, the mediation of pre-digested views, as part of a bargaining process, where "consensus" reflects what a traditional liberal rationalist would regard as a stalemate or a stand-off. If there is "real" debate, it is secretive and takes place within these groupings. The public sphere is refeudalised by formalistic acts of self-representation by these groups, struggling for the prestige and reputation.

Id. at 24 (citations omitted) (referring to JÜRGEN HABERMAS, L'ESPACE PUBLIC 208-09 (1986)).

99. HUGO GROTIUS, DE JURE BELLI AC PACIS Bk. II, ch. xv, § xii; H. Lauterpacht, *The Grotian Tradition in International Law*, 23 BRIT. Y.B. INT'L L. 1, 26-30 (1946); Douglas M. Johnston, *The Heritage of Political Thought in International Law*, *in* THE STRUCTURE AND PROCESS OF INTERNATIONAL LAW: ESSAYS IN LEGAL PHILOSOPHY DOCTRINE AND THEORY 179, 188 (R. St.J. Macdonald & Douglas M. Johnston eds., 1983) [hereinafter STRUCTURE AND PROCESS]; MARTTI KOSKENNIEMI, FROM APOLOGY TO UTOPIA: THE STRUCTURE OF INTERNATIONAL LEGAL ARGUMENT 7, 68-73, 117-18 (1989) (discussing the analogy as part of a larger project of deconstructing the liberal foundations of international law).

law rules.[100] For instance, Grotius conceived of the very notion of sovereignty as being like property,[101] and various authors have documented the heavy influence of the private law of property on the development of international law rules for the acquisition of territorial sovereignty.[102] In the course of a recent, quixotic argument for jettisoning the term "sovereignty" while retaining its traditional attributes, Louis Henkin develops the analogy as follows:

> [W]ith much *mutatis mutandis*, states are to be seen like individuals in the state of nature. Like all men (and women), all states are equal, equal in status and rights (as well as duties). Like individuals, states have "personhood", including moral status and "will"—the ability to decide, to agree, to offer and accept moral commitment. All states have rights, implying reciprocal duties. A state's rights include the right to life, *i.e.*, the right to continue to exist. It has a right to liberty, to internal autonomy, and to be let alone, which we sometimes call political independence. A state has a right to pursue happiness. A state also has the right to property, including its territory, which implies territorial integrity.
>
> ....
>
> ...Like individuals forming a society, states that enter into relations with each other create a political system reflecting a social contract.[103]

Nevertheless, the true meaning of this essential identity, Sir Hersch Lauterpacht maintains, is not

> that states *are like* individuals; it is due to the fact that states *are composed of* individual human beings; it results from the fact that behind the mystical, impersonal, and therefore necessarily irresponsible personality of the metaphysical state there are the actual subjects of rights and duties, namely, individual human beings.[104]

We are left, then, with two ways of understanding how States relate

---

100. *See generally* H. LAUTERPACHT, PRIVATE LAW SOURCES AND ANALOGIES OF INTERNATIONAL LAW (1927).

101. Lauterpacht, *supra* note 99, at 29.

102. LAUTERPACHT, *supra* note 100, at 91-119; ANTHONY CARTY, THE DECAY OF INTERNATIONAL LAW? A REAPPRAISAL OF THE LIMITS OF LEGAL IMAGINATION IN INTERNATIONAL AFFAIRS 43-64 (1986) (discussing critically the limits this analogy imposed on the international legal imagination of the nineteenth century).

103. Louis Henkin, *The Mythology of Sovereignty*, *in* STATE SOVEREIGNTY, *supra* note 9, at 15, 18.

104. Lauterpacht, *supra* note 99, at 27.

to individuals. One is an analogy (States are like individuals) and the other a theory about the ultimate bearer of rights (States are composed of individuals).

Part IV explores the limitations of the analogy between States and individuals. It indicates the weaknesses both of particular, feminist versions of the analogy and of the analogy itself. These two types of limitation may be distinguished briefly as follows. By treating States as if they were individuals, the analogy projects a certain view about human nature onto the nature of the State. Because the essence of the analogy is this mapping function, rather than what is mapped onto what, it does not require any particular view of human nature. Substituting other assumptions about human nature will lead to other assumptions about the nature of the State without altering the analogy itself. If an incomplete account of human nature and the human condition results in an equally incomplete account of how States operate in the international system, this is not a weakness of the analogy as such, but of a particular version which considers only a subset of similarities.

Instead, the limitation of the analogy as such lies in the dissimilarities of States and individuals. Namely, the analogy cannot take into account that States are not like individuals in the significant respect that they are not unified beings, they are not irreducible units of analysis. It follows that the analogy renders problematic any consideration of the status of individuals and groups in international law, other than as part of a monolithic State. This difficulty does not exist if the State is viewed as composed of individuals or, modifying Lauterpacht's reading of Grotius on this point, as composed of individuals and groups.

Part IV consists of two sections, corresponding loosely to the two ways of understanding the essential identity of States and individuals. Section A examines the analogy of sovereign State to individual as it exists in feminist international legal literature. Section B discusses the ways that the sovereign State might be broken down and whether they permit the direct participation of individuals and groups in international law, that is, unmediated by the State. It also speculates on how feminist theory might relate to this inquiry and what the difference might be to women's participation in international law.

A. The State as Individual

In the short time since feminist critiques of international law first caused a commotion in scholarly circles,[105] the methods most often used in this new literature tend to assume the analogy of States and individuals. Whether the topic is international legal norms that govern relations between States or those norms that regulate international legal intervention in matters belonging to a State's domestic jurisdiction, the problem is assumed to be analogous to that of the autonomous individual in liberal thought. If the assumption is sometimes obscured, this is in part because the *impetus* for the critique is the condition of women within States; in part because much of the work is more accurately situated within the fields of international human rights or international relations, which are less concerned with challenging the analytical framework of international law; and in part because feminist international legal scholarship, at least in its initial phase of deconstruction, may consciously use incompatible levels of analysis and methodologies in order to reveal the ubiquity of gendered divisions in international law.[106]

In Section A, I show that a number of feminist approaches to international law are predicated on the analogy between the sovereign State and the unified self. At the same time, these feminist scholars seek to substitute a different view of the self for the liberal view mapped onto the State in classical international law. They see the self as connected to others through a web of relationships, instead of as separate and surrounded by solid boundaries that protect its autonomy.[107] Based on their version of the analogy, some of these feminist scholars suggest that conceptually, the solid boundaries around the State be replaced with permeable boundaries, while others propose that certain of these notional boundaries be removed altogether.

Section A also argues that feminist analyses of the sovereign State as a unified self have drawn attention only to the negative aspects of State sovereignty for women, as Karen Engle comments,[108] whereas sovereignty must be understood as a more profoundly ambivalent institution. I make this point differently from Engle, namely, by showing that the metaphors for sovereignty used in these

105. For an account of the first conference on feminist approaches to international law, held in 1990, see Charlesworth, *supra* note 2, at 1.

106. Hilary Charlesworth characterizes the feminist project in law as a dig through layers of masculinist constructions which demands different techniques at different levels. *Id.* at 2. Her comments are made, however, in the context of deconstructing international law. Reconstructing international law, which the analysis in the current Article anticipates, may demand a different standard of coherence.

107. *See generally* Jennifer Nedelsky, *Law, Boundaries, and the Bounded Self*, *in* LAW AND THE ORDER OF CULTURE 162 (Robert Post ed., 1991).

108. Engle, *supra* note 7; Engle, *supra* note 9.

analyses are problematic for feminism, inconsistent, or both.

My contention is that feminist approaches to international law actually proceed from two distinct versions of the analogy between State and individual: the territory of the State as the physical body of the individual and the territory of the State as the individual's private property. Without claiming any causal linkage, I suggest that this distinction is clarified by considering the similar if not identical distinction that Sir Hersch Lauterpacht makes between rival theories of sovereignty in early twentieth century international legal thought. Lauterpacht differentiates notably two theories of the relationship between a State and its territory.[109] Although he designates them as the space theory and the object theory, I shall refer to them as the body theory and the property theory respectively, so as to facilitate the comparison. According to the body theory,

> The territory...is an *element* of the State, and it can no more be regarded as the object of a State's right, than the body of a man can be said to be his property...The State rules *within* the territory, not *over* it.[110]

Alternatively, the property theory regards the relationship of a State to its territory "as identical with or analogous to the private law right of property."[111] According to the property theory, which had become dominant by the time that Lauterpacht wrote, international law cannot control what a State does on its territory any more than domestic law can control what an individual property owner does with her property.

As Section A demonstrates, each of these metaphoric understandings, in and of itself, invokes contested imagery in feminist thought. Moreover, since each metaphor captures only certain aspects of how the sovereign State functions in international law, replacing one with another in any given critique of State/self may result in quite a different analysis of women's relationship to the sovereign State. Juxtaposing the partial insights of the two metaphors creates an ambivalent impression of the relationship, thereby making the case for the alternative methods of analysis introduced in Section B.

Section A is divided into two subsections. Each subsection looks at feminist perspectives on a different set of norms in international law. Subsection 1 treats norms governing relations between States, and Subsection 2 discusses certain norms determining the jurisdiction of international law. Or, in analogic terms, Subsection 1

---

109. LAUTERPACHT, *supra* note 100, at 91-96 (footnotes omitted).

110. *Id.* at 93.

111. *Id.* at 92.

treats norms governing relations between individuals, and Subsection 2 discusses the relationship between the State and the individual, that is, the public/private distinction.

1. Relations Between States

In feminist analyses of norms governing relations between States, the metaphor for the State tends to be the body. Through an acceptance of the embodied individual as the metaphor for the sovereign State embedded in international law, some feminist scholars have translated the feminist ethic of care or theories of connectedness[112] from relations between individuals to relations between States. Moira McConnell[113] and Isabelle Gunning[114] both use the feminist ethic of care to make sense of what they perceive to be the nature of relationships between States, thereby claiming for it an explanatory power[115] as well as presumably a prescriptive power.

McConnell argues that developments in international law, primarily international environmental law, represent a movement towards the notions of morality observed in little girls by psychologist Carol Gilligan[116] and advocated by feminist theorists such as Joan Tronto[117] and Robin West.[118] She defines this morality as grounded in an ethic of care, an understanding of connectedness that takes

112. In feminist historiography, these theories are sometimes grouped together as the second stage of feminist theorizing, termed "difference" feminism or "cultural" feminism. In the context of feminist legal theory, see, e.g., Bartlett, *supra* note 1, at 872-77; Menkel-Meadow, *supra* note 1, at 1499-1501.

113. McConnell, *supra* note 6. Although McConnell does refer to McDougal, Lasswell, and Reisman's arguments in favor of enabling the individual to take active part in decision-making at all levels from the municipality to the global community, her own analysis focuses on the relations between States.

114. Gunning, *supra* note 6. *See also* Keohane, *supra* note 6.

115. As was discussed in Part III, Gunning maintains that her argument does no more than modernize international law to reflect the reality of international relations. Gunning, *supra* note 67. McConnell states that "the so called 'new' analysis of international relationships described by women is in many respects merely a description of international law as it actually operates." Moira L. McConnell, *The Relationship Between Theories About Women and Theories About International Law*, *in* STATE SOVEREIGNTY, *supra* note 9, at 68, 75-76. *See also* Moira McConnell, *Feminist Analysis as the Embodiment of Marginalization*, *in* RECONCEIVING REALITY, *supra* note 2 (manuscript at 12, on file with author).

116. GILLIGAN, *supra* note 46.

117. Joan C. Tronto, *Beyond Gender Difference to a Theory of Care*, 12 SIGNS 644 (1987).

118. Robin West, *Jurisprudence and Gender*, *in* FEMINIST JURISPRUDENCE 493 (Patricia Smith ed., 1993).

context and an experience of powerlessness into account. While McConnell is addressing powerlessness in the face of diminishing global natural resources, she also adverts to the power imbalances in the world community that, one could argue, leave some States in the vulnerable, dependent position often occupied by women in society and other States in the position of strength often associated with men.[119] For McConnell, the international law concept of global or environmental stewardship is most likely to embody the feminist morality she describes, as it "embraces a notion of caretaking and accountability, presumably to ourselves and future generations."[120]

Like McConnell, Gunning sees the cooperative dimension of inter-State relations as corresponding to a feminist understanding–and in many respects also an Afrocentric understanding–of the individual as connected to others by relationships and community. Seen through this alternative lens, rules become contextual, rather than fixed and universal, and power changes from control over others to Arendt's notion of action in concert with others. As we have already seen,[121] Gunning then uses this reconception of power to argue that the range of actors whose actions can contribute to the creation of customary international law be broadened to include international organizations, the U.N. General Assembly for example, and broadly-based NGOs such as the International Committee of the Red Cross. For her, any action that is the product of a sufficient degree of global concert should be taken into consideration in deciding whether a new norm of customary law has come into existence. The difficulty with Gunning's thesis, however, is that her analogic reasoning cannot hold for both international organizations and NGOs. If the actions of an international organization whose members are States, such as the U.N. General Assembly, can consistently be analogized to the coordinated actions of individuals, the analogy breaks down in the case of NGOs, whose members actually *are* individuals. If Gunning accepts the international order as populated by States, then she has depicted

---

119. *See* Charlesworth et al., *supra* note 3, at 618 (discussing similarities between the position of Third World States and that of women); Jane S. Jaquette, *Power as Ideology: A Feminist Analysis*, *in* WOMEN'S VIEWS OF THE POLITICAL WORLD OF MEN 9, 22 (Judith H. Stiehm ed., 1982) (discussing similarities between female strategies of persuasion and the strategies of small States operating from positions of weakness in the international system).

120. McConnell, *supra* note 6, at 27. *But cf.* McConnell, *The Relationship Between Theories About Women and Theories About International Law*, *supra* note 115, at 71; McConnell, *Feminist Analysis as the Embodiment of Marginalization*, *supra* note 115, at 12 (While McConnell continues to subscribe to this analysis, she now refuses to acknowledge it as "feminist" on the grounds that to do so would perpetuate the marginalization of women.).

121. *See supra* pp. 314-16.

international society, at least for the purpose of international law-making, in such a way that there is no room for the individual, or even individuals acting in concert. She needs to furnish a reason for rejecting or modifying this picture. If we cannot look beyond the overlay of the analogy for some purposes, why can we for others, such as creation of international law? In international law, unlike international relations, the construct of subjects of international law calls for either an account of why the analogy of States and individuals breaks down in some places, or–moving toward international relations–the outright rejection of the notion of subjects.[122]

In terms of a feminist rethinking of State sovereignty, McConnell's and Gunning's arguments may be cast as critiques of the bounded State/self. Their focus on relationships and connectedness implies that fixed, rigid boundaries between States fail–both conceptually and physically, as the example of international environmental law illustrates–to reflect patterns of interaction and responsibility, or, worse, prevent the formation of patterns that are seen as desirable.

This, however, is not the only possible feminist reading of the State as embodied individual. For McConnell and Gunning, the relationship between States, like the relationship between self and Other, is partially or potentially a caring and nurturing one. The approach of the cultural feminists whose work they cite may be summarized as abstracting from the biological, sociological, or psychoanalytic experience of the maternal relationship to create an actual or aspirational ethical vision. Radical feminism has quite a different vision of relationships.[123] Encounters between self and Other inevitably reproduce the invasion and intrusion suffered physically by women in heterosexual intercourse. Far from valuing the dissolution of boundaries, radical feminists dread it. Andrea Dworkin writes:

> A human being has a body that is inviolate; and when it is violated, it is abused.
>
> ....
>
> Physically, the woman in intercourse is a space inhabited, a literal territory occupied literally: occupied even if there has been no resistance, no force;
>
> ....

122. *See* Rosalyn Higgins, *Conceptual Thinking About the Individual in International Law*, 24 N.Y.L. SCH. L. REV. 11, 15-16 (1978).

123. On this contrast, see West, *supra* note 118, at 499-509.

> ...**In the experience of intercourse, she loses the capacity for integrity because her body–the basis of privacy and freedom in the material world for all human beings–is entered and occupied; the boundaries of her physical body are–neutrally speaking–violated.**[124]

Dworkin thus analogizes the body to the inviolable State, the woman in intercourse to occupied territory, and intercourse to the violation of boundaries. Inversely, the violation of a State's territorial integrity is transformed into the imagery and reality of rape in a number of ways:[125] by the psychological transference of identity to the State through the machinery of patriotism[126] and the language used to describe the event,[127] as well as by the actual abuse suffered by women in the wake of an invasion.[128]

These different types of transformation may be illustrated by a trio of examples. First, Abouali Farmanfarmaian hypothesizes that growth in American popular support for the Gulf War can be correlated with the Pentagon's increased association of Iraq's violation of Kuwaiti sovereignty at international law not only with the imagery of rape--the "rape" of Kuwait–but with actual sexual atrocities committed by Iraqi soldiers.[129]

A second illustration is provided by Edward Morgan's case comment[130] on the decision of the U.S. Supreme Court in *Alvarez-Machain*, a case of the accused's forcible abduction by U.S. law enforcement officials on Mexican territory contrary to an existing United States-Mexico Extradition Treaty. In a mischievous *tour de force* of psychoanalysis and post-modern word play, Morgan constructs, in the act of deconstructing, the idea that international law both is and renders all sovereign States hermaphroditic. Like other critical international legal scholars, he examines how the

124. ANDREA DWORKIN, INTERCOURSE 122, 133, 137 (1987).

125. *See generally* Chinkin, *supra* note 3, at 2-11.

126. *Id.* at 6-8; Jean Bethke Elshtain, *Sovereignty, Identity, Sacrifice*, 58 SOC. RES. 545 (1991).

127. RUTH SEIFERT, WAR AND RAPE: ANALYTICAL APPROACHES 8-9 (Women's Int'l League for Peace and Freedom, 1993); Chinkin, *supra* note 3; Abouali Farmanfarmaian, *Did You Measure Up? The Role of Race and Sexuality in the Gulf War*, *in* COLLATERAL DAMAGE: THE NEW WORLD ORDER AT HOME AND ABROAD 111 (Cynthia Peters ed., 1992); Edward M. Morgan, *The Hermaphroditic Paradigm of International Law: A Comment on Alvarez-Machain*, *in* STATE SOVEREIGNTY, *supra* note 9, at 78.

128. *See* sources cited *supra* note 4; SUSAN BROWNMILLER, AGAINST OUR WILL: MEN, WOMEN AND RAPE 31-113 (1975).

129. Farmanfarmaian, *supra* note 127, at 113, 115, 120.

130. Morgan, *supra* note 127.

discourse of international law simultaneously requires and obfuscates the normative contradiction that lies at its heart: that sovereign States are both above and subject to international law.[131] Through his comment on *Alvarez-Machain*, Morgan argues that international law's shifting style of argumentation is replicated in the alternating sexual roles played by international law and by sovereign States:

> The paradox of male sovereignty is that nations cannot be both assertive and submissive as they confront one another, the dilemma of female universality is that the law cannot both engulf sovereigns and be their underpinning.[132]

In a final example, Betty Reardon chillingly summarizes the reality for women of the parallel between a State's territorial integrity and a woman's bodily integrity:

> Rape...is to male-female relations what the behaviour of conquering troops is to occupied territories, what the trappings of imperial authority are to colonialism. Rape in various forms has been a traditional war system device used for symbolic or deterrent purposes as well as the basic intimidating mechanism to maintain submission.[133]

Although the implications of the radical feminist vision for rethinking State sovereignty have not been explored in the international legal literature, it is clear that by underlining women's security interest in the bounded State/self,[134] such a vision contradicts the dissolving of boundaries implicit in the work of feminists such as McConnell and Gunning.

Alternative accounts of sexuality have been strikingly absent from the above discussion of inter-State relations as sexually constructed. Without pursuing this point, since I will ultimately argue that the analogy between State and individual is analytically limiting, I note the project of *écriture féminine* to reimagine the

---

131. *See, e.g.*, KOSKENNIEMI, *supra* note 99, at 40-42.

132. Morgan, *supra* note 127, at 90. For a similar distinction between male sovereignty and female universalism, see Elshtain, *supra* note 7, at 1361.

133. BETTY A. REARDON, SEXISM AND THE WAR SYSTEM 39 (1985). *See also* SEIFERT, *supra* note 127, at 6-7.

134. The security interest emphasized by the analogy of State and individual is a static one in that it is predicated on the current international legal system. Quite another question is whether State sovereignty in reality offers much protection against military aggression, that is, whether the salient units are not actually regional defense organizations or interlocking transnational interests. Still another question is whether State sovereignty does not inevitably cause conflict such that in a more fundamental sense, it ill serves women's security interest.

female body so as to escape the phallic dualism of a female body constructed by male desire.[135] As Luce Irigaray, one of its practitioners, explains:

> if [women's] aim were simply to reverse the order of things, even supposing this to be possible, history would repeat itself in the long run, would revert to sameness: to phallocratism. It would leave room neither for women's sexuality, nor for women's imaginary, nor for women's language to take (their) place.[136]

Irigaray calls woman's "geography...far more diversified, more multiple in its differences, more complex, more subtle than is commonly imagined–in an imaginary rather too narrowly focused on sameness."[137] The metaphor of sexual penetration and the thrust of sovereign power[138] would be replaced by the continuous contact of skin and the everywhereness of *jouissance*, the French term used to denote women's specifically feminine, total sexual pleasure. It remains to be explored whether such imagery would throw into relief certain qualities of boundaries between States–the contact and interaction that occurs at every point on a boundary[139] as opposed to the discrete points of entry and relationships emphasized by the international system–or whether its larger lesson revolves around the potential of metaphor both for expansion of meaning and for reinterpretation.[140]

2. *Jurisdiction in International Law*

The preceding Subsection examined how feminist approaches to the international law norms governing relations between States rely

---

135. For an introduction to *écriture féminine*, see, e.g., DRUCILLA CORNELL, BEYOND ACCOMMODATION: ETHICAL FEMINISM, DECONSTRUCTION, AND THE LAW 152-64 (1991); Arleen B. Dallery, *The Politics of Writing (the) Body: Ecriture Féminine*, *in* GENDER/BODY/KNOWLEDGE: FEMINIST RECONSTRUCTIONS OF BEING AND KNOWING 52 (Alison M. Jaggar & Susan R. Bordo eds., 1989).

136. LUCE IRIGARAY, THIS SEX WHICH IS NOT ONE 33 (Catherine Porter trans., 1985).

137. *Id.* at 28.

138. *Cf.* Morgan, *supra* note 127, at 84 ("[I]n the *Alvarez-Machain* decision, the Court fails to restrain the thrust of American power, and Mexico gets penetrated in a non-consensual way.").

139. *See* IRIGARAY, *supra* note 136, at 213.

> No surface holds. No figure, line, or point remains....Where top and bottom, inside and outside, in front and behind, above and below are not separated, remote, out of touch. Our all intermingled. Without breaks or gaps.

140. *See* CORNELL, *supra* note 135, at 165-96.

on the analogy between State and unified self, more particularly, the version of the analogy that analyzes the State as an embodied individual. By fleshing out the State, certain authors were able to apply critiques of individual autonomy developed in the context of domestic law to State sovereignty. Implicit in their work is a move away from the rigid boundaries of the sovereign State toward boundaries permeated by relationships and responsibilities. In contrast, the application of other feminist interpretations of intercourse between individuals to the sovereign State might suggest women's interest in maintaining or reimagining boundaries. The preceding Subsection shows that if the emerging feminist literature on the basic norms of international law is premised on the analogy between State and self, it may simply transport the feminist debate over the nature of the self and the relationship to others to the level of the State. The treatment of Isabelle Gunning's work in that Subsection also illustrates the proposition that the analogy itself, by treating the State as a unified facade, forecloses or renders problematic any consideration of individuals and groups in international law.

In this Subsection, I reach a similar result by considering how a different boundary–the line between international and domestic jurisdiction–is treated in feminist international legal scholarship. By applying feminist critiques of the boundary between public and private to the boundary between international and domestic jurisdiction, many feminist scholars conclude either that this rigid boundary should become permeable or that at least in certain cases, the boundary should be eliminated altogether. What has gone unnoticed, I show in this Subsection, is that this conclusion depends on switching the underlying metaphor for the State from the embodied individual to the propertied individual, whether propertied in the concrete sense of owning private property or in the abstract sense of limits or fences around the individual's private domain or family.[141] Once the interplay of metaphors is revealed, Karen Engle's caution that the public/private critique ought not necessarily to lead women away from the private is seen to flow from her consideration of examples that switch metaphors again, replacing the property metaphor for the State with the body metaphor. This Subsection discusses how the choice of metaphor for the State, as distinct from the interpretation given to the metaphor, affects a feminist analysis of State sovereignty.

One of the public/private dichotomies central to feminist critiques of domestic law is the dichotomy between the public world of work and commerce, and the private world of home and family. In much

---

141. *See* Jennifer Nedelsky, *Reconceiving Autonomy*, 1 YALE J. L. & FEMINISM 7, 15-18 (1989).

of classical liberalism, these two spheres are based on different principles of association: participation in the public sphere is governed by universal and impersonal criteria such as rights, equality, and property, whereas participation in the private sphere is determined by ties of blood and affection, and by the status of husband and wife, or mother and father, thereby preserving the inequality and vulnerability of women within the family.[142] Feminist scholarship has stressed that the very jurisdiction of international law is divided along these same public/private lines.[143] International law regulates relations between States, which take place in the public sphere, whereas a State's treatment of its nationals occurs in the State's private sphere, away from the scrutiny of international law. Many would argue that while the emergence of international human rights law has shifted the boundary between public and private–international and domestic jurisdiction–it has not called into question the concept of the boundary.

Understood in terms of public and private, humanitarian assistance as an exception to the international legal principle of nonintervention[144] may be treated in the same way as state intervention in the family.[145] If the moderate feminist response to the classical "family privacy" argument[146] is that "the state *should* intervene in the family to protect weaker members from isolated instances of abuse,"[147] Louise Lussier formulates the dilemma of humanitarian assistance as one of protecting

> les groupes qui, sans statut ni pouvoir, sont démunis face aux plus forts qui, en raison de leur sexe, détiennent non seulement la force, l'arrogance, et la puissance politique mais également la possibilité de désigner les autres comme étant les plus faibles.[148]

---

142. *See, e.g.*, Carole Pateman, *Feminist Critiques of the Public/Private Dichotomy*, *in* PUBLIC AND PRIVATE IN SOCIAL LIFE 281 (Stanley I. Benn & Gerald F. Gaus eds., 1983).

143. *See* sources cited *supra* note 7.

144. U.N. CHARTER art. 2, ¶ 7.

145. Frances Olsen, *in* RECONCEIVING REALITY, *supra* note 2 (manuscript at 4-8, on file with author); Wright, *supra* note 7, at 14.

146. For a summary of the "family privacy" argument, see Frances E. Olsen, *The Family and the Market: A Study of Ideology and Legal Reform*, 96 HARV. L. REV. 1497, 1504-07 (1983).

147. Olsen, *supra* note 145, at 6. *See also* Frances E. Olsen, *The Myth of State Intervention in the Family*, 18 U. MICH. J.L. REF. 835, 838-42 (1985).

148. "[T]he groups that, with neither status nor power, are unequipped in front of the stronger who, by virtue of their sex, possess not only force, arrogance and political power, but equally the possibility of designating others as being the weaker." (author's trans.). Louise Lussier, *Réflexions juridiques et éthiques sur l'assistance humanitaire*, *in*

A more radical response is illustrated by Judith Gardam's gendered perspective on the law of armed conflict. Gardam argues for a breakdown of the distinction between "public" international conflicts and "private" internal conflicts[149] which grounds the greater protection afforded combatants and non-combatants in international conflicts.[150] This rigid distinction, she argues, reflects neither women's experience nor their perception of conflict.

If women's security interest in the sovereign State supports rigid boundaries between States/bodies,[151] it supports equally the removal of the boundary between international jurisdiction/public and domestic jurisdiction/private in situations of armed conflict. We are caught here in the tension between particularism and universalism, the conceptual opposition of Apology and Utopia that critical legal scholars identify as central to international legal discourse.[152]

Karen Engle describes her misgivings in the context of international human rights law:

> I agree with [advocates of women's rights] that the "private" sphere should be open to public scrutiny, but this cannot be done without attention to the particularities of women's lives in various cultures and sub-cultures. Ironically, then, it seems that women's rights advocates may even learn from classical public international law–from its attention to notions such as self-determination and relativism.[153]

Engle's concern with the protection of culture is echoed in the work of other authors such as Isabelle Gunning[154] and Sharon Hom.[155]

STATE SOVEREIGNTY, *supra* note 9, at 187, 187.

149. *Cf.* John F. Burns, *Renegades Help Bosnia By Helping Themselves*, N.Y. TIMES, July 5, 1993, at 3 (Lieutenant General Philippe Morillon, commander of the U.N. forces in Bosnia, described fighting between Bosnian army units as "domestic violence.").

150. Judith G. Gardam, *The Law of Armed Conflict: A Feminist Perspective*, *in* HUMAN RIGHTS IN THE TWENTY-FIRST CENTURY: A GLOBAL CHALLENGE, *supra* note 40, at 419, 422-24, 430. *See also* Gardam, *supra* note 5, at 278 ("The false barriers of state sovereignty should be lowered to facilitate the development of a genuinely humanitarian system...of armed conflict.").

151. *See supra* pp. 326-28.

152. KOSKENNIEMI, *supra* note 99, *passim*. *Cf.* West, *supra* note 118, at 517-20 (discussing the relevance of the Critical Legal Studies argument of contradiction to feminist legal theory).

153. Engle, *supra* note 7, at 254.

154. Isabelle R. Gunning, *Arrogant Perception, World-Travelling and Multicultural Feminism: The Case of Female Genital Surgeries*, 23 COLUM. HUM. RTS. L. REV. 189 (1991-92).

155. Sharon K. Hom, *Female Infanticide in China: The Human Rights Specter and Thoughts Towards (An)Other Vision*, 23 COLUM. HUM. RTS. L. REV. 249 (1991-92).

If Engle is equivocal about incursions into the private sphere of the self/State,[156] her tentativeness stems more from the body metaphor for the State than from the property metaphor. Although she does not make this distinction, her examples of abortion, the right to wear the veil as protection from sexual harassment, and the right to participate in or be free of clitoridectomies, sati, breast implants, and the wearing of spike-heeled shoes go to the issue of women's control over their bodies.[157]

In summary, feminist scholarship in international law has not yet set itself the task of rethinking State sovereignty, preferring to work within or–perhaps more aptly–around it. While criticizing the premise of the State as bounded, it has nevertheless accepted the premise of the State as unified. I have attempted to show that such an approach does not and cannot yield a clear direction for rethinking State sovereignty. Instead the result is to project onto State sovereignty what Jennifer Nedelsky has described as the "powerful, yet ambivalent, feminist rejection of liberalism,"[158] the simultaneous demand for respect of women's selfhood, and rejection of much of the language and many of the assumptions of individual rights that have been the primary means of expressing and enforcing respect for selfhood.[159]

B. Breaking Down the State

> Historically, much of the power of the concept of sovereignty lay precisely in its encoding of the absolute, perpetual, indivisible power of a masculinized deity, a deity whose power was absolute and from everlasting to everlasting, as a penultimate political form.
>
> Jean Bethke Elshtain[160]

Grotius wrote during a period when the European order was changing and territorial States were beginning to take shape. The naturalness of his analogy between sovereign State and individual stemmed from the historical fact that these emerging territorial States were creatures of personal rule. At that time, European history could still be conceived of as embodied in dynasties and dynastic ambitions, the marriage settlements and testamentary

156. *See also* Engle, *supra* note 9.

157. *Id.* at 9.

158. Nedelsky, *supra* note 141, at 8.

159. *Id.*

160. Elshtain, *supra* note 126, at 557-58.

dispositions of monarchs, and the policies of the ruling princes.[161]

In the post-modern cacophony of the late twentieth century, it is clear that whatever the analogic conventions of international law, the State is not a unified self. It encompasses a variety of groups and performs a variety of functions. These functions do not necessarily serve the interests of all groups. For some functions, the advantaged group may be the entire population, while for others, a group within the State or spread across State boundaries may be disadvantaged. International law deals with this issue of "fit" between State and population by giving peoples the right of self-determination, most often realized as statehood, while international human rights law takes different groups' interests into account through a limited notion of minority rights within the State. The division between the sovereignty solution and the rights solution is becoming increasingly blurred, however, as the right of self-determination is being reinterpreted as something less than full sovereignty and "minorities" are claiming the right of self-determination limited in positive law to "peoples." These demands for sovereignty may involve territorially-based sovereignty within the State or non-territorially-based sovereignty in the sense of control over certain essential aspects of the group's collective identity or well-being.

These developments create a new problem for sovereignty in international law. The dilemma has long been *who* should practice sovereignty. As we saw in Part II, a number of publicists have been tracking the evolution from State sovereignty to popular sovereignty and its implications for international law. The more recent quandary, however, is *what* sovereignty should be. Regardless of whether sovereignty ultimately resides in the government or the people, why should there be a single sovereign order coterminous with the State? Why not have overlapping sovereignties, fragmented sovereignties, layered sovereignties?

Kathleen Jones asks a parallel question about authority. She contends that feminists have been unaware of the continued connection between authority defined as sovereignty and masculinity.[162] In the struggle over who should practice authority, feminists have ignored what authority should be.[163] The selection of women over men as rulers will not transcend the principle of authority as sovereignty, that is, the unitary and universal ability to command obedience.[164] The challenge of race, class, and sexuality to gender as a sovereign category leads Jones to conclude:

---

161. Lauterpacht, *supra* note 99, at 28-29.

162. Kathleen B. Jones, *The Trouble With Authority*, 3 DIFFERENCES 104, 108 (1991).

163. *Id.* at 109.

164. *Id.* at 114.

> We can replace the voice of the sovereign master not with babble, but with efforts to recognize and admit responsibility for patterns of relationships that sovereign boundaries aim to negate....[165]

As the parallel between my question about sovereignty in international law and Kathleen Jones' question about authority in feminism suggests, there is space for a conversation between international law and feminism here.[166] International legal theory, on my reading, has developed two main types of approach to the question of what sovereignty should be: a number of well-established, policy-oriented or functionalist approaches and several newer, still tentative, normative approaches. While there is no ready-made body of feminist literature relevant to sovereignty, the beginnings of such a contribution are visible in the work of Jean Bethke Elshtain,[167] Denise Réaume,[168] and Iris Young.[169]

In Section B, I introduce the two types of approach to reconceptualizing sovereignty in international legal theory, interspersed with some thoughts on where feminist theory has or might contribute to the project and what difference the project might make to women's participation in international law.

1. Policy-Oriented and Functionalist Approaches to Sovereignty

From a policy-science,[170] sociological,[171] or functionalist[172] perspective on international law, the idea of State sovereignty is a

165. *Id.* at 123.

166. *Cf.* V. Spike Peterson, *Introduction* to GENDERED STATES, *supra* note 10, at 1 (opening spaces for feminist-international relations conversations).

167. Elshtain, *supra* note 7; Elshtain, *supra* note 126.

168. Réaume, *supra* note 49.

169. Young, *supra* note 54, at 257-60.

170. *E.g.*, MYRES S. MCDOUGAL ET AL., HUMAN RIGHTS AND WORLD PUBLIC ORDER: THE BASIC POLICIES OF AN INTERNATIONAL LAW OF HUMAN DIGNITY (1980) [hereinafter MCDOUGAL ET AL., HUMAN RIGHTS AND WORLD PUBLIC ORDER]; Myres S. McDougal & W. Michael Reisman, *International Law in Policy-Oriented Perspective, in* STRUCTURE AND PROCESS, *supra* note 99, at 103 [hereinafter McDougal & Reisman, *Policy-Oriented Perspective*]; Myres S. McDougal et al., *Theories About International Law: Prologue to a Configurative Jurisprudence*, 8 VA. J. INT'L L. 188 (1968) [hereinafter McDougal et al., *Theories About International Law*].

171. JULIUS STONE, VISIONS OF WORLD ORDER: BETWEEN STATE POWER AND HUMAN JUSTICE (1984) [hereinafter STONE, VISIONS OF WORLD ORDER]. For a summary of the relevant portions, see Julius Stone, *A Sociological Perspective on International Law, in* STRUCTURE AND PROCESS, *supra* note 99, at 263 [hereinafter Stone, *A Sociological Perspective*].

172. Johnston, *supra* note 56.

distraction. By fetishizing sovereignty, international law has ignored what is actually happening in the international legal community, who the actors really are, and what each one does. Besides acting as an empirical corrective to international law, scholars working within these perspectives break down sovereignty into its functional components and ask of each one whether it is best performed by the State or by other actors. At the theoretical level, these schools of international law liberate us from a take-it-or-leave-it approach to State sovereignty–we can take some functions and leave others. At the practical level, they envisage the direct participation of individuals and groups, conceivably women individually and collectively, in international law-making.

The policy-oriented perspective on international law developed by Myres McDougal and his associates, principally Harold Lasswell and later Michael Reisman,[173] stands as one of this century's monumental contributions to international jurisprudence. It is perhaps indicative of its stature that the McDougal framework of analysis cannot be understood other than in its own terms. A number of the basic features of their policy-oriented theory about international law are introduced in the following statement by McDougal and Reisman:

> [T]here is urgent need for a framework of theory and intellectual procedures which might more effectively and economically relate authoritative decision *to its larger context* and *to a preferred world public order*...International law would be conceived of not merely in terms of the rules that officials and others use in explaining and justifying decision, but rather as *decision itself, combining both authority and control*, and constituting a continuous flow of decision of trans-national origin and impact.[174]

This densely written passage reveals three aspects of the McDougal conception of international law. First, international law is seen as decision itself, rather than merely rules. Second, international law unites "authority" and "control," where authority signifies community expectations about how decisions should be made and who should make them, and control refers to a decision backed by

---

173. The McDougal-Lasswell approach to international law is known by its academic site (e.g., New Haven school or Yale school of international law), as well as by its features (e.g., world public order or policy science). For the purposes of this preliminary exposition, I rely chiefly on McDougal & Reisman, *Policy-Oriented Perspective, supra* note 170, and the excellent introduction to the McDougal-Lasswell jurisprudence by John Norton Moore, *Prolegomenon to the Jurisprudence of Myres McDougal and Harold Lasswell*, 54 VA. L. REV. 662 (1968).

174. McDougal & Reisman, *Policy-Oriented Perspective, supra* note 170, at 112 (emphasis added).

effective sanctions.[175] Third, international law is but one process situated in a larger framework of interpenetrating global processes. Against this trio of elements, the McDougal designation of international law as the "global process of authoritative decision" assumes a highly specific meaning.

The passage tells us as well that the McDougal theory of international law is "policy-oriented" in that it seeks to evaluate international law in terms of its furtherance of a preferred world public order. The dual role of the McDougal theory of international law–explanatory and prescriptive, methodology and instrumentalist jurisprudence[176]–is also apparent from the intellectual demands that McDougal and his associates make of a theory of international law, including creating a map of inquiry for relating authoritative decision to the larger social and community processes and postulating a set of basic public order goals.[177] To understand their view of the sovereign State's function in international law, then, it is necessary to understand both the current law-making dynamic as they see it and the system that their preferred policies on participation in international law might yield.

McDougal and his colleagues employ sets of mapping concepts, developed initially by Lasswell, which can be crossed to describe completely any event related to authoritative decision, be it the event giving rise to a group's claim to some value, the claim itself, or the choice made by the relevant decision-maker. One set of concepts is designed to comprehend all the principal values that might be sought;[178] another, which describes institutional practices, includes participation (individual and group, governmental and non-governmental), perspectives (demands, identifications, and expectations), and arenas.[179]

The institutional practice of participation is further refined according to the type of authoritative decision and the stage of the decision-making process. The global process of authoritative decision, which we recognize as international law, is divided into "constitutive decisions" which establish and maintain the process of authoritative decision, and "public order decisions" which emerge from this process and regulate the process of securing the various

175. Moore, *supra* note 173, at 666.

176. *See, e.g.*, TERRY NARDIN, LAW, MORALITY, AND THE RELATIONS OF STATES 200-01 (1983).

177. McDougal & Reisman, *Policy-Oriented Perspective*, *supra* note 170, at 113-28.

178. *Id.* at 118.

179. *Id. See* MCDOUGAL ET AL., HUMAN RIGHTS AND WORLD PUBLIC ORDER, *supra* note 170, at xi (listing "arenas" in preferred policies relating to the world constitutive process).

principal values.[180] Within the global constitutive process, the traditional division of decision-making into legislative, executive, and judicial branches is replaced by division into such functions as intelligence gathering, promotion and advocacy of policy, formulation of policy, application of prescription, and appraisal of the decision in terms of goals and performance.[181] These functions enable participation to be analyzed more precisely, for example, as participation in gathering, processing, and distributing information relevant to constitutive decision. This exactness permits the conclusion that broadly based participation in the intelligence gathering function is clearly less problematic for the State than participation in the application of prescription function would be.

In describing participation in the global constitutive process of authoritative decision, McDougal, Lasswell, and associate Lung-Chu Chen criticize the exaggerated role of the nation-state as the principal subject of international law in the face of "ever-growing pressures of global interdependences that defy artificial and arbitrary national boundaries."[182] They write:

> The choice in features of world constitutive process is not one of simple dichotomy: either of a world controlled solely by "sovereign" nation-states or of a world government supplanting all the existing nation-states. Ours is a world of pluralism and diversity, a global arena in which various participants–groups (territorial and functional, governmental and nongovernmental) and individual human beings–constantly interact under ever-changing conditions. All of the above-mentioned group participants–nation-states, international governmental organizations, political parties, pressure groups, and private associations–are forms of associations through which individuals cooperate to achieve fulfillment of their demands. They are, in the ultimate analysis, highly malleable instruments....[183]

The McDougal interpretation of the current world legal order thus represents a move away from international legal theory's preoccupation with sovereign States as the paradigmatic subjects of international law. It describes a world of plural identities and interactions which all contribute to the process of decision. But this is only half of the picture. The other half is the goal of participation

180. McDougal & Reisman, *Policy-Oriented Perspective*, *supra* note 170, at 119-21.

181. *Id.* at 120-21.

182. McDOUGAL ET AL., HUMAN RIGHTS AND WORLD PUBLIC ORDER, *supra* note 170, at 179 (footnote omitted).

183. *Id.*

that McDougal and his colleagues are moving towards.

McDougal, Lasswell, and Chen's overriding policy on participation is one of universality, whereby "all who are affected by, or who can affect, authoritative decisions should, or should be made to, participate in the making of such decisions."[184] Their preferred policy on arenas stresses the openness of all structures of authority to the parties affected, be they individuals, governments, or private groups.[185]

These policy objectives, however, do not seem to suggest a fundamentally different participatory structure for international law. Generally speaking, while the work of McDougal and his associates is, to quote Richard Falk, "transitional, deriving substance from the state system as well as moving beyond it,"[186] it is noncommittal as to the shape of a global system most likely to realize their preferred policies.[187] As regards the forms that individual and group participation might take, McDougal and his associates consider the individual's participation in international law to be limited as much by "his passive acquiescence and ignorance of the potentialities of his participation as [by] the structures of the complex human organizations of the contemporary world."[188] The essential problem, then, is not the structure of participation, but a lack of knowledge on the part of the participant, which the development of a configurative jurisprudence by McDougal and his associates is designed to address. Although McDougal and Reisman were to observe in a later piece that participation in all stages of decision-making is diversifying,[189] they do not revisit in that piece their earlier claim that participation in some stages of decision-making, notably the "prescription" stage of formulating and projecting policies as authoritative for the community, is necessarily restricted.[190]

I have set out in some detail the policy-oriented perspective on international law because it represents one of the few sustained attempts to develop a theory of international law that recognizes overlapping identities and multiple forms of participation. At the same time, some feminists may see the McDougal-Lasswell approach as seriously, if not fatally, flawed by its methodological

184. *Id.* at 400.

185. *Id.* at 402.

186. RICHARD FALK, *A New Paradigm for International Legal Studies: Prospects and Proposals*, *in* REVITALIZING INTERNATIONAL LAW 3, 38 (1989).

187. *Id.* at 39.

188. McDougal et al., *Theories About International Law*, *supra* note 170, at 193.

189. McDougal & Reisman, *Policy-Oriented Perspective*, *supra* note 170, at 108.

190. McDougal et al., *Theories About International Law*, *supra* note 170, at 192-93.

premises and assumptions about participation. Quite apart from McDougal and his colleagues' espousal of classical liberal notions of equality,[191] feminists may be troubled by their reliance on objectivity,[192] rationality,[193] and universalism.[194] Also problematic is the assumption that knowledge, in and of itself, might be sufficient to empower women as participants in the international legal process.

Richard Falk characterizes his contribution to the World Order Models Project (WOMP)[195] as an attempt to adapt the McDougal world order framework to a strategy for the transition from a world order system of sovereign States to a world order system of central guidance.[196] According to Falk's blueprint, this change in world order systems would begin with global consciousness-raising aimed at building consensus on the nature of the challenges facing the current world order and orienting values toward peace, economic equity, social and political dignity, and ecological balance. In a system where these values had largely been realized, central guidance would consist of four functional systems corresponding to the four values. Each functional system would be linked with technical organs of coordination and political organs of oversight, the latter being composed equally of representatives of peoples, NGOs, and governments. Efficiency, Falk writes, would be sacrificed to widely-based participation. The tendency toward centralization of functional control in order to allocate scarce resources equitably would be offset by the tendency toward decentralization of political structures together with increasingly localized loyalties and

191. MCDOUGAL ET AL., HUMAN RIGHTS AND WORLD PUBLIC ORDER, *supra* note 170, at 612-52. It is noteworthy that an earlier version of this chapter, which appeared as Myres S. McDougal et al., *Human Rights for Women and World Public Order: The Outlawing of Sex-Based Discrimination*, 69 AM. J. INT'L L. 497 (1975), ranks among the early works published on women's international human rights. *See* Rebecca J. Cook, *Women's International Human Rights: A Bibliography*, 24 N.Y.U. J. INT'L L. & POL. 857 (1992).

192. For example, McDougal and his colleagues believe that an observational standpoint can be established "in identification with the whole of humankind" or that the scholar can "make appropriate discount for the biases of his cultural background, class and group memberships, personality formation, and previous experience." McDougal & Reisman, *Policy-Oriented Perspective*, *supra* note 170, at 113, 115. For one feminist critique of objectivity, see Catharine A. MacKinnon, *Feminism, Marxism, Method, and the State: Toward a Feminist Jurisprudence*, 8 SIGNS 635 (1983).

193. SANDRA HARDING, THE SCIENCE QUESTION IN FEMINISM (1986).

194. *See* Gunning, *supra* note 154; Hom, *supra* note 155.

195. On WOMP, see generally Saul Mendlovitz, *General Introduction* to RICHARD FALK, A STUDY OF FUTURE WORLDS xvii (1975).

196. FALK, *supra* note 186, at 39. *See generally* FALK, *supra* note 195.

identities.[197] While the universalist orientation of Falk's project may be incompatible with some schools of feminist thought,[198] Falk's attention to global consciousness-raising, his conception of the role of an international civil society, creates at a conceptual level an important space for the formation and participation of non-State groups.[199]

Julius Stone agrees with what he takes to be presuppositions of Falk's project; namely, that international law as a coordinated system of sovereign States cannot satisfy even demands for human survival, that a broader spectrum of decision-making elites cannot remedy this failure of the system, and that "state entities by their very existence prevent the spontaneous emergence across frontiers of the planetarywide general awareness of people necessary to support institutions performing essential planetary functions."[200] At the same time, scholars such as Stone and Douglas Johnston seek to separate the functional values of sovereignty and ask of each whether it is better achieved by other actors. In a passage that recalls Karen Engle's concerns,[201] Stone writes:

> [W]e must still remember that [State sovereignty] *can* serve functions that are not *merely* a rationalization of human greed, folly, or madness. It still corresponds, in measures varying from state to state, to certain basic human interests and values, originating in the fact that cultural inheritance is itself usually territorial.[202]

Cultural inheritance, Stone argues, is a complex of functional values that Falk's project of a nonterritorial central guidance system should be designed to leave intact.[203]

Johnston's account of functionalism in contemporary international law conveys functionalism's willingness to discard the conventions of sovereignty and allow the direct participation of sub-State actors such as individuals, minorities, and indigenous peoples in international legal processes where this would enhance human

197. FALK, *supra* note 186, at 24 fig. 1.1, 28 tbl. 1.1, 40-41.

198. For an analysis contrasting two feminist perspectives on peace research and world order studies such as WOMP, see Christine Sylvester, *Some Dangers in Merging Feminist and Peace Projects*, 7 ALTERNATIVES 493 (1987).

199. *See supra* p. 310.

200. STONE, VISIONS OF WORLD ORDER, *supra* note 171, at 34, 38. Stone's discussion of Falk is summarized in Stone, *A Sociological Perspective*, *supra* note 171, at 277-84.

201. *Supra* note 153 and accompanying text.

202. STONE, VISIONS OF WORLD ORDER, *supra* note 171, at 40.

203. *Id.*

welfare.[204] While functionalism does not consider gender specifically, its reasoning would apply to women's individual and collective participation in international law, whether on the basis of gender or gender in combination with nationality, ethnicity, culture, or other forms of identification.

The perspectives on international law surveyed in this Subsection offer a number of insights into how feminism might go about reconceiving sovereignty and how women might participate in international law-making. The policy-oriented perspective on international law pioneered by Myres McDougal and Harold Lasswell draws our attention to the wide range of actors on the world stage and the diverse ways in which they interact. It recognizes that individuals can participate in international law-making both as individuals and through their membership in different, potentially overlapping groups. Richard Falk's study of the transition to a world order system of central guidance points to the possibility that a global awareness of issues can be fostered other than through States. By identifying the different functional values of sovereignty, the sociological perspective of Julius Stone provides a method of isolating and retaining those functions of sovereignty beneficial to women. Finally, Douglas Johnston's functionalist perspective can be used to argue, for example, that women should be guaranteed a place at the table when international treaties on subjects of particular concern to women are being negotiated, provided that this measure enhances human welfare.

2. *Normative Approaches to Sovereignty*

This Subsection looks at normative approaches to reconceiving sovereignty in international law. Unlike the literature discussed in the previous Subsection, these writings cannot be seen as an ongoing exchange between scholars who draw on one another's work. Instead, this rubric brings together relatively preliminary work from a number of scholars working in quite different fields and contexts. The similarity lies in the normative inquiry into sovereignty, a normative inquiry that I have grouped around the questions of limited sovereignty and overlapping sovereignty.

The question of limited sovereignty is the question of why the State should have a monopoly on representation in international fora when it may not decide the issue at hand domestically. As groups such as ethnic minorities are claiming greater autonomy within the State, the argument is being made that this autonomy should be

---

204. Johnston, *supra* note 56 , at 29-30, 29 n.91. Among the effects of functionalist logic on core concepts of international law is "to reduce dependency on abstractions, particularly in issue contexts and problem situations where they seem obstructive of co-operative behaviour." *Id.* at 40.

reflected in their direct participation in international law-making on issues that come within their decision-making power domestically.[205] This issue is already familiar to international law in the context of treaty-making and other forms of participation in international relations by federal sub-units.[206]

Limited sovereignty assumes that if the State loses some of its sovereignty, another entity must gain it; for example, the sovereignty lost by the member States of the European Community is gained by the Community itself. Overlapping sovereignty is at odds with this monocular view of sovereignty.[207] It envisages instead the recognition of overlapping legal orders. Feminist Jean Bethke Elshtain argues that the sharply bounded, unified sovereign State/self should be replaced by the "co-existence of overlapping, porous sovereignties," with communities and groups–as well as sovereign selves–having rights, and mediating institutions having more power than in statist constructions.[208] Taking the legal framework of the European Community and its member States as his point of departure, Neil MacCormick asks:

> Can we think of a world in which our normative existence and our practical life are anchored in, or related to, a variety of institutional systems, each of which has validity or operation in relation to some range of concerns, none of which is absolute over all the others, and all of which, for most purposes, can operate without serious mutual conflict in areas of overlap?[209]

In the context of indigenous peoples and religious groups, Perry Dane explores the asymmetric questions of when the State should recognize the non-State sovereignty or separate legal order of such a community and, inversely, when the community should recognize the State.[210] Indeed, it is indigenous peoples, frustrated by the denial of collective forms of representation in the international legal system, who increasingly are demanding recognition as subjects of international law so that they can represent their own interests

205. *See* McRae, *supra* note 36, at 21.

206. *See, e.g.*, IVAN BERNIER, INTERNATIONAL LEGAL ASPECTS OF FEDERALISM 13-17 (1973) (summarizing the debate on the treaty-making power of federal sub-units leading up to the Vienna Convention on the Law of Treaties).

207. The term is that of Neil MacCormick, *Beyond the Sovereign State*, 56 MODERN L. REV. 1, 5 (1993).

208. Elshtain, *supra* note 7, at 1377.

209. MacCormick, *supra* note 207, at 17.

210. Perry Dane, *The Maps of Sovereignty: A Meditation*, 12 CARDOZO L. REV. 959 (1991).

directly in international fora.[211]

Underlying the normative reconception of sovereignty in international law is a concern with difference and diversity, voice and representation, pluralism and multiple viewpoints that is also fundamental to much of feminist legal scholarship. At the same time, using women's participation as a practical yardstick, these emerging approaches to sovereignty theory will not immediately affect the ways that women influence international law. Women's aspirations do not always lie in the direction of autonomy and sovereignty; indeed they are sometimes trapped in a contest between the order of the sovereign State and the alternative order struggling to survive.[212] I suggest that this measure points not to the irrelevancy of sovereignty theory for women, but instead to the importance of developing women's perspectives on sovereignty theory.

V. CONCLUSION

International law, with what sceptics consider to be only a simulacrum of coercive mechanisms and organization, is either not "law" or is the very essence of "law." Either characterization reduces it to core concepts and ways of reasoning. Perhaps no concept is more fundamental to international law than State sovereignty. This Article has outlined three aspects of State sovereignty: statism, the centrality of the State to international law-making, and the State as a bounded, unified self. It has proceeded by asking what altering each of these assumptions might mean for women in terms of participation in international law and where feminist theory might join, borrow from, or criticize the existing debates in international legal scholarship. Paradoxically, if the Article appears to rely more on international law than on feminism, one of its themes has been that emerging feminist approaches to international law have not yet challenged the deep structures of international law.

Part II introduced the trend in some recent international theory and practice away from statism toward a readiness to condition the status of the State in international law on its respect domestically for the rights constitutive of liberal democracy. If the recognition, territorial integrity, and legitimacy of the State are increasingly tied to notions of equal representation and participation in democratic

211. *See, e.g.*, Maivân Clech Lâm, *Making Room for Peoples at the United Nations: Thoughts Provoked by Indigenous Claims to Self-Determination*, 25 CORNELL INT'L L.J. 603, 621-22 (1992).

212. *E.g.*, Native Women's Association of Canada v. Canada, [1992] 3 F.C. 192 (F.C.A.) (application for leave to S.C.C. granted, Mar. 12, 1993) (place of aboriginal women in the recent Canadian constitutional negotiations).

governance, I suggested that it is open to women to argue for one of several feminist interpretations of these ideas.

Part III discussed international civil society as an alternative space for women's participation in international law, analyzing several examples of the growing involvement of NGOs in the creation of "soft" law. It also examined different types of arguments that could be made for treating the actions of some women's NGOs as contributing directly to the formation of customary international law.

Part IV explored the analogy of State to individual, in particular as it has appeared in the feminist international legal literature. In Section A, I showed that feminist critiques of the State/self equation tend to argue against the bounded nature of the State/self without questioning its unitary nature. I distinguished between body and property metaphors for the State, tracing how different feminist arguments in international law personify the State differently. Section B attempted to go beyond the contradictory metaphoric understandings of state sovereignty by breaking down the unified conception of the State. To that end, it presented a series of functionalist and normative approaches to reconceptualizing sovereignty in international law, commenting on how they might engage feminism and what effect they might have on women's direct participation, instead of or separate from State participation, in international law.

If the international system is "nothing other than a structure of ideas," as Philip Allott has written,[213] then it is at this level that the system must be challenged–but with the abstract anchored in the concrete, the real transformed by the imagination.

213. PHILIP ALLOTT, EUNOMIA: NEW ORDER FOR A NEW WORLD xv (1990).

[15]

VOLUME 40, NUMBER 1, WINTER 1999

Finding the Peripheries: Sovereignty and Colonialism in Nineteenth-Century International Law

Antony Anghie*

I. INTRODUCTION

International law is universal. It is a body of law that applies to all states regardless of their specific cultures, belief systems, and political organizations. It is a common set of doctrines that all states use to regulate relations with each other. The association between international law and universality is so ingrained that pointing to this connection appears tautological. And yet, the universality of international law is a relatively recent development. It was not until the end of the nineteenth century that a set of doctrines was established as applicable to all states, whether these were in Asia, Africa, or Europe.

The universalization of international law was principally a consequence of the imperial expansion that took place towards the end of the "long nineteenth century."[1] The conquest of non-European[2] peo-

* Associate Professor of Law, University of Utah College of Law. S.J.D., Harvard Law School, 1995; LL.B., Monash University, 1987; B.A., Monash University, 1986. My thanks are due to Nathaniel Berman, Robert Chu, Mitchel Lasser, Vasuki Nesiah, Kunal Parker, Ileana Porras, Annelise Riles, Uta Roth, Michael Schwalb, and Lee Teitelbaum; to the Summer Stipend Program of the College of Law, University of Utah, the participants at the Dighton Writers Workshop, and my colleagues at the College of Law at the University of Utah who offered encouragement and comment when this work was presented to the Faculty; and to B.S. Chimni, Karen Engle, Thomas Franck, James Gathii, and Balakrishnan Rajagopal who painstakingly read and commented on earlier drafts of this Article. I am especially grateful to David Kennedy for his comments, insight, encouragement, and provocation over the years that I have been working on the issues explored in this Article. I am indebted to C.G. Weeramantry; I have had the privilege of being, over the years, his student and research assistant, and the themes animating this work emerged for me out of the experience of working for the Nauru Commission of Inquiry in 1987-88 as his Research Assistant.

This Article is based on a chapter of my S.J.D. dissertation, Creating the Nation-State: Colonialism and the Making of International Law (1995) (unpublished S.J.D. dissertation, Harvard Law School) (on file with the author), and is part of a larger and ongoing project examining the relationship between international law and colonialism.

1. Historians of the period tend to see the 19th century as ending in 1914 with the commencement of the Great War that marks the end of the century. *See* ERIC HOBSBAWM, THE AGE OF EMPIRE: 1875–1914, at 8 (1987).

2. By "non-European" I refer to the areas that were the subject of colonial expansion in the late 19th century, that is, principally, Asia, Africa, and the Pacific. The impact of the Americas on the development of international law gives rise to an important and distinct set of issues, which I do

ples for economic and political advantage was the most prominent feature of this period, which was termed by one eminent historian, Eric Hobsbawm, as the "Age of Empire."[3] By 1914, after numerous colonial wars, virtually all the territories of Asia, Africa, and the Pacific were controlled by the major European states, resulting in the assimilation of all these non-European peoples into a system of law that was fundamentally European in that it derived from European thought and experience.

The late nineteenth century was also the period in which positivism decisively replaced naturalism as the principal jurisprudential technique of the discipline of international law.[4] Positivism was the new analytic apparatus used by the jurists of the time to account for the events that culminated in the universalization of international law and the formulation of a body of principles that was understood to apply globally as a result of the annexation of "unoccupied" territories such as the Australian continent, the conquest of large parts of Asia, and the partitioning of Africa.

This Article focuses on the relationship between positivism and colonialism. My interest lies in examining the way in which positivism dealt with the colonial confrontation. Particularly, this is an attempt to examine how positivism sought to account for the expansion of European Empires and for the dispossession of various peoples stemming therefrom. In studying this relationship, I seek not only to outline an architecture of the legal framework, but also to question extant understandings of the relationship between colonialism and positivism and the significance of the nineteenth-century colonial encounter for the discipline as a whole.

Positivist jurisprudence is premised on the notion of the primacy of the state. Despite subsequent attempts to reformulate the foundations of international law, the fundamental positivist position, that states are the principal actors of international law and they are bound only by that to which they have consented, continues to operate as the basic premise of the international legal system. Positivism, furthermore, has generated the problem that governs the major theoretical inquiries into the discipline: how can legal order be created among sovereign states? Attempts to resolve this problem, as well as the critiques of these attempts, have, on the whole, constituted the central theoretical

---

not address here.

3. HOBSBAWM, *supra* note 1.

4. As to the emergence of positivism, Henkin et al. provide a useful summary and a historical periodization: "The rise of positivism in Western political and legal theory, especially from the latter part of the 18th century to the early part of the 20th century, corresponds to the steady rise of the national state and its increasingly absolute claims to legal and political supremacy." LOUIS HENKIN ET AL., INTERNATIONAL LAW at xxv (3d ed. 1993).

debate of the discipline over the last century.[5] The defining character of this problem to the discipline of international law is further reflected by the structure of many of the major textbooks of international law, which introduce the subject by outlining the problem and offering some sort of solution to it.[6]

Colonialism features only incidentally within this scheme. This appears inevitable, because the colonial confrontation was not a confrontation between two sovereign states, but between a sovereign European state and a non-European state that, according to the positivist jurisprudence of the time, was lacking in sovereignty. Such a confrontation poses no conceptual difficulties for the positivist jurist who basically resolves the issue by arguing that the sovereign state can do as it wishes with regard to the non-sovereign entity, which lacks the legal personality to assert any legal opposition. This resolution was profoundly important from a political point of view as its operation resulted in the universalization of international law. Nevertheless, it seemingly poses no theoretical difficulties; consequently, the colonial world is relegated to both the geographical and theoretical peripheries of the discipline.

Certainly, colonies were often exasperatingly troublesome, both in terms of their governance and international jurisprudence. But for the international lawyers, colonial problems constituted a distinct set of issues that were principally not of a theoretical, but rather a political character: how the colonized peoples should be governed and, later, what role international law should play in decolonization.

Even when the colonies were perceived to challenge some of the fundamental assumptions of the discipline, as in the case of the doctrine of self-determination, which was used in the 1960s and 1970s to effect the transformation of colonial territories into sovereign states, such challenges were perceived, mainly in political terms, as a threat to a stable and established system of international law, which was ineluctably European and was now faced with the quandary of accommodating these outsiders. The conceptualization of the problem in this way

5. I am indebted to a number of important recent works that examine the importance of the 19th century to international law, as seen within this framework. *See, e.g.*, ANTHONY CARTY, THE DECAY OF INTERNATIONAL LAW: A REAPPRAISAL OF THE LIMITS OF LEGAL IMAGINATION IN INTERNATIONAL AFFAIRS (1987); David Kennedy, *International Law and the Nineteenth Century: History of an Illusion*, 17 QUINNIPIAC L. REV. 99 (1997) [hereinafter Kennedy, *History*]; MARTTI KOSKENNIEMI, FROM APOLOGY TO UTOPIA (1989) [hereinafter KOSKENNIEMI, APOLOGY]; Martti Koskenniemi, *Lauterpacht: The Victorian Tradition in International Law*, 2 EUR. J. INT'L L. 215 (1997) [hereinafter Koskenniemi, *Lauterpacht*]. I am also indebted to major works that deal with the entry of colonial states into the international system. *See, e.g.*, JAMES CRAWFORD, THE CREATION OF STATES IN INTERNATIONAL LAW (1979), GERRIT W. GONG, THE STANDARD OF 'CIVILIZATION' IN INTERNATIONAL SOCIETY (1984).

6. This problem is usually posed as one of "Is International Law Really Law?" HENKIN ET AL., *supra* note 4, at 10–18. As discussed below, international lawyers, for over a century, have adopted the same practice.

suggested again that the non-European world was completely peripheral to the discipline proper; and it was only the disconcerting prospect of Africans and Asians acquiring sovereignty in the 1950s and 1960s that alerted international lawyers to the existence of a multicultural world.[7]

Scholars focusing on the colonial world naturally adopted a very different approach. The principal concern of these scholars was to show how positivist international law subordinated non-European peoples. The naturalist international law that had applied in the sixteenth and seventeenth centuries asserted that a universal international law deriving from human reason applied to all peoples, European or non-European. By contrast, positivist international law distinguished between civilized states and non-civilized states and asserted further that international law applied only to the sovereign states that composed the civilized "Family of Nations." The important work of these scholars focused, then, on the complicity between positivism and colonialism.[8] Although the traditional view of the discipline downplays the

---

7. For an examination of this period, see ADDA BOZEMAN, THE FUTURE OF LAW IN A MULTICULTURAL WORLD (1971); THE FUTURE OF INTERNATIONAL LAW IN A MULTICULTURAL WORLD (R.J. Dupuy ed., 1983). The axiomatically European character of international law has been often proclaimed. In his monumental work on the history of the discipline, Verzijl states:

> Now there is one truth that is not open to denial or even to doubt, namely that the actual body of international law, as it stands today, not only is the product of the conscious activity of the European mind, but has also drawn its vital essence from a common source of beliefs, and in both of these aspects it is mainly of Western European origin.

J.H.W. VERZIJL, INTERNATIONAL LAW IN HISTORICAL PERSPECTIVE 435–36 (1968). It is not entirely surprising, then, that colonialism features only incidentally even in important recent works. *See, e.g.*, JENS BARTELSON, A GENEALOGY OF SOVEREIGNTY (1995).

8. The most notable scholar in this area is C.H. Alexandrowicz, whose extensive and pioneering body of work includes AN INTRODUCTION TO THE HISTORY OF THE LAW OF NATIONS IN THE EAST INDIES (1967) [hereinafter ALEXANDROWICZ, EAST INDIES]; THE EUROPEAN-AFRICAN CONFRONTATION: A STUDY IN TREATY MAKING (1973) [hereinafter ALEXANDROWICZ, TREATY MAKING]. Many scholars from developing nations have examined the effect of the 19th century in their broader treatment of the relationship between colonialism and international law. *See, e.g.*, R.P. ANAND, NEW STATES AND INTERNATIONAL LAW (1972); TASLIM O. ELIAS, AFRICA AND THE DEVELOPMENT OF INTERNATIONAL LAW (1972); MOHAMMED BEDJAOUI, TOWARDS A NEW INTERNATIONAL ECONOMIC ORDER (1979). These works were written at a time when the newly independent states of Africa and Asia were assessing the history of the international system of which they were now full members.

Other recent important works that deal with the issue of the significance of 19th-century colonialism to international law include Georges Abi-Saab, *International Law and the International Community: The Long Road to Universality*, *in* ESSAYS IN HONOUR OF WANG TIEYA 31 (Ronald St. John Macdonald ed., 1994); Annelise Riles, *Aspiration and Control: International Legal Rhetoric and the Essentialization of Culture*, 106 HARV. L. REV. 723 (1993); SIBA N'ZATIOULA GROVOGUI, SOVEREIGNS, QUASI SOVEREIGNS AND AFRICANS: RACE AND SELF-DETERMINATION IN INTERNATIONAL LAW (1996); James Thuo Gathii, *International Law and Eurocentricity*, 9 EUR. J. INT'L L. 184 (1998); Makau wa Mutua, *Why Redraw the Map of Africa: A Moral and Legal Inquiry*, 16 MICH. J. INT'L L. 1113 (1995). I have also drawn upon the important work of scholars writing more generally in the tradition of developing nations. *See generally* B.S. CHIMNI, INTERNATIONAL LAW AND WORLD ORDER: A CRITIQUE OF CONTEMPORARY APPROACHES (1993); M. Sornarajah, *Power and Justice in International Law*, 1 SINGAPORE J. INT'L & COMP. L. 28 (1997). For a case study of the way in which international law dealt with colonial territories, see the sustained ex-

importance of the colonial confrontation for an understanding of the subject as a whole, it is clear that much of the international law of the nineteenth century was preoccupied with colonial problems. It is explicitly recognized that special doctrines and norms had to be devised for the purpose of defining, identifying, and categorizing the uncivilized, and this was what the jurists of the period proceeded to do, for instance when listing "conquest" and "cession by treaty" among the modes of acquiring territory. While analyzing and critiquing these doctrines and their effects, however, even distinguished scholars such as Alexandrowicz implicitly tend to treat the colonial encounter as marginal by studying it principally in terms of the effects of positivism on the colonized peoples.

My approach both borrows from and differs from these two broad approaches to the relationship between international law and the colonial confrontation. My argument is that the colonial confrontation is central to an understanding of the character and nature of international law, but that the extent of this centrality cannot be appreciated by a framework that adopts as the commencing point of its inquiry the problem of how order is created among sovereign states. In attempting to demonstrate this centrality I have focused instead on how order is created among entities characterized as belonging to entirely different cultural systems.[9] I suggest that the maneuvers engaged in by positivist jurists with respect to colonialism may be best understood in terms of what might be termed the dynamic of difference. Jurists, using the conceptual tools of positivism, postulated a gap, understood principally in terms of cultural differences, between the civilized European and uncivilized non-European world. Having established this gap they then proceeded to devise a series of techniques for bridging this gap—of civilizing the uncivilized.

Such an approach enables an exploration of both the relationship between ideas of culture and sovereignty, and the ways in which sovereignty became identified with a specific set of cultural practices to the exclusion of others. By adopting this framework, I hope to inquire into a series of related problems: what does it mean to say that international law consists of rules to which sovereigns have acquiesced when certain societies were denied sovereign status? What are the processes by which this denial was justified and enforced? How does an under-

amination provided in CHRISTOPHER WEERAMANTRY, NAURU: ENVIRONMENTAL DAMAGE UNDER INTERNATIONAL TRUSTEESHIP (1992).

9. I have adopted a similar framework in analyzing an international dispute involving questions of colonial exploitation and in discussing the works of a naturalist jurist, Francisco de Vitoria. *See* Antony Anghie, *"The Heart of My Home": Colonialism, Environmental Damage, and the Nauru Case*, 34 HARV. INT'L L.J. 445 (1993) [hereinafter Anghie, *Nauru*]; Antony Anghie, *Francisco de Vitoria and the Colonial Origins of International Law*, 5 SOC. & LEGAL STUD. 321 (1996) [hereinafter Anghie, *Vitoria*].

standing of these processes of denial offer a means of reinterpreting contemporary understandings of sovereignty doctrine and of positivism itself? Exploring these issues might enable an appreciation of the distinctive and unique character of sovereignty as it developed in the non-European context. Such an appreciation is important for an understanding of the subsequent histories of the non-European states, even after decolonization.

My broader goal is to contest the received and traditional understandings of positivism and of sovereignty doctrine, which treat each of these concepts as independently and completely constituted within European thought and history. Within this framework, the relationship between positivism and colonialism is understood principally in terms of the crippling effect that an already established positivism had on non-European peoples. Similarly, sovereignty doctrine is understood as a stable and comprehensive set of ideas that was formulated in Europe and that extended inexorably and imperiously with empire into darkest Africa, the inscrutable Orient, and the far reaches of the Pacific, acquiring control over these territories and peoples and transforming them into European possessions. The effects of the operation of these doctrines are not insignificant. My interest lies, however, not only in the important point that positivism legitimized conquest and dispossession, but also in the reverse relationship—in identifying how notions of positivism and sovereignty were themselves shaped by the encounter. In contrast to the view that the colonial confrontation illuminates a minor and negligible aspect of sovereignty doctrine, my argument is that no adequate account of sovereignty can be given without analyzing the constitutive effect of colonialism on sovereignty. Colonialism cannot be accounted for as an example of the application of sovereignty; rather, sovereignty was constituted and shaped through colonialism.[10]

---

10. This follows, with a little adaptation, Edward Said's concern to "regard imperial concerns as constitutively significant to the culture of the modern West." EDWARD W. SAID, CULTURE AND IMPERIALISM 66 (1993). Many of the themes and concerns of this essay are derived from the profoundly important work done by a group of scholars loosely and problematically termed "post-colonial." Some of the major works that have emerged from these scholars and that have shaped my approach in this Article are EDWARD SAID, ORIENTALISM (1978) GAYATRI CHAKRAVORTY SPIVAK, IN OTHER WORLDS (1987). For general works on these scholars, see BART MOORE-GILBERT, POSTCOLONIAL THEORY: CONTEXTS, PRACTICES, POLITICS (1997). For the purposes of this essay, my major concern is to explore, in the context of international law, the broad idea developed by these theorists that Europe cannot be understood without reference to the non-European world and that there was an intimate connection between the development of various disciplines in the West and the colonial project. Important collections of essays that develop and apply different aspects of this body of theory include SELECTED SUBALTERN STUDIES (Ranajit Guha & Gayatri Chakravorty Spivak eds., 1988); COLONIALISM AND CULTURE (Nicholas B. Dirks ed., 1992); TENSIONS OF EMPIRE: COLONIAL CULTURES IN A BOURGEOIS WORLD (Frederick Cooper & Ann Laura Stoler eds., 1997). I am also indebted to the pioneering work done by critical race theorists on the relationship between law and race, particularly PATRICIA J. WILLIAMS, THE ALCHEMY OF RACE AND RIGHTS (1991); Kimberlé Williams Crenshaw, *Race, Reform and*

My argument is that what passes now as the defining dilemma of the discipline, the problem of order among states, is a problem that has been peculiar, from the time of its origin, to the specificities of European history. Additionally, the extension and universalization of the European experience, which is achieved by transmuting it into the major theoretical problem of the discipline, has the effect of suppressing and subordinating other histories of international law and the people to whom it has applied. Within the axiomatic framework of positivism, which decrees that European states are sovereign while non-European states are not, there is only one means of relating the history of the non-European world, and this the positivists proceed to do: it is a history of the civilizing mission, the process by which peoples of Africa, Asia, the Americas, and the Pacific were finally assimilated into a European international law. This is the history I am examining, not with a view to furthering it, but in an attempt to point to the "ambivalences, contradictions, the use of force, and the tragedies and ironies that attend it."[11] In attempting this sort of a history, I depart from the tendency, present even among writers such as Alexandrowicz who are sympathetic to the injustices of colonialism, to focus on positivism's triumphant suppression of the non-European world. The violence of positivist language in relation to non-European peoples is hard to overlook. Positivists developed an elaborate vocabulary for denigrating these peoples, presenting them as suitable objects for conquest, and legitimizing the most extreme violence against them, all in the furtherance of the civilizing mission—the discharge of the white man's burden.[12] Despite this, it is incorrect to see the colonial encounter as a series of problems that were effortlessly resolved by the simple application of the formidable intellectual resources of positivism. Rather, I argue, positivists were engaged in an ongoing struggle to define, subordinate, and exclude the uncivilized native; my argument is that colonial problems posed a significant and ultimately insuperable set of challenges to positivism and its pretensions to develop a set of doctrines that could coherently account for native personality, a task that

---

Retrenchment: Transformation and Legitimation in Anti-Discrimination Law, 101 HARV. L. REV. 1331 (1988). For important recent works that apply critical race theory and post-colonial theory to various problems of international law, see Ruth Gordon, *Saving Failed States: Sometimes a Neocolonialist Notion*,12 AM. U. J. INT'L L. & POL'Y 903 (1997); Dianne Otto, *Subalternity and International Law: The Problem of Global Community and the Incommensurbility of Difference*, 5 SOC. & LEGAL STUD. 337 (1996).

11. Dipesh Chakrabarty, *Postcoloniality and the Artifice of History: Who Speaks for "Indian" Pasts?*, REPRESENTATIONS, Winter 1992, *extracted in* THE POST-COLONIAL STUDIES READER 386 (Bill Ashcroft et al. eds., 1995).

12. This corresponds exactly with Said's notion of Orientalism: "Orientalism can be discussed and analyzed as the corporate institution for dealing with Orient—dealing with it by making statements about it, authorizing views of it, describing it, by teaching it, settling it, ruling over it: in short, Orientalism as a Western style for dominating, restructuring, and having authority over the Orient." SAID, ORIENTALISM, *supra* note 10, at 3.

was crucial to the positivist self-image. The brutal realities of conquest and dispossession can hardly be ameliorated by asserting that the legal framework legitimizing this dispossession was contradictory and incoherent. But it is perhaps by pointing to these inconsistencies and ambiguities, by interrogating how it was that sovereignty became the exclusive preserve of Europe, and by questioning this framework, even while describing how it came into being, that it might be possible to open the way not only towards a different history of the discipline, but to a different understanding of the workings and effects of colonialism itself.[13] This in turn is part of a larger project that has been the preoccupation of many jurists of the non-European world: to understand the relationship between international law and colonialism in order to formulate more adequately the potential of the discipline to remedy the enduring inequities and imbalances that resulted from the colonial confrontation.

The subject of this Article is colonialism in the nineteenth century. And yet, it is also part of a larger project that focuses on international law as a whole and seeks to understand the entire complex, convoluted, and fraught relationship between colonialism and international law. I am concerned with understanding the strategies by which international law rewrites its history, in different phases, and, in particular, how it seeks to suppress the colonial foundations of the discipline. The systematic neglect of the centrality of colonialism for the whole project of international law is far from coincidental. Rather, it is a consequence of a powerful set of attitudes and juristic techniques that need to be identified, understood, and contested. Thus the final sections of this Article use the nineteenth century as a means for examining the broader question of how international law, even while relying on the colonial past and the legal and political relations it created, nevertheless presents that past as inconsequential, both in terms of the theory of international law and the systems of power and inequality it brought into being. The conventional approach studies the nineteenth century in order to show how it has been overcome. My argument is that central elements of nineteenth-century international law are reproduced in current approaches to international law and relations.

This inquiry is conducted through an analysis of the works of prominent jurists of the nineteenth century, including James Lorimer,[14]

13. The broad attempt, then, is to begin in some way the problematic task, which Dipesh Chakrabarty has formulated, of "provincializing 'Europe.'" Chakrabarty, *supra* note 11, at 383. To attempt this project is paradoxical given that what I am examining is the process by which European international law became universal; as Chakrabarty notes, "The project of provincializing 'Europe' refers to a history which does not yet exist." *Id.* at 385.

14. 1 James Lorimer, LL.D., The Institutes of the Law of Nations: A Treatise of the Jural Relations of Separate Political Communities 22 (London, Blackwood and Sons 1883).

W.E. Hall,[15] John Westlake,[16] Thomas Lawrence,[17] and Henry Wheaton.[18] I have also considered the works of later jurists, such as Lassa Oppenheim[19] and M.F. Lindley,[20] who wrote in the 1920s, but whose work adopts and elaborates the nineteenth-century framework.[21]

Part II of this Article focuses on the basic elements of positivism—the analytical tools, methods, and ambitions of positivist jurists—in order to examine how issues of race and culture were always central to the very conceptualization and project of positivism, rather than a set of issues for which an established positivism developed an ancillary vocabulary. Furthermore, in studying the ambitions and methods of positivists, it becomes possible to appreciate their preoccupation with establishing the intellectual coherence and rigor of their discipline and, therefore, the significance of successfully overcoming the challenges colonialism posed to such ambitions.

---

15. WILLIAM EDWARD HALL, M.A., A TREATISE ON INTERNATIONAL LAW (1880). The first edition of this work was published in 1880 and was revised on numerous occasions. It was the major English treatise on the subject prior to the appearance of L. OPPENHEIM, M.A., LL.D. INTERNATIONAL LAW: A TREATISE (1912), *infra* note 19.

16. John Westlake was Whewell Professor of International Law at the University of Cambridge in 1894, at the time of the publication of his work, CHAPTERS ON THE PRINCIPLES OF INTERNATIONAL LAW (Cambridge, Cambridge Univ. Press 1894). The book's 11 chapters deal mainly with jurisprudential aspects of international law (the distinctiveness of international law and its status as "law") and the history of international law from the time of the Greeks to the 18th century. There are also several chapters discussing "colonial problems," as suggested by the titles "The Equality and Independence of States," "International Rights of Self-Preservation," "Territorial Sovereignty, Especially with Relation to Uncivilised Regions," "The Empire of India"; and a final chapter succinctly entitled "War." It is notable that, for a work which purports to be general in scope, 3 of the 11 chapters deal quite explicitly with issues regarding the status and treatment of colonies and natives.

17. THOMAS LAWRENCE, THE PRINCIPLES OF INTERNATIONAL LAW (London, Macmillan 1895).

18. HENRY WHEATON, ELEMENTS OF INTERNATIONAL LAW (George Grafton Wilson ed., The Carnegie Institute of Washington photo. reprint 1964) (1866). Wheaton's work, which has passed through several editions, was widely respected and used at this time.

19. The first edition of Lassa Oppenheim's magisterial work was published in 1905 and could be regarded as a superb embodiment of positivist jurisprudence. The analysis of this Article is based on LASSA OPPENHEIM, INTERNATIONAL LAW (2d ed., 1912), perhaps the last great international law text of the long 19th century. Subsequent editions have been edited by a series of extremely distinguished international lawyers, and Oppenheim's INTERNATIONAL LAW continues to be, in all likelihood, the most authoritative and distinguished treatise on international law in the English language.

20. M.F. LINDLEY, THE ACQUISITION AND GOVERNMENT OF BACKWARD TERRITORY IN INTERNATIONAL LAW: BEING A TREATISE ON THE LAW AND PRACTICE RELATING TO COLONIAL EXPANSION (photo. reprint 1969) (1926).

21. For comprehensive accounts of the broader political contexts in which these judicial developments occurred, see GONG, *supra* note 5; THE EXPANSION OF INTERNATIONAL SOCIETY (Hedley Bull & Adam Watson eds., 1984); ADAM WATSON, THE EVOLUTION OF INTERNATIONAL SOCIETY: A COMPARATIVE APPROACH (1992). For other useful but shorter works dealing with the same themes, see David Strang, *Contested Sovereignty: The Social Construction of Colonial Imperialism*, *in* STATE SOVEREIGNTY AS SOCIAL CONSTRUCT 22, 22–50 (Thomas J. Biersteker & Cynthia Weber eds., 1996).

Part III explores the first step in the dynamic of difference, the process by which a gap was postulated between European and non-European peoples; it examines how cultural distinctions became the basis for establishing a legal status, and how sovereignty doctrine was constituted by the elaboration of these distinctions so as to exclude non-European peoples from the realm of sovereignty.

Part IV examines the process by which the gap was bridged and the non-European world was brought into the realm of international law. It focuses, first, on the techniques of assimilation and, second, on the Berlin West Africa Conference of 1884–85, which provides an example of the broader diplomatic and political contexts in which these doctrines were applied.

Part V offers a reinterpretation of the significance of the nineteenth century to the discipline in the context of the previous analysis.[22]

II. ELEMENTS OF POSITIVIST JURISPRUDENCE

A. *Introduction*

The philosophy of positivism provided the primary jurisprudential resource for the jurists of the late nineteenth century. In the naturalist scheme, the sovereign administered a system of natural law by which it was bound. Positivism, by way of contrast, asserts, not only that the sovereign administers and enforces the law, but that law itself is the creation of sovereign will. The sovereign is the foundation of positivist jurisprudence, and nineteenth-century positivist jurists essentially sought to reconstruct the entire system of international law based on their new version of sovereignty doctrine. Two additional factors are important to an understanding of the positivist project. Positivist international lawyers were heavily influenced by the English jurist, John Austin, who questioned whether international law could be regarded as law at all. Accordingly, international legal positivists attempted to develop a jurisprudence that could address these objections. Moreover, they sought to present their discipline as "scientific" in character. Each of these factors was important to the positivist self-image and played a significant role in the development of positivist jurisprudence. Not only did positivism establish the legal framework that dealt with international disputes, but it also established the vocabulary and the set of constraints and considerations, that both shaped and was shaped by sovereignty doctrine.

22. The language of the period is replete with racial references to the "uncivilized," "natives," "backward," and so forth but I have refrained from placing these terms in quotations. I hope it is understood that the appearance of these terms in this essay does not reflect my acceptance of them.

B. Positivism and the Shift from Natural Law

Positivist jurists generally commenced their campaign of articulating new, distinctive versions of international law by employing the traditional technique of sketching the histories of their discipline up to their own time, and then distinguishing themselves from their naturalist predecessors. In broad terms, natural law consisted of a set of transcendental principles that could be identified through the use of reason. Still, even early jurists such as Francisco de Vitoria, a sixteenth-century scholar, made a distinction between "natural law" and "human law."[23] Human law, as the term suggests, was created by secular political authorities, and positivism was an extended elaboration of this framework. Natural law, by contrast, was strongly identified with principles of justice and the notion that all human activity was bound by an overarching morality. Thus within the naturalist framework, sovereign states were bound by the principles of natural law.

The techniques of naturalists are illustrated by jurists such as Grotius who argued that reason revealed a set of rules that governed relations between nations.[24] Nineteenth-century writers such as Wheaton understood Grotius's science[25] to have been,

> *First*, to lay down those rules of justice which would be binding on men living in a social state, independently of any positive laws of human institution; or, as is commonly expressed, living together in a *state of nature*; and,
>
> *Secondly*, to apply those rules, under the name of Natural Law, to the mutual relations of separate communities living in a similar state with respect to each other.[26]

Naturalist jurists such as Grotius and Pufendorff continuously debated the questions of whether rules emanated from reason or custom, or whether custom could be regarded as a manifestation of reason.[27]

23. Vitoria makes distinctions between three categories of law: divine, human, and natural law. *See* FRANCISCO DE VITORIA, DE INDIS ET DE IVRE BELLI REFLECTIONES [ON THE INDIANS LATELY DISCOVERED] ¶ 342, at 131 (Ernest Nys ed. & J.P. Bate trans., The Carnegie Institute of Washington 1917) (1696). For an extended discussion of Vitoria's use of these categories of law, see Alfred P. Rubin, *International Law in the Age of Columbus*, 39 NETH. INT'L L. REV. 5 (1992).

24. Earlier jurists such as Vitoria identified "international law" as natural law. Vitoria writes of "the law of nations *(jus gentium)* which either is natural law or is derived from natural law." VITORIA, *supra* note 23, ¶ 386, at 351.

25. The discussion here of naturalist jurisprudence is based on 19th-century understandings of this jurisprudence, rather than on my own analysis of the original works of jurists such as Grotius.

26. WHEATON, *supra* note 18, ch. 1.2.

27. As Wheaton notes, Grotius himself recognized that "natural law" was by no means a universal, self-evident category and that it was understood in different ways in different communities. Hence he makes the distinction between "natural law" and the "law of nations." "For if a

Essentially, however, custom was still approached through the naturalist framework, which examined and assessed the validity of state behavior with reference to the transcendent principles originating from the "state of nature," the model society whose laws could be identified and elaborated by reason and that, ideally, governed state behavior. A gradual shift in this approach is evident from the mid-seventeenth century onwards. Vattel, whose major work, *The Law of Nations*,[28] first appeared in 1758 is a pivotal figure in this shift towards positivism; while Vattel retained many aspects of naturalist thinking, he emphasized the power and authority of the sovereign to an extent that raised doubts as to whether international law could ever bind the sovereign.[29] Jurists in the late eighteenth century and early nineteenth century combined positivism and naturalism in various ways, noting that while a certain universal natural law applied to all nations without distinction between civilized and non-civilized, this system had to accommodate a considerable and emerging body of positive law specific to Europe.

Positivist law consisted of those rules that had been agreed upon by sovereign states, either explicitly or implicitly, as regulating relations between them.[30] Several late-eighteenth-century jurists such as von Ompteda, Moser, Surland, and Martens, noting the powerful emergence of positivist law, attempted to reconcile positivism and naturalism into an overall scheme of international law.[31] Traces of this reconciliatory approach may be found in some nineteenth-century jurists such as Lorimer who accepted that the law of nations comprised treaties and customs, but who argued that the overall purpose of the law of nations, derived from the law of nature,[32] was that of securing and furthering liberty.[33] Overall, however, the most influential late-

---

certain maxim which cannot be fairly inferred from admitted principles is, nevertheless, found to be everywhere observed, there is reason to conclude that it derives its origins from positive institutions." *Id.*, ch. 1.4. Within this scheme, consent is of importance, as it is the consent of the states which leads to the creation of "positive law" (the law of nations), which cannot be attributable to principles derived from the state of nature. *See id.*

28. EMER DE VATTEL, THE LAW OF NATIONS OR PRINCIPLES OF NATURAL LAW (C. Fenwick trans. & ed., 1916) (1758).

29. *See* KOSKENNIEMI, APOLOGY, *supra* note 5, at 85–98; CARTY, *supra* note 5, at 71–74. For a short and general treatment of Vattel, see ARTHUR NUSSBAUM, A CONCISE HISTORY OF THE LAW OF NATIONS, 156–58 (rev. ed. 1954).

30. *See generally* C.H. Alexandrowicz, *Doctrinal Aspects of the Universality of the Law of Nations*, 37 BRIT. Y.B. INT'L L. 506 (1961).

31. *See id.*

32. Lorimer insisted on "the exceptional dependence of the law of nations on the law of nature." LORIMER, *supra* note 14, at 22.

33. *See id.* at 15–27. Lorimer's basic argument was that the positive law of nations was directed towards the goal, identified in natural law, of securing liberty. In this way, Lorimer was adopting the sort of teleological approach which Wheaton would have dismissed. In arguing for the "exceptional dependence of the law of nations on natural law," Lorimer asserts:

nineteenth-century positivists such as Westlake and Hall were emphatically and exclusively positivist. This trend was such that by 1908, Oppenheim, probably the most eminent scholar of his time, emphasized that "we are no longer justified in teaching a law of nature and a 'natural' law of nations."[34]

For positivists, the sovereign state was the foundation of the whole legal system, and their broad project was to reconstitute the entire framework of international law based on this premise. Thus positivists rejected completely the naturalist notions that sovereign states were bound by an overarching natural law or that state action had to be guided by a higher morality. The sovereign was the highest authority and could only be bound by that to which it had agreed to be bound. Thus, for positivists, the rules of international law were to be discovered, not by speculative inquiries into the nature of justice or teleology, but by a careful study of the actual behavior of states and the institutions and laws that those states created.

Thus Westlake, for example, outlines his own approach in criticizing Pufendorff's argument that the rules relating to the immunities of ambassadors may be sought in natural law. Pufendorff,

> while insisting much on the social nature of man as the source of his duties . . . missed the essential facts that, if society is to exist, it must establish rules free from such undefinable elements as the principal purpose of an ambassador's residence, and those rules must be acquiesced in by the members of the society.[35]

The teleological basis of Pufendorff's rule was unacceptable to positivists, for whom treaties and custom had replaced natural law as the exclusive and primary source of international law. Treaties were an expression of sovereign will. Furthermore, positivists argued, the practice of states was also a manifestation of sovereign will and could suggest consent—either expressly or implicitly—to a set of customary laws. Thus, for positivists, treaties and the developing body of custom were the best guides to the proper rules of international behavior.

C. *Reactions to the Austinan Critique of International Law*

In focusing on the sovereign as the exclusive and ultimate source of law, positivist international jurists were following a long tradition that

---

> In dealing with the law of nations, the jurist has always a preliminary function to perform, and as it is natural law that determines the objects of positive law in all its departments, the function is one which he can perform only by keeping it steadily in view.

Id. at 22.

34. Lassa Oppenheim, *The Science of International Law: Its Task and Method*, 2 AM. J. INT'L L. 313, 328 (1908).

35. WESTLAKE, *supra* note 16, at 63.

had been notably developed by eminent political philosophers such as Thomas Hobbes and Jean Bodin. The English jurists of the late nineteenth century, however, were most influenced by John Austin, the foremost spokesman for positivism at the time,[36] who asserted famously that "[l]aws properly so called are a species of *commands*. But, being a *command*, every law properly so called flows from a *determinate* source."[37] The source is, for Austin, as for international jurists, a sovereign.

International law could conform in many respects to Austin's notion of law: international lawyers based their legal framework on sovereign behavior and, like Austin, insisted on the distinction between law and morality or justice. Problematically, however, the international system lacked the global sovereign crucial to Austin's scheme. Given his premise that all authority derived from a determinate source and the acknowledged absence in international relations of an overarching international sovereign, Austin argued that "the law obtaining between nations is not positive law: for every positive law is set by a given sovereign to a person or persons in a state of subjection to its author."[38]

Positivist international lawyers prided themselves on having rid the discipline of insupportable arguments regarding "natural law" and its associated idea of a higher morality. Austin, on the other hand, intent on defining law in such a manner as to establish a sound basis for a science of jurisprudence, and rescuing it from the muddy speculations of naturalists, threatened such pretensions by categorically asserting that international law itself was nothing more than morality.

Austin's challenge was taken up, not only by the international lawyers of succeeding generations, but also by his contemporaries. Westlake,[39] Lawrence,[40] Oppenheim,[41] and Walker,[42] for example, commence their works with attempts at refuting or qualifying Austin. In effect, these responses present a modified and more specific version of what law and positivism meant to international lawyers, who set about establishing why international law was law despite its failure to meet Austinian criteria.

---

36. The primary works of Austin are LECTURES ON JURISPRUDENCE (London, J. Murry 1879), LECTURES IN JURISPRUDENCE (1885), and THE PROVINCE OF JURISPRUDENCE DETERMINED 101 (David Campbell & Philip Thomas eds., Ashgate 1998) (1832) [hereinafter AUSTIN, JURISPRUDENCE DETERMINED].

37. AUSTIN, JURISPRUDENCE DETERMINED, *supra* note 36, at 101.

38. *Id.* at 152.

39. *See* WESTLAKE, *supra* note 16, at v–16.

40. *See* LAWRENCE, *supra* note 17, at 1–25.

41. *See* OPPENHEIM, *supra* note 19, at 4–5.

42. *See* 1 THOMAS ALFRED WALKER, A HISTORY OF THE LAW OF NATIONS 1–20 (Cambridge, Cambridge University Press 1899).

International jurists used both analytical and historical arguments,[43] often in combination, to refute Austin. The analytical argument questioned the adequacy of Austin's definition of law itself. Lawrence, for example, meets Austin's objection by arguing that Austin's definition of law is not authoritative and that alternative definitions should also be taken into account. Thus Lawrence argues, "If we follow Austin and hold that all laws are commands of superiors, International Law is improperly so called. If we follow Hooker and hold that whatever precepts regulate conduct are laws, International Law is properly so called."[44] Lawrence seems to argue, in effect, that law can be said to exist as long as states observe a set of norms; it is irrelevant whether or not these norms are enunciated by some supreme, sovereign authority. Oppenheim similarly argued that Austin failed to take into account the reality of unwritten or customary law.[45] This law did not originate from a sovereign and hence failed to meet Austin's definition. And yet, even within national systems, such customary laws were recognized and administered by municipal courts.[46]

The reality and efficacy of customary law was further illustrated by the historical work of writers such as Sir Henry Maine. Maine had been a consistent critic of Austin and Austin's fellow positivist Jeremey Bentham, and his works such as *Ancient Law* suggested powerfully that Austin's view of law was rather limited and that societies had generally been governed by conceptions of law that differed markedly from those defined by Austin.[47] International jurists such as Walker[48] and Lawrence[49] seized upon Maine's researches, the "hard facts of History"[50] to point to the inadequacy of Austin's definition. International jurists had a particular interest in stressing the importance of customary law, furthermore, as customary law was one of the principal, if not the principal, sources of international law.

Austin had anticipated such criticisms by explicitly arguing that custom was not a proper source of law. Referring to the existence of custom in a domestic setting, Austin argued:

> At its origin, a custom is a rule of conduct which the governed observe spontaneously, or not in pursuance of a law set by a politi-

43. Analytical arguments focused on the consistency and adequacy of definitions; historical arguments drew on what had been revealed by historical researches into other societies. For an outline of what the two approaches constituted for international jurists, see WESTLAKE, *supra* note 16, at vii–ix.

44. LAWRENCE, *supra* note 17, at 25.

45. *See* OPPENHEIM, *supra* note 19, at 5.

46. *See id.*

47. SIR HENRY SUMNER MAINE, ANCIENT LAW 6 (1864).

48. WALKER, *supra* note 42, at 8–19.

49. For a discussion of Lawrence's use of Maine, see Riles, *supra* note 8, at 726.

50. WALKER, *supra* note 42, at 8.

> cal superior. The custom is transmuted into positive law, when it is adopted as such by the courts of justice, and when the judicial decisions fashioned upon it are enforced by the power of the state. But before it is adopted by the courts and clothed with the legal sanction, it is merely a rule of positive morality: a rule generally observed by the citizens or subjects but deriving the only force, which it can be said to possess, from the general diapprobation falling on those who transgress it.[51]

This passage illustrates not only the indispensability of a sovereign to Austin's scheme, but the extent to which his whole concept of law is based on a rather specific idea of society and political arrangements. The debate remained—and remains—unresolved. But to the extent that international jurists could make a case, it depended largely on establishing that a functioning system of rules governed the behavior of states, as exemplified by the operation of customary international law. This raised a further question for the jurist: in what circumstances, among which actors, could custom be said to arise in the dispersed international context? Custom, to international jurists, presupposed the existence of society. And "society" is the metaphor used elsewhere by Lawrence and by virtually all international lawyers of this period in their efforts to posit the existence of rules that are observed even in the absence of a supreme authority. "International law," proclaims Westlake, "is the body of rules prevailing between states."[52] He proceeds to explain this to mean that

> states form a society, the members of which claim from each other the observance of certain lines of conduct, capable of being expressed in general terms as rules and hold themselves justified in mutually compelling such observance, by force if necessary; also that in such society the lines of conduct in question are observed with more or less regularity, either as the result of compulsion or in accordance with the sentiments which would support compulsion in case of need.[53]

Within this scheme, sovereignty is important, inasmuch as society is constituted by sovereign states. Equally, however, it is because these states exist in society that international law can claim to be law. The interaction of the members of this society gives rise to rules that are regularly observed and enforced by sanctions. Consequently, "without society no law, without law no society." It is through a complicated interplay between law and society that the result, the maintenance of

51. Austin, Jurisprudence Determined, *supra* note 36, at 21.
52. Westlake, *supra* note 16, at 1.
53. *Id.* at 2.

international order and creation of international law, is circularly achieved. "Without society no law, without law no society. When we assert that there is such a thing as international law, we assert that there is a society of states: when we recognise that there is a society of states, we recognise that there is international law."[54]

When focusing on the idea of law, Westlake writes that

> perhaps no better account can be given of what is commonly understood by law than that it is a body of rules expressing the claims which, in a given society, are held to be enforceable and are more or less commonly observed.[55]

Westlake unsurprisingly deviates here from the Austinian approach of looking to the source of these laws in order to locate the single authority, the sovereign, from whom they should all properly emanate. Law is not imposed from above by a sovereign but agreed upon by the relevant entities. Law exists where there is regularity in dealings, when the members of the society regard themselves as bound by the rules, and where sanctions of some sort would follow a breach. The notion of a "community," "society," or a "family"[56] becomes fundamental to the definition of law, as illustrated by Oppenheim's argument that "law is a body of rules for human conduct within a community which by common consent of this community shall be enforced by external law."[57]

Thus, society, rather than sovereignty, is the central concept used to construct the system of international law. Despite the positivist claims that the sovereign was the exclusive basis for the international system, it was only if society was introduced into the system that positivists could approximate the idea of "law" to which they urged adherence. Society, therefore, provides the matrix of ideas, the analytical resource that, allied with sovereignty, could establish a positivist international legal order. This is an important shift, for implicit in the idea of society is membership; only those states that are accepted into society and agree upon principles regulating their behavior can be regarded as belonging to society. The concepts of society, furthermore, enabled the formulation and elaboration of the various cultural distinctions that were crucial to the constitution of sovereignty doctrine.

---

54. *Id.* at 3.

55. *Id.* at 2.

56. The terms "family of nations" or "community of nations" are used quite interchangeably by positivist jurists.

57. OPPENHEIM, *supra* note 19, at 8. For Oppenheim's general discussion on "community," see *id.* at 8–9. "Innumerable are the interests which knit all the individualised civilised States together and which create constant intercourse between these States as well as between their subjects." *Id.* at 10.

D. International Law as Science

The decisively important status accorded to natural sciences such as physics and biology profoundly influenced both domestic and international law. The epistemological validity of the scientific method was demonstrated, not only by the triumph of Darwin's ideas[58] on natural selection, but by the massive success of the industrial revolution that had been made possible by scientific discoveries.[59] While jurists understood that jurisprudence could not achieve the same results as the natural sciences, it was important for them to be engaged in a "scientific inquiry"; this involved redefining their discipline in ways that appeared compatible with the scientific framework in an attempt not only to elevate their discipline, but their profession.[60] The human sciences, of which international law was a part, could not, of course, be studied in the same way as natural sciences. But while asserting that international law is not a natural science, Westlake nevertheless, introduces his work as considering "the place of international law among the sciences,"[61] and international lawyers of the period invariably refer to the "science" of international law.[62] The positivist self-image of being engaged in a scientific inquiry—and all that suggested in terms of rigor, consistency, and precision—played an important role in the method, elaboration, and application of nineteenth-century jurisprudence.

58. On the importance of Darwin for validating the new "scientific method," see J.M. ROBERTS, A HISTORY OF EUROPE 344 (1996). As Roberts points out, Darwin's ideas were extended to a number of fields. Darwinism could justify colonialism on the basis that it was because they were the "fittest" that the white races dominated the colored races. *Id.* The French historian Auguste Comte was one of the most forceful early proponents of science and positivism and stressed the importance of knowledge based on empirically verifiable facts rather than religious speculation. *Id.* at 342–43.

59. On the place of science in society at the end of the 19th century, see generally HOBSBAWM, *supra* note 1, chs. 10–11.

60. This issue is explored by David Sugarman, *'A Hatred of Disorder': Legal Science, Liberalism and Imperialism*, *in* DANGEROUS SUPPLEMENTS 47 (Peter Fitzpatrick ed. 1991). Sugarman's essay is also valuable as it clearly traces the importance that legal scholars attached—in a domestic context—to establishing law as a science in order to establish their disciplinary and professional status. In the international law context, as Koskenniemi notes, "By early 19th century, international law has become a science, an academic discipline taught separately from, on the one hand, theology, philosophy and natural law and, on the other, civil law." KOSKENNIEMI, APOLOGY, *supra* note 5, at 98 (footnotes omitted). For the attempts of more recent generations of international lawyers to establish the viability of their discipline, see David Kennedy, *A New Stream of International Law Scholarship*, 7 WIS. INT'L L.J. 1 (1988). For an illuminating examination of the relationship between the writing of history and disciplinary renewal, see Outi Korhonen, *Liberalism and International Law: A Centre Projecting a Periphery*, 65 NORDIC J. INT'L L. 481 (1996).

61. WESTLAKE, *supra* note 16, at vi.

62. Thus Oppenheim's notable attempt to define the project of international law is titled *The Science of International Law: Its Task and Method*, *see* Oppenheim, *supra* note 34. For a very illuminating examination of the relationship between the writing of history and disciplinary renewal, see Outi Korhonen, *Liberalism and International Law: A Centre Projecting a Periphery*, 65 NORDIC J. INT'L L. 481 (1996).

The positivists sought to develop a scientific methodology to identify and interpret relevant forms of state behavior in the midst of the general flux and confusion of international relations. Thus Lawrence writes that the great international lawyers of the nineteenth century produced "order from chaos, and made International Law into a science, instead of a shapeless mass of undigested and sometimes inconsistent rules."[63]

The term "science" was used in varied and complex ways by different international lawyers, but some of the core ideas as to the science of international law are illustrated by Lawrence, who

> regard[ed] International Law, not as an instrument for the discovery and interpretation of a transcendental rule of right binding upon states as moral beings whether they observe it or not in practice, but as a science whose chief business it is to find out by observation the rules actually followed by states in their mutual intercourse, and to classify and arrange these rules by referring them to certain fundamental principles on which they are based.[64]

Order could be established through classification, both of the legal phenomena of state behavior and of the rules of international law itself. Law is concerned, according to Westlake, with the "classification of institutions or facts";[65] furthermore, it is "with law as an institution or fact that the legal student has to deal."[66] Facts having been classified and the rules of international law having been identified, the further and broader task was to "classify and arrange these rules" in an effort to develop a coherent and overarching international law.

This endeavor pointed to a further tension in positivist jurisprudence. On the one hand, as its reliance on custom demonstrated, this jurisprudence encompassed the idea of flux and development. As the needs of states changed, so too would the treaties they entered into and the practices in which they engaged. The positivist differed from the naturalist precisely in asserting that there were no immutable, tran-

---

63. LAWRENCE, *supra* note 17, at 94.

64. *Id.* at 1.

65. WESTLAKE, *supra* note 16, at 12. For the jurist who seeks to classify complex forms of state behavior that may fall, arguably, into several different categories, a certain blurring and inaccuracy may arise. Nevertheless, overall, the stability and coherence of international law is dependent, notwithstanding these inevitable confusions, on developing, maintaining and strictly applying a system of classification, by placing the appropriate species in the correct genus. Horwitz's comments on the American jurisprudence of the period apply no less accurately to the international jurists of the time: "Nineteenth-century legal thought was overwhelmingly dominated by categorical thinking—by clear, distinct, bright-line classifications of legal phenomena. Late nineteenth-century legal reasoning brought categorical modes of thought to their highest fulfillment." MORTON J. HORWITZ, THE TRANSFORMATION OF AMERICAN LAW 1870–1960: THE CRISIS OF LEGAL ORTHODOXY 17 (1992).

66. WESTLAKE, *supra* note 16, at 12.

scendent laws. At the same time, however, positivists argued that whatever the changes in international law, all the rules emerging from such developments referred back to certain "fundamental principles," to use Lawrence's terminology. Thus, whatever the haphazardness, flux, and uncertainty of state practice, it was ordered and understood by a fixed set of principles that classified and processed the raw material of practice and reconstituted it into a coherent and complete legal framework.[67]

The origins and character of ordering mechanisms that performed these vital tasks, however, assumed a transcendental quality that seemed beyond history and inquiry. Indeed, to adopt any approach that denied the fixed quality of these principles could undermine the entire system of law. For many jurists, it was only by adopting an historical approach that international law could overcome Austinian objections. Nevertheless, once established as a discipline, international law repudiated the historical approach, which had the potential to challenge the implicit assumption that the principles used by jurists to order the world of legal phenomena were in some way eternal, beyond history. The danger of adopting such an approach was evident even to lawyers in the domestic sphere. Adoption of the historical or literary approach would result in a debilitating awareness of flux and contingency, warned Frederick Harrison, Professor of Jurisprudence at the Inns of Court in 1879.

> It would lead to the utmost confusion of thought . . . if we come to regard historical explanations as the substantial or independent part of jurisprudence. From history we always get ideas of . . . constant development, of instability. But in law, at any rate for the purposes of the practical lawyer, what we need are ideas of fixity, of uniformity . . . .
>
> It is so great a strain upon the mind to build up and retrace the conception of a great body of titles reducible to abstract and symmetrical classification, and capable of statement as a set of

67. An analogy might be drawn here with natural selection. Species evolved over time; but whatever the nature of the changes, they took place in accordance with the fundamental laws that had been identified by Darwin. Ideas of progress and evolution were embodied in international law thinking, and biological metaphors were often used by international lawyers. *See, e.g.*, WESTLAKE, *supra* note 16, at 14–15. The same tension is manifested in thinking at the time about the English common law and is well encapsulated by Sugarman: "Scientific rationality was forever being mediated, refracted and sustained by an omnipresent irrationality: thereby lies the peculiar rationality of the common law mind. Thus the legal community could, with seeming effortlessness, eulogize the haphazard, particularistic, unsystematic evolution of the common law—and also trumpet its intrinsic rationalism." Sugarman, *supra* note 60, at 45. The positivist idea that law was autonomous, comprehensive and scientific was also important in shaping the Classical Legal Thought which dominated American jurisprudence in the late 19th century. *See* HORWITZ, *supra* note 65, at 9–32.

consistent principles—and this is what I take jurisprudence to be—that we are perpetually in danger of giving to law a literary instead of a scientific character, and in slipping in our thoughts from what the law is into speculating upon the coincidences which make it what it once was.[68]

This scientific methodology favored, then, a movement towards abstraction—a propensity to rely upon a formulation of categories and their systematic exposition as a means of preserving order and arriving at the correct "solution" to any particular problem. Legal science in the latter half of the nineteenth century was conceived of, even in the municipal sphere, as a struggle against chaos that could only be won by ensuring the autonomy of law, and establishing and maintaining the taxonomies and principles that existed in fixed relations to each other. What Harrison warns against is any attempt to examine the manner in which a particular mode of classification or system of law came into being; it is precisely this inquiry, however, that the "historical approach" that he condemns would advocate.[69] Thus, within the analytic approach, the myth of the state of nature is replaced, in positivist jurisprudence, with the myth of a fixed set of principles and a scheme of classifications that reveals itself to the scrutiny of the expert jurist who uses this scheme to establish and develop international law.

While thus outlining a sophisticated scientific technique, however, the question remained as to how these positivist jurists related these techniques (this emphasis on taxonomy and on the juridical character of state behavior) with the idea of "society," which was indispensable to any claim that international law possessed the status of law and was the basis of the defense presented by Westlake and Lawrence against Austin's charges. In order for the reconstructed system of positivism with all its claims to being a science to work, international lawyers had to develop a sociological vision, an understanding of various attributes of societies and their customs and the way in which they functioned, both internally and externally, in relation to each other. Society and history thus became the subject of positivist scrutiny. For positivists, consequently, the concepts and classifications they employed could be

68. *Id.* at 51.

69. It must be noted that other 19th-century writers such as Lawrence espoused the historical approach. See LAWRENCE, *supra* note 17, at 16, where he raises the issue of whether the inquiry into international law should be based on an historical method. As Lawrence himself makes clear, however, he uses these terms to signify the distinction between "what the rules of international intercourse ought to be, or an historical investigation of what they are." *Id.* There is no inconsistency between Lawrence and Harrison, then, as they use the term "historical" in different respects. The larger historical challenge was presented by writers such as Sir Henry Maine, who pointedly criticized Austin's attempt to outline a system of law based on logic rather than history. Maine himself elaborated the historical approach in his own famous works ANCIENT LAW, *supra* note 47 and EARLY HISTORY OF INSTITUTIONS (1875).

used to order history and society, but these same concepts and classifications were outside and beyond history. This was one means by which positivism presented itself as universal and eternal, existing in a realm beyond the reach of historical scrutiny. Positivism, in this way, sought to suppress its own past. How could the positivist insistence on the primacy of concepts and on the autonomy of law accommodate and encompass this sociological aspect upon which it was so curiously and ambivalently dependent for its functioning?

The tensions and ambivalence generated by positivist attempts to articulate a new and scientific jurisprudence were as important a part of that body of thought as its self-consciously proclaimed modernity and rigor.

III. DEFINING AND EXCLUDING THE UNCIVILIZED

A. *Positivism, Society, and the Uncivilized*

A further central feature of positivism was the distinction it made between civilized and uncivilized states. The naturalist notion that a single, universally applicable law governed a naturally constituted society of nations was completely repudiated by jurists of the mid-nineteenth century.[70] Instead, nineteenth-century writers such as Wheaton claimed that international law was the exclusive province of civilized societies. Wheaton's brief discussion of earlier jurists such as Grotius suggests a trend that culminated in Wheaton's own stance; Grotius states that law (*jus gentium*) "acquires its obligatory force from the positive consent of all nations, or at least of several."[71] While this emphasis on the consent of nations foreshadows a central characteristic of positivism, Wheaton notes that Grotius makes no further distinction between different types of nations; nor does he suggest, while acknowledging these differences, that some nations should be granted priority as opposed to others, that some nations participate in the law of nations while others do not.[72] No distinction is made between the civilized and the uncivilized.

70. Hence Wheaton's critique of Wolf, who argued that the law of nations was something to which all nations had consented, basing this theory on "the fiction of a great commonwealth of nations (*civitate gentium maxima*) instituted by nature herself, and of which all the nations of the world are members." WHEATON, *supra* note 18, at 10 (footnote omitted).

71. *Id.*, *ch.* 1.11.

72. This is an aspect of one of the central questions of Grotius's great work—the relationship between natural law and the law of nations. The tension is introduced in his preface, as cited by Wheaton. *Id.* at 10. That such is the condition of mankind that the strict law of nature cannot always be applied to the government of a particular community, but it becomes necessary to resort to laws of positive institution more or less varying from the natural law, so in the great society of nations it becomes necessary to establish a law of positive institution more or less varying from the natural law of nations.

The relative cosmopolitanism of Grotius contrasts with the narrower approaches of jurists such as Bynkershoek, who argued that only the practice of civilized states acquires legal currency. He states that "the law of nations is that which is observed, in accordance with the light of reason, between nations, if not among all, *at least certainly among the greater part, and those the most civilised.*"[73]

Despite this trend towards excluding the uncivilized states, non-European states were recognized as part of the law of nations even in the early part of the nineteenth century. In a decision handed down in 1825, *The Antelope*, the Supreme Court of the United States confronted the issue of whether slavery was an acceptable practice according to the law of nations. Chief Justice Marshall, in examining this issue, asserted:

> The parties to the modern law of nations do not propagate their principles by force; and Africa has not yet adopted them [the modern principles relating to the abolition of slavery]. Throughout the whole of that immense continent, so far as we know its history, it is still the law of nations that prisoners are slaves.[74]

The passage is notable for its gesture towards including Africa within the law of nations and for suggesting that European states, indeed America itself, had to respect the law of nations as practiced within Africa.[75]

By the latter part of the nineteenth century, however, whatever the systems of law existent on that "immense continent," they are made irrelevant; the custom that counts as law is that which is practiced only among the "civilized countries." By 1866, Wheaton argued:

> Is there a uniform law of nations? There certainly is not the same one for all the nations and states of the world. The public law, with slight exceptions, has always been, and still is, limited to the civilized and Christian people of Europe or to those of European origin.[76]

---

73. WHEATON, *supra* note 18, ch. 1.11 (emphasis in original). Montesquieu offers a further variation on these themes; even while dismissing the practices of non-European peoples, he suggests that all nations have some sort of "international law," which governs their relations with their neighbors: thus "even the Iroquois, who eat their prisoners, have one. They send and receive ambassadors; they know the laws of war and peace; the evil is, that their law of nations is not founded upon true principles." *Id.*

74. The Antelope, 23 U.S. (10 Wheaton) 5, 66 (1825).

75. Marshall seems to be suggesting the existence of a regional African custom, which must be accepted as part of international law. Alternatively, of course, it seems as though the abolition of slavery was the "new custom" observed by certain states and that the legality of slavery was the older and more widely accepted principle of international law.

76. WHEATON, *supra* note 18, at 15.

Naturalists such as Vitoria recognized the existence of important cultural differences between, for example, the Spanish and the Indians of the Americas.[77] Nevertheless, they asserted that all societies were bound by a universal natural law. The gap between the European and non-European worlds was as evident to Wheaton as it was to Vitoria. For Wheaton and the jurists who succeeded him, however, this gap was to be bridged, not by a universal natural law, but by the explicit imposition of European international law over the uncivilized non-Europeans. It was simply and massively asserted that only the practice of European states was decisive and could create international law. Only European law counted as law. Non-European states were excluded from the realm of law, now identified as being the exclusive preserve of European states, as a result of which they lacked both membership and the ability to assert any rights cognizable as legal. In its most extreme form, positivist reasoning suggested that relations and transactions between the European and non-European states occurred entirely outside the realm of law.[78]

Thus the state of nature that naturalists such as Grotius used as a basis for the formulation of rules of international law was unsatisfactory, not only because it was subjective, imprecise, and based on transcendental principles rather than the realities of state behavior, but because it failed to make the distinction between the civilized and uncivilized. Westlake writes:

> No theorist on law who is pleased to imagine a state of nature independent of human institutions can introduce into his picture a difference between civilised and uncivilised man, because it is just in the presence or absence of certain institutions or in their greater or less perfection, that that difference consists for the lawyer.[79]

The existence of a distinction between the civilized and the uncivilized was so vehemently presupposed by positivist jurists, that the state of nature—and therefore naturalism—becomes epistemologically incoherent because lacking this central distinction. Positivist jurisprudence was so insistent on this distinction that any system of law that failed to acknowledge it was unacceptable. In crude terms, in the naturalist world, law was given; in the positivist world, law was created by human societies and institutions. Once the connection between "law" and "institutions" had been established, it followed from this premise that jurists could focus on the character of institutions, a shift that

77. *See* Anghie, *Vitoria*, *supra* note 9.
78. *See* GONG, *supra* note 5, at 53–57.
79. WESTLAKE, *supra* note 16, at 137. For an important examination of the relationship between law and myth, see PETER FITZPATRICK, THE MYTHOLOGY OF MODERN LAW (1992).

facilitated the racialization of law by delimiting the notion of law to very specific European institutions.

As for the political implications following adherence to this distinction, Westlake himself immediately suggests how this distinction could be deployed by justifying his claim that "the occupation by uncivilised tribes of a tract, of which according to our habits a small part ought to have sufficed for them, was not felt to interpose a serious obstacle to the right of the first civilised occupant."[80] Once the distinction is made, then, completely different standards could be applied to the two categories of people. Whatever the practices of the "uncivilized tribes," in a situation where these practices conflict with the assessment made by the civilized as to the "real needs" of the uncivilized in relation to land, it is the latter which prevails. Broadly, once non-European states were excluded from the realm of sovereignty, they were precluded from making any sort of legal claim in the realm of international law because only sovereign states were able to participate as full members with all the attendant rights and powers.

In summary, the distinction between the civilized and uncivilized was a fundamental tenet of positivist epistemology and thus profoundly shaped the concepts constituting the positivist framework. The racialization of positivist law followed inevitably from these premises—as demonstrated, for example, by the argument that law was the creation of unique, civilized, and social institutions and that only states possessing such institutions could be members of "international society." In distinguishing between the civilized and uncivilized on all these different levels, positivist jurisprudence created the first element of what I have termed the "dynamic of difference," the postulation of a gap between the European and non-European worlds that had to be bridged by positivist international law.

B. *The Uncivilized and Defining Sovereignty*

The task of defining sovereignty was fundamental to positivist jurisprudence—and not merely because definition was such an integral part of positivist reasoning and methodology. The positivist insistence that sovereignty was the founding concept of the international system led naturally to a careful scrutiny of what entities could be regarded as sovereign. This was an important theoretical and practical issue, given the positivist argument that the sovereign had supreme authority. Such a project of definition was not so fundamental to the naturalist framework, since that jurisprudence proposed a system of law that applied to all human activity, whether that of an individual or of a sovereign.[81]

80. *Id.*

81. The state was not recognized as an independent, clearly defined entity in works of the

By contrast, the jurisprudence of "personality," which dealt with the question of defining the proper subjects of international law was one of the central issues explored by positivist jurists.[82] Given that the civilized/non-civilized distinction expelled the non-European world from the realm of law and society, the question arose: what was the status of non-European societies with regard to sovereignty? It was simple enough to assert that the civilized possessed sovereignty while the uncivilized did not, but positivist jurisprudence had to establish plausibly that cultural difference translated into legal difference. Positivists were equipped with a number of analytical tools to arrive at such a conclusion, but, given the positivist preoccupation with consistency and coherence, they had to do so in a manner consistent with the broad complex of ideas and systems of thinking that constituted sovereignty doctrine and positivist jurisprudence.

The practical task of identifying the "sovereign" and defining sovereignty were interrelated tasks that posed a number of complex problems for jurists. The task involved distinguishing sovereigns proper from other entities that also seemed to possess the attributes of sovereignty, such as pirates, non-European states, and nomads.[83] How could it be claimed within this jurisprudence that the barbarian nations, "a wandering tribe with no fixed territory to call its own," a "race of savages," and a "band of pirates"[84] were not sovereign? This question posed a dilemma to nineteenth-century jurists, whose understanding of positivism was ineluctably affected by Austin: simply, these entities satisfied the essential Austinian criteria of sovereignty. As Lawrence acknowledges, even the wandering tribe might "obey implicitly a chief who took no commands from other rulers";[85] pirates, similarly, "might be temporarily under the sway of a chief with unrestricted power."[86]

For positivists, the general answer was that sovereignty could be most clearly defined as control over territory. Thus Lawrence states:

---

early naturalists such as Vitoria, for example. It is arguable that the absence of a clear distinction between the municipal and international realms may also be attributed to the overarching character of natural law. *See* David Kennedy, *Primitive Legal Scholarship*, 27 HARV. INT'L L.J. 1 (1986).

82. Thus the major treatises of the period, such as Hall and Oppenheim, discussed the "law of persons" in either the first or second chapter of their works. Hall begins his work with a chapter titled "Persons in International Law, and Communities Possessing A Character Analogous to Them," HALL, *supra* note 15, ch. 1, while Oppenheim provides a theory and history of international law in his introductory chapter and titles the next part of his work "The Subjects of the Law of Nations," OPPENHEIM, *supra* note 19, Table of Contents.

83. For an examination of the political dimensions of state building, see THE FORMATION OF NATIONAL STATES IN WESTERN EUROPE (Charles Tilly ed. 1975). The challenge that pirates posed to the nation-state and its response is examined in JANICE E. THOMSON, MERCENARIES, PIRATES AND SOVEREIGNS: STATE BUILDING AND EXTRATERRITORIAL VIOLENCE IN EARLY MODERN EUROPE (1994).

84. LAWRENCE, *supra* note 17, at 58.

85. *Id.*

86. *Id.*

> International Law regards states as political units possessed of proprietary rights over definite portions of the earth's surface. So entirely is its conception of a state bound up with the notion of territorial possession that it would be impossible for a nomadic tribe, even if highly organised and civilized, to come under its provisions.[87]

Whatever the extent to which an entity may have satisfied the other criteria of statehood, a failure to occupy territory would preclude that entity from being treated as sovereign. The primacy of territory is again emphasized by Lawrence when, after considering two possible bases for the exercise of jurisdiction by a state, he decides finally that jurisdiction over territory takes precedence over jurisdiction over citizens. Thus Lawrence argues, "Modern International law, being permeated throughout by the doctrine of territorial sovereignty, has adopted the latter principle as fundamental."[88]

Territorial control is thus fundamental to sovereignty, whatever the exceptions established to this rule—in the form of the principle, for example, that foreign sovereigns and diplomats are not completely subjected to a state's jurisdiction although they may be present within the territory of that state.[89] Accordingly, wandering tribes could not be sovereign because they failed the territorial requirement; they were not in sole occupation of a particular area of land. But the problem then confronting the jurists was that many of the uncivilized Asian and African states easily met both the Austinian definition of sovereignty and the requirement of control over territory. The historical reality, as Alexandrowicz points out regarding the Indies, for example, was that "[a]ll the major communities in India as well as elsewhere in the East Indies were politically organized; they were governed by their Sovereigns, they had their legal systems and lived according to centuries-old cultural traditions."[90] In Africa, as scholars such as Elias have argued, the kingdoms of Benin, Ethiopia, and Mali, for instance, were sophisticated and powerful political entities that were accorded the respect due to sovereigns by the European states with which they established diplomatic relations.[91]

---

87. *Id.* at 136.

88. LAWRENCE, *supra* note 17, at 190. The theme is reiterated throughout the work. "The rules of modern International Law are so permeated from end to end with the idea of territorial sovereignty that they would be entirely inapplicable to any body politic that was not permanently settled upon a portion of the earth's surface which in its collective capacity it owned." *Id.* at 59.

89. *See id.* at 221.

90. ALEXANDROWICZ, EAST INDIES, *supra* note 8, at 14.

91. *See* ELIAS, *supra* note 8, at 6–15. For a detailed study of the early history of treaty making between African and European states, see ALEXANDROWICZ, TREATY MAKING, *supra* note 8.

Positivist jurists could hardly disregard these facts, especially given that European powers had entered into treaties with such communities. The works of eighteenth-century jurists, for instance, gave accounts of diplomatic usages in countries such as Persia, Siam, Turkey, and China, analyzed the negotiations that led to the making of various treaties, and included these treaties within larger collections of international treaties.[92] Confronted with this dilemma, positivists resorted once more to the concept of society. The broad response was that Asian states, for example, could be formally "sovereign"; but unless they satisfied the criteria of membership in civilized international society, they lacked the comprehensive range of powers enjoyed by the European sovereigns who constituted international society.[93]

Therefore, the distinction between the civilized and uncivilized, crucial to the intellectual and political validity of positivist jurisprudence, was to be made, not in the realm of sovereignty, but of society. Society, and the constellation of ideas associated with it, promised to enable the jurist to link a legal status to a cultural distinction. Thus positivists argued that sovereignty and society posed two different tests, and the decisive issue was whether or not a particular entity—even a sovereign—was a full member of international society. Lawrence makes this point when considering the legal status of a wandering tribe. "[Y]et none of these communities would be subject to International Law, because they would want various characteristics, which, though not essential to sovereignty, are essential to the membership of the family of nations."[94]

The tribes remain outside the realm of international law, not so much because they lack sovereignty, but because they are wanting in the other characteristics essential for membership in international society. It follows, despite positivist preoccupations with sovereignty doctrine, that "society" and the "family of nations" are the essential foundations of positivist jurisprudence and of the vision of sovereignty that it supports. In the final analysis, non-European states are lacking in sovereignty because they are excluded from the family of nations. The novel maneuver of focusing on society enabled positivist jurists to overcome the historical fact that, by and large, non-European states were previously regarded as sovereign, that they enjoyed all the rights accompanying this status, and that their behavior constituted a form of

92. *See* Alexandrowicz, *supra* note 30; *see also* Jeremy Thomas, *History and International Law in Asia: A Time for Review?*, *in* ESSAYS IN HONOUR OF WANG TIEYA 813 (Ronald St. John Macdonald ed. 1994).

93. On the problems of categorizing these entities, see Oppenheim: "No other explanation of these and similar facts [the fact that these non-entities engaged in sovereign behavior] can be given except that these not-full Sovereign States are in some way or another International Persons and subjects of International Law." OPPENHEIM, *supra* note 19, at 110. *See id.* at 154–56.

94. LAWRENCE, *supra* note 17, at 58.

practice and precedent that gave rise to rules and doctrines of international law.

The concept of society enabled positivists to develop a number of strategies for explaining further why the non-European world was excluded from international law. One such strategy consisted of asserting that no law existed in certain non-European, barbaric regions. According to this argument, the distinction between the civilized and uncivilized was too obvious to require elaboration. Thus Lawrence, for example, stated, "It would, for instance, be absurd to expect the king of Dahomey to establish a Prize Court, or to require the dwarfs of the central African forest to receive a permanent diplomatic mission."[95] Such powerful evocations of the backward and barbaric confirmed the incongruity of any correspondence between Europe and these societies. Law did no more than maintain an essential and self-evident distinction.

And yet, a closer examination of primitive societies suggested disconcerting parallels. Westlake described the inquiries of the "historical school" into societies "remote from our own."

> We learn from them how the different peoples whom we study usually conducted themselves with regard to family, property, or any other matter which in our actual England is regulated by law; by what beliefs and motives, and by what commands or compulsion if any, their conduct was kept to its usual lines. And by accumulating a number of such investigations we learn how what we now know as the law of a country has arisen. But the analytical school are certainly right in maintaining that, if we give the name of law to anything which we so discover in a remote state of society before we have fixed in our minds what we mean by that name, we beg the question, and have no security that our language has any consistent, or therefore useful, sense.[96]

The passage reflects many of the techniques of positivism analyzed earlier. The "analytical school" establishes a definition, adheres to it, and applies it rigorously and unyieldingly. Any conflict between the realities disclosed by the historical researchers and the definition must be resolved in favor of the definition, in order to maintain its "consistent or therefore, useful sense." Language, it would seem, cannot yield to acknowledged empirical reality where this could lead to destabiliz-

95. *Id.* For an insightful study of this rhetoric, see Riles, *supra* note 8. Riles points out in her important study, "Lawrence's polemic participated on a number of levels in the creation of an essentialized and coherent European community defined in dichotomous opposition to non-European 'savages.'" *Id.* at 736. As Riles further elaborates, "This essentialized European identity depended, however, upon an opposition of Europe to non-Europe that articulated in symbolic terms inequalities of power between Europeans and their colonial subjects." *Id.* at 737.

96. WESTLAKE, *supra* note 16, at viii.

ing the concepts and categories on which the system is based. In the final analysis, it would seem, the matter is decided by the simple assertion that whatever the commonality between European and non-European societies, European societies are civilized and sovereign, while non-European societies are not. Thus Westlake, even while acknowledging the fact that "different peoples" could possess a system that disconcertingly parallels that of England, quickly proceeded to affirm that "our actual England is regulated by law."[97]

Law, accordingly, is the preserve of England. While other remote societies may appear to have their own laws, any tendency to affirm this similarity must be immediately repulsed as it could result in the collapse of the language of sovereignty and, therefore, of international law itself. Simply and summarily, within nineteenth-century jurisprudence, law cannot be defined in such a way as to encompass the practices that historical research demonstrates as serving the same function as "law" in Western society.

Thus the methodology of the analytical school was important, not merely in terms of the broad theoretical debate it was engaged in with the historical school, but because it was through the suppression of implications arising from the historical school that the analytical school could make the distinction between the civilized and non-civilized. This demarcation was central to positivist attempts to preserve the coherence of their jurisprudence in the face of the problems posed by the non-European world.

A second strategy used to distinguish the civilized from the uncivilized consisted of asserting the fact that while certain societies may have had their own systems of law these were of such an alien character that no proper legal relations could develop between European and non-European states. Positivist jurists such as Westlake made further distinctions between the Asian states, for example, which were characterized as being in certain respects civilized but "different,"[98] and the uncivilized tribes, who were more severely denounced as completely backward.[99]

In this way, positivists formulated different classifications for the non-Europeans, and distinctions were made for certain purposes between the societies of Asia, Africa, and the Pacific.[100] Basically, how-

---

97. *Id.* The word "actual" is used in a curious fashion, almost as though to add reassurance. It seems to be suppressing the suggestion, which Westlake himself provokes, that there could be some other England which compares with the savage societies which Westlake is intent on separating from England.

98. WESTLAKE, *supra* note 16, at 102. For Westlake, government is the test of civilization; Asian states satisfy this test as they comprise of populations "leading complex lives of their own" with their own systems of family relations, criminal law, and administration. *Id.* at 141.

99. *See id.* at 143–55.

100. *See* discussion *infra* notes 148–155 and accompanying text.

ever, these classifications were irrelevant in terms of the broad issue of the central distinction between the civilized and uncivilized. All non-European societies, regardless of whether they were regarded as completely primitive or relatively advanced, were outside the sphere of law, and European society provided the model that all societies had to follow if they were to progress.

The positivist attempt to distinguish between the civilized and uncivilized was fraught with unresolved complications. Westlake's analytic approach sought to extinguish any suggestion of correspondence between advanced European and primitive non-European peoples; but seen from a broader perspective, there was a complete irony in this insistence that only one form of law could accurately be given the term law. After all, it was precisely by relativizing and contesting Austin's rigid definition of law, a strategy used by members of both the analytical and historical schools, that international law could claim to be law at all.[101] If states could be regarded as governed by "law," they were governed by law in the same way that the primitive societies described by Maine were governed by law, notwithstanding the lack of a determinate sovereign who issued laws enforced by controls.[102] Seen from this perspective, there is an identity between primitive societies and international law; it is by asserting the validity of primitive societies governed by custom, the principal source of international law, that international law is established as a scientific discipline. Having been so established, however, international law then emphatically disassociates itself from the primitive by becoming the authoritative, master discipline that identifies, places, expels, and civilizes the primitive. The implications of the disconcerting identity between the international and the primitive are suppressed. For if the uncivilized non-European societies were to be expelled from the field of international society because they were barbaric and primitive, it followed that in-

101. The analytic approach relativized Austin by arguing that his definition was only one possible definition of law. This is the approach taken by WESTLAKE, *supra* note 16, at viii–ix. Walker went further and argued that Austin's defintion was philologically inaccurate. *See* WALKER, *supra* note 42, at 14–17. The historical approach suggested that Austin's definition of law applied only to modern European society. Others such as Bryce went further and argued that Austin's definition did not apply accurately to *any* societies. *See* Wilfrid E. Rumble, '*Introduction*' to JOHN AUSTIN, THE PROVINCE OF JURISPRUDENCE DETERMINED, vii, xxii. (1995). In essence, both the analytic and historical schools, in attempting to rescue the discipline of international law, were attacking Austin for privileging one rather specific meaning of the word "law."

102. Walker, in his attempt to refute Austin, could, with little modification, be describing the international system when pointing to Maine's research:

> But in such a state of society as that described by Maine, there is rule, and rule effectively enforced, but it is not command set by a determinate author to a human being formerly [sic] obliged to obey; there, while we may identify no determinate legislator, so neither may we point out any one person, or body of persons, *less than the whole,* as at once representing the unity of the race, and admittedly and habitually supreme within.

WALKER, *supra* note 42, at 12.

ternational law occupied a similar status with respect to domestic law, law properly so called. If this was so, then international law was an inferior discipline just as non-European peoples were inferior peoples. It followed, furthermore, that international law, rather than possessing any integrity and coherence of its own, bore only a faint and subordinate relationship with domestic law and could only hope to evolve by imperfectly mimicking the definitive institutions and practices of domestic law. Conformity with the master model of Europe, after all, was the path to progress prescribed by positivist international lawyers for the non-European peoples. These implications are evaded by the positivist jurists, desperately intent only on establishing their discipline and demonstrating its usefulness.

Even at the theoretical, jurisprudential level, alien societies were a primary threat to the integrity of the overall structure. Consequently, the international law of the period can be read, not simply as the confident expansion of intellectual imperialism, but a far more anxiety-driven process of naming the unfamiliar, asserting its alien nature, and attempting to reduce and subordinate it.

Within the positivist universe, therefore, the non-European world is excluded from the realms of sovereignty, society, and law. Each of these concepts, which acted as founding concepts to the framework of the positivist system, was precisely defined, correspondingly, in ways that maintained and policed the boundary between the civilized and uncivilized. The whole edifice of positivist jurisprudence is based on these initial exclusions and discriminations. Furthermore, it is clear that, notwithstanding positivist assertions of the primacy of sovereignty, the concept of society is at least equally central to the whole system.

Quite apart from the fact that the concept of society was crucial to any refutation of Austin's criticisms, it was only by recourse to this concept that jurists could divide the civilized from the uncivilized and thereby demarcate in legal terms the exclusive sphere occupied by European states. This distinction having been established, it was possible for jurists to draw upon disciplines such as anthropology to elaborate on the characteristics of the uncivilized. Finally, the constitution of sovereignty doctrine itself is based on this fundamental distinction because positivist definitions of sovereignty rely on the premise that civilized states are sovereign and uncivilized states are not.

Afflicted by all the insecurities generated by Austin, positivist jurists nevertheless attempted to present international law as a coherent and autonomous scientific discipline that could play an important role in the management of international relations. For an international law anxious to establish itself and make good on its claims to be both scientific and practical, colonialism could be seen as an ideal subject. This was not merely because "colonial problems" had become a central preoccupation of European powers to whom the acquisition of colonies was fundamental to their prestige and whose consequent competition for colonies threatened to lead to the first great European war since the defeat of Napoleon, but also because the colonial problem appeared, at least initially, to be free of many of the central complications raised by Austin. Both the analytical and historical schools pointed to the deficiencies of Austinian thinking, but the real power of his critique of international law emerged whenever a dispute developed between two sovereign states. How was such a dispute to be resolved in the absence of an overarching sovereign to articulate the appropriate law, adjudicate the dispute, and enforce the verdict? The absence of any such system was made explicit by the efforts during the late nineteenth and early twentieth centuries to institute a system of international arbitration and to codify international law—efforts that could be seen as attempts to address exactly these problems.[103] By contrast, the colonial encounter did not directly pose such problems: it was an encounter, not between two sovereign states, but between a sovereign European state and an amorphous uncivilized entity. And enforcement posed no real difficulties because of massively superior European military strength. Having stripped the non-European world of sovereignty, the positivists in effect constructed the colonial encounter as an arena in which the sovereign made, interpreted, and enforced the law. In this way, the colonial arena promised international jurists a chance to develop a jurisprudence that demonstrated the efficacy, coherence, and utility of international law free of the ubiquitous and unanswerable Austinian objections.[104] In short, the colonies offered international law the same opportunity they traditionally extended to the lower classes—and the dissolute members of the aristocracy—of the imperial center: the opportunity to make something of oneself, to prove and rehabilitate oneself.[105]

The division between the civilized and the uncivilized was central to this project; however, efforts to effect this crucial distinction were disrupted by the complication that the uncivilized resembled the civilized in important respects, while the discipline of international law

---

103. On these efforts and the importance attached to them, see Oppenheim, *supra* note 34; KOSKENNIEMI, APOLOGY, *supra* note 5, at 123–29.

104. As Riles notes, jurists such as Lawrence "diverted attention from the positivist vision of law as *force*, and reorganized international law around the theme of *order* to reassure the reader of viability of the discipline's project." (Footnotes omitted, italics in original). Riles, *supra* note 8, at 726. Further, it was particularly in the colonial context that the idiom of order could acquire an especially compelling significance. *See id.* at 727. The discussion below demonstrates, however, the problem of order among sovereign states emerged even in the colonial context, as when two European states claimed title to the same colonial territory.

105. This is an important theme of much of Victorian literature including Rudyard Kipling's KIM, and Charles Dickens's GREAT EXPECTATIONS. As the experiences of Magwitch demonstrate, rehabilitation does not always lead to acceptance.

itself bore disconcerting connections with the primitive. The primitive was not outside international law awaiting its ordering ministrations, but rather was within the very heart of the discipline. The subsequent efforts of the international jurist to define and manage the primitive served to conceal this fundamental connection.

IV. NATIVE PERSONALITY AND MANAGING THE COLONIAL ENCOUNTER

A. *Introduction*

Whatever the positivist assertions as to the legal absence of non-European societies during the second half of the nineteenth century, contact between European Empires and the societies of Asia, Africa, and the Pacific was intensifying at precisely the same period. Indeed, the expansion of colonial empires was one of the defining features of the international relations of the period. Jurisprudentially, positivists confronted the task of formulating the doctrines that could legally account for this expansion of Europe. The interaction between European and non-European societies, which had been taking place for more than four centuries, had, by this time, generated a significant and complex body of treaties.[106]

Despite this, the positivists purported to expel the non-European world from the realm of legality by insisting on the distinction between civilized and non-civilized states and then proceeded to effect the re-admission of non-European states into "international society" by the use of the modern and distinctive analytic tools of positivism. Basically, just as positivists sought to reconstitute the discipline according to prevailing ideas of modernity and science, so too they endeavored to recast entirely the legal basis of relations between the civilized and uncivilized by framing the project as though the colonial encounter was about to occur, as opposed to having already taken place. This was accomplished by basing the inquiry on the premise that the uncivilized were outside the law; thus the positivist task was to define the terms and methods by which they were to be assimilated into the legal framework. Positivist jurists made little attempt to acknowledge, much less engage with, the naturalist past and the techniques used by the naturalists to account for the preceding centuries of contact between European and non-European peoples. The principal importance of this maneuver was that the re-entry of non-European societies into the sphere of law could now take place on terms that completely sub-

106. *See* ALEXANDROWICZ, EAST INDIES and TREATY MAKING, *supra* note 8; Ian Brownlie, *The Expansion of International Society: The Consequences for the Law of Nations*, *in* THE EXPANSION OF INTERNATIONAL SOCIETY, *supra* note 21, at 358, 358–61.

ordinated and crippled non-European societies. This was achieved by deploying the new, racialized scientific lexicon of positivism, which, it was asserted, represented a higher and decisive truth. The language of positivism made up only one part of an extremely elaborate vocabulary of conquest that had been developing in many of the disciplines of the late nineteenth century. Anthropology, science, economics, and philology, while purporting in various ways to expand impartial knowledge, in fact participated crucially in the colonial project.[107] International law relied upon, reinforced, and reflected this larger body of thought from which it could borrow when required to further its own project.

This section explores this positivist project by focusing on three closely related and intersecting concerns. First, I examine how the positivist method, with its ambitions to be scientific and coherent, effected the assimilation of the non-European world into international society, and the different doctrines and techniques it developed for this purpose. Second, I focus particularly on the concept of sovereignty and the variations of sovereignty embodied in the doctrines of assimilation and, in particular, the notion of "quasi-sovereignty" that positivists developed in order to remedy problematic aspects of their theory of assimilation. This was only one example of sovereignty doctrine mutating in the confusions arising from the colonial encounter. Third, I examine how positivists characterized the different peoples of Asia, Africa, and the Pacific, and the effects and function of these characterizations within the overall positivist framework. I then seek to place these jurisprudential developments within a broader context, as diplomatic, political, and ideological considerations inevitably affected the development and application of these doctrines. For these purposes, I focus on the Berlin Africa Conference of 1885, which sought to deal with the native problems attendant upon the partitioning of Africa.

B. *Doctrines of Assimilation*

In somewhat simplistic terms, non-European peoples could be brought within the realm of international law through four basic, and often interrelated, techniques. First, treaty making constituted the basic technique for regulating relations between European and non-European peoples. Treaties provided for a broad set of arrangements ranging from agreements governing trading relations between the two entities, to treaties by which the non-European entity ostensibly ceded complete sovereignty to the European entity. Second, non-European peoples were colonized and thus subjected to the control of European

107. This is one of the central themes of Said's work, *See* SAID, ORIENTALISM, *supra* note 10, at 7–8.

sovereignty. Colonization took place by a number of methods including by a treaty of cession, by annexation, or by conquest. Third, independent non-European states such as Japan and Siam could be accepted into international society by meeting the requirements of the standard of civilization and being officially recognized, by European states, as proper members of the family of nations. Fourth, European states, particularly in the late nineteenth century, often acquired control over Asian and African societies by way of a special type of treaty: protectorate agreements. While these four categories are crudely distinct, they are nevertheless far from mutually exclusive: protectorates were established through treaties, for example, and sometimes became colonies.

1. Treaty Relations Between Europeans and Non-Europeans

a. The Historical Context

The juridical problems that positivists faced in developing a jurisprudence that would account for colonialism were attributable not only to the analytic limitations of positivism but also to the particular character of colonial expansion in the latter part of the nineteenth century. It is hardly controversial that one of the primary driving forces of nineteenth-century colonial expansion was trade. The right to enter other territories to trade and the freedom of commerce asserted so powerfully and inevitably even in Vitoria's time, was a principal rule of nineteenth-century legal and diplomatic relations.[108] Historically, much of the early trade had been conducted by trading companies such as the British East India Company and the Dutch East India Company.[109] The characteristics and functions of such companies had been clearly summarized by M.F. Lindley:

> Formed in most cases, at all events from the point of view of the shareholders, for the purpose of earning dividends, these corporations have proved to be the instruments by which enormous areas have been brought under the dominion of the States under whose auspices they were created, and in this way they have been util-

108. The reverberations of such policies have powerful legacies reaching into the modern era. Covering Hong Kong's transition in 1997, for example, THE ECONOMIST, first having noted that the Chinese were intent on stopping the British opium trade, writes that

> China had a deep suspicion of all outside "barbarians"; it insisted that trade with the outside world be conducted only through Canton (modern day Guanghzou) and only on its own, capricious terms. Britain thought it had a right to trade freely and a God-given right to pummel with canon any nation that thought otherwise.

1898 and All That—A Brief History of Hong Kong, ECONOMIST, June 1997, at 22.

109. *See generally* D.K. FIELDHOUSE, THE COLONIAL EMPIRES: A COMPARATIVE SURVEY FROM THE EIGHTEENTH CENTURY (1966).

> ized by all the important colonizing Powers. The special field of their operations has been territory which the State creating them was not at the time prepared to administer directly, but which offered good prospects from the point of view of trade or industrial exploitation.[110]

All these factors inevitably affected the international law of the period. Doctrines were developed to give trading companies some measure of legal personality by characterizing them as extensions of the Crown by virtue of royal charter.[111] Thus trading companies were capable of asserting sovereign rights over non-European peoples who were deprived of any sort of sovereignty.[112] Company charters granted them not merely the right to trade in particular areas, but also the right to make peace and war with natives and the power to coin money.[113] The control of territories by companies that were established for the explicit purpose of making money, meant, inevitably, that the territories were administered simply for profit.[114] Unsurprisingly, governance driven by such imperatives resulted in excesses that led to wars between the companies and the African and Asian peoples they purported to govern. As a consequence these companies often embroiled their chartering sovereigns in complex foreign wars.

By the end of the nineteenth century, European states were assuming direct responsibility for colonial territories. Thus, the East India Company was dissolved and the British Crown took direct control over India in 1858.[115] The direct involvement of European states in the whole process of governing resulted in a shift in the ideology justifying Empire from the vulgar language of profit to that of order, proper governance, and humanitarianism. This new synthesis was articulated at the Berlin Conference in 1884–85, where humanitarianism and profit seeking were presented in proper and judicious balance as the European powers carved up Africa. The Berlin Conference marked a new phase in the colonial enterprise not only because it formulated a

110. LINDLEY, *supra* note 20, at 91.

111. For a discussion of the powers and status of the British East India Company, see Nabob of Arcot v. The East India Company, 3 Bro. C. C. 292; 29 Eng. Rep. 544 (Ch. 1791), *reprinted in* 6 BRITISH INTERNATIONAL LAW CASES 281 (1967).

112. Thus, as Lindley notes of the British East India Company, "what was at first a mere trading Corporation came in the course of time to exercise sovereign rights over an immense area which afterwards passed under the direct administration of the British Crown." LINDLEY, *supra* note 20, at 94.

113. *See id.*

114. *See* LAWRENCE, *supra* note 17, at 174–75. As Fieldhouse points out, these trading companies changed their modes of operation rather significantly over the years. From being intent simply on trading in the 16th and 17th centuries, these companies increasingly engaged in acquiring and governing territories in order to protect their interests in the 18th and 19th centuries. For a discussion of the East India Company and England's colonization of India, see FIELDHOUSE, *supra* note 109, at 149–52, 161–73.

115. Pursuant to the Government of India Act of 1858. *See* LINDLEY, *supra* note 20.

new ideological basis for the expansion of European Empires, but because it attempted to establish a firm and clear framework for the management of the colonial scramble that otherwise threatened to exacerbate inter-European rivalries.[116]

The direct involvement of European states in the scramble for colonies led to a number of complications. Legal niceties were hardly a concern of European states driven by ambitions of imperial expansion. The positivists insisted on the supreme power of the sovereign state: but if everything a state did was "legal," then law had no place at all in the scheme of international relations. Thus, in order to assert the existence and relevance of the discipline, positivism had to balance its emphasis on sovereign power with the formulation of a clear set of rules that were observed and obeyed by sovereign states. This familiar problem of the relationship between law and politics in positivist international law manifested itself uniquely in the colonial encounter. State behavior was the basis of positivist jurisprudence; but it was difficult to detect any consistent and principled behavior in the flux, confusion, and self-interest of the colonial encounter. Consequently, there was every danger that law would degenerate into expediency.

A further problem was posed by the fact that although positivists asserted that non-European societies were officially excluded from the realm of international law, numerous treaties had been entered into between these supposedly non-existent societies and European states and trading companies in the period from the fifteenth century onwards. Furthermore, these treaties, and the state practices that followed, suggested that both the European and non-European parties understood themselves to be entering into legal relations.[117] Moreover, many doctrines of international law, accepted even by the nineteenth-century jurists, had been produced by this intercourse. For example, as Alexandrowicz's comprehensive account of the relations between the European and East Indian states prior to the nineteenth century points out, "the details of mutually agreed principles of inter-State dealings can be ascertained from the texts of treaties and documents relating to diplomatic negotiations which took place before and after their conclusion."[118]

The status of these treaties became problematic as a result of the emergence of positivism. Indeed, several jurists of the eighteenth cen-

116. The Berlin Conference, however, hardly succeeded in eliminating such rivalries. Britain and France nearly went to war over the "Fashoda incident," for example. *See generally* DAVID LEVERING LEWIS, THE MARCH TO FASHODA: EUROPEAN COLONIALISM AND AFRICAN RESISTANCE IN THE SCRAMBLE FOR AFRICA (1987).

117. A detailed account of these exchanges and the international law created both by European and non-European states in the course of these exchanges is given by ALEXANDROWICZ, EAST INDIES, *supra* note 8.

118. *See id.* at 2.

tury had anticipated the problem that now confronted the nineteenth-century positivists. Noting that positive law—the custom and treaty law developing among European states—was becoming increasingly significant, these jurists raised the problem of the implications of these developments for the "universal" international law, which applied to all states and regulated centuries of interaction between Europe and Asia.[119]

This history of treaty making posed a challenge to the positivist framework since the fundamental premises of positivism, when extended to their logical conclusion, implicitly suggested that treaties with non-Europeans were impossible. After all, the treaty is a legal instrument; it presupposes, at least, a sense of mutual obligations and an overarching system of law that would both recognize the treaty as a legal instrument and be applied in any dispute as to the meaning of the treaty. The existence of a treaty, in this way, presupposed a legal universe to which both parties adhered.[120] This presupposition, however, contradicted the powerful positivist claim that non-Europeans were uncivilized, that they were lacking in any understanding of law at all, or else, that their understanding of law was so fundamentally different from that of the Europeans that the two parties existed in incommensurable universes.

Despite this, the positivists were compelled by practical realities to apply their science to a legal institution, the treaty, whose existence seemed an aberration within the positivist conceptual universe. Positivists prided themselves on their empiricism—on their focus on state practice as opposed to the subjective metaphysical speculations of the naturalists. The nineteenth-century European states, however, relied very heavily on treaties with non-European societies in expanding their colonial empires, and in so doing, demonstrated a lamentable disregard for the systematically established and elaborated positivist assertion that non-European peoples were outside the scope of law.

For example, European states intent on creating colonies in Africa often claimed to derive their title rights from treaties with African chiefs. Thus positivists had to formulate a way of incorporating the inescapable phenomenon of treaty relations between these entities within their system. Furthermore, it was not merely unrealistic but also dangerous to ignore the many detailed treaties between European and non-European states. Many states had conducted themselves on the basis that these treaties were valid. International stability would

119. *See* Alexandrowicz, *supra* note 30. Alexandrowicz's general argument, presented in this Article and in his book on the Asian-European encounter, is that treaties in the period from the 15th to the 18th centuries were generally more equal than the imposed, unequal treaties of the 19th century.

120. Further, as Carty notes, "treaty-making capacity was a vital mark of sovereignty and independence." CARTY, *supra* note 5, at 65.

have been severely undermined if it suddenly became possible for states to question the arrangements, titles, and interests that had been ostensibly established by these treaties.[121] It was precisely the fear of disputes over title to colonial territories among European powers that inspired the Conference of Berlin of 1885.[122] Consequently, the non-European world had to be located in the positivist system, not merely for purposes of control and suppression, but to prevent its ambiguous status from undermining European solidarity.

Treaties between European and non-European states thus became the objects of positivist scrutiny. But the methodology used by positivists to examine these treaties had the paradoxical effect of erasing the non-European side of the treaty even when claiming to identify and give effect to the intentions of that party. This was a consequence of the positivist practice of focusing on the words of the treaty to the complete exclusion of the circumstances under which the treaty had been arrived at. In this way, the positivists ignored the massive violence inflicted on non-European peoples and the resistance of these peoples against that violence.

Anti-colonial resistance took a number of complex and singular forms: the rulers of Ethiopia used both diplomatic and military techniques to maintain Ethiopian independence;[123] the Kings of Thailand played rival European powers against each other;[124] and Chinese authorities relied on translations of Vattel and Wheaton to try and protect their interests against European states.[125] Almost invariably, furthermore, African and Asian states resorted to war in an attempt to stem colonial expansion. Defeat was inevitable given the superior military power of the European states, and it was principally by using force or threatening to use force that European states compelled non-European states to enter into "treaties" that basically entitled the European powers to whatever they pleased. Coercion and military superiority combined to create ostensibly legal instruments. Under the positivist sys-

---

121. European and non-European states had entered into a great number of such treaties. *See* C.H. Alexandrowicz, *The Theory of Recognition in Fieri*, 34 BRIT. Y.B. INT'L L. 176 (1958); ALEXANDROWICZ, EAST INDIES, *supra* note 8.

122. For a discussion of this see WESTLAKE, *supra* note 16, at 137–40. The Berlin Conference, apart from dividing up Africa among the European powers, sought to establish a system by which European powers making claims to African territories had to notify the Conference of their claims; it was then open to other members to make objections. *See id.*

123. *See* K.V. Ram, *The Survival of Ethiopian Independence*, *in* CONQUEST AND RESISTANCE TO COLONIALISM IN AFRICA 51 (Gregory Maddox ed. 1993).

124. *See* GONG, *supra* note 5, at 210–11, for an account of King Mongkut's dealings with the British.

125. *See* Wang Tieya, *International Law in China: Historical and Contemporary Perspectives*, *in* 221 ACADÉMIE DU DROIT INTERNATIONAL, RECUEIL DE COURS [COLLECTED COURSES OF THE HAGUE ACADEMY OF INTERNATIONAL LAW] 195, 232–37 (1990-II).

tem, it was legal to use coercion to compel parties to enter into treaties that were then legally binding.[126]

The resulting "unequal treaties"—unequal not only because they were the product of unequal power, but because they embodied unequal obligations—were humiliating to the non-European states, which sought to terminate such treaties at the earliest opportunity.[127] Rights to trade were an important part of such treaties. Thus the Treaty of Nanking[128] required the Emperor of China to cede Hong Kong to Great Britain,[129] open five Chinese ports for trade,[130] and establish a "fair and regular" tariff for British goods.[131] In addition, it required the Emperor to pay approximately $21 million to the British for various losses suffered by the British government and citizens as a result of the Opium War. As a consequence of these developments, non-European peoples were governed not by general principles of international law, but by the regimes created by these unequal treaties.[132]

The history of violence and military conquest, which led to the formation of these treaties, plays no part in the positivists' approach to the treaty.[133] Moreover, the positivists, on the whole, accepted the treaties as expressing clearly and unproblematically the actual intentions of the non-European party. Thus positivists regarded as perfectly authentic and completely natural treaties such as those in which the Wyanasa Chiefs of Nayasaland apparently stated:

---

126. *See* GONG, *supra* note 5, at 43.

127. On the origins of capitulations, see *id.* at 64–65.

128. The Treaty was, in effect, imposed on the Emperor of China after the Chinese defeat in the Opium Wars of 1839–1842. The war broke out as a result of Chinese attempts to halt the trade in opium, which had been a source of immense wealth to European traders in China. *See generally* JONATHAN D. SPENCE, THE SEARCH FOR MODERN CHINA 147–64 (1990). For details about the legal aspects of trading with China in the era preceding the Opium Wars, see Randle Edwards, *The Old Canton System of Foreign Trade*, *in* LAW AND POLITICS IN CHINA'S FOREIGN TRADE 360, 362–63 (Victor Li ed., 1977). As the works of Spence and Edwards make clear, the metaphor of barbarity was used by both the Chinese and the Europeans. Many of the legal complications that early European traders confronted in China were attributable to the Chinese view that the traders were barbarians and that no direct communication was to occur between the traders and the Emperor. *See id.* at 364–65.

129. Treaty of Nanking, Treaty of Peace, Friendship, and Commerce Between Her Majesty the Queen of Great Britain and Ireland and the Emperor of China, Aug. 29, 1842, G.B.-Ir.-P.R.C., art. III, 93 Consol. T.S. 467.

130. This allowed British merchants and their families to reside in these cities for purposes of trade. *See id.*, art. II, at 467.

131. *See id.*, art. X, at 468.

132. Tieya describes the collapse of the traditional Chinese view after the attack of the European powers: "It was not replaced by the modern international order of the system of sovereign States, but by a new order of unequal treaties. In China's foreign relations, what applied were not principles and rules of international law, but unequal treaties." Tieya, *supra* note 125, at 251.

133. Although a treaty obtained by coercion would be invalid under contemporary international law, it is difficult to find an example of an unequal colonial treaty set aside on the basis of it being obtained by force.

> We . . . most earnestly beseech Her Most Gracious Majesty the Queen of Great Britain and Ireland, Empress of India, Defender of the Faith, &c., to take our country, ourselves, and our people to observe the following conditions:
>
> I. That we give over all our country within the above described limits, all sovereign rights, and all and every other claim absolutely, and without any reservation whatever, to Her Most Gracious Majesty . . . and heirs and successors, for all time coming.[134]

Lindley cites this, apparently without any irony, as an example of a treaty of cession. The parties most knowledgeable about treaty making had no illusions about the legal status of these treaties, recognizing them to be simple manifestations of military superiority. Lord Lugard, doyen of colonial administrators,[135] made short shrift of the hypocrisy surrounding the issue:

> The frank assertion of the inexorable law of progress, based on the power to enforce it if need be, was termed "filibustering". It shocked the moral sense of a civilisation content to accept the naked deception of "treaty-making," or to shut its eyes and ears and thank God for the results.[136]

Lugard himself thought it far preferable for the European powers to "found their title to intervention on force," rather than in treaties, "which were either not understood, or which the ruler had no power to make, and which rarely provided an adequate legal sanction for the powers assumed."[137]

Jurists had some perception of the fraudulence of such treaties; however, they made no contribution to revealing the deceptions of treaty making. Instead, they applied all their considerable scholarship, insight, and learning towards identifying the proper import of such treaties and giving them effect. The acceptance of Lugard's argument, after all, would simply confirm the absence of any coherent or effective in-

134. *Cited in* LINDLEY, *supra* note 20, at 186.

135. Lugard's extraordinary life was inextricably interwoven with Empire: born in India in 1858, he was the son of a chaplain of the East India Company; he trained for soldiering at Sandhurst; and was employed for several years in the Imperial British East African Company. In that capacity he "annexed" large parts of Uganda and explored the Niger in an attempt to fend off French competition. His appointment as High Commissioner of Northern Nigeria, led him to write the classic work on colonial administration, THE DUAL MANDATE. Recognized internationally as the foremost colonial expert of his time, Lugard served on the Permanent Mandates Commission of the League of Nations. *See* Margery Perham, *Introduction* of LORD LUGARD'S THE DUAL MANDATE (5th ed. 1965).

136. *Id.* at 17.

137. *Id.*

ternational legal system and the irrelevance of international lawyers to the great project of Empire.

Rather than confront this possibility, positivists turned to the judicial arena. The broad question raised was: if the non-European world did not exist for the purposes of international law until properly incorporated into international society, what was to be made of the many treaties between European and non-European states?[138] Although evading this larger issue, Westlake confronts a part of the problem when writing of Europeans entering alien territories:

> We find that one of their first proceedings is to conclude treaties with such chiefs or other authorities as they can discover: and very properly, for no men are so savage as to be incapable of coming to some understanding with other men, and wherever contact has been established between men, some understanding, however incomplete it may be, is a better basis for their mutual relations than force. But what is the scope which it is reasonably possible to give to treaties in such a case, and what the effect which may be reasonably attributed to them?[139]

In attempting to resolve this difficulty, positivists resorted to concepts of recognition and quasi-sovereignty.

b. Doctrines of Quasi-Sovereignty and Recognition

Recognition doctrine was one technique for accounting for the metamorphosis of a non-European society into a legal entity. In broad terms, the doctrine stipulated that a new state came into being when its existence was recognized by established states.[140] The fact that a non-European society may have constituted a state was not in itself sufficient, because of the civilized/non-civilized distinction, to belong to the realm of international law.[141] In its particular application to uncivilized states, recognition takes place when "a state is brought by increasing civilisation within the realm of law."[142] But until this stage

138. This problem would not arise in the Groatian universe, where these treaties would be interpreted as the understanding between different societies governed by universal natural law. This is the problem posed by authorities on the 19th century such as Gong. "How could treaty relations with these 'backward,' non-European countries be made consistent with the fact that such relations might be construed as recognition of legal personality?" GONG, *supra* note 5, at 60.

139. WESTLAKE, *supra* note 16, at 143–44.

140. *See* W.E. HALL, A TREATISE ON INTERNATIONAL LAW 82–83 (2d ed. 1884). *See also* OPPENHEIM, *supra* note 19, at 116: "For every State that is not already, but wants to be, a member, recognition is therefore necessary. A State is, and becomes, an International Person through recognition only and exclusively."

141. "As the basis of the Law of Nations is the common consent of the civilised States, statehood alone does not include membership in the Family of Nations." OPPENHEIM, *supra* note 19, at 116.

142. HALL, *supra* note 140, at 83.

was reached, non-Europeans were excluded from the proper application of the doctrine as it operated in the European realm.[143]

Westlake and other positivists attempted to resolve the problem of whether or not the native states were part of international law by arguing that such states, although not proper, sovereign members of international society, were nevertheless partial members.[144] Hence, Westlake proposed, "Our international society exercises the right of admitting outside states to parts of its international law without necessarily admitting them to the whole of it."[145] The non-European states thus existed in a sort of twilight world; lacking personality, they nevertheless were capable of entering into certain treaties and, to that extent, were members of international law.[146]

But how was the determination made as to who was to be admitted into international society, to what extent, and for what purposes? The answers to these questions were extremely vital as it was common for European states to challenge the claims made by rival states that they had acquired property rights or even sovereignty over territory by way of treaty with, for example, an African chief. A European state attacking a rival claim to sovereignty over territory would argue, for instance, that the chief who had entered into the treaty had no authority to do so, that he was not properly a chief, or that the land covered by the treaty was not within the chief's authority to transfer. It was important, then, to devise rules that could resolve all these disputes and would fix and stabilize the personality of non-European entities; failure to achieve this would lead to an exacerbation of inter-European tensions. Moreover, positivists regarded the successful resolution of such problems as a test of the coherence and value of positivist international law. Indeed, it was precisely this accomplishment that distinguished the positivist from his less able naturalist predecessor. Thus Lawrence dismissed the law of the Middle Ages, when the European expansion

143. As Lorimer asserts, "The right of undeveloped races, like the right of undeveloped individuals, is a right not to recognition as to what they are not, but to guardianship—that is, to guidance—in becoming that which they are capable, in realising their special ideals." LORIMER, *supra* note 14, at 157. Thus it was only through "guardianship" that the non-Europeans could achieve any status.

144. As Lorimer put it, "He [the international jurist] is not bound to apply the positive law of nations to savages, or even to barbarians, as such; but he is bound to ascertain the points at which, and the directions in which, barbarians or savages come within the scope of partial recognition." LORIMER, *supra* note 14, at 102.

145. WESTLAKE, *supra* note 16, at 82. Westlake presents this flexibility as an advantage offered by the system: "This is an instance of the way in which all human institutions, being free and not mechanical products, shade off from one to another." *Id.*

146. Oppenheim also developed a similar doctrine, asserting, in relation to treaties between Christian and non-Christian states, "when they [Christian states] enter into treaty obligations with them, they indirectly declare that they are ready to recognise them for these parts as International Persons and subjects of the Law of Nations." OPPENHEIM, *supra* note 19, at 155. See also the opinion of Arbitrator Max Huber in Island of Palmas Case (U.S. v. Neth.), 2 R.I.A.A. 829, 852 (1928).

commenced, claiming "it was powerless to decide what acts were necessary in order to obtain dominion over newly discovered territory, or how great an extent of country could be acquired by one act of discovery or colonisation."[147]

The basic method of resolving the problem of personality comprised a complex process of determining the status of the non-European entity through the doctrine of recognition and then examining whether the right the European state claimed with respect to that entity was consistent with its legal status.[148] For example, if the entity was recognized as having a personality that enabled it to alienate its lands, then European states that had entered into a treaty with that entity regarding rights to the land could claim to possess valid title. But the use of recognition for these purposes raised further tensions. On the one hand, recognition was bestowed by a state at its own discretion; on the other, positivists argued that recognition could only take place within certain confines that were juridically established.[149] Positivists such as Westlake argued that the legal capacity of the entity was predetermined by the degree of civilization it had attained. Thus African tribes, according to Westlake, could not transfer sovereignty because they were incapable of understanding the concept;[150] whereas Asian states possessed this capacity, having attained a higher level of civilization.[151] Within this scheme, the jurist's task was to develop a system of classification, of taxonomy, which could properly categorize every entity encountered in the course of colonial expansion. The implication is that the often self-interested recognition bestowed by a European state was invalid if it disregarded the inherent capacities of the entity in question, capacities that were legally and objectively established by the entity's position on the scale of civilization. In short, international law had established general rules defining the capacities of native peoples, and individual states had to exercise their discretion within the boundaries of such rules.

147. LAWRENCE, *supra* note 17, at 52. Lawrence characterizes Grotius as being engaged in the task of solving this problem by an application of the Roman law of property. It was from this prism, then, that doctrines of sovereignty were formulated.

148. It was vital for these purposes that some agreement be established between international lawyers from different backgrounds. Hence Westlake is at pains to point out that his views on some of these issues correspond with those of Portuguese jurists. *See* WESTLAKE, *supra* note 16, at 146.

149. This is a familiar problem with respect to recognition doctrine as a whole.

150. Thus, for Westlake, sovereignty was acquired by other procedures, some of which had been formalized at the Berlin Conference. While natives could alienate property, sovereignty was obtained, "not in treaties with natives, but in the nature of the case and compliance with conditions recognized by the civilised world." WESTLAKE, *supra* note 16, at 145. Westlake's argument, however, was completely contrary to actual state practice. *See* ALEXANDROWICZ, TREATY MAKING, *supra* note 8, at 48–50.

151. *See* OPPENHEIM, *supra* note 19, at 286.

Each of these elements of the positivist framework, intended to establish objective legal standards whose application could resolve international disputes, faced insuperable problems. The project of classification, for example, faced a formidable challenge. Essentially, positivist jurisprudence sought to combine anthropological insight with taxonomic precision: each entity was to be studied, its degree of civilization ascertained, and its legal status accordingly allocated. This was the system used to account for a proliferation of entities ranging from "Amerindian and African kings and chiefs, Muslim sultans, khans and emirs, Hindu princes, and the empires of China and Japan."[152] Given the range of societies and practices with which the system had to deal, however, it is hardly surprising that positivist jurists themselves finally acknowledged the limitations of their own methods. Lawrence asserts, in discussing the question of whether or not an entity should be admitted into international membership, that "a certain degree of civilization is necessary, though it is difficult to define the exact amount."[153] The willingness of a non-European to be bound by international law would not in itself suffice to ensure membership; but beyond this, Lawrence suggests that "[i]n matters of this kind, no general rule can be laid down."[154]

State practice, likewise, did not reveal a consistent set of principles as to questions of admittance and capacity. Recognition was granted by states, not in accordance with any international principle, but according to the powerful and unpredictable expedience of competition for colonies. Certainly, there were occasions on which unanimity prevailed among European states, as when Turkey was ceremoniously admitted into the circle of European nations.[155] In such a case, the collective act of recognition established the existence of an entity whose capacity was accepted and agreed upon by European states. This, however, was a relatively rare occurrence.

Colonial expansion, by contrast, involved a haphazard and chaotic series of encounters between rival European states, trading companies, and Asian and African societies. European states adopted different views of native personality, depending on their own interests. The problem was that native personality was fluid since it was created through the encounter with a European state that would inevitably "recognize" the capacity of the non-European entity according to its own needs.[156] A European state that had been granted particular treaty

152. Hedley Bull, *The Emergence of a Universal International Society*, *in* THE EXPANSION OF INTERNATIONAL SOCIETY, *supra* note 21, at 117.

153. LAWRENCE, *supra* note 17, at 58.

154. *Id.* at 59.

155. *See id.* at 84. On this occasion, by the Treaty of Paris of 1856, Turkey was "admitted to participate in the advantages of the public law and system of Europe."

156. Oppenheim appears to accept this. *See supra* note 146.

rights by an African chief would insist on the validity of the treaty and on the capacity of the chief to enter into such an agreement.[157] Yet, acceptance of this approach meant that any action undertaken by an individual state created law, which, as Lorimer points out, "deprives international law of permanent basis in nature and fails to bring it within the sphere of jurisprudence."[158] Acceptance of this solution dispensed with the idea of law and privileged state sovereignty. In the final analysis, international law failed to establish any clear limits to the exercise of state discretion in matters of recognition, as a consequence of which the subjective and self-interested views of states appeared to prevail.[159]

In an attempt to establish standards independent of arbitrary state will, Westlake was prepared, ironically,[160] to base the capacity of non-European peoples on the degree of understanding of the non-European party entering into a treaty. "We have here a clear apprehension of the principle that an uncivilised tribe can grant by treaty such rights as it understands and exercises, but nothing more."[161] He states that cession of this sort "may confer a moral title to such property or power as they [the natives] understand while they cede it, but that no form of cession by them can confer title to what they do not understand."[162] As a consequence, "it is possible that a right of property may be derived from natives, and this even before European sovereignty has existed over the spot."[163]

If the degree of native understanding was the test, the question then naturally arose: how was a jurist to ascertain what these natives were capable of understanding? Westlake addresses this problem in his examination of two treaties that concerned disputes between Portugal

157. It was a common tactic among states disputing one other's claims to argue, for example, that the chieftain who entered into a treaty ceding a disputed territory was not the proper chief. *See* S.E. CROWE, THE BERLIN WEST AFRICAN CONFERENCE 1884–1885, at 158–59 (Negro Universities Press 1970) (1942).

158. LORIMER, *supra* note 14, at 104.

159. As Gong notes, "The subjective nature of the recognition process and the political element within the standard of 'civilization' put the European powers in the always powerful and sometimes awkward position of having to be judge in their own cases." GONG, *supra* note 5, at 61.

160. Ironically because the basic positivist premise is that natives are entirely outside the law.

161. WESTLAKE, *supra* note 16, at 149.

162. *Id.* at 145.

163. *Id. See also* Johnson v. McIntosh, 21 U.S. (8 Wheat) 543, 593 (1823) *quoted in* WESTLAKE, *supra* note 16, at 148: "The grant derives its efficacy from their [the Amerindians'] will, and if they choose to resume it and make a different disposition of the land, the Courts of the United States cannot interpose for the protection of the title." The suggestion of this quotation from Chief Justice Marshall's opinion in Johnson v. McIntosh is that land rights of the natives were recognized in international law (thus enabling the natives to alienate their lands) and that these rights continued even when the natives were incorporated into the sovereignty of the colonial state. Hence Marshall's statement that the Indians could go so far as to modify the terms on which the land may have been "granted."

and England. In these disputes, both states claimed rights over the same territory. In order to decide this issue, Westlake is compelled to resort to his conjecture as to native understanding. He dismisses one treaty as "mixed with a farrago which must have been mere jargon to him [the Chief]." As opposed to another where "there is nothing beyond the comprehension of the Makololo chiefs."[164] Having initially insisted that non-Europeans were absent from the legal universe, Westlake now effectively acknowledges the inadequacies of positivism by resorting to constructing the Makololo chiefs and divining their consciousness in order to give his scheme *some* semblance of coherence.

It is almost superfluous to note that while European powers claimed to derive rights from treaties entered into with non-European states, they refused to accept the obligations arising from them. Thus Hall, noting the tendency on "the part of such [non-European] states to expect that European countries shall behave in conformity with the standard which they themselves have set up," concludes that treaties only create obligations of "honour" on the part of the European states.[165] Similarly, Oppenheim argues that European states interacted with non-European states on the basis of "discretion, and not International Law."[166]

Positivism claimed to provide, through a precise examination of state behavior and the employment of a comprehensive and clearly defined system of classification, a definitive answer to any legal problem with which it was confronted. Once the actualities of applying positivism to resolving problems of native title are examined, however, it becomes evident that such claims were hardly well-founded. Ultimately, the matter is resolved not in accordance with these detailed and elaborate principles, but rather on an almost completely ad hoc basis, by a process that is reduced to attempting to reconstruct that to which Makololo chiefs imagine themselves to be agreeing. The randomness of this process is acknowledged by the jurists themselves. Lawrence, for instance, acknowledges that "[e]ach case must be judged on its own merits by the powers who deal with it."[167] Jurists simply could not account for the ambiguous position occupied by the non-European world, which is simultaneously capable of entering into treaty relations, yet lacking in any cognizable international personality. Positivists grandiosely claimed that while their system was based on

---

164. WESTLAKE, *supra* note 16, at 153.

165. W.E. HALL, A TREATISE ON INTERNATIONAL LAW 43–44 (3d ed.), *quoted in* GONG, *supra* note 5, at 61. See also Crawford's summary of statehood doctrine in the 19th century in CRAWFORD, *supra* note 5, at 12–15.

166. OPPENHEIM, *supra* note 19, at 34–35. "The moral rights of all outside the international society against the several members of that society remain intact, though they have not and scarcely could have been converted into legal rights. . . ." WESTLAKE, *supra* note 16, at 140.

167. LAWRENCE, *supra* note 17, at 85.

empirical science, it nevertheless remained autonomous from the messy world of politics, society, and history that it imperiously and decisively ordered. The complex realities of late nineteenth-century politics overwhelmed the positivist system. Its failure to coherently place and incorporate the non-European entity into its overall scheme completely invalidated its much vaunted claims of being comprehensive, systematic, and consistent. The ambivalent status of the non-European entity, outside the scope of the law and yet within it, lacking in international personality and yet necessarily possessing it, was never satisfactorily defined or resolved. As Oppenheim acknowledges, "No other explanation of these and similar facts [the fact that these non-sovereign entities engaged in sovereign behaviour] can be given except that these not-full Sovereign States are in some way or another International Persons and subjects of International Law."[168]

2. Colonization

The problem of the legal personality of non-European peoples could be most simply resolved by the actual act of colonization, which effectively extinguished this personality. Once colonization took place, the colonizing power assumed sovereignty over the non-European territory, and any European state carrying on business with that territory would deal with the colonial power. In this way, legal relations would once again take place between two European powers. The tension that existed between these European states (for example, over access to markets or resources of a colony) was in many respects less jurisprudentially complicated than relations between European and non-European entities were.

Nevertheless, questions of native personality played an important role in determining whether colonization had properly taken place in the first instance. The jurisprudence concerning the issue of how sovereignty was acquired over non-European peoples was controversial and unsettled because, once again, states took very different views depending on their own interests.[169] Broadly, however, discovery,[170] occupation, conquest,[171] and cession[172] were some of the doctrines his-

168. OPPENHEIM, *supra* note 19, at 110.

169. *See id.* at 283.

170. The basic idea underlying the method of discovery to acquire property rights was that the mere "discovery" of a territory sufficed to provide title. Discovery was used as a basis for title in the 15th and 16th centuries, but was generally discredited by international lawyers as a valid basis for establishing title because it was so prone to abuse. *See* LINDLEY, *supra* note 20, at 128–38.

171. *See* HALL, *supra* note 140, at 522–29. "Conquest consists in the appropriation of the property in, and of the sovereignty over, a part or the whole of the territory of a state, and when definitively accomplished vests the whole rights of property and sovereignty over such territory in the conquering state." *Id.* at 522.

172. In 1912, Oppenheim listed five modes of acquiring territory: cession, occupation, accre-

torically devised to deal with this issue. The conceptual framework offered by private law, particularly property law, played an influential role in the jurisprudence regarding the acquisition of territory.[173] In order to prevent a state from claiming that it had acquired valid title over an entire territory simply by landing there, positivist analysis focused on questions such as what acts were sufficient to show that the European state had acquired control over the territory or that occupation had been "effective."

Conquest generally involved militarily defeating an opponent and thus acquiring sovereignty over the defeated party's territory.[174] Conquest was one of the most ancient ways of acquiring title; within the nineteenth-century framework, it was a completely legal and valid way of expanding territory. Recognition of such a right of conquest is completely contrary to the very concept of law as it legitimizes outcomes dictated by power rather than legal principle. Nevertheless, conquest received legal sanction. Given the military weakness of the non-European states and the absence of any legal limitations on a state's ability to commence a war, it was inevitable that European colonial empires expanded by the conquest of large parts of Asia and Africa.[175] As Korman notes, furthermore, European states quite openly relied on the doctrine of conquest as a basis for their title.[176]

Furthermore, the emphasis on the concept of property and the positivist view that uncivilized peoples were not legal entities contributed towards doctrines such as "occupation" erasing the existence of many non-European peoples.

> Only such territory can be the object of occupation as is no State's land, whether entirely uninhabited, as e.g. an island, or inhabited by natives whose community is not to be considered as a State. Even civilised individuals may live and have private property on a

---

tion, subjugation, and prescription. *See* OPPENHEIM, *supra* note 19, at 284.

173. *See generally* CARTY, *supra* note 5, for a study of the complex ways in which these analogies were made. Although territory was spoken of as property, this did not mean that, at the end of the 19th century, the modes of acquiring territory were treated as identical to the modes of acquiring private property; however, it is notable that the international law of Grotius's time had apparently relied on Roman law concepts of private property in describing how states acquired property, and this schematization had a continuing influence. *See* OPPENHEIM, *supra* note 19, at 283.

174. For a comprehensive and detailed study of conquest, see SHARON KORMAN, THE RIGHT OF CONQUEST: THE ACQUISITION OF TERRITORY BY FORCE IN INTERNATIONAL LAW AND PRACTICE (1996).

175. For an outline of conquest, see OPPENHEIM, *supra* note 19, at 302–07. Conquest seems to have been officially outlawed in contemporary international law as a means of acquiring title to territory, even though certain events suggest that it remains a part of international law. The Indonesian assertions of sovereignty over East Timor, which have been, implicitly, if not explicitly, recognized by countries such as Australia, can be principally explained in terms of conquest. *See* Case Concerning East Timor (Portugal v. Australia), 1995 I.C.J. 90 (June 30).

176. *See* KORMAN, *supra* note 174, at 66.

> territory without any union by them into a State proper which exercises sovereignty over such territory. And natives may live on a territory under a tribal organisation which need not be considered a State proper.[177]

This meant that the territory of "tribal" peoples could be appropriated simply through occupation by the European state on the basis that tribal organization did not correspond with a "State." Thus, British title to the Australian continent was based on occupation of uninhabited territory, *terra nullius*; it was irrelevant that Aboriginal peoples had occupied the continent for more than forty thousand years and had developed sophisticated forms of political and social organization in this time.[178]

Each of these doctrines relied upon different notions of native personality, as the particular means of asserting title depended on the positivist assessment of the degree of civilization of the peoples occupying the land. Using this scale, the positivists asserted, for example, that in the case of merely tribal peoples occupation itself would suffice. Still, if the natives belonged to what positivists regarded as an uncivilized, but organized, polity, European powers would have to assert title through some other means such as conquest or cession.[179] The issue of cession raised the problems discussed earlier as to treaty relations between European and non-European peoples. The legitimacy of conquest as a mode of acquiring control, together with the positivist argument that resort to force was a valid expression of sovereign will, meant that few restrictions were imposed on imperial expansion. This, coupled with the fact that municipal courts of the colonized countries were precluded from inquiring into sovereign behavior, effectively meant that the attempts made by colonized peoples to question the legality of actions taken by the colonizing state or other entities vested with sovereignty by the colonizing state were bound to fail.[180]

---

177. OPPENHEIM, *supra* note 19, at 292.

178. *See* LINDLEY, *supra* note 20, at 40–41. British courts which made such rulings essentially relied on reports of the Aborigines which asserted that "so entirely destitute are they even of the rudest forms of civil polity, that their claims, whether as sovereigns or proprietors of the soil, have been utterly disregarded." *Id.* at 41, *quoting* 7 PARL. PAPERS NO. 425, at 82 (1837).

179. For discussion of the various ways in which title could be obtained over territories occupied by primitive peoples, see WESTLAKE, *supra* note 16, at 155–66. British acquisition of title over India presented a different set of problems by virtue of the existence of a complex political system there. *See id.* at 191.

180. This is illustrated by a series of cases regarding the validity of concessions obtained by colonial powers and affiliated companies, with respect to colonial territories. These took place in India, where it was once declared by the municipal courts that even the actions of the East India Company were to be regarded as the acts of a sovereign and therefore immune from scrutiny. As a consequence, colonized peoples could not bring any claims in the international arena. *See* 2 Y.B. INT'L L. COMM'N 117–18, UN Doc.A/CN.4/Ser.A./1963/ Add.1.

3. Complying with the Standard of Civilization

States such as Japan and Siam succeeded in retaining their nominal independence. For such states, acceptance into the Family of Nations could only occur if they met the "standard of civilization," which amounted, essentially, to idealized European standards in both their external and, more significantly, internal relations.

These standards presupposed and legitimized colonial intrusion in that a non-European state was deemed to be civilized if it could provide an individual, a European foreigner, with the same treatment that the individual would expect to receive in Europe.[181] The development of this framework appears to correspond with the changing nature of European penetration of the non-European world and the legal regimes that had been devised to promote this. As discussed earlier, the first phase of contact took place through trading companies, which confined their activities principally to trade. As they gradually adopted a more intrusive role in the governance of the non-European state in order to further their trading interests, more demands were made on non-European states, which were compelled under threat of military action to make increasing concessions to the interests of the traders. Apart from demonstrating some of the characteristics of an unequal treaty, the Treaty of Nanking suggests how different European practices and policies were gradually introduced into non-European societies and then expanded. Once it had been established by way of treaty that a European had a right to reside and trade in a particular state, it was not altogether surprising that international jurists would use this as a measure of whether a country was civilized or not. Westlake presents the basic test: "When people of European race come into contact with American or African tribes, the prime necessity is a government under the protection of which the former may carry on the complex life to which they have been accustomed in their homes . . . ."[182]

Westlake argued that the "Asian Empires" were capable of meeting this standard, provided that Europeans were subject to the jurisdiction of a European consul rather than subject to the local laws; but even so, this meant only that European international law had merely to "take account" of such Asian societies rather than accept them as members of the Family of Nations.[183] For the European states, the local systems of justice were completely inadequate, and there was no question of submitting one of their citizens to these systems. Thus, non-European states were forced to sign treaties of capitulation that gave European powers extra-territorial jurisdiction over the activities of their own

181. *See* WESTLAKE, *supra* note 16, at 102–03, 141–42.
182. *Id.* at 141.
183. *See id.* at 142.

citizens in these non-European states.[184] This derogation from the sovereignty of the non-European state was naturally regarded as a massive humiliation by that state, which sought to terminate all capitulations at the earliest opportunity.[185] Capitulations were an aspect of the unequal treaty regime imposed on these states and usually comprised just one part of these treaties, which also granted rights to trade and to establish residences, for example.[186] Once these treaties allowed for a trading presence, it was almost inevitable that the scope of the rights demanded by the European powers to enable them effectively to carry on their trade expanded.

Both external and internal reform had to be carried out by a state seeking entry into the family of nations. In the external sphere, the state had to be capable of meeting international obligations and maintaining the diplomatic missions and channels necessary to enable and preserve relations with European states. In the internal sphere, the state was required to reform radically its legal and political systems to the extent that they reflected European standards as a whole. Put in another way, this test in effect suggested that the project of meeting the standard of civilization consisted of generalizing the standards embodied in the capitulation system, which was specific to aliens, to the entire country.[187] In the domestic sphere, then, the non-European state was required to guarantee basic rights relating to dignity, property, and freedom of travel, commerce, and religion, and it had to possess a court system that comprised codes, published laws, and legal guarantees.[188] All these rules compelling domestic reform essentially required profound transformations of non-European societies in ways that negated the principle of territorial sovereignty. Oppenheim states the principle in its fullest form:

> In consequence of its internal independence and territorial supremacy, a State can adopt any Constitution it likes, arrange its

184. *See* OPPENHEIM, *supra* note 19, at 395. This jurisdiction was exercised by European consuls in the non-European states; the competence of these consuls comprised "the whole civil and criminal jurisdiction, the power of protection of the privileges, the life, and property of their countrymen." *Id.* at 497.

185. *See* ANAND, *supra* note 8, at 23–24; Tieya, *supra* note 125, at 195. Alexandrowicz argues that originally capitulations were voluntarily undertaken by Asian states who were sympathetic to the problems faced by traders in a foreign culture and who sought to facilitate trade by means of the capitulation, which, in the early stage of the colonial encounter, took place on equal terms. Capitulations at that stage did not signify inequality or inferiority; that occurred by the 19th century. *See* ALEXANDROWICZ, EAST INDIES, *supra* note 8, at 97.

186. *See* GONG, *supra* note 5, at 211, *citing* Treaty of Friendship and Commerce between Her Majesty and the Kings of Siam, Apr. 18, 1855 (the Bowring Treaty).

187. Thus it was only after Japan had extensively revised its civil and criminal codes that it was admitted to the Family of Nations. *See* GONG, *supra* note 5, at 29.

188. *See id.* at 14–15. Gong provides a clear and useful summary taken from various texts, of what the standard of civilization required.

> administration in a way it thinks fit, make use of legislature as it pleases, organise its forces on land and sea, build and pull down fortresses, adopt any commercial policy it likes and so on.[189]

While positivist jurisprudence insisted that states were formally equal and that states possessed extensive powers over their own territory, a different set of principles applied in the case of non-European states, which significantly compromised their internal sovereignty and their cultural distinctiveness in order to be accepted as legal subjects of the system. It was not open for non-European states to exercise the far ranging freedoms over their internal affairs suggested by Oppenheim, principally because it was only if the non-European states had adopted Western forms of political organization that they were accepted into the system. Essentially the actions that non-European states had to take to enter into the system negated the rights that they were supposed to enjoy formally upon admittance.

4. Protectorates

Toward the latter part of the nineteenth century, protectorates were a rather common technique by which European states exercised extensive control over non-European states, while not officially assuming sovereignty over those states.[190] Although used to regulate relations within Europe itself, the protectorate was a device modified by European states and used in unique ways in furthering their colonial empires. The protectorate was ostensibly a means of protecting vulnerable states from "great power politics" by entrusting those same great powers to look after the interests of these vulnerable states.[191] Thus the "protectorate" was essentially a treaty by which uncivilized states placed themselves under the "protection" of European states. Under this regime, a European state would acquire complete control over the external affairs of the non-European state, which was prohibited from communicating with any other European state without the permission of its protector.[192] In theory, the non-European states retained their sovereignty over internal affairs. Indeed, a number of disputes heard by the British courts established and affirmed this proposition.[193]

---

189. OPPENHEIM, *supra* note 19, at 178.

190. On protectorates in general, *see* LINDLEY, *supra* note 20, at 181–206; OPPENHEIM, *supra* note 19, at 296–98.

191. *See* ALEXANDROWICZ, TREATY MAKING, *supra* note 8, at 62.

192. *See id.* at 62–83. Alexandrowicz defines a protectorate as "a split of sovereignty and its purpose is to vest in the Protector rights of external sovereignty while leaving rights of internal sovereignty in the protected entity. In this way the Protector shelters another entity against the external hazards of power politics." *Id.* at 62. *See also* CRAWFORD, *supra* note 5, at 187–88.

193. *See, e.g.*, Duff Development Co. v. Kelentan Govt. 470 A.C. 797 (1924). See LINDLEY, *supra* note 20, at 194–200 for discussion of the status of Malay and Indian protectorates.

Nevertheless, the technical distinction between internal and external sovereignty was porous. As Westlake remarks, "[T]he institution of protectorates over uncivilised nations has given greater freedom to the initial steps towards their acquisition."[194] This was legally justified by protectorate provisions, which enabled the protecting power to assume control over internal affairs because this was explicitly provided for in the agreement,[195] or else because the native ruler was incapable, for example, of maintaining "good government" within the protectorate.[196] The artificiality of the supposed distinction between external and internal sovereignty is suggested by the fact that even questions of succession, which were the very core of native sovereignty, often had to be answered by the protecting power.[197] As Maine points out, regimes such as the protectorate were a complete aberration of Austin's idea of sovereignty:

> It is necessary to the Austinian theory that the all-powerful portion of the community which make laws should not be divisible, that it should not share its power with anybody else, and Austin himself speaks with some contempt of the semi-sovereign or demi-sovereign states which are recognised by the classical writers on International Law. But this indivisibility of Sovereignty, though it belongs to Austin's system, does not belong to International Law. The powers of sovereigns are a bundle or collection of powers and they may be separated one from another.[198]

Significantly, then, the protectorate mechanism enabled European states to exercise control over a state with respect to both its internal and external affairs, even while asserting that sovereignty was properly located in the native ruler. As Lindley notes, "By such an arrangement, one State could acquire complete control over another, so far as third

194. WESTLAKE, *supra* note 16, at 184. Lindley goes further in saying, "The more modern protectorates [i.e., protectorates established with respect to non-European states] . . . have been usually intended or destined to result in the incorporation of the protected region into the dominions of the protecting Power, or, at all events, in an increasing control by that Power over the internal affairs of the protected country." LINDLEY, *supra* note 20, at 182. Later Lindley states, "In both India and Africa, the tendency has been for the protecting Power to increase its control over internal affairs. In India this has been effected mainly by emphasizing and regularizing the duties which the native princes owe to the paramount Power; in Africa by more direct action in the various branches of administrative government." *Id.* at 200–01. *See also* Island of Palmas Case, *supra* note 146.

195. *See* LINDLEY, *supra* note 20, at 184 (discussing the Warsangali treaty between Warsangali chiefs, near the Somali coast, and Britain). The Warsangali agreed to act upon the advice of British Officers "in matters relating to the administration of justice, the development of the resources of the country, the interests of commerce, or in any other matter in relation to peace, order, and good government, and the general progress of civilization." *Id.*

196. *See id.* at 196.

197. *Id.* at 196–98.

198. HENRY SUMNER MAINE, INTERNATIONAL LAW 58 (1888).

nations were concerned, without necessarily assuming the burden of its administration, and it was this feature of the protectorate which favoured its extensive adoption by European Powers in the spread of their dominion."[199]

The protectorate was a wonderfully flexible legal instrument because it could be used for a number of different purposes. It could, as Lindley suggests, be used to exclude competing European powers. Equally, it could be used to acquire control over the interior realm of the native state when that was considered desirable. The existence of a protectorate enabled European states to regulate the degree of sovereignty a local ruler had. Thus in terms of some issues, the local ruler could be characterized as having the capacity to transfer property to the Protecting power. For example, where the Protecting power wished to assert its own power, it could declare that the matter in question was within the its sphere of authority.[200] In analyzing British practice as a protecting state with respect to Indian princely kingdoms, it is asserted that

> [t]here *is* paramount power in the British Crown, of which the extent is wisely left undefined. There *is* a subordination in the native states, which is understood but not explained. The paramount power intervenes only on grounds of general policy, where interests of the Indian people or the safety of the British power are at stake.[201]

What is notable is that, at a time when sovereignty was generally regarded as fixed, stable, and monolithic,[202] colonial jurists self-consciously grasped the usefulness of keeping sovereignty undefined in order that it could be extended or withdrawn according to the requirements of British interests. It is also notable in this passage that Britain had by now assumed responsibility for the well being of the natives and used this as a further basis for intervention. In the final analysis, the distinction between protectorates and colonies was gradually eroded, and the protectorate became a vehicle by which the European power controlled both the internal and external relations of the native state.[203] As in the case of Vitorian jurisprudence, intervention

---

199. LINDLEY, *supra* note 20, at 182.

200. For the complications that could arise regarding which rights attributable to sovereignty were being exercised, see The King v. Crewe, 2 Eng. Rep. 576 (2 K.B. 1910).

201. WESTLAKE, *supra* note 16, at 206 (*citing* WILLIAM LEE-WARNER, THE PROTECTED PRINCES OF INDIA 37–40 (1894)).

202. For an analysis of this image of 19th-century sovereignty, see Kennedy, *supra* note 5, at 119: "By century's end, international law would countenance but one form of political authority, absolute within its territory and equal in its relations with other sovereigns."

203. Lindley asserts that the protectorate was intended to lead to "an increasing control by that [protecting] Power over the internal affairs of the protected country. The sovereignty is to be

was endorsed by a number of techniques, such as the powerful invocation of disorder and lawlessness within the non-European territory, which necessitated the imposition of an order that could only take place through conquest posited as unwillingly undertaken.[204] The protectorate, then, demonstrated yet another variation on sovereignty as it developed in the colonial encounter. The use of the protectorate as a flexible instrument of control corresponded with a growing appreciation for the uses of the "informal Empire" and the realization that an important distinction could be made between economic and political control.[205] While it was desirable to exploit the raw materials of Asian and African countries and develop new markets in these countries, these goals could be achieved without assuming political control over the territory or incurring the costs and problems of managing a colony. Seen from this perspective, the ideal situation enabled Britain to exercise economic control over a non-European state that was nominally "sovereign." The protectorate arrangement, as a legal instrument, was ideally suited for the implementation of such a policy.[206]

C. *The Berlin Conference on West Africa of 1884–85*

1. Introduction

Given the conceptual inadequacies of the positivist framework for dealing with the colonial encounter, it was hardly surprising that international law contributed little towards the effective management of the colonial scramble. This scramble generated such grave tensions that the European powers held the Berlin Conference of 1884–85 in an attempt to resolve matters. Here diplomacy and traditional balance of power politics combined with international law, as the imperial powers of Europe attempted to create a legal and political framework that would ensure that colonial expansion in the Congo Basin took place in an orderly way that minimized tensions among the three most powerful European states at the time: England, France, and Germany. This Part of the Article focuses on the legal attempts to define and domesticate the native and place him securely within the authoritative framework of positivist jurisprudence, and on the related theme of the com-

---

acquired piecemeal, the external sovereignty first." LINDLEY, *supra* note 20, at 182.

204. *See* Anghie, *Vitoria*, *supra* note 9, at 326–27.

205. *See* John Gallagher and Ronald Robinson, *The Imperialism of Free Trade*, 6 ECON. HIST. REV. 1 (1953). For a discussion of the role of informal empire in the larger context of empire, see MICHAEL W. DOYLE, EMPIRES (1986).

206. In the final analysis, however, the British, for example, found it necessary to assume political control over most of the territories which they initially treated as protectorates. It was only in this way that they could create the political conditions and stability that enabled economic expansion.

plex ways in which law and politics intermingled in the grand project of colonial management.

African peoples played no part at all in these deliberations,[207] which determined in important ways the future of the continent and continue to have a profound influence on the politics of contemporary Africa.[208] This exclusion was reiterated and intensified in a more complex way by the positivist argument that African tribes were too primitive to understand the concept of sovereignty and, hence, were unable to cede it by treaty. Consequently, any claims to sovereignty based on such treaties were invalid.[209] This proposition may have been advanced not only for theoretical consistency, but also to preclude European adventurers from abusing the treaty mechanism as a means to acquire sovereignty. Nevertheless, its effect was to transform Africa into a conceptual *terra nullius*; as such, only dealings between European states with respect to those territories could have decisive legal effect. The Berlin Conference was a unique event because it was the first occasion on which European states[210] sought to address the "colonial problem." Although primarily concerned with the division of Africa, the deliberations of the Conference illuminated many aspects of the broader question of colonialism as a whole. The management of the division of Africa by systematizing the colonial scramble and the articulation of a new ideology of colonialism were two of the major projects of the Conference.

2. Partitioning and Managing Africa

Trade was the central theme of the Conference. Issues concerning free trade in the Congo basin[211] and free navigation of the Congo and Niger rivers were intensely discussed.[212] The implicit failure of international law to devise a coherent framework for regulating the European-African encounter became evident in their deliberations. As the previous discussion on treaties suggests, the modes of acquiring trading rights and control over non-European territory were easily open to

---

207. *See* ELIAS, *supra* note 8, at 18–20, 33.

208. *See generally* Mutua, *supra* note 8.

209. See OPPENHEIM, *supra* note 19, at 285–86 for the general proposition that cessions of territory by native tribes to states fall outside the Law of Nations. For the application of the doctrine to Africa specifically, see WESTLAKE, *supra* note 16, at 149–55.

210. France and Germany first developed the idea of holding the Conference. Invitations were issued in three stages: first to Great Britain, Belgium, the Netherlands, Portugal, Spain, and the United States; later, to Austria, Russia, Italy, Denmark, Sweden, and Norway; and finally to Turkey. *See* CROWE, *supra* note 157, at 220. Elias asserts that China was a party to the Treaty, *see* ELIAS, *supra* note 8, at 20, but no Chinese representative appears on the list of Signatories appearing in the preamble to the original Treaty. *See* General Act of the Berlin Conference on West Africa, Feb. 26 1885, *translated in* Official Documents, 1909 AM. J. INT'L L. 7 (Vol. 3, Supp.) [hereinafter General Act].

211. *See* CROWE, *supra* note 157, at 105–18.

212. *See* General Act, *supra* note 210, art. 1.

abuse as European trading companies or adventurers such as Henry Morton Stanley[213] could enter into "treaties," which they claimed provided them with rights, if not actual sovereignty, to vast areas of land. Thus the Berlin Conference, in addition to focusing on trade issues, sought to create a unified system by which claims could be asserted and recognized.

The underlying and crucial issue in this debate was the legal personality of African tribes. Despite the objections of jurists such as Westlake,[214] treaties with African tribes were the basis on which claims were made to African territory. This raised the familiar, and by now apparently insurmountable, problems of deciding the capacity of the African entity and the status of that entity within the overall political structure of the tribe.

The American representative to the Berlin Conference, Mr. Kasson, made an alternative proposal arguing that

> [m]odern international law follows closely a line which leads to the recognition of the right of native tribes to dispose freely of themselves and of their hereditary territory. In conformity with this principle my government would gladly adhere to a more extended rule, to be based on a principle which should aim at the voluntary consent of the natives whose country is taken possession of, in all cases where they had not provoked the aggression.[215]

Kasson's proposal was greeted cautiously; the conference "hesitated to express an opinion" on such a delicate matter,[216] and scholarly opinion was divided as to whether Kasson's proposal nevertheless reflected the practice of states.[217] On the one hand, Kasson's proposal would have severely and unacceptably curtailed colonial powers if the principle had indeed been implemented so as to require scrupulous evidence of proper consent.[218] On the other hand, absent such an inquiry into the validity of the ostensible consent, it simply offered a

213. Stanley, acting on behalf of the International Association of the Congo headed by King Leopold II, King of the Belgians, made hundreds of treaties with native "sovereigns" in the region and thus gained control over large portions of the Congo basin that eventually formed the Congo Free State. Leopold was the personal sovereign over the State whose existence was recognized by the powers at the Berlin Conference. *See* LINDLEY, *supra* note 20, at 112; CROWE, *supra* note 157, at 158–60.

214. Westlake argued that African tribes were too simple to understand the concept of sovereignty and hence were incapable of transferring it by treaty. *See* WESTLAKE, *supra* note 16, at 144–46.

215. WESTLAKE, *supra* note 16, at 138. For an illuminating discussion of this passage, see CRAWFORD, *supra* note 5, at 178–79. For Kasson's contribution to the Conference, see CROWE, *supra* note 157, at 97–98.

216. WESTLAKE, *supra* note 16, at 138.

217. *See* CRAWFORD, *supra* note 5, at 179. Incidentally, Mr. Kasson's proposal was never officially accepted. *See id.*

218. *See* WESTLAKE, *supra* note 16, at 139.

justification for entering into more treaties with African states, claiming that such treaties conformed with the scheme Kasson outlined.

Several jurists such as Westlake pointed out that Kasson's scheme was impractical and dangerous. Its proper implementation raised questions to which there were no clear answers.

> Is any territorial cession permitted by the ideas of the tribe? What is the authority—chief, elders, body of fighting men—if there is one, which those ideas point out as empowered to make the cession? With what formalities do they require it to be made, if they allow it to be made at all?[219]

There is more than a suggestion in Westlake that the individuals characterized as African chiefs in these treaties exploited all of these confusions for their own purposes.[220]

Overall, no clear procedure for acquiring valid title was laid down by the Conference. This same vagueness afflicted its attempt to clarify the issue of "effective occupation." The Conference basically stipulated that any party taking possession of a tract of land in Africa was required to notify all other members of this possession[221] and, further, was required to exercise its authority in its possessions so as to protect existing rights within the territory.[222] This was intended to prevent countries from making claims to territory based only on the most tenuous connections with that territory and to ensure that control was accompanied by international responsibility. The Conference was only partially successful in achieving these ambitions because Britain, which had the largest interests in Africa, opposed all efforts to impose greater responsibility on the colonizing powers.[223] These attempts to formulate rules for effective occupation acknowledged the lack of any precise, accepted, and workable principles regulating the colonial encounter. The best that could be achieved was to proceduralize the matter[224] by requiring states acquiring territorial interests to notify other signatories of their claims, which would enable these states to lodge

219. *Id.* at 139–40.

220. *See id.*

221. *See* General Act, *supra* note 210, ch. 6, art. 34. For discussion as to the problem of effective occupation, see CROWE, *supra* note 157, at 176–91.

222. *See* General Act, *supra* note 210, art. 35.

223. *See* CROWE, *supra* note 157, at 176–91. In particular, Britain sought to restrict the application of these principles to the coastal states in Africa and further prevented these principles from applying to protectorates.

224. This could be read as an example of a tendency that was noted by Koskenniemi: "The problem of order becomes a procedural problem. If only advanced mechanisms for sovereign cooperation and settlement are developed, material disagreements can be prevented from threatening the system." KOSKENNIEMI, APOLOGY, *supra* note 5, at 123.

any objections.[225] No clarity existed as to how or in which forum such claims were to be resolved.

This unsatisfactory resolution represented a fundamental irony for positivist jurisprudence. At various levels of their jurisprudence, positivists had sought to erase the problematic native from their scheme; the native was expelled from the family of nations and excised from history by positivist disregard for the four preceding centuries of diplomatic relations and was thereby excluded from the process of treaty making. Native resistance was silenced by the positivist practice of reading a treaty without regard to the violence and coercion that led to its formation. Despite all attempts to exclude Africans from the Conference, however, the identity of the African native became the central preoccupation of its deliberations over the question of systematizing territory. And despite positivist attempts to assume complete control over the identity of the native, the native remained unknowable in a way that threatened the stability and unity of Europe. Conventional histories of the Conference make the powerful point that Africans were excluded from its deliberations. The story of the Conference may also be written, however, from another perspective that focuses on the complex way in which the identity of the African was an enduring problem that haunted the proceedings of the Conference.[226]

The existence of unassimilability, the problems of native identity, and their effect in bringing to crisis the colonial will to power may well be worth examining and celebrating. Still, such a celebration must be tempered with the knowledge that whatever the disruptions inflicted on the logic of colonial narratives, these did little to ameliorate the real and violent consequences that followed for African societies.

Although Kasson's approach was criticized, subsequent practice suggests that *any* remotely legal explanation for the partition of Africa was inevitably based on his proposal.[227] Seen from the perspective that accepted the possibility of treaties between Africans and Europeans, consent as ostensibly granted by Africans became a complete reversal of what it was supposed to mean. Consent, rather than an expression of the free will of the relevant African party, was instead created in accordance with the exigencies of the situation. Consent was the basis of positivist jurisprudence, and the science of jurisprudence precisely determined whether such consent had led to the formation of certain rules that would then be binding on the state that had given consent. A rich and complex set of ideas—which are still an integral aspect of

225. The term used in the Act is "reclamations" rather than protest. General Act, *supra* note 210, art. 34.

226. *See* WESTLAKE, *supra* note 16, at 139–40.

227. *See* CRAWFORD, *supra* note 5, at 178–79 and sources cited therein, which include Lugard.

contemporary international legal jurisprudence—developed out of this set of considerations. Still, with regard to native consent, a completely different set of issues arose. Here, the jurist created consent and the writer created agency, as African chiefs, Indian princes, and Chinese emperors were attributed with powers to consent to various measures that benefited the European states. They were excluded from personality; when granted personality, this was in order to enable the formulation of a consistent jurisprudential system or to transfer the entitlement that the Europeans sought. Having articulated a legal framework for acquiring sovereignty over African territory, which was radically disconnected from the actual practice on which they purported to base their system,[228] positivists, in a now familiar reversal, discarded several important elements of their jurisprudence. Whereas previously they insisted that treaties could not be the basis for acquiring sovereignty over African territory, they now applied their science to the interpretation and application of treaties.

3. Justifying Colonialism: Trade, Humanitarianism, and the Civilizing Mission[229]

The Berlin Conference was perhaps the first occasion on which Europe went some way towards articulating a philosophy of colonialism that was appropriate for the late nineteenth century. This was a time when the colonial project went through a new phase because of the direct involvement of states in the furtherance of colonialism and because of the systematic economic exploitation of the colonies, which had led not only to intense inter-state rivalries, but also to the increasing importance of the colonies for the European economy.[230] The idea of the civilizing mission—of extending the Empire for the higher purpose of educating and rescuing the barbarian—had a very ancient lineage.[231] All imperial powers used versions of the civilizing mission. While this was always an important aspect of European attitudes to-

228. See CRAWFORD, *supra* note 5 at 178–79, on this issue.

229. "The conquest of the earth, which mostly means the taking it away from those who have a different complexion or slightly flatter noses than ourselves, is not a pretty thing when you look into it too much. What redeems it is the idea only. An idea at the back of it . . . ." JOSEPH CONRAD, HEART OF DARKNESS 21 (Ross C. Murfin ed., Bedford Books 1996) (1902).

230. There is a vast amount of literature regarding the economics of imperialism, ranging from the early work of J.A. Hobson to that of contemporary dependency theorists. For an overview, see, for example, SAMIR AMIN, IMPERIALISM AND UNEQUAL DEVELOPMENT (1977); MICHAEL BARRATT BROWN, THE ECONOMICS OF IMPERIALISM (1974); WALTER RODNEY, HOW EUROPE UNDERDEVELOPED AFRICA (1972).

231. For a study of how the modern European Empires modeled themselves after the Roman Empire and the Roman idea of what may be termed the civilizing mission, see ANTHONY PAGDEN, LORDS OF ALL THE WORLD: IDEOLOGIES OF EMPIRE IN SPAIN, BRITAIN AND FRANCE C.1500–C.1800 (1995). In particular, for his discussion of Cicero's version of the civilizing mission, see *id.* at 22–23.

wards imperial expansion in the preceding centuries,[232] it was in the nineteenth century that states took a particular and renewed interest in articulating the goals of their colonial project, which was now carried out principally by the state itself, as opposed to trading companies. Consequently, new challenges were posed to the way in which imperial states conceived of themselves and their colonies when the United Kingdom dissolved the East India Company and assumed direct responsibility for its Indian subjects.[233]

The humanitarian treatment of inferior and subject peoples was a further issue addressed by the Conference. Over the previous two centuries, international law had gradually abolished the slave trade. The Conference, while reiterating the necessity to stamp out the trade, went further. In his opening speech at the Conference, Prince Bismarck noted that "all the Governments invited share the wish to bring the natives of Africa within that pale of civilization by opening up the interior of the continent to commerce."[234] The British representative made similar remarks, warning of the dangers of completely unregulated trade and arguing for that type of trade that would "confer the advantages of civilization on the natives."[235] The Conference concluded that it had properly embodied these concerns in Article 6 of the Conference, which read, in part:

> All Powers exercising rights of sovereignty or an influence in the Said territories [the conventional basin of the Congo] engage themselves to watch over the conservation of the indigenous populations, and the amelioration of their moral and material conditions, and to strive for the suppression of slavery and especially the negro slave trade.[236]

These vaguely expressed concerns were only sporadically implemented;[237] indeed, the most notable achievement of the Conference was the creation of the Congo Free State, which was subsequently recognized as belonging to the personal sovereignty of King Leopold II of Belgium and soon became the setting of mass atrocities.[238] Nevertheless, the humanitarian rhetoric of the Conference was extremely important because it refined the justification for the colonial project. Trade

232. See, for example, the work of Vitoria in the 16th century.

233. This led Queen Victoria to declare that the Crown was as responsible toward its native Indian subjects as it was to all its other subjects. *See* QUINCY WRIGHT, MANDATES UNDER THE LEAGUE OF NATIONS 11 n.18 (1930).

234. LINDLEY, *supra* note 20, at 332.

235. *Id.*

236. General Act, *supra* note 210, art. 6.

237. Crowe, for example, asserts quite forcefully that humanitarian issues played only a small part in the Conference. *See* CROWE, *supra* note 157, at 3, 103–04.

238. *See* LINDLEY, *supra* note 20, at 112–13.

was not what it had been earlier, a means of simply maximizing profit and increasing national power. Rather, trade was an indispensable part of the civilizing mission itself; the expansion of commerce was the means by which the backward natives could be civilized. "Moral and material well-being" were the twin pillars of the program. This gave the whole rhetoric of trade a new and important impetus. Implicit within it was a new world view; it was not simply the case that independent communities would trade with each other. Now, because trade was the mechanism for advancement and progress, it was essential that trade be extended as far as possible into the interior of all these societies.

D. *Recognition and the Reconstruction of Positivism*

I have stressed and reiterated the importance of the concept of society because its significance for the whole edifice of positivist jurisprudence has not been properly appreciated. Although a fundamental part of the nineteenth-century positivist vocabulary, "society" has ceased to be a legal concept of any importance in contemporary discussions of international law. This is because recognition doctrine serves to obscure the role and function of "society" by presenting it as a creation of sovereignty. This maneuver is important for the purpose of this Article, since it obscures an understanding of society's operational role as a mechanism by which cultural assessments could be transformed into a legal status. Furthermore, presenting society as a creation of sovereignty suggests another way in which international law suppresses the colonial past at the doctrinal level. Recognition doctrine was fundamental not only to the task of assimilating the non-European world, but also to the very structure of the positivist legal system. Lorimer points to this in arguing that "recognition, in its various phases, constitutes the major premise of the positive law of nations when stated as a logical system."[239] The link between positivism and recognition may be traced both historically[240] and logically. In logical terms, Lorimer's assertion appears correct, in that the positivist emphasis on the sovereign as the fundamental basis of international law suggests that only the phenomena recognized by the sovereign become part of the legal universe.

Recognition doctrine is implicitly based on the assumption that a properly constituted sovereign exists. Only those principles created

239. LORIMER, *supra* note 14, at 103. Indeed, Lorimer commences his work by stating that the Law of Nations is divided into three leading doctrines: (1) recognition; (2) normal relations that result from the doctrine of recognition; and (3) abnormal relations that result from the doctrine of recognition. *See id.* at 3–4.

240. For an account of the beginnings of the doctrine of recognition in the 18th and early 19th centuries and how it corresponded with the emergence of positivism, see Alexandrowicz, *supra* note 121.

and accepted by sovereigns constitute law, and only those entities granted legal personality by the sovereign exist within the legal universe. Once established, the sovereign can reconstitute the legal universe. This view of recognition doctrine, however, conceals the complex process by which the sovereign is constituted in the first place.

The origins of sovereignty have always posed a major problem for the discipline, as suggested, for example, by contemporary debates about the right of self-determination. Within the framework of the colonial encounter, however, it is possible to trace how a self-conscious effort was made to constitute sovereignty in ways that were explicitly racialized. Austin argued that law was the command of the sovereign.[241] Positivists also focused on sovereignty, but, for them, the idea that sovereignty was the exclusive preserve of Europe was enabled by an elaboration of the concept of "society." Law only properly prevailed among the members of society, so for the positivists, the concept of law was intimately linked with the concept of society, rather than that of sovereignty as outlined by Austin.[242] The concept of society was crucial to the positivist scheme because it enabled a distinction to be made between different types of states. The effect of the distinction was to exclude non-European states from the family of nations and, hence, from the realm of sovereignty itself.[243] Seen in this way, the scope of "sovereignty" principally depended on the development of the "society doctrine." Reliance on the concept of society to establish sovereignty casts doubt on the claim that sovereignty is the core principle of international law and that everything within the international legal system derives from sovereignty.

The sovereign European state was established through reliance on the concept of society. Once constituted, however, the relationship is reversed and the sovereign asserts its supremacy by presenting itself as the means by which society comes into being and operates. Through recognition doctrine, sovereignty doctrine is reconstructed and presents itself as self-contained, coherent, comprehensive, and all-encompassing. A structure of power and decision-making is implicit in

241. *See* discussion *supra* notes 36–57 and accompanying text.

242. *See* HALL, *supra* note 140, at 40.

> It is scarcely necessary to point out that as international law is a product of the special civilisation of modern Europe, and forms a highly artificial system of which the principles cannot be supposed to be understood or recognised by countries differently civilised, such states only can be presumed to be subject to it as are inheritors of that civilisation. They have lived, and are living, under law, and a positive act of withdrawal would be required to free them from its restraints.

Id.

243. Crawford summarizes the situation in the 19th century as "[s]tates as such were not therefore necessarily members of the Society of Nations. Recognition, express or implied, solely created their membership and bound them to obey international law." CRAWFORD, *supra* note 5, at 13.

recognition doctrine because the power to "recognize" new states is vested in the states that are already "sovereign." The doctrine is premised on the existence of a sovereign state, whose will establishes law and whose actions may be subject to lawyers' inquiry.

Once the existence of the state is presumed, positivist jurisprudence is completely consistent. Once a particular group of states wins the title of "sovereign," an authoritative interpretive framework, employing clearly established categories of "backward" and "advanced," is established and used to determine the status of other, excluded states. Simple acceptance of this framework precludes inquiries into how this distinction was made and why one set of states becomes sovereign while the other does not, even though anthropological and historical research subversively suggests various disconcerting parallels between these apparently disparate societies.

My argument is that recognition doctrine was not merely, or even primarily, concerned with ascertaining or establishing the legal status of the entity under scrutiny; rather, it was about affirming the power of the European states to claim sovereignty, to reinforce their authority to make such determinations, and, consequently, to make sovereignty a possession that they could then proceed to dispense, deny, create, or grant partially. The history of sovereignty doctrine in the nineteenth century, then, is a history of the processes by which European states, by developing a complex vocabulary of cultural and racial discriminations, set about establishing and presiding over a system of authority by which they could determine who was and was not sovereign. Recognition does not so much resolve the problem of determining the status of unknown entities as obscure the history of the process by which this decision-making framework came into being.

Sovereignty is explicitly identified with particular cultural characteristics and a particular cultural process: that of Europe. The history of sovereignty, then, is equated with the creation of European civilization, and at the same time this becomes the conventional history of how international law became universal.

V. RECONCEPTUALIZING SOVEREIGNTY

A. *Colonialism and the Racialization of Sovereignty*

An examination of the foundations of positivist views of sovereignty and their complex relationship with colonialism suggests new ways of approaching traditional understandings of sovereignty doctrine and the character of sovereignty as it was inherited by the non-European world.

In attempting to formulate a new, scientific international law, the jurists of the nineteenth century articulated a formalist model of sovereignty: an absolute set of powers bound by no higher authority and properly detached from all the imprecise claims of morality and justice. This model of sovereignty has been the subject of considerable and important critique. The fundamental problem with this model, which was evident from the time it was first articulated, was how order could be created among sovereign states in the absence of an overarching sovereign to articulate and enforce the relevant law authoritatively. The conundrum of this image of sovereignty has been, in one way or another, the central preoccupation of the discipline. This is suggested not merely by scholarly works, but by the manner in which the discipline is introduced in standard textbooks such as Henkin's *International Law*.[244] Important theoretical works by scholars such as Franck, Carty, Kennedy, and Koskenniemi elaborate in various ways on problems arising from this framework.[245]

A major concern of this Article is to identify what this model of sovereignty excludes. Although this framework plays a significant role in international legal thinking, the relationship between sovereignty and the non-European world cannot be properly understood within it. The interaction between European and non-European societies in the colonial encounter was an interaction not between equal sovereign states, but rather between sovereign European states and non-European states denied sovereignty. The conventional way to account for this relationship is by recourse to recognition doctrine[246] and to the "Expansion of International Society," an ambiguous, euphemistic, and somewhat misleading term that refers not to an open process by which the autonomy and integrity of non-European states were accepted, but to the colonial process by which Asian and African societies were made to comply with European standards as the price of membership into the family of nations.

The paradigm of "order among sovereign states" excludes from critical inquiry the processes that I have attempted to trace here: (1) the process by which non-European states were deemed lacking in sovereignty and thus excluded from the family of nations and of law; and (2) the racialization of the vocabulary of the period, not only in the explicit distinctions between civilized and uncivilized, advanced and barbaric, but also in the integration of these distinctions into the very

244. *See* HENKIN ET AL., *supra* note 4.

245. *See* THOMAS FRANCK, THE POWER OF LEGITIMACY AMONG NATIONS (1990); CARTY, *supra* note 5, at 4; Kennedy, *supra* note 5, at 4; KOSKENNIEMI, APOLOGY, *supra* note 5, at 4. The innovative contributions of these scholars concern the analysis of the ingenious (Kennedy) but ultimately unconvincing and indeterminate (Koskenniemi) ways in which this problem is resolved. Carty focuses on the failure of international law to meet the essential requirements of the positivist notion of a legal system.

246. *See* discussion *supra* notes 239–243 and accompanying text for the way in which recognition doctrine restores the integrity of the positivist framework.

foundations of the discipline, namely the ostensibly neutral concepts of "law," "society," and "sovereignty." The "order" paradigm fails to account for the role of race and culture, not only in the application of these concepts, but also in their very formation. I argue, by contrast, that sovereignty can only be understood in terms of its complex relationship with colonialism and the racial and cultural distinctions it generated and reinforced. At the simplest level, the connection between sovereignty and culture was embodied by the fundamental positivist proposition that only European states could be sovereign. This complete identification of Europe with sovereignty was maintained, reiterated, and reinforced at a number of different levels. Not only was the non-European excluded from the realm of sovereignty, but European culture and society were naturalized. Hence Lawrence argued that European states had belonged to the family of nations "since time immemorial."[247] Lawrence continues, "[M]any of them existed before the great majority of [modern international law's] rules came into being. There was no need for them to be received formally among its subjects. Anything like a ceremony of initiation would have been wholly inapplicable to their case."[248]

The naturalist notion of a mythic state of nature is replaced by a positivist notion of a mythic age when European states constituted a self-evident family of nations. Lawrence emphatically argues that the origins of European supremacy are beyond history and inquiry and incapable of identification. The appeal to "time immemorial" precludes inquiry into how European states were deemed sovereign in the first place.[249] Under this scheme, history is disregarded, and all of the interactions between European and non-European societies in the previous four centuries, which suggested the existence of a family of nations that included non-European societies, are largely dismissed.

In effect, Europe was the subject of sovereignty and the rest of the world was the object of European sovereignty. Acceptance of these premises—the primacy of sovereignty and the identification of Europe as exclusively sovereign—creates a conceptual framework that dictates that the only possible history of the non-European world is the history of its absorption into the European world in order to move towards acquiring sovereignty. Two different dimensions of sovereignty can be seen when studied from this point of view: since European sovereignty is presumed, the European issue is how conflicts between sovereign states may be resolved in the absence of an overarching sovereign; the problem for the non-European world, by contrast, is how to acquire

247. LAWRENCE, *supra* note 17, at 84.

248. *Id.*

249. Writers such as Westlake were insistent that the origins of sovereignty could not subjected to inquiry. *See* WESTLAKE, *supra* note 16, at 134–36.

sovereignty. This argument creates, in effect, something like a linear, evolutionary scheme in which the non-European world is the past and the European world the future. Thus, while the non-European world may illuminate aspects of the past of the European world that may otherwise remain hidden, the complex work of the future lies in the elaboration of established sovereignty, an elaboration that takes the form of the conceptual problems generated by the interaction of sovereign European states.

Sovereignty manifested itself quite differently in the non-European world than in the European world. First, since the non-European world was not "sovereign," virtually no legal restrictions were imposed on the actions of European states with respect to non-European peoples. European states could engage in massive violence, invariably justified as necessary to pacify the natives and followed by the project of reshaping those societies in accordance with their particular vision of the world. Sovereignty was therefore aligned with existing European ideas of social order, political organization, progress, and development. This points to a second and implicit difference between sovereignty in Europe and sovereignty in the non-European world. In Europe, nineteenth-century positivism created a situation in which sovereignty was supreme and a sovereign's actions within its own territory were beyond scrutiny. In contrast, lacking sovereignty, non-European states exercised no rights recognizable by international law over their own territory. Any legal restrictions on the actions of European states towards non-European states resulted from contentions among European states regarding the same territory, not from the rights of the non-European states. This is evident in the partition of Africa, which was determined in accordance with the needs of the major European states.

The intent to erase any independent identity or sovereignty in the non-European world pervades positivism at virtually every level of its jurisprudence: in the distinction between civilized and non-civilized states; in the doctrine of *terra nullius*; in the attempt to suppress the long history of treaty practice between European and non-European peoples; and inevitably, as Westlake points out, in the very process of acquiring sovereignty.

> The form which has been given to the question, namely what facts are necessary and sufficient in order that an uncivilised region may be internationally appropriated in sovereignty to a particular state? implies that it is only the recognition of such sovereignty by the members of the international society which concerns us, that of uncivilised natives international law takes no account.[250]

---

250. WESTLAKE, *supra* note 16, at 136.

As a consequence of the positivist conception of sovereignty, the character of sovereignty in the non-European world was profoundly different from its character in the European world. Sovereignty represents at the most basic level an assertion of power and authority, a means by which a people may preserve and assert their distinctive culture. For the non-European world, however, sovereignty was the complete negation of independent power, authority, and authenticity. This was not only because European sovereignty was used as a mechanism of suppression and management but also because acquiring sovereignty was equated with adopting European civilization. In effect, for the non-European society, personhood as recognized internationally was achieved precisely when the society ceased to have an independent existence, when it was absorbed into European colonial empires or when it profoundly altered its own cultural practices and political organizations. This paradox and irony is nicely if unselfconsciously suggested by Oppenheim's discussion of the transfer of sovereignty by cession. "[C]ession of territory made to a member of the Family of Nations by a State as yet outside that family is real cession and a concern of the Law of Nations, since such State becomes through the treaty of cession in some respects a member of that family."[251] The sovereignty acquired by the non-European state, then, was only tenuously connected with its own identity. This artificially created sovereignty reflected the interests and world view of Europe, and it emerged and is inextricably linked with the exploitation and domination of non-European peoples.[252]

Sovereignty for the non-European world consisted of alienation and subordination rather than empowerment. This point emerges powerfully from a study of positivist approaches to treaty-making which clearly demonstrate that the only occasion on which native "sovereignty" or "personality" was bestowed or recognized was in a context where that personality enabled the native to transfer title of territory or to grant rights to sovereignty itself. The basic point is that the development of the idea of sovereignty in relation to the non-European world occurs in terms of its ability to alienate its lands and rights.[253] This is a radical contrast with the elaboration of sovereignty in the European world where the question is: are there any limits at all on state sovereignty? Sovereignty in the European and non-European

251. OPPENHEIM, *supra* note 19, at 286.

252. For a powerful argument as to the continuing effects of this artificiality on African states, see Mutua, *supra* note 8. The problem remains as to whether it is possible or desirable to return to some "natural" identity.

253. This same maneuver is evident even in naturalist works. For example, Vitoria's apparently novel argument that the Indians of the New World are human beings and thus possess personality results in the Indians being bound by a universal "natural law" that in effect reflects European standards and values. *See* Anghie, *Vitoria*, *supra* note 9.

worlds are characterized, then, in two conceptual frameworks that are inverses of each other and, in important ways, are mutually exclusive.

The peculiar character of sovereignty in the non-European context is further evident in protectorate arrangements. At first glance, it may appear that such arrangements recognized and gave effect to native sovereignty. It is clear, however, that native sovereignty was accommodated largely to the extent that this was compatible with the interests of colonial powers. When vital issues were at stake, European states simply assumed sovereignty over that issue. Simply put, granting sovereignty to the natives was precisely the means by which protecting states extended their authority and control over the natives. Similar arguments may be made with regard to consent; consent was the very bedrock of the positivist system, and the whole science of positivism was dedicated to identifying whether in fact a state had consented to be bound by a particular principle. In the case of the non-European world, Kasson's apparently well-meaning attempt to make native consent an integral part of the scheme facilitated the construction of the pretence that natives had in fact consented to their own dispossession.[254] In reality, native consent was not so much an expression of an independent will as a construct dictated by the colonial scramble. Rather than providing the stable foundation of the international legal system, in the non-European context, native consent was a variable entity that could be manipulated to give the system an appearance of coherence.

These inversions of sovereignty were a manifestation of a more profound change in the jurists' understanding of sovereignty resulting from the colonial encounter. Since European sovereignty was placed beyond scrutiny and inquiry, it was principally through the operations of sovereignty in the non-European world that European states acquired a new, self-conscious understanding of the origins of sovereignty and its potential operations. Some sense of this was conveyed by Westlake in his discussion of the acquisition of territorial sovereignty, "[T]he title to territorial sovereignty in old countries not being capable of discussion apart from the several dealings, as cession or conquest, which transfer it, we must turn to new [i.e., non-European] countries."[255]

As in evolutionary theory, it was by examining the primitive that the modern acquires a better, clearer sense of itself. The history of the

254. It is difficult to know what to make of Kasson's position. On the one hand, it could suggest the importance of proper treaty making based on genuine consent, on the other, as the representative of the United States, Kasson knew of the types of treaties that had been entered into, and they were absurdly one-sided. One can only assume that Kasson's view of the world was such that he thought it only natural that African tribes would wish to surrender their sovereignty to the "International Association of the Congo," King Leopold's vehicle of conquest.

255. WESTLAKE, *supra* note 16, at 134.

origins of sovereignty could now be written through an examination of its operations in the non-European world. And with the peculiar thrill that accompanies the magnification and universalization of the self, the history that emerged from this inquiry confirmed that the history of sovereignty was the coming into being and expansion of European civilization and, moreover, that progress suggested an inevitable evolution towards that highest point.

Furthermore, Westlake suggests that the colonies played an important role in the discipline of international law, not simply because they offered an arena in which sovereignty could exercise itself in ways that were denied to it in Europe, but also because it was through an examination of the acquisition of sovereignty—whether through protectorates, annexation, or meeting the standard of civilization—that jurists could self-consciously grasp sovereignty as a *mechanism*, the characteristics of which could be both theoretically understood and practically developed precisely through its operation in the "new countries" of the non-European world. Sovereignty, in the case of non-European societies, did not arise "naturally"; rather, it had to be bestowed. Law was the creation of "positive institutions," and international law is a "highly artificial system," argues Hall.[256] The nineteenth century was the age of science, during which industry was applied for the betterment and progress of human society. We see here the suggestion that international law is not merely a science but a technology.[257] As a technology, it could help realize the Victorian ideals of progress, optimism, and liberalism,[258] which, when applied specifically to the non-European world, meant the civilizing of the benighted native peoples.

In summary, there are two distinctive models of sovereignty that developed in the nineteenth century: one, the standard model, which focuses on the problem of order among sovereign states, cannot satisfactorily account for the process by which European sovereignty became "universalized"; the other, which I have attempted to develop here, focuses on the problem of cultural difference. This Article has attempted to elaborate the uniqueness of the second model, and I argue that it is a fundamental mistake to see the second model as subsumed in some way by the first. These two models cannot be seen in isolation; rather, they are inextricably interrelated because they emerged at the same period out of the same philosophical matrix of positivism. Any attempt to outline a comprehensive theory of sovereignty surely must take this interdependence into account and resist

256. HALL, *supra* note 140, at 40.

257. But it is a technology of legal norms; the major advance with pragmatism is the understanding that the technology could be elaborated by using legal norms to create institutions that had a far greater range and flexibility.

258. For a searching study of the "Victorian tradition," see Koskenniemi, *Lauterpacht*, *supra* note 5.

the prevailing tendency to assimilate the unique history of the non-European world into the conventional model.

B. The Legacy of the Nineteenth Century

The jurisprudence of the nineteenth century has had profound and enduring consequences for the non-European world. Basically, it presented non-European societies with the fundamental contradiction of having to comply with authoritative European standards in order to win recognition and assert themselves. The implications of this situation are powerfully summarized by Fanon:

> Man is human only to the extent to which he tries to impose his existence on another man in order to be recognized by him. As long as he has not been effectively recognized by the other, that other will remain the theme of his actions. It is on that other being, on recognition by that other being, that his own human worth and reality depend. It is in that other being in whom the meaning of his life is condensed.[259]

Consequently, for the non-European world, the achievement of sovereignty was a profoundly ambiguous development, as it involved alienation rather than empowerment, and presupposed the submission to alien standards rather than the affirmation of authentic identity.

Furthermore, as R.P. Anand has argued, "having lost their international personality, the Asian states could not play any active role in the development of international law during the most creative period of its history."[260] Anand refers to many rules of international law, such as the rules of state responsibility, which were explicitly devised to facilitate the economic exploitation of non-European territories.

The question of the enduring effects on non-European societies of the history of exclusion is related to the issue of the legacy of the nineteenth century for the discipline as a whole. Lawrence's definition of international law reflects both the view prevalent at the time and the fundamental nexus between race and law: "International law may be defined as the rules which determine the conduct of the general body of civilized states in their dealings with one another."[261] A century later, international law is defined as "the law of the international community of states" by Henkin and his colleagues in their major textbook on the subject.[262] The notion of community is retained, but no

259. FRANTZ FANON, BLACK SKIN, WHITE MASKS 216–17 (Charles Lam Markham trans., Grove Press 1967) (1952).

260. ANAND, *supra* note 8, at 20.

261. LAWRENCE, *supra* note 17, at 1.

262. *See* HENKIN ET AL., *supra* note 4, at xvii.

distinctions are made between civilized and non-civilized states. The international community of the late twentieth century appears open, cosmopolitan, accommodating, and neutral; sovereignty today is a set of powers and competencies that can be enjoyed by all states regardless of their particular cultural identities.

Profound changes in international law have occurred in the intervening years, and the nineteenth century is something of an embarrassment to the discipline for a number of reasons. Its monolithic view of sovereignty, its formalism, and its rigidity, were important causes of the First World War in the view of a number of distinguished inter-war jurists such as Lauterpacht and Alvarez, who set about the task of constructing a New International Law.[263] Its complete complicity with the colonial project has led to its denunciation as an international law of imperialism. Subsequent generations of international lawyers have strenuously attempted to distance the discipline from that period in much the same way that positivists distanced themselves from naturalists. And, as with that previous attempt at distancing, the results are ambiguous.

My argument has been that the modern discipline operates very much within the framework it has inherited from the nineteenth century. The problem of how to establish order in the absence of an overarching sovereign is a problem that arises with the articulation of the positivist framework. Since its articulation, it has been and continues to be a problem that has preoccupied both mainstream and critical theorizing about the discipline. In making this point I am not in any way seeking to diminish the extraordinary or defining importance of this body of work. Rather, I am arguing that an exclusive focus on this framework cannot provide an understanding of the history of the relationship between international law and the non-European world. The non-European world, relegated to the geographical periphery, is also relegated to the margins of theory. The specific historical experience of European states is generalized and universalized by its metamorphosis into the defining theoretical preoccupation of the discipline.[264]

Nor does it appear sufficient to me to claim that the racism of the nineteenth century has been transcended by the achievement of sovereign statehood by the non-European world. It is true that international law is now more open and cosmopolitan; moreover, international law has promoted the process of decolonization by formulating doctrines of self-determination where once it formulated doctrines of annexation

263. *See* Kennedy, *supra* note 5, at 102.

264. Underlying the conventional approach to the universalization of international law is the tendency to simply treat it as an accomplished historical reality of no larger theoretical significance. Thus there appears to be in operation a further dichotomy whereby Europe constitutes the "theory," and what occurs in the non-European world is simply secondary.

and *terra nullius*. Still, this movement towards the decolonization of international law was by no means universally acclaimed. In the 1960s, when it was clear that the emergence of developing nations would change radically the character of the international system, a number of eminent international lawyers voiced concern about the dilution effect of these new states on an international law that was, in the final analysis, European.[265]

The question that remained was the possibility and effectiveness of reversing the consequences of colonialism. The optimistic international lawyers of the 1960s, even those notable scholars from developing nations, who were the most trenchant critics of the Eurocentric character of international law, were hopeful that the acquisition of sovereignty by developing nations and participation in international legal forums would result in the creation of a truly universal, just, and equal international system.[266] Thus Guha-Roy, while pointing to the obvious inequities of the doctrines of state responsibility, argued that developing nations were intent, not on repudiating the whole of international law, but on repudiating those rules that facilitated colonialism. The civilized/non-civilized distinction featured in the doctrines and treaties of the nineteenth century was generally expunged from the vocabulary of international law.[267] It is clear that scholars from developing nations never achieved the significant reforms that they desired. For instance, the drive by developing countries to create a "New International Economic Order" ended, on the whole, in failure.

The alternative position is that the nineteenth century remains an integral part of contemporary international law. On a material level, the systems of economic and political inequality created by colonialism under the auspices of nineteenth-century international law continue to operate despite the ostensible change of legal regime.[268] It is doubtful whether a discipline whose fundamental concepts, "sovereignty" and

265. *See* ANAND, *supra* note 8, at 6–9. The scholars discussed include J.H.W. Verzijl, Josef Kunz, and Julius Stone. The implicit view was that international law should continue to be European despite the repressive effects of such a policy. On the other hand, a number of Western-based lawyers, such as Richard Falk, were consistently and forcefully sympathetic to the cause of decolonization. *See* Richard Falk, *The New States and International Legal Order*, 118 Recueil de Cours 1 (1966-II).

266. I rely here on the distinction developed by James Gathii between weak and strong forms of anti-colonial scholarship. Gathii elaborates:

> The *weak* form of anti-colonial scholarship is basically integrationist: meaning that it is largely complimentary of the liberatory claims of principles such as self-determination as uncompromising tenets of world peace and indicators of the rejection of the colonial experience and specifically as an expression of the value these principles uphold against the unacceptable repression of non-European humanity under colonialism, slavery, and other forms of discrimination and repression of the non-European personality.

Gathii, *supra* note 8, at 189.

267. Some vestiges are still evident, as in art. 38(1)(c) of the Statute of the International Court of Justice.

268. *See* Gathii, *supra* note 8.

"law," had been so explicitly and clearly formulated in ways that embodied distinctions and discriminations that furthered colonialism could be readily reformed by the simple expedient of excising or reformulating the offending terminology.[269] Thus, the International Court of Justice may theoretically draw upon "the general principles of law recognized by civilized nations," where "civilized" must now be understood to mean all nations. But an examination of the recent jurisprudence of the Court suggests that little effort has been made to draw upon the legal traditions and systems of non-Western peoples in the administration of international justice.[270] International law remains emphatically European in this respect, regardless of its supposed receptivity to other legal thinking.

The legacies of the nineteenth century appear in even more fundamental ways: despite recognizing that the treaties were unequal and often extracted by force, these treaties continue to be legally binding. The doctrine of *terra nullius* is now understood to have been used over the centuries to dispossess and destroy indigenous peoples throughout the non-European world. Nevertheless, these doctrines are not so much confronted as evaded through reinterpretation of the relevant facts. For example, the argument is made that more recent anthropological evidence suggests the Aboriginal peoples of Australia had a form of "political organization," as a consequence of which the *terra nullius* doctrine could not be said to apply to Australia. While the operation of the doctrine is thus denied, the doctrine itself is rarely dismissed as outmoded because of the racist ways in which it has been almost invariably deployed.[271] Similarly, in the Western Sahara Case, the International Court of Justice asserted that the Western Sahara could not have been *terra nullius* because the people who lived there did in fact have a form of political organization.[272] Thus, the doctrines consolidated by nineteenth-century jurists continue, in important ways, to

269. I have tried to argue this point at greater length in the context of an actual international dispute in which the use of the supposedly empowering language of "self-determination" and "permanent sovereignty over natural resources" limit the character of the claims that can be made. *See* Anghie, *Nauru*, *supra* note 9. Critical race theory provides a perceptive and powerful analysis of the continuation of racist and discriminatory practices through the application of a legal vocabulary that has been ostensibly sanitized. *See* Crenshaw, *supra* note 10; WILLIAMS, *supra* note 10.

270. Certain notable exceptions to this are evident. Judge Weeramantry's decisions, in particular, have made far-reaching attempts to incorporate non-European legal traditions into the jurisprudence of the Court.

271. *See, e.g.*, Anthony Mason, *The Rights of Indigenous Peoples in Lands Once Part of the Old Dominions of the Crown*, 46 INT'L & COMP. L.Q. 812 (1997); Gerry Simpson, Mabo, *International Law*: Terra Nullius *and the Stories of Settlement: An Unresolved Jurisprudence*, 19 MELB. U. L. REV. 195, 196 (1993); Nehal Bhuta, Mabo, Wik *and the Art of Paradigm Management*, 22 MELB. U. L. REV. 24, 36 (1998). As Bhuta and Simpson point out, even when jurists reject *terra nullius* as a proper basis for obtaining title, they have great difficulties in articulating a legally coherent alternative account of how sovereignty was acquired.

272. Western Sahara (Advisory Opinion) 1975 I.C.J. 12, 39 (Oct. 16).

establish the framework within which indigenous peoples struggle to assert their rights. Jurists and courts attempting to reverse the effects of these laws are often compelled to do so within these established frameworks.

The question is not so much whether the nineteenth century has been transcended but how its continuing effects within the contemporary legal system may be obscured. Any tendency to treat the nineteenth century as being only of historical interest must be treated cautiously. As I have attempted to argue, there appears to be an inherent reflex within international law to conceal the colonial past on which its entire structure is based. The same reflex may be seen at the doctrinal level, for example, in the way that the construction of "law" depends on a notion of "society." Once that construction has served its purpose, it is inverted by way of a reconstructed jurisprudence in which "society" has been successfully constituted as a function of law. On a larger scale, as discussed earlier, positivists vehemently set out to detach themselves from their naturalist past. The process of distancing and suppressing the past is a common feature of the discipline, and a ritual enacted whenever it attempts to renew and revive itself. The nineteenth century exists within the discipline in a way suggested by Freud, who asserted in *Civilization and Its Discontents*:

> But have we a right to assume the survival of something that was originally there, alongside of what was later derived from it? Undoubtedly. There is nothing strange in such a phenomenon, whether in the mental field or elsewhere. In the animal kingdom we hold to the view that the most highly developed species we have proceeded from the lowest; and yet we find all the simple forms still in existence today.[273]

Positivism and the nineteenth century are an integral part of the contemporary discipline. Simplifying considerably, the nineteenth century could be said to embody a particular set of attitudes and methods: it posits an essentialist dichotomy between the non-European and the European; it characterizes relations between these entities to be inherently antagonistic; it establishes a hierarchy between these entities, suggesting that one is advanced, just, and authoritative while the other is backward and barbaric; it asserts that the only history that may be written of the backward is in terms of its progress towards the advanced; it silences the backward and denies it any subjectivity or autonomy; it assumes and promotes the centrality of the civilized and legitimizes the conquest and dispossession of the backward; and it con-

273. Sigmund Freud, CIVILIZATION AND ITS DISCONTENTS 15 (James Strachey ed. & trans. 1961) (1930).

templates no other approaches to solve the problems of society than those that the civilized have formulated. Many of these elements are evident in the work of prominent international relations scholars, from Samuel Huntington's influential argument regarding "The Clash of Civilizations,"[274] to Francis Fukuyama's assertions as to "The End of History."[275] There is a danger that the suggestive work being done on the liberal peace, which relies on the distinction between liberal and non-liberal states, could embody and reproduce some of the elements and attitudes of the nineteenth century.[276]

Equally important, it must be noted that nineteenth-century attitudes are by no means peculiar to relations between European and non-European peoples. Many of the Asian and African societies colonized in the nineteenth century had previously been involved in imperial projects themselves. Further, it appears to be an enduring and unfortunate truth that non-European states that have been the victims of colonialism often have no inhibition from themselves becoming colonial oppressors.

VI. CONCLUSION

The interpretation of nineteenth-century international law, as developed in this Article, is based on a departure from two of the basic premises of the period's conventional understandings. First, I have argued that the colonial encounter, far from being peripheral to the making of international law, has been central to the formation of the discipline. By this I mean not merely the specific doctrines of the discipline, but its informing philosophy: positivism. Second, I have departed from the dominant theoretical paradigm of the discipline, which focuses on the problem of order among sovereign states in an attempt to reflect the realities of the colonial encounter. By adopting the model of cultural difference, it becomes possible to examine the complex relationship between culture and sovereignty and, specifically, the manner in which sovereignty became identified with the cultural practices of Europe. I have argued that a failure to appreciate this relationship results in a rather limited understanding of sovereignty and

---

274. SAMUEL P. HUNTINGTON, THE CLASH OF CIVILIZATONS AND THE REMAKING OF WORLD ORDER (1996).

275. FRANCIS FUKUYAMA, THE END OF HISTORY AND THE LAST MAN (1992).

276. Notwithstanding the respect they accorded one another, liberal states have historically engaged in colonial wars and justified them as advancing the liberal values embodied in the civilizing mission. This phenomenon of "liberal imperialism" was recognized by Michael W. Doyle in a seminal article on the subject of liberal peace. *See* Michael W. Doyle, *Kant, Liberal Legacies, and Foreign Affairs, Part 2*, 12 PHIL. & PUB. AFF. 323, 331 (1983). On the implications of the enormous body on the liberal peace on international law, see Anne-Marie Slaughter, *International Law in a World of Liberal States*, 6 EUR. J. INT'L L. 503 (1995).

its operations, as well as a deficient grasp of the processes and mechanisms that resulted in the universalization of international law.

This alternative framework may clear the way for a new and different interpretation of the period and a subtler understanding of its enduring effects, not merely on non-European societies, but also on the discipline itself. This in turn may assist in the important and as yet unaddressed task of writing alternative histories of the discipline. These histories might focus, for example, on the resistances of the non-European peoples and the strategies they used to combat colonialism. Despite its pretences to coherence and comprehensiveness, positivist jurisprudence was riddled with contradictions and uncertainties and, I argue, never succeeded in properly defining and placing native personality. It is in the contradictions of conventional jurisprudence that alternative histories responsive to the non-European voices excluded from traditional histories may be written.

The alternative framework developed here calls also for a deeper examination of the question of how sovereignty could be used by the non-European world to advance its own interests. As a number of eminent scholars have argued, positivism and nineteenth-century international law crippled the non-European world. For these scholars, the problem arises because of the selective and discriminatory application of the neutral concept of sovereignty. According to this view, the problem is not embodied in the concept of sovereignty itself, but rather in the fact that non-European people are denied sovereignty. My argument is, by contrast, that the concepts themselves are far from neutral, that they are racialized and contain within them the discrimination that non-European people have attempted to contest. An appreciation of the way in which the very vocabulary of international law was racialized from its inception raises important questions about the ways in which sovereignty operates.

Furthermore, this Article is an attempt to make the experience and the specificity of the colonial encounter a subject of theoretical scrutiny as opposed to historical interest. It is unclear to me how a comprehensive understanding of the discipline could be achieved otherwise, given that the encounter was, as I have attempted to demonstrate, central to the formation of the discipline.

More generally, the nineteenth century offers us an example of a much broader theme: the importance of the existence of the "other" for the progress and development of the discipline itself. Seen from this perspective, the nineteenth century is both distinctive and conventional. Its method, focus, and techniques are in many ways unique. But in another respect, the nineteenth century is simply one example of the nexus between international law and the civilizing mission. The same mission was implemented by the vocabulary of naturalism in sixteenth-century international law. Furthermore, the succeeding paradigm of pragmatism, which developed in the inter-war period, was similarly preoccupied with furthering the civilizing mission even as it condemned nineteenth-century positivism for being formalist and colonial. Thus, the only thing unique about the nineteenth century is that it explicitly adopted the civilizing mission and reflected these goals in its very vocabulary. The more alarming and likely possibility is that the civilizing mission is inherent in one form or another in the principal concepts and categories that govern our existence: ideas of modernity, progress, development, emancipation, and rights. The enormous task of identifying these biases and ridding the discipline of them continues, as does the related task of constructing an international law that fulfils its promise of advancing the cause of justice.

I have argued that because sovereignty was shaped by the colonial encounter, its exercise often reproduced the inequalities inherent in that encounter. But the broader point is that sovereignty is a flexible instrument that readily lends itself to the powerful imperatives of the civilizing mission, in part because through that mission, sovereignty extends and expands its reach and scope. For this reason, the essential structure of the civilizing mission may be reconstructed in the contemporary vocabulary of human rights, governance, and economic liberalization. In this larger sense, then, the jurisprudence of the nineteenth century is both a distinctive and yet entirely familiar part of international law.

Part VI
Is International Law Just?

[16]

Is Justice Relevant to the International Legal System?*

*Thomas M. Franck***

When speaking of law, it is usual for the student of legal teleology to focus on its *legitimacy* and its *justice*. I have elsewhere[1] proposed a set of indicators by which to measure the legitimacy of the system of rules among states.[2] In that discourse legitimacy was defined as the perception that a rule or rule-making or rule-applying institution was derived or acting in accordance with agreed principles of right process. I also argued that the extent to which a rule is perceived to be legitimate by those to whom it is addressed will affect the rule's capacity to exert a pull towards voluntary compliance. This observed effect of legitimacy is particularly germane to the international system because of the absence of superior coercive force to compel obedience to rules. In the *domestic* legal system of nations, justice is seen to join legitimacy in exerting a pull towards voluntary compliance. That is, persons tend to be more willing to obey laws when those laws have been enacted, applied and interpreted legitimately, in accordance with agreed notions of right process *and when the rules are seen to promote fairness in the distribution of rights, entitlements, benefits and duties*. By contrast, the *international* system differs from the *domestic* legal order of states not only because of the former's relative lack of institutionalized rule-supportive coercion, but because, in the international community, justice does not seem to exert a pull to compliance on states comparable to its effect on individuals in national communities. If this is a correct observation, legitimacy is the dominant and perhaps sole factor in the international system capable of creating a genuine sense of obligation.

The exposed role of legitimacy and the minimal role of justice distinguish the international rule system from its domestic counterparts. It is not entirely an agreeable task to argue that justice is largely irrelevant to the international rule system, but it is necessary to do so if the dynamic of that system is to be understood, studied, and, gradually, reformed. That is this essay's enterprise. This limited relevance of justice is demonstrable both theoretically and functionally or operationally. The *theoretical* reasons are derived from the priority which states still attach to certainty, predictability and order—as opposed to fairness—in their interactions in a world in which the dangers of uncertainty, unpredictability and chaos are better understood and appreciated than those of unfairness. The

* This essay is based in part on materials in a forthcoming book: T. Franck, The Power of Legitimacy Among Nations (to be published by Oxford in 1990). For an earlier draft of this essay, see Franck & Hawkins, *Justice in the International System*, 10 MICH. J. INT'L L. 127 (1989).

** Professor of Law and Director, Center for International Studies, New York University School of Law.

1 Franck, *Legitimacy in the International System*, 82 AM. J. INT'L L. 705 (1988).

2 These indicators are: determinacy, symbolic validation, coherence and adherence. *See id.* at 712.

very notion of the *state* embodies unfair inequalities in life-prospects which are controlled and preordained by the rules of nationality. These arbitrary inequities are accepted, however, by the masses of all states as a trade-off for the peace, order and good government which they believe are attainable objects of a system of sovereign states. That such belief may well be quixotic romanticism does little to undermine its contemporary power, not least in the newly decolonized nations that are most egregiously deprived by its operation. The *operational* reasons will be considered in this essay. In it we will examine justice theory, as it has developed in modern jurisprudence, demonstrating its inapplicability to the community of nations at its present condition of evolution. Both the theoretical and operational analyses end with the same conclusion: that a state system is inherently inconsistent with the idea of justice.

Operationally, it comes to this: *justice can only be said to be done to persons, not to such collective entities as states*. Of course, it is possible to say that the Treaty of Versailles did an "injustice" to Germany at the end of the First World War. To the extent that all Germans suffered from the inflation, unemployment and social unravelling which followed the treaty's imposition of huge reparations and their concomitant deprivations, the statement may be useful as metaphorical shorthand for the wrongs imposed on the people. Even so, the metaphor of a suffering Germany is misleading, if only because some Germans prospered and profited at the same time others were being severely deprived. An aggregate concept of justice and injustice thus distorts reality. The real injustice of Versailles can only be accounted in units of suffering by individuals, not by some imaginary suffering of that inanimate aggregation known as "the state."

Since one can only talk metaphorically of justice among states, it is difficult to say anything meaningful or true about the justice of the international rule system. At its present stage of development, most systemic rules command not persons but states, allocating duties and benefits on an aggregate basis. To say that the rules operate justly among nations, however, is to say little about the rules' actual impact on those who matter: the individuals who, unlike states, are capable of pleasure and pain.

In this essay the discussion will focus on the operational obstacles to devising principles of justice applicable to the rules of the international system. Before proceeding, however, it may be helpful to relate our inquiry to the idea of legitimacy and to establish certain commonalities between the notions of legitimacy and justice. The power of legitimacy lies in its capacity to pull those addressed by commands—primarily states—towards noncoerced compliance. This is of peculiar importance in the rule system of states because otherwise, without legitimate rules, there could be no normative system and the community would not have the means to meet, cooperatively, the contemporary challenges of nuclear arms, ozone depletion, desertification, hunger and virulent disease. The community would also be incapable of promoting systematic development, commerce, science, culture and transportation. Nevertheless, it is surely true that compliance with rules should not be the sole or ultimate goal of any decent social structure, including the global one. If, as may happen in any society, the rules are unjust, reflecting the society's imperfect social values; there may even be a good case for noncompliance. Nevertheless, in the international system the first task, for now, is to build a rule system of such manifest legitimacy as to engender a broad base of uncoerced habitual *compliance*. Lexically, the task of ensuring the *justice* of that rule system is the second, not the first order of business on the urgent, but still largely unfinished, global agenda.

While legitimacy therefore enjoys a degree of priority in the international system which it may not have in domestic systems of law, justice need not be eliminated from thought about the international system. It is simply more difficult to do so. Thinking about international justice can be facilitated, however, by comparing its properties to those of the more familiar notion of legitimacy, which it resembles in important structural aspects. For example, the *effect* of justice on a rule is quite a bit like that of legitimacy. Like legitimacy, the perception that a rule is just pulls those addressed by a rule towards voluntary compliance, whereas a strong sense of its injustice encourages noncompliance. And, again like legitimacy, the justice of a rule or institution can be measured by a set of principles which, like the Greenwich "foot" or the Paris "metre" bar is the agreed hypothetical standard employed by a *community* to make discourse, decision and action possible. The differences between legitimacy and justice arise not from such aspects of their respective structures but from the degree to which the international system has evolved as a community with common assumptions about each measure. While there is significant agreement as to what makes an international rule or institution legitimate, a common measure of justice is still in its most rudimentary stage of evolution in the global community.

With that caveat, let us now examine further the *operational* problems and prospects of justice as these relate to the international rule system. As noted above, the operational problems derive initially from the fact that justice can only be said to be done to persons, not to collectivities or corporate fictions, unless, as rarely happens, a rule has precisely the same effect on all individuals in the collective or corporate entity. A few rules of the global system, particularly the new obligations pertaining to human rights, do address individuals, thereby surmounting this initial obstacle. Nevertheless, there are others which are even more daunting and which derive from the fact that even when the rules address *persons*, they are still made by and for *states*.

In the system of Western natural law, with a Christian God as the ultimate source of all commands, the problem of law's justice did not arise, or, at least, it was not perceived as a problem so long as God spoke through one tradition and a single church-state hierarchy within a circumscribed, abbreviated international community. It is only more recently, with the emergence of a positivist rule system and social pluralism such as we find in America and, especially since the decolonization and inclusive expansion of the global community, that the problem of justice has become difficult. When different belief systems contend and none are universally accepted as definitive, what can one say about the justice of rules? A brief look at the way in which the legal philosophy of John Rawls has tried to deal with the problem of justice in the context of American moral-pluralist society may help to clarify thinking about justice in the global community. It may thus advance an understanding of the formidable operational problems inherent in devising a commonly accepted global measure of justice.

Modern American theories of justice, particularly those of Rawls, the leading thinker in the field, have been shaped by the positivist and pluralist assumptions of American constitutionalism. Like the Constitution itself, the American philosophers have been attracted to notions of social contract first developed by Europeans. However, contract theory, originally, did not claim to be a theory of justice but of social order. In the national, as in the international community, order was the first concern of those whose lives were still too frequently nasty, brutish and short. While justice was never, even then, entirely without its champions, its coming to the fore awaited an era in which the legitimacy of rules and institutions had become a relatively well-understood requisite of goverance. That evolution occurred gradually without much notice. Beginning with Hobbes' *The Leviathan*,[3] social contract doctrine has been refined by Locke's *Two Treatises of Government*,[4] Rousseau's *The Social Contract*,[5] and Kant's *Fundamental Principles of the Metaphysics of Morals*.[6] Professor John Rawls, in his principle work, *A Theory of Justice*, has brought Locke, Rousseau and Kant together to shape the social contract tradition in modern American justice theory.[7]

Locke, like Hobbes, maintained that we are by our nature free, equal and independent beings.[8] Consequently, it follows that persons can only be deprived of their estates and liberty, and subjected to the political control of another, if, and to the extent that, each agrees to empower such authority. We do this, Locke said, "by agreeing . . . to join and unite into a community for [our] comfortable, safe, and peaceable living, one amongst another, in a secure enjoyment of [our] properties, and a greater security against any that are not of it."[9] The theory of social contract thus reinforces the power of rules and the obligation to obey constituted authority, sweeping aside any lingering belief in the divine right of kings or the natural (God-given) authority of laws and substituting a volitional act of freely determined association for the greater good of all.

---

3 T. HOBBES, THE LEVIATHAN (1651), *reprinted in* 3 THE ENGLISH WORKS OF THOMAS HOBBES (W. Molesworth ed. 1839).

4 J. LOCKE, TWO TREATISES OF GOVERNMENT 1690 (W. Carpenter ed. 1924).

5 J. ROUSSEAU, ON THE SOCIAL CONTRACT 1762 (D. Cress trans. ed. 1983).

6 I. KANT, FUNDAMENTAL PRINCIPLES OF THE METAPHYSICS OF MORALS 1785 (T. Abbott trans. 1873), *reprinted in* THE ESSENTIAL KANT 295-360 (A. Zweig ed. 1970).

7 J. RAWLS, A THEORY OF JUSTICE 11 n.4 (1971).

8 Locke describes our natural condition—i.e., our status as free and equal beings—as the state of nature. It is a state of perfect freedom, whereby we order our actions and dispose of our possessions as we see fit. It is a state of equality, "wherein all the power and jurisdiction is reciprocal" and creatures of the same species are "equal one amongst another, without subordination or subjection." *See* Locke, *supra* note 4, at 118. The state of nature is only bound by the laws of nature, which proscribe each person from divesting another of the alienable rights of life, liberty and property. *Id.* at 119-20.

9 *Id.* at 164.

This, although conceived as an explanation of national governance, is also quite relevant to the notion of community as it emerges in the international system. Its relevance to legitimacy is apparent. Its relation to justice, however, is less so.

The community formed by the consent of each individual, according to Locke, acts as one body, obeying the will and determination of the majority.[10] Each person, in consenting to join an association of politics, is thereby obliged to submit to the "determination of the majority, and to be concluded by it."[11] Were it otherwise, the original social compact would be meaningless, and we would "be left free and under no other ties than [those existing] before in the state of Nature."[12] Moreover, where the majority cannot make a determination or draw a conclusion, it cannot act as one body, and therefore dissolves.[13]

Nearly a century later, Rousseau validated the social compact as "a form of association which defends and protects with all common forces the person and goods of each associate . . . ."[14] The compact calls for "the total alienation of each associate, together with all of his rights, to the entire community."[15] Rousseau believed that the social contract actually increases the value of each person and property in the association.[16] They gain back whatever they give and benefit from membership in an augmented collective force for the preservation of what they have.[17] This, too, is relevant to any analysis of legitimacy, not least as it operates in the international community of states. It is also relevant to justice.

Rousseau understood the first virtue of social contract to be its capacity to organize a collective defense of liberty and order. Secondly, the social contract also establishes a community with potential for doing justice. Rousseau explained that associates have obligations both to themselves and to every member of the union. These obligations civilize and socialize the members. As they move "from the state of nature to the civil state . . . duty replaces [their] physical impulse."[18] Notions of justice replace instinct as guides to their conduct, thereby giving their actions the morality that had been wanting in the state of nature. "[They are] forced to act upon other principles and to consult [their] reason before listening to [their] inclinations."[19]

Kant, too, observed that the individual, in a social contract, tends to act in accordance with general principles which are intuitively recognized and not self-contradictory: that is, are understood as a "categorical imperative."[20] Examples include the keeping of promises or the telling of

10 *Id.* at 165.
11 *Id.*
12 *Id.*
13 *Id.* at 166.
14 Rousseau, *supra* note 5, at 24.
15 *Id.*
16 Rousseau states that in our corporate capacity "we receive each member as an indivisible part of the whole." *Id.*
17 *Id.*
18 *Id.* at 26.
19 *Id.* at 27.
20 For an explication of the categorical imperative, see Kant, *supra* note 6, at 317-24.

the truth. In other words, each individual will act according to "that maxim whereby thou canst at the same time will that it should become a universal law."[21]

In all of this, it is apparent that social contract theory came to rely on a rationale in which justice and legitimacy are mingled, rather than clearly distinguished. Citizens should want to obey the rules, the writers contend, because of the evident benefits derived from membership in the community and because the rules will be fair to all in a free association of equals, working in a principled manner by treating likes alike. Only rarely is there recognition of the potential for conflict between the operation of the social contract as a means of ensuring order and security and its regard for individuated liberty and fairness in allocating obligations and rights. Little is made of the capacity of a majority of free and equal citizens to use the law to oppress minorities or to organize the distribution of scarce resources unfairly.

To be sure, Kant and Rousseau emphasized human dignity and equality. For Kant, rational beings exist as ends in themselves, and not merely as the means to an end.[22] Because persons are ends, and may not be used merely as means, they are above all price. They possess dignity.[23] In this can be seen emerging a sort of secular morality, a concept of associational justice.

Nevertheless, it remained for Rawls to build a modern theory of *justice* on these contractarian notions of Locke, Rousseau, and Kant, adapting the idea of the social compact to formulate moral principles.[24] Rawls' project was to devise a formula for measuring the presence or absence of justice in the basic rule structure of a society where the social compact operates as it should. While Rawls does not seek to advance any particular form of government, his theory is intended to facilitate justice, understood as fairness. His attention is directed almost entirely to the rules and institutions of a closed social system strongly resembling the liberal secular and pluralist United States. But because even that model has its serious defects—the failure of the Constitution to abolish slavery, or enfranchise women and the unpropertied class, are the most obvious examples—Rawls uses an idealized social contract model, rather than demonstrate his principles by reference to any system in actual existence. More precisely, he defines justice not in terms of a particular kind of association capable of producing a designated social good, but as one based on an ideal rule of procedure, of decision. Rawls' principles of justice are whatever "free and rational persons concerned to further their own interests would accept in an initial position of equality as defining

21 *Id.* at 324.

22 *Id.* at 329-30.

23 *See generally* I. KANT, THE PHILOSOPHY OF LAW (2d ed. 1798) (W. Hastie trans. ed. 1887). Kant viewed equality before the law as an *a priori* principle of a civil state. *See* 2 I. KANT, *On the Common Saying: "This May be True in Theory, but it does not Apply in Practice,"* in KANT'S POLITICAL WRITINGS 74-77 (H. Reiss ed., H. Nisbet trans. 1970); I. KANT, *Perpetual Peace: A Philosophical Sketch*, in KANT'S POLITICAL WRITINGS 113-14 (H. Reiss ed., H. Nisbet trans. 1970).

24 For a discussion of the relevance of Rawls' theory to the "society" of states, see D'Amato, *International Law and Rawls' Theory of Justice*, 5 DEN. J. INT'L L. & POL'Y 525 (1975).

the fundamental terms of their association."[25] It is the *process* by which principles of justice are defined which assumes pivotal importance. What the principles produce in the way of "goods" is not irrelevant, but secondary.

Rawls' process-oriented concept of justice as an idealized social contract is formulated as a negotiation among anonymous equals in the "original position," a purely metaphoric construct. Those who enter this negotiation to devise principles of justice do not know their identity or even their social or class status. They are to choose principles of justice behind a *veil of ignorance*, which

> ensures that no one is advantaged or disadvantaged in the choice of principles by the outcome of natural chance or the contingency of social circumstances. Since all are similarly situated and no one is able to design principles to favor his particular condition, the principles of justice are the result of a fair agreement or bargain.[26]

They are also charged with negotiating in socio-economic conditions of moderate scarcity[27] and will assert conflicting claims to limited resources that reflect their various conceptions of the social good.[28] As they negotiate, the participants will discover common ground where the preferences may be seen to overlap, enabling general principles to emerge.[29] Rawls believes that, acting rationally[30] and in compliance with the formal constraints of the concept of right,[31] the parties would agree on principles for ordering the basic institutional structure of society: *The Principle of Liberty* ("[E]ach person is to have an equal right to the most extensive basic liberty compatible with a similar liberty for others"[32]) and *The Principle of Equality* ("Social and economic inequalities are to be arranged so that they are both (a) to the greatest benefit of the least advantaged and (b) attached to offices and positions open to all under conditions of fair equality of opportunity."[33])

Rawls speaks, essentially, to justice in the national community, to which he refers as "a special case of the problem of justice."[34] He admits that "the law of nations may require different principles arrived at in a somewhat different way."[35] This does not altogether preclude his venturing some preliminary views on the problem of justice in the interna-

---

25 Rawls, *supra* note 7, at 11. For an attempt to convert Rawls' test of the parties' subjective preferences into objective mandates of justice, see Scanlon, *Preference and Urgency*, 72 J. PHIL. 655 (1975).

26 Rawls, *supra* note 7, at 12.

27 *Id.* at 128.

28 *See id.* at 22, 126-30.

29 Rawls explains that generality and universality are distinct. For example, if everyone has to serve the interests of a dictator, there exists the latter but not the former. *See id.* at 132.

30 *See id.* at 24-25, 142-50.

31 *See id.* at 23, 130-36.

32 *Id.* at 60.

33 *Id.* at 83.

34 *Id.* at 7.

35 *Id.* at 8.

tional arena.[36] For example, he proposes an international analog to the original position behind a global veil of ignorance:

> [O]ne may extend the interpretation of the original position and think of the parties as representatives of different nations who must choose together the fundamental principles to adjudicate conflicting claims among states. Following out the conception of the initial situation, I assume that these representatives are deprived of various kinds of information. While they know that they represent different nations each living under the normal circumstances of human life, they know nothing about the particular circumstances of their own society. . . . Once again the contracting parties, in this case representatives of states, are allowed only enough knowledge to make a rational choice to protect their interests but not so much that the more fortunate among them can take advantage of their special situation. This original position is fair between nations; it nullifies the contingencies and biases of historical fate. Justice between states is determined by the principles that would be chosen in the original position so interpreted.[37]

This leads Rawls to suggest that, in such a metaphorical negotiation, states might agree to principles that are already familiar to us. Citing Professor Brierly, he expresses the view that they would agree that all states are endowed with certain fundamental equal rights, including a right to "liberty," which could translate into the principles of *nonintervention* and *self-determination*.[38]

Here we have two concrete principles of potential use in assessing justice in the international rule system. Let us see whether they work in the way Rawls hoped they might. In so doing, we may discover more about the problem of devising any yardstick for measuring justice globally.

To make this examination, we will use Rawls' methodology, assuming that representatives of the world's states have gathered to try to agree on an applicable principle of justice without knowing which nations they represent, but aware of an actual crisis to which a just rule could be applied if one could be negotiated to everyone's satisfaction. The first crisis implicates the principle of *nonintervention* and the second the principle of *self-determination*, the two which Rawls himself thought likely to result from the operation of his model.

Scenario #1 (nonintervention): Suppose control of the state of Malarkey, with a population of seven million, had been seized by an army coup. In a reign of terror a million civilians have been executed. The economy was destroyed and two million starving refugees have fled to neighboring states. The foreign ministers of the nations have gathered to discuss what, if anything, should be done. Should they intervene col-

36 *See id.* at 57-58, 377-82. (Rawls considers the situation of a conscientious objector to a war he considers in violation of international law. This leads him to regard the moral basis of the law of nations.)

37 *Id.* at 378.

38 *Id.* Rawls relies upon J.L. BRIERLY, THE LAW OF NATIONS chs. IV-V (6th ed. 1963) in stating these basic principles. *See* Rawls, *supra* note 7, at 378 n.27. In addition to nonintervention and self-determination, Rawls also notes the right of collective self-defense, the sanctity of treaties and principles applicable to *jus in bello*. *Id.* at 378-79.

lectively to stop the killing? Should neighboring states intervene to stanch the flow of refugees across their borders? Or should Malarkey be left alone to resolve its own problems? Is it possible for states' representatives, in the original position, negotiating behind the veil of ignorance, to arrive at an applicable principle of justice to guide their actions? What might such a principle look like?

Rawls, addressing this problem, has visualized anonymous *representatives of states* arriving at a general principle of *nonintervention*.

In his conception of the international original position, Rawls postulates a world of separate and equal states, sovereign and autonomous entities, analogous to those persons Kant defined as ends in themselves.[39] Representatives of these nations, negotiating behind the veil of ignorance, naturally would arrive at a principle of justice which recognized a fundamental *equality* between "[i]ndependent peoples organized as states,"[40] because *that is what the negotiators represent*. Using Rawls' model, one would also expect the negotiators to agree on this principle of nonintervention as justice for the further good reason that, being ignorant of whether "their" states are powerful or weak, threatened or threatening, they would seek first to preserve their governments' autonomy in a world of gross power disparity.

Nonintervention as a principle of justice, however, requires that the foreign ministers, meeting the backdrop of the Malarkey cases, *do nothing*. But that cannot be right. Doing nothing looks suspiciously like the Hobbesian understanding of the state of nature. For Hobbes, the state of nature is populated by persons who are equal and autonomous. In it, he said, *no* moral principles can govern.[41] If nations exist in the state of nature, then, similarly, no moral rules apply to them because "in states, and commonwealths not dependent on one another, every commonwealth . . . has an absolute liberty, to do what it shall judge . . . most conducing to [its] benefit."[42] Professor Charles Beitz characterizes this not as justice but as "international moral skepticism,"[43] although Professor Antonio Cassese has noted that the desire of states to be seen as autonomous and equal has become more prevalent than ever, with a hundred new nations jealously guarding their hard-won sovereign prerogatives.[44]

While the state of nature may, indeed, describe one tendency in contemporary realpolitik, it would be exceedingly odd if that were to coin-

39 Rawls here follows the thoughts of early theorists like Wolff, who wrote in 1749 that "[n]ations are regarded as individual free persons living in a state of nature." C. WOLFF, JUS GENTIUM METHODO SCIENTIFICA PERTRACTATUM (J. Drake trans.) in 2 THE CLASSICS OF INTERNATIONAL LAW 9 (1934). Upon this view, "states might be conceived as moral beings which are organic wholes with the capacity to realize their nature in the choice and pursuit of ends." *See* C. BEITZ, POLITICAL THEORY AND INTERNATIONAL RELATIONS 76 (1979).

40 Rawls, *supra* note 7, at 378.

41 Hobbes, *supra* note 3, at 116-17.

42 *Id.* at 201.

43 Beitz, *supra* note 39, at 13. For Beitz's analysis of moral skepticism in the international state of nature *see id.* at 27-34.

44 A. CASSESE, INTERNATIONAL LAW IN A DIVIDED WORLD 144-46 (1986). *See also* M. HALPERN, THE MORALITY AND POLITICS OF INTERVENTION, in 1 THE VIETNAM WAR AND INTERNATIONAL LAW 39 (R. Falk ed. 1968).

cide with an ideal of justice. Such coincidence between what the negotiators in the original position agree upon, and Hobbes' state of nature, should warn us that something must be wrong with the model producing that result.

According to such an idiosyncratic account of justice, no state would ever be justified in intervening in the international affairs of any other. The agreement reached behind the veil of ignorance would require states to leave Malarkey alone to sort out its own problems. Applying such a principle, justice would have been served when the world left Hitler free to kill the Jews of Germany and Field Marshal Idi Amin or Pol Pot free to decimate the populations of Uganda and Kampuchea. Before these recent developments, John Stuart Mill could still plausibly extol the virtue of nonintervention on the ground that leaving nations alone to deal with their own problems of misgovernment builds their moral character.[45] With today's hindsight, that seems rather unfeeling or jejune.

Intuitively, we know these to be untenable results. The principle of nonintervention cannot lead both to Hobbes' brutish state of nature and also to Rawls' community of just principles. That the principle of nonintervention compels noninterference in Malarkey should instill doubts not only about Rawls' proposed principle, but about the process by which it was reached: the metaphorical negotiation of representatives of *governments* behind the veil of ignorance. Perhaps this is the wrong way to think about principles of justice in the international community.

We have already observed that a negotiation between governments inevitably would favor a principle of nonintervention because it liberates governments, within their own borders, to do largely as they please. This might seem *just* to governments, but does not necessarily do justice to their citizens. Nevertheless, it is important to note that the principle treats governments equally, and undoubtedly meets the moral expectations of many who govern. Governments do share the belief that they have a moral right to govern without interference from "outside." Secondly, the representatives of governments, negotiating principles of justice, are also likely to choose nonintervention, because, not knowing which governments they represent, the weak or the powerful, it would be rational for them to agree on a principle which best protects an autonomy professed by all. The negotiators, acting rationally, would suspect that a principle *permitting* intervention, even if limited to particularly egregious regimes, could easily be abused by the powerful, who would be tempted to see it as a license to intervene in the affairs of the weak for their own parochial purposes. Thirdly, governments concerned with maintaining the delicate balance on which rests the aspiration for world peace, would favor a rule which precludes the use of force in ways that could lead to unpredictable and unmanageable consequences.

Thus, rational governmental representatives would agree upon an absolute principle of nonintervention; and they would agree because the negotiators would have the shared moral perspective of *governments*. It is

45 J.S. MILL, 3 DISSERTATIONS AND DISCUSSIONS: POLITICAL, PHILOSOPHICAL AND HISTORICAL 238-63 (1873).

the special self-interest of governments—all governments—to protect their authority against external intervention, and to prefer order above other virtues. It is this shared governmental perspective which would shape the international principle of justice if we proceed to define it by the metaphorical process developed by Rawls. The result, however, is not a principle which yields justice for the people of Malarkey.

The false result, alone, does not render inoperable the veil of ignorance as a useful way to think about justice. But it does invalidate the assumption that one can think about principles of international justice by imagining a negotiation between representatives of *states*. The metaphor would become more useful if one were to substitute as the metaphorical negotiators all *persons*, or *representatives* of all persons *who are not engaged in governing states*. The characteristics of such nongovernmental persons would provide us with clues as to what principles those individuals would probably agree upon. They would choose principles advancing *personal*—not governmental—autonomy and equality. They would imagine the possibility that, emerging from behind the veil, they might find that they were prisoners of conscience, disappeared persons, or torture victims of their own governments. Presumably they would balance those personal concerns with their concerns for national security and independence.

This difference in the perspective of governments and citizens is fully born out by examining contemporary state practice. Real nations, not behind Rawls' veil but, rather, practicing actual multilateral diplomacy, tend to prefer to act in accordance with a principle which elevates nonintervention above such humanitarian concerns as are evident in the Malarkey case. For this reason, when contemplating military intervention, the United Nations (U.N.) usually has preferred not to differentiate between just and unjust reasons to intervene.[46] Instead, the nations have favored treating all states as autonomous entities entitled to be left alone, and doing so on grounds of maintaining international peace and order, rather than advancing justice. At least in their public posture, nations seem almost to agree with Hobbes that, in the world "nothing can be unjust. The notions of right and wrong, justice and injustice have there no place."[47] This receives some implicit support from article 2(4) of the U.N. Charter (Charter),[48] which categorically proscribes the "threat or use of force against the territorial integrity or political independence" of any nation, without distinguishing between Malarkey and Denmark. Moreover, the Charter pointedly prohibits the international community from "interven[ing] in matters which are essentially within the domestic jurisdiction of any state."[49] The U.N. Declarations on Principles of International Law Concerning Friendly Relations and Cooperation Among States,[50] and on Inadmissibility of Intervention[51]—both relatively recent

46 T. Franck, Nation Against Nation 224-31 (1985).
47 Hobbes, *supra* note 3, at 115.
48 U.N. Charter art. 2, para. 4.
49 *Id.* art. 2, para. 7.
50 G.A. Res. 2625, 25 U.N. GAOR Supp. (No. 28) at 121, U.N. Doc. A/8028 (1970).
51 G.A. Res. 2131, 20 U.N. GAOR Supp. (No. 14) at 11, U.N. Doc. A/6014 (1965).

formulations of global normative consensus—also give high priority to the principle of nonintervention.

What the texts suggests, the behavior of states confirms. Despite ample, credible reports of government-sanctioned genocide in Kampuchea, the nations did not act,[52] choosing, instead to deplore the Vietnamese military intervention which ended the tenure of the offending regime.[53] Governments reacted out of concern for national autonomy, and fear of the destabilizing effect of any recourse to military force, not concern for justice. They seem to have preferred to rally around a rule perceived as advancing not justice but orderliness and to bar violence against governments rather than against *persons*.

Similarly, in 1971, the U.N. called on India to withdraw its troops and observe a cease-fire after its army had joined Bengali insurgents to end Pakistan's bloody repression in the territory that became the state of Bangladesh.[54] Both the Vietnamese and Indian humanitarian interventions undeniably relieved what, in any defensible conception of justice, must surely be recognized intuitively as injustice. Yet the U.N.—the community of states—unblinkingly chose to reaffirm the norm of nonintervention in circumstances that must make justice weep.

Regrettably, yet understandably, states seem reluctant to distinguish between interventions that may be said to advance human rights—as in the cases of Kampuchea or Bangladesh—and interventions, such as those of the Soviets in Afghanistan[55] and the United States in Nicaragua,[56] which—arguably—do not. Where regimes have slaughtered tens of thousands of their own citizens, as in Kampuchea, Uganda and Burundi, the U.N. has remained mute and passive. It is, after all, a community of *governments*.

This preference of those who govern for order over justice is exemplified by Abraham Lincoln's letter to Horace Greeley of August 22, 1862, more than a year after the commencement of the civil war:

52 This is not surprising since "[t]he Assembly has never been able to bring itself to address the extirpation of entire populations—some seven to nine million persons—in Burundi, Kampuchea and Pakistani Bengal." *See* Franck, *Of Gnats and Camels: Is There a Double Standard at the United Nations?*, 78 AM. J. INT'L L. 811, 825 (1984).

53 G.A. Res. 34/22, 34 U.N. GAOR Supp. (No. 46) at 209, U.N. Doc. A/34/46 (1979).

54 The resolution was addressed to both India and Pakistan, but since Pakistani troops were not on Indian soil, it was obviously aimed at New Delhi. G.A. Res. 2793, 26 U.N. GAOR Supp. (No. 29) at 3, U.N. Doc. A/8429 (1971).

55 The Security Council, unable to reach a unanimous consensus among its permanent members, called upon the General Assembly to conduct an emergency special session concerning Soviet intervention in Afghanistan. *See* S.C. Res. 462, 35 U.N. SCOR (Res. & Dec.) at 2, U.N. Doc. S/INF/36 (1980). Thereafter, the General Assembly "[s]*trongly deplore*[d] the . . . armed intervention in Afghanistan" and "[c]*all*[ed] for the immediate, unconditional and total withdrawal of the foreign troops." G.A. Res. ES-6/2, U.N. GAOR (6th Emer. Spec. Sess.) Supp. (No. 1) at 2, U.N. Doc. A/ES-6/7 (1980).

56 The World Court ruled that the United States, "by training, arming, equipping, financing and supplying the *contra* forces or otherwise encouraging, supporting and aiding military and paramilitary activities in and against Nicaragua . . . acted . . . in breach of its obligation under customary international law not to intervene in the affairs of another State." *See* Military and Paramilitary Activities in and against Nicaragua (Nicar. v. U.S.), 1986 I.C.J. 14, 146 (Judgment of June 27). The General Assembly subsequently passed a resolution calling for "full and immediate compliance" with the judgment. G.A. Res. 41/31, 41 U.N. GAOR Supp. (No. 53) at 24, U.N. Doc. A/41/53 (1986).

> My paramount object in this struggle *is* to save the Union, and is *not* either to save or to destroy slavery. If I could save the Union without freeing *any* slave I would do it, and if I could save it by freeing *all* the slaves I would do it; and if I could save it by freeing some and leaving others alone I would also do that.[57]

So, too, in the international system. Even the most enlightened of those who govern first seek to preserve an orderly, predictable state system. Only to the extent order can be advanced by justice will justice be done. This leaves the international system some leeway to make, or interpret, rules in consonance with their intuitive notions of justice. In confronting a case of extreme injustice, it may even bend the rules a little. For example, Tanzania was not criticized by the members of the U.N. for its invasion of Uganda, which toppled Idi Amin at last. India, while told to withdraw its troops, was not actually condemned for invading East Pakistan (Bangladesh). France escaped uncensured when its troops ousted Emperor Bokassa of the Central African Empire after he had begun to murder large numbers of children. Israel was not penalized, or even seriously reprimanded, for its invasion of Uganda to liberate hostages hijacked to Entebbe.[58] Still, in the eyes of most states, just and unjust interventions tend to be lumped together as posing manifestly unacceptable risks to states' autonomy and safety.[59]

That is the *governmental* perspective. In defense of Rawls' model, it should be noted that his negotiators, although representing the regimes of the world, could be expected to have a different perspective because they would reach issues of international justice only *after* agreeing on the principles of justice applicable to their domestic systems of governance. They would represent only *just* governments.

This might produce quite a different negotiating dynamic. Professor David Richards has concluded that such *just* negotiators,

> where there is a grave violation of equal liberty within institutions, . . . will view war . . . [as] a justified means in stopping this. . . . [They] are concerned not with the well-being of institutions . . . but with the well-being of persons; and thus, it is perfectly natural that the contractors may approve the destruction of a certain nation, if it severely frustrates the interests of its populace.[60]

This version of Rawls' model permits us to imagine rules of justice for a world of *just* states. Unfortunately, this is a formidable barrier to theoretical speculation, requiring us—counter-intuitively—to imagine two things at once: just nations making a just world. It does not much help in the task of defining principles of justice for the real world. On the other hand, any version of Rawls' model which shifts the perspective

57 Letter from Abraham Lincoln to Hon. Horace Greeley (August 22, 1862), *reprinted in* 5 THE COLLECTED WORKS OF ABRAHAM LINCOLN 338 (R. Basler ed. 1953).

58 The Security Council failed to act in response to Uganda's complaint. *See* 31 U.N. SCOR (1943d mtg.) at 1, U.N. Doc. S/PV. 1943 (1976); 31 U.N. SCOR (1942d mtg.) at 1, U.N. Doc. S/PV. 1942 (1976); 31 U.N. SCOR (1941st mtg.) at 1, U.N. Doc. S/PV. 1941 (1976); 31 U.N. SCOR (1940th mtg.) at 1, U.N. Doc. S/PV. 1940 (1976); 31 U.N. SCOR (1939th mtg.) at 2, U.N. Doc. S/PV. 1939 (1976).

59 Franck, *supra* note 52, at 811-19.

60 D. RICHARDS, A THEORY OF REASONS FOR ACTION 137-38 (1971).

to that of nongoverning persons will encounter much the same problem of unreality. What would be the relevance of the principles arrived at from that perspective? Very few secular rules of the international system apply to individuals, while almost all apply to states. This makes it virtually inevitable that these rules, made by and for governments, would not be congruent with principles of justice devised by the governed, or by an assemblage of perfectly just governments.

To put it another way, if we were to apply a measure of justice derived from the perspective of *persons*, the international rule system is likely to appear more unjust than almost any nation's legal system, precisely because the structure of the international system is that of a concert of rules rather than a parliament of humanity. The priorities and sensibilities of rulers, not the people's shared (or intersecting) notions of justice, usually determine the contents of the rules and also determine their compliance pull.

Scenario #2 (self-determination): Imagine a sovereign state of Euphoria with a population consisting of two different ethnic groups: the *Sucrose* and the *Lactose* peoples. The former inhabit the northern region, the latter the south. Sucrose people make up sixty per cent and Lactose forty per cent of the population. For generations, the Sucrose have dominated the Lactose. By virtue of their numerical superiority, the Sucrose have dominated Euphoria's elected parliament and used this majority to impose various restrictions on the Lactose minority. Lactose citizens are restricted to twenty per cent of jobs in the public sector of the economy, twenty per cent of the land, and that in the inclement mountains of the country, and twenty per cent of places in the public schools and universities. Legislation enacted ten years ago by the parliament has imposed a stiff poll tax on Euphoria's voters which effectively disenfranchises most Lactose citizens, who are poor. Sucrose has been made the sole official language of the nation. The effect of all this has been to create a Lactose secessionist movement, with a political wing which campaigns peacefully for a Lactose homeland, and an underground army, which fights for the same objectives.

The political and military struggle in Euphoria has been underway for a decade, since the enactment of the poll tax. It has disrupted life not only in Euphoria, but also in the neighboring states, where thousands of refugees from Euphoria's civil strife—both Sucrose and Lactose—are now camped. The war is also causing severe economic, social and political dislocation throughout Euphoria. The world's foreign ministers are meeting to try, in Rawls' original position, to devise a principle of justice relevant to this crisis. Do the Lactose people have a moral right to secede and should such a right be recognized by the international community?

As we have seen, Rawls did briefly address this problem, too. Behind the veil of ignorance, he suggested, rational state representatives would agree upon a right of *self-determination* as a general principle of justice. In this he could be right only if the nations whose representatives were negotiating the applicable principle of justice were themselves models of justice.

Professor Beitz has observed that the concept of self-determination can be regarded as the "positive" aspect of state autonomy.[61] While the principle of intervention protects the rights of states already independent, self-determination protects the independence option of nations under foreign control. Nonintervention is conservative, tending to preserve the international status quo. Self-determination, however, is dynamic in that it sanctions change in the structure of the international order. It is apparent that the two principles, rather than invariably supporting one another, actually may sometimes conflict.

The idea that national or ethnic groups are entitled to "self-determination" began to be applied in the settlement of post-World War I European land claims. After World War II, the principle of self-determination was expanded to include colonial possessions in Africa, Asia and the Americas. It was spelled out in the U.N. Charter which obliges the colonial powers to "develop self-government, to take due account of the political aspirations of the peoples, and to assist them in the progressive development of their free political institutions. . . ."[62] Between 1947 and 1977, nearly one billion people benefitted from this right.

However, while the European application of the principle of self-determination in the 1920's had encouraged the breakup of multi-ethnic nations like Austro-Hungary and the Ottoman Empire and led to wholesale rearrangement of boundaries as various groups elected to shift allegiances, the principle operated differently in Africa and Asia in the period following World War II. In the latter, self-determination was defined in almost every instance as a right exercisable collectively by all the inhabitants of an existing colony within the colony's sacrosanct borders. Many of these colonies, however, had been created quite arbitrarily by the imperial powers, lumping together disparate races, cultures and religions. Applied in this way, self-determination did not advance but actually frustrated the ambitions of various tribes and other groups. The resultant denials of self-determination—for example, by Nigeria to the secessionist Ibo tribal state of Biafra[63]—were vigorously defended on grounds not of fairness but of order and legitimacy. The application of the principle to permit tribal secession, it was argued, would create chaos throughout Africa and end in an economically and politically devastating balkanization. Besides, each new multi-tribal nation was itself legitimate: usually it had come into being by a recognized, well-established process with determinate procedural rules and had been validated by pedigreed

61 Beitz, *supra* note 39, at 92-93. *See also* Cassese, *supra* note 44, at 131-37; L.C. BUCHHEIT, SECESSION: THE LEGITIMACY OF SELF-DETERMINATION 43-137, 216-45 (1978), and, for an early effort to create a legal category of those entitled *see* Interpretation of the Convention Between Greece and Bulgaria Respecting Reciprocal Emigration (Question of the "Communities") (Adv. Op.), 1920 P.C.I.J. (ser. B) No. 17.

62 U.N. CHARTER art. 73, para. b.

63 Biafra had declared its independence on May 30, 1967. 14 THE WORLD BOOK ENCYCLOPEDIA 326h (1986).

institutions such as the United Nations, the parliament of the colonial power and by the political process of the colony itself.

This change of circumstance was soon making its consequences felt in the rule system. The new states of the Third World, drafting the U.N. Declaration on the Granting of Independence to Colonial Countries and Peoples,[64] proclaimed the principle that "[a]ll peoples have the right to self-determination"[65] but also carefully added the order-and-legitimacy-based caveat that "[a]ny attempt aimed at the partial or total disruption of the national unity and the territorial integrity of a country is incompatible with the purposes and principles of the Charter of the United Nations."[66] This contradiction was reenforced, rather than resolved, in subsequent General Assembly iterations.[67] Soon powerful African and Asian states, themselves only recently freed from alien rule, felt free to send military aid to sister governments forcibly repressing disaffected minorities seeking to secede. Most remarkable is the recent spectacle of India providing troops to suppress the secessionist movement in Sri Lanka mounted by Tamils of Indian origin. There are other such paradoxes. Nigeria sought and received military assistance from its former colonial masters, the British, to extinguish secessionist Biafra. Zimbabwe, having only recently gained control of the country from its white settlers,[68] vigorously used a large white-led militia to suppress secessionism among the Ndebele tribe in its western region.[69] As for the United Nations, it actually despatched a large multinational military force led by Irish and Swedish troops to prevent a populist tribal secession in the Katanga province of newly independent Zaire.[70]

Against this background of state practice can be set Rawls' belief that self-determination is a general principle of justice at which representa-

64 G.A. Res. 1514, 15 U.N. GAOR Supp. (No. 16) at 66-67, U.N. Doc. A/4684 (1960).

65 *Id.* para. 2.

66 *Id.* para. 6.

67 *See, e.g.*, G.A. Res. 3382, 30 U.N. GAOR Supp. (No. 34) at 84, U.N. Doc. A/10034 (1975).

68 Zimbabwe came into official existence at midnight on April 17, 1980, thus bringing to a close the former white-ruled government of Rhodesia, which was first established by the United Kingdom under the Constitution of the Federation of Rhodesia and Nyasaland. *See* 518 PARL. DEB., H.C. (5th ser.) 899-965, 1505 (1953). More generally, *see* M. POMERANCE, SELF-DETERMINATION IN LAW AND PRACTICE (1982), and Blay, *Self-Determination versus Territorial Integrity in Decolonization*, 18 N.Y.U.J. INT'L L. & POL'Y 441 (1986).

69 After a new outbreak of killings by anti-government rebels in late 1982, the Zimbabwean government deployed the army's Fifth Brigade in Matebeleland North in late January, 1983. Amnesty International reported allegations of executions, torture and detention carried out by the Brigade against the Ndebele in its effort to quash the dissidents. *See* AMNESTY INT'L, COUNTRY DOSSIERS: AFRICA 137 (1984). Yet, to Robert Mugabe's credit, his ruling Zimbabwe African National Union (ZANU) party has made peace with the Zimbabwe African People's Union (ZAPU), the opposition party led by the Ndebele leader, Joshua Nkomo. Their alliance, hopefully, spells the end to ethnic division that has plagued Zimbabwe since independence. *See Rival Zimbabwe Parties Agree to Merge*, N.Y. Times, Dec. 23, 1987, at A3, col. 4. Indeed, a promising sign is seen in the fact that with Mugabe's inauguration as Zimbabwe's first Executive President, Nkomo has also been named Vice President and Second Secretary of Mugabe's party. *See Mugabe Now President of a One-Party Zimbabwe*, N.Y. Times, Jan. 1, 1988, at A3, col. 4.

70 For a discussion of U.N. action in Katanga, *see* T. Franck & J. Carey, *The Role of the United Nations in the Congo—A Retrospective Perspective*, in THE HAMMARSKJOLD FORUMS: THE LEGAL ASPECTS OF THE UNITED NATIONS ACTION IN THE CONGO 40-51 (The Ass'n of the Bar of the City of New York Working Paper 525/62/2, 1962). *See also* S.C. Res. 169, 16 U.N. SCOR (Res. & Dec.) at 3-5, U.N. Doc. S/5002 (1961); 16 U.N. SCOR (982d mtg.) at 1-3, U.N. Doc. S/5002 (1961).

tives of nations would arrive in a negotiation behind the veil of ignorance. If this were so, the meeting of foreign ministers, addressing the problems of Euphoria, would formulate a principle of justice that would recognize the right of the Lactose people to choose independence. By validating the Lactose cause, the community of nations would give it reenforcement even without recourse to military intervention. It would probably justify states taking measures, individually or collectively, to help the Lactose achieve justice.

However, we know that this is not the principle upon which the Foreign Ministers would agree. States—that is, governments, *all* governments—would hesitate to adopt so dynamic and centrifugal a principle. Like Lincoln, they would give priority to preserving the union—*any* union. As governments, they would favor cohesion, unity and order. We know this because such post-colonial secessionist movements as those in Biafra and Kashmir have met with almost no support from any governments. This tells us something about governments: that it is generally in their nature to abhor secession. It would follow that a negotiation in the original position, among persons who knew that they represented governments, would very quickly agree on a principle not of self-determination but of something else: that sovereign, equal *states* have a right to "territorial integrity." In plainer words, they have the same "right" the United States exercised when it crushed the Confederacy. Such a principle of justice would have almost nothing to do with justice as *people* might understand it, but everything to do with the way governments naturally think.

It is highly unlikely that government negotiators would agree on the Wilsonian principle that every discrete ethnic group is entitled to self-determination "on demand" and regardless of circumstances. Even Wilson compromised the principle in such cases as the Rhineland.[71] In its purest form, the principle has been championed by John Stuart Mill, who wrote: "Where the sentiment of nationality exists in any force, there is a *prima facie* case for uniting all the members of the nationality under the same government, and a government to themselves apart."[72] In practice, however, few, if any, genuine representatives of governments, even behind the veil of ignorance, would subscribe to a principle of justice defined with so little regard for the national security, economic well-being and stability of nations.

If, on the other hand, Rawls' negotiators were representatives of people, rather than governments, they would be able—indeed might even be compelled by prudence—to imagine themselves as the Lactose

71 The separation of the Saar Basin or Rhineland from Germany posed a clear conflict with the Wilsonian principle of self-determination, since its four million inhabitants were ethnic Germans. However, the President submitted to geopolitical logic—the creation of a buffer Rhenish Republic would help prevent a German resurgence. The compromise eventually worked out by the powers at the Versailles Peace Conference led to the formation of a Saar territory which was not to be independent but administered through the League of Nations. *See* C. SEYMOUR, 4 THE INTIMATE PAPERS OF COLONEL HOUSE 334-35, 345 (1926). *See also* H.W.V. TEMPERLEY, 2 A HISTORY OF THE PEACE CONFERENCE OF PARIS 1 2 (1920).

72 J.S. MILL, *Considerations on Representative Government*, in 19 COLLECTED WORKS OF JOHN STUART MILL 547 (J. Robson ed. 1977).

people, or other oppressed, disentitled minorities around the globe, and all might therefore choose a principle which sought to respond to the most basic concerns of victims. For example, they might agree that minorities should be given as much liberty to secede as was compatible with the rights of the non-seceding majorities to live within secure, defensible boundaries and with a viable economy. Or they might agree that justice entitles minorities *persistently denied equal rights* to separate from the oppressing state and form their own nation. They might also concede that neighboring peoples have a right to help victims achieve separation where such intervention *is the only, or the fastest, least costly and painful, way to realize that just result*. Some similar principle of justice might also have been reached if one had imagined a negotiation among the foreign ministers of all states which, as a precondition, had already satisfied all the conditions of justice in the organization of their national societies. Even existing governments might be imagined as moving towards enunciating a new, coherent concept of self-determination which is both legitimate and also just; but they have not yet done so, which is why the concept is in danger of falling into desuetude.

In the real world, nations have not reached the state of perfect domestic justice, and the interests of governments often do not accord with the justice-based claims of its citizens. Thus, the international system, based on rules made among states to suit the overlapping priorities of governments, cannot be expected consistently to generate real principles of justice.

The metaphorical use of justice to describe a fair arrangement between states may reflect the identity of citizens' interest in some instances. For example, all citizens of Russia and the United States may be said to benefit alike when Soviet and American governments obey the just—and, as it happens, very legitimate—rule against initiating nuclear aggression. In that instance, it is possible to say that the rule is just because all persons benefit as equals. But the 1988 free trade agreement between Canada and the United States,[73] while it imposes the same terms of commerce on both nations, is only metaphorically just to all Americans and all Canadians. In actual operation, it benefits some citizens of each nation more than others. This may be the result of a deliberate decision to promote not justice but efficiency. Whatever that treaty's rationale, its justice cannot be demonstrated by comparing the aggregate gains and losses of each country, but only by examining the fairness of the way those collective benefits and costs are allocated among all individuals. Since few institutions and rules of the international system address individuals—human rights constitute one important exception—their justice in the literal, as opposed to metaphorical, sense is irrelevant. Moreover, if the legitimacy of these institutions and rules were conditioned on their justice, most would be found sadly wanting. That is the gist of the operational reason for not including justice among the indicators of legitimacy.

73 Free Trade Agreement, Dec. 22, 1987-Jan. 2, 1988, United States-Canada, —— U.S.T. ——, T.I.A.S. No. —— (text available at 27 I.L.M. 281 (1988)).

An especially dramatic example of this is the set of rules by which the system determines and recognizes nationality. These rules are certainly legitimate. They are determinate (the ground rules are quite clearly fixed), symbolically validated by long usage, coherent and reenforced by adherence to a hierarchy of rules about rules. But there is nothing about the rules of nationality which is just in the sense of being fair to persons. On the contrary, the rules governing bestowal and recognition of nationality severely distort individual life chances by their deference to place of birth and parentage. The egregious unfairness these rules promote, however, but little undermines states' perception of their legitimacy.

The rules applicable among states cannot be expected to embody principles of justice because the notion of *states*, itself, is an arbitrary and unfair suspension of personal equality. It embodies a difference principle no student of justice would accept.

Rawls himself conceded that his justice principles apply only within the borders of a nation-state.[74] His Harvard colleague, Robert Keohane, contends that "states cannot be considered independent subjects of moral theory; a justification of the morality of states . . . must ultimately be made in terms of the rights or interests of individual human beings."[75] The evolution of a system of global justice, therefore, must await, and go hand in hand with, the system's transformation from one based on states to one based on the primacy of world government and global citizenship. Universal *individual* rights may be a historic imperative whose day will come; but it is not yet fully upon us.

In summary, the system of states, which is the basic contemporary circumstance of the international community, vastly complicates the task of discerning applicable principles of justice. The best model is the one devised by John Rawls; but when it is translated from the national to the international political context, it yields odd, counter-instinctive results. It can be applied, if at all, only by replacing the foreign ministers who Rawls would summon to negotiate in the original position with an entirely different set of nongovernmental representatives, or with negotiators representing not states as we know them, but delegates of infinitely more graceful—and unreal—regimes. The difficulty in using Rawls' model of negotiating foreign ministers merely illustrates the difficulty in applying the test of justice to rules devised by, and for, states.

74 *See* Rawls, *supra* note 7, at 457.

75 R. Keohane, After Hegemony: Cooperation and Discord in the World Political Economy 249 (1984). A useful critique of states as subjects of a jurisprudence of justice is found in Skubik, *Two Models for a Rawlsian Theory of International Law and Justice*, 14 Den. J. Int'l L. & Pol'y 231, 236-37, 248-51 (1986).

[17]

Law, justice and the idea of a world society

DAVID ARMSTRONG

International law has traditionally been seen as concerned with the relations among states rather than among people and with order rather than justice. Because of its emphasis on sovereignty, it was, furthermore, regarded as dependent on the consent of states rather than as being capable of being derived from any form of democratic principle, still less from any kind of hierarchical structure of normative authority. Its societal grounding—something that any system of law requires—was, therefore, a presumed society of states: a loose and limited association among sovereign entities whose primary purpose was to enable orderly relations among states without in any way diminishing their sovereign statehood and rights. In the past 30 years this view has been increasingly challenged by interpretations of recent developments in international law that envisage gradual progress towards something that might more properly be called 'world law', since it extends legal personality beyond the state, it derives increasingly from consensus rather than consent and it reflects a growing concern with justice rather than with order. In short, it is a form of law appropriate to a world society of people rather than a society of states. This article first discusses the kinds of reasoning and forms of evidence employed in such an interpretation, then considers the main critiques of it, before, finally, advancing a perspective that differs in certain respects from both the progressivist interpretation and its rebuttal, while drawing some inspiration from each.

The progressivist case

Academic international lawyers, like their IR counterparts, may be grouped into three loosely associated clusters. The first is usually to be found with labels such as 'realist' or 'positivist' (in the juridical rather than the epistemological sense, denoting a belief that international law must be grounded in state consent). The second is variously termed 'liberal–humanist' or 'progressivist'. The third embraces such categories as 'radicals', 'critical theorists', and 'post-modernists', sometimes all classed together under the umbrella term 'Newstream'.

David Armstrong

Even the most optimistic idealist would find it hard to maintain that international law has made steady, unbroken progress towards a world society governed by principles of justice. Nonetheless, there is a plausible progressivist story to be told about the evolution of international law. It might begin with the assertion that what Franck calls a 'fairness discourse' has been present in international law from the beginning.[1] Terms like 'equality', 'reciprocity' and 'balance'—all commonplace in eighteenth-century treaties—might be derided by some as doing little more than placing a mask of gentility over what in reality was no more than a relentless struggle for power.[2] But they also delineated an intersubjective social reality in which states shared not only mutually acceptable defining characteristics but also a common language and a normative structure founded on shared assumptions about the rights and duties of states.

Of course, fairness to states in the anarchical European international society of the eighteenth century involved quite different principles and even modes of reasoning from those commonly employed in any other ethical discourse. *Raison d'état* permitted acts of treachery and violence abroad that would be unconscionable at home; the unassailable principle of non-intervention gave governments the freedom to do as they chose with their populaces; states might enjoy an equality in international law but in no material sense; and the 'just balance' they sought in some of their treaties was a balance only of power, not one of any deeper harmony. Yet the fact that their formal communications with each other involved the constant use of a language of diplomacy constructed in terms appropriate to civilized social interaction within a society of sovereign equals meant that the struggle for power was accompanied by the development of a normative and discursive framework that did not simply reflect the naked realities of power.

In the nineteenth century this minimal ethical component became more firmly institutionalized in many international treaties, and also broadened to a limited extent beyond aristocratic courtesy to touch upon issues that related to larger and more communally based questions of justice than those embraced by the esoteric morality of the society of states. As in the previous century, this was partly just a matter of linguistic conventions—the term 'family of nations' became commonplace, for example, but there were also developments that are less easy to dismiss as mere window dressing. From 1815 the Great Powers assumed a privileged status that undermined the formal equality that had prevailed in the previous century and enabled them to set norms and lay down rules for international society as a whole. The sacred principle of sovereignty was further eroded around the edges by treaties and other international instruments according rights to non-state entities such as slaves, Jews, and some

[1] Thomas M. Franck, *Fairness in international law and institutions* (Oxford: Clarendon, 1995), p. 9.

[2] The Peace of Westphalia declared that in the Empire, there should be 'an exact and reciprocal Equality amongst all the Electors, Princes and States of both religions...so that what is just of one side shall be so of the other'. Cited in David Armstrong, *Revolution and world order: the revolutionary state in international society* (Oxford: Clarendon, 1993), p. 34.

minorities. Humanitarian principles were written into the laws of war, international law imposed increasing obligations on states to notify outbreaks of disease and take measures to deal with them, a war crimes tribunal was held in Crete in 1898[3] and the dominant European states insisted that full membership of international society required the ability to demonstrate that internal governance measured up to a 'standard of civilisation'.[4]

In the first half of the twentieth century the League of Nations saw a further extension of such institutionalized norms. Once again these reflected the influence of a fairness discourse that went significantly beyond the traditional rights of states. In the Covenant itself, the 'well being and development' of the peoples of the former enemy colonies were deemed a 'sacred trust of civilisation', while the signatories also undertook 'to secure just treatment' for their own colonial peoples and 'to secure and maintain fair and humane conditions of labour' wherever they had influence. The territorial settlement also had various guarantees written into it of minority rights, including, in Upper Silesia, the first ever right for individuals to appeal to an international court.[5]

The UN Charter represented a further stage in this evolutionary process. Human rights, justice, social progress and 'better standards of life in larger freedom' were all affirmed as fundamental norms, while strict limitations were placed on the resort to force. The General Assembly was charged with the progressive development of international law and far more extensive commitments were undertaken in respect of all colonial peoples. Non-governmental organizations were given consultative status with the Economic and Social Council. There was, however, only one sop to distributive justice: the richer countries paid a higher proportion of the costs of the UN than the poorer. But it is to the normative explosion after 1945 that progressivists turn in support of their thesis about fundamental change in international law. Three particular progressivist claims about this profusion of legal material are worth considering: that it has significant implications for distributive justice; that it has given rise to one generally accepted new norm—sustainable development—with profound consequences for the issue of justice in international relations; and that the new norms, taken as a whole and viewed in the light of their application by various international legal agencies, may be interpreted as involving a clear shift from an international society to a world society.

Distributive justice is a novel principle in the international context. It was only at the beginning of this century that international law was amended to the effect that states could not use force in pursuit of debts owed by foreign governments. By that measure, today's legal regime in trade and finance looks positively generous, with agreements like the Lomé Convention and other compensatory and stabilizing schemes or the GATT's Generalised System of

[3] R. John Pritchard, *Gunboat diplomacy* (ECPR/ISA Joint Conference, Vienna, 1998).

[4] Gerrit W. Gong, *The standard of 'civilization' in international society* (Oxford: Oxford University Press, 1984).

[5] David Armstrong, *The rise of the international organisation* (Basingstoke: Macmillan, 1982), pp. 37–44.

David Armstrong

Preferences.[6] The 'right to development' has been asserted in numerous UN resolutions and declarations, although normally accompanied by disclaimers from the United States to the effect that it does not recognize the principle, and there may have been some marginal shift from the rigorous principle that compensation to foreigners for nationalised assets should be 'prompt, adequate and effective', a standard hard to meet for poor countries and one enshrining an intrinsic unfairness given that foreign property rights were frequently obtained during the colonial period.[7] Mention might also be made of the requirement in several treaties relating to maritime or watercourses disputes for 'economic and social needs' to be taken into account by tribunals.[8]

Complex issues of distributive justice have also been raised in the debates accompanying the emerging environmental regime. Developing countries have advanced several different kinds of justice claims in environmental negotiations: that they have the right to exploit their own resources, that their own sovereignty should not be infringed, that the costs of an environmental regime should fall primarily on the developed world, and that the more environmentally friendly technology should be freely transferred to them, rather than being subject to current rules about intellectual property rights.[9] On the other hand, Western states have expressed concern that unequally applied environmental standards might unfairly damage the interests of their economic enterprises. The precise status and even the meaning of contemporary environmental norms where they touch upon such North–South issues is far from clear, with one important document, the Rio Declaration, managing to incorporate several distinct and partially contradictory principles. The 'right to development' was formally acknowledged for the first time in a consensus agreement, although the United States entered its traditional dissenting statement and, in one commentator's words, 'the nature and extent of that right is left open, as is the question of whether such a right attaches to states, peoples or individuals'.[10] The formula that states had 'common but differentiated responsibilities' for the environment appeared in Principle 7 of the Declaration but Principle 2 gave states 'the sovereign right to exploit their own resources pursuant to their own environmental and developmental policies'. Principle 6 gave 'special priority' to developing countries but also called for the 'interests and needs of all countries' to be recognized. Principle 11 acknowledged that environmental standards 'applied by some countries may be inappropriate and of unwarranted economic and social cost' to developing countries but Principle 12 insisted that trade measures taken for environmental reasons should not 'constitute a means of

6 Antonio F. Perez, 'WTO and UN law: institutional comity in national security', *The Yale Journal of International Law* 23, 1998, p. 368.

7 Malcolm M. Shaw, *International law* (Cambridge: Cambridge University Press, 1991), p. 521.

8 Ximena Fuentes, 'The criteria for the equitable utilization of international rivers', *British Yearbook of International Law* (Oxford: Clarendon, 1996), pp. 337–412.

9 See Shanna I. Halpern, 'The United Nations Conference on Environment and Development: Process and Documentation', *The Academic Council on the United Nations System, Reports and Papers*, 1993, no.2.

10 Philippe Sands, *Principles of international environmental law*, Vol.1, *Frameworks, standards and implementation* (Manchester: Manchester University Press, 1995), p. 51.

Law, justice and the idea of a world society

arbitrary or unjustifiable discrimination or a disguised restriction on international trade'. The 1997 Kyoto Protocol on climate change is mainly concerned with setting out several detailed requirements on the emission of greenhouse gases but, in terms of this progressivist narrative, the Protocol (which has much stronger legal status than the Rio Declaration) might be regarded as a small advance for distributive justice. It repeats the 'common but differentiated responsibilities' formula of Rio, but adds relatively stronger requirements for all to implement their commitments 'in such a way as to minimize adverse social, environmental and economic impacts' on developing countries and for new resources, including the transfer of technology to be provided to meet the costs of developing countries.

In 1987 the semi-official Bruntland Report declared that existing international law 'is being rapidly out-distanced by the accelerating pace and expanding scale of impacts on the ecological basis of development',[11] thus aligning itself with those who were beginning to argue that the existing rules and institutions of the society of states were inadequate to cope with the new forces unleashed by globalization. More significantly, it played an important catalytic role in bringing into prominence the term 'sustainable development', which contains the implied principle of 'intergenerational equity', adding another dimension to the fairness discourse, namely that future generations have rights that need to be taken account of in legal instruments. Unlike some new would-be norms, this principle experienced a remarkably rapid progress from declaration to fundamental norm, appearing in numerous subsequent international documents.[12] Of particular interest to international lawyers, the principle was also cited, as if it were already an accepted norm of international law, in the International Court of Justice's (ICJ) decision in the 1997 *Case Concerning the Gabcikovo–Nagymaros Project*, a dispute between Hungary and Slovakia over their proposed navigational regime along the Danube, from which Hungary had withdrawn, citing environmental concerns among other reasons.[13]

The deep seabed mining provisions of the 1982 UN Law of the Sea Convention were widely seen as going much further in the direction of distributive justice than any previous international regime. A fundamental conceptual conflict, arising from Pardo's original 1967 assertion that the seabed was the 'common heritage of mankind', needed to be resolved before any progress could be made in the negotiations. Pardo rejected the concepts of '*laissez-faire* freedom beyond national jurisdiction' and 'the unfettered sovereignty of the State within national jurisdiction'. There was a need, therefore, for 'strong and equitably balanced international institutions with powers to administer ocean space beyond national jurisdiction and to manage its living and non-living

[11] Sands, *Principles of international environmental law*, p. 46.

[12] Guenther Handl, 'The legal mandate of multilateral development banks as agents for change towards sustainable development', *American Journal of International Law* 92: 4, October 1998, pp. 642–65.

[13] 'Report on ICJ decision, 25 September 1997, on Gabcikovo–Nagymaros Project', *American Journal of International Law* 92: 2, April 1998, p. 278.

David Armstrong

resources on behalf of the international community'. But so far as 'common heritage' was concerned, the developing countries (in alliance with the 'landlocked and geographically disadvantaged' group of states) wanted this to be interpreted to mean that the relevant resources should be exploited for the benefit of mankind as a whole; the developed countries' first riposte was that the 'common heritage' was available for all on a first come first served basis. In the event, the agreed regime was a compromise, but one that—until the United States reopened the issue as discussed later—on balance reflected developing countries' notions of justice in the following important respects:

- Article 150 called for exploitation of deep seabed minerals to take place in a manner consistent with the interests of developing countries and specifically required existing land based producers of the relevant minerals in the developing world to be compensated for any fall in revenue resulting from exploitation of the seabed.
- The proposed seabed Authority was to control all exploitation of the seabed 'on behalf of mankind as a whole', with its 'parallel access' system designed to ensure that its own mining company, the Enterprise, received the rights to mine half of the available sites. The Authority was also to receive a revenue from its licensing activities, making it the only international organization with a potentially large income not dependent on governments.
- A Review Conference, to be held 15 years after the commencement of commercial exploitation, was to have the capacity to amend the Convention by a three-quarters majority. The Review Conference was specifically charged to ensure that the seabed had been exploited 'for the benefit of all countries, especially the developing states'.[14]
- Companies wishing to conduct mining operations were required to transfer their technological know-how to the Enterprise and to developing country companies that had received mining licences.

Apart from specific developments such as those cited here, the progressivist case rests on a particular way of interpreting the evolution of the international legal system over the last few decades. The nature of the evolution is neatly encapsulated in statements from two noted cases, the first the 1927 *Lotus Case* in which the judgment of the Permanent Court of International Justice included a strong assertion that since international law derived from the will of states, 'Restrictions upon the independence of States cannot therefore be presumed'.[15] The second is from the ICJ President's Declaration in relation to a controversial ICJ Advisory Opinion in 1996 concerning the *Legality of the Threat or Use of Nuclear Weapons*:

[14] Bradley Larschan, 'The international legal status of the contractual rights of contractors under the Deep Sea-Bed Mining Provisions (Part XI) of the Third United Nations Convention on the Law of the Sea', *Denver Journal of International Law and Policy* 14: 2–3, 1986, pp. 218–21.

[15] Richard A. Falk, *The status of law in international society* (Princeton, NJ: Princeton University Press, 1970), p. 177.

Law, justice and the idea of a world society

Despite the still modest breakthrough of 'supra-nationalism', the progress made in terms of the institutionalization, not to say integration and 'globalization' of international society is undeniable. As proof of this, one may cite the multiplication of international organizations, the progressive substitution of an international law of cooperation for the classical international law of coexistence, the emergence of the concept of an '*international community*' ... The resolutely positivist, voluntarist approach of international law still current at the beginning of the century ... has been replaced by an objective conception of international law, a law more readily seeking to reflect a collective juridical conscience and respond to the social necessities of States organized as a community.[16]

These statements lead into one of the arguments used in support of the case that international law is evolving towards a 'world law', whose subjects are individuals and whose purpose is justice as well as order: the role played by the ICJ itself. Strictly speaking, international law does not have a doctrine of precedent—one case is not binding upon subsequent cases, so there is, theoretically, no possibility for 'judge-made law'. In practice, if only to achieve some consistency, ICJ decisions are generally seen as having a relevance beyond the immediate case to which they relate, if not actually as definitive statements of the state of law at that point. Hence if, as some argue, ICJ judges have taken an increasingly 'progressivist' view of their role and responsibilities, this would have significant legal consequences. Evidence of such an evolution might include (apart from the environmental and nuclear weapons cases already cited) a comparison of the ICJ's 1966 Decision in relation to South Africa's right to continue its possession of South-West Africa (Namibia) under its League of Nations Mandate with its 1971 Advisory Opinion on the same subject. In 1966 the Court had bluntly rejected the Liberian and Ethiopian case against South Africa with the assertion:

Humanitarian considerations were not in themselves sufficient to generate legal rights and duties. A court of law could not take account of moral principles unclothed in legal form.[17]

In 1971, by contrast, the Court took a far more liberal view of its capacities, arguing that it could take account of the evolution in thinking about issues like colonialism since 1919.[18]

If the ICJ is indeed playing a more prominent and proactive role in promoting new, 'progressive' norms, this, it might be argued, is essentially because it is merely reflecting, if not following a long way behind, developments taking

[16] Bruno Simma and Andreas L. Paulus, 'The "international community": facing the challenge of globalization', *European Journal of International Law* 9: 2, 1998, p. 277. See also, Handl, 'The legal mandate of multilateral development banks', p. 662, n. 148.

[17] 'South-West Africa Cases (Ethiopia v South Africa; Liberia v South Africa)', Second Phase, 18 July 1966, ICJ Reports 1966, 4, *International Law Reports*.

[18] ICJ Reports, 1971, para. 54, *International Law Reports*.

place elsewhere in the international legal order. In 1969, the Vienna Convention on the Law of Treaties invoked the notion of *jus cogens* —a peremptory norm of international law which would render void any treaty that conflicted with it, such norms being defined as ones 'accepted and recognised by the international community of States as a whole'.[19] In this way the Convention laid the foundations for a clear hierarchy of norms, including a category that had the power to negate even such a fundamental positivist principle as the pre-eminence and binding nature of treaties.

Other developments appeared to challenge the exclusive legal personality claimed by the state. Non-governmental organizations had influenced the creation of new legal norms, especially in relation to the environment. The growing body of international economic and environmental law was increasingly obliged to recognize the rights of various non-state entities, including individuals.[20] An even more significant breakthrough came with the war crimes tribunals in the 1990s, together with the creation of an international criminal court. However richly deserved was the fate of the defendants at Nuremburg, the trials were seen as deeply flawed in legal terms, meting out a retroactive justice to individuals in the defeated states only. The more recent developments in establishing the principle of individual accountability for certain kinds of violations of international norms were built upon much firmer juridical foundations.

At a more general level, some have argued that globalization has had a positive effect in promoting certain values that were seen to be inseperable from its central ideology of trusting markets, deregulating and privatizing.[21] These values included limiting the role of governments, providing equality of opportunity for women and disadvantaged groups in the interests of economic efficiency, and promoting good governance norms including democracy and human rights. All of these norms are explicitly or implicitly in evidence in international economic law and in particular in the interpretation and application of this by agencies such as the World Bank, the IMF and the Development Banks. The combined effect of changes of this kind, some argue, has been to shift international law increasingly from a concern with 'coexistence' to an emphasis on 'cooperation' and its societal base from a limited association to a more fully developed community. Some would even go so far as to suggest that we are witnessing the emergence of a body of law appropriate to a nascent international civil society.[22]

19 'The Vienna Convention on the Law of Treaties, 1969', Article 53, Malcolm D. Evans, *Blackstone's International Law Documents* (London: Blackstone, 1994), pp. 168–9.

20 Dominic McGoldrick, 'Sustainable development and human rights: an integrated conception', *International and Comparative Law Quarterly* 45, October 1996, p. 805.

21 Philip Alston, 'The myopia of the handmaidens: international lawyers and globalisation', *European Journal of International Law* 8: 3, 1997. See also Thomas M. Franck, 'Is personal freedom a Western value?', *American Journal of International Law* 91: 4, October 1997.

22 Simma and Paulus, 'The international community', p. 270. See also Jonathan I. Charney, 'Universal international law', *American Journal of International Law* 87: 4, October 1993.

Law, justice and the idea of a world society

The sceptic's tale

Needless to say, progressivist narratives of the kind sketched above have not gone unchallenged. Traditional realists, who have argued with John Austin for many years that international law is not true law, or with Dean Acheson that it is merely 'a body of ethical distillation', have seen little to cause them to amend their views.[23] This of course is an ancient and mostly inconclusive debate that will not be entered into here, except in so far as the pragmatic approach that concentrates on law's actual role in international affairs rather than the real nature of law as such will be utilized in this article's conclusion.

The more sophisticated positivist case tends not to deny any validity to international law as such but to suggest that progressivists are clutching at straws in their attempt to demonstrate fundamental change rather than a very limited fraying around the edges of traditional doctrine. Positivists would point to the many instances where the ICJ and other courts have not strayed very far from traditionalism. For example, in several continental shelf and water course disputes the ICJ has in practice paid very little attention to social and economic need in its decisions. In the 1982 Tunisia–Libya continental shelf case, the Court explicitly refused to take account of Tunisia's argument that its greater poverty should be a factor in the Court's delimitation. The Court responded that 'a country might be poor today and rich tomorrow as the result of an event such as the discovery of a valuable economic resource', so that a temporary phenomenon such as a state's relative wealth should not be allowed to influence a permanently applicable legal finding.[24] Even this refusal did not satisfy conservative judges who felt that the Court had gone too far in applying equitable principles, as Judge Oda argued:

> ... the consideration of socio-economic elements involves questions on global resource policies and world politics which should not be solved by international tribunals because these questions go well beyond equity as a norm of law into the realm of social organization.[25]

In a similar case between Malta and Libya in 1985 the Court also rejected Malta's argument that its status as a developing country without resources should be taken into account:

> ... neither the rules determining the validity of legal entitlement to the continental shelf, nor those concerning delimitation between neighbouring countries leave room for any considerations of economic development of the States in question.[26]

[23] See G. L. Williams, 'International law and the controversy concerning the word "law"', *British Yearbook of International Law* (Oxford: Clarendon, 1945), pp. 146–63 and Percy E. Corbett, *The growth of world law* (Princeton, NJ: Princeton University Press, 1971), p. 18.
[24] Fuentes, 'The criteria for equitable utilization', p. 343.
[25] Ibid., p. 341.
[26] Ibid., p. 343.

David Armstrong

More generally, the Court has never invoked *jus cogens* in any dispute, nor even used its statutory right to apply *ex aequo et bono* principles of equity in reaching its decisions. Moreover, far from *jus cogens* being the apex of a hierarchical normative structure, with the ICJ heading a similar jurisdictional hierarchy, the reality is that international law is applied in several quite disinct jurisdictional areas, so that, for example, the kind of criteria employed in a trade dispute by a WTO panel would be different from those operating over an environmental issue.[27].

Similar points might be made in respect of the Law of the Sea. Although the seabed mining provisions contain a radical redistributive principle it is one that operates in respect of a resource which may take many decades to become economically viable, if it ever does. In the first phase of negotiations an offer was on the table from the Nixon administration that would have had far greater practical effect: namely that coastal states might share revenues from the much more lucrative area closer to their coasts, which became in the end an Exclusive Economic Zone (EEZ) of 200 miles reserved for the coastal states alone.[28] The Nixon proposal failed essentially because coastal developing states could see more benefit to themselves from an EEZ than from a regime that offered some measure of fairness to all, so were happy to line up with richer coastal states such as Canada.[29] When the Law of the Sea Convention was concluded in 1982, its deep seabed mining provisions were then rejected by the United States and other Western countries. The American case rested on one important constitutional problem—the possibility that a Review Conference might technically be able to bind the United States without the consent of Congress—and a fundamental set of ideological objections arising from the strongly pro-market convictions of the Reagan administration. These generally worked against the redistributive intent of the Convention, for example, by insisting on greater protection for 'pioneer investors' and rejecting the provisions for compulsory transfer of technology, for measures to protect the interests of land-based developing country mineral producers, and for a powerful, independently resourced international organization working mainly in the interests of developing countries. In the event the seabed mining provisions were effectively renegotiated and a new Implementation Agreement devised in 1994 that took much greater account of the market principles that were by then reigning supreme over the regulatory emphasis of the original Convention. The provisions for the Review Conference were in effect abandoned, as were those relating to mandatory transfer of technology.[30] It should be noted, however, that the Implementation Agreement still embraces the principles of redistribution to developing countries

[27] Jonathan I. Charney, 'Third party dispute settlement and international law', *Columbia Journal of Transnational Law* 36, 1997, p. 89.
[28] Bernard H. Oxman, 'Human rights and the United Nations Convention on the Law of the Sea', *Columbia Journal of Transnational Law* 36, 1997, p. 412.
[29] Franck, *Fairness in international law*, p. 397.
[30] Marti Koskenniemi and Marja Lehto, 'The privilege of universality: international law, economic ideology and seabed resources', *Nordic Journal of International Law* 65: 3–4, 1996, p. 550.

as well as compensation for their land-based producers: its main aim is to place these within a free market framework rather than a centrally controlled one.

Realist cold water might also be thrown on other aspects of the progressivist case. For example, a more common evaluation of the GATT/WTO trade regime than the optimistic interpretation presented above is that its 'bias toward trade values ignores other human values that are ordinarily a central part of the political processes of most communities...'.[31]

Even where attempts have been made to inject considerations of distributive justice into trade matters, these have frequently failed to have the desired effect. The International Tin Agreement collapsed in 1985[32] and the UN's Common Fund for Commodities has had little impact.[33] Even the most ambitious scheme to support developing countries' trade, the Lomé Convention's STABEX, has not lived up to expectations with its developing country members' share of EU trade actually declining since the scheme was established.

In the case of sustainable development, this norm might in some respects actually work against the interests of developing countries, however 'progressive' its intentions. The richer developed nations are leading the drive to prevent further environmental and ecological damage and, to that end, are establishing relatively strict domestic regimes in certain areas. But in the numerous trade–environment negotiations that have taken place in recent years, clear differences have begun to emerge between regional regimes dominated by major powers, such as the EU and NAFTA, and those in which there is a stronger developing country presence, such as WTO.[34] This clearly reflects the differing interests between developed and developing blocs, and the fact that the developed countries have not been willing to pick up the bill for a truly global environmental regime. For instance, the richer states have strongly resisted proposals to amend the Agreement on Trade-Related Aspects of Intellectual Property Rights to make environmentally friendly technology more accessible to developing countries.[35] Finally, notwithstanding the excitement in the international legal community following the *Gabcikovo–Nagymaros* case, this was mainly concerned with the law of treaties and the law of state responsibility, with its pronouncements on the environment being essentially marginal and also of only limited general applicability.

Newstream international lawyers will typically reject both positivist and progressivist approaches (each of which they will, in any case, tend to see as parts of the same spectrum and subject to the same fundamental criticism that they sustain a discourse and its associated practices that are, at root, oppressive and need radical rethinking). Without going into detail about Newstream

[31] Perez, 'WTO and UN law', p. 376.
[32] Franck, *Fairness in international law*, p. 422, n. 65.
[33] Ibid., pp. 423–4.
[34] Richard H. Steinberg, 'Trade–environment negotiations in the EU, NAFTA and WTO: regional trajectories of rule development', *American Journal of International Law* 91: 2, April 1997.
[35] Ibid., p. 243.

perspectives,[36] the following central points may be briefly noted, since they will play a part in the concluding argument.[37] First, international law has played a central part in determining who is included and who excluded or marginalized in international society. Terms such as 'civilization', commonly used up to the time of the League Covenant, are far from being value-neutral and could easily help to underpin an unjust international order, excluding colonies, indigenous peoples and others from any legal entitlements. Second, where more conventional perspectives see international law as arising from state practice, Newstream theorists see it as being constituted by language, and hence as a system of 'linguistic manoeuvres' rather than rules. Law as 'discursive practice' contributes to global social exclusion, for example through its central term 'sovereignty', which defines legal personality in such a way as to prevent the emergence of a global legal order in which non-state entities might have rights. Third, both positivist and progressivist writers subscribe to a flawed Enlightenment view of history in which international law helped to constrain the worst excesses of an anarchical state system, or, in the progressivist view, assisted in a steady evolution towards a more just world community. This conceals the extent to which international law consistently reflected the interests and preoccupations of the most powerful states: from legitimizing territorial conquest in the past to institutionalizing an unjust international economic order today. War crimes tribunals, for example, are merely the latest instrument to uphold Great Power dominance. In either version of the sceptical narrative we remain a considerable distance from anything resembling a world society.

The socialization of states

It is my contention in this concluding section that neither the progressivist thesis nor the positivist or Newstream critiques quite capture the nature of contemporary international society or the role of international law in it. For, while a world society is clearly not taking shape on the back of developments of the kind described by the progressivists, neither is the society of states unchanged from its nineteenth-century form. Globalization and other forces may well have created a structure of economic, social, political and cultural interactions that cannot fully be understood within a framework defined solely by the state and the relations among states, but they have not replaced that framework. Rather, they have altered the way in which it operates primarily by redefining our understanding of what it means to be a state at the end of the millennium. That redefinition and reformulation, in turn, have influenced the social interaction

[36] See the excellent discussion of these approaches in Deborah Z. Cass, 'Navigating the Newstream: recent critical scholarship in international law', *Nordic Journal of International Law* 65: 3–4, 1996, pp. 341–83. See also David Kennedy, 'A New Stream of international law scholarship', in Robert J. Beck, Anthony Clark Arend and Robert D. Vander Lugt, *International rules: approaches from international law and international relations* (Oxford: Oxford University Press, 1996), pp. 230–52.

[37] This summary is derived from Cass, 'Navigating the Newstream'.

among states, including the processes by which international society arrives at its rules, and the nature of the rules themselves. Such changes have, in turn, fed into the fairness discourse in international relations.

It is, perhaps, time to call a halt to one of the more pointless (if most popular) games in academic IR: pronouncing the end of sovereignty. Sovereignty has a legal meaning, and only a legal meaning. It denotes constitutional or jurisdictional independence and has nothing to do with a state's actual power to perform specific functions or the ways in which its freedom to act may be constrained by non-legal forces outside its control.[38] As such it is a term with only limited worth, but it is not valueless: in particular it is of central importance in comprehending the nature and role of formal rules in international society. A sovereign state cannot formally be subject to any external jurisdiction except by its own consent. One implication of this is that the sole source of legitimate authority inside or outside the state is the state itself. However profound the changes in international relations in the past 50 years have been, they have not altered this central fact. This does not mean that the ICJ or WTO or other such agencies may not sometimes be able to play a quasi-independent role in world affairs, merely that the ultimate source of such capacity they possess is the state, and they function within the limits of state tolerance of their freedom.

International law, therefore, remains the law of states associated in a society of states, not of people who are members of some larger community. As such it inevitably reflects the interests of the more powerful members of international society, much as the Newstream critics maintain. But where both the Newstreamers and realists show a curious blindness is in refusing to take much account of changes in the nature of those powerful states since the last century. Less than one hundred years ago all major states were in a posture of permanent readiness for war with each other and, more importantly, were able to carry their societies with them into two world wars. They dominated the rest of the world and, again, had few problems in mobilizing their societies to uphold their domination by force. International legal texts reflected this reality, being as much concerned with legal issues arising from war as those governing peace. Indeed, international law may be said to have evolved through three stages rather than two, with a law of competition preceding a Cold War law of coexistence and what may be today's law of cooperation. But today both war among the major powers and straightforward colonial domination by them of other states look less and less plausible. There are many reasons for this, but two of particular importance are the increasing interdependence and multi-level interaction among the major powers, and the fact that all of them are subject to far greater degrees of popular scrutiny and accountability. The first has given them an ever longer list of common interests and problems requiring settled rules and norms to bring some predictability and stability to the international

[38] Alan James, *Sovereign statehood* (London: Allen and Unwin, 1986), p. 25.

system. The second has meant that popular demands for greater welfare and continuing economic growth, combined with a greater distaste for the amoral ways of the old politics, have both determined to a great extent the domestic political agenda for most leaders and constrained to some degree their international options. These developments are of course interrelated: popular demands for prosperity are increasingly dependent upon what happens in the international economic order. Today's liberal democracies are kinder, gentler things than they used to be, organised at least as much to provide justice as order or security.

A further effect of globalization is that the major powers constantly watch each other, not, as in the past, out of fear of military threat but because they face the same kinds of economic, social and political problems and are interested in observing how others deal with them. International society is not just a juridical association but a framework within which multifaceted social interaction among states takes place—most intensively among the major liberal democracies. In the course of such interaction, states are subject to a constant process of socialization in which they internalize each others' policies and practices across a wide spectrum, including economic, financial, educational and social policies. One consequence of this continuing process has been a redefinition in the West of collective understandings of what being a legitimate state entails. Where once legitimacy in international society required primarily the ability to demonstrate control over a specified territorial area and to perform certain limited international obligations, international legitimacy today is coming increasingly to involve considerations that were once deemed to be entirely matters of domestic concern for states, considerations that may be summed up by the term 'good governance': a set of norms embracing democracy, human rights, the rule of law and deregulated economies. With the end of the Cold War Western states have been less constrained by the perceived need to prop up regimes that fell far short of good governance standards and consequently far readier to press other states to move towards such objectives through attaching political conditions to loans and so forth. They have also perceived it to be in their self-interest to do so. If their own publics impose increasingly high standards on Western governments in areas like the environment or welfare provisions, they risk pricing themselves out of the international market place unless they can ensure that such norms spread. Furthermore, there is increasing recognition that capital finds its most secure and profitable homes in states that are reasonably well governed, with well educated work forces. Hence, while the most thoroughgoing processes of international socialization operate among the major Western powers, any state participating or aspiring to participate in the international politico/economic order encounters pressures to internalize the norms, institutions and practices that are now believed to characterize the fully legitimate state.

International society, therefore, remains a society of states, but one dominated by states that bear little resemblance to their imperial predecessors.

Law, justice and the idea of a world society

They have also become increasingly confident that their own liberal democratic capitalist societies constitute the norm towards which other states should gravitate and international law has essentially reflected that conviction. Newstreamers would have no problems in interpreting this development as simply the latest stage in a long history of Western imperial domination. Where once the 'standard of civilization' provided the respectable cloak behind which the West oppressed weaker countries, now the standard of governance plays the same part. But not all Newstream propositions lead to negative interpretations. For example, the argument that language constitutes reality is invariably used to show how a certain terminology sustains oppressive and unjust structures. But it has never been entirely clear why language need necessarily function in such a negative fashion: as good governance terminology permeates the international discourse, and becomes institutionalized in legal documents, is it not possible that it might help to constitute a more just reality?

A similar argument about the importance of language may be used to answer the realists' claims that international law does not matter much, if indeed we can accept that it is a form of law in the first place. Constant reiteration of good governance doctrines in legal documents gives them a taken-for-granted quality that leads eventually to their institutionalization as basic norms of international society. Even so, can they affect state behaviour in the absence of powerful sanctions to enforce them, such as those that operate within states? This brings us perilously close once again to the debate about the essential legality or otherwise of international law, and indeed the nature of law as such. It will suffice here to employ the pragmatic case: that most states, most of the time act as if they perceive themselves to be operating within a framework of legal norms and react strongly when states are seen to be violating basic rules. To repeat, this is far from claiming that we live in a world society where justice is a fundamental objective. Globalization, like any process of rapid change, has produced winners and losers and the institutions of international society can have only the most limited impact on this state of affairs while they remain based on the doctrine of state sovereignty. But international society has always played a crucial role in determining the criteria for full membership, or for legitimate statehood. Its current criteria include requirements that, if adopted, will inevitably push states towards a greater responsiveness to justice claims from their own peoples. Insofar as progress may be made in ameliorating some of the unfairnesses arising from globalization, it will be made within each individual state rather than the international community, but the latter, by institutionalizing good governance norms in international law, can have a significant effect upon the fairness discourse inside states.

Part VII
Is International Law Democratic?

[18]

THE KANTIAN THEORY OF INTERNATIONAL LAW

*Fernando R. Tesón**

INTRODUCTION

This Article defends the view, first developed by Immanuel Kant, that international law and domestic justice are fundamentally connected.[1] Despite the recent prominence of the international law of human rights, the dominant discourse in international law fails to recognize the important normative status of the individual. Traditional international legal theory focuses upon the rights and duties of states and rejects the contention that the rights of states are merely derivative of the rights and interests of the individuals who reside within them. Accordingly, international legitimacy and sovereignty are a function of whether the government politically controls the population, rather than whether it justly represents its people. This statist conceptualization of international law argues for a dual paradigm for the ordering of individuals: one domestic, the other international. Justice and legitimacy are conceptually separate. It may well be that domestic systems strive to promote justice; but international systems only seek order and compliance.

International law thus conceived, however, is incapable of serving as the normative framework for present or future political realities.[2]

---

* Professor of Law, Arizona State University. J.D., University of Buenos Aires; Licencié en Droit International, Université Libre de Bruxelles; S.J.D., Northwestern University. This article is excerpted from my book The Philosophy of International Law (Westview Press, forthcoming). My thanks to Kirsten Spalding, David Kaye, and to the members of the Moral, Political, and Legal Philosophy Research Group here at Arizona State: Jeffrie Murphy, David Kader, Larry Winer, Peter de Marneffe, Joan McGregor, Richard Dagger, Jack Crittendon, Charles Dresser, and Al D'Amico. All these people contributed helpful comments and criticisms. My thanks also to Harold A. Neu from the Columbia Law Review for his excellent suggestions.

1. Immanuel Kant's most important work on international relations is Immanuel Kant, To Perpetual Peace: A Philosophical Sketch [1795], *in* Perpetual Peace and Other Essays 107 (Ted Humphrey trans., 1983) [hereinafter Kant, Perpetual Peace]. Kant elaborates on his international theory elsewhere, see Idea for a Universal History with a Cosmopolitan Intent [1784], *in* Perpetual Peace and Other Essays, supra, at 29, 34–39 [hereinafter Kant, Universal History]; On the Proverb: That May be True in Theory, But Is of No Practical Use [1793], *in* Perpetual Peace and Other Essays, supra, at 61, 85–89 [hereinafter Kant, Theory and Practice]. The best summary of Kant's moral theory by Kant himself is Immanuel Kant, Groundwork of the Metaphysic of Morals (H.J. Paton trans., Harper Torchbook ed. 1964) [hereinafter Kant, Groundwork]. A very useful secondary source for Kant's moral theory is Roger J. Sullivan, Immanuel Kant's Moral Theory (1989). This article relies extensively on Professor Sullivan's account.

2. I am referring to the liberal revolutionary changes in the last 20 years, including the Iberian Peninsula in the 1970s; Latin America (led by Argentina) in the middle 1980s; and Central Europe since 1989. See Dankwart A. Rustow, Democracy: A Global Revolution?, Foreign Aff., Fall 1990, at 75. On Latin America, see 4 Democracy In De-

While it is understandably hard for lawyers to forsake the statist assumptions of classic international legal discourse, new times call for a fresh conceptual and ethical language.[3] A liberal theory of international law can hardly be reconciled with the statist approach.[4] Liberal theory commits itself instead to *normative individualism*, to the premise that the primary normative unit is the individual, not the state.[5] The end of states and governments is to benefit, serve, and protect their components, human beings; and the end of international law must also be to benefit, serve, and protect human beings, and not its components, states and governments. Respect for states is merely derivative of respect for persons. In this way, the notion of state sovereignty is redefined: the sovereignty of the state is dependent upon the state's domestic legitimacy; and therefore the principles of international justice must be congruent with the principles of internal justice.[6]

Immanuel Kant was the first to defend this thesis,[7] and for that reason it will be called the Kantian theory of international law. This Article reconstructs and examines Kant's theory as put forth in his famous essay *Perpetual Peace*. Part I addresses the controversy regarding the essay's structure and organization, ánd argues that Kant developed a normative philosophy of international law, not merely a practical political program. Part II shows that Kant's reason for respecting states stemmed from concerns about individual freedom, not from holistic claims about the state as a moral person. Part III presents and defends

veloping Countries: Latin America (Larry Diamond, et al. eds., 1989); on Europe, see Vents D'Est: Vers l'Europe des Etats de droit (Pierre Grémion & Pierre Hassner eds., 1990).

3. The growing number of legal scholars who are challenging the statist paradigm include Anthony D'Amato, The Invasion of Panama Was a Lawful Response to Tyranny, 84 Am. J. Int'l L. 516 (1990); W. Michael Reisman, Sovereignty and Human Rights in Contemporary International Law, 84 Am. J. Int'l L. 866 (1990).

4. The word "liberal" is notorious for its multiple meanings in politics and political theory. I mean "liberal theory" here simply as a theory of politics founded upon individual freedom, respect for individual preferences, and individual autonomy. As such, it encompasses a broad spectrum of actual political positions, from social democrats to libertarians.

5. For a survey of the different meanings of "individualism," see Steven Lukes, Individualism (1973). The notion of individualism defended in this Article is both methodological and normative. Methodological individualism contends that social science explanations should only be made in terms of individuals, see id. at 110–22. Normative individualism insists that our moral concepts should be referred in the last analysis to individual rights and interests—this is *not* to be confused with ethical egoism, which is a substantive moral doctrine, see id. at 99–106.

6. I have elsewhere argued for the same thesis using a modified Rawlsian model. See Fernando R. Tesón, International Obligation and the Theory of Hypothetical Consent, 15 Yale J. Int'l L. 84, 109–18 (1990).

7. Kant was the first to suggest human rights as the basis of international law, but not the first to propose an international alliance or organization. In this latter sense, the pioneer work is C.I. Castel de Saint-Pierre, Selections from the Second Edition of the Abrégé du Projet de Paix Perpétuelle (H. Hale Bellot trans., 1927), reprinted in Peace Projects of the Eighteenth Century (Garland ed., 1974).

the two Kantian arguments for the international human rights imperative. First, an international community of just, democratic states is the best guarantee for international peace because internal freedom at home is causally related to peaceful behavior abroad. Second, international law requires respect for human rights because the just civic society is the ultimate goal of all political arrangements. The argument for human rights is universal since it is derived from the Kantian categorical imperative.[8] These two arguments link international law to human rights and individual autonomy, not to national interest, rights of governments, or other notions similarly rooted in the primacy of state sovereignty. Part IV examines the nature of the liberal alliance proposed by Kant. Kant's choice of a decentralized system of international authority and enforcement is discussed and defended. This Part also examines the place of war within the theory, showing an inconsistency in Kant's views on war, and proposing a modified version. Part V defends the Kantian theory of international law against recent challenges to the idea that justice should be a component of international legitimacy. This Part also sets forth some conclusions and suggestions for practical reforms in accordance with the theory.

While offering a modern reconstruction of Kant's thesis rather than a meticulously faithful account of what Kant meant, the interpretation of Kant suggested in this Article is accurate, whether one wants to confine oneself to the text of *Perpetual Peace*, or one views his discussion of international law against the backdrop provided by Kant's general moral theory. To be sure, this Article departs from Kant on a few important points,[9] but the main thrust of his account remains intact.

It is not surprising that Immanuel Kant's philosophy is cited with renewed frequency in many international fora. He is conventionally seen as the pioneering advocate of an international organization capable of securing a lasting peace. Commentators have justly praised Kant as the one philosopher who, in his effort to contest the prevailing views upholding the absolute right of governments to wage war, foreshadowed modern conceptions of international law associated with the United Nations.[10] The novelty of his proposals explains why Kant's contribution has been regarded as *avant la lettre* political advocacy for the United Nations and peaceful world order.[11] Nevertheless, Kant accomplished far more. He developed a subtle, rich, and innovative the-

---

8. For a discussion of Kant's categorical imperative, see infra notes 48–71 and accompanying text.

9. See notes 65–68, 167–170, 199–220 and accompanying text.

10. For a comparison between Kant's proposals and the precepts of the U.N. Charter, see Carl J. Friedrich, Inevitable Peace 33 (1948) (U.N. Charter in many respects mirrors Kant's conditions for world order); Wolfgang Schwarz, Kant's Philosophy of Law and International Peace, 23 Phil. & Phenomenological Res. 71, 76–78 (1962).

11. See A.C. Armstrong, Kant's Philosophy of Peace and War, 28 J. Phil. 197, 201–04 (1931) (Kant's proposals for world peace "run closely parallel to those of 20th century"); see also W.B. Gallie, Philosophers of Peace and War 11–12 (1978) (Kant's

ory of international law, one that was so much ahead of its time that even admirers were blind to its importance. Kant's originality stems not so much from predicting the rise of a global international organization, but from having been the first to show the strong links between international peace and personal freedom, and between arbitrary government at home and aggressive behavior abroad. Not only did he have the vision to predict modern international organization for the maintenance of peace; he also explained, for the first time, the connection between domestic freedom and the foundations of international law. In essence, he foresaw the human rights revolution of the twentieth century.

I. The Structure of *Perpetual Peace*

Perpetual Peace was published in 1795 and was one of Immanuel Kant's last philosophical works.[12] It is a relatively short essay that was meant for popular reading.[13] Kant was not very good at writing for the general public, however, and the essay suffers as a consequence: the arguments are at times too concise and the writing often obscure.[14] Nonetheless, Kant's genius pervades the essay.[15] It had immediate success, and Kant's authority has been invoked frequently by advocates of pacifism and internationalism throughout the nineteenth and twentieth centuries.[16] While there are many interpretations of *Perpetual Peace*, almost all commentators agree that in this short essay Kant made a subtle, rich, and lasting contribution both to the theory of international law and to the causes of justice and peace. The themes developed in *Perpetual Peace* have extraordinary contemporary relevance. It is no surprise that interest in the essay has been revived recently. Even the President of the former Soviet Union referred to Kant's work in his speech accepting the Nobel Peace Prize.[17]

Perpetual Peace contains six "Preliminary Articles," three "Definitive Articles," and two long "Addenda," the most important of which is "On the Guarantee of Perpetual Peace."[18] The structural organization

vision was both "original" and "unique"). Although I differ with Professor Gallie in important ways, I have benefitted greatly from reading his excellent discussion of Kant.

12. See supra note 1.

13. See Gallie, supra note 11, at 8–9.

14. For an account of Kant's background and the history of his interest in political philosophy, see Gallie, supra note 11, at 12–17.

15. In the words of Kenneth Waltz, Kant's mode of analysis is "rigorous and yet subtle, his style difficult but clear, his writing crabbed and still, as Goethe said, sometimes slyly ironic and even eloquent." Kenneth N. Waltz, Kant, Liberalism, and War, 56 Am. Pol. Sci. Rev. 331, 331 (1962).

16. See Armstrong, supra note 11, at 197–98.

17. See Gorbachev Skips Nobel Awards, Chi. Trib., Dec. 11, 1990, at 4.

18. The text of the Articles with their headings is as follows:

First Section Which Contains the Preliminary Articles for Perpetual Peace Among Nations

of *Perpetual Peace* raises two questions, the answer to which may provide insight into Kant's intent: Why is the essay put in the form of articles, like a treaty? What meaning, if any, should we ascribe to the categories of "preliminary" and "definitive" articles?

The selection of the format indicates that Kant intended to offer a programmatic formula for peace, rather than a philosophical analysis of the nature of international law and relations. Indeed, he wanted politicians to follow his advice—he specifically enjoins governments to take advice from philosophers.[19] Thus, the form of the essay, at least in part, suggests that Kant wanted to draft a model treaty of some sort,[20] with specific provisions to be honored by all signatories. However, he only partially succeeded: *Perpetual Peace*, as written, seems to suffer from a fundamental ambiguity. While the essay can be viewed as an unattainable moral ideal to which states ought to aspire in their international relations,[21] it is preferably treated as an attempt to explicate international moral principles—the principles that should underlie the

---

1) No treaty of peace that tacitly reserves issues for a future war shall be held valid.

2) No independent nation, be it large or small, may be acquired by another nation by inheritance, exchange, purchase, or gift.

3) Standing armies (*miles perpetus*) shall be gradually abolished.

4) No national debt shall be contracted in connection with the foreign affairs of the nation.

5) No nation shall forcibly interfere with the constitution and government of another.

6) No nation at war with another shall permit such acts of war as must make mutual trust impossible during some future time of peace: Such acts include the use of *Assassins* (*percussores*), *Poisoners* (*venefici*), *breach of surrender*, *instigation of treason* (*perduellio*) in the opposing nation, etc.

Second Section Which Contains the Definitive Articles for Perpetual Peace Among Nations

1) The civil constitution of every nation should be republican.

2) [International law] shall be based on a federation of free states.

3) Cosmopolitan [Law] shall be limited to conditions of universal *hospitality*.

Kant, Perpetual Peace, supra note 1, at 107–18. In the Second and Third Definitive Articles, I prefer to use the word "law" rather than Humphrey's "right." The word "*Recht*" used in the original is ambiguous (as are the words "*derecho*" in Spanish and "*droit*" in French) and it may be translated as "law" or as "right," depending on the context. It is clear from the context in Perpetual Peace that Kant is referring to the objective international order, the "law," and not to "right" in the subjective sense. The German word "Volkerrecht" is ordinarily translated as "international law," not "international right." A better translation is offered by Carl Friedrich in Immanuel Kant, The Philosophy of Kant 441 (Carl J. Friedrich ed., 1949) ("law of nations").

19. Kant, Perpetual Peace, supra note 1, at 126. But cf. Waltz, supra note 15, at 339–40 (Kant "was not engaged in the puerile task of telling men of affairs to stop behaving badly").

20. See F.H. Hinsley, Power and the Pursuit of Peace 66 (1963).

21. See Waltz, supra note 15, at 334, 339–40. This ambiguity is quite distinct from differences of interpretation about the essay's substantive content, discussed below. See infra notes 23–34 and accompanying text.

relations among nations. Kant was a philosopher, not a mere pamphleteer.[22] There is also a call for political action, to be sure: it is the one that flows naturally from his normative theory of international law. Thus, the essay is both conceptual and normative; it attempts to draw applied international legal principles from an understanding of the underlying philosophical nature of international relations.

The second organizational issue is what meaning to attribute to the categories "preliminary" and "definitive." Some commentators have interpreted the Preliminary Articles to be those which might have served as the legal foundation of international peace, or as a statement of international law as it ought to be; whereas the Definitive Articles are interpreted to be the political premises and safeguards, without which no state could be expected to comply with the earlier articles.[23] For these writers, the Preliminary Articles are the solution, not a statement of the necessary preconditions to establishing the framework for a lasting peace.[24]

The reader may think that this debate is highly formalistic, exegetic, and overly textual. On the contrary, the debate over the purpose of Kant's choice of structure for *Perpetual Peace* is critical to an analysis of the work itself. Commentators in the realist tradition, who emphasize the primacy of the state as the international actor, exalt the Preliminary Articles.[25] Indeed, the key pro-government rule, nonintervention, is embodied in one of the Preliminary Articles. In addition, Kant's commentary ostensibly relies on the analogy of the state as a moral person, which is a favorite theoretical device of realists.[26] In contrast, each of the three Definitive Articles enshrines in different ways the primacy of individual freedom and the logically consistent unity of purpose of international and domestic law.[27] Thus, a reading of *Perpetual Peace* that emphasizes the Preliminary Articles leads to a realist or statist interpretation that gives primacy to states and governments over individuals; whereas a reading that relies on the Definitive Articles leads to an interpretation that gives the priority to human rights over the power of the state as a foundation of international law.

---

22. See Karl Jaspers, Philosophy and the World 113-17 (E.B. Ashton trans., 1963) (Kant sets forth principles underlying international law, not political program). But see Waltz, supra note 15, at 334 ("Kant does set forth 'shoulds' and 'oughts' of state behavior.").

23. See Hinsley, supra note 20, at 69; Gallie, supra note 11, at 9–10.

24. See Hinsley, supra note 20, at 66-69.

25. See id. at 69 (arguing that Preliminary Articles are "a statement . . . of Kant's solution"). Hinsley flatly rejects the First Definitive Article—the requirement that all states be republican—by observing that "[i]t is impossible to overlook the lameness of [Kant's] conclusion [that republican states are more likely to be peaceful]." Id. at 71. His views are characteristic of the discomfort felt toward Kant's revolutionary humanism by those who cling to a statist world view and as a result adopt a statist reading of Kant.

26. For further discussion, see infra Part II.D.

27. See infra Parts II and III.

The realist interpretation seems dubious. According to Kant, no perpetual peace can be achieved unless states are internally free and agree on an alliance or federation;[28] therefore, it does not seem that adherence to the Preliminary Articles alone would have sufficed to maintain peace even among the 18th century European powers. The better interpretation of the Preliminary Articles is that they are those urgent agreements that should enter into force if the state of nature[29] among states is to progress toward the formation of a federation that mirrors the relation of men under a civil constitution. The Preliminary Articles describe the most pressing steps to be taken if we want subsequently to proceed toward the lasting solution.[30]

In contrast, the substantive solutions, the institutional features of an effective and just international organization, are contained in the Definitive Articles. When Kant wrote "definitive," he meant what the word implies—a structure providing the final and conclusive solution to the problem of international relations. The Preliminary Articles do not even provide for the everlasting peace that Kant envisioned, which is included in the Second Definitive Article. Moreover, the Definitive Articles—which, as conceded by one of the above mentioned realist commentators, contain "Kant's most original political thinking"[31]—are

28. See infra Part III.

29. Commentators have emphasized how much Kant owed to Rousseau. See Gallie, supra note 11, at 17. Yet, Kant's conception of the state of nature as the pre-civil state of human beings before the formation of the state is, in different ways, closer to that of Hobbes and Locke. There are striking similarities and contrasts between Kant's conception of the state of nature and that of each of the great English philosophers. Kant shares with Hobbes the belief in the evil propensities of men and their tendency to immoral social conduct. See, e.g., Kant, Universal History, supra note 1, at 31; see also Sullivan, supra note 1, at 238–39 (Kant believed that "everyone is infected by the tendency to evil"). But Kant did have tremendous faith in reason. See Kant, Universal History, supra note 1, at 31 ("[A]s a class of rational beings . . . [humanity] is destined to develop its capacities to perfection."). In contrast, Rousseau believed that man in the state of nature was ignorant of vice. See Jean-Jacques Rousseau, A Discourse on the Origin of Inequality, *in* The Social Contract and Discourse, 27, 66 (G.D.H. Cole trans., 1973). On the other hand, Kant shares with Locke the belief in morality *predating* the social contract (contrary to Hobbes). In Locke this takes the simple form of natural rights; whereas in Kant this innate morality is anchored in individual reason and autonomy. See Kant, Universal History, supra note 1, at 29–31. Finally, for both Kant and Locke, but not for Hobbes, the purpose of the state is to protect the citizen's freedom. See Thomas Hobbes, Leviathan 98–102 (Michael Oakeshott ed., 1962) (1651); David P. Gauthier, The Logic of Leviathan: The Moral and Political Theory of Thomas Hobbes 134–46 (1969); John Locke, Two Treatises of Government 350–53 (Peter Laslett ed., student ed. 1988) (1698). The analogy for the state of nature in international relations is qualified, however. The Kantian theory insists that *individual* morality, and therefore individual freedom, not "state" morality, predates the creation of international law.

30. See Schwarz, supra note 10, at 75; Thomas L. Carson, *Perpetual Peace*: What Kant Should Have Said, 14 Soc. Theory and Prac. 173, 174 (1988); Michael W. Doyle, Kant, Liberal Legacies, and Foreign Affairs (pt. 1), 12 Phil. & Pub. Aff. 205, 225–32 (1983).

31. See Gallie, supra note 11, at 10.

preceded by a very important paragraph in which Kant writes that the state of peace must be founded or established; hence the need for the federation or alliance proposed in the Second Definitive Article.[32]

The most natural interpretation, then, is that the Definitive Articles are the foundation of perpetual peace; they contain the institutional arrangements that directly reflect the precepts of international justice. They are the ones that are designed to eliminate war from the face of the earth for all time.[33]

The defining characteristics of the Preliminary Articles are that they are the first steps that governments must take to end international lawlessness; those points upon which they must agree first in order to agree subsequently on the definitive and fundamental principles of international law. Here, Kant is trying to lay down the preliminary conditions conducive to definitive peace. These norms are designed to govern the intermediate status of international relations after the lawless state of nature is ended, but before the definitive law of nations is established.[34] Yet, the important point to remember is that they are meant to be permanent; they are preliminary, but not provisional. Standing armies must disappear; peace treaties should not contain reservations for future wars; states should not intervene in other states' affairs; states should not be acquired by conquest; and abject means of conducting war should be permanently prohibited. The Preliminary Articles will not suffice to guarantee peace unless the Definitive Articles are agreed upon.

II. The Requirement That States Be Liberal Democracies

The first principle of international ethics, embodied in the First Definitive Article, is: "The civil constitution of every nation should be republican."[35] The requirement of a republican form of government must be read in conjunction with the Second Definitive Article: "The

32. Kant writes:

> The state of peace among men living in close proximity is not the natural state (*status naturalis*); instead, the natural state is one of war, which does not just consist in open hostilities, but also in the constant and enduring threat of them. The state of peace must therefore be *established*, for the suspension of hostilities does not provide the security of peace, and unless this security is pledged by one neighbor to another (which can happen only in a state of *lawfulness*), the latter, from whom such security has been requested, can treat the former as an enemy.

Kant, Perpetual Peace, supra note 1, at 111 (footnotes omitted).

33. The interpretation suggested by Gallie and Hinsley is not consistent with the meaning of the words "preliminary" and "definitive." See Webster's Third New International Dictionary 592, 1789 (1981). Hinsley tries to meet this objection by suggesting that the word "preliminary" is used in the sense of the law of treaties, see Hinsley, supra note 20, at 69; Gallie, supra note 11, at 9–10. Even if this is true, it does not provide or explain the contextual meaning of the word "definitive."

34. See Hinsley, supra note 20, at 69; Gallie, supra note 11, at 9–10.

35. Kant, Perpetual Peace, supra note 1, at 112.

law of nations shall be based on a federation of free states."[36] Together, these first two articles stipulate that international law should be based upon a union of republican states.[37] Kant asserts that adherence to these requirements will result in an alliance of free nations that will maintain itself, prevent wars, and steadily expand.[38] Contrary to the predominant belief of his time, and to conventional present legal thinking, international law and the peace it intends to secure can only be based upon a union or an alliance of participant states that protect freedom internally and whose governments are representative. Kant for the first time linked arbitrary government at home with aggressive foreign policies.

By "republican," Kant means what we would call today a liberal democracy, a form of political organization that provides full respect for human rights.[39] This is so notwithstanding Kant's assertion that a *pure* democracy is a form of despotism.[40] Kant's explanation of a republican constitution[41] strongly suggests the idea of a constitutional democracy, conceived as a participatory political process constrained by respect for rights. Kant correctly points out that a system of pure democracy, if unconstrained by rights, will result in the tyranny of the majority. Kant writes:

> Among the three forms of government, *democracy*, in the proper sense of the term, is necessarily a *despotism*, because it sets up an executive power in which all citizens make decisions about and, if need be, *against one (who therefore does not agree); consequently, all, who are not quite all, decide, so that the general will contradicts both itself and freedom*.[42]

Plainly, Kant wanted to set constraints upon majoritarian decisions.[43] So, only a *pure* democracy ("in the proper sense of the term") is despotic. In contrast, the republican constitution is a form of political organization that allows people to govern themselves and to legislate by majority vote, provided that the rights of everyone are

36. Id. at 115.

37. The word "free" in the Second Definitive Article may be a reiteration of the requirement of the republican constitution: a federation of *free* states. See Friedrich, supra note 10, at 45. However, it is possible also to interpret the word "free" in that article as meaning "politically independent," thus suggesting that states enter the alliance voluntarily. See infra part III. This second interpretation is suggested by Kant's commentary to this article. See Kant, Perpetual Peace, supra note 1, at 115–18.

38. See Kant, Perpetual Peace, supra note 1, at 117–18.

39. I wish to avoid terminological debate about the meaning of the words "liberal" and "democracy." The word "liberal," as used in this Article, is broad and refers to a political theory centered around the notion of individual autonomy, individual preferences, or individual rights. A liberal democracy is one in which individual rights are honored and rulers are appointed by the people.

40. See Kant, Perpetual Peace, supra note 1, at 114.

41. See infra notes 45–47, 72–73, 88 and accompanying text.

42. Kant, Perpetual Peace, supra note 1, at 114.

43. See infra notes 45–47, 72–73, 88 and accompanying text.

respected—in short, a *constitutional* democracy. Thus, the Kantian idea of republicanism is best understood as being in opposition to the idea of despotism, whether exercised by a minority (one person or a junta), or by the majority enforcing its decisions in violation of the rights of dissenters.[44] Kant envisions the republican state as one defined by a constitution based upon three principles: freedom, due process, and equality.[45]

A. *Freedom*

The principle of freedom[46] consists of the liberal principles of respect for individual autonomy and government neutrality of ends:

> No one can compel me (in accordance with his belief about the welfare of others) to be happy after his fashion; instead, every person may seek happiness in the way that seems best to him, if only he does not violate the freedom of others to strive toward such similar ends as are compatible with everyone's freedom under a possible universal law . . . .[47]

One can hardly overemphasize the importance of this highly innovative Kantian thesis. Kant includes freedom—respect for individual autonomy under the rule of law—as the first tenet of international ethics. He is not committing the fallacy of transposing the notion of individual freedom into the conceptual framework of nationalism: freedom here is not the right *to* a nation-state, but primarily claims *against* it, claims against fellow citizens and against the government established by a social contract to implement social cooperation.

In order to understand Kant's discussion of the principle of freedom in the republican constitution, it is necessary to analyze in some detail Kant's categorical imperative. In his writings on moral philosophy, Kant attempted to demonstrate the possibility of human freedom and autonomy in the face of the deterministic laws of nature.[48] Only a

---

44. See Kant, Perpetual Peace, supra note 1, at 114 ("government is either *republican* or *despotic*").

45. The requirements of a republican constitution, merely summarized in Perpetual Peace, are eloquently put forth in Kant, Theory and Practice, supra note 1, at 71–84.

46. See Kant, Perpetual Peace, supra note 1, at 112.

47. Kant, Theory and Practice, supra note 1, at 72. In his *Critique of Pure Reason*, Kant argues for the proposition that

> [a] constitution allowing the greatest possible human freedom in accordance with laws by which the freedom of each is made to be consistent with that of all others . . . is at any rate a necessary idea, which must be taken as fundamental not only in first projecting a constitution but in all its laws.

Immanuel Kant, Critique of Pure Reason 312 (B373) (Norman Kemp Smith trans., 1929) [hereinafter Kant, Critique of Pure Reason].

48. Within the general framework of Kant's Critical program, the categorical imperative constitutes the solution to the third antinomy of pure reason, to wit, the apparently irresolvable conflict between the ideas of freedom and causal determinism. Kant, Critique of Pure Reason, supra note 47, at 409–15. (A445/B473–A451/B479); Immanuel Kant, Critique of Practical Reason 3–8 (4–8) (Lewis W. Beck trans., 1956)

free and autonomous being is capable of acting morally and can be said to have dignity and be worthy of respect. Thus Kant's primary aim in the *Groundwork* was "to seek out and establish the supreme principle of morality."[49] This he calls the categorical imperative, a universal law that all rational beings can make and act upon for themselves as free, self-determining agents whose actions are morally good.[50] Kant offers three different formulae of the categorical imperative, yet contends that they are "at bottom merely so many formulations of precisely the same law."[51]

The first formula is the most abstract. It emphasizes the impartiality and universal nature that moral principles ought to exhibit: "Act only on that maxim through which you can at the same time will that it should become a universal law."[52] While initially this formula seems empty of content, there is good reason for that. Kant insists that moral philosophy must have an *a priori* foundation, which in turn necessarily must be formal.[53] In this way, the violation of the categorical imperative is not only morally reprehensible, but irrational and self-contradictory.[54] Additionally, while this maxim is formal, it is not entirely devoid of content, for it enjoins us to "act autonomously and respect the right and obligation of everyone else to do the same."[55] From the standpoint of a theory of international law, the first version of the cate-

---

[hereinafter Kant, Critique of Practical Reason]; Kant, Groundwork, supra note 1, at 123-29.

49. Kant, Groundwork, supra note 1, at 60. Kant defines the categorical imperative and explicates the complex ideas contained within it in the Groundwork. In his two later works on moral philosophy, Critique of Pure Reason and The Metaphysics of Morals, Kant demonstrates the binding force of the categorical imperative on human beings who are only imperfectly rational and employs the categorical imperative to derive the whole system of human duties. It is important to note that, for Kant, the categorical imperative cannot be proved but can be deduced from pure practical reason. In the Critique of Practical Reason, Kant presents this deduction and demonstrates "the unity of practical and theoretical reason in [the] common principle" that is the categorical imperative. Kant, Groundwork, supra note 1, at 59. See Kant, Critique of Practical Reason, supra note 48, at 43-51 (42-50).

50. Kant, Groundwork, supra note 1, at 98-103.

51. Id. at 103. Paton identifies five interrelated but distinct formulations of the categorical imperative in the Groundwork. H.J. Paton, The Categorical Imperative: A Study in Kant's Moral Philosophy 129-30, 133-98 (1971).

52. Id. at 88.

53. See Kant, Groundwork, supra note 1, at 55; Sullivan, supra note 1, at 151-53.

54. See Kant, Groundwork, supra note 1, at 90; Sullivan, supra note 1, at 151-53. Most philosophers agree that Kant has provided a *necessary* condition for the validity of moral judgment. See, e.g., Marcus G. Singer, Generalization in Ethics: An Essay in the Logic of Ethics, with the Rudiments of a System of Moral Philosophy 34 (1971) (explaining that generalization is presupposed in every genuine moral judgment). However, doubt has been expressed by commentators as to whether Kant has provided a *sufficient* condition for such validity. Indeed, many principles which we intuitively regard as unacceptable comply with the formal requirement of this first version of the categorical imperative.

55. See Sullivan, supra note 1, at 165-66.

gorical imperative provides crucial support for the universality of human rights.[56]

The emphasis on the agent's autonomy and the respect for the autonomy of others leads naturally to the second version, the formula of respect for the dignity of persons: "Act in such a way that you always treat humanity, whether in your own person or in the person of any other, never simply as a means, but always at the same time as an end."[57] This second formula is a specification of the first in that here Kant identifies the class of moral agents: all human beings. The term "humanity" denotes the "functional complex of abilities and characteristics that enables us to set ends and make rational choices."[58] Because rationality defines the moral agent and because the categorical imperative requires universalization, we must presuppose rationality in the persons on whom the agent's behavior impinges. Kant's crucial step in the argument is that this rationality makes persons objects that are worthy of respect, ends in themselves. Things are instrumental and have only extrinsic value. Human beings, on the other hand, have *intrinsic* value. In Kant's words:

> Now I say that man, and in general every rational being, *exists* as an end in himself, *not merely as means* for arbitrary use by this or that will: he must in all his actions, whether they are directed to himself or to other rational beings, always be viewed *at the same time as an end*.[59]

The consequences for *political* philosophy of this view of respect for the dignity of human beings as the ultimate basis for the moral justification of our conduct are self-evident. If in our everyday behavior we should never consider fellow human beings merely as means, it follows *a fortiori* that the constitution of the state, an artificial creation to serve human needs, must embody and incorporate a formula of respect for persons—a bill of human rights.[60] Thus, in the Kantian vision, mechanisms for guaranteeing traditional civil and political rights, which act as barriers against the abuse of state power, form the basis of a republican constitution because such mechanisms implement the respect for autonomy and dignity of persons. [61]

---

56. For a development of this argument, see infra Part III.B.

57. Kant, Groundwork, supra note 1, at 96 (footnotes omitted).

58. Sullivan, supra note 1, at 193; cf. Kant, Groundwork, supra note 1, at 105 ("So act in relation to every rational being (both to yourself and to others) that he may at the same time count in your maxim as an end in himself."). Kant here attempts to demonstrate how the second version is logically equivalent to the first.

59. Kant, Groundwork, supra note 1, at 95.

60. See supra note 47.

61. The second version of the categorical imperative is not just a logical equivalent of the first. Rather, it adds substantive content to the formal requirements for moral judgement. Cf. John Rawls, A Theory of Justice, 251 & n.29, 251–57 (1971) (arguing that one should avoid interpretation of Kant's writings as merely providing formal elements of moral theory). See generally Jeffrie G. Murphy, Kant: The Philosophy of Right 60–86 (1970) (arguing that Kant's moral point of view is not strictly formal but contains

It would be a serious mistake, however, to conclude that the Kantian notion of freedom entails only negative duties, the duties to leave others alone to pursue their own happiness in accordance with their ideal of individual excellence. While Kant was against what he called "paternal government,"[62] the second version of the categorical imperative entails positive duties as well.[63] We must go beyond negative duties to make human beings our end. This command leads both to the perfection of our virtues of character and to acting benevolently toward others.[64]

A modern reconstruction of Kantian political theory should make room for what we would today call positive socioeconomic rights alongside the traditional negative, civil and political rights.[65] Respect for the dignity of persons requires, in addition to respecting their moral space, doing our best to secure an adequate level of material well-being for every member of society. Two reasons militate in favor of requiring that socioeconomic rights be recognized by domestic and international law. First, socioeconomic rights allow individuals to flourish and fully develop their uniquely human potential.[66] Second, a certain material well-being is necessary for persons fully to enjoy their civil and political rights and thus value and take advantage of liberty to its full extent. In an ideal society individuals are not only free; for them, liberty has high and roughly equal worth.[67]

There are, of course, problems of priority between these two generations of rights. From the standpoint of Kantian theory, the focus should be respect for individual autonomy. Securing socioeconomic rights is necessary for individuals to flourish as autonomous persons. Indeed, a neglect of the less favored will result in a lesser possibility for many to lead meaningful and fulfilling lives in freedom. Yet, sometimes a legitimate government may enforce socioeconomic rights in such a way that it ends up thwarting, instead of stimulating, individual autonomy. The neglect of civil and political rights for the benefit of socioeconomic equality may result, as it has often done, in outright tyranny. The question of priority can be resolved by applying a Kantian

ends, purposes, and values); O. Nora Nell, Acting on Principle: An Essay on Kantian Ethics 59–93 (1975) (discussing practical application of categorical imperative). For a defense of the Rawlsian reading of Kant, see Arnold I. Davidson, Is Rawls a Kantian?, 66 Pac. Phil. Q. 48 (1985).

62. See Kant, Theory and Practice, supra note 1, at 73.

63. See Paton, supra note 51, at 171–72; Sullivan, supra note 1, at 194.

64. See Paton, supra note 51, at 171–72; Sullivan, supra note 1, at 194.

65. The best modern reconstruction of Kant in this sense is, of course, Rawls, A Theory of Justice, supra note 61, at 60–75.

66. For an analysis of the place of socioeconomic rights in Rawlsian theory, see Frank I. Michelman, Constitutional Welfare Rights and *A Theory of Justice*, *in* Reading Rawls: Critical Studies on Rawls' *A Theory of Justice* 319 (Norman Daniels ed., 1973) [hereinafter Reading Rawls].

67. See Norman Daniels, Equal Liberty and Unequal Worth of Liberty, *in* Reading Rawls, supra note 66, at 253, 256–57.

standard: the ideal combination of rights is the one that yields the maximum possible individual autonomy under the coercion presupposed by the social contract. This is the point of equilibrium, as it were: any move from that curve would result in a reduction of individual autonomy.[68]

The third version of the categorical imperative is also highly revealing for its justification of the republican constitution and international human rights: "So act as if your maxims had to serve at the same time as a universal law (for all rational beings)."[69] This formulation points to an ideal vision of a moral community, where each individual is his own judge and the members obey only laws they can rationally prescribe.[70] Such a moral community describes an ideal just state and, consistently with *Perpetual Peace*, a world community of just states.[71]

B. *Due Process*

The second basic principle of a republican system is the derivation of all legal acts from, or dependence of all subjects on, a single common legislation.[72] The legitimacy of a legal act therefore depends upon whether it is in harmony with the constitution, procedurally and substantively.[73] Kant's formulation resembles the juridical definition of a state developed by Hans Kelsen.[74] Kelsen's system provides a valuable counterpoint to Kant's understanding of a legitimate republican regime. For Kelsen, all legal acts must derive from a single basic norm which in turn legitimizes the first positive norm, the constitution. How-

68. These important questions of priority between positive and negative duties and between civil-political rights and socioeconomic rights are beyond the scope of this Article. However, I join Rawls in defending the priority of liberty. See Rawls, supra note 61, at 243–51. Civil and political rights are definitive of freedom and individual autonomy, whereas socioeconomic rights, on the Kantian conception, are instrumental to freedom.

69. Kant, Groundwork, supra note 1, at 106. In the *Groundwork*, Kant treats the first formulation of the categorical imperative as primary, while the third version is given the position of priority in the *Critique of Practical Reason*. See Kant, Critique of Practical Reason, supra note 48, at 30; Paton, supra note 51, at 130.

70. See Sullivan, supra note 1, at 214.

71. There are important differences, however, between an ethical commonwealth, in which individuals self-legislate by obedience to moral duty, and a state in which duties are imposed by statute. See Sullivan, supra note 1, at 214–18.

72. See Kant, Perpetual Peace, supra note 1, at 112; Kant, Theory and Practice, supra note 1, at 75–77.

73. The Kantian position is neutral toward different forms of constitutional government, the legitimacy of judicial review, and similar questions. As the diversity of solutions to these issues in actual liberal democracies shows, a republican constitution, in Kant's sense, is compatible with many different mechanisms for distributing political power within the state. For a useful survey of the different ways in which constitutionalism has been implemented, see Mauro Cappelletti, Judicial Review in the Contemporary World (1971).

74. See Hans Kelsen, General Theory of Law and State 181–92 (Anders Wedberg trans., 1946).

ever, such derivation provides only formal legitimacy because the basic norm has no *a priori*, or objective, status. For Kelsen, the basic norm is "presupposed to be valid . . . . It is this presupposition that enables us to distinguish between individuals who are legal authorities and other individuals whom we do not regard as such, between acts of human beings which create legal norms and acts which have no such effect."[75]

Kant's system also mandates obedience to law that depends upon a single constitution. However, Kant's constitution, unlike Kelsen's basic norm, is not presupposed to be valid, but rather is the result of a rational choice by free agents as expressed in the legitimate social contract which requires that every citizen be a co-legislator.[76] The validity of the constitution is based on the fact that it proceeds from the exercise of rational cognitive faculties by the members of the body politic. Individual members of the state will insist that the principles of the constitution comport with the categorical imperative. For Kant, the constitution ceases to be valid when it no longer reflects this aggregate rationality. Thus, allegiance to the state by individuals is based upon their rationally believing that such allegiance is right, and the fact that a rational individual will not adhere to an irrational constitution.

The requirement of a dependence of all upon a common constitution is yet another instance of Kant's strong reliance on, and reverence for, the idea of law.[77] For him, an institution is justified only insofar as it has legally protected status.[78] This means, domestically, that both freedom from, and subjection to, the power of the state must be legally regulated: freedom and coercion under law, or freedom and coercion according to reason.[79] In a lengthy footnote, Kant explains that external lawful freedom means "the privilege not to obey any external laws [i.e., laws prescribed by someone else] except those to which I have been able to give my consent."[80] In line with the commands of the categorical imperative,[81] the laws enacted by the legislature must pass the test of rational deliberation to be deserving of compliance. It follows that only in the *Rechtstaat*, that is, under the rule of law, is allegiance to the law rational.

Kant's political theory, however, has one weakness. His thesis of

75. Id. at 115.

76. See Kant, Theory and Practice, supra note 1, at 75–76.

77. See, e.g., Kant, Groundwork, supra note 1, at 71 ("[R]evernce is the assessment of a worth which far outweighs all the worth of what is commended by inclination, and the necessity for me to act out of *pure* reverence for the practical law is what constitutes duty, to which every other motive must give way because it is the condition of a will good *in itself*, whose value is above all else.").

78. See Kant, Perpetual Peace, supra note 1, at 127–31; see also Gallie, supra note 11, at 22 (explaining Kant's view that anything of value must have legally protected status).

79. See Sullivan, supra note 1, at 247–52; Waltz, supra note 15, at 331–33.

80. Kant, Perpetual Peace, supra note 1, at 112–13.

81. See supra notes 48–64 and accompanying text.

rational allegiance to the law is not easily reconciled with his strong opposition to a right to revolution.[82] The proposition that citizens may revolt as a last resort against arbitrary power, when the sovereign has broken the agency contract,[83] follows logically from any liberal political theory.[84] Perhaps Kant was trying to make a purely formal point, namely that for citizens to have a *legal right* to revolution is self-contradictory, because there can be no higher judge to resolve the dispute between the citizens and the government.[85] Nevertheless, Kant's views on civil disobedience and revolution are inconsistent with his own moral theory and with the common-sense judgments of ordinary morality.[86] If government breaches the social contract, then the people may dismiss the government, by violence if all other means have failed.

The recognition of the right to resist tyranny is extremely important in international law. Beyond the consequences for the law of international human rights itself, it is significant with respect to developing a theory of humanitarian intervention. If citizens did not have a right to revolt against their tyrants, foreigners *a fortiori* would not have a right to help them, even by noncoercive measures, in the struggle against despotism. Humanitarian intervention can be defended as a corollary to the right to revolution: victims of serious human rights deprivations, who have rationally decided to revolt against their oppressors, have a right to receive proportionate transboundary assistance, including forcible assistance.[87]

---

82. See Kant, Perpetual Peace, supra note 1, at 136; Kant, Theory and Practice, supra note 1, at 79–80; Sullivan, supra note 1, at 244–45; see also Lewis W. Beck, Kant and the Right of Revolution, 32 J. Hist. of Ideas 411, 413–15 (1971) (attempting to reconcile Kant's denial of right to revolution with his enthusiasm over French and American revolutions).

83. See infra note 100 and accompanying text.

84. See, e.g., John Locke, An Essay Concerning the True Origin, Extent, and End of Civil Government, *in* Social Contract 1, 122–43 (Sir Ernest Barker ed., 1962) (1690).

85. In Kant's own words:

> For suppose they had such a right, and, indeed, that they opposed the actual judgment of the nation's leader, then who would determine on which side the right lies? Neither of them can serve as judge in his own case. Thus, there would have to be still another head above the head to decide between the latter and the people—and that is contradictory.

Kant, Theory and Practice, supra note 1, at 79. This is not the only reason that Kant offers to explain his belief that citizens cannot have a legal right to revolution, however. The other reasons include his obsession with the danger of reverting to the "lawless state of nature" and the prudential reason that since revolution is violent, citizens living under an unjust regime must go to the furthest extent to achieve liberal reforms peacefully. See Sullivan, supra note 1, at 244–45.

86. See Sullivan, supra note 1, at 245.

87. See Fernando R. Tesón, Humanitarian Intervention: An Inquiry into Law and Morality 5, 87–88 (1988); D'Amato, supra note 3, at 519. A growing minority of writers shares this view. See, e.g., Robert M. Chilstron, Humanitarian Intervention Under Contemporary International Law, 1 Yale J. World Pub. Ord. 93, 121–26 (1974); Anthony D'Amato, Nicaragua and International Law, 77 Am. J. Int'l L. 657, 659 (1985), reprinted in International Law: Process and Prospect 223, 225 (1987); W. Michael Reisman, Coer-

C. *Equality*

The third principle that defines a republican system is the principle of equality of all as citizens, that is, equality before the law.[88] The requirement of equality follows analytically from Kant's definition of law. Law is universal in form,[89] therefore every person must have exactly the same rights as every other person.[90] In *Perpetual Peace*, Kant reaffirms his long-standing rejection of nobility or birth as a basis for assigning rights and duties under a republican constitution.[91] Despite the fact that his writings were hardly accessible to the public, Kant reveals himself, in an historical context, as a philosopher of the ordinary people. Indeed, as Sullivan argues, "Kant's entire moral philosophy can be understood as a protest against distinctions based on the far less important criteria of rank, wealth, and privilege, and perpetuated by religious and political force and fear."[92] Kant's vision of society based upon a republican constitution is one that combines respect for moral autonomy and the individual, with the need for social order. It applies equally to classical laissez-faire and welfare states in the modern European tradition.

Observance of human rights is a primary requirement to join the community of civilized nations under international law. It follows that there cannot be a federation or peace alliance with tyrannical states. Domestic freedom is a primary credential required of any state before it may become a legitimate member of the international community. Yet, an important qualification is necessary here with respect to the question of democratic representation. In principle, both respect for human rights and democratic representation are needed to fulfill the requirements of the Kantian theory of international law. The main requirement of the First Definitive Article, however, is that *domestic freedom* be observed within each state. Because domestic freedom encompasses the right to elect the government, normally respect for human rights entails, and results in, representative government of the kind found in

---

cion and Self-Determination: Construing Charter Article 2(4), 78 Am. J. Int'l L. 642, 645 (1984); M. Sornarajah, Internal Colonialism and Humanitarian Intervention, 11 Ga. J. Int'l & Comp. L. 45, 75–77 (1981). Among those opposed to the legality or wisdom of humanitarian intervention, see, e.g., Louis Henkin, The Use of Force: Law and U.S. Policy, *in* Right v. Might: International Law and the Use of Force 37, 41–42, 61 (1989); Oscar Schachter, In Defense of International Rules on the Use of Force, 53 U. Chi. L. Rev. 113, 117–19, 145 (1986). For a scathing critique of Henkin's article, see Anthony D'Amato, Book Review, 85 Am. J. Int'l L. 201, 202 (1991).

88. See Kant, Perpetual Peace, supra note 1, at 112; Kant, Theory and Practice, supra note 1, at 73–75.

89. See supra notes 52–56 and accompanying text.

90. This is not inconsistent with the sorts of inequalities in wealth and power that arise in every society from a combination of talent, industry, and luck. See Sullivan, supra note 1, at 256.

91. See Kant, Perpetual Peace, supra note 1, at 112–13 & n.*.

92. Sullivan, supra note 1, at 197; accord Kant, Perpetual Peace, supra note 1, at 113 & n.*.

liberal democracies.[93] Thus, for example, we may assume that an originally unrepresentative monarchy that nevertheless respects human rights will naturally mature into a constitutional monarchy, much like those found in Western Europe today. Therefore, for the purpose of international law, the central requirement is respect for human rights. Governments that respect those rights, even if they are not representative in form, are entitled to a *presumption* of agency. Individuals who are free are presumed to consent to their government, much as citizens in a liberal democracy are presumed to consent to the governance of the administration brought to power through the electoral system, even if they did not vote for that government. It follows that governments that fully respect human rights are deemed to represent their citizens internationally.[94]

D. *The Normative Status of Nations*

Kant's understanding of the normative status of the state proceeds logically from the three criteria he proposed as the organizing principles of just republican states. The state when viewed as a unit interacting with other states does not acquire moral value greater than its components. Kant's Second Preliminary Article demonstrates that the moral standing of the state must be anchored in individual freedom. It provides that "[n]o independent nation be it large or small, may be acquired by another nation by inheritance, exchange, purchase, or gift."[95] For Kant, a state is not a possession or a piece of property, and since, like a tree, the state has its own roots, "to incorporate it into another nation as a graft, denies its existence as a moral person, turns it into a thing, and thus contradicts the concept of the original contract, without which a people [*Volk*] has no rights."[96]

At first blush, Kant seems to conceive of the state in a holistic way as a moral person, with rights and duties above and beyond the individuals who make up the state.[97] Such a view would regard the state as deserving respect because it is an autonomous moral being and enjoys

93. Again, a rights-constrained, as opposed to a pure, democracy is intended here by "liberal democracy." As indicated above, Kant thought that the latter was a form of despotism. See supra notes 39–44 and accompanying text.

94. This is very different from Michael Walzer's assertion that *all* governments are presumed to represent their people unless they render themselves guilty of genocide or similar atrocious and widespread crimes. See Michael Walzer, The Moral Standing of States, 9 Phil. & Pub. Aff. 209 (1980).

95. Kant, Perpetual Peace, supra note 1, at 108.

96. Id.

97. See Hinsley, supra note 20, at 66–67; see also Carson, supra note 30, at 183–84 (discussing Kant's idea of world federation in which states have duty to "higher authority"); Sullivan, supra note 1, at 257 (describing Kant's characterization of states as "moral persons" in *Perpetual Peace*). But see Tesón, supra note 87, at 53–76 (criticizing "Hegelian myth," in which states are entitled to autonomy as "moral beings" making choices).

sovereignty in its own right. This interpretation misunderstands Kant's argument. Kant maintains that a state is not a piece of territory, but rather a civil society created by a social contract. The state as moral person is just an analogy, except insofar as violating the state "contradicts the concept of the original contract."[98] What is important for Kant, and is captured by this analogy, is that the normative value of the individual not be violated by another state. Indeed, he emphasizes several times in the same paragraph the nature of the state as a society of men and how acquisition of the state violates that association.[99] The dichotomy established is between the state as a moral-political entity created by autonomous persons and the state as a mere piece of territory that can be bought and sold, not between rights of the state and rights of individuals, in which the community would hold a preeminent position at the expense of the individual. The state, for Kant, has moral standing *qua* the creature of a social contract.

The distinction often drawn between the horizontal and vertical contracts nicely illustrates why Kant maintains that the fundamental unit and, at the same time, fundamental end of both domestic and international law is the individual human being. The horizontal contract is the social compact entered into by citizens among themselves. The vertical contract is the agency contract between the individual beings, who comprise the state and are bound together by the horizontal contract, and their government. The vertical contract exists at the sufferance of, and for the purpose of maintaining, a healthy horizontal contract.[100] If a community of individuals is founded upon a legitimate social contract—horizontal and vertical—then foreigners must respect that community and accept its rulers as the legitimate representatives of that community. This principle can be extended to hold that the reason international aggression should be condemned is that the aggressor is using citizens of the victim state as mere things; in Kant's words, "subjects are used and wasted as mere objects to be manipulated at will."[101] Kant is not thinking about protecting governments unless they are legitimately appointed by their people, that is, unless there is a legitimate vertical contract. In spite of his metaphorical description of the state as a moral person, Kant is no Hegel.

Kant's international ethics follow from the categorical imperative. Just as individuals may not use human beings as mere means to an end, so foreigners, and especially foreign governments, may not use the persons that form another state by disrupting their free civil association in order to pursue the foreigners' own ends such as national glory, exer-

98. Kant, Perpetual Peace, supra note 1, at 108.

99. See id.

100. See Hannah Arendt, Crises of the Republic 85–87 (1969); see also Tesón, supra note 6, at 99–107 (arguing that "vertical contract" theory requires that government hold no autonomous rights).

101. Kant, Perpetual Peace, supra note 1, at 108.

cise of political power, material enrichment, or the aggrandizement of territory. All communities freely constituted are deserving of respect because they come into existence as a result of the rational exercise of free choice by autonomous agents. Thus, a government is not deserving of respect *per se*, but only insofar as it is the agent empowered by free individuals to make the law (legislative power), apply the law (executive power), and adjudicate claims among citizens (judicial power).[102] The state is the institution created to implement social cooperation grounded on the inviolability of liberty and must be honored because failure to respect the freely constituted state would be to deny the validity of the categorical imperative.

Kant's emphasis on the individual rather than the state is also apparent in his commentary to the Third Definitive Article, where Kant writes that "originally no one had a greater right to any region of the earth than anyone else."[103] Such a statement is hardly compatible with the idea of the state as the primary moral unit. For Kant, national borders are contingent features of social life. Kant never loses sight of the second version of the categorical imperative: persons should always be treated as ends in themselves, not merely as means.[104] Here we have the outline of a liberal theory of self-determination—one that relies not on mystical properties of the state or the prerogatives of enlightened rulers but, properly, on the rational pursuit of freedom by autonomous agents.[105]

But why must states guarantee internal freedom in order to be legitimate members of the international community? One could argue that, provided international peace and stability are secured, the fundamental goal of international law according to Kant,[106] the internal organization of states is irrelevant. Certainly it ought not be the indispensable starting point of a theory of international law. This argument has been repeatedly made; indeed, it is one of the tenets of the statist or realist school of thought.[107] Some commentators even em-

102. See, e.g., Kant, Theory and Practice, supra note 1, at 71–84.

103. Kant, Perpetual Peace, supra note 1, at 118. Kant also suggests here, along the same lines, that all men have a "common ownership of the earth's surface." Id.

104. See supra notes 57–61 and accompanying text.

105. I return below to Kant's liberal defense of a world divided into separate states, as opposed to world government, see infra Part III.

106. See Kant, Perpetual Peace, supra note 1, at 111; supra notes 35–38 and accompanying text.

107. Statism and realism overlap but are not coextensive. Statism is the view that the basic unit of analysis is the nation-state, not the individual. Realism is the view that nation-states act in the international arena motivated by national interest. Thus, all realists are statists, but not all statists are realists. For example, the "legalists" would argue that international law *conceived in a statist way* is a major component of foreign policy, thus rejecting the realist emphasis on national interest. The targets of this Article are *both* statists, because their version of international law is morally impotent, and realists, because they tend to be moral skeptics and because their explanation of international behavior is flawed.

brace such a reading of Kant.[108] All we can aspire to, it is argued, is balance of power, or peace. Except as an occasional political tool, concern for freedom or human rights does not belong in the realm of international relations because there is no centralized authority or superstate that can guarantee the rights of subjects.[109] There are of course several variations on this theme. Subtle realists would not discard the importance of human rights and democracy altogether.[110] But, characteristically, realists regard such concerns as subordinate to the national interest.[111] National interest is seen as an interest of the state that endures regardless of political or socioeconomic changes within the state, and extends over and above individual interests and the internal organization of the state. Conventional political theory, realists argue, addresses relations between government and governed—usually centering around individuals and their claims against the state—and is therefore incapable of accounting for the national interest as the key component of foreign policy. Only an international theory built around the state as the primary actor can do the job. The consequence of this approach is to overlook or downplay human rights in the study, formulation, and implementation of international law and policy.

One can legitimately ask how the notion of national interest is different from the understanding reached by citizens in the horizontal social contract. Why is it that national interest persists over and above changes in the actual interests of the citizens? The idea of national interest in the realist sense is incompatible with a view of the state as a creation of men and women to serve their needs. The only enduring collective interest is the preservation of freedom; political issues are issues of how to establish a fair, efficient, and mutually beneficial system of social cooperation consistent with the protection of everyone's liberty interests.[112]

The connection between freedom and international peace, however, runs even deeper than these considerations suggest. The realist challenge can be met by arguments proving that the link between peace and freedom is genuine and indisputable. Kant showed for the first

---

108. Classic works in the realist tradition include Hedley Bull, The Anarchical Society: A Study of Order in World Politics (1977); Kenneth N. Waltz, Man, the State, and War (1959). For an extended critical discussion of the realist view, see Marshall Cohen, Moral Skepticism and International Relations, 13 Phil. & Pub. Aff. 299 (1984).

109. See infra notes 117–120 and accompanying text. Kant seems to make a similar argument in his discussion of the right to revolution. I have argued Kant's views on revolution ought to be rejected wholesale. See supra notes 82–87 and accompanying text.

110. See, e.g., Stanley Hoffmann, Duties Beyond Borders: On the Limits and Possibilities of Ethical International Politics 95–140 (1981).

111. See authorities cited supra note 108.

112. It is not surprising that many of the goals that pass as national interest are, when closely examined, morally dubious: for example, territorial gains, economic gains, national glory, national unity, and ethnic pride.

time that we cannot aspire to a lasting international peace if individual freedom is not secured within every state's borders.

III. Freedom and Peace

A. *The Empirical Argument*

Kant's work on international law begins with the premise that peace is the fundamental purpose of international law, and that under normal circumstances war is an intrinsic evil that must be avoided. Kant does not furnish separate arguments for this maxim,[113] and his views on war are indeed complicated.[114] Kant believed that an international order could be established only when governments freely abjured their right to make war on each other, despite his emphasis on the necessity of coercion to sustain the law within a state.[115] From the peace premise, he attempts to design international law so that peace will be forever secured.

Kant gives several reasons why peace is likely to be achieved when individual rights and political participation are secured. His central argument is that if people are self-governed, citizens on both sides of any dispute will be very cautious in bringing about a war whose consequences they themselves must bear.[116] Those who will be eventually exposed to the horrors of the conflagration will decide whether or not to go to war. This central theme can be expanded in several directions.

In a liberal state, the government is elected and rotates periodically. These two factors are crucial restrictions on the power of the government to initiate war, both for reasons of self-interest (incumbency) and outright political and logistical limitations. In contrast, it is relatively easy for a despot to start a war. As Kant points out, the tyrant does not suffer the consequences; his privileges and prerogatives remain intact.[117] Crucially, the despot does not have the benefit of objective advice and debate. He rules by force, which means that within his own *entourage* he is feared and vulnerable to adulation. Advisors are not likely to tell the tyrant the harsh truths, but rather only what he wants to hear. More generally, because a despotic regime does not tolerate free-

113. Kant writes that "reason absolutely condemns war as a means of determining the right and makes seeking the state of peace a matter of unmitigated duty." Kant, Perpetual Peace, supra note 1, at 116; cf. Gallie, supra note 11, at 9 (opening section of Perpetual Peace "a *tour de force*, without any preliminary discussion of why or in what circumstances war is an unacceptable evil").

114. As we shall see, Kant had peculiar views, not all negative, about the role that war has played in the "Design of Nature." See infra notes 199–220 and accompanying text.

115. See Gallie, supra note 11, at 20.

116. See Kant, Perpetual Peace, supra note 1, at 113.

117. See id. Kant contends that the ruler does not act here as a fellow citizen, but as the nation's owner. See id. Kant's prudential reasons are always permeated by the theme of the categorical imperative: never use persons simply as means, which of course applies with even more strength to the government.

dom of expression, public opinion has no significant impact on the government's decisions; consequently, there is no opportunity for public debate on the moral and prudential reasons to make war. Psychologically, insulation of tyrannical rulers from criticism and debate fuels in them a sense of megalomania. Tyrants acquire a feeling of invincibility. They become accustomed to getting away with murder (literally) internally and no doubt reach a point of self-delusion where they become convinced that they can get away with external aggression as well.[118]

From an institutional standpoint, the separation of powers inherent in a liberal democracy creates a system of mutual controls and relative diffusion of power that complicates and encumbers governmental decisions about war.[119] No all-powerful sovereign exists who can by himself initiate hostilities. For Kant, that a multiplicity of decision-makers will participate in decisions to make war is implicit in the notion of autonomy inherent in the republican form of government.[120] The law-maker does not administer the law. Thus, liberal constitutions attempt to impose institutional limits on power, including the power to conduct foreign relations, through the checks and balances inherent in the separation of powers and through freedom of speech—notably freedom of the press.[121]

Another reason Kant believes that there is an increased likelihood of an enduring peace among free republics is that in a liberal democracy citizens will be educated in the principles of right, and therefore war will appear to them as the evil that every rational person knows it is.[122] Kant had a rich and exciting theory of cosmopolitan education, the main theme of which is that we must cultivate universal virtues that will prevail over the bellicose instincts that we also have.[123] Similar to the authors of some of the modern peace-education projects,[124] Kant saw clearly that peace education aimed only at inculcating fear of war

118. I suggested this explanation of the Malvinas war, see Fernando Tesón, 81 Am. J. Int'l L. 556, 558 (1987) (reviewing Crisi Falkland-Malvina e Organizzazione Internationale (Laura Forlati & Francisco Leita eds., 1985)) ("Dictators inevitably become persuaded that they can get away with anything."). The continuing validity of this explanation to the conduct of the Iraqi ruler in the recent Gulf crisis is painfully obvious.

119. See Kant, Perpetual Peace, supra note 1, at 114; Doyle, supra note 30, at 228.

120. See supra notes 35–45 and accompanying text.

121. See Sullivan, supra note 1, at 244.

122. See id. at 258. Citizens in a liberal democracy would not necessarily oppose *all* war. Some wars waged for liberal causes will be recognized as just. See infra notes 199–220 and accompanying text.

123. See Sullivan, supra note 1, at 287; see also Joseph M. Knippenberg, Moving Beyond Fear: Rousseau and Kant on Cosmopolitan Education, 51 J. Pol. 809, 815–19 (1989) ("Kant's proposed education is avowedly 'cosmopolitan.' . . . He advocates a process aiming successfully, at four goals: discipline, the acquisition of a trade, 'cleverness,' and morality.").

124. See generally Education for Peace and Disarmament: Toward a Living World (Douglas Sloan ed., 1983) (arguing that modern peace movement ought not be "impelled solely by fear").

and its instrumentalities was insufficient. Fear alone is demoralizing and may lead people to surrender to a tyrant, rather than act on behalf of a morally good and peaceful world.[125] A proper moral education should include instruction on the principles that underlie a just constitution from a cosmopolitan perspective, that is, on the value of human rights generally, not only as they relate to *our* domestic constitution.[126] Because this kind of moral education emphasizes rationality as a universal trait of persons, it will induce citizens in a liberal democracy to see individuals in other nations as deserving equal respect, and thus treat them as ends in themselves, not as mere objects for the satisfaction of local preferences.[127]

The final reason why liberal states are likely to be peaceful is that liberal democracies foster free trade and a generous system of freedom of international movement that Kant calls the Cosmopolitan Law.[128] Kant remarks that by observing a rule of hospitality for foreigners facilitating commerce with indigenous peoples, "distant parts of the world can establish with one another peaceful relations that will eventually become matters of public law, and the human race can gradually be brought closer and closer to a cosmopolitan constitution."[129] Kant reaffirms this idea by observing that peoples' mutual interests unite them against violence and war, for "the spirit of trade cannot coexist with war."[130]

He was cognizant, of course, that "peace to do business"[131] is a nonmoral reason to want peace, but that such pecuniary interests provide an additional argument for requiring a liberalization of trade and freedom of movement. Free trade and freedom of movement[132] are sufficiently linked to the principles of a liberal constitution to make leaders in liberal democracies much more prone to weigh economic

125. See Knippenberg, supra note 123, at 810.

126. Kant maintains that cosmopolitan education is aimed at the universal good and the perfection for which humanity is destined. Immanuel Kant, Education 15 (Annette Churton trans., 1960); Knippenberg, supra note 123, at 815.

127. Indeed, Kant thought that the moral law, the categorical imperative, was already present in a sound moral understanding and required not so much to be taught but clarified. See Kant, Groundwork, supra note 1, at 71–72.

128. See Kant, Perpetual Peace, supra note 1, at 118–19, 125; see also Doyle, supra note 30, at 231–32 ("The cosmopolitan right to hospitality permits the 'spirit of commerce' sooner or later to take hold of every nation, thus impelling states to promote peace and to try to avert war" if only out of fear of jeopardizing the benefits of trade).

129. Kant, Perpetual Peace, supra note 1, at 118; see also Kant's remarkable condemnation of colonialism, id. at 119.

130. Id. at 125.

131. "For among all those powers (or means) that belong to a nation, financial power may be the most reliable in forcing nations to pursue the noble cause of peace (though not from moral motives) . . . ." Id. at 125.

132. The rule of hospitality requires that "an alien not . . . be treated as an enemy upon his arrival in another's country." Id. at 118.

costs before initiating a war.[133] There is no question that free trade is a strong, if not dispositive, influence over external behavior. Free trade inclines diplomacy toward peace because international business transactions require stability and predictability to be successful. Kant's views have been confirmed by the success of the European Economic Community and even by the global system of international trade regulated by GATT and similar institutions. It is not by coincidence that the European Economic Community requires democracy as a prerequisite for membership, as does the more recent Mercosur, the Argentine-Brazilian free market agreement.[134]

Recent research by Michael Doyle and R.J. Rummel bolsters Kant's argument for the causal link between domestic freedom and peace.[135] These modern versions of Kant's argument have shown that Kant's prediction of a gradual expansion of the liberal alliance has been confirmed by events of the last 200 years, and notably the last 45 years. These authors' research has demonstrated that Kant was essentially right. Events since the publication of these articles provide splendid supplementary confirmation of the Kantian thesis.[136]

Liberal states have shown a definite tendency to maintain peace among themselves, while nonliberal states have shown themselves to be generally prone to make war. The historical data since 1795 seems to indicate that even though liberal states have become involved in numerous wars with nonliberal states, liberal states have yet to engage in war with one another.[137]

Doyle concedes that liberal states have behaved aggressively toward nonliberal states, but he attributes this fact precisely to the difference in regimes.[138] Conversely, nonliberal states have frequently behaved aggressively among themselves. Therefore, only a community of liberal states has a chance of securing peace, as Kant thought. Should people ever fulfill the hope of creating such a liberal international community, the likelihood of war will be greatly reduced.

Alternative hypotheses have not been forthcoming to explain the

---

133. One could expand this theme by saying that liberal citizens tend to be more cosmopolitan and less nationalistic, except concerning the defense of freedom, precisely because they place the individual at the origin and end of political arrangements.

134. For the European Economic Community, see 1978 Bull. Eur. Communities, No. 3, at 5–6; for the Argentine-Brazilian free trade agreement, see Shirley Christian, Argentina and Brazil Sign Pacts, N.Y. Times, July 31, 1986, at D18.

135. See Doyle, supra note 30, at 213; Michael W. Doyle, Kant, Liberal Legacies, and Foreign Affairs (pt. 2), 12 Phil. & Pub. Aff. 323 (1983) [hereinafter Doyle, Liberal Legacies (pt. 2)]; Michael W. Doyle, Liberalism and World Politics, 80 Am. Pol. Sci. Rev. 1151, 1162 (1986) (reprinted in substantially the same form as Michael W. Doyle, Liberal Institutions and International Ethics, *in* Political Realism and International Morality 185, 190–91 (Kenneth Kipnis & Diana T. Meyers eds., 1987)); R.J. Rummel, Libertarianism and International Violence, 27 J. Conflict Resol. 27 (1983).

136. See supra note 2.

137. See Doyle, supra note 30, at 209–17.

138. See Doyle, Liberal Legacies (pt. 2), supra note 135, passim.

liberal peace. I have not seen serious challenge to the evidence provided by Doyle and Rummel. Doyle's assertion that constitutionally secure liberal states have never engaged in war with one another is indeed bold.[139] Writers who take issue with this view contest only the thesis—held by Rummel but not by Doyle—that liberal democracies are *generally* peace-prone, regardless of the nature of the other regimes.[140] Nevertheless, everyone concurs in the factual assertion that democratic states rarely go to war amongst one another.[141] To be sure, there are some difficult cases.[142] Yet, even if those cases are treated as genuine instances of war between liberal states, the correlation is still so strong that it begs explanation. The argument is not that war between liberal states is impossible, but that it is highly unlikely. Kant warns that there will be regressive wars and setbacks in the establishment of the liberal alliance. Nevertheless he was confident that the alliance would expand and solidify with time.[143]

Some commentators have challenged the plausibility of the causal connection between freedom and war. They have treated the correlation as spurious, either the result of pure coincidence or, more likely, of an underlying common factor unrelated to the nature of the domestic regimes. Professor Diana Meyers has taken such a position: while she agrees that liberal states by and large have maintained peaceful relations, she raises questions about the explanation offered by Kant and Doyle.[144] Meyers offers two considerations to deny the premise that liberal democracies provide mechanisms through which aggregated self-interest is translated into national policy.[145] First, state bureaucra-

139. See Doyle, supra note 30, at 213.

140. See Chan, Mirror, Mirror on the Wall: Are the Freer Countries More Pacific?, 7 Peace Res. Soc'y Papers 31 (1984); Melvin Small & J. David Singer, The War Proneness of Democratic Régimes, 1816–1965, 1 Jerusalem J. Int'l Rel. 50 (1976); Erich Weede, Democracy and War Involvement, 28 J. Conflict Resol. 649 (1984). As indicated above, Doyle concedes, and the evidence seems to show, that liberal states behave aggressively toward nonliberal states.

141. See David Garnham, War-Proneness, War-Weariness, and Régime Type: 1916–1980, 23 J. Peace Res. 279, 283–84 (1986); authorities cited supra note 140. For another challenge to Rummel's methodology, see Jack Vincent, Freedom and International Conflict: Another Look, 31 Int'l Stud. Q. 103, 103–05, 111–12 (1987). But see R.J. Rummel, On Vincent's View of Freedom and International Conflict, 31 Int'l Stud. Q. 113, 113–17 (1987).

142. Two hard cases are the 1812 war between England and the United States, and the First World War. As to the first, arguably the United States became a liberal republic only after 1865; as to the second, Doyle's explanation is that Imperial Germany, although largely a liberal republic for domestic issues, did not allow any popular participation in foreign affairs decisions. See Doyle, supra note 30, at 216–17, n.8.

143. See Kant, Perpetual Peace, supra note 1, at 118.

144. See Diana T. Meyers, Kant's Liberal Alliance: A Permanent Peace?, *in* Political Realism and International Morality, supra note 135, at 212, 219.

145. Id. at 215. Similarly, Professor Hinsley opines that "[i]t is impossible to overlook the lameness of th[e] conclusion" that republican forms of government are more likely to lead to international peace. Hinsley downplays Kant's emphasis on internal

cies often distort public opinion, and thus "liberal democracy does not in any straightforward way place state action under the control of majority interests."[146] Second, people are deceived about their self-interest, and therefore express preferences that may militate for or against peace.[147] Public opinion in a liberal democracy, it is argued, may also be bellicose. Neither a free press nor a constitutional system with checks and balances has prevented leaders of liberal democracies from waging aggressive wars for spurious liberal causes.[148]

This reply to Kant and Doyle is unconvincing. The general skeptical position that liberal democracies do not provide a true outlet to majority opinions and preferences proves too much. To accept the argument one must believe that there is no real difference, in any respect—not just in the formulation of foreign policy or the initiation of wars— between liberal democracies and despotisms. While threats to popular participation posed by bureaucracies should be a matter of concern, this does not equate all political systems in terms of the degree to which popular will is expressed. Liberal democracies provide better mechanisms for political participation, to put it mildly, than do tyrannies. While there are surely hard cases, free political systems and despotic ones can be distinguished. We draw the distinction precisely in terms of how human rights are protected, how the citizen's interests are served, and the degree of their participation in the political process.

More importantly, this objection misses Kant's central point: peace is likely to be maintained only among liberal societies and, consequently, the likelihood of world peace will increase as the liberal alliance expands. All the examples of liberal aggression involve confrontations against nonliberal states.[149] Yet, the Kantian theory insists that the difference in regimes is the cause of instability. Liberal states do engage in aggressive behavior against nonliberal states, but this fact cannot support the claim that official duplicity could serve just as well to rationalize an attack on a bothersome liberal state.[150]

The argument seems to be that the psychology of power is the same regardless of which political system is in place and, therefore, both tyrannical and democratic rulers are equally prone to deceiving the people and waging war for dishonorable reasons such as the ruler's self-aggrandizement. However, the Kantian hypothesis is precisely that

---

freedom and emphasizes instead the freedom of the state and the "design of Nature" as Kant's main causes of peace. See Hinsley, supra note 20, at 71. Professor Hinsley's view on this point is empirically implausible and unfaithful to Perpetual Peace and to Kant's philosophy generally.

146. Meyers, supra note 144, at 215.

147. See id.

148. See id. at 216 (using the Vietnam War as an example).

149. Plausible candidates are the force used in Vietnam, Grenada, and Panama by the United States, and in Chad and Congo by France and Belgium, and in Pakistan by India.

150. See Myers, supra note 144, at 216.

in a liberal democracy there are intrinsic limitations on the ability and discretion of governments to deceive and manipulate. It is not enough to say that democratic governments are also capable of deceit and manipulation; the very point of democratic institutions is to keep political power, with all its corrupting potential, under check.[151] While the psychology of power may be the same across political systems, there is little question that in liberal societies institutional constraints are more likely to prevent bad governments from doing too much damage, both at home and abroad.

Other commentators have accepted the evidence, but have nevertheless attempted to explain the liberal peace by different hypotheses. The realist school of thought in international relations has long maintained that war is caused by prudential reasons that affect all state actors equally in the international arena. These reasons are not related to the difference in regimes. Doyle summarizes the realist theory of war:

> Specific wars . . . arise from fear as a state seeking to avoid a surprise attack decides to attack first; from competitive emulation as states lacking an imposed international hierarchy of prestige struggle to establish their place; and from straightforward conflicts of interest that escalate into war because there is no global sovereign to prevent states from adopting that ultimate form of conflict resolution.[152]

Thus, the realist explains peace through purely prudential factors that motivate state decision-makers. Realists downplay the importance of the difference in domestic regimes and emphasize features of states and governments that derive from the condition of international anarchy.[153]

151. There are countless real and counterfactual examples to illustrate the Kantian hypothesis. My favorite one is: there would have been no Malvinas war between the United Kingdom and Argentina had there been a democratic government installed in Buenos Aires. While there is no indication that irredentist sentiments have subsided in Argentina, the two countries, with Argentina now a member of the liberal alliance, are pursuing peaceful means to solve the conflict. See, e.g., the UK-Argentine Joint Statement on Relations and a Formula on Sovereignty with Regard to Falkland Islands, South Georgia, and South Sandwich Islands, 29 I.L.M. 1291 (Sept. 1990); see also BBC Summary of World Broadcasts, The Monitoring Report, Part 4 (Dec. 29, 1990) (Argentine Foreign Minister downplaying British Prime Minister's comparison of Iraqi invasion of Kuwait with 1982 Argentine invasion of Malvinas).

152. Doyle, supra note 30, at 219. As Doyle notes, this tradition goes back to Thucydides and Hobbes. See id.; authorities cited supra note 108. Other realist explanations of the liberal peace discussed and rejected by Doyle are based on hegemony or equilibrium, along the lines suggested by Raymond Aron. In refuting Aron, Doyle notes that the liberal peace persisted in the inter-war period when there was no hegemony. Doyle, supra note 30, at 223. Doyle also points out that hegemonic control is overestimated in both the pre-war and post-war periods. It is argued that in a situation of international equilibrium aggressive attempts at hegemony will deter wars. However, bipolar equilibrium is insufficient because it only explains peace among the polar powers, not proxy or regional wars. See id. at 224.

153. See id.

Realists have failed to explain the undeniable peace that has reigned among liberal states for so long. To suggest that relations among states with similar domestic regimes, liberal or not, would be peaceful, conflicts with the evidence regarding relations among feudal, communist, and fascist societies.[154] To say that the liberal peace only reflects the absence of deep conflicts of interest among liberal states simply begs the question of why liberal states have fewer or less fundamental conflicts of interest with other liberal states than liberal states have with nonliberal states, or nonliberal states have among themselves.[155]

But let us concede, *gratia argumentandi*, that the real reason for peace is the similarity in regimes, so that a community of despotic states could equally maintain peace. In that case, since peace is our ultimate goal and since uniformity of regimes is the only guarantee for peace, we have a choice of designing a system of international law that would either require respect for human rights or require despotism. On any defensible theory of morality, if that is our choice, we would prefer an international legal system that required states to secure human rights and political representation and thus be uniform on the side of liberty.

There is a strong factual correlation between internal freedom and external peaceful behavior toward similarly free societies; the causal dynamics that underlie the correlation seem very plausible; and those who disagree with this explanation have failed to provide convincing alternative explanatory hypotheses. The conjecture that internal freedom is causally related to peaceful international behavior is as safe a generalization as one can make in the realm of political science. Kant's empirical argument therefore shows that, if only for prudential reasons, international law must require full respect for human rights.

B. *The Normative Argument*

The second Kantian argument for including a requirement of respect for human rights as a foundational principle of international law is even more straightforward: Governments should be required by international law to observe human rights because that is the right thing to do. Because international law is rooted in the categorical imperative, it must likewise require respect for human rights if it is to be universal.

Kant commentators have overlooked the fact that Kant expressly offers this argument along with the empirical one. In *Perpetual Peace*, Kant defends the universal requirement of human rights and democracy as grounded in "the purity of its origin, *a purity whose source is the pure concept of right*."[156] The empirical argument is then offered in addition to this normative one. Writers who felt uncomfortable with Kant's

154. See id. at 22.
155. See id. at 224.
156. Kant, Perpetual Peace, supra note 1, at 113 (emphasis added).

First Definitive Article have attacked the plausibility of the empirical argument,[157] without realizing that it was just a reason given to reinforce the main argument, which alone suffices: that a global requirement of a republican constitution logically follows from the categorical imperative.[158] Thus, Kant's complete argument for democracy and human rights as a requirement of international law is far stronger than many of his critics thought. The normative argument is addressed to those who rank justice over peace; the empirical argument, to those who rank peace over justice.

Protecting human rights is the reason why governments exist in the first place.[159] The reasons that support internal freedom are universal, they derive from the categorical imperative, therefore, they should be embodied in the law of nations which also purports to be universal. Because Kantianism relies on rationality as a universal trait of persons, it is incompatible with relativism. It is not possible to defend simultaneously Kant's theory of human nature and morality, and the view that liberal democracy and respect for persons is good only for certain societies. The categorical imperative is universal and holds for every civil society regardless of history and culture. Liberal democracies, ranging from laissez-faire states to welfare states, are the only ones that are likely to secure individual freedom, thereby allowing human beings to develop their potential fully. Therefore, the only way in which international law can be made fully compatible with the freedom of individuals to pursue and act upon rational life plans is if it contains a strong obligation for governments to respect human rights. International law must be congruent with individual autonomy; the trait, for Kant, that sets human beings apart from other species.

Kant insists that pure ethics, or pure duty, be separated from historical and cultural contingencies. The whole enterprise of moral philosophy, for Kant, is based on that part of practical knowledge that is pure, perceived by human beings *a priori*, that is, independent of their experiences and traditions.[160] The nonrelative character of Kantian philosophy is easy to see in the realm of *individual* or personal morality. Indeed, the examples that Kant gives are of this type.[161] Yet, there is every reason to extend Kant's moral universalism to *political* morality as well. The contingent division of the world into discrete nation-states

---

157. See, e.g., Hinsley, supra note 20, at 71.

158. See Kant, Perpetual Peace, supra note 1, at 112–15; Kant, Universal History, supra note 1, at 34–36. In addition, Kant's general moral theory logically leads to the proposition, see authorities cited supra note 1.

159. See Tesón, supra note 6, at 99–120.

160. See Kant, Groundwork, supra note 1, at 55–56. Kant asks: "Do we not think it a matter of the utmost necessity to work out for once a pure moral philosophy completely cleansed of everything that can only be empirical and appropriate to anthropology?" Id. at 57.

161. See id. at 84–86.

does not transform political freedom[162] from an ethical imperative into a mere accident of history. Just as rational, albeit fallible, beings are capable of selecting the morally correct action out of a pure sense of duty, so too are the same rational beings creating the law of nations capable of selecting the morally correct form of political organization.

International law is concerned, at least in part, with the incorporation of those rules and principles that are deemed just on a global scale. First among them is the principle of a republican constitution proposed by Kant. This is not generated by a desire to impose an idiosyncratic system of values upon groups in other parts of the globe who have different traditions. The republican constitution of the liberal-democratic society, far from being idiosyncratic, is *objectively* right; it is not tied to empirical circumstance or historical accident. The republican constitution derives from the categorical imperative, from the exercise of rational faculties by autonomous agents capable of articulating the pure concept of right, as Kant expressly says in *Perpetual Peace* on this very issue.[163] To be consistent with justice, therefore, international law must require that states respect human rights. An international legal system that authorizes individuals to exercise despotic political power is morally deficient in a fundamental way. It disregards ethics that are central to Kant's "kingdom of ends,"[164] in which humans are defined by their aptitude to become members of the same moral community, worthy of dignity and respect.[165] Such is the notion that the international law of human rights attempts to vindicate.[166] In the Kantian vision, human rights are not mere privileges graciously granted by individuals in power—for example, by signing an international human rights convention. They are constitutive of the international definition of a legitimate nation-state.

The Kantian normative argument for the primacy of human rights can be reconstructed or extended using modern social contract theory.[167] The just civic constitution is the one that would be agreed upon by parties in an original position of uncertainty. The just world order likewise is the one that would be agreed upon by rational individuals in an original position of uncertainty, that is, knowing neither which country they will be part of nor what socioeconomic position they will occupy in that country. Under this model, and contrary to what John

162. See supra part II.A.

163. See supra notes 38–46 and accompanying text.

164. See supra notes 69–71 and accompanying text.

165. See Kant, Groundwork, supra note 1, at 95–96.

166. State-oriented international lawyers persistently disregard the fact that the respect for human dignity was a major concern of the international community after 1945. See, e.g., U.N. Charter pmbl.

167. See Rawls, supra note 61, at 11–17 (developing modern Kantian-contractarian theory). The passage that follows summarizes the arguments made in Tesón, supra note 6, at 109–20, and in Tesón, supra note 87, at 58–71.

Rawls himself has suggested,[168] the parties in the original position are individuals, not governments. They will agree on, among other principles of global justice, an international bill of human rights and on strong mechanisms to protect them against their governments, such as international human rights courts and even humanitarian intervention in cases of extreme human rights deprivations. They will include the notion of just constitutions as the fundamental requirement for a just world order. The contractors, however, will agree on a world of separate nations, thus stopping short of creating a global super-state, for reasons discussed below.[169] The original contractors will not risk their liberty interests by gambling on a law of nations that would permit governments to adopt tyrannical methods, because they might end up as citizens of tyrannical states.[170] Thus, the very principles of rational choice suggested by Rawls exclude a purely statist conception of international law.

IV. The Problem of Authority and Enforcement

Kant's Second Definitive Article provides that international law must be based on a federation of free states. Kant refers first to international law. We have seen already how important the idea of law is for Kant.[171] Domestically, civil society, the just civic constitution, results, as in Hobbes and Locke, from citizens surrendering their unlimited freedom in the state of nature in order to create the rule of law, the *Rechtstaat*, which alone can rationally secure individual freedom. The moral and civilized nature in us thus overcomes our evil instincts of lawlessness and destruction. We accept coercion and the idea of law and order to secure freedom for all.[172] Only then can we pursue the higher forms of life which define our essential humanity.

The human propensity to master our evil nature with reason[173] and reliance on law holds internationally as well. Governments, even in times of Kant's international state of nature, want to see their actions, no matter how self-interested and destructive, as legally justified. Far from reaching a skeptical conclusion from this crude reality of world

168. See Rawls, supra note 61, at 378.

169. See infra notes 182–197 and accompanying text.

170. See Tesón, supra note 6, at 109–20; Tesón, supra note 87, at 58–71; see also Mark R. Wicclair, Rawls and the Principle of Nonintervention, *in* John Rawls, Theory of Social Justice 289, 299–301 (H. Gene Blocker & Elizabeth H. Smith eds., 1980) (parties to contract in original position would choose limited intervention rule over nonintervention rule).

171. See supra notes 77–81 and accompanying text.

172. See Kant, Perpetual Peace, supra note 1, at 111–12 & n.† ("For by entering into civil society, each person gives every other . . . the requisite security.").

173. See Gallie, supra note 11, at 16 ("The intensity of feeling which Kant focused upon this hope for Reason in human life is unparalleled in the history of political thought, anyhow since Plato.").

politics, Kant saw this reliance on legal discourse as evidence of rationality:

> The homage that every nation pays (at least in words) to the concept of [law] proves . . . that there is in man a still greater, though presently dormant moral aptitude to master the evil principle in himself (a principle he cannot deny) and to hope that others will also overcome it.[174]

Therefore, according to Kant, the international order logically ought to mirror the domestic order; just as individuals would choose to create a civic constitution to solve the problems posed by the ruthless state of nature, so too would the same individuals, organized in nation-states, agree upon a system of international law to solve the problems posed by the international state of nature.

The analogy to domestic ordering raises the question of whether a successful system of international law must also be centralized into a super-state with a world government. This question is, of course, an old acquaintance of international lawyers: the view that there cannot be international law without an international sovereign has long since been discredited in international legal circles.[175] In addition, the controversy over whether international law is "really" law seems to be primarily semantic.[176] Yet, the objection is still worth examining, for it could well be that critical philosophical reflection will lead us to reconsider world government as a better alternative.[177]

In order fully to understand Kant's proposed solution to this dilemma, one must remember that Kant was writing at a time when war was the main method of settling international disputes and when the right of princes to make war was not seriously in dispute.[178] Politicians, scholars, and other educated persons living in that climate of interna-

174. Kant, Perpetual Peace, supra note 1, at 116. The word "law" has been substituted for "right" in this Article; see supra note 18.

175. See, e.g., Anthony D'Amato, International Law: Process and Prospect 1–26 (1987) (rejecting idea that international law must be centrally enforced to be considered law); W. Michael Reisman, Sanctions and Enforcement, *in* International Law Essays 381, 386 (Myres S. McDougal ed., 1981) (discussing community and group sanctions as distinguished from state-imposed); see also Eiichi Fukatsu, Coercion and the Theory of Sanctions in International Law, *in* The Structure and Process of International Law 1187 (R. St.J. Macdonald & Douglas M. Johnston eds., 1983) (discussing diplomatic, economic, and military coercion by individual state as international law sanctions).

176. See Glanville L. Williams, International Law and the Controversy Concerning the Word "Law," 22 Brit. Y.B. Int'l L. 146, 158–62 (1945).

177. See Carson, supra note 30 at 184–91 (arguing that "ultra-minimal" world government could preserve world peace).

178. For an account of international law allowing the right of states to wage war prior to the United Nations Charter, see 2 L. Oppenheim, International Law 177–78 (H. Lauterpacht ed., 7th ed. 1952); see also Hubert Thierry et al., Droit International Public 538–41 (1975) (discussing development of ideas of pacifism and just war from early Christianity to absolute monarchies of the 18th century). Kant has numerous references in his writings to international lawlessness and the international state of nature. See, e.g., Kant, Perpetual Peace, supra note 1, at 115–16; Kant, Theory and Practice, supra

tional lawlessness were his audience. Therefore, the idea of an international legal system that would outlaw war was revolutionary. Of course, today the presumption is against the right to make war, not in favor of it, and so many of Kant's arguments and assumptions might seem to us outmoded or taken for granted.

Both Hobbes and Rousseau faced the problem of authority before Kant. Hobbes, of course, thought that international relations were the state of nature par excellence.[179] Some commentators of Kant's work followed his argument to its seemingly logical conclusion: they read "federation" in the modern sense, as meaning a federated republic with a unified sovereign.[180] These commentators mistakenly argued that just as a constitutional government is the answer to the problems of social cooperation, freedom, and order within civil society; so too, world government should be the answer to similar problems internationally. Others believed that world government is what Kant should have argued for and that anything less is either useless, because it does not solve the problem of the international state of nature, or logically inconsistent with Kant's own arguments in *Perpetual Peace* and elsewhere.[181]

Most modern commentators, however, agree that Kant did not support world government.[182] Not only does Kant expressly disavow the creation of a centralized world government,[183] but the Third Definitive Article, establishing the Cosmopolitan Law, or the rules of free trade and universal hospitality, is inexplicable outside the context of a world of independent nation-states.[184]

Kant's answer (or, rather, the best Kantian answer) to this problem is to propose instead *an alliance of separate free nations, united by their moral commitment to individual freedom, by their allegiance to the international rule of law, and by the mutual advantages derived from peaceful intercourse*. The global distribution of authority proposed by Kant is thus quite close to the modern international legal system: states have rights and duties under international law, because they represent autonomous moral beings. However, there is no sovereign to enforce them; enforcement is

---

note 1, at 67; see also Waltz, supra note 15, at 334 (discussing Kant's conception of states in international system).

179. See Thomas Hobbes, On Dominion, ch. XIII, cited by Hinsley, supra note 20, at 51. The problem of authority confounded Rousseau. Consequently his works contain some inconsistencies about the appropriate resolution. See Hinsley, supra note 20, at 46–51 (discussing Rousseau's works on international relations).

180. See, e.g., Friedrich, supra note 10, at 45.

181. See Carson, supra note 30, at 179–84.

182. See Hinsley, supra note 20, at 62–70; Gallie, supra note 11, at 20–21; Waltz, supra note 15, at 335–37; Jean-Michel Besnier, Le Droit International Chez Kant et Hegel, 32 Archives De Philosophie Du Droit: Le Droit International 85, 91 (1987).

183. See Kant, Perpetual Peace, supra note 1, at 117.

184. See id., at 118–19.

decentralized.[185] Kant was ahead of modern international law in requiring that states observe human rights as a precondition for joining the alliance.

Quite apart from textual evidence, and notwithstanding the serious problem of the lack of centralized enforcement, there are good reasons to prefer a loose organization of separate states subject to international law to a centralized world government. Kant defended separate states not only because he thought that in this way his proposal would be more realistic, but because he thought that such a loose system was morally justified.[186]

First, he decided that world government presents too great a threat to individual freedom. Liberty is better secured when political power is relatively diluted. Kant wrote:

> [A world consisting of separate nations] is rationally preferable to [its] being overrun by a superior power that melds them into a universal monarchy. For laws invariably lose their impact with the expansion of their domain of governance, and after it has uprooted the soul of good a soulless despotism finally degenerates into anarchy.[187]

Kant was aware that while world government may be an attractive idea in theory, it carries the danger of degenerating first into a world tyranny and ultimately back into international anarchy.[188] Under a centralized world government, resisting the tyranny of a corrupt leadership would present an overwhelming logistical problem for individuals struggling to reestablish human rights and representative democracy. Freedom fighters would not have safe refuge, nor the fiscal and political support of independent representative governments. Nor would free states exist to moderate the excesses of despots through diplomacy and coercive intervention when appropriate.[189]

Second, a system of separate states allows individuals to associate with those that share their same culture, customs, history, and language. Such a system is more likely to respect the individuals' "community" interests and contribute to the affirmation of their self-respect that ultimately leads to the flourishing of individual autonomy. From a practical standpoint, a decentralized system minimizes conflicts originating as a result of those cultural differences.

Kant supports his view with a curious argument, mixing a Hobbes-

185. See infra notes 187–197 and accompanying text.

186. See Hinsley, supra note 20, at 63.

187. Kant, Perpetual Peace, supra note 1, at 125.

188. After suggesting the possibility that nations might consider world government, Kant writes: "But they do not will to do this because it does not conform to their idea of the [law] of nations, and consequently they discard in *hypothesis* what is true in *thesis*." Id. at 117; see also Gallie, supra note 11, at 23–24 (discussing Kant's rejection of both peace-by-empire and peace-by-federation).

189. See Terry Nardin, Law, Morality, and The Relations of States 238–39 (1983).

ian perspective with a sort of evolutionary determinism.[190] He argues that nature has used war as an instrument to force people to live in all sections of the globe, and eventually to reach the situation of separate nations in a state of (potential) war. On the other hand, nature has used the same features that divide peoples—differences in language and religion—to create an "equilibrium of the liveliest competing powers" which alone can control the danger of the deceptive peace that despotism brings—as he writes, "in the graveyard of freedom."[191] Despite Kant's dubious deterministic parlance,[192] the argument is based on Kant's original theory of the "asocial sociability" of human beings.[193]

In the international arena, the Kantian analysis shows how decentralized enforcement can take the place of a world police force, and underscores the subtlety of international mechanisms to secure compliance.[194] Of course, the idea that communities with a strong sense of cultural identity should be allowed to be autonomous is a relative assessment. It springs from the empirical conjecture that if subject to world government, different groups and minorities would tend to see their claims for identity ignored by a huge bureaucracy, whereas local government might appear to be more responsive to such claims. Yet by no means must all cultures live under separate governments; there are a number of successful examples of multicultural states. Furthermore, cultural differences should not preclude nations from voluntarily merging into larger political units, such as the European Economic Community. Finally, principles of respect for individual human rights trump the right to self-determination.[195]

---

190. See Kant, Perpetual Peace, supra note 1, at 120–25.

191. Id. at 125.

192. Why should the champion of free will talk about the Laws of Nature forcing people to do things? Professor Besnier rightly criticizes Kant's abuse of the notion of the Design of Nature. See Besnier, supra note 182, at 93–94 (calling the argument "la ruse de la nature"); see also Robert K. Faulkner, Liberal Plans for the World: Locke, Kant, and World Ecology Theories, Int'l J. World Peace, March 1990, at 61, 77–79 (1990) (critiquing Kant's "strangely ruthless humanitarianism" that assumes war will eventually dictate progress toward a rational world).

193. See George Modelski, Is World Politics Evolutionary Learning?, 44 Int'l Org. 1, 2–6 (1990) (Kant's historicist argument confirmed by recent studies on nature of international cooperation); Hinsley, supra note 20, at 72 (Kant's international philosophy combined "the historical sense, the moral element in politics, and the irrational element in man"); Gallie, supra note 11, at 28–29 (for Kant, idea of human reason excludes use of war); see also Sullivan, supra note 1, at 235–41 (summarizing Kant's philosophy of history).

194. Gallie eloquently summarizes the Kantian tension between man's rational powers: Reason is "that tendency, in all human thought and conscious effort, towards, at one and the same time, ever greater unity, system and necessity, and *equally* towards ever sharper and more constant self-criticism and self-control." Gallie, supra note 11, at 14.

195. The question of the interplay between self-determination and individual human rights is an extremely complex one, and is beyond the scope of this Article. See

Kant argues for the maintenance of separate nation-states as a balance between the dangers to freedom posed by centralized world government and the state of nature.[196] An alliance of liberal democracies subject to international law will provide the exact point of equilibrium for world order. Compliance will hopefully be achieved gradually by operation of subtle decentralized systemic mechanisms.[197]

If a morally justified international law is the result of such a liberal alliance, the question arises as to the legal status of those states that are not liberal democracies. First, tyrannical governments are outlaws. However, they are not outside the law of nations. Like domestic criminals, they are still bound by elementary principles, such as the rules that prohibit crimes of aggression and war crimes. While outlaw governments do not benefit from the rights conferred by membership in the alliance, they retain some rights. For example, if they are accused of human rights violations or war crimes, they have a right to be tried by an independent and impartial tribunal in accordance with well-established international rules.[198]

Second, a liberal theory of international law seeks to protect individuals. Therefore, actions, even by legitimate governments, that violate the rights of individuals in tyrannical states are prohibited. Citizens in undemocratic states lack representation, but they have not lost their rights. It follows that agreements creating obligations that benefit individuals should be respected. Such agreements include conventions inspired by elementary considerations of humanity and, in some cases, treaties that establish boundaries. However, agreements that dictators enter into to benefit themselves are binding neither upon members of the alliance nor upon the citizens of the tyrannical state. Because dictators do not represent their people, they cannot create obligations for their subjects. Such agreements are not respected because of the traditional principle *pacta sunt servanda*, but rather for prudential reasons or because they protect oppressed individuals.

Similarly, a liberal theory of international law must account for the role of force and war. Force may be used in defense of persons and, derivatively, in defense of representative governments and states.[199] Because members of the liberal alliance are in compliance with the First

Avishai Margalis & Joseph Raz, National Self-Determination, 87 J. Phil. 439, 454–61 (1990).

196. According to Kant, the state of nature exists when states are at war or a threat of war exists. See Kant, Perpetual Peace, supra note 1, at 111. Yet, the establishment of the liberal alliance, while a dramatic improvement, will still harbor dangers of war *against nonmembers*, i.e., despotic states. See infra text accompanying notes 199–220. Perpetual peace will be finally achieved when all nations become democratic and join the alliance.

197. See supra note 175.

198. See, e.g., European Convention for the Protection of Human Rights and Fundamental Freedoms, art. 6, 213 U.N.T.S. 221, 228 (1955).

199. See Tesón, supra note 87, at 111–23 (arguing that intervention is appropriate only if (1) force is used to thwart human rights violations, (2) nonhumanitarian motives

Definitive Article, force will never need to be used to exact compliance with their international obligations. However, force will sometimes have to be used against nonliberal regimes as a last resort in self-defense or in defense of human rights. Liberal democracies must seek peace and use all possible alternatives to preserve it. In extreme circumstances, however, violence may be the only means to uphold the law and to defend the liberal alliance against outlaw dictators that remain nonmembers. Such, I believe, is the proper place of war in the Kantian theory.

However, Kant seems to disagree. In his commentary to the Sixth Preliminary Article, Kant dismisses the idea that there could be a just war. War, Kant writes, is "a sad necessity in the state of nature [where] the outcome of the conflict (as if . . . it were the so-called 'judgment of God') determines the side on which justice lies."[200] Kant was troubled by the impossibility of rationally making a judgment of right prior to the conflict itself, since in international relations there is "no tribunal empowered to make judgments supported by the power of law."[201] Kant returns to the theme of justice as identified with law and legal adjudication.[202] Because in the international arena there can be no courts backed by force, there can be no rational decision about the justice of a particular war.[203]

How can we reconcile the extreme pacifism voiced in these passages with Kant's acceptance of a decentralized law of nations[204] and with the analysis of the causes of war as intimately related to the difference in regimes?[205] As to the first point, Kant's argument for rejecting the possibility of a just war proves too much. For if the absence of international courts with compulsory jurisdiction means that no war can ever be just, then there can be no law of nations at all. There would be no courts to render enforceable judgments about *any* disputes among nations. There seems to be an inconsistency here. We saw that in the addendum entitled "On the Guarantee for Perpetual Peace," Kant accepted a definition of international law that did not require a sovereign power, courts, legislators, or police—in short, world government.[206] Perhaps Kant fell prey to his obsession with the definition of law in *civil society*, which indeed requires courts rendering decisions

do not detract from paramount human rights objective, (3) means used is rights-inspired, and (4) victims welcome intervention).

200. Kant, Perpetual Peace, supra note 1, at 110.

201. Id. Kant concludes that a war of extermination, which extinguishes all rights, is absolutely prohibited because it would achieve perpetual peace only "in the vast graveyard of humanity as a whole." Id.

202. See supra notes 77–81 and accompanying text.

203. Kant reiterates this point in his commentary to the Second Definitive Article. See Kant, Perpetual Peace, supra note 1, at 116–17.

204. See supra notes 182–185 and accompanying text.

205. See supra part III.A.

206. See Kant, Perpetual Peace, supra note 1, at 120–25.

backed by the power of the state. In his discussion of international authority, in contrast, Kant addressed the difficulty and dangers of creating world government by the incorporation of the notion of decentralized enforcement. Yet, decentralized enforcement means that, while war is absolutely banned within the alliance, force will sometimes need to be used by individual states or members of the alliance acting in concert against enemies of the alliance. Therefore, a war of self-defense by a democratic government and its allies against a despotic aggressor is a just war.[207]

The central difficulty with Kant's rejection of just war is the status of tyrannical regimes that have not yet joined the alliance. If the analysis in Part III is correct, the difference in domestic regimes will be a permanent threat to peace. Perhaps one could devise principles of political prudence designed to moderate the historical intolerance of liberal governments toward despots,[208] but there are at least two thorny problems with Kant's view. The first, already mentioned, concerns the reaction of liberal democracies against aggressive despots. There is no doubt that democratic governments should retain their inherent right of self-defense,[209] which in Kantian terms is nothing more than the defense of persons by their government against foreign attack.[210] Second, similar perplexities arise in the case of intervention to stop serious violations of human rights in other states. Kant's Fifth Preliminary Article provides that "no nation shall forcibly interfere with the constitution and government of another."[211] In a very succinct commentary, Kant justifies this precept by saying that "[g]enerally, the bad example that one free person furnishes for another . . . does not injure the latter."[212] For example, a tyrant who tortures his citizens does not injure citizens in neighboring nations.

Leaving aside for the moment the patent inconsistency of this view with the universalist thrust of Kant's thesis, there remains the question whether such an absolute rule of nonintervention can be reconciled with Kant's First Definitive Article, the requirement that states be lib-

207. In his commentary to the Third Preliminary Article, Kant seems to justify war in cases of self-defense. See id. at 108 (distinguishing between "paying men to kill or be killed," which Kant deems "inconsistent with the rights of humanity," and "the *voluntary*, periodic military training of citizens so that they can secure their homeland against external attack.") (emphasis added); see also Gallie, supra note 11, at 24 (discussing Kant's advocacy of a confederation of common defense against aggression).

208. See, e.g., Doyle, Liberal Legacies (pt. 2), supra note 135 at 343–49.

209. U.N. Charter art. 51 ("Nothing in the present Charter shall impair the inherent right of individual or collective self-defence [sic] if an armed attack occurs against a Member of the United Nations, until the Security Council has taken measures necessary to maintain international peace and security.").

210. See Kant, Perpetual Peace, supra note 1, at 108; cf. Michael Walzer, Just and Unjust Wars 21–32 (1977) (war is crime because it forces people to fight for their rights).

211. Kant, Perpetual Peace, supra note 1, at 109.

212. Id.

eral democracies. A possible answer would be that nations join the alliance voluntarily, not as a result of intervention, however benign, by liberal members of the alliance.[213] Voluntary adherence to the alliance means allowing citizens in nonliberal states to resolve their differences among themselves, through their own efforts. In this way, citizens of a nonliberal state could eventually upgrade their society, as it were, so it could become a liberal democracy and qualify as a member. Only through the unfolding of such a process of self-determination will a decision to join the liberal alliance be voluntary; and members of the alliance should patiently wait until that occurs spontaneously and not force the process by intervening.

This reading of Kant is certainly possible. A reading more consistent with the rest of Kant's views, however, is that the nonintervention principle is dependent upon compliance with the First Definitive Article. Internal legitimacy is what gives states the shield of sovereignty against foreign intervention. Since morally autonomous citizens hold rights to liberty, the states and governments that democratically represent them have a right to be politically independent and should be shielded by international law from foreign intervention.[214] The liberal version of nonintervention and self-determination thus emphasizes respect for human rights and true representation. Political legitimacy is thus seen as the proper foundation of state sovereignty.[215] The question of internal legitimacy must be resolved prior to the question of nonintervention.[216] Noninterventionism, therefore, follows from whatever theory of internal legitimacy one adopts. If the only just political arrangement is the republican constitution, state sovereignty reacquires its shielding power only in states that have adopted and implemented such a constitution. Sovereignty is to be respected only when it is justly exercised.[217]

---

213. See, e.g., id. at 115 ("[E]ach nation can and should demand that the others enter into a contract resembling the civil one and guaranteeing the rights of each.").

214. See Doyle, supra note 30, at 213.

215. The nonintervention principle seems to us a permanent feature of international law, and so it might seem peculiar to see it included by Kant among the Preliminary Articles. Unlike Woodrow Wilson, for example, Kant was indeed a noninterventionist liberal, but what commentators have failed to emphasize is that his being liberal is a precondition of his being noninterventionist. See Waltz, supra note 15, at 339–40.

216. Even Hinsley, who repeatedly underscores the importance of state sovereignty, writes: "Just as [Kant] derived the right to freedom of the individual from the dictates of a moral law, so he derived the right to freedom of the state—*the route to and the guarantee of the freedom of the individual*—from the same moral law." Hinsley, supra note 20, at 63 (emphasis added). The moral law mandates freedom of the individual and freedom of the state as but a means to that end. See Kant, Universal History, supra note 1, at 34 (problem of just civic constitution cannot be solved without solving international problem).

217. See, e.g., Tesón, supra note 87, at 82; Charles R. Beitz, Political Theory and International Relations 80–83 (1979).

This suggests that Kant's Fifth Preliminary Article (the prohibition of forcible intervention) might be misplaced. If the protection against intervention is a consequence of domestic legitimacy, then nonintervention holds *only* among liberal states, and therefore the nonintervention principle should be seen as a definitive precept that governs the liberal alliance, not as a step that must be taken before the alliance is formed.

It follows from these considerations that citizens in a liberal democracy should be free to argue that, in some admittedly rare cases, the only morally acceptable alternative is to intervene to help the victims of serious human rights deprivations.[218] However, even if Kant is correct on the issue of humanitarian intervention, his rejection of the possibility of just wars is not consistent with the normative individualism underlying the rest of his theory of international law.[219] While aggression by members against other members of the alliance will be banned forever, in some cases democratic nations must resort to self-help to enforce their rights against outsiders.[220] At the very least, Kant's view does not account for the case of aggression by despots against members of the alliance. More generally, Kant's reason for rejecting just wars—that there are no courts to determine the justice of the cause—is unconvincing. Kant himself advocates an international law among separate nations that entails a decentralized system of authority. Judgments on the legality of wars are no different from judgments of legality generally, so if there are no courts available for the former, there are no courts available for the latter. Yet, Kant's whole purpose is precisely to show that a law of nations, and judgments of legality in conformity with it, are possible notwithstanding such a decentralization of power.

V. Why Justice: The Neo-Positivist Theory of Legitimacy

The attempt to use theories of justice, such as Kantian or Rawlsian social contract theory, as the basis for international law has been recently criticized. Professor Thomas M. Franck argues that theories of justice should not be used as a springboard for determining the legiti-

218. See Tesón, supra note 87, at 111–23.

219. Kant's view here is also inconsistent with his own rejection of the right to revolution. See supra notes 82–87 and accompanying text. For it is often the case that the only way for a tyranny to become a liberal democracy, and thus qualify for the alliance, is for citizens violently to overthrow the tyrant. Of course, I have rejected Kant's views on revolution; someone may still salvage Kant's views on the nonintervention issue by disagreeing with him on the revolution issue. My own position is that the right of humanitarian intervention in appropriate cases is an extension of the right to revolution.

220. There is yet another case: the use of force by a nonliberal state against another nonliberal state. The justice of that will depend on whose rights are being violated. Even an illegitimate government may defend citizens against aggression by foreigners. However, despotic governments do not have any right to defend themselves against external force used to remove them from power, provided that such foreign help is welcomed by the victims themselves. See Tesón, supra note 87, at 119–23.

macy of international rules.[221] He maintains that an international rule is deemed legitimate if the governments upon which it operates accept the rule and agree that it accords with generally accepted principles of "right process."[222] Professor Franck's definition of "right process" is quite rich, a blend of traditional positivism, critical legal studies, and natural law *á la* Fuller. According to Franck, legitimacy has four components: determinacy, symbolic validation, coherence, and adherence.[223]

Franck rejects the inclusion of principles of justice as a component of legitimacy. He asserts an operational and a theoretical objection. The operational problem is that justice applies to individuals, while international law addresses states and governments. The theoretical problem with global justice raised by Franck is an old tenet of positivism, namely that the concepts of justice and legitimacy are conceptually distinct.[224] On this view, justice and legitimacy are two separate concepts which should be carefully kept apart, even though their normative commands may sometimes overlap.[225] That a rule is legitimate does not mean that it is just and, conversely, many just rules may not be legitimate. This is so even in domestic systems.[226] Under Franck's theory, the first task is for nations to comply with international law, even if many of its rules are unjust. An international legal system seeks compliance with the rules that participating governments have created, mostly through custom and treaty.[227]

There is much to commend in this account of legitimacy. Professor Franck should be applauded for tackling long-neglected foundational issues in international law. In particular, the notion of right process seems useful as a method for identifying legitimate norms when the international legal system as a whole is just. However, by and large, this view is an extension of the traditional positivist belief that international law is created exclusively by the acts of governments. As such, his theory of international legitimacy is open to a number of objections.[228]

---

221. See Thomas M. Franck, The Power of Legitimacy Among Nations 208–46 (1990).

222. Id. at 19.

223. Id. at 49. He develops each of these ideas in chapters four through twelve. Franck explains that "symbolic validation" only obtains once the "cues" or symbols that confer legitimacy are perceived to be true which occurs as a result of historical practice and custom.

224. See id. at 208–09.

225. See id. at 242.

226. See id. at 236. Regarding domestic organization, Franck confines his analysis to "secular democracies" maintaining that this bifurcation may not apply to nonwestern "moral communities," see id. at 235.

227. See id. at 210.

228. For a general critique of consent theory (or positivism), see Tesón, supra note 6, at 99–107.

The contention that international law emphasizes compliance, not justice, does not merely describe the way international law works, it states a normative proposition. The theory *recommends* that international lawyers emphasize compliance and order to the detriment of moral considerations.[229] By requiring that a legitimate norm satisfy the four part test of determinacy, symbolic validation, coherence, and adherence, Franck constructs his own principle of international justice that sacrifices morality and the primacy of respect for individual autonomy in favor of procedural regularity. The idea that order and compliance are a good in and of themselves and, consequently, a valid end of international law is insufficient. Franck's theory amounts to a normative decision that law deserves allegiance irrespective of its substantive content, who created the law, and the extent to which rulers represent their citizens. Franck substitutes political power as the basic determinant of international legitimacy without explanation; he does so at the expense of more important and basic values, such as respect for human rights and fair representation of members of the state.

Second, the operational objection that justice may work among individuals, but not among nations, presupposes the statist paradigm. Professor Franck is correct that the idea of justice among nations seems awkward, but because states are merely representatives, not persons, international justice must also focus on the rights of individuals—the central claim of the Kantian theory of international law. Take, for example, the question of human rights. Kant argued that a world order is just if, and only if, the governments themselves are legitimate, which can only be true if the state's constitution is republican. Despots, who by definition represent no one but themselves, should not play a role in forming international rules. There is no reason why dictatorships ought to be protected under international law and accorded the honorific label of legitimate governments for the purpose of participating in the international legal process.[230] The first precept of the Kantian theory of international justice is quite simple: international law should not sanction a rule that permits the exercise of tyrannical power. One would think this a basic precept of legitimacy, yet Franck's view claims that domestic rule is a matter of justice which is not, and should not, be addressed by the international system. Once one accepts normative individualism, not statism, Franck's premise must be rejected.

Professor Franck reveals his adherence to the statist paradigm in his discussion of Rawls' theory. Rawls argued that international principles of justice are the ones that would be agreed upon by representatives of nations. These representatives would adopt the principles of equality of nations, self-determination, and nonintervention.[231] Using the hypothetical example of a genocidal government, Franck correctly

229. See Franck, supra note 221, at 210.
230. See Tesón, supra note 6, at 99–103.
231. See supra notes 167–170 and accompanying text.

observes that the absolute principle of nonintervention suggested by Rawls leads to unacceptable results from the standpoint of justice.[232] However, he then reproduces Rawls' mistake of postulating governments as the original contractors and understandably concludes that such a model, which he believes is also supported by the practice of states, would yield the almost absolute nonintervention principle. Furthermore, because noninterventionism is incompatible with elementary notions of justice, at least in extreme cases, he argues that *justice*, not the absolute nonintervention rule, should be discarded as a component of legitimacy.

This is a rather stunning conclusion in Franck's own positivist terms, because reasoning from state practice yields an inconsistent rule on the question of humanitarian intervention.[233] Even within the positivist paradigm, in some instances state practice supports intervention.[234] It is obvious that governments interested in incumbency and preserving their power and privileges will agree on rules of international law that protect the political space in which they can do as they please. Examples of such rules that protect governments[235] are the principle of nonintervention, as opposed to humanitarian intervention, and the preservation of territorial integrity, as opposed to the right of secession.[236] Professor Franck, like several Rawls commentators before him,[237] acknowledges the problem with considering states and not individuals as the primary subjects of justice. However, he concludes that since rulers insist that international law be couched in statist terms, the precepts of justice should not count as components of international legitimacy. His conclusion does not follow logically.

The logical conclusion should be that current international law is wrongly conceptualized in terms of prerogatives of rulers, and that we should move toward a theory of international law that has the individual, not the state, as its subject and basic moral unit. The point that justice makes sense only among individuals not among states is correct, but the conclusion that we must discard justice is incorrect. Instead, the logical corollary should be that international law must be made con-

232. See Franck, supra note 221, at 221. The same point is argued at length in Tesón, supra note 87, at 58–71.

233. See Tesón, supra note 87, at 155–200.

234. See Richard Lillich, Humanitarian Intervention: A Reply to Ian Brownlie and Plea for Constructive Alternatives, *in* Law and Civil War in the Modern World 229, 235–37 (John N. Moore & Wolfgang G. Friedman eds., 1974).

235. Such rules serve to protect governments although they often use euphemistically collective nouns such as "the people" or "the state." See Fernando R. Tesón, Le Peuple, C'Est Moi! The World Court and Human Rights, 81 Am. J. Int'l L. 173, 181–82 (1987).

236. See the hypothetical example in Franck, supra note 221, at 226–30.

237. See Wicclair, supra note 170, at 297-98; Thomas Pogge, Rawls and Global Justice, 18 Can. J. Phil. 227, 238–39 (1988); Tesón, supra note 87, at 58–64.

gruent with justice, and thus be conceived in terms of individuals, not states or governments.

By modifying the Rawlsian model in which the contracting parties are individuals or representatives of individuals, not representatives of states, the logical problem of applying the requirements of justice to states is solved. Professor Franck, however, rejects such a model. He concludes that a social contract among individuals or their legitimate representatives,[238] far from eliminating the rules suggested by Rawls' model that conflict with our moral intuition, would yield an unjust system and fail to accord with reality because it requires that we "imagine two things at once: just nations making a just world."[239] Franck maintains that such a system could never appear just from the perspective of the individual because "[t]he priorities and sensibilities of rulers, not the people's shared (or intersecting) notions of justice, usually frame the contents of [international] rules and also have the most say in determining their compliance pull."[240] His reasoning misses the point. If the Rawlsian model with governments in the original position yields results incompatible with justice, such as precluding intervention in case of a genocidal government, then we should alter the model to accommodate our moral intuitions, rather than forsake justice.

The statist paradigm is precisely what is wrong. To say that a theory of international justice centered on the individual is unjust because current international law is created by and for governments begs the question of why justice should be a component of legitimacy. If part of what a normative theory of international law wants to do is evaluate the behavior of states in the light of what is right, then the standard cannot be the very behavior of states. What the Kantian thesis suggests is that domestic justice must be the first priority of the international system both because that is intrinsically right and because it is causally linked to peace and, by extension, to all other important global challenges.[241]

Franck's theory is also open to the objection raised by Kant's empirical argument.[242] If international law validates tyrannical governments as legitimate members of the international community, it interferes with the purpose of achieving peaceful cooperation needed to meet pressing global challenges. If Kant and Doyle are right that nonliberal governments are naturally prone to aggression, the chance of getting them to work for peace and mutual understanding is indeed

238. See supra note 195 and accompanying text; see also David A. J. Richards, International Distributive Justice, 24 Nomos 275, 282 (1982) (arguing for plausibility of contractarian theory to provide foundations for moral duties in international area).

239. Franck, supra note 221, at 226, 233.

240. Id.

241. Professor Franck includes among these challenges the control of arms, ozone depletion, desertification, hunger, and virulent disease. See id. at 210. One would think that all these tasks are instrumental in achieving the two most important global ends: freedom and peace.

242. See supra part III.A.

slim. The international community would be admitting a Trojan Horse in its midst. Franck's deceptively realistic approach, obsessed with compliance, will in the end result in the defeat of the very ends that international law was supposed to pursue.

The more natural approach is this: Insofar as international law addresses governments, it does so in their capacity as agents of persons, as representatives. This in turn raises the question of representation as an international matter. The agency relationship itself must be subject to international scrutiny. Individuals who claim to represent a nation but in fact have seized power by brute force should not be accepted as members of the community that makes the law. There is every reason to extend these common sense notions of justice to international relations and include them in a definition of international legitimacy.

State-oriented theories of international law like Franck's propose a double paradigm for the ordering of individuals: one for international law and the other for domestic law.[243] Justice and legitimacy are always conceptually separate,[244] but whereas in domestic law justice permeates legitimacy, in the international legal system the main goals are order and compliance. In contrast, the Kantian theory of international law rejects this dual paradigm and dual purpose, attempts to unify our theory of justice, and makes legitimacy depend on justice.[245] Thus, there is only one theory of justice, embracing both global and national institutional arrangements.[246]

Any theory of international or domestic justice attempts to put forward principles which amount to an ideal standard for adjudicating competing claims in a scheme of social cooperation. Thus, the Kantian theory of international law contends that a morally just world order comprises nation-states that are internally just and whose governments therefore represent individuals. The rights and interests of individuals form the ultimate touchstone of the theory. Along with this substantive thesis, the theory must provide a notion of formal justice or legitimacy not altogether different from the one Professor Franck suggests.

Once one leaves the domain of ideal theory, many rules enacted by

243. See Franck's discussion of *pacta sunt servanda*: for domestic law, in which justice reigns, he argues that principle is justified by moral sacredness of promises. For international law, in which order controls, the justification is stability. See Franck, supra note 221, at 234–36.

244. See id. at 242.

245. Franck does appreciate the importance of justice. He writes: "As the firm outlines of world order become readily apparent, and as that order increasingly focuses on the individual's place in global society, a keener understanding of the theory, function, and power of justice must surely move to the top of the agenda." Id. at 246. Yet, he settles for the statist paradigm and rejects the view that justice should be the basis of legitimacy and international law.

246. Cf. Lea Brilmayer, Justifying International Acts 157, 159 (1989) (agreeing with unity of domestic and international theory from methodological standpoint but rejecting notion that justice underlies theory of legitimacy).

governments, even representative governments that respect human rights, may be unjust. What is the role of ideal theory in those cases? First, international rules enacted through right process are legitimate provided that the system as a whole is just.[247] For example, if just governments agree by treaty to a uniform tax, which upon reflection is considered contrary to notions of distributive justice, the tax may be collected legitimately nonetheless, because the basic requirement of justice that the rule be agreed upon by representative governments that respect basic human rights has been fulfilled. The Kantian theory, far from rejecting right process, makes it a central feature of international law second only to the elementary precepts of justice.

The second function of an ideal theory, such as the Kantian theory, is to achieve determinacy of the rules of international law.[248] Treaties and custom should be interpreted in the light of appropriate principles of justice; there is no such thing as objective state practice. The behavior of governments cannot be normatively understood without presupposing a moral-political judgment.[249] In order to glean a normative pattern or a rule from diplomatic history, one must interpret that history and draw from it the best normative teachings. Thus, ideal theory, far from being "wishful thinking,"[250] performs the double role of being an impulse for reform in those cases in which the behavior of states conflicts with the theory's basic tenets; and, in hard cases, of providing standards of interpretation that will make international law consistent with the precepts of justice.

On the other hand, the Kantian theory of international law cannot be seen merely as a rational reconstruction of the actual rules and principles of international law. Some rules may be so much in conflict with the theory that all we can say is that they ought to be repealed or ignored. Yet in those cases in which the practice of states can be interpreted in accordance with the theory, justice becomes the major component of legitimacy.

Coda

The Kantian theory is not limited to a rarified philosophical domain. The theory yields practical solutions in many fields. First, the theory mandates the creation of compulsory judicial mechanisms to settle controversies arising from the three Definitive Articles: an Interna-

247. See Rawls, supra note 61, at 350–55 (discussing "the duty to comply with an unjust law").

248. See Tesón, supra note 87, at 6, 11, 200 (arguing that countries do not disagree on whether to follow international law, but rather on what that law dictates); Tesón, supra note 6, at 85–89 (same).

249. See sources cited supra note 248; Charles de Visscher, Theories et Realités en Droit International Public 171 (1970) (normative force of custom is result of lawyer "reconstituting" facts in light of moral imperatives).

250. See Franck, supra note 221, at 233.

tional Court of Human Rights, the International Court of Justice, and an International Court of Trade (roughly corresponding to Kant's three Definitive Articles respectively). Second, the Kantian theory also necessitates amendment of the conditions of admission and permanence in the United Nations. Articles 4 and 6 of the Charter of the United Nations should be amended to include the requirement that only democratic governments that respect human rights should be allowed to represent members, and that only democratic states will be accepted as new members.[251] Third, the law of treaties must undergo important changes. Representatives of dictators must be disenfranchised for the purposes of expressing the state's consent to be bound by the treaty.[252] Fourth, the law of diplomatic relations should be amended to deny diplomatic status to representatives of illegitimate governments.[253] Finally, the law of recognition should prohibit recognition of illegitimate governments, along the lines suggested by President Woodrow Wilson in the beginning of this century[254] and by the International Court of Justice for South Africa in the *Namibia* opinion.[255] These and other reforms will have to be worked out in detail, and many variations consistent with the Kantian theory are possible.

---

251. Article 4 of the U.N. Charter reads: "Membership in the United Nations is open to all other peace-loving states which accept the obligations contained in the present Charter and, in the judgment of the Organization, are able and willing to carry out these obligations." U.N. Charter art. 4, ¶ 1. While article 4 may conceivably be read as requiring respect for human rights from prospective members, the main organs of the United Nations have not interpreted it so. For a summary of the practice, see Guy Feuer, Article 4, *in* La Charte Des Nations Unies 171–72, 177–79 (Jean-Pierre Cot & Alain Pellet eds., 1985).

252. See, e.g., article 7 of the Vienna Convention on the Law of Treaties, in which the only requirement for considering a person as representing a state for the purposes of expressing the consent to be bound by a treaty is that such person produce "appropriate full powers." Vienna Convention on the Law of Treaties, art. 7, U.N. Doc. A/ Conf. 39/27, 5, 8 I.L.M. 683 (1969).

253. Articles 2, 4 and 7 of the Vienna Convention on Diplomatic Relations give almost unlimited discretion to sending and receiving states, so in theory it allows for the receiving state either to refuse to establish diplomatic relations with a tyrannical government, or to deny *agrément* to representatives of illegitimate governments. Vienna Convention on Diplomatic Relations, Apr. 18, 1961, art. 2, 4, 7, 23 U.S.T. 3227, 500 U.N.T.S. 95. There is a difference between denying *agrément* to the individual because of his or her past or other circumstances, and denying the *agrément* because the envoy is not representative of the sending state. The practice of states, however, has not shown much concern for true representativeness, with one exception: South Africa. The General Assembly recommended members to sever diplomatic relations with South Africa as early as 1962. See Ludwik Dembinski, The Modern Law of Diplomacy 92 (1988). South Africa is a clear case of *internal* illegitimacy for lack of representativeness and serious human rights deprivations. The principle governing that case should be extended to other cases of tyranny.

254. See Wilson's famous Mobile statement, 7 Am. J. Int'l L. 331 (1913) (discussing United States' desire only to deal with just governments in Central and South America).

255. See *Namibia* Opinion, 1971 I.C.J. 16, 58, ¶ 133 (June 21) (obligation by states not to recognize South Africa's illegal occupation of Namibia because of South Africa's human rights violations in Namibia).

One of the most remarkable developments since the end of the Second World War has been the exponential growth of individual liberty—the impressive expansion of human rights and democracy to societies that had been excluded from the benefits of freedom. This extraordinary and, for many, unexpected development disproves the claim that human rights and democracy are just the luxury of industrial societies and lends credence to the assumption that every rational person, regardless of historical or cultural circumstance, is apt to value and pursue freedom both as an intrinsic good and as the necessary means to formulate and act upon rational plans of life.

This enlightened moral and political global reality is ill-served by the statist model of international law. The model promotes states and not individuals, governments and not persons, order and not rights, compliance and not justice. It insists that rulers be permitted to exercise whatever amount of coercion is necessary to politically control their subjects. Yet, the reasons to prefer a world of free nations are strong enough to place the burden of proof on international lawyers who cling to the traditional statist paradigm that privileges power-holders and ignores people. If some empirical confirmation is required, recent events in the Persian Gulf should teach us at least the lesson that things would have been very different had the states in the region been liberal democracies of the kind defended here.

Perhaps there is no necessary link between the political triumph of human rights and democracy and the theoretical foundations of international law and politics. Perhaps all we can say is that the wind is blowing now in the direction of individual freedom and that the historical cycle will before long see nations return to despotism and gross injustice. It is indeed possible that the optimism caused by the triumph of human rights is hasty and that the celebration is therefore premature.[256] Yet, if the tide is going to turn against individual freedom, it will be the product of human design, not of the forces of nature pushing us around. It follows that we have to construct and defend our global institutions if we want them to last.

International law can make an important contribution in this respect. We must rethink and reconstruct international law in a way that incorporates and recognizes that the ultimate aim of global institutional arrangements is to foster the development of each individual's full po-

256. Recall the warnings of former Soviet Foreign Minister Shevardnadze, who resigned in protest of Gorbachev's courtship of the hardliners which he felt would lead toward the reestablishment of totalitarianism in the U.S.S.R., Tom Wicker, An Ominous Warning, N.Y. Times, Dec. 23, 1990, at O11. These warnings proved to be accurate: in the last week in August 1991, a coup d'état in the Soviet Union succeeded in reestablishing a dictatorship for a couple of days. Freedom and democracy, however, re-emerged with renewed force after the restoration of the legitimate government. The adherence to the liberal alliance by the nations that succeeded the now extinct Soviet Union will be perhaps the most encouraging event of the century.

tential as an autonomous human being, to protect freedom. This is so even if pessimist forecasters are right that we should expect significant setbacks to freedom globally in the years to come. Moreover, international law does not merely describe international behavior, so that our conceptual model would be more or less statist depending on the progress or restriction of human rights around the world. Rather, international law purports to set standards of international behavior. Judgments of legality are evaluations of diplomatic history according to that standard. It is insufficient to verify that many governments ignore the precepts of justice and conclude that justice should be discarded. The better view includes moral analysis as an integral part of international law. The alternative positivist paradigm, by clinging to the deceptively simple notion of the unrestrained practice of states as the touchstone for legitimacy, ends up surrendering to tyranny and aggression, the evils that international law was intended to control in the first place.

Kant's accomplishment in the field of international theory and ethics is magnificent. Few other thinkers have successfully combined so many disparate elements of morality, politics, epistemology, and history in a theory of international law. The community of free nations envisioned by Kant will hopefully expand gradually and maintain itself, as it has done for the past two hundred years, and the aim of perpetual peace will be achieved the moment when the liberal alliance comprises every civil society. It is never too late to replace the grim view of a world order in which naked political power is the standard of legitimacy with Kant's inspired cosmopolitan vision of moral progress in which tribute is paid to the definitive traits of humanity—freedom and reason.

[19]

The End of History? Reflections on Some International Legal Theses

*Susan Marks**

Democracy used to be a word that international legal commentators preferred to avoid. At least by the second half of the present century, this was not because too few governments identified themselves as democratic. It was rather because too many did so. The world's most repressive regimes joined their more representative counterparts in claiming a title that had become synonymous with praiseworthy and justified politics. In some cases modifying adjectives were used ('one-party democracy', 'people's democracy', etc.); in other cases the appropriation was unmodified. Either way, observers found normative inferences difficult to draw, for democracy appeared to mean everything, and therefore nothing.

What put an end to the commentators' reticence was, of course, the demise of communism and the turn in all regions of the world to multi-party electoral politics. For many, these events confirmed both that democracy was the foundation of political legitimacy, and that repressive regimes, whatever they chose to call themselves, lacked that legitimacy. Influential international legal scholars felt able to declare that a 'right of democratic governance' was now 'emerging',[1] and that international law was, or at any rate should now be, beginning to take in the lessons of 'liberal internationalism'.[2]

* Fellow, Emmanuel College, Cambridge, CB2 3AP, United Kingdom. I would like to thank Professor James Crawford for his invaluable assistance and support in the writing of the PhD dissertation on which this article draws.

1 The leading exponent of this is Thomas Franck. See, esp., 'United Nations Based Prospects for a New Global Order', 22 *NYUJ. Int'l L. & Pol.* (1990) 601; 'The Emerging Right to Democratic Governance', 86 *AJIL* (1992) 46 (hereinafter Franck 1992); 'Democracy as a Human Right', in L. Henkin and J. Hargrove (eds.), *Human Rights: An Agenda for the Next Century* (1994) 73 (hereinafter Franck 1994); and *Fairness in International Law and Institutions* (1995) (hereinafter Franck 1995), Ch. 4 (largely reproducing Franck 1992).

2 See esp. Slaughter (Burley), 'Revolution of the Spirit', 3 *Harv. Hum. Rts J.* (1990) 1 (hereinafter Slaughter 1990); 'Towards an Age of Liberal Nations', 33 *Harv. Int'l L.J.* (1992) 393 (hereinafter Slaughter 1992a); 'Law Among Liberal States: Liberal Internationalism and the Act of State Doctrine', 92 *Columbia L.R.* (1992) 1907 (hereinafter Slaughter 1992b); 'Law and the Liberal Paradigm in International Relations Theory', *Proc. ASIL* (1993) 180 (hereinafter Slaughter 1993); and 'International Law in a World of Liberal States', 6 *EJIL* (1995) 503 (hereinafter Slaughter 1995). For a related theme, see Tesón, 'The Kantian Theory of International Law', 92 *Columbia L.R.* (1992) 53 (hereinafter Tesón 1992).

3 EJIL (1997) 449–477

This article examines these claims.[3] The concern here is not to affirm or deny that state practice and *opinio juris* square with an emerging right of democratic governance. The evidence relevant to deciding that doctrinal question will not be presented, and no conclusion will be offered with respect to it. Nor does this article seek to maintain that democracy is a Western artefact, with limited relevance outside the West. On the contrary, the premise of what follows is that, *provided* it is understood to refer to a general concept or ideal of self-rule on a footing of equality among citizens,[4] rather than to particular conceptions of democratic politics and their institutional manifestations, democracy is an idea of potentially universal pertinence. Its historical roots may be localized. But the worldwide struggles being waged in democracy's name leave little room for doubt that democracy has today become globalized.

The previous paragraph's proviso is, however, a very large one, and points to the central question addressed in this article. What is the understanding of democracy that informs the claims concerning the right of democratic governance and liberal internationalism? The argument advanced here is that the international legal scholars who put forward these claims precisely *do not* identify democracy with a concept or ideal of self-rule on a footing of equality among citizens. Rather, they, along with many of their critics, for the most part elide democracy with certain liberal institutions. This serves, in ways to be highlighted, to attenuate the emancipatory and critical force that democracy might have. In doing so, it limits the contribution that international law (should it develop along the lines the scholars suggest) might make with respect to anti-authoritarian politics, whether in countries yet to embrace democracy, in countries newly embracing democracy, in countries of long-standing democratic commitment, or indeed in the innumerable other non-national settings of contemporary political life.

The elision of democracy with certain liberal institutions can be linked to a more general perspective evinced in the claims concerning the norm of democratic governance and liberal internationalism. This perspective will be referred to as 'liberal millenarianism' (an expression which hopefully makes up in salience for what it

3 For elaboration of these claims, see also Fox, 'The Right to Political Participation in International Law', 17 *Yale Int'l L.J.* (1992) 539; Fox and Nolte, 'Intolerant Democracies', 36 *Harv. Int'l L.J.* (1995) 1; and Cerna, 'Universal Democracy: An International Legal Right or a Pipe Dream of the West?', 27 *N.Y.U. J. Int'l L. & Pol.* (1995) 289. For arguments refuting the claims, see Carothers, 'Empirical Perspectives on the Emerging Norm of Democratic Governance', *Proc. ASIL* (1992) 261; Koskenniemi, '"Intolerant Democracies": A Reaction', 37 *Harv. Int'l L. J.* (1996) 231; and Roth, 'Democratic Intolerance: Observations on Fox and Nolte', 37 *Harv. Int'l L.J.* (1996) 235. For discussion of the claims, see Panel 'National Sovereignty Revisited: Perspectives on the Emerging Norm of Democracy in International Law', *Proc. ASIL* (1992) 249–71.

4 Amongst the vast literature on the subject of democracy, D. Held, *Models of Democracy* (2nd ed., 1996) and J. Dunn (ed.), *Democracy: The Unfinished Journey 508 BC to AD 1993* (1992) provide exceptionally valuable overviews of the roots and vicissitudes of this ideal. In evoking the ideal, this article seeks not to define democracy (the contestability of which resists definition), but rather to associate itself with a venerable and powerful strand of democratic thought. For an exemplary distillation of that strand, see Beetham, 'Key Principles and Indices for a Democratic Audit', in D. Beetham (ed.), *Defining and Measuring Democracy* (1994) 25.

lacks in euphony). Liberal millenarianism is the analytical framework adopted in this article, and the first section sketches the key features that are here associated with it. The second section then reviews the international legal scholarship in which the claims under discussion are elaborated. The final section considers to what extent, and with what consequences, that scholarship exhibits a liberal millenarian perspective. This article's conclusion is that, if international law is to lend its support to ongoing efforts to extend and deepen democracy's purchase, the emerging norm of democratic governance and liberal internationalism offer, at best, a partial agenda.

I. Liberal Millenarianism

Liberal millenarianism finds its most extreme, and certainly its best known, expression in the work of Francis Fukuyama in the late 1980s and early 1990s.[5] Fukuyama undoubtedly set out to provoke, and this he very effectively did. His work of this period attracted many critics and few unqualified supporters.[6] One is tempted to dismiss him as isolated, a passing gadfly not to be taken too seriously. To do that would, however, be to ignore his many qualified supporters. It would be to overlook that his premises and argument found resonance – and continue to find resonance – in the work of a broad spectrum of commentators, including many whose outlooks are considerably more moderate than his. Liberal millenarianism refers to this whole spectrum. That said, precisely because he articulates in bold, telegraphic fashion, and even at times rhetorically overstates, that which others more delicately bury or hedge, Fukuyama's work offers an excellent vantage point for surveying the shared terrain.

A. Fukuyama and the End of History

Fukuyama's central thesis is that the end of the Cold War confirms a worldwide consensus in favour of liberalism, including not just capitalism but liberal democracy as well. As he sees it, liberalism has conquered all rival ideologies, most recently communism, and liberal democracy is now the sole legitimate system of gov-

5 Fukuyama's thesis, discussed below, was first advanced in an article published in 1989, and then elaborated in a further article and in a book published three years later. See Fukuyama, 'The End of History', *The National Interest* (Summer 1989) 16 (hereinafter Fukuyama 1989); 'A Reply to My Critics', *The National Interest* (Winter, 1989/90) 18; and *The End of History and the Last Man* (1992) (hereinafter Fukuyama 1992).

6 For a sampling of critiques, see Huntington, 'No Exit: The Errors of Endism', *The National Interest* (Fall, 1989) 3; Holmes, 'The Scowl of Minerva', *New Republic* (March 23, 1992) 27; Macey and Miller, 'The End of History and the New World Order: The Triumph of Capitalism and the Competition between Liberalism and Democracy', 25 *Cornell Int'l L.J.* (1992) 277; and Held, 'Liberalism, Marxism and Democracy', 22 *Theory and Society* (1993) 249 and 'Anything But A Dog's Life? Further Comments on Fukuyama, Callinicos and Giddens', 22 *Theory and Society* (1993) 293.

ernment. This marks the 'triumph of the West'.[7] More than that, it heralds – he proposes – the 'end of history'.

> What we may be witnessing is not just the end of the Cold War, or the passing of a particular period of postwar history, but the end of history as such; that is, the end point of mankind's ideological evolution and the universalisation of Western liberal democracy as the final form of human government.[8]

This claim obviously relies on a distinctive notion of 'history'. If most scholars today conceive history as without grand design, Fukuyama considers this an understandable response to the abominations of the first half of the twentieth century. But he holds that this conception now requires rethinking. In the events of the century's closing decades he finds warrant for returning to the teleological notion of history that can be found in the work of Hegel and Marx, their secular reworkings of the pre-modern deterministic understanding. According to this perspective, history is purposive, directional, progressive, and oriented towards a particular goal. Fukuyama endorses the view, which he identifies especially with Hegel,[9] that the goal towards which history is oriented is rationality and freedom, and that human societies progress towards it dialectically, through the clash of ideologies. The culmination – or 'end' – of history is eventually reached when perfect freedom and rationality are attained, and the clash of ideologies is resolved. This is what Fukuyama argues may now have occurred. Ideological competition appears to be over. Whereas Marx thought democracy in the shape of communism was our final destiny, it turns out – so Fukuyama holds – to be liberal democracy that has emerged from the fray, to await us at the end of history. It turns out to be liberal democracy that overcomes all the defects, irrationalities and contradictions of earlier forms of government, and promises to bring the historical dialectic to a close.

Fukuyama recognizes, of course, that not all countries of the world have embraced liberal democracy, and that those which have done so face continuing challenges. His point, he insists, is that history may have ended in the sense that the *ideology* of liberal democracy represents the final stage of political evolution. By this he means that the idea of liberal democracy cannot be improved upon. Ideology and ideas are one thing; practice is quite another, and in this case lags far behind. Thus, the end of history does not entail that there may, or will, be no further events and no further conflict. Nationalism and religion, in particular, appear to Fukuyama likely to remain sources of violence. Many societies have not yet begun, or have scarcely begun, to realize liberal democracy, and will face turbulent times before they do. In particular, he remarks, 'the vast bulk of the Third World remains very much mired in history'.[10] Even 'post-historical', Western societies have incom-

7 Fukuyama 1989, at 3.
8 Fukuyama 1989, at 4.
9 A consideration of whether this is accurate is beyond the scope of this article. Fukuyama acknowledges, in any event, that his understanding of Hegel is strongly influenced by the interpretation of French philosopher Alexandre Kojève (himself introduced in English translation by Allan Bloom).
10 Fukuyama 1989, at 15.

pletely implemented liberal democratic principles. For this reason they are likely to experience continuing internal strife. In their relations with one another, however, war has – so Fukuyama holds – become 'unthinkable'.[11] In this connection, he argues that the post-historical West should actively defend its gains through a 'league of democratic nations', 'capable of forceful action to protect its collective security from threats arising from the non-democratic part of the world', and 'inclined also to expand the sphere of democracy, where possible and prudent'.[12]

Why is it that liberal democracy has achieved such a victory, at least at the level of ideas or consciousness? On what basis does Fukuyama claim that liberal democracy embodies perfect rationality and freedom? He takes the view that the main engine of progress in the modern world is what he terms the 'logic of modern natural science'.[13] By this he means instrumental rationality, especially calculations of economic cost and benefit. According to Fukuyama the logic of modern natural science accounts for the triumph of capitalism and the establishment of a 'universal consumer culture'. It also accounts for the decline of traditional forms of social organization and the profound worldwide impact of technological innovation. But of itself this logic cannot account for liberal democracy's privileged place in history. While liberal democratic countries generally fare best economically, and while economic modernization may help create the material conditions for liberal democracy, such as urbanization and education, economic efficiency may in some contexts militate in favour of authoritarian-bureaucratic government, rather than liberal democracy. Economics alone cannot explain liberal democracy's consummate status. In his words, the logic of modern natural science 'gets us to the gates of the Promised Land of liberal democracy, but does not quite deliver us to the other side'.[14]

Fukuyama believes that liberal democracy may represent the ultimate form of government because it satisfies certain fundamental human psychological needs. These he refers to (drawing again on Hegel) as the desire for 'recognition', a desire he takes to be manifested in such feelings as self-respect, self-esteem, dignity, ambition, pride and concern for prestige. For Fukuyama 'the problem of human history can be seen ... as the search for a way to satisfy the desire of both masters and slaves for recognition on a mutual and equal basis; history ends with the victory of a societal order that accomplishes that goal'.[15] As he sees it, liberal democracy is that order; it offers a framework for mutual and equal recognition of all citizens.

11 Fukuyama 1992, at 283.

12 Fukuyama links this idea with Kant and the tradition of liberal internationalism, as to which see *infra*, sections II and III. He considers that the league of democratic nations he recommends – a 'Kantian liberal international order' (Fukuyama 1992, at 283) – already exists to an degree under the umbrella of organizations such as NATO, EC, OECD, Group of Seven and GATT. He contrasts such a league with other organizations and alliances, such as the UN, which are not limited to liberal democratic nations. See Fukuyama 1992, at 276–284 (quotations are at 283 and 280 respectively).

13 This is explained further in Fukuyama 1992, ch. 6.

14 Fukuyama 1992, at 134.

15 Fukuyama 1992, at 152.

And yet, if liberal democracy awaits us at history's end, there is another sense in which, according to Fukuyama, the human desire for recognition will be left profoundly unfulfilled, even debilitated. There is an aspect of that desire that can only find fulfilment in the context of ideological competition. Whereas those – he refers to them as the 'first men' – who began the struggle for liberal democracy had to exhibit courage, take risks, and aim high, the 'last men' at the end of history will have no further need of heroism.[16] Indeed, they will be encouraged not to stand out. Fukuyama worries about the mediocrity, ignobility and materialism of liberal democracy's 'last men'. Following in the tradition of Tocqueville and others,[17] his enthusiasm for democracy is tinged with regret for the decline of aristocracy, and a belief that too much equality, rather than too little, may pose liberal democracy's greatest challenge.

B. Liberal Millenarianism

This thesis was widely interpreted – and Fukuyama himself confirms that it was intended – as an attempt to provide an antidote to the prevailing 'declinist' mood of American political analysis in the 1980s.[18] Those 'pessimists' who were continuing to assert that the power and influence of the United States were in decline had failed to notice the 'good news'[19] that a 'liberal revolution' was underway worldwide. Those 'intellectuals who believe they grasp the world in all its complexity and tragedy'[20] had failed to see that history has a pattern, and that, posturing aside, '[t]oday ... we have trouble imagining a world that is radically better than our own'.[21]

Patently, Fukuyama's antidote was strong stuff. Though not without ambivalences, his work makes few concessions to those who do not share his outlook, and is almost ostentatious in its disdain for those he takes to be left-liberal or, perhaps, un-American. And yet, his themes are not confined to what has been called the New Right. Rather, they appear, as noted at the outset, to exemplify a more widely held perspective. It is this perspective to which liberal millenarianism refers. Its key features may be summarized as follows.

In the first place there is the notion that history has a *telos*. This involves a view of historical change as directional, linear and evolutionary, with identifiable developmental stages and an end-point that can be known, and potentially reached. Secondly, there is the supposition that history's *telos* is liberalism, or at any rate liberal

16 Concerning the 'last man', see F. Nietzsche (R. Hollingdale, trans.), *Thus Spoke Zarathustra* (1969) 45–47.

17 See A. de Tocqueville (G. Lawrence trans.; J. Mayer. ed.), 2 *Democracy in America* (1994) 690–95. Fukuyama's contemporary influences are conservative-elitist thinkers, Leo Strauss and Allan Bloom.

18 See, e.g., R. Keohane, *After Hegemony* (1984) and P. Kennedy, *The Rise and Fall of Great Powers* (1988).

19 Fukuyama 1992, at xiii.

20 Fukuyama 1992, at 69.

21 Fukuyama 1992, at 46.

democracy in association with a market-oriented economy. This is based both on an empirical assertion that all alternatives to liberalism have been eliminated, and on a normative assertion that liberalism is superior to all alternatives. A third feature is a distinctive voice, a 'we' who (fine tuning aside) *have* liberal democracy and experience no serious – or, at any rate, no intractable – problems, in contradistinction to a non-liberal 'they' (in the Third World and elsewhere) for whom things will necessarily remain more complicated and more unpleasant. Finally, there is a distinctive tone, a call to celebrate the present, tempered perhaps by nostalgia for the past, but nonetheless optimistic, confident and flushed with a sense of victory over the forces of regression.

Millenarianism refers in Christian doctrine to the belief that Christ will return to reign on earth for a thousand years. More generally, it is applied to premonitions of global futures of diverse kinds, but especially redemptive ones.[22] Liberal millenarianism's *millenarianism* thus consists in its perception that the world may stand on the brink of an unprecedented era of peace and good government, a perception which is millenarian also in the more literal sense that it pertains to the millennium about to begin.[23] Reinforcing the millenarian character of this vision in Fukuyama's work is the annunciatory, exalted, sometimes even ecstatic, language in which it is expressed, and the evocation of eschatological, especially evangelical,[24] themes. The *liberal* character of liberal millenarianism derives obviously from the fact that this is presented as a vision of a liberal world. But what sort of liberal world? To pursue this question, and also to explore further liberal millenarianism's implications for the meaning of democracy, it is helpful to draw into the discussion some of Fukuyama's critics.[25]

22 Fredric Jameson contrasts this with 'inverse millenarianism' – claims about 'the end of this or that' – which he associates with postmodernism. See F. Jameson, *Postmodernism, or The Cultural Logic of Late Capitalism* (1991), at 1. The difference between millenarianism and 'inverse millenarianism' appears to be principally one of emphasis, however, for both look at once backwards and forwards. Liberal millenarianism, in any event, has this ambivalence.

23 James Crawford refers to 'the facile millenarianism that was an immediate product of 1989'. See J. Crawford, *Democracy and International Law: Inaugural Lecture* (1994) 25.

24 Jacques Derrida finds a specifically Christian resonance in Fukuyama's work, thus buttressing the present characterization of Fukuyama as 'millenarian'. When Fukuyama says that economics takes us 'to the gates of the promised land but does not quite deliver us to the other side', and when he finds a spiritual basis for his 'good news' concerning liberal democracy in the human desire for recognition, Derrida suggests that Fukuyama is not only choosing Hegel in preference to Marx, but is also (in so doing) choosing a Christian account in place of a Jewish one. The other great religion of the 'promised land', Islam, does not feature in Fukuyama's allusive repertoire; he observes that the Islamic world falls outside the consensus he finds in favour of liberalism. See J. Derrida (P. Kamuf, trans.), *Specters of Marx* (1994), at 59–61 and 66.

25 The following discussion draws mainly on Held, *supra* note 6; Macey and Miller, *supra* note 6; Huntington, *supra* note 6; and Derrida, *supra* note 24. These critiques proceed, it should be noted, from widely divergent standpoints and reach widely divergent conclusions from their analysis of Fukuyama.

C. Liberal Millenarianism and Democracy

One striking feature of Fukuyama's argument is that it largely proceeds as if there is, and can be, only one liberalism, one democracy and one liberal democracy. While recognizing a certain diversity of institutional arrangements, Fukuyama fails to consider the diversity of values and beliefs that contributes to producing divergent understandings of the meaning of liberalism and democracy, and of their interrelation. Liberal democracy cannot spell the end of ideological struggle because it is itself the subject of ideological contestation, and will continue to be so.

What, then, of Fukuyama's own understanding of liberalism, democracy and liberal democracy? A number of critics highlight Fukuyama's failure to address the tension between liberalism and democracy. The liberal preoccupation with rights and freedom from government control, and the democratic preoccupation with equal participation in, and accountability of, public power, may point in different directions. Rights and freedoms justified by reference to liberalism may compromise the extent to which all citizens are equally enabled to participate in politics; political decisions justified by reference to democracy may compromise individuals' rights and freedoms. On this point David Held observes that Fukuyama endorses economic liberalism, without examining the extent to which the 'free market' constrains democratic processes, by generating and sustaining systematic inequalities of wealth that involve systematic inequalities of power.[26] Thus, without addressing the implications of doing so, Fukuyama effectively resolves the tension between liberalism and democracy in favour of liberalism (especially in its neo-liberal economic aspect). This leads him, Jonathan Macey and Geoffrey Miller remark, to proclaim a victory for liberal democracy wherever he sees economic liberalism.[27]

Also of concern is Fukuyama's 'uncritical affirmation'[28] of liberal democracy. He neglects to investigate alternatives to prevailing liberal democratic practices, and gives little sign of grasping the limitations of those practices. Indeed he leaves largely unexplained the basis on which an evaluation might be made. His celebration of liberal democracy, thus ungrounded, overlooks the obvious failures of liberal democracy, its omissions with respect to the historic promise of self-rule on the basis of equality among citizens. These omissions find reflection in the pervasiveness of unaccountable power and the persistence of asymmetrical life chances between sexes, ethnic groups and classes.[29] At the same time, Fukuyama's celebration

26 Held, *supra* note 6, at 257–58.

27 Macey and Miller, *supra* note 6, at 282. This comment finds support in Fukuyama's inclusion, in a list of countries he characterizes as liberal democratic, of Singapore, South Korea, Honduras and Mexico. See Fukuyama 1992, at 49–50. (But see also his later discussion of, e.g., Singapore's authoritarianism, Fukuyama 1992, at 241.)

28 Held, *supra* note 6, at 295.

29 An illustrative summary of democracy's 'broken promises' and 'unforeseen obstacles' can be found in N. Bobbio (R. Griffin, trans.; R. Bellamy, ed.), *The Future of Democracy* (1987), at 27–39. (The conclusions Bobbio draws are, however, at variance with the position adopted in the present article.)

also overlooks that liberal democracy has never been under so much strain. He considers the challenges posed to liberal democracy by nationalist and religious movements. But, as Held and others observe, he fails to address the far-reaching challenges posed by the diffusion of decision-making power and political activity in the contemporary world.[30] This arises from a wide range of developments, among them innovations in the media and communications and information technology, economic globalization, and the rising importance of social movements (the environmental and women's movements, etc.).[31] In profound and diverse ways, these developments put in doubt the tenability of an account of liberal democratic politics that focuses solely on national governments, and treats periodic elections, the rule of law and civil and political rights as not just necessary but largely sufficient. Yet this is the account that informs Fukuyama's claims.

Fukuyama's uncritical approach to liberal democracy is accompanied by a portrayal of the world that is hard to locate in actuality. Like Voltaire's Pangloss, he insists on an account of this 'best of all possible worlds' that defies, rather than attends to, contemporary realities. Jacques Derrida puts this point starkly:

> [N]ever have violence, inequality, exclusion, famine, and thus economic oppression affected as many human beings in the history of the earth and humanity. Instead of singing the advent of the ideal of liberal democracy and of the capitalist market in the euphoria of the end of history, ... let us never neglect this macroscopic fact, made up of innumerable singular sites of suffering: no degree of progress allows one to ignore that never before, in absolute figures, have so many men, women and children been subjugated, starved or exterminated.[32]

These sites of suffering, of course, cross-cut the distinction Fukuyama draws between 'historical' and 'post-historical' states, and serve to assure the continuance of ideological divergences in both categories of countries.

A further problematic element in Fukuyama's argument is his premise that a 'liberal revolution' is underway. He acknowledges that the Islamic world stands outside the consensus that he takes to be forming concerning liberal democracy, but discounts the significance of resistance there and elsewhere. Commentators have countered that, while few profess to reject the basic ideas associated with democracy and while some form of capitalism characterizes most economies, there is little evidence of support in many countries for liberal values more generally. Fukuyama exaggerates the scope of the consensus by finding liberal democracy almost – though not invariably – wherever he locates some variant of capitalism.

Fukuyama's defence is that his thesis about the end of history posits the end of *ideological* contestation, and is not an empirical claim. Thus it is not falsifed by the

30 For a wide-ranging and instructive discussion of the implications of globalization for democracy, see D. Held, *Democracy and the Global Order* (1995).

31 Amongst the many accounts of globalization and associated developments, from diverse perspectives, M. Waters, *Globalization* (1995) is especially instructive. A valuable corrective to over-enthusiastic accounts of globalization, especially economic globalization, can be found in P. Hirst and G. Thompson, *Globalization in Question* (1996).

32 Derrida, *supra* note 24, at 85.

obvious fact that not all societies have embraced liberal democracy. But does this thesis not presuppose compelling evidence as regards aspirations, even if not as regards political practices and institutions? What precisely is Fukuyama's 'good news'? Derrida calls attention to the way Fukuyama characterizes liberal democracy both as an ideal and as an occurrence, alternating between the two to suit his argument.[33] On the one hand, Fukuyama refutes evidence that contradicts his thesis, insisting that he is speaking of an ideal that transcends events. On the other hand, he maintains that events have occurred – the death of communism, the establishment of liberal democracy and capitalism as ideologies of near-universal choice, the recognition accorded by Western liberal democracies to their citizens – which represent the realization of this ideal. Fukuyama's 'good news' thus intends to refer, Derrida shows, both to an accomplished fact and to a vision of the future.

This leads to a final observation. Inasmuch as Fukuyama's linear conception of history admits of only one future, it reduces and oversimplifies the processes of historical change. While Fukuyama acknowledges that reversals are possible, he assumes that the trends he identifies will broadly continue. In this, Samuel Huntington observes, Fukuyama overstates the predictability of history and the permanence of the moment. Current trends may continue, but experience suggests that they may well not.[34] The historical record to date offers little support for Fukuyama's notion of progress. Held too finds that Fukuyama has failed to appreciate the contingency of events and the complexity of social processes. Held highlights that Fukuyama's essentialized conception of 'man' and his two master engines of modernity (instrumental rationality and the desire for recognition) cannot adequately explain such central historical phenomena as classes, gender inequalities and the international division of labour.[35] If this is the case, then the predictive value of his conceptual framework must likewise be open to question.

To summarize, it can be argued that the thesis of the end of history – as the ideological triumph of capitalist economics and liberal democracy – attaches insufficient importance to a number of matters which render ideological divergences inescapable and, indeed, vital. These include the following points: the meaning ascribed to the terms involved is itself at least partly a matter of ideology; the enduring tension between liberalism and democracy invites continuing contestation concerning liberal democracy; liberal democracy is subject to profound – increasingly profound – challenge; at the end of the twentieth century progress is far from obvious; the scope of support for any version of liberal democracy, even at the level of ideas, is not clear; history follows not a single path but multiple and diverse trajectories that proceed and interact in complex and imponderable ways.

Critics draw diverse conclusions from their analyses of Fukuyama's thesis, though almost all find in it a dangerous inducement to complacency. Huntington's worry is that it may encourage Americans to underestimate the contemporary sources of

33 *Ibid*, at 62–63.
34 Huntington, *supra* note 6, at 10.
35 Held, *supra* note 6, at 296–97.

political instability, and on this basis to relax their vigilance in foreign relations. Declinism, in Huntington's view, was, in contrast, a useful warning and goad to action.[36] Held has a different concern. Only fifty years after nazism, fascism and Stalinism almost eclipsed liberal democracy, Fukuyama prematurely pronounces a secure future for liberal democracy, and glosses over the most serious challenges that currently confront it.[37] Derrida shares this anxiety that Fukuyama masks the fragility of liberal democracy, and thus reduces the possibilities for strengthening and improving it. In this regard Derrida expresses particular disquiet at the way Fukuyama seeks to deny (while himself, however, in key respects exemplifying)[38] the continuing relevance of ideas and critical practices that draw inspiration from Marx.[39] Like a number of other scholars,[40] Derrida takes the view that these ideas and practices are rendered more, not less, pertinent by liberalism's gains.

The points discussed here arise in relation to Fukuyama's writings. But most apply with equal force to liberal millenarianism generally. This is because most stem from the features of Fukuyama's work that have been characterized as, more broadly, liberal millenarian: the progressivist notion of history; the identification of liberal democracy as history's *telos* ; the distinctive 'post-historical' voice; the celebratory tone. Indeed, the critical perspectives just reviewed highlight the extent to which these features are interrelated and mutually reinforcing. With respect to the progressivist conception of history that is a central pillar of liberal millenarianism, Fukuyama's critics echo insights that can be found in the work of many other scholars. Among these, Michel Foucault's well-known account of history and genealogy is worth briefly recalling at this point.[41] Foucault shows how progressivist history

36 Huntington, *supra* note 6, at 4.

37 Held, *supra* note 6, at 296.

38 A number of commentators make this argument on the basis, e.g., of Fukuyama's teleological notion of history and his turn to 'grand theory'. See, e.g., Huntington, *supra* note 6, at 9–10. Others, however, disagree. See, e.g., A. Callinicos, *Theories and Narratives* (1995), ch. 1.

39 Derrida, *supra* note 24, at 68–69 and 86–94. Derrida has an intriguing explanation for why Fukuyama does this. He proposes that, in advancing the thesis of the end of history, Fukuyama is engaging in a kind of 'mourning work' following the death of 'actually existing socialism'. Out of fear and 'bereavement' as Marx's unacknowledged heir (for, Derrida insists, we are all Marx's heirs, whether we wish it or not), Fukuyama is denying the continued relevance of socialist critique. As Derrida puts it, adapting Marx and Engels' own immortal image, Fukuyama is attempting to 'conjure away' the 'spectre of Marx' that has long haunted liberalism. Yet, Derrida maintains, this work of mourning cannot succeed. It can displace, but it cannot efface, the spectre of Marx, for that spectre is liberalism's necessary accompaniment. In this regard Derrida refers not only to Marx and Marxian thought. He evokes the spectre – or, as he prefers to say, spectres (for he stresses the extent to which Marx's legacy is plural and diverse) – of Marx *metonymically* to stand for *all* the forms of critique that can help to evaluate ideals, grasp realities, and reduce the gap between them. In view of the importance of these forms of critique, Derrida urges instead a 'counter-conjuration', a strategy of active engagement, rather than disavowal. In this, he contends, scholars have a particular role. Quoting (at 176) a line in connection with another famous ghost, Derrida recalls Hamlet's injunction: 'Thou art a scholar; speak to it, Horatio.' See Derrida, *supra* note 24, at 61 and 68–75.

40 See, e.g., the essays in R. Blackburn (ed.), *After the Fall* (1991).

41 M. Foucault (P. Rabinow, ed.), 'Nietzsche, Genealogy, History', in *The Foucault Reader* (1984) 76. I am grateful to Professor Gerald Frug, Harvard Law School, for calling my attention to this text, and for an illuminating discussion of it.

confirms rather than unsettles established power relations. It represses dissension, struggle, and domination, rather than articulating and addressing them. It presents the world comfortingly, as simple, coherent and ordered, rather than challengingly, as complex, heterogeneous and contingent. In seeking to hold onto things as they are, it asserts blithely, but also impotently, that things must be as they are. What this puts in relief is the sense in which liberal millenarianism, for all its professed optimism, is ultimately pessimistic, not – as Fukuyama suggests – because it envisions a world of excessive equality, but because it evokes a world of enduring and immutable inequalities.

II. The 'Norm of Democratic Governance' and Other Theses

Insofar as the thesis of the emerging norm of democratic governance and related claims share the liberal millenarianism of Fukuyama's end of history narrative, the foregoing discussion is rich in implications. Before addressing the issue of these theses' liberal millenarianism, however, it is necessary to set out the arguments involved. For this purpose a distinction may be drawn between those which discuss democracy primarily as a right and those which discuss democracy primarily in more instrumental liberal internationalist terms.

A. Democracy as a Right

The right-oriented theses involve the claim – first advanced by Thomas Franck,[42] but subsequently taken up and developed by others as well[43] – that international law is beginning to embrace a 'norm of democratic governance' or 'global democratic entitlement'. Such a norm or entitlement would mean three things. First, it would entail that the legitimacy of governments is judged by international, rather than purely national, rules and processes. Second, it would connote that those international rules and processes stipulate democracy; that is to say, only democratic governments are legitimate. And third, it would establish that democracy is an internationally guaranteed human right, in respect of which international procedures of monitoring and enforcement are justified and, indeed, required.

How has this norm or right come to 'emerge'? Franck offers the fullest explanation. He traces the normative and customary evolution of the global democratic entitlement by reference to three overlapping phases or 'generations'[44] of international rule-making and implementation. The first generation, born after the First

42 See the references cited at note 1. The thesis has earlier roots, which can be found, e.g., in Steiner, 'Political Participation as a Human Right', 1 *Harv. Hum. Rts Ybk* (1988) 77.

43 See *supra* note 3.

44 Franck 1992, at 52. Franck is not referring to the three-generational scheme used (and debated) in human rights commentary, according to which civil and political rights are the first generation; economic, social and cultural rights are the second; and peoples' rights are the third.

World War (but with older antecedents), is the right of self-determination. The plebiscites, popular consultations and commissions of inquiry that were mandated at the Versailles Peace Conference in connection with the redrawing of European boundaries gave rise to the idea that 'a people organised in established territory [has the right] to determine its collective political destiny in a democratic fashion'.[45] At the same time, a body of practice concerning plebiscite-holding and international supervision was initiated. This was further developed when self-determination was applied outside Europe in the context of decolonization.

The second generation, born after the Second World War, is the international legal recognition of human rights. With this the idea was established that all human beings have the right to freedoms of expression, thought, assembly and association (among other rights). Procedures for holding governments to their obligations in this regard, and for clarifying the scope of the rights and correlative obligations, were also elaborated. The third generation, still in its infancy, is the right to free and open elections. This was effectively born with the transformations of the late 1980s. While the right to vote and stand for election had been recognized in key human rights instruments decades before, it was not until those transformations occurred that this right began to be taken seriously as a norm of universal application. It was not until those transformations occurred, in other words, that it became possible to consider this right an emerging norm of customary international law. That it has begun to be taken seriously is reflected in the fact that a substantial majority of states now actually practise 'a reasonably credible version of electoral democracy'.[46] This is also reflected in international efforts to establish and define the 'principle of genuine and periodic elections'; in the increasingly common provision of 'technical assistance' by the UN and other organizations and agencies to governments holding democratic elections for the first time; and in the expanding practice of international and regional election monitoring. Varying his metaphor so as to emphasize the way that the right to free and open elections extends, and depends on, international legal developments with respect to self-determination and human rights, Franck sometimes refers to these as three 'building stones'[47] in the edifice that is the global democratic entitlement.

Other scholars likewise hold that, while the global democratic entitlement has had a basis for decades in international human rights instruments, and before that in the principle of self-determination of peoples, it has only recently begun to be respected, monitored and enforced to a significant extent.[48] Thus, it has only recently begun to acquire the status of a norm of customary international law. In addition to the evidence of this to which Franck calls attention, Christina Cerna notes the procedures elaborated in the 1990s within the framework of the Council of Europe and the Or-

45 Franck 1992, at 52.
46 Franck 1992, at 64.
47 Franck 1992; Franck 1995, ch. 4; and Franck 1994, *passim*.
48 See, e.g., Fox, *supra* note 3 and Cerna, *supra* note 3.

ganisation of American States for conditioning admission or continued participation on democratic government.[49]

As this suggests, these scholars take free and fair elections to be the decisive criterion of democracy, though they in no way underestimate the extent to which the right to such elections presupposes other rights, especially freedoms of expression, thought, assembly and association. Elections are in this perspective decisive because they legitimate governance. Thus, the expressions 'democratic entitlement', 'right to democracy', 'norm of democratic governance', 'entitlement to a participatory electoral process', 'right to political participation', 'electoral rights', and the 'right to free and open elections' are employed with relative interchangeability. Franck explains:

> The term 'democracy', as used in international rights parlance, is intended to connote the kind of governance that is legitimated by the consent of the governed. Essential to the legitimacy of governance is evidence of *consent to the process by which a populace is consulted* by its government.[50]

Franck acknowledges that this is a limited conception of democracy. 'This definition', he observes, 'is not ambitious, it is not necessarily unambiguous, and it is almost certainly not the one Americans would prefer'.[51] But given the diversity of polities and traditions in the world, and given the inbuilt resistance of the states system to the international regulation of national affairs, he considers that this conception or something like it 'probably represents the limit of what the still frail global system of states can be expected to accept and promote as a right of peoples assertable against their own, and other, governments'.[52]

Gregory Fox and Georg Nolte, while sharing the view that elections are the central issue in a norm of democratic governance, have highlighted that holding regular elections which are free and fair may not always be sufficient to protect the democratic entitlement.[53] Where candidates are opposed to liberal democracy, and are committed to the establishment in its place of, for instance, a theocratic political order, the question arises whether those candidates should be allowed to stand.

49 Cerna, *supra* note 3. In connection with applications for membership from Central and Eastern European States, the Council of Europe has begun to require evidence of commitment to democracy. See, e.g., 'Report on the Legal Order of the Russian Federation', Council of Europe Doc. AS/Bur/Russia 7 (1994), reprinted at 15 *Hum. Rts L. J.* (1994) 249. The Organisation of American States has long had this as a formal – though, for much of the OAS's life, unenforced – requirement for OAS member states. See the Declaration of Santiago, adopted at the Fifth Meeting of Consultation of Ministers of Foreign Affairs, August 1959, reprinted in T. Buergenthal and R. Norris (eds.), *Human Rights: The Inter-American System* (hereinafter Buergenthal and Norris), Binder 1, Booklet 6, 134. More recently, the OAS has sanctioned the further step of engaging in collective action to secure the installation, or reinstatement, of democratic government in the event that a coup occurs. See OAS General Assembly Resolution 1080 (adopted 5 June 1991) reprinted in Buergenthal and Norris, Binder 2, Booklet 7.6, 43; and Protocol of Amendments to the Charter of the OAS ('Protocol of Washington') (adopted 14 December 1992), OAS AG/DOC.11 (XVI-E/92).

50 Franck 1994, at 75.

51 Franck 1994, at 75.

52 Franck 1994, at 75.

53 Fox and Nolte, *supra* note 3. They have in mind particularly the case of Algeria.

Based on a survey of constitutional laws and traditions of diverse democratic states, Fox and Nolte contend that in customary international law the exclusion of such candidates is warranted, and perhaps even required. This reflects, they observe, a conception of democracy as not simply a set of procedures for ascertaining majority preferences, but rather as a means by which citizens are enabled to enjoy basic rights. Thus, Fox and Nolte find support in customary international law for an account of democracy that tolerates only the tolerant, and that in this respect insists on the value of 'political liberalism'.[54] More generally, they find support for an account of democracy that rests on the liberal notion that government is legitimated not just procedurally but also to the extent that it fulfils its side of the social contract and protects citizens' rights.

Those who advance the thesis of the emerging norm of democratic governance give close attention to the question of how compliance might be monitored and enforced. As noted, existing election-monitoring efforts and innovations with respect to participation in regional organizations are among the developments which persuaded the scholars that the norm was emerging in the first place. They consider a number of possible ways of strengthening enforcement. Franck proposes that the 'older democracies' might volunteer to have their elections monitored, so as to encourage a custom of election-observation that might eventually evolve into an obligation.[55] In the longer term, he proposes that democratic government might be set as a precondition to participation in all international organizations, including the United Nations, a proposal also developed by Fox.[56] Franck suggests additionally that democratic government might be made a precondition for fiscal, trade and development benefits, and for the protection of UN and regional collective security measures. He strongly rejects as a means of enforcement unilateral intervention to install or reinstate elected governments, though he finds acceptable collective action at UN or regional level, even, in extreme cases, involving the use of force. Franck considers that, while the question of the scope and incidents of the norm of democratic governance is likely to remain on the international law agenda, the more pressing problem is the monitoring and enforcement of compliance. He urges that the future emphasis of international efforts should be laid accordingly.[57]

B. International Law and the 'Liberal Peace'

The writers so far considered base their case for the emerging democratic entitlement on, above all, developments with respect to the holding of elections, international and regional election monitoring, and democratic conditionality in regional organizations. Those whose work will now be reviewed are also impressed with these developments. What strikes them as even more significant, however, is the

54 See J. Rawls, *Political Liberalism* (1993).
55 Concerning this and the other proposals considered here, see Franck 1992.
56 Fox, *supra* note 3.
57 Franck 1994.

correlation between liberal democracy and peace.[58] This forms the basis of an argument that there should be a norm of democratic governance, and that the signs that it is emerging confirm this. The theorists of the right to democratic governance also draw support from the correlation between liberal democracy and peace to help explain and vindicate the right.[59] Thus, the difference between the two sets of theses is largely one of emphasis. Both sets are at once empirically-based claims that a norm is emerging, speculations concerning its future as *lex lata*, explanations of why it is emerging, and justifications for its recognition in international law. And in both sets the so-called 'liberal' or 'democratic' 'peace' plays a part.

Among the leading proponents of theses of this second type are Fernando Tesón[60] and Anne-Marie Slaughter.[61] In presenting the correlation between liberal democracy and peace, they take account of both speculative and empirical literature. With respect to the former, the key figure is Kant. These scholars, like the international relations analysts on whose work they draw, look to Kant for the insight that liberal states are likely to maintain peaceful relations with one another. As is well known, Kant held that 'perpetual peace' would depend on three things: every state having a 'republican' constitution; a 'pacific federation' being established among states, in the shape of an agreement to refrain from war against one another; and extensive international commerce, underpinned by 'cosmopolitan law'. Republican government would discourage warfare, he believed, because, if government was accountable to citizens, the fact that citizens would suffer the consequences of war – as soldiers, bereaved civilians, taxpayers, etc. – would serve to engender caution in waging it.[62]

Internationalists have long attended to the points about the pacific federation and extensive international commerce. Particularly compelling in the aftermath of the twentieth century's two World Wars, these ideas are reflected in the League of Nations, the Kellogg-Briand Pact, the United Nations, and the General Agreement on Tariffs and Trade. Indeed, they inform the whole enterprise of modern international law and institution-building. But what, according to Tesón, Slaughter and the international relations analysts, has *not* received sufficient attention is Kant's insight about republican government. For these scholars the sort of 'republican' state Kant had in mind corresponds in contemporary terms to a liberal democratic state.[63] The

58 The scope of the correlation that is claimed to exist will be discussed below.

59 See, e.g., Franck 1995, at 134–137, and Fox and Nolte, *supra* note 3 , at 61–63.

60 See esp. Tesón 1992.

61 See the references to Slaughter's work cited at note 2. Slaughter 1995 develops a more general 'Liberal model' of international law. 'Liberalism' is presented as an account of how some – liberal – states 'do behave rather than how they should behave' (at 508). But 'Liberal' theory appears to be envisaged as serving a normative function as well, inasmuch as Slaughter evokes the possibility that this theory might become 'normatively applicable to all States even if positively descriptive of only some' (at 538). See further *infra*, section III.

62 See I. Kant (H. Nisbet, trans.), 'Perpetual Peace: A Philosophical Sketch' (1795), in H. Reiss (ed.), *Kant: Political Writings* (1991), at 93 *et seq.*

63 If Kant himself drew a sharp distinction between a republican constitution and a democratic one, this was because his conception of democracy was a pre-modern one. His frequently quoted definition of a 'republican' constitution entails three principles: 'firstly, the principle of *freedom* for all

Second World War, along with the bitter ideological rivalries of the Cold War, fuelled a realist outlook which got in the way of a proper appreciation of Kant's idea. Now that many countries of the world have embraced this liberal model, a fresh appraisal is called for. The notion that the prospects for peace may be greatest among liberal states should, these scholars maintain, no longer be ignored.

Slaughter and Tesón observe that international relations scholars have presented evidence which appears to back up this notion. Based on analysis of international wars since 1817, Michael Doyle, among others, has argued that a separate 'zone of peace' does indeed exist among liberal states.[64] This zone has steadily expanded as the number of liberal states has increased. Doyle has reported that throughout this period liberal states, while they have engaged in wars with non-liberal states, have remained at peace with one another. From this he has drawn the inference that liberal states are likely to be more pacific than non-liberal ones, not in general, but at least in their relations with other liberal states. The scope of this claim, the precise character of the link it posits, and the reasons for that link, remain the subject of debate. In its broad lines, however, the 'democratic' or 'liberal' 'peace' is spoken of as a 'fact'[65] and 'as close as anything we have to an empirical law in international relations'.[66] It is an empirical law that, according to Slaughter and Tesón, has profound implications for international law.

The first implication is that international law should place the question of the legitimacy of governments on its agenda. It should abandon the idea that this is an exclusively national issue. The second implication is that international law should accept as legitimate only liberal democratic governments. It should stipulate that a legitimate government – one that has a right to exercise sovereign authority – is not just any government that wields factual power; it is a liberal democratic one. Tesón calls this a 'Kantian theory of international law'. Slaughter employs the name given by international relations scholars, 'liberal internationalism'.[67] *Internationalism* evokes the second and third dimensions of Kant's formula for perpetual peace noted above, those that find reflection in international cooperation; *liberal* internationalism includes also the first dimension, 'republican government'. Against an international law that is in thrall to realism and power politics, Slaughter counterposes a vision of an international law that takes seriously the connection between national political

members of society (as men); secondly, the principle of *dependence* of everyone upon a single common legislation (as subjects); and thirdly, the principle of legal *equality* for everyone (as citizens)'. He wrote that 'republicanism [is] that political principle whereby the executive power . . . is separated from the legislative power', and that 'republican' government is, in principle, 'representative'. *Ibid*, at 99–102.

64 Doyle, 'Kant, Liberal Legacies and Foreign Affairs', 12 *Philosophy & Public Affairs* (1983) 205 (Part 1) and 323 (Part 2). For a survey of relevant empirical literature, see B. Russett, *Grasping the Democratic Peace* (1993), ch. 1.

65 Russett, *supra* note 64 (Ch.1: 'The Fact of Democratic Peace').

66 Levy, 'Domestic Politics and War', 18 *J. Interdisciplinary History* (1988) 653, 662.

67 For her general 'model' of international law, developed in recent work, Slaughter prefers the term 'Liberal', and distinguishes a 'Liberal' theory of international relations from 'Wilsonian liberal internationalism'. See Slaughter 1995, at 508 *et seq.* for her definition of 'Liberal' in this context.

ideology and international relations, and in this way dedicates itself to (in the phrase of one international relations scholar) 'grasping the democratic peace'.[68]

In effect this is a vision of a norm of democratic governance along the lines proposed in the first category of theses considered, though without the same emphasis on the notion of democracy as a human right.[69] Slaughter thus finds signs that her vision is beginning to materialize in the developments to which Franck and others call attention. She also finds signs that the 'zone of peace' is accompanied and reinforced by a 'zone of law', in that transnational disputes involving only liberal states are more readily resolved through judicial procedures than is the case where non-liberal states are involved. She presents evidence that courts of liberal states cooperate with one another, and take into account each other's national interests, in a way that courts of non-liberal states do not, and in a way that courts of liberal states themselves do not where a dispute involving a non-liberal state is at issue.[70]

On the question of how this norm might be enforced, Tesón concurs with Franck and Fox that the UN and other international organizations might change their rules to admit only states with liberal democratic governments, and to allow only such governments to participate. In his view the unilateral use of force might even be justified in some circumstances, especially where violation of the norm is associated with gross abuses of human rights. Tesón also proposes that the law of treaties might be made to reflect the illegitimacy of non-liberal governments; such governments might, for instance, be deprived of the competence to create binding obligations in their own favour. Diplomatic law too might be changed so as to deny diplomatic status to representatives of non-liberal regimes.[71] Slaughter differs in rejecting the right of unilateral intervention, and generally distances herself from Tesón's professed anti-statism. Nonetheless, she shares the view that liberal democracies have a 'leadership' role to play in relation to liberal internationalist international law.[72]

As this discussion indicates, these claims revolve around a distinction between 'liberal' or 'liberal democratic' states and 'non-liberal' states. It is worth pausing at this point to note more fully how the theorists understand this distinction. Slaughter defines a liberal state as, in broad terms, a state with 'juridical equality, constitutional protections of individual rights, representative republican governments, and market economies based on private property rights'.[73] This uncontroversial defini-

68 Russett, *supra* note 64.

69 Tesón does, however, argue that international law should accord legitimacy only to liberal democratic states not just for prudential reasons but also because this is morally justified. His 'Kantian theory' includes the idea that governments should be required to respect liberal rights because this is the right thing to do. See Tesón 1992, esp. 81–84.

70 Slaughter 1992b. See Slaughter 1995 for further development of this argument. Slaughter claims, for instance, that interaction between the executive and legislative branches of government is also greater among liberal states than among non-liberal states or between liberal and non-liberal states.

71 Tesón 1992, at 100.

72 Slaughter 1992a, at 404 and 394. Doyle for this reason expresses concern at what he takes to be the decline of the United States from hegemonic status. See Doyle, *supra* note 64, at 233–235.

73 Slaughter, 1992b, at 1909. This is largely reiterated, though the need for market economies based on private property rights is separately stated, in Slaughter 1995, at 511–152.

tion corresponds closely to that used by Doyle and other international relations analysts in their work on the 'liberal peace'.[74] Tesón adopts a similar approach, variously referring to the legitimate state of his 'Kantian theory of international law' as a 'democratic state', 'free state', 'liberal democracy' and 'form of political organisation that provides full respect for human rights'.[75] For both scholars the key feature of a liberal state, which explains its irenic character (at least *vis-à-vis* other liberal states), is the fact that there are powerful checks on the exercise of public power – constraints that operate principally through the periodic recall of legislators, the separation of powers and the protection of civil and political rights.

III. Liberal Millenarianism and International Law

It is now possible to return to the question of the relationship between these international legal theses and liberal millenarianism. In this context, the implications for the understanding of democracy that underpins these claims can be brought into view. It will be valuable at the end of this discussion to take stock of the fact that, if these international legal scholars are right, democracy has, will have, or at any rate ought to have, far-reaching significance in international law, as determinant of the legitimacy of governments.

A. Liberal Millenarian Perspectives

Most likely, all the international legal scholars discussed in this article would locate themselves at some considerable distance from Fukuyama on almost every issue. Certainly, none shares the narrow, elitist outlook that pervades his account of the 'end of history'. A number explicitly dissociate themselves from that account. Franck, for instance, states that he does not consider that '[exulting] in smug satisfaction at the "end of history"' is an appropriate response to the post-Cold War juncture, which he sees rather as an occasion for 'seizing the moment to rethink the basic structure and processes of the international system'.[76] Slaughter explains that liberal internationalism promises a result that is 'neither utopia nor the end of history, but holds out the hope of at least a small measure of progress toward individual rights and the global rule of law'.[77] There are some grounds for believing that liberal millenarianism may, nonetheless, be built into the form and structure of these scholars' arguments. As discussed earlier, liberal millenarianism includes, but extends beyond, Fukuyama. It is characterized by a progressivist notion of history, coupled with a conceptualization of history's *telos* in terms of liberalism, and a distinctive voice and tone. On what basis, and to what extent, can it be said that the international legal theses considered here exhibit these features?

74 See, e.g., Doyle, *supra* note 64, at 206.
75 Tesón 1992, *passim*.
76 Franck 1990, 601. See also Franck 1995, at 141.
77 Slaughter 1992a, at 405.

A progressivist view of historical change is evident in Franck's history of the development of the norm of democratic governance. His account is divided into developmental phases, beginning with the principle of self-determination and culminating in the right of free and open elections, now evolving from lip service into widely respected normative commitment. 'The transformation of the democratic entitlement from moral obligation to prescription has evolved gradually', he explains, but 'in the past decade the tendency has accelerated'.[78] Each phase pushes further along the course to eventual prescription. The fact that the phases overlap does not detract from, but rather reinforces, the impression of progress and directionality, as do the metaphors of generations and building blocks. The norm of democratic governance appears to be growing out of, or building on, earlier developments. This evolutionary logic also informs the work of scholars who put forward liberal internationalist and Kantian theses. Slaughter, for instance, in seeking to connect international law with developments in international relations, offers an unmistakeably progressivist account of the history of international relations. This account starts with Wilsonian internationalism (or idealism, in the phraseology of those who later called themselves realists), passes through the stage of realism, and reaches its conclusion with liberal internationalism, which is said to combine the strengths, but also to overcome the shortcomings, of both its forerunners. Since these forerunners are presented as the only alternatives, liberal internationalism is made naturally to appear as an advance.[79] The notion of the 'liberal peace', liberal internationalism's central premise, likewise posits that historical change is incremental and directional. The image is one of an expanding zone of peace among liberal states that will reach the end of its expansion when all are included within it.

The second aspect of liberal millenarianism is that history's *telos* is taken to be liberal democracy, along with a market-oriented economy. It hardly needs restating that this is indeed the goal envisaged in the international legal theses examined here. That this should be so is believed, in the liberal millenarian perspective described earlier, to be supported empirically by the elimination of all ideological alternatives. And it is also believed to be supported normatively. That is to say, these ideological alternatives have been eliminated because they were flawed, as democracy and capitalism – at least in principle, if not in current practice – are not. Both points are alluded to in a memorable passage by Franck:

> [T]he [global democratic] entitlement now aborning is widely enough understood to be almost universally celebrated. It is welcomed from Malagache to Mongolia, in the streets, the universities and the legislatures, not only because it portends a new, global political culture supported by common rules and communitarian implementing institutions, but also because it opens the stagnant political economies of states to economic, social and cultural, as well as political, development.[80]

78 Franck 1992, at 47.

79 See, e.g., Slaughter 1993. For a further narrowing of alternatives to 'Realism' and 'Liberalism', see Slaughter 1995.

80 Franck 1992, at 90.

For Slaughter, 'the geopolitical framework for the millennium is ... liberal internationalism'.[81] An eventual 'world of liberal states' is the sole alternative to '[sacrificing] the values of universalism ... to the realism of recognising that States in the international system inhabit very different worlds'.[82] The choice, in her account, is either liberal universalism or realist difference, either grasping the liberal-democratic peace or living perpetually on the edge of war. The embrace of liberal democracy in every country thus appears as humanity's ultimate salvation.[83]

Liberal millenarianism involves, thirdly, a 'post-historical' voice or standpoint that figures the non-liberal world, still mired in 'history', as radically 'other'. Progress towards the full achievement of liberal democracy is taken to be more or less straightforward in liberal societies, while elsewhere the almost total transformation of prevailing realities will be required. This is, again, apparent in the thesis of the emerging norm of democratic governance. Such governance is portrayed as something some largely have, and the rest almost entirely lack. Thus, Franck writes that for the citizens of some states this norm will 'merely embellish rights already protected by their existing domestic constitutional order. For others it could be the realization of a cherished dream'.[84] A similar standpoint orients the liberal internationalist and neo-Kantian approaches. Slaughter envisions that her model of international law for a one-world order of liberal states might be 'normatively applicable to all States even if positively descriptive of only some'.[85] In practice, she observes, the distinction between liberal and non-liberal states may be difficult to apply, especially in the context of 'quasi-liberal' and 'transitional states'. Certainly, it cannot be treated as an 'absolute divide'.[86] But the point of the 'liberal peace', around which her argument turns, is that, as Doyle explains, liberal states are not just relatively but 'fundamentally different' from non-liberal states. Hence the 'separate peace' among them.[87] If this is the reason for the 'separate peace', it is, of course, also the consequence. In any event, the claim of liberal internationalism, as of the norm of democratic governance, is that this fundamental difference should, and is beginning to, be reflected in international law.

There is, finally, the issue of liberal millenarianism's distinctive tone, its momentous, celebratory, and apparently optimistic, key. Liberal millenarianism seeks

81 Slaughter 1992a, at 393. (emphasis omitted)
82 Slaughter 1995, at 538.
83 It also appears as *international law's* salvation, inasmuch as liberal universalism also represents an option in favour of law, rather than politics. Liberal internationalism thus seems to rescue international law from realist irrelevance. Fukuyama suggests this too, arguing that, while 'international law in general' (Fukuyama 1992, at 281) became discredited owing to the failure of the League of Nations and the United Nations, the 'states making ... up [the "league of democratic nations" which he proposes] would be able to live according to the rules of international law in their mutual dealings' (Fukuyama 1992, at 283).
84 Franck 1992, at 50.
85 Slaughter 1995, at 538.
86 Slaughter 1992b, at 1988–89.
87 Doyle, *supra* note 64, at 235. Slaughter takes up Doyle's phraseology, noting the 'fundamental difference in the nature of relations among liberal States as compared to relations between liberal and non-liberal States'. Slaughter 1995, at 537.

to call attention to events which augur that history's destination may finally be in sight. The discussion in the previous section gave only a slight indication of the tone of these international legal arguments. The quotation from Franck above is, however, typical of the terms in which his claims, and those of some of the other international legal scholars, are expressed.[88] Thus, for instance, Franck goes on to speak of a 'cosmic but unmysterious change' in which governments, 'no longer blinded by the totalitarian miasma' have come to recognize the advantages of democracy.[89] Slaughter likewise writes emphatically of revolutions that 'liberated millions. *Millions* ...', and occasioned a 'human rights victory on an unprecedented scale, a triumph of human dignity and the human spirit'.[90] On the basis of those events she proposes liberal internationalism as a new vision of peace and good government for a new age.

If the thesis of the emerging norm of democratic governance and related claims share key features of liberal millenarianism, they also give rise to a number of the concerns raised by Fukuyama's critics. In accounts of the norm of democratic governance and the order of liberal states envisioned by the liberal internationalist and Kantian theories, liberal democracy is presented largely as an identifiable, coherent and stable system. It is stressed that a great variety of practices and institutions is consistent with liberal democracy, but little attention is drawn to the diversity of the values, ideas and principles that might animate those practices and institutions. In particular, little attention is given to the enduring tensions within liberal democracy between liberal and democratic preoccupations, and to the implications for that tension of different models of liberal democracy. While the international legal theorists are less apt than Fukuyama to mistake capitalism for liberal democracy, their arguments nonetheless tend, like his, towards an attenuation of the democratic dimension.

The democratic component of liberal democracy comes to revolve, principally, around elections. That what is denoted is a particular method of producing governments is made particularly clear in the thesis of the emerging norm of democratic governance. Democracy's part there is adjectival; it is a procedure for securing the acquiescence of citizens in their governance by others.[91] The same holds, however, whether democracy is understood in these terms, or in terms of a social contract to protect citizens' rights (as by Fox and Nolte), a mechanism to ensure that government acts not just in its own interests but in the interests of society as a whole (as by Slaughter) or a system of government that is not just prudentially but also morally justified (as by Tesón). The shared assumption is that democracy refers to the 'process by which the people choose those they entrust with the exercise of power',[92] the

88 But not all express themselves in this way. Cf. the more cautious tone of, e.g., Fox and Nolte, *supra* note 3.
89 Franck 1995, at 85–86.
90 Slaughter 1990, at 1.
91 Franck 1992, at 51 and *passim*.
92 Franck 1992, at 50.

right 'to participate in the selection of one's own national government'.[93] Yet, according to some political theorists, democracy entails not just the right to participate in the selection of national governments, but also the right to participate directly in decision-making affecting one.[94] For other theorists, democracy involves not just the process of selecting governments, but also the process of connecting people with their governments through civil society.[95] Still other theorists emphasize that democracy requires not just the right to vote and stand for election and associated civil liberties, but also the whole range of further rights that actually enable participation in public life on a footing of equality.[96] While Franck, Fox and Nolte take their position to be dictated by that which customary international law will support,[97] what is being suggested here is that it is also embedded in the structure of their argument. Inasmuch as elections stand at the narrative's climax, democracy is made to appear to have nowhere further to go. Issues of citizenship, accountability and equality, and their respective significance and relative importance – along with other issues at the heart of democratic debate – are thus removed from view.

An additional, related concern is these theses' uncritical, affirmative approach towards liberal democracy. Franck's reference, cited above, to the embellishment of rights in existing liberal states suggests a perception that such states are already satisfactory; the rest is ornament. Depicting democratic political practice as entailing a 'genuine [openness] to meaningful political choice'[98] and a 'free market in ideas',[99] Franck puts to one side the many grounds for doubting the meaningfulness of political choice and the freedom of the market in ideas. Slaughter attaches much importance to what she refers to as the 'paradox of liberal states'. By this she intends that 'as a factual rather than a legal matter, liberal states are likely to have a lesser capacity for autonomous economic and political action than non-liberal states'.[100] But she too neglects to consider how well these constraints on power work, whether they work better for some social groups than others, and whether further constraints might be valuable. With liberal democracy the pinnacle of political development – and with dictatorship, communism and 'forced march modernization' the only alter-

93 Fox, *supra* note 3, at 542.
94 See, e.g., B. Barber, *Strong Democracy* (1984).
95 See, e.g., J. Cohen and A. Arato, *Civil Society and Political Theory* (1992).
96 Amongst the innumerable different ways and contexts in which this argument has been advanced, see, e.g., A. Phillips, *Engendering Democracy* (1991) and *Democracy and Difference* (1993).
97 Fox also emphasizes that his position is dictated by that which is feasible, elections being the most readily monitored dimension of democratic politics. See Fox, concluding comments in panel 'National Sovereignty Revisited: Perspectives on the Emerging Norm of Democracy in International Law', *Proc. ASIL* (1992) 249, 270–71, and *infra* text at note 121 for discussion of this point.
98 Franck 1995, at 86. Franck lists 130 states which as of late 1994 were 'legally committed to permit open, multiparty, secret-ballot elections with a universal franchise'. Of these he remarks that '[w]hile a few may arguably be democracies in form rather than substance, most are, or are in the process of becoming, genuinely open to meaningful political choice'. Franck 1995, at 85–6.
99 *Ibid*, at 138.
100 Slaughter 1992a, at 395–96 (emphasis omitted). The sense in which this is a paradox is unclear. If the thought is that the freedom associated with liberal states entails in another sense greater constraint than is the case with non-liberal states, then the paradox remains obscure, inasmuch as the freedom is that of citizens and the constraint is that of the state.

natives ever mentioned[101] – questions concerning liberal democracy's limitations can scarcely arise, let alone be addressed. It is not only issues of the kind just noted that are left out of account, however. The whole matter of liberal democracy's tenability in a world of intensified globalization is largely passed over. While globalizing processes are certainly registered,[102] the ways in which they are putting democracy under strain receive limited attention.[103] These scholars evoke a liberal democracy that is triumphant, vigorous, redemptive.

They also evoke a liberal democracy that provides the key to expanded prospects for peace. In this respect too, however, limitations are glossed over. The 'peace', which some international relations analysts claim is now a 'fact', is a '*liberal* peace'; it is said to hold *among liberal states*. Relations between liberal and non-liberal states are not claimed to be especially pacific, and may, according to the analysts, even be especially aggressive.[104] In finding warrant in this for a norm of democratic governance, the international legal scholars give little attention to the implications of the fact that democratic governance does not appear to induce pacific relations with non-liberal states.

But there is also a much larger limitation of which these writers take insufficient cognizance. The *'peace'* that is postulated among liberal states is an absence of armed conflict between them. Yet the Clausewitzean paradigm of war between nation-states to which this refers today fits only a minority of violent conflicts, even large-scale ones. Mary Kaldor highlights that much contemporary conflict arises out of the break-up of states, and centres on issues of 'identity politics' (ranging from religious communalism, to ethnic nationalism, to 'tribalism').[105] Support frequently comes from overseas diasporas, along with foreign governments and 'experts'. State actors are often hard to distinguish from non-state actors. Fighting is commonly sporadic, scattered within and across borders, and focused to a large extent on civilian targets.[106] Is this peace or war? Civil war or international war? The boundaries between these categories – like those between violent crime and armed conflict, public aims and private aims, combatants and civilians – are becoming blurred. She concludes that

> the prognosis is grim. The breakdown of the distinction between war and peace, the re-privatisation of violence, implies more or less continuous and geographically pervasive low-level violence, ranging from individual criminality to organised warfare.[107]

101 See, e.g., Franck 1995, at 86.
102 See, esp. Slaughter 1995.
103 A rare example of such attention can be found in the final eight pages of Franck's 484-page study of 'fairness' in international law and institutions. Franck 1995, at 477–484.
104 See Doyle, *supra* note 64, at 323 *et seq.*
105 Kaldor, 'Introduction', in M. Kaldor (ed.), *New Wars* (forthcoming).
106 For a similar account of war in the 1990s, see *Supplement to an Agenda for Peace: Position Paper of the Secretary-General on the Occasion of the Fiftieth Anniversary of the United Nations*, UN Doc. A/50/60; S/1995/1 (1995), esp. para. 10 *et seq.*
107 Kaldor, *supra* note 105.

Alongside these considerations concerning the character of war are further questions concerning the character of peace. There is, for instance, the question of whether peace can be held to prevail where certain forms of non-forcible coercion are occurring, arising (*inter alia*) from the exploitation of relations of dependency. There is also the broader issue of whether systemic inequalities of power, resources and opportunities, between and within nation-states, may in themselves constitute a type of ongoing 'structural violence'.[108] The identification of peace with an absence of armed conflict leaves out of account the possibility that peace may entail more than the failure to resort to arms.

It follows that the scope of the claims associated with the 'liberal peace' is highly circumscribed. Even assuming those claims are justified on their own terms, they miss important contemporary sources of violence, and important questions that arise in connection with that violence.

Moreover, Derrida's 'macroscopic fact, made up of innumerable singular sites of suffering' cited earlier finds scarcely greater resonance in these arguments than does Kaldor's 'grim prognosis'. These international lawyers are undoubtedly no Panglosses. Yet the progressivist premises of their claims, buttressed by the celebratory tone and 'post-historical' voice, do tend to shift attention away from the scale, character and sources of deprivation, oppression and conflict in the contemporary world. To read this international legal literature is to be filled with enthusiasm about the state of, or at any rate prospects for, human flourishing.

Also arguably overestimated is the extent to which there is evidence to support an emerging norm of democratic governance. For Franck and the other theorists of the emerging norm, this empirical issue – raised by some of Franck's critics[109] – has a different significance than it does for Fukuyama. While Fukuyama might shift between the empirical and the ideal, the international legal commentators cannot avoid confronting state practice if they are to make good their claim that the norm is emerging in international law. Or maybe Fukuyama's move, or something like it, is precisely what they intend. Perhaps characterizing the norm as 'emerging' allows it to remain poised between occurrence and prediction.

Finally, the international legal arguments are inclined to overstate the significance of the present moment, as an indication of the future. While the possibility of setbacks is certainly acknowledged, the evolutionary logic of the arguments tends to signal that contemporary trends will continue in a more or less linear fashion. As Fukuyama's critics highlight, the processes of historical change appear to be far more complex and contingent than this logic allows.

The observations made by Fukuyama's critics are also worth recalling as regards the consequences of these concerns. There is a danger of inducing complacency, and of prematurely pronouncing liberal democracy's future secure. In masking the limi-

108 The notion of 'structural violence' is elaborated in the work of Johan Galtung. See, e.g., 'Violence, Peace and Peace Research', 1 *Essays in Peace Research* (1975), ch. 4.

109 See, e.g., Carothers, *supra* note 3.

tations of liberal democracy, the prospects that those limitations might be addressed are correspondingly reduced. Inequalities may be made to seem, and to become, unalterable. And, to the extent that Kaldor's 'grim prognosis' is inadequately heeded, there is a danger of attaching insufficient importance and urgency to the medicine she prescribes. This entails re-establishing legitimate control of violence at a transnational level.[110]

To these points might be added further misgivings expressed by international legal commentators. Thomas Carothers argues that '[a]dvocacy of a democratic norm actually highlights [the] West versus non-West division and the tension in international law concerning the fact that it is at root a Western system that Western countries are seeking to apply to the whole world'.[111] He worries, furthermore, about the harm that might be done, via sanctions or armed intervention, in the 'implementation' of such a norm. Is the way opened up for the waging of 'just wars' or neo-colonial adventures? All the international legal scholars whose work is discussed here recognize the force of this concern.[112] With the exception of Tesón, none accepts unilateral intervention as a legitimate means of enforcing the norm, though each does appear to accept collective action by regional organizations and the United Nations.

Carothers here echoes a widely shared apprehension as regards the division of the world into liberal democratic and non-liberal democratic states. This is an apprehension that cannot forget all the other notorious divisions of history: between civilized and barbarian, Christian and heathen, European and oriental, developed and underdeveloped. Given the historical record, there is a case to be answered that a norm of democratic governance, like Fukuyama's 'league of democratic nations', would express a 'new ideology of imperialism'.[113] This article's premise is that democracy's universal relevance can indeed be defended.[114] The question is whether it is likely to be defensible within the framework of liberal millenarianism.

That it is not is highlighted in some observations by Martti Koskenniemi.[115] Like Carothers, Koskenniemi warns that a universal norm of democracy will 'always be suspect as a neocolonialist strategy'. 'The nation-State and its democratic forms may not be for export as pure form', he suggests. 'They may equally well constitute a specific product of Western history, culture and, especially, economy.'[116] What Koskenniemi appears to have in mind here is the sort of liberal world envisioned in liberal millenarianism. He seems to confirm this when he voices the further concern that a universal norm of democracy is 'too easily used against revolutionary politics

110 Kaldor, *supra* note 105.
111 Carothers, *supra* note 3, at 264. Derrida likewise discerns the outlines of a renewed European Christian alliance. Derrida, *supra* note 24, at 60–61.
112 See, e.g., Franck 1992, at 84.
113 F. Füredi, *The New Ideology of Imperialism* (1994). Franck and others acknowledge the concern. See, e.g., Franck 1992, at 80, 82.
114 See text at *supra* note 4.
115 Koskenniemi, *supra* note 3.
116 *Ibid*, at 234.

that aim at the roots of the existing distributional system and it domesticates cultural and political specificity in an overall (Western) culture of moral agnosticism and rule by the market'.[117]

If Koskenniemi's objections are informed by the same vision of democracy as that of the commentators he criticizes, then perhaps the source of his disquiet is not democracy *per se* but that particular (liberal millenarian) vision of it.[118] At any rate, his objections are unlikely to be refuted by arguments appealing to such a vision. However, from this it does not follow that those objections are unlikely to be refuted by *any* arguments. The simple point which this article has sought to recall is that the vision of democracy on which Koskenniemi (in common with Franck, Slaughter and others) relies is not the only one conceivable. Defenders of democracy's universal relevance have a wide range of *alternative* democratic possibilities upon which to draw. Among these are many that are substantially more congenial to redistribution and difference, and substantially less subordinate to the market and its mangers, than is liberal millenarianism.

B. Conclusion

The thesis of the emerging norm of democratic governance, and the liberal internationalist and neo-Kantian perspectives considered here, grapple with the significance for international law of profound transformations. They call attention to important normative and institutional developments, and connect subject matters more commonly treated in isolation from one another: international law and international relations; self-determination, human rights, and electoral assistance; political theory and international law. In doing so, however, they adopt a narrow understanding of democracy, largely equating it with certain liberal institutions. Franck expresses regret that this is all customary international law will currently support.[119] Fox recognizes that democracy entails much more than periodic national elections, but considers that elections, being easier for international organizations to monitor than other facets of democratic life, are international law's most appropriate starting point. 'It is much more difficult', he observes, 'to stay in a country after elections, for the long haul, to monitor all institutions of government and attempt to secure key elements of democracy ... Elections ... must not end the push to a democratic society, but they are an essential first step'.[120]

Yet it is not self-evident either that elections are democracy's first step or that ease of monitoring by international organisations should determine international

117 *Ibid.*

118 *Ibid.* Koskenniemi appears to recognize this, inasmuch as his 'most fundamental problem' is that these international legal commentators position themselves 'as possessing a transparent view of the essential meaning of democracy...'.

119 This is what Franck appears to suggest when defending a conception which, he acknowledges, is 'not ambitious, not unambiguous, and ... almost certainly not the one Americans would prefer'. Franck 1994, at 75.

120 Fox, *supra* note 97, at 270–71.

law's priorities. Democracy involves no necessary order of events, and difficulties of monitoring have all too frequently served in international law to make chosen priorities seem unavoidable.[121] This is not to suggest that periodic elections and related institutions lack value.[122] It is just to highlight the way democracy's further dimensions may be eclipsed. This article has sought to show that, whatever may be the constraints of the international legal system, they are not the only constraints in operation here. The scholars' liberal millenarian standpoint also plays a part in shaping the account of democracy that informs their claims.

At the same time, the theses provide powerful reasons for being concerned about this. If a norm of democratic governance indeed 'emerges', this will entail – to reiterate earlier discussion – that international law lays down criteria of governmental legitimacy, and that those criteria require democracy. It may also entail that individuals can claim a human right to democracy. The international legal scholars suggest that the norm should be enforced by making admission to, and participation in, international organizations conditional on democratic government (as is currently the case with some regional organizations). Franck proposes that financial and trade benefits and development assistance, and even the protection of UN and regional collective security measures in the event of an invasion, might likewise be made conditional on democratic government. Tesón advocates modifications of treaty and diplomatic law that would place further pressure on governments which do not meet the criteria of liberal democracy. Though Tesón alone would be prepared to sanction unilateral intervention, the other scholars appear to support collective enforcement.

Dire consequences could thus follow where legitimacy is denied. From the perspective of citizens, dire – perhaps even direr – consequences could also follow where legitimacy is accorded. This latter danger is easy to overlook. Yet if, in line with the international legal scholarship discussed in this article, liberal millenarianism shapes the criteria used, international law may find itself according legitimacy for what may in some circumstances be the most cosmetic democracy. In so doing, the law may undercut efforts to deepen democracy's purchase in the countries concerned. To the objection that any step in the direction of democracy is better than unmitigated repression, it may be replied that this is not necessarily so if the conditions upon which power is exercised remain essentially unchanged. Where international law confers on a repressive regime a legitimacy that it formerly lacked, the regime is strengthened and counter-authoritarian forces correspondingly debilitated.

According to former United Nations Secretary-General Boutros Boutros-Ghali, democracy is today an 'ideal that belongs to all humanity'.[123] To characterize de-

121 An example is the case of economic, social and cultural rights, and the way their relative deemphasis is routinely linked to undeniable, but exaggerated, difficulties of monitoring and enforcement.

122 However, for an intriguing critique of the 'reality' of elections, see J. Baudrillard (P. Foss *et al.*, trans.), *In the Shadow of Silent Majorities, or The End of the Social and Other Essays* (1983).

123 'Democracy: A Newly Recognized Imperative', 1 *Global Governance* (1995) 3, 4. See further B. Boutros-Ghali, *An Agenda for Democratization* (1996).

mocracy as an ideal is to highlight that it is an engine of criticism and change, necessarily at odds with prevailing realities. To label it as the property of all humanity is to recall, amongst other things, that its institutional complements necessarily reflect the huge diversity of social circumstances to which it is applied. Should international law seek to vindicate efforts animated by such an ideal, then a framework of ideas that posits liberal institutions as history's end scarcely seems an adequate basis on which to proceed.

Name Index

For Product Safety Concerns and Information please contact our EU representative GPSR@taylorandfrancis.com Taylor & Francis Verlag GmbH, Kaufingerstraße 24, 80331 München, Germany

Batch number: 10726322

Printed by Printforce, the Netherlands